RE-FORMING THE CENTER

Re-Forming the Center

American Protestantism, 1900 to the Present

Edited by

Douglas Jacobsen
and
William Vance Trollinger, Jr.

WILLIAM B. EERDMANS PUBLISHING COMPANY
GRAND RAPIDS, MICHIGAN / CAMBRIDGE, U.K.

© 1998 Wm. B. Eerdmans Publishing Co.
255 Jefferson Ave. S.E., Grand Rapids, Michigan 49503 /
P.O. Box 163, Cambridge CB3 9PU U.K.

Printed in the United States of America

03 02 01 00 99 98   7 6 5 4 3 2 1

Library of Congress Cataloging-in-Publication Data

Re-forming the center: American Protestantism, 1900 to the present /
    edited by Douglas Jacobsen and William Vance Trollinger, Jr.
        p.   cm.
    Includes bibliographical references and index.
    ISBN 0-8028-4298-4 (pbk. : alk. paper)
    1. Protestantism — 20th century. 2. United States — Church history — 20th
century. 3. Protestant churches — United States — History — 20th century.
4. Liberalism (Religion) — Protestant churches — History — 20th century.
5. Evangelicalism — United States — History — 20th century.
I. Jacobsen, Douglas. II. Trollinger, William Vance.
BR525.R35 1998
280'.4'09730904 — dc21   98-6059
                                                                              CIP

For Kate, Anna, and Grant
For Abby and Bekah

Contents

CONTENTS

Acknowledgments

This book grows out of a larger project, "Re-Forming the Center: Beyond the Two Party System of American Protestantism." As has been the case with so many other studies of American religion, this project was generously funded by the Lilly Endowment. In fact, it is rather sobering to consider what we would not know about religion in the United States if it were not for this institution. Thanks to Lilly, and thanks especially to Craig Dykstra for his unwavering support of the Re-Forming the Center project. We must also thank the Louisville Institute for its generous support of the project in its planning stages, and, in particular, Jim Lewis for helping us to refine our ideas and turn them into a viable plan of action.

The Re-Forming the Center project began in 1990 as a series of conversations with Harold Heie, then the academic dean at Messiah College. Heie pushed and prodded us to consider turning our private discontents with the two-party paradigm into a public discussion, and he graciously provided us with the time and the resources to begin that work. Rodney Sawatsky, who became Messiah's president in the middle of this project, has also been highly supportive of this project. In general, Messiah College has provided an enormous amount of institutional assistance for Re-Forming the Center, and it is a mark of the school's institutional maturation that it has come to see its educational mission as including projects such as this one which extend beyond the confines of the campus.

In the early stages of this project we turned to numerous scholars of American religion to help us in our theoretical formulations and in our logistical planning. The list is far too long to give here (and we would certainly be guilty of leaving out some individuals who were very helpful). But of all the persons with whom we spoke, Robert Handy was particularly generous in his encouragement and gracious in his advice. We also need to mention three other people who served as "project commentators" throughout this work: Ronald J. Sider, Harold Dean Trulear, and Barbara G. Wheeler. Representing rather different viewpoints, and not always agreeing with our conclusions, these three persons helped us with their combined wisdom to maintain a course of research and analysis that threaded a way between the shore and shoals of the two-party paradigm. (See the Appendix for a complete list of persons who have been formally involved in this research endeavor.)

As part of the "Re-Forming the Center" enterprise we held three national conferences at Messiah. The first (June 1994) dealt with American Protestantism, 1900-1960; the second (June 1995) dealt with the years since 1960; the third (May 1996) concentrated on what a (re)formed and constructive Protestant "center" or "middle ground" might look like in America. Many of the essays included in this book were originally presented (in truncated form) by the authors at the first two conferences. But we thank all of the hundreds of scholars and church leaders and interested laypeople who attended one or more of these conferences; these conferences were really extended conversations, and all who attended contributed to this discussion about Protestantism in America. Thanks in particular to Nancy Ammerman, Randall Balmer, Virginia Brereton, and Grant Wacker, who served as conference commentators, and to Peggy Shriver for her input and advice.

As regards this book, we owe much to Chuck Van Hof at Eerdmans, who has supported Re-Forming the Center from its early days, and who has patiently encouraged us as we engaged in the long process to complete this manuscript. Thanks also to Faculty Services at Messiah College for massive amounts of secretarial assistance, and to Messiah College and the University of Dayton for providing us with the time to finish the task.

Finally, we need to say a word about ourselves and the nature of our collaboration. We, with our families, are both active members of Protestant churches, but neither of us has ever been particularly beholden to any one denomination. Congregational life has always been more important than denominational. (For the record, however, one of us is currently a member of the United Church of Christ and the other is now a member of the General Conference Mennonite Church.) We also both tend to be more pietistic and ethical in our faith than doctrinal. This disposition has, no doubt, encouraged us down the road we have taken in this project. But the connections between faith and scholarship are complex, and there is no simple cause and effect relationship between our own strong Christian convictions and the academic dimensions of Re-Forming the Center. We do hope, however, that the essays included in this volume will open new possibilities of Christian friendship and understanding that transcend the numerous boundaries that still separate us.

By the time this book comes out we will have been working together on Re-Forming the Center for eight years. For the first six years (until Trollinger departed for the University of Dayton) we met for bagels once a week at a Mechanicsburg delicatessen, to converse, argue, dream, and complain about this project. For the last two years the conversation has continued over the phone and via e-mail. The point is that this project has been a collaboration in the truest sense of the word. This includes our writing. We have joint ownership of and responsibility for everything that bears both of our bylines, including the introductory and concluding essays in this book. And despite all of the horror stories we heard, and despite quite different work habits (one of us hates deadlines, one of us craves them) and writing styles (one of us adds, one of us deletes), we have found writing together to be a remarkably smooth, even enjoyable process. We started this project as friends. As the project begins to wind down, we are even better friends.

Our last word of thanks and appreciation is reserved for those closest to us: our families. Put simply, we think our families are great. Our wives, Rhonda Hustedt Jacobsen and Gayle May Trollinger, are both scholars in their own fields and wonderful human beings. More than any other persons they know precisely how to encourage us when that is called for and how to critique our work when and where it is most needed. They clearly deserve part of the credit for this volume and for the Re-Forming the Center project as a whole. Finally, our children are constant sources of joy for both of us, and constant reminders that we are more blessed than we deserve. We hope that the Christian future they inherit from us and our generation will be more peaceable and caring than it is today. This book is for them.

Contributors

Edwin David Aponte is Assistant Professor of Hispanic Christianity and Culture at the Perkins School of Theology, Southern Methodist University, and author of "Coritos as Active Symbol in Latino Protestant Popular Religion," *Journal of Hispanic/Latino Theology* 2:3 (1995).

Margaret Bendroth is Director of the Women and Twentieth-Century Protestantism project at Andover Newton Theological School and Professor of History at Calvin College. She is the author of *Fundamentalism and Gender, 1875 to the Present* (1993).

N. J. Demerath, III is Professor of Sociology at the University of Massachusetts, Amherst, and current (1998) President of the Society for the Scientific Study of Religion. His article here is drawn from his forthcoming book, *Crossing the Gods: Religion, Violence, Politics, and the State across the World.*

Nancy L. Eiesland is Assistant Professor of Sociology of Religion at the Candler School of Theology and the Graduate Division of Religion at Emory University. She is the author of *A Particular Place: Exurbanization and Religious Response* (forthcoming).

Mark Ellingsen is Associate Professor at the Interdenominational Theological Center. He is author of six books, including *The Evangelical Movement* (1988) and *A Common Sense Theology* (1995).

J. Samuel Escobar is the Thornley B. Wood Professor of Missiology at

Eastern Baptist Theological Seminary and Theological Education Consultant for Baptist International Ministries in Lima, Perú. Recent publications include *De la misión a la teologia* (1998) and *Desafios da Igreja na America Latina* (1997).

Nancy G. Garner is Assistant Professor of History at Wright State University. She is author of "A Prayerful Public Protest: The Significance of Gender in the Woman's Crusade of 1874," *Kansas History* (winter 1997/1998).

Mark Granquist is Assistant Professor of Religion at St. Olaf College, Northfield, MN. He has published a number of articles on the history of American Lutheranism and the religious institutions of Scandinavian-American immigrants.

Michael S. Hamilton is Coordinator of the Pew Scholars Programs at the University of Notre Dame and is currently completing a book tentatively entitled *The Fundamentalist Harvard: Wheaton College and the Continuing Vitality of American Evangelicalism in the Twentieth Century.*

David Edwin Harrell, Jr. is Daniel F. Breeden Eminent Scholar in the Humanities at Auburn University. He is the author of six books about American religion, including *Oral Roberts: An American Life* (1975) and *Pat Robertson: A Personal, Religious and Political Portrait* (1987).

D. G. Hart is Director of the Library and Associate Professor of Church History at Westminster Theological Seminary in Philadelphia. He has written *Defending the Faith, J. Gresham Machen and the Crisis of Conservative Protestantism in Modern America* (1994).

Richard T. Hughes is Distinguished Professor of Religion at Pepperdine University. He has recently edited *The Primitive Church in the Modern World* (1995) and authored *Reviving the Ancient Faith: The Story of Churches of Christ in America* (1997).

James Juhnke is Professor of History at Bethel College (North Newton, KS) and author of numerous books and articles on Mennonite denominational history, including *Vision, Doctrine, War: Mennonite Identity and Organization in America, 1890-1930* (1989).

Albert Keim is Professor of History and Director of the Honors Program at Eastern Mennonite University. His publications include *The Politics of Conscience: The Historic Peace Churches and America at War, 1917-1955* (1988) and *Harold S. Bender, 1897-1962* (1998).

Fred Kniss is Associate Professor of Sociology at Loyola University (Chicago, IL) and the author of numerous articles addressing aspects of the relationship between culture, religion, social change, and conflict, including *Disquiet in the Land: Cultural Conflict in American Mennonite Communities* (1997).

Donald A. Luidens is Professor of Sociology and Chair of the Department of Sociology and Social Work at Hope College. Among his recent publications are two coedited volumes, *Rethinking Secularization: Reformed Reactions to Modernity* (1997) and *Reformed Vitality: Continuity and Change in the Face of Modernity* (1998).

Martin E. Marty is Fairfax M. Cone Distinguished Service Professor Emeritus at the University of Chicago and the Director of the Public Religion Project. His most recent book is *The One and the Many* (1997).

Roger J. Nemeth is Professor of Sociology at Hope College. His recent publications include studies of the intergenerational transmission of religious practices, and he is currently involved in a major research project entitled "One Hundred and Fifty Years of Congregational Change: Church Life in the Reformed Church in America."

Steven M. Nolt is currently a doctoral student in History at the University of Notre Dame. His publications include *A History of the Amish* (1992) and the coauthored book *Amish Enterprise* (1995).

Richard V. Pierard is Professor of History at Indiana State University. He is coauthor of *Two Kingdoms: The Church and Culture through the Ages* (1993) and "Shaking the Foundations: World War I, the Western Allies, and German Protestant Missions," *International Bulletin of Missionary Research* (January 1998).

Mary R. Sawyer is Associate Professor of Religious Studies at Iowa State University in Ames, IA. She is the author of *Black Ecumenism: Implementing the Demands of Justice* (1994).

CONTRIBUTORS

Gerald T. Sheppard is Professor of Old Testament Literature and Exegesis at Emmanuel College of Victoria University and the Toronto School of Theology in the University of Toronto. Among his publications is "How Do Neoorthodox and Post-Neoorthodox Theologians Approach the Doing of Theology Today," in *Doing Theology in Today's World*, ed. J. Woodbridge and T. E. McComiskey (1991).

David Sikkink is currently a doctoral student in Sociology at the University of North Carolina/Chapel Hill. He is coauthor with Christian Smith of *American Evangelicalism* (1998). His dissertation investigates relationships between religious identities, views of public schools, and schooling choices for children.

Susie C. Stanley is Professor of Historical Theology at Messiah College and Convener of Wesleyan/Holiness Women Clergy, Inc. She has authored *Feminist Pillar of Fire: The Life of Alma White* (1993) and numerous articles and chapters on the Wesleyan/Holiness movement.

William J. Weston is Associate Professor of Sociology at Centre College (Danville, KY) and author of *Presbyterian Pluralism: Competition in a Protestant House* (1997).

Ronald C. White is Dean and Professor of Church History at San Francisco Theological Seminary. He is the author or editor of five books, including *Liberty and Justice for All: Racial Reform and the Social Gospel* (1990). The chapter in this volume grows out of a larger study of youth ministry and youth cultures in America funded by the Lilly Endowment.

Introduction

This book deals with the structure and identity of Protestantism in the United States in the twentieth century. The standard picture of these years portrays Protestantism as divided into two diametrically and bitterly opposed camps. On the one side of the divide stands fundamentalist/evangelical Protestantism; on the other, liberal/mainline Protestantism. This book challenges this two-party thesis. It questions it both on the basis of empirical validity and on the basis of contemporary usefulness. That is to say, we are convinced that the two-party model provides an inadequate map of American Protestantism, 1900-present, while at the same time distorting Protestant hopes for the future.

Central to the Re-Forming the Center project, and central to this book, has been the desire to move beyond a bipolar model and toward the formulation of a more nuanced and accurate understanding of the past and present state of Protestantism in America. It thus behooves us to begin this work with a brief but critical discussion of the place of the two-party paradigm in American religious historiography.[1]

*   *   *

According to the now standard two-party view, there are really only two kinds of Protestants in America — at least, only two kinds that count. On the one side of this alleged divide are mainline, liberal, and progressive Protes-

---

1. For an earlier and expanded version of this historiographical discussion, see Douglas Jacobsen and William Vance Trollinger, Jr., "Historiography of American Protestantism: The Two-Party Paradigm, and Beyond," *Fides et Historia* 25 (Fall 1993): 4-15.

tants. On the other side are conservatives, evangelicals, charismatics, and fundamentalists. Sometimes the metaphor has been geological, with a fault line running through the middle of American Protestantism. Sometimes the explanation has been theological, i.e., orthodoxy versus heresy. Sometimes the distinctions have been cultural and culinary: the polyester, punch and crackers people contrasted with the 100% cotton, wine and cheese crowd.

Whatever the illustrative metaphor, the pervasive assumption is that Protestants in the United States are almost wholly divisible into two distinct and relatively hostile camps, and that the story of this bipolar division forms the primary plot of twentieth-century American religion. This notion was first articulated at the beginning of this century by church leaders who were involved in the Modernist-Fundamentalist controversy, and who used two-party language to depersonalize and demonize their opponents, and to advance their own standing and agendas within their respective denominations or parachurch organizations. But in the last three decades this pugnacious rhetoric has been adopted by a number of leading scholars, who have refashioned it into an academic paradigm of American religion. These academic interpreters have toned down the language of that older conflict, but they have essentially retained the same confrontational categories; in fact, some scholars (most notably James Davison Hunter) have actually made claims significantly greater than their ecclesiastical forbearers as to how broadly the two-party paradigm can be applied to American life.

While the two-party paradigm has become deeply entrenched in the language of and the literature about American Protestantism, this paradigm has also proven itself to be extraordinarily plastic. Few scholars or religious leaders mean precisely the same thing when they talk of two parties, to the point that the whole paradigm seems to be a rapidly moving target. That is, the ways in which the two parties are defined in one article or book often seem to bear only slight resemblance to the ways in which they are defined in another article or book. This malleability helps explain the prominence of the paradigm, given that it can be adjusted so easily to fit new (even seemingly contradictory) data. But it also suggests that the simple principle of twoness might actually be more significant than the specific content that is assigned to either side of the supposed divide. To the degree that this is the case, however, we have moved beyond empirical analysis to dualism as a mythic construct of life.

What might account for this power of twoness? The biologist Lynn Margulis has argued that we may be drawn almost irresistibly toward twoness, given the importance of pairs in our experience: two sexes are needed to procreate, we have two hands and feet and eyes, our lives are divided into the day and the night, and so forth. Margulis is certainly well aware of how tenaciously we hold onto binary visions of the world. Her proposal (now canonized) that there are five basic divisions of living things, not two (the old plant and animal kingdoms), was met with tremendous opposition when first suggested.[2]

This kind of biological grounding, however, is probably not necessary to explain the penchant to think about American Protestantism in dualistic terms. For religious leaders, it is much easier to mobilize people and raise money by dividing the world into two, presenting one's own group, the good and the true and the pure, as standing in the gap against an easily identified and unified enemy. Such simplistic and moralistic dualisms play particularly well on television. But even in the academy, where substance is supposed to outweigh form, the two-party model has prevailed. For those of us who teach about American religion, the primary reason for this may be quite mundane: the two-party model is easy to present, and simple for our students to understand. It works in the classroom, even if it misrepresents the real world.

*   *   *

In tracing the historical development of this interpretive paradigm, the best place to start is with one of the earliest and clearest academic statements of the two-party thesis: Martin Marty's *Righteous Empire* (1970). Building on the work of his graduate student, Jean Miller Schmidt, Marty argues that since the late nineteenth century two Protestant parties (the "private" party and the "public" party) have dominated the American religious landscape, in much the same way that Republicans and Democrats have dominated the American political scene. In other works, including *A Nation of Behavers* (1976) and *Pilgrims in Their Own Land* (1984), Marty has developed a more pluralistic model of American religious history — and perhaps this pluralistic vision is more quintessentially "Marty" — but the two-party influence of *Righteous Empire* has been enormous nonetheless.[3]

2. Tyler Volk, *Metapatterns* (New York: Columbia University Press, 1995), 91.

3. Martin E. Marty, *Righteous Empire: The Protestant Experience in America* (New York: Dial Press, 1970), esp. 177-187; *A Nation of Behavers* (Chicago: University of Chicago Press, 1976); and *Pilgrims in Their Own Land: 500 Years of Religion in America* (Boston: Little, Brown and Company, 1984); Jean Miller Schmidt, *Souls or the Social Order: The Two-Party System in American Protestantism* (Brooklyn: Carlson Publishing, 1991).

The heart of Schmidt's research is an analysis of the rhetoric used by religious leaders during the modernist-fundamentalist controversy; moreover, as she has forthrightly explained, her study was designed to serve as a usable history that would help make sense of the divide she saw in the Protestantism of the 1960s. Given this motivation, and given that she examined the public rhetoric of conflict, which is typically couched in "we/they" terms, it is no surprise that much of her own interpretation is framed in binary terms. Marty kept Schmidt's twoness, but he more explicitly rooted his analysis in a broad perspective that made the issue of modernity the key to understanding twentieth-century American religion. There is certainly a grandness to this interpretive vision, which is enhanced by the clarity of Marty's prose. Such an approach, however (and Marty is by no means alone here), almost inevitably leads to dualism, as persons and movements are lined up as either for or against modernity. While there is room for individuals and groups to exist between the extremes in this metavision of modernity and its discontents, that middle ground is often either ignored or explained only briefly as a muddled mix of the more logically consistent positions at the poles.

It should be noted that, far from being partisan, both Marty and Schmidt have tried to be peacemakers between the two supposed parties, a redemptive concern most clearly expressed in Marty's *The Public Church* (1981).[4] Irenic impulses notwithstanding, the two-party interpretation of Protestant life articulated by Marty and Schmidt still carries significant interpretive weight in the academic community and still helps reinforce a bifurcated and oppositional approach to Protestant history, even though American religious historiography has gone in a variety of directions in the three decades since the publication of *Righteous Empire*.

In this regard, three trends bear noting. The first is the tremendous growth in scholarship about fundamentalism and evangelicalism. Most of the literature in this rapidly expanding field has been written by self-declared evangelicals who are writing from a bipolar perspective. That is to say, most of these scholars have accepted, either explicitly or implicitly, the two-party paradigm of American Protestantism, and in their scholarship they have sought to establish the importance of the conservative side of this alleged Protestant divide. Most significant of these works is George Marsden's *Fundamentalism and American Culture*

---

4. Martin E. Marty, *The Public Church: Mainline-Evangelical-Catholic* (New York: Crossroad, 1981).

(1980). In many ways this elegant study is a careful and nuanced interpretation of the rise and flowering of American fundamentalism. In fact, Marsden takes great pains to point out the internal divisions within the fundamentalist movement. This said, there is also no question that he sees himself as dealing with one side of a conflict that divided into two parties the previously unified evangelicalism of the late nineteenth century. He carries a similar dualistic scheme through his more recent works: *Reforming Fundamentalism* (1987) and *The Soul of the American University* (1994).[5]

Clearly Marsden, like Marty and Schmidt before him, is on to something. He is absolutely correct to emphasize the importance of the previously slighted fundamentalist movement and evangelical subculture. But to say this is not to accept with Marsden that fundamentalism/evangelicalism is one party in a two-party Protestant world. Marsden's own bipolar convictions are, however, quite strong. In this regard, the most revealing section of *Fundamentalism and American Culture* may well be the two-page Afterword, in which Marsden asserted that: "I find that a Christian view of history is clarified if one considers reality more or less like the world portrayed in the works of J. R. R. Tolkien. We live in the midst of contests between great and mysterious spiritual forces, which we understand only imperfectly and whose true dimensions we only occasionally glimpse. Yet, frail as we are, we do play a role in this history, on the side either of the powers of light or of the powers of darkness. It is crucially important then, that, by God's grace, we keep our wits about us and discern the vast difference between the real forces for good and the powers of darkness disguised as angels of light."[6]

Many Christians affirm some sort of cosmic dualism in their vision of the world. What is significant here, however, is the way in which Marsden suggests that this dualism should be converted into historical methodology. But once this methodological move is made, it is difficult to see how one could ever write history in a way that would not involve dividing the world into two parties, the one tending toward the light, and the other veering toward darkness. While we have concentrated on Marsden's work here, many other self-consciously "evangelical" historians (but

---

5. George M. Marsden, *Fundamentalism and American Culture: The Shaping of Twentieth-Century Evangelicalism, 1870-1925* (New York: Oxford University Press, 1980); *Reforming Fundamentalism* (Grand Rapids: Eerdmans, 1987); and *The Soul of the American University* (New York: Oxford University Press, 1994).

6. Marsden, *Fundamentalism and American Culture*, 229-30.

not all) have adopted a similar bipolar style. In this regard, it is interesting to note that evangelical scholar Mark Noll has recently argued for "modifying the evangelical tendency to Manichaeism" so that evangelicals can better "worship God with [their] mind[s]." We hope that this anti-Manichaeism will grow as a leavening force within "evangelical" historiography.[7]

A second recent trend in American religious historiography has been the expansion of the pluralist model of American religion. This model has shifted the focus of study away from the "center" of American religion and society to a more careful analysis of all the diverse religious traditions found in America, giving special attention to those groups that were previously ignored as "outsiders." One of the most prominent historians articulating this approach is Catherine Albanese, who is known for her influential text, *America: Religions and Religion*, which was originally published in 1981 (a significantly revised edition was published in 1992). Historian R. Laurence Moore (who has also advocated a pluralistic model vis-à-vis American religion) has referred to Albanese's survey as "a splendidly convincing text that manages to ignore Protestants until the fourth chapter."[8]

Given Albanese's attention to substantive religious diversity, one would not expect to find anything approaching the two-party paradigm in this sterling example of the pluralist approach to American religion. But when it comes to Protestantism, Albanese perpetuates the bipolar model. It may be that it is precisely *because* Albanese so emphasizes religious diversity in America that she does not look more intently at Protestant diversity, given that, when placed against the backdrop of American religion as a whole, most Protestant divisions do not merit detailing. Whatever the reason, in *America: Religions and Religion* Albanese repeatedly emphasizes that "the twentieth century brought firm lines of separation between [Protestant] liberals and conservatives"; looking toward the future, she notes that "a liberal-fundamentalist split seemed a permanent feature of the Protestant landscape."[9] Albanese's use of a two-party paradigm is clearest in the 1992 edition of her text, where she has divided the discussion of Protestantism into two chapters, "American Protestant

7. Mark Noll, *The Scandal of the Evangelical Mind* (Grand Rapids: Eerdmans, 1994), 245.

8. R. Laurence Moore, *Religious Outsiders and the Making of Americans* (New York: Oxford University Press, 1986), 20.

9. Catherine L. Albanese, *America: Religions and Religion*, 2nd ed. (Belmont, CA: Wadsworth Publishing Co., 1992), 139-40.

Origins and the Liberal Tradition" and "The Protestant Churches and the Mission Mind."[10] These two chapters rather neatly correspond with the two-party view of American Protestantism.

A third pertinent trend in American religious scholarship has been the increasing number of historical studies written by sociologists. In keeping with the aforementioned approaches to American religious history, some of the most important of these socio-historical works reinforce the two-party paradigm of American Protestantism, and even promote it with new vigor. The best example here is Robert Wuthnow's *The Restructuring of American Religion* (1988). In this work Wuthnow argues that, since World War II, a great divide has emerged in American Protestantism, with American believers polarized along the lines of left and right. Wuthnow argues that this division is not between denominations, but, instead, runs straight through the middle of almost all American mainstream churches. According to Wuthnow, numerous factors have contributed to this development, including the expansion of the federal government, the rise and rapid growth of parachurch organizations, and the lessening of old denominational ties. Perhaps the most telling factor, however, is education. The higher the level of education, the more likely one will be a "liberal"; the lower the level of education, the more likely one will be a "conservative."[11]

Wuthnow's insights are important, and yet there are questions as to how he has chosen to interpret his data. In *The Struggle for America's Soul* (1989) — a revealingly prescriptive title — Wuthnow writes: "To state that American religion is divided neatly into two communities with sharply differentiated views is, of course, to ride roughshod over the countless landmarks, signposts, hills, and gullies that actually constitute the religious landscape."[12] But it is precisely this roughshod path that Wuthnow chooses to take, rather than dwelling on the nuances and complexities of American religion. Perhaps this is because he, like almost all grand-scale sociologists since Max Weber, finds himself irresistibly drawn to the "ideal types" that can be found at the extremes of any social situation. Wuthnow himself has said: "The work of the poles is to define the issues in terms of clear oppositions. These oppositions set the outer limits of debate and

---

10. Albanese, *America: Religions and Religion*, 102-192.

11. Robert Wuthnow, *The Restructuring of American Religion: Society and Faith Since World War II* (Princeton, NJ: Princeton University Press, 1988), esp. 3-14, 133-72, 297-322.

12. Robert Wuthnow, *The Struggle for America's Soul: Evangelicals, Liberals, and Secularism* (Grand Rapids: Eerdmans, 1989), 23.

they unmask any false consensus that may inhibit an honest rethinking of public values."[13]

It should be noted that, as with Marty and Schmidt, Wuthnow has sought to be a peacemaker between the parties he describes. He has made very clear that he wants to help develop "a stronger middle-of-the-road position as a distinct alternative to both the extreme right and the extreme left." What is more, many of his more recent publications have posited a more complex matrix of Protestant faith where two-party conflict is either absent or functions as only one among several dynamics that need to be analyzed.[14] Nevertheless, the strong two-party narrative of *The Restructuring of American Protestantism* has helped reinforce a bifurcated picture of American Protestantism.

Without a doubt, however, it is in the work of sociologist James Davison Hunter that we find the most recent and the most outspoken defense and enlargement of the two-party thesis. In his influential book, *Culture Wars* (1991), Hunter explicitly expands upon Wuthnow's thesis, asserting that the bitter warfare within American Protestantism has now spilled over the religious banks and has infected the entirety of American culture. A bitter conflict now exists in the United States between an "orthodox" party committed to belief in "an external, definable, and transcendent authority," and a "progressive" party seeking to "resymbolize historic faiths according to prevailing assumptions of contemporary life." For the author of *Culture Wars* (and for many of the commentators who have followed in his wake) there is something frighteningly ominous about this conflict. His 1994 book, dramatically entitled *Before the Shooting Begins* (1994), even suggests that we just might be on the brink of a religious civil war.[15]

Hunter has said that, while "as a Christian" he would like to hope

13. Wuthnow, *Struggle for America's Soul,* 186.
14. See, e.g., his *Christianity in the Twenty-First Century* (New York: Oxford University Press, 1993), *Acts of Compassion* (Princeton: Princeton University Press, 1993), *God and Mammon* (New York: Free Press, 1994), *Sharing the Journey* (New York: Free Press, 1996), *Christianity and Civil Society* (Valley Forge: Trinity Press International, 1996), and *The Crisis in the Churches* (New York: Oxford University Press, 1997).
15. James Davison Hunter, *Culture Wars: The Struggle to Define America* (New York: Basic Books, 1991), 329n. and 44-45; and *Before the Shooting Begins: Searching for Democracy in America's Culture War* (New York: Free Press, 1994). Hunter had actually adopted a two-party thesis well before the publication of *Culture Wars.* See his *American Evangelicalism: Conservative Religion and the Quandary of Modernity* (New Brunswick: Rutgers University Press, 1983) and *Evangelicalism: The Coming Generation* (Chicago: University of Chicago Press, 1987).

for a less conflictive future, "as a sociologist" he has no choice but to predict increasing tensions and violence in an America wracked by cultural warfare.[16] But for all of his heated rhetoric about an America splitting into two bitterly hostile camps, a careful reading of his work reveals that Hunter concedes that "most Americans occupy a vast middle ground" between the poles. Some Americans lean one way or the other; some are pulled in both directions; some are "altogether oblivious" of either camp; few Americans would fully "embrace" one of Hunter's two competing moral visions. To put it another way, most Americans do not possess "coherent, clearly articulated, sharply differentiated world views."[17] Whatever the intellectual and emotional state of people who do not measure up to the "ideal types" at each end of the spectrum, and however Hunter argues that what matters most is the polarized rhetoric of elites representing the two camps, the fact that most Americans are in neither camp undermines the whole notion of a "culture war." Of course, it is true that the prophecies of Hunter and similar commentators have a certain self-fulfilling potential; still, it seems clear that Hunter has simply gotten his facts and his theory all jumbled up.

The point of this brief survey is simple: even in the hands of our most sophisticated and intelligent scholars of religion in the United States, the two-party model is a limited and flawed means by which to understand the past and present of American Protestantism. This is not to claim that a bipolar interpretation never applies. On occasion, and particularly when issues have become politicized within a particular group of Protestants, there may be merit in the notion that there were/are two distinct camps in conflict with each other. This said, the reality is that the two-party model does not and cannot do justice to the bewildering complexity of American Protestantism. Not only were and are there numerous Protestants who do not truly fit in either party, but the fault lines within Protestantism are both multiple and constantly shifting, hence ensuring that conflicts did not and do not reflect a single bifurcated division. That James Davison Hunter acknowledges that most Americans fall into neither of his two warring factions is evidence that the bipolar paradigm is woefully inadequate.

*   *   *

16. James Davison Hunter, Messiah College Annual Lectures on Religion and Society (March 3, 1994).

17. Hunter, *Culture Wars*, 43.

If we are to move forward in our understanding of American Protestantism, we must rein in the two-party model and allow other stories to be told. The Re-Forming the Center project is part of that telling of other stories. But we are certainly not alone. For example, there is the work of Thomas Tweed and associates, who are trying to "de-center" the story of American religious faith so that no one plot is allowed to marginalize all others.[18] There is also the phenomenal growth in the study of women's religious faith, which is forcing a reexamination of the interpretive categories we use to make sense of Protestant history and life. This is also true for the growing body of literature dealing with African-American and Hispanic churches which is now being augmented by a spate of scholarship concerning America's emerging "new ethnic" churches.[19] Finally, there is a resurgent interest in both congregational and denominational history, which may provide another set of data challenging two-party interpretations.[20]

This collection of essays, however, has its own distinctive identity. The specific purpose of this volume is to advance our understanding of American Protestantism beyond the two-party model, in the process creating space for the development of more accurate and sophisticated understandings of Protestantism in the United States in the twentieth century. This work entails both a critical and a constructive dimension. Critically, many of the essays in this book explicitly attack the inadequacies and inaccuracies of the two-party model. Constructively, this collection of es-

18. Thomas A. Tweed, ed., *Retelling U.S. Religious History* (Berkeley: University of California Press, 1997).

19. See especially R. Stephen Warner and Judith G. Wittners, eds., *Gatherings in Diaspora* [tentative title] (Philadelphia: Temple University Press, forthcoming).

20. The growth in literature on congregations has been especially significant. See, e.g., James P. Wind and James W. Lewis, eds., *American Congregations*, 2 vols. (Chicago: University of Chicago Press, 1994); and Nancy T. Ammerman et al., eds., *Congregation and Community* (New Brunswick: Rutgers University Press, 1997).

With regard to denominational history see, among others, the six-volume *Presbyterian Presence*, ed. Milton J Coalter, John M. Mulder, and Louis B. Weeks (Louisville: Westminster/John Knox, 1990-92). See also D. Newell Williams, ed., *A Case Study of Mainstream Protestantism: The Disciples' Relation to American Culture, 1880-1989* (Grand Rapids: Eerdmans, 1991); Russell E. Richey, Kenneth E. Rowe, and Jean Miller Schmidt, *Perspectives on American Methodism: Interpretive Essays* (Nashville: Kingswood Books/Abingdon, 1993); and the four-volume *Mennonite Experience in America* published by Herald Press in Scottdale, PA: Richard K. MacMaster, *Vol. I: Land, Piety, Peoplehood* (1985), Theron F. Schlabach, *Vol. II: Peace, Faith, Nation* (1988), James C. Juhnke, *Vol. III: Vision, Doctrine, War* (1989), and Paul Toews, *Vol. IV: Mennonites in American Society, 1930-1970* (1996).

says tries to line out alternative readings of American Protestantism, especially with regard to groups, organizations, and individuals often thought to be prime examples of the older two-party paradigm.

It should be noted that we do not claim that this volume comes close to covering the entirety of American Protestantism. In particular, we readily acknowledge that the bulk of this volume focuses on white Protestantism as opposed to other ethnic groups. The reason for this is simple. The two-party paradigm was developed to categorize and explain Euro-American Protestantism. Even the staunchest defenders of the bipolar model will acknowledge that, to refer to the most obvious example, the experience of the Black Church falls outside the two-party paradigm of American Protestantism. But it would be insufficient for this volume to concentrate only on developments within white Protestantism, and a number of essays included here do discuss developments outside of that arena.

Granting the limitations of this volume, we would nevertheless maintain that these essays, in their topical breadth, analytical depth, and variety of disciplinary perspectives, provide a good starting point for reexamining the question of how best to understand American Protestantism in the twentieth century. We begin this volume with a section devoted to general analyses of the two-party paradigm. David Edwin Harrell leads off with a vigorous essay in which he asserts that to insist on "reducing the variegated theological and cultural diversity in American Protestantism to two poles simply distorts history beyond recognition." A second essay by Jay Demerath then examines America's cultural conflicts in comparative context. This exercise leads Demerath to conclude that the notion of a "culture war" in the United States is more hyperbole than reality. David Sikkink bolsters Demerath's argument by providing evidence that most Americans do not view themselves as being in a culture war, and do not identify themselves according to some national "liberal/conservative symbolic boundary." Looking for a new means of categorization, sociologist Fred Kniss develops an insightful alternative to the two-party paradigm that includes four groupings of American religious faith. We conclude this first section with an essay by Martin Marty, the dean of American religious history, who provides a spirited (and qualified) defense of his notion that there were and are two parties in American Protestantism.

From general analyses we move to a section of essays devoted to denominational case studies. The first three pieces deal with the northern Presbyterians and northern Baptists in the early twentieth century: shaken by the fundamentalist-modernist controversy, these two denominations have been held up as the paradigmatic historical examples of the two-party thesis, and yet all three contributors take issue with this claim. William Weston asserts that while fundamentalists and modernists have garnered most of the historical attention, it was a third group (denominational loyalists) who held the balance of power among Presbyterians. D. G. Hart points to a fourth group among the Presbyterians, the confessionalists, who, under the leadership of J. Gresham Machen, eventually broke away to found the Orthodox Presbyterian Church, a denomination that cannot really be classified as fundamentalist. Finally, Richard Pierard argues that, contrary to past and present descriptions as modernist, many Presbyterian and Baptist missionaries and agency leaders often combined commitments to ecumenism and social action with evangelical passion and theological orthodoxy.

The next five essays in this section deal with denominations and traditions that cannot be, and did not want to be, squeezed into one of the two parties; in fact, as these essays make clear, many of these groups were/are not so much between the two parties, as simply outside of them. Susie Stanley contends that, while observers have often assumed that the churches of the Wesleyan/Holiness movement were/are in the fundamentalist camp, the reality is that the differences are so great that it can be fairly stated that "Wesleyan/Holiness fundamentalism is an oxymoron." Richard Hughes makes a similar argument regarding the Churches of Christ, but with a caveat: while their desire to create churches patterned after first-century churches put them squarely at odds with evangelicalism, as the century progressed the Churches of Christ slowly abandoned their restorationist commitments and gradually moved toward evangelicalism. Regarding another restorationist group, James Juhnke and Albert Keim assert that the Mennonites never fit in either the modernist or fundamentalist camp, and that E. G. Kaufman (General Conference Mennonites) and Harold Bender (Mennonite Church) worked hard to ensure that this remained the case in their respective denominations. Mark Granquist examines the conflicts that grew out of mid-century efforts to consolidate American Lutheranism, in the process concluding that, in keeping with Darryl Hart's argument regarding Orthodox Presbyterians, "models of confessional Lutheranism go much further than the 'two-party' model in explaining the course of American Lutheranism." Finally, Don Luidens and Roger Nemeth find not two but four parties within the Reformed Church in America, four parties that cannot be neatly laid out on a clearly delineated theological or ideological continuum.

Section three continues the focus on case studies, but here the attention is on parachurch, interdenominational, and local organizations. We begin with Nancy Garner's examination of the Woman's Christian Temperance Union, in which she argues that the WCTU is a prime example of how the two-party paradigm ignores women's organizations and obscures issues of gender within American Protestantism. Mary Sawyer's essay expands this theme into the issue of race, using black ecumenical organizations to show that, throughout the twentieth century, the Black Church has been able to hold together both the personal and the social justice–oriented facets of faith. Michael Hamilton and Margaret Lamberts Bendroth turn our attention to the Winona Lake Bible Conference as an evangelical yet ecumenical organization, emphasizing personal piety and fundamentalist doctrine while at the same time allowing enormous room "for variation in spirituality, theology, and church affiliation." In somewhat the same vein, Steven Nolt discusses the Biblical Seminary in New York, an influential and irenically evangelical institution which promoted a radically inductive approach to the Bible that made the school impossible to situate in two-party terms. Continuing this theme, Samuel Escobar examines two Protestant missionary organizations, InterVarsity Christian Fellowship and the Latin American Mission, that promoted an evangelical theology while at the same time maintaining an ecumenical posture that minimized or disregarded conservative-liberal (and Protestant-Catholic) divisions. Making a similar point, Ron White tells the story of Young Life, a youth ministries organization that emphasized a "friendship evangelism" that transcended theological and denominational divisions.

At the local level, Ed Aponte points out that the Hispanic Protestant churches of Philadelphia simply do not fit the "middle class 'Anglo'" two-party model, particularly given that the more theologically conservative Hispanic churches are where one finds a heightened commitment to social activism. But if Nancy Eiesland is correct, the bipolar paradigm does not even apply where it is supposed to: her examination of a United Methodist church near Atlanta reveals church members with eclectic, dynamic faith commitments who cannot be located on "maps of religious geography which attend primarily to two parties."

The fourth and rather short section of the book focuses on issues of theology and biblical scholarship. While these two essays, by Mark Ellingsen and Gerald Sheppard, differ somewhat from the more sociological and historical pieces that precede them, this collection of essays dealing with twentieth-century Protestantism would be incomplete without them. At the heart of both essays is an understanding that postliberal narrative theology provides the means by which we can get beyond the two-party paradigm: Ellingsen sees this approach to Scripture and theology as salvaging the pre-Enlightenment hermeneutic of the old Protestant center, while Sheppard argues that this approach opens the door to a "positive, postmodern criticism of modern criticisms" that may allow Protestants to envision a new kind of center.

Most of these contributors agree that the two-party paradigm is, at best, an insufficient means by which to understand American Protestantism. They are at some pains to establish that the individuals and/or groups under examination cannot be easily shoehorned into one of the alleged Protestant camps or the other. Of course, it may be argued that some of the essayists are engaging in definitional quibbling, splitting hairs in an effort to argue that "their group" does not belong in one of the two alleged parties. But to say blithely that, to take examples from the essays on Presbyterians, Orthodox Presbyterians were part of the fundamentalist party or Robert Speer was in the liberal camp is to engage in intellectual misrepresentation. To "flatten" the past and present of American Protestantism in this fashion means that all sorts of distinctions are ignored and, as noted above, all sorts of stories are left out of the larger narrative. The result is an inaccurate, distorted, and, well, duller account of the history of religion in twentieth-century America.

It should be acknowledged that while some of these essayists are more radical in their critique of bipolar analyses of American Protestantism and lean toward having it done away with altogether, other contributors are willing to accept a continued (albeit, in most cases, severely limited and appropriately nuanced) use of the two-party model. There is no "party line" in this regard. This does not alter the fact that virtually all of the contributors to this volume have lent their pens to the effort to get beyond the two-party paradigm, and to tell the whole Protestant story, in all of its complexity and subtleties.

Finally, we would be remiss if we did not affirm that, as the above paragraphs may suggest, our concerns here are not simply for historical and sociological accuracy. As we see it, the two-party paradigm not only has been a limited and distorted descriptor of American Protestant realities, but, in a sense, it may have (in self-fulfilling fashion) contributed to present tensions and polarizing tendencies within Protestantism. If twentieth-century Protestantism can be understood in less divisive and in more accurate and nuanced terms than those of the two-party system, then perhaps it will be easier for contemporary American Protestants themselves to come together in constructive new ways.

CHAPTER 1

Bipolar Protestantism: The Straight and Narrow Ways

DAVID EDWIN HARRELL, JR.

Asians harbor two major misconceptions about religion in America. First, they presume that the United States is a comprehensive, secularized den of iniquity. Much of the Asian image of America is based on reading novels and viewing American film and television. "Dallas," "Santa Barbara," and "MTV" have found their ways into middle-class living rooms from Colombo to Kathmandu. In that context, most Asians are surprised to hear that there is another, ostensibly more devout, side to American culture.

A second misconception has to do with the uniformity of American religion. Viewed from the Indian subcontinent, religion in American looks deceptively uncomplicated: the United States is a Christian nation. Compared to India's long heritage of religious rivalry between Hindu, Muslim, Sikh, Buddhist, Jain, Parsi, and Christian — groups that continue to exist as legal, political, and cultural enclaves in a truly multicultural society — American diversity seems trifling.

Often I have found myself explaining to Asian audiences that the term "Christian" has limited explanatory value in America. Of course, Indians know that Catholics and Protestants maintain separate schools and churches around the world, but the doctrinal differences seem sufficiently trivial, and Catholic-Protestant relationships sufficiently placid, to make even that schism second-rate in the context of the Hindu-Muslim-Sikh tensions that threaten the fabric of Indian society. But, as I have also explained to Asians, while Americans are several centuries removed from killing one another in the name of Christ on a large scale, they cling tenaciously to their God-given right to question one another's morality and sanity. Political and cultural confrontation in modern America make sense only when viewed within this context of religious diversity.

Of course, in these days of self-conscious multiculturalism, most academics know that American religion is not unipolar. We know that American Catholics, Protestants, and Jews still have distinguishing marks that seem unlikely to vanish within the next few years, and that religious diversity has become even more noticeable with the influx of Asian immigrants during the past two decades. More to the point in this discussion of bipolar models of Protestantism, it is commonly accepted among scholars of American religion that in the twentieth century Protestantism divided into two warring camps: modernists and fundamentalists, conservatives and liberals, mainstream and evangelical. To Asians, this fact is an unsettling complication, though one that seems to have parallels in their own society; to Americans, the bipolarization of Protestantism in the twentieth century in some ways simplified the sectarian chaos of earlier times.

From Denominational Diversity to Unipolar Protestantism

American Protestantism was not always portrayed as divided into two neat parties. Until less than a century ago, historical narratives about American religion chronicled mostly the histories of scores of competing denominations. The unique American religious settlement at the end of the revolution, which protected the freedom of individual conscience and separated church and state, was plausible only in a society of competing minority sects with no dominating church. Nineteenth-century American Protestantism drank deeply of democratic ideals, and flourished in an arena of sectarian conflict and debate.

In the nineteenth century competing Protestant denominations could and did unite in various causes in the face of serious common threats, most notably the perceived menace of Roman Catholic immigration and the related evil of demon rum. By the end of the century these alliances seemed to many to have established a virtual national religion. However, the nineteenth-century Protestant alliances, powerful as they were, hardly destroyed the denominational patchwork in the American countryside. Many groups, including Lutherans, Mormons, Adventists, Christian Scientists, Churches of Christ, and virtually all southern churches both white and African-American, were never a part of the WASP empire. Nonetheless, by the end of the nineteenth century a mighty alliance of older denominations had come to speak for American Protestantism, and, they believed, for America.

The First Articulation of the Bipolar Myth

This unipolar Protestant universe, conventional wisdom tells us, was shattered in the early twentieth century by the fundamentalist-modernist controversy, creating a bipolar American Protestantism. Despite the complexity of the theological debate within the churches in the early twentieth century, and the variety and inconclusiveness of the pragmatic denominational settlements negotiated between 1920 and 1960, by the end of the 1920s a bipolar myth was firmly entrenched in American historiography. It has obscured and distorted the history of American Protestantism for more than half a century.

How was such a simplistic notion born and how did it gain currency? In part, bipolar Protestantism was created by journalists and popularizers to clarify for their customers and peers the murky and confusing Protestant infighting of the early twentieth century. Of course, no one performed that task more eloquently or with greater relish than the elitist, proudly prejudiced, and wonderfully quotable H. L. Mencken. Mencken's descriptions of the bipolarization of Protestantism surpassed even his witty, entertaining, and equally ahistorical parodies of Puritanism. In 1926, he wrote:

> That Protestantism in this great Christian realm is down with a wasting disease must be obvious to every amateur of ghostly pathology. One half of it is moving, with slowly accelerating speed, in the direction of the Harlot of the Seven Hills: the other is sliding down into voodooism. The former carries the greater part of Protestant money with it; the latter carries the greater part of Protestant libido. What remains in the middle may be likened to a torso without either brains to think with or legs to dance — in other words, something that begins to be professionally attractive to the mortician. . . . There is no lack of life on the higher levels, where the more solvent Methodists and the like are gradually transmogrified into Episcopalians, and the Episcopalians shin up the ancient bastions of Holy Church, and there is no lack of life on the lower levels, where the rural Baptists, by the route of Fundamentalism, rapidly descend to the dogmas and practices of the Congo jungle. But in the middle there is desiccation and decay. Here is where Protestantism was once strongest. Here is the region of the plain and godly Americano, fond of

devotion but distrustful of every hint of orgy — the honest fellow who suffers dutifully on Sunday, pays his tithes, and hopes for a few kind words from the pastor when his time comes to die. Today, alas, he tends to absent himself from pious exercises, and the news goes about that there is something the matter with the churches, and the denominational papers bristle with schemes to set it right, and many up-and-coming pastors, tiring of preaching and parish work, get jobs as the executive secretaries of these schemes, and go about the country expounding them to the faithful.[1]

Mencken and his smart set companions were hardly enamored with highbrow Protestantism, but given the two options, modernism was the clear winner. "Viewed from a tree," Mencken confided, the emergence of a more genteel, liberal Protestantism meant that the "stock of nonsense in the world is sensibly diminished and the stock of beauty augmented." The fundamentalist option was sheer madness: "In all those parts of the Republic where Beelzebub is still real — for example, in the rural sections of the Middle West and everywhere in the South save a few walled towns — the evangelical sects plunge into an abyss of malignant imbecility, and declare a holy war upon every decency that civilized men cherish. . . . They constitute, perhaps, the most ignorant class of teachers ever set up to guide a presumably civilized people; they are even more ignorant than the county superintendents of schools."[2]

Journalists did not single-handedly create the myth of a bipolar Protestantism in the early twentieth century. Indeed, they got most of their ammunition from ambitious clerics on the left and right who coveted the attention of the press, their admiring Christian supporters, and their fellow Americans. Hundreds of preachers — educated and uneducated, enlightened and proudly obscurantist — postured and jockeyed for position, offering their services as the voice of American Protestantism. Spokespersons on both the left and the right posed strikingly similar options: agree with me or go to hell. There were two straight and narrow ways.

Much was at stake in this battle for Protestantism. First, of course, was souls, but, incidentally, there were also churches, jobs, bureaucracies, money, power, and prestige. And the fundamental question (at least as fundamental as some of "the fundamentals") was: Who speaks for that great body of God-fearing Americans who occasionally visit the tens of

1. H. L. Mencken, ed., *A Mencken Chrestomathy* (New York: Alfred A. Knopf, 1978), 76-77.
2. Ibid., 78-79.

thousands of Protestant churches gracing the countryside? Harry Emerson Fosdick or Billy Sunday, Shailer Mathews or Bob Jones? A question of weighty political and social import. Even the underdogs in the conflict, as historian R. Laurence Moore has pointed out, had much to gain on earth as well as in heaven by fighting a valiant rearguard action. At different times, actors on both sides played the role of prophet and savior of the remnant.[3]

The bipolar war within American Protestantism, declared by religious leaders and described by the press, has been chronicled from beginning to end by a generation of social scientists. In the years after the Scopes trial in 1925, most observers agreed that fundamentalism had been routed, hopelessly embarrassed, and discredited. Asked his assessment of William Jennings Bryan after the Scopes trial, Mencken replied: "We killed the son-of-a-bitch."[4] By the 1950s, many believed that all that remained of Protestantism was a relatively benign and tolerant mainstream. In 1940, Roman Catholic Theodore Maynard wrote: "American Protestantism is now so doctrinally decayed as to be incapable of offering any serious opposition to the sharp sword of the Spirit. . . . Except for isolated 'fundamentalists' — and these are pretty thoroughly discredited and without intellectual leadership — Catholicism would cut through Protestantism as through so much butter."[5]

The False Unipolarity of Mid-Century Protestantism

In his 1955 book *Protestant, Catholic, Jew,* Will Herberg described a triumphant post–World War II Protestantism that had come to terms with its former enemies based on a shared ethical idealism and biblical theism. The booming, prosperous, mainstream denominations of the 1950s seemed to be indisputable evidence that Protestantism had become a powerful single-minded force in American society. Careful observers were aware that the centrist Protestantism of the 1950s contained serious divisions, but most made little of these differences.

Since 1960, historians and sociologists have routinely described a

3. R. Laurence Moore, "Insiders and Outsiders in American Historical Narrative and American History," *American Historical Review* 87 (1982): 405-7.

4. Quoted in William Manchester, *Disturber of the Peace* (New York: Harper & Brothers, 1950), 185.

5. Quoted in Thomas Clancy, "Fundamental Facts about Evangelicals," *America* 31 (May 1980): 454.

bipolar religious warfare in the early twentieth century that ended with the demise of fundamentalism. In 1978 a widely distributed text on religious history assured that "the defeats suffered by the Fundamentalists in the 1920s insured that few Protestants would ever again call themselves fundamentalists."[6] More recently, Robert Wuthnow argued that fundamentalism was pretty well spent by the 1950s. In *The Restructuring of American Religion*, Wuthnow wrote: "By the time World War II ended . . . fundamentalism had largely ceased to exist as an organized movement. . . . The organizational and cultural identity of fundamentalism had become largely that of an isolated fringe group comprised of separatist eccentrics."[7] In 1993, based on a statistical survey entitled *One Nation Under God, Newsweek* magazine reported that there are nearly twice as many Scientologists in the United States as the 27,000 "self-styled fundamentalists" discovered in the survey.[8]

Obviously, such statements beg for a definition of the word "fundamentalist." It is true that older fundamentalist organizations have been succeeded by a new generation of organizations, many of them regional and local rather than national. It is also true that fundamentalist is not as fashionable a word as it once was — and neither is modernist. Even so, how could an investigator come up with 27,000 "self-styled fundamentalists" without pretty seriously distorting the questions? I have attended congregations with the word "fundamentalist" on the marquee that claimed more than 27,000 members. In the 1980s, the hard-core fundamentalist paper, the *Sword of the Lord,* had a circulation of more than 100,000.

The idea of a one-party American Protestantism in the 1950s simply cannot account for what may well be the two most portentous Protestant movements in the United States in the second half of the century: the booming evangelical revival led by Billy Graham (who at least in the early 1950s had the blessings of those who still called themselves fundamentalists), and a less visible, but equally powerful Pentecostal healing revival that by 1960 had reshaped world Protestantism almost without notice. Most Pentecostals both in the 1950s and the 1990s would be reasonably comfortable with the "fundamentals," though they are not "self-styled fundamentalists."

6. *Student's Guide to the Long Search: A Study of Religions* (Dubuque, IA: Kendall/Hunt Publishing Company, 1978), 197.

7. Robert Wuthnow, *The Restructuring of American Religion: Society and Faith Since World War II* (Princeton: Princeton University Press, 1988), 137.

8. Kenneth L. Woodward, "The Rites of Americans," *Newsweek,* November 29, 1993, 81.

The New Bipolar Model

Not everyone believed that the Protestant struggle of the early twentieth century was quite so neatly concluded after the Scopes trial. Even Mencken doubted that the modernist victory was complete. In 1934, he warned: "Religion is sick, but it is by no means dead, and on some calamitous tomorrow it may enjoy something of a revival. . . . Let us remember that a man who casts off his hereditary articles of faith does not become thereby, at one stroke, a scientist comparable to Darwin or Huxley."[9] In a series of popular articles in the 1950s Henry Van Dusen noted the vitality of conservative Christianity, and *Life* and *Look* published occasional stories about Graham and Oral Roberts. But not until the 1970s did the notion of a two-party Protestantism once again draw public attention. By that time, the clues had begun to mount: the curious faith of Jimmy Carter, the rise of the televangelists, the appearance of the Moral Majority and the New Religious Right, and the spectacle of seemingly rational people in respectable churches raising their hands and whispering "hallelujah."

Where did these sons of Bible thumpers come from? American Protestantism seemed headed once again for a bipolar holy war. Was this a new war? If fundamentalism was dead at mid-century, the events of the 1970s heralded the emergence of a new bipolarity. Much that has been written in recent years by sociologists has set out to explain the origins and distinctiveness of this new bipolar Protestantism. Robert Wuthnow and James Davison Hunter have thus described a Protestantism newly divided into two parties delineated by shared articles of faith and cultural values.[10] These two horizontal Protestant communities have replaced or diminished historic denominational distinctives, leaving behind a conservative-liberal bipolarization. This re-bipolarization of Protestantism is highlighted by the cooperation among conservatives and among liberals in the advocacy of social and political objectives. Thus, Protestants are once again left with two choices. All of this sounds and looks like the religious/cultural dichotomy of the 1920s, but, we are told, the modern confrontation is an unrelated phenomenon.

9. Mayo DuBasky, *The Gist of Mencken* (Metuchen, NJ: The Scarecrow Press, 1990), 196.

10. Wuthnow, *The Restructuring of American Religion;* James Davison Hunter, *Culture Wars: The Struggle to Define America* (New York: Basic Books, 1991).

DAVID EDWIN HARRELL, JR.

The Distortions of Bipolar Models

Let me suggest three broad reasons why both old and new bipolar models distort the history of American Protestantism. My first two objections grow out of my own research and writing, the third relies more on the writings of such scholars as William Trollinger, Virginia Brereton, Joel Carpenter, Grant Wacker, George Marsden, Edith Blumhofer, Richard Hughes, Richard Pierard, Douglas Frank, Darryl Hart, Randall Balmer, and others.

First, I believe that it is still premature to write the hundreds of obituaries necessary to properly bury denominationalism in a bipolar Protestant world. Denominations die hard. It is true that many of the more civilized Protestant churches contain fewer and fewer members who would die in defense of episcopal or presbyterian forms of church government, or even know what the words mean. It is also true that many of the mainstream denominations are beset by internal squabbles caused by an increasing social heterogeneity, making them, as Wuthnow points out, "resemble more closely the cultural diversity in the society at large."[11] Declining memberships certainly imply that denominational affiliation has become less critical in defining the religious conscience of the members of those churches. Nonetheless, mainstream Protestant churches have shown considerable staying power in recent years.

These patterns of denominational attrition are hardly new. In every period of American history some denominations have grown in grace and favor with man and woman, becoming more culturally diverse with each decade of success. At the same time, they waned in distinctiveness and separatist zeal, and they sometimes united with other upwardly mobile denominations. In the first half of the twentieth century mainstream churches ranging from Congregationalists to Disciples of Christ found more and more in common and less and less that seriously divided them. In short, during these years denominationalism became less important to all of those for whom denominationalism seemed less important.

But millions of other Americans in the first half of the twentieth century still regarded their denomination as their religious family. They were Mormons, Adventists, members of Churches of Christ, Southern Baptists, Landmark Baptists, Primitive Baptists, Jehovah's Witnesses, Christian Scientists, Nazarenes, and Pentecostals — not to mention older outsiders such as Amish, Mennonites, Hutterites, and Free Will Baptists. If the names "Episcopal" and "Presbyterian" came to tell less and less

---

11. Wuthnow, *Restructuring*, 85.

about the beliefs and identities of the people who wore those titles, every word in the name Fire-Baptized Pentecostal Holiness Church was laden with theological import. Millions of American Protestants continued to live their religious lives within the framework of tight-knit denominational boundaries, believing the denominational creeds and ordering their daily lives in tune with denominational calendars.

Is it possible that the dynamic processes of sect formation in the twentieth century have somehow escaped the attention of the framers of bipolar theories? Has anyone noticed the rising independent mega-churches in every American city wearing such names as Abundant Life Tabernacle, Word of Life Assembly, or Faith Assembly? In 1993, the *New York Times* reported that 60,000 Hispanic Americans each year left the Roman Catholic Church to join new evangelical groups, an exodus that the *Times* blandly and correctly described: "As one church declines, others reap success."[12] Thousands of new churches and Protestant denominations are covering the earth; they glory in their distinctive theologies and they are forming worldwide denominational fellowships. They would be astonished to learn that they must either be fundamentalists or liberals. Outside of the United States, where the real Protestant action is, in Latin America, Africa, and Asia, in Paul Yongii Cho's Yoido Full Gospel Church in Seoul and Brother D. S. Dinakarian's booming healing ministry in Madras, churches are bulging and the religious demography is visibly changing week by week. In that world, indigenous church leaders are organizing vibrant new Protestant families that know nothing of bipolar models. And much of what they are doing is modeled on the American experience in the twentieth century.

Second, it is simplistic to say that cultural issues in the twentieth century have created unique parachurch and interdenominational pressure groups that transcend denominations and thus produce a bipolar Protestantism. It is true, of course, that conservative and liberal Protestant coalitions in the twentieth century have often generated wide support across denominational lines. Thus, the anti-evolution campaign (or, more properly, the battle for control of the public schools) rallied millions of Protestants in common cause in the early twentieth century, just as abortion, school prayer, and family issues have become foci for alliances in the late twentieth century.

However, a number of factors complicate the story of cultural bipolarization in early twentieth-century Protestantism. First, most reli-

---

12. Roberto Suro, "Switch by Hispanic Catholics Changes Face of U.S. Religion," *New York Times* (14 May 1989): 1, 14.

gious-cultural alliances were neither complete nor stable. Real Protestant outsiders, such as the Churches of Christ and many Pentecostals, sympathized with the cultural causes supported by other conservatives, but rarely supported parachurch organizations; real outsiders often considered all social reforms worldly and irrelevant. Often, conservative Protestant denominations, such as the conservative Christian Church, "supported fundamentalism," according to Kevin Kragenbrink, but their allegiance was "qualified and cautious."[13]

Furthermore, cultural tensions in the first half of the twentieth century forged not one conservative alliance but a series of shifting coalitions. Well into the 1950s anti-Catholicism found support across a broad front of American Protestants. The leadership of the prohibition movement came mostly from mainstream churches, not from fundamentalists, and its success depended on support from educated, middle-class church members. On the other hand, the leaders of the anti-evolution campaign were mostly fundamentalists who received, at best, token and grudging support from more sophisticated evangelicals.

Quite clearly, cultural causes have repeatedly united segments of American Protestantism. Sometimes, denominational animosities were momentarily subordinated in view of the supreme importance of a social crusade. Differences within denominations on these crucial issues might even seem more important than differences between them.

None of this is new. Modern advocates of a bipolar interpretation of Protestantism acknowledge that there have been past instances when "special interest groups have arisen for the express purpose of combating, restraining, or promoting certain types of government action."[14] But the present polarization, they insist, is different. Pressure groups have "grown to such large proportions that they now appear to cast their imprint heavily on the character of American religion more generally."[15] Furthermore, the modern cultural war is disconnected and qualitatively different from earlier cultural divisions in Protestantism, separated from the fundamentalist-modernist clash of the early twentieth century by the collapse of fundamentalism and the period of Protestant unity in the 1950s. The plethora of evangelical special interest groups that appeared in the 1950s

---

13. Kevin R. Kragenbrink, "Cooperation with Compromise: Fundamentalism among the Disciples of Christ, 1920-1928" (unpublished paper in possession of the author), 25.

14. Wuthnow, *Restructuring*, 114.

15. Wuthnow, *Restructuring*, 107.

were nothing more than "a cluster of loosely integrated special purpose groups devoted to the cause of evangelism."[16] The post-1970s clashes were different, James Davison Hunter writes, because "the last decades of the twentieth century constitute . . . a time of societal change and transition."[17]

Is it plausible to believe that the current cultural-religious-political coalitions are different in kind from the abolition, nativist, prohibition, anti-evolution, and anticommunist crusades of the past? It is difficult to take seriously a theory that divorces the evangelical revival of the 1950s from the moral imperative to save the American way of life from communism. Ideological issues have always cut across institutional lines in American history, and I presume that "societal change and transition" have contributed to all of the religious and political tensions of the twentieth century, and of every previous century.

Furthermore, in the late twentieth century, as in the first half of the century, there are not two neat religious/cultural alliances in America. Rather, there are a number of tenuous and shifting coalitions. The pro-life and creationist movements do not appeal to the same clienteles. Jerry Falwell's Moral Majority received substantial contributions from four communities in the early 1980s: fundamentalists, Roman Catholics, Orthodox Jews, and Mormons. But that coalition was neither stable nor lasting. The level of cooperation was always highly circumscribed (for instance, they never prayed together in public). Each of those communities remains a distinctive religious presence in modern America with its own religious agenda and political peculiarities. Furthermore, Jerry Falwell and Pat Robertson notwithstanding, in the 1980s many conservative Protestant religious groups (perhaps a majority) remained either politically passive or apolitical, including most of the leading television ministries.

One final caveat about the modern bipolar culture wars. We are told that there is a new ferocity and intensity about the modern debate; it is marked by a penchant for trivializing the issues and caricaturing the opposition. Anyone who believes that rhetorical courtesy and theological seriousness typified popular political and religious debate in the nineteenth century has simply not read the papers. Misrepresentation, calumny, oversimplification, and insider-outsider rhetoric are persistent themes in American political and religious debate. Does anyone seriously believe that the debate over abortion is more bellicose or lacking in civility

16. Wuthnow, *Restructuring,* 177.
17. Hunter, *Culture Wars,* 62.

than the clash over slavery, or more given to caricature than the popular literature circulated by prohibitionist and anti-Catholic organizations?

Thirdly, and finally, reducing the variegated theological and cultural diversity in American Protestantism to two poles simply distorts history beyond recognition. As R. Laurence Moore has pointed out, such portrayals cause "a good chunk of the American population to disappear."[18] All religious historians are tempted to try to locate denominations on a theological and cultural continuum, but even denominations defy such classifications. Oral Roberts, always a keen observer of what was going on under his tent, noticed in the late 1950s that his healing line included nearly as many Methodists as Pentecostals, and sandwiched between them was a smattering of Baptists, Catholics, and other nonpolarized Christians. All of which set him thinking about becoming a Methodist and led him to quite correctly anticipate the worldwide charismatic explosion a decade before it happened.

The majority of American Protestants in the first half of the twentieth century were neither fundamentalists nor modernists. Most Protestants, like most Americans, struggled to find a balance between modern realities and inherited beliefs. Some lived lives of faith within churches that had presumably been captured by their adversaries; many were members of denominations that to a remarkable degree ignored the heated fundamentalist-modernist rhetoric.

Of course, poles do appear from time to time in American Protestantism, and in Southern Baptist and other churches. Because of its history of intellectual independence and lack of denominational authority, the Disciples of Christ movement furnishes an admirable model for churches intent on schism. R. Laurence Moore suggested a few years ago that the Disciples of Christ and Churches of Christ "may be the most seriously overlooked and underestimated groups in the standard surveys of American religious history" — a fact I had suspected based on the sale of my books.[19] Within the Disciples of Christ movement schisms have historically revolved not around two poles, but around three or more. As theological, sectional, and cultural tensions increased in the first half of the twentieth century, the Disciples clustered around conservative, moderate, and liberal poles to form the Churches of Christ, the Independent Christian Church, and the Christian Church (Disciples of Christ). These divisions were polar, but they were not neat. Each of the three separated wings was

18. Moore, "Insiders and Outsiders," 407.
19. Moore, "Insiders and Outsiders," 420.

itself a continuum, and people and churches crossed the boundaries between the polar churches easily and regularly.

New Extensions of the Two-Party Model

The bipolar model has gained new influence because it has lately taken on global significance. Diana L. Eck, professor of comparative religion at Harvard, recently summarized the bipolar model for world religion: "Are we then at the beginning of a new era of religious extremism, chauvinism, and fundamentalism, or one of religious pluralism based on the recognition of interdependence and the necessity of interreligious cooperation? While the georeligious world today is too complex to assert that either of these two powerful currents predominates, one can safely say that fundamentalism and pluralism pose the two challenges that people of all religious traditions face."[20]

Eck's pluralism is not precisely the modernism of the early twentieth century; it sometimes sounds like nothing more than an appeal for religious tolerance and separation of church and state. On the other hand, Eck's pluralism is pretty hegemonic itself, the sole rational and sane religious answer for the twentieth century. Fundamentalism, on the other hand, remains pretty much where Mencken left it. It is easy to separate the good guys from the bad guys in Eck's bipolar world: "Fundamentalists reaffirm the exclusive certainties of their own traditions, with a heightened sense of the boundaries of belonging that separate 'us' from 'them.' Pluralists, without giving up the distinctiveness of their own tradition, engage the other in the mutual education and, potentially, the mutual transformation of dialogue. To the fundamentalist, the borders of religious certainty are tightly guarded; to the pluralist, the borders are the good fences where one meets the neighbor. To many fundamentalists, secularism, seen as the denial of religious claims, is the enemy; to pluralists, secularism, seen as the separation of government from the domination of a single religion, is the essential concomitant of religious diversity and the protection of religious freedom."[21]

So, the battle is rejoined between the two Protestant armies of the Lord in America and, indeed, between similar factions all over the world.

20. Diana L. Eck, "In the Name of Religions," *Wilson Quarterly* 17 (Autumn 1993): 92.

21. Ibid.

Not everyone is as clear as Eck in separating the sheep and the goats, but all bipolar theorists offer a simple either/or religious choice — my way and their way. James Davison Hunter calls for a "principled pluralism and a principled toleration," from both parties, so that those who "disagree with each other on principle, do not kill each other over these differences, do not desecrate what the other holds sublime, and do not eschew principled discourse with the other."[22] In asking American Protestants not to kill one another, Hunter seems to be on safe ground; killing in the name of religion has probably reached a low ebb in American history. His other two pleas, for mutual respect and principled discourse, highly commendable to be sure, have little to do with the American past. Not only has American Protestantism never been in two camps, but the non-existent two camps have never behaved like sanitized, sanctified Christians in dealing with one another.

Bipolar thinking serves a number of different interests in modern America. Conservative evangelicals and pluralists use the dualism to serve their purposes as did fundamentalists and modernists. Bipolar models make the world easier to explain to the uninformed, and they seem to point toward a better future so long as your party is the final victor.

The directors of the Re-Forming the Center project have posed a question: "Does 'two-party' language retain some value when it comes to understanding American Protestantism, or should we abandon it completely for a different model of understanding?" Bipolar language describes those who use it; it reveals much about the religious and academic communities who find it a believable description of the past. But it is a history, as R. Laurence Moore points out, "that many Americans cannot recognize as their own."[23] Much of American history will remain buried, Moore argues, hidden by labels like "fringe" and "marginal," until we "stop assessing these contests solely for their impact on sociopolitical conflicts affecting American egalitarian principles." Many religious movements in America have been neither "nice" nor composed of "egalitarian-minded people,"[24] but they have been as American as apple pie. Over-simplifying them out of existence can only open the door for lots of future surprises.

In these postmodern times when historians are constantly reminded of a truth that I presume we all understood — that all historical and social

---

22. Hunter, *Culture Wars*, 325.
23. Moore, "Insiders and Outsiders," 407.
24. Moore, "Insiders and Outsiders," 411.

science constructs are products of the cultural imaginations of the writers — we are bound to inquire about the hegemonic interests that shape the American Protestant experience into two choices. Bipolar models generally point toward unipolar solutions. Fundamentalism vanished from the American historical narrative, Moore argues, because historians who were "proponents of secularization theory" judged fundamentalism not to be "helpful to a rational political order. Given all of the other troubles that stood in the way of the political enlightenment of Americans, historians wanted to write Americans beyond their religious backwardness as quickly as possible."[25] So, those who write the stories decide who won and who lost, and who ought to win and who ought to lose, and most American Protestants think they are reading someone else's history.

The Reality of Multiple Untidy Categories

All descriptions of the past are flawed and have limited explanatory value, but I believe that there is much to be gained by paying more attention to the historic and continuing diversity within American Protestantism, looking honestly at the irregularities and complexities. American intellectuals have been bushwhacked repeatedly in the twentieth century by the alleged rebirth of a conservative Protestantism that has been declared dead, buried, and forgotten. Bipolar duels to the death simply do not predict the future very well.

Let me return to an Indian perspective for a final remark about the two-party view. I believe that such thinking conceals the central contribution that the American religious experience has to offer to a troubled religious world. Americans learned to live together not in a unipolar or bipolar religious society, but in a nation filled with religious competition, debate, and dissent, even as it was filled with political and social dissent. American society has always accommodated religious insiders and outsiders; it not only tolerates proselyting, it thrives on it; freedom of religious speech is our most cherished icon, and as a result American Protestantism constantly re-democratizes itself. The American experiment in religious liberty is not neat, it is often not pretty, it is sometimes zany and outrageous, but (at least for us) it works. This is how Protestantism makes its way through American history, not in a series of bipolar wars that end in unconditional surrender. It is this model of earnest debate, pungent but

25. Moore, "Insiders and Outsiders," 406.

bloodless contention, and political compromise that may offer the most promise for India and other tense religious societies in Asia and Africa. They are no more likely than Americans to buy into a bipolarity that forces them to choose between wild-eyed fanaticism and the latest formula devised in western comparative religion classes.

Most American Protestants neither wish to be nor can be compartmentalized into two, or three, or four neat categories. I agree with Randall Balmer that what is "so remarkable about the history of American Protestantism in the twentieth century is that, despite all of the institutional contortions and the ebb and flow of ideology, the center has held."[26] So it has. Extremists have warned incessantly that the broad middle highway leads straight to hell, and they divert a part of the traffic from time to time into one of the narrow ways on the left and right. But it takes serious scholars to make the expansive middle-of-the-road disappear.

---

26. Randall Balmer, "Culture Wars: Views from the Ivory Tower," *Evangelical Studies Bulletin* 10 (Spring 1993): 2.

CHAPTER 2

America's Culture Wars
in Cross-cultural Perspective[1]

N. J. DEMERATH, III

"It was after the catastrophe, when they shot the president and machine-gunned the Congress and the army declared a state of emergency. They blamed it on the Islamic fanatics, at the time. Keep calm, they said on television. Everything is under control. I was stunned. Everyone was, I know that. It was hard to believe. The entire government, gone like that. How did they get in, how did it happen?

That was when they suspended the Constitution. They said it would be temporary. There wasn't even any rioting in the streets. People stayed home at night, watching television, looking for some direction. There wasn't even an enemy you could put your finger on."

Margaret Atwood, *The Handmaid's Tale*[2]

Just as the present is often condemned to repeat the past, so social analysis frequently is pressed in the molds of fiction — our interpretations of life imitate art. Margaret Atwood's recent nightmarish novel, *The Handmaid's Tale*, depicts life in the United States after the nation has been taken over

---

1. A slightly different version of this essay appears in Rhys H. Williams, ed., *Culture Wars in American Politics: Critical Reviews of a Popular Myth* (Hawthorne, NY: Aldine De Gruyter, 1998).
2. Margaret Atwood, *The Handmaid's Tale* (New York: Fawcett Crest, 1985), 225.

31

by right-wing religious fanatics, and the "culture war" she portrays in her fiction is now reflected with increasing frequency in sociological literature. Just the titles of two recent books by James Davison Hunter, *Culture Wars* and *Before the Shooting Begins*,[3] carry ominous connotations of a looming pitched battle of a sort not seen in this country for almost a century and a half. In pointing toward a bloody contest between liberals and conservatives, progressives and the orthodox , modernists and fundamentalists, the rhetoric suggests that Americans who have not yet chosen sides will have to soon. And some would say that this is no longer a war of mere words or government policy options, since the violence has already begun.

But I demur. Call me Thomas Jefferson, Yankee Doodle, or Richard J. Daley, but what some pundits now see as cultural warfare, I see as cultural democracy at work. It is true that cultural discord over abortion, school prayer, family and gender roles, and racial and ethnic status have led to cultural hostilities, violence, and even murders, as recent events in Pensacola, Boston, and Oklahoma City attest. But while a minuscule minority has seized the right to bear both arms and witness, all of this falls short of what I would define as a true culture war: namely, *concerted violence over governmental legitimacy and control in the pursuit of non-economic interests*.

Of course, every definition is an invitation to quibble, and this one is no exception. To clarify it further, I mean by "concerted violence" a strategic use of collective force on a large scale as opposed to aberrant actions that are more individualized and sporadic; neither isolated murders of abortionists nor a consensually condemned militia-type bombing qualifies. My concern with "governmental legitimacy and control" is intended to distinguish conflicts where real power is at stake from other forms of violent confrontations, however tragic. Finally, I specify "noneconomic interests" to distinguish culture wars from the more conventional forms of class conflict, though in truth there are few "pure" forms of social conflict.

Like some Horatio at the bridge to semantic inflation, I feel impelled to insist that if this definition of a culture war is accepted, the United States hardly qualifies. Recent research by Yonghe Yang makes the point internally on the basis of a careful analysis of recent General Social Surveys from the National Opinion Research Center.[4] American opinions on flash

---

3. James Davison Hunter, *Culture Wars: The Struggle to Define America* (New York: Basic Books, 1991) and *Before the Shooting Begins* (New York: Free Press, 1994).
4. Yonghe Yang, "The Structure and Dynamics of Ideological Pluralism in American Religion," Unpublished Ph.D. Dissertation, University of Massachusetts, 1996. See

point issues are not neatly divided in culture war fashion. But the argument against the American culture war thesis can also be made on the basis of external, comparative evidence. Applying the phrase "culture war" to the United States makes a mockery of the situations that prevail in numerous other countries where those criteria are fulfilled all too well. And these examples are not hard to find. For example, the same issue of *USA Today* which reported 170 deaths in the Oklahoma City bombing also reported side by side on the front page the discovery of some 2,000 bodies in a mass grave in Rwanda. The Oklahoma bombing is an exceptional event in America; the discovery of a mass grave in Rwanda is an all too frequent occurrence. One of these two nations is involved in a culture war; the other clearly is not.

A 1993 United Nations Report lists some thirty-two ethnic and religious civil wars, each involving more than 1,000 deaths in 1989-1990 alone. And Charles Tilly has reviewed a spate of literature on "state-incited violence" (including both state-sponsored and state-seeking violence) that would fairly describe the twentieth century as "the most virulently violent ten decades in human history."[5]

As part of my current comparative research on religion, politics, and the state,[6] I have recently visited some fourteen countries around the globe, including a number where cultural warfare has become a way of life. Space constraints force me to set aside some of the more obvious cases (e.g., China, Egypt, Indonesia, and Turkey) and dramatically truncate my discussion of the other examples. However, brief personal reports from the cultural trenches of Northern Ireland, Guatemala, Israel, and India are sufficient to paint an impressionistic landscape of the global culture war scene. What we find in these countries is cultural conflict that is both much more intense than anything in America and, even in the most extreme

also Yonghe Yang and N. J. Demerath, III, "What American Culture War? A View from the Trenches As Opposed to the Command Posts and the Press Corp," in Rhys H. Williams, ed., *Cultural Wars in American Politics* (Hawthorne, NY: Aldine De Gruyter, 1997).

5. United Nations Department of Economic and Social Development, *Report on the World Situation, 1993* (New York: United Nations, 1993); Charles Tilly, "State-Incited Violence, 1900-1999," New School for Social Research Working Paper Series, No. 177, 1993, 1. See also: Ruth Leger Sivard, *World Military and Social Expenditures, 1991* (Washington: World Priorities Press, 1991); Ted Robert Gurr, *Minorities at Risk: A Global View of Ethnopolitical Conflicts* (Washington: U.S. Institute of Peace Press, 1993).

6. N. J. Demerath, III, "The Moth and the Flame: Religion and Politics in Comparative Blur," *Sociology of Religion* 55 (March 1994): 105-17.

cases, more complicated than any two-party religious model can explain. Against this international comparative backdrop, I will develop five conceptual distinctions in the second half of this essay that help to explain the differences between those countries where culture warfare is both deep-seated and routine, and those countries, like our own, where such conflict is less common and less extreme.

Four International Case Studies

Northern Ireland

If there was any country in my travels where I should have been able to pass for a native, it was Northern Ireland. After all, my own religious legacy is part Protestant and part Catholic, and there is certainly no dearth of men in Ireland who look just like me — in their fifties with round faces, bifocals, and rapidly receding white hair. But even in Belfast in the fall of 1993, I was spotted as a stranger and accorded liberties that no local enjoyed — for example, the ability to walk naively from the Falls Road (Catholic) to the Donegal Road (Protestant) neighborhoods. And when the British commandos came down the street in full battle regalia, darting from doorway to doorway, it was not unusual for one to look up at me, smile, and say cheerily, "Good Morning, Suh." There was a culture war going on here, but it was clear to all that I was not one of the players in that conflict.

Surely Northern Ireland is a country where religion is a prime mover. This was the case in the past; today the religious determinant may be becoming even more primary as Catholics have begun to catch up with Protestants in economic terms, a fact which is mitigating the effect of class factors that previously complicated the picture. And yet, many of my informants cautioned me not to overplay the religious dimension. True, they said, there are small groups of religious zealots clustered around centers such as Ian Paisley's Martyr's Memorial "Presbyterian" Church, but old-line theological differences have lost much of their salience after some three hundred years of conflict. Most people are now more "culturally" Protestant or Catholic than they are "religiously" so identified. By now most of the citizenry is also weary of a war that has, if one extrapolates the numbers over the past twenty years, cost more lives in Northern Ireland than the Vietnam War did for the United States. Nonetheless, religion remains a basic fault line in this society, and it continues to fuel a violent dispute that seems rightly labeled a culture war.

And yet when I returned from Northern Ireland in October 1993, I brought with me cheerier news than most of my colleagues were used to hearing. The reason is demographic. At the time of partition in 1921, Catholics constituted roughly one quarter of the Northern Irish population; Catholics are now closing fast on the majority they would need for a vote to leave Great Britain for the somewhat reluctant embrace of the Irish Republic — and given the state of the Northern Irish economy, a dependent affiliation with the Irish Republic appears necessary if the connection to Great Britain is severed. The change is only partly and decliningly a matter of differential fertility. Many Protestants have seen the political writing on the wall and are leaving for England and the United States. Indeed, the Protestants remaining in Northern Ireland resemble the Catholics remaining in South Boston: both are on the losing side of a process of social transformation, and, in the time-honored tradition of losers everywhere, they tend to see violence as one of their few remaining options. The fact that most of the recent deaths in this conflict have been Catholic rather than Protestant may be a perverse harbinger of better times to come. The peace agreement of 1998 has opened the possibility of an end to the violence. Clearly many citizens of Northern Ireland are tired of the bloodshed. In culture wars, however, one should never assume too quickly that guarantees of peace are permanent.

Guatemala

Here "passing" was out of the question for me. But so would it have been for the alabaster Virgin Mary looking down in stunning whiteness from her wall pedestal high above the dark-skinned women in their brightly woven "huipiles" who had come to attend a memorial mass in honor of a local agrarian reform counsellor killed by the military the previous year. Indeed, because of the military's killing of one priest and threats against others in the early 1980s, this Quiche parish had been formally closed for several years.

Estimates of the number of war deaths in Guatemala over the past twenty-five years range from 20,000 to 100,000, with uncounted others missing or in exile. Much of this conflict is undeniably economic as part of Latin America's continuing battle over land, agricultural control, and capitalist profiteering. But the struggle also has sharp cultural edges that reflect the ethnic, linguistic, and religious differences sketched in such detail by Guatemala's 1992 Nobel laureate, Rigoberta Menchu.[7] Religion in Guatemala is no longer a single Catholic monolith but rather a series of conflicting movements, often at each others' throats as well as souls.

Although the Catholic Church was officially disestablished in 1871, it took more than one hundred years to mount an effective challenge to its place at the head of the state table. The challenge finally came from two directions. First, in Guatemala as throughout Latin America, various forms of "evangelical" (mostly Pentecostal) Protestantism are surging both among the affluent and the working class. Second, again in keeping with other countries, there is currently in process a resurgence of traditional Mayan religion, culture, and identity. This is especially strong among the "indigenos" in the rural countryside and mountains to the north, including members of the anti-government guerilla movement still active there.

All of this has produced kaleidoscopic changes. The guerilla movement now has a traditional cultural agenda to complement its radical thrusts on behalf of economic rights, gender equity, and relief from political terror. Since General Rios Montt's regime of the early 1970s, the government and the military have become increasingly Protestant, bringing Latin America's first elected Protestant chief of state, Jorge Serrano, to office in 1990. Meanwhile, Guatemala's Catholic Church, led by arch-reactionary archbishops until late in the 1980s, has begun to move to the left. Recently its criticism of the government and its human rights abuses have come to resemble the Liberation Theology that began in Brazil thirty years ago. And many small-town Catholic parishes in Guatemala have become surprisingly syncretic as their services reflect both Mayan and Pentecostal Protestant elements, including a greater role for women. There may be good news in the peace accords negotiated between the government and the guerilla movement in late 1996. But once again, nothing is certain, as the recent assassination of Bishop Gerari indicates.

Israel

Here perhaps the name alone is so evocative that I need scarcely elaborate. Israel's culture conflicts have even perhaps been accorded more American media time than our own, so we are all eyewitnesses of a sort to this conflict. Recent events have been somewhat encouraging. Despite the

7. Rigoberta Menchu, *I, Rigoberta Menchu* (London: Verso Publishers, 1983).

efforts of obstructionist groups on both sides, the Israeli-Palestinian peace agreements were successfully concluded and a quasi-independent Palestinian territory has been set up. What's more, Israel's borders with Egypt and Jordan, if not yet with Syria, appear more secure. New tensions are in evidence with the Netanyahu government that is now in charge, but guarded optimism may still be appropriate.

Here as elsewhere, however, deaths and casualties due to this conflict have been enormous and elude precise counts. Good data are in scarce supply concerning the number of thousands of "internal" deaths related to the Arab-Israeli conflict over the country's near half-century of formal existence (and the same lack of precision holds true for the "external" casualties produced by the region's several Arab-Israeli wars). There are even fluctuating figures for the number of deaths that have occurred just in the past several years since the activation of Hamas and the Oslo accord.

But in addition to the obvious culture war of long standing, there are several other less obvious culture battles only now developing. Once Israel and the Palestinians settle their respective borders for good, their internal conflicts will be just beginning. These will not only continue to pit Jew against Muslim, but Jew against Jew and Muslim against Muslim, as Israel begins again to shape itself as a state. Having postponed a formal Constitution in 1948, Israel has operated in the interim with a half-dozen "Basic Laws" on important issues. But as circumstances change, so may the laws themselves.

In all of this, religion is a deceptive factor. Among Muslims, the continuing dispute between Hamas and the PLO represents an internal power struggle that is only partly a function of their relative religious zealotry. And to say that Israel is a Zionist state is not necessarily to say that it is a Jewish state. Many members of the most passionately pro-Zionist movement, the Gush Emunim, are themselves secular. On the other hand, the most fervently religious, ultra-orthodox Jewish group, the Haredim of the Mia Sharim, oppose the very notion of the Israeli state; given the state's support for their educational and family systems, they are often perceived as hypocritical in their efforts to avoid military duty and other forms of state service.

Since the Haredim and Israeli Arabs each account for roughly eighteen percent of the Israeli population, it is difficult to know which group may be the greater instigator of cultural warfare within the state of Israel in the future. Insofar as Israel proclaims its civil religion to be Jewish, it faces obvious problems from within the growing Muslim ranks; to the extent that it opts for a more secular self-conception, as many would like, it would face a wholly different kind of opposition. It might be preferable for Israel to engage in battles on both fronts at once, since at least a tri-cornered conflict would head off the escalation of a fully polarized war.

India

As one last example of cultural warfare, we turn to India. Of course, the partition of India and creation of Pakistan in 1948 was one of the most tragic and grotesque moments in world history, with estimates of 250,000 to 500,000 deaths in that episode alone. However, for some thirty years following independence India was generally successful in avoiding the culture wars threatened by its uneasy pluralism. In large part, this was due to its religiously neutral constitution. But beginning in the early 1980s, the secularity of Indian politics and statecraft began to give way. As too many political moths got too close to the religious flames — and vice versa — official religious neutrality was caught in surging communal strife. Cultural violence broke out in Kashmir between Hindus and Muslims, in the Sikh mobilization within the Punjab, among Tamil nationalists in Southeastern India, and in many other troubled areas across the nation.

As one case in point, consider the recent episode involving contested sacred land claimed both by Hindus and by Muslims in the north-central city of Ayodyah. Here the very site that a Moslem mosque has occupied for some 400 years is also revered by Hindus as the putative birthplace of the mythical God-like figure, Rama. The competing claims are not new, and actual legal disputes date back to the 1860s. The mosque had been closed for years as a way of forestalling the dispute and quelling the violence associated with it. However, in the late 1980s this controversial Muslim mosque was re-opened, and it was here that tensions so escalated over the succeeding five years that in December 1992, at an Ayodyah rally of the Hindu right-wing Bharatiya Janata Party (BJP), thousands broke away and razed the mosque entirely. Yet another round of violence ensued, especially across the north of India and most particularly in Bombay. (These internal tensions are sure to be exacerbated as a result of the nuclear weapons detonated earlier this year by the new BJP government in India and, in response, by Pakistan.)

Who is really to blame? It may surprise you to learn that in the eyes of a number of prominent Indian intellectuals these days, we — or at least, the intellectual legacy represented by Western social science — are to blame.[8] The argument goes this way: India would never have secularized except under the influence of men like Gandhi, Ambedkar, and Nehru, all of whom were originally influenced by Western scholars and political figures who were themselves largely secular. Once the Indian state became secular, it really became both anti-religious and anti-Hindu. Hence, the only way for Hinduism to survive was by taking extreme action. These people argue that since India is eighty-five percent Hindu, a Hindu government would be not only well deserved but the only way to end the culture war now raging. Other Indians, of course, are skeptical of this broad line of reasoning (and I tend to agree with them). They suggest that a truly secular government, not a religiously Hindu one, would most likely provide the only "salvation" for a culture that is both as deeply religious and as religiously pluralistic as India.

Five Distinctions Pertinent to Culture Wars

Embedded in the four cases I have sketched are a number of reasons why many other countries have experienced full-fledged culture wars, but the United States has not. These reasons pivot around five critical distinctions:

1. Civil Religion vs. the Religion of the Civil

The concept of "civil religion" as a nationally binding religious common denominator has been a major preoccupation of American sociologists of religion at least since Robert Bellah's 1967 article in *Daedalus*.[9] The theory assumes a relatively homogenous society in which a shared commitment emerges from an underlying consensus. Some recent accounts suggest that America may now be developing two conflicting civil religions[10] (though one might wonder if the phrase "two civil religions" isn't an oxymoron if national unity is a prime criterion of civil religion itself). If I thought that the cohesion of American society depended upon some kind of civil reli-

8. See Ashish Nandy, "The Politics of Secularism and the Recovery of Religious Tolerance," in Veena Das, ed., *Mirrors of Violence* (Delhi: Oxford University Press, 1990).
    9. Robert Bellah, "Civil Religion in America," *Daedalus* 26 (1967): 1-21. See also N. J. Demerath, III and Rhys H. Williams, "Civil Religion in an Uncivil Society," *Annals* 480 (1987): 154-66.
    10. See Robert Wuthnow, *The Restructuring of American Religion* (Princeton: Princeton University Press, 1988); Hunter, *Culture Wars* and *Before the Shooting Begins*.

gious consensus, I would certainly agree that this country is increasingly in trouble. This is not just because of disputes between orthodox and progressive Christians, but also because of rapidly increasing diversity within the nation, including Jewish, Muslim, Hindu, and secular voices. But I am not at all convinced that it is necessary to have a civil religious consensus to maintain cultural peace within the nation.

Compared to most other countries, our religious discord remains generally civil and little involved with a struggle to overturn the current political system. Our civil religion, such as it is, is largely non-political, emerging from the bottom up. In many other countries, however, we find that those who have recently achieved power and are eager to solidify it often seek to impose a kind of civil religion on the people from the top down. Such cynical uses of religion, applying a thin sacred veneer to often quite profane realities, are more likely to begin culture wars than to end them.

We should be careful, however, not to locate the cause of America's lack of cultural strife in a too literal interpretation of the phrase "civil religion." In basically stable societies like the United States, it is not that religion forms the necessarily civil glue of society but rather that "the civil" itself has become religious to some degree. That was not Bellah's point, but it was most assuredly Durkheim's in *The Elementary Forms of the Religious Life*.[11] What strikes me about America whenever I am abroad is the extent to which our most basic common culture exists neither prior to nor independent of our system of governance. Instead, that basic common culture is significantly derived from our system of governance and is largely coterminous with it. Such quintessential American cultural values as democracy, freedom, individualism, and equality are grounded in the Constitution and other politically "sacred" documents and institutions. The legitimacy of our governance system stands virtually without question and without threat because our culture and political structures demand a certain level of civility from all who are involved in governing the nation.

In many other countries, by contrast, political governance is seen as an intrusive reality that is often at odds with the host culture. Consequently, political governance is constantly scrambling for legitimacy. This offers not only an incentive to culture wars, but an opportunity for them to succeed. And to the extent that imposed governments and uncivil

11. Emile Durkheim, *The Elementary Forms of the Religious Life* (New York: Free Press, 1915).

ruling elites overplay their ties to religion and other cultural forms in the search for legitimacy, this sets an inviting precedent for marginalized religious and cultural movements to do the same in pursuing power for themselves.

2. Nationalism vs. Tribalism

One major structural constraint to cultural conflict has been the nation-state itself. For more than two hundred years, and especially within the twentieth century, international politics has seen the spoils of war served up with the bittersweet garnishings of statecraft. The United States is one of the very few "new" nations to prosper on its own terms. Each of the four cases described earlier provides a counter instance, since each is a created nation unable to sustain itself easily. Northern Ireland, Guatemala, Israel, and India are all products of *realpolitik* in which structural strait-jackets have been imposed upon diverse and conflicting cultural subjects. While these structural restraints secured order in the short run, they tended only to postpone longer-term cultural struggles. Indeed, such struggles were often exacerbated by forced political confinement under a shared national banner.

Further examples around the globe are conspicuously, often tragically, abundant. In the West they include not only the former Yugoslavia and the USSR, but "devolution" movements in Canada's Quebec, Britain's Wales and Scotland, France's Brittany, and Spain's Basque region. Examples elsewhere stretch from Liberia and Rwanda to Iraq, Burma, Sri Lanka, and Indonesia.[12]

The common term for such movements these days is "nationalism," but it is only half accurate. Yes, these are national movements insofar as they seek for themselves a distinctive national political identity. On the other hand, they are also "tribal" movements insofar as they are shucking off the unity of a nation-state designed specifically to defuse differences rather than inflame them. Today we see far more tribalism than nationalism, and it is tribalism that is especially responsible for culture wars.

Of course, cultural identities of all sorts deserve respect, and culture becomes a more salient source of identity as structural entities and ar-

---

12. See, e.g., Benedict Anderson, *Imagined Communities* (London: Routledge, Chapman and Hall, 1983); and Rogers Brubaker, *Citizenship and Nationalism in France and Germany* (Cambridge: Harvard University Press, 1992).

rangements break down. But it is difficult to imagine a world in which every cultural group would become its own nation. The challenge here is one of sophisticated statecraft that can construct and maintain nations without merely cobbling them together insensitively. Successful nation-states can accommodate cultural differences, but this is far more likely to occur when nation building results from a willing embrace than from a coercive hammer-lock.

Nation-states that have successfully dealt with cultural diversity, countries that have successfully defused their own internal cultural tribalisms have typically been secular states. And they have been "secular" not only with respect to religion but with respect to all other "sacred" cultural matters as well. This has certainly been a major key in the United States' success as the oldest constitutional democracy and federated nation-state still standing. Our First Amendment not only guarantees the free exercise of religion and the prohibition of undue state entanglements with religion, but stipulates the same separation, by implication, for all other forms of cultural identity. Nation-states flourish best when no power-seeking or power-wielding group can use cultural dominance as a weapon to control others.

This returns us to the importance of the political constraints inherent in the modern nation-state. Without such constraints, power can become both more absolute in the short run and more fluid over the longer haul. Cultural movements are more inclined to pursue power directly and even illicitly when the rules of the political game are made up as the game proceeds. Under these conditions, ends truly justify means, and it is often tempting to eschew conventional politics in favor of a down-and-dirty tribal grab for power. This, of course, is a prime source of culture warfare.

A significant complicating factor concerns the advisability of allowing constitutionally guaranteed democratic procedures to run their course even if such a process would threaten the future of democratic politics in a given nation-state. During the past thirty years, we have seen the elite leadership of Brazil, Indonesia, Pakistan, and most recently Algeria send in the military and suspend elections when a culturally insurgent movement seemed poised to win an election. Western and Western-influenced liberals were understandably affronted by such cases; after all, free contests are the essence of democracy, and cancelling elections is a betrayal of the system itself. And yet, sometimes the question can become more complex. Sometimes the issue is not just one of following particular electoral rules but of following the rules of governance itself. Thus, the Algerian ruling party canceled elections largely because of its concern that a winning Islamic movement would suspend the government as a whole to follow the example of the Iranian Republic under the Ayatollah Khoumeini. Of course, the oligarchic elite in charge was hardly democratic in its own right, and some might reply, "better the devil you *don't* know than the devil you do."

It is clear that democratic shibboleths can be applied at several different levels with sometimes conflicting results. When democratic nation-states work well, culture wars can hardly ever get off the ground. When democracy fails to overcome tribal tensions, however, culture wars can and do easily flare up.

3. Stacked vs. Cross-cutting Grievances and Identities

One possible reason to doubt the American culture wars thesis is the argument that culture itself lacks the power required to provoke and sustain such combat. This hard-core "structuralist" perspective is still in vogue in some circles, but not with me. As Rhys Williams and I have demonstrated, "cultural power" can be a great reservoir of movement passion, resolve, resources, and tactical advantages — at least under certain conditions.[13]

For one thing, cultural claims become exponentially more compelling when they are arithmetically aggregated, i.e., stacked on top of each other. Of course, this is the obverse of American pluralism where cross-cutting divisions of class, race, region, and religion prevent any one stacked set of grievances from serving as the catalyst for a single axis of polarization within society. From the standpoint of conflict alone, not always the only or most morally defensible standpoint, situations are less disruptive when natural partisans are divided among themselves by other factors, for example, when the lower classes are comprised of both Irish and Italians, whites and blacks, Protestants and Catholics, and urban and rural residents. These kinds of ethnic, racial, religious, and geographic differences can prevent any one group from serving as a single basis of coalescence as, for example, Marx envisioned in the emerging proletariat but saw lacking among the rural peasantry.

While the United States has had some experience with stacked grievances among, say, our religious right, this phenomenon is actually declin-

---

13. N. J. Demerath, III, and Rhys H. Williams, "Civil Religion in an Uncivil Society," *Annals* 480 (1987): 154-66.

ing with the current increase in the right's internal diversity. This kind of de-stacking of concerns makes it both easier and more difficult for cultural movements to organize themselves. Thus, for example, the pro-life movement can no longer mobilize along dominantly Catholic lines, but it also no longer has to organize itself in that way. Now the single issue of abortion can be excerpted from other religious and cultural supporting contexts and can stand alone.

In contrast to the United States, large-scale cultural divisions between aggregated cultural camps are likely elsewhere. Stacked class grievances, political disenfranchisement, and cultural defensiveness have long been true of Northern Ireland's Catholics, Guatemala's indigenos, Israel's Palestinians, and India's Muslims. In these nations, a spark in one area can spread flames everywhere. The result is not always a pure culture war, if such a thing can ever exist, but cultural identities in these countries do produce important issues in their own right and often provide critical symbolic fuel and moral weaponry for use with other causes. And of all the different kinds of cultural identities, religion can be the most urgent and intense, thus providing a foundation upon which to stack other concerns.[14]

4. Fundamentalisms vs. Fundamentalists

From a Western secularist perspective, there was a time when imagining religion as a source of power was like imagining lead as a source of gold. But over the past fifteen years, religion has been so politically resurgent around the globe that some anti-secularists have seized the development as a categorical disproof of secularization itself. Here one must be wary of the ultimate folly of simply substituting one erroneous trend for another — in this case, exchanging the fallacy of an all-dominant secularization for the fallacy of an all-dominant re-sacralization.

A word that crops up frequently in these matters is one I have so far avoided: fundamentalism. Concern over "fundamentalism" has produced a veritable growth industry among scholars of religion.[15] Virtually defined to death, the term has been given so many meanings that it now means

14. Mark Juergensmeyer, *The New Cold War: Religious Nationalism Confronts the Secular State* (Berkeley: University of California Press, 1993).

15. See, e.g., Martin E. Marty and R. Scott Appleby, eds., *The Fundamentalism Project*, 6 vols. (Chicago: University of Chicago Press, 1992ff.).

all too little. Originally coined some eighty years ago to refer to a group of Protestant leaders intent on defending what they saw as certain "fundamental" Christian beliefs against the threat of "modernist" reinterpretation, it has recently become a synonym for religious extremism of any form in whatever setting. The result has been such a muddying of the waters that one can practically walk upon them with no faith at all.

Of course, there is no question that religious movements now occupy a front and center place on many of the world's cultural and political stages that was unthinkable just a few short decades ago, and many of these movements are anti-secularist, responding to a perceived decline in the importance of religion at both the public and private levels. Moreover, as noted earlier, the mobilization of these movements has been enhanced when and where religious commitments are reinforced by shared ethnic, class, or other cultural bonds. This has been the case even more when religious movements have found themselves in conflict with each other, whether structurally in a contest for real power, or culturally in conflict over sacred texts, sacred pedigrees, or (perhaps most strikingly) sacred space. Contested sacramental land is a major source of religious violence, as evidenced especially at Ayodyah in India, and Jerusalem and Hebron in Israel. While this geographic factor does apply to some Native American religious conflicts with the United States government, it has mercifully been absent from most of our religious conflicts.

But contrary to prevailing perceptions, not all who march under the banner of religious extremism are deeply or principally religious. Some find religious movements either supportive or intoxicating even without believing deeply. Others are downright cynical in using movements for personal gain. Many participants in these fundamentalist movements locate their deepest and most abiding commitments in a basically secular agenda, but find that their inherited religious faith provides a certain legitimacy for their public activities. This is especially likely in countries where outright political opposition is illegal. In such settings, so-called culture wars may be far less religious and much more conventionally political than they appear at first blush. Fundamentalism is also nowadays a not infrequent proxy for movements opposed to political corruption, Western imperialism, and a whole series of other forms of exploitation and predation. Finally, the fundamentalist banner can be a surrogate for movements that would merely replace one form of oppression with another.

Certainly the United States is not immune to fundamentalism in any of these myriad forms i.e., as reactionary Protestantism, as general religious extremism, or as cultural extremism that may have little to do with religion at all except for the borrowing of symbols. And yet these latter forms are more in the minority in America than in many other countries, and in America different kinds of fundamentalists have tended to shift their bases and agendas over time. For example, as noted earlier, one's attitude on abortion is no longer a fail-safe litmus test of one's religious affiliation. The pro-life movement has lost much of its distinctively religious flavor to become a more secular moral movement that cross-cuts various religious denominations.

Along the same lines, one hears a great deal these days about how the "New Christian Right" is on the move both in local politics and within the Republican Party. However, there are ample reasons to be skeptical about its chances of becoming a prime contender for national political dominance.[16] Despite the popular image, traditional American fundamentalists remain split in their membership between the Democrats and Republicans. What's more, there seems to be a naturally operative ceiling effect that limits the power of extreme religious movements in both parties. While religion can be effective in mobilizing a given minority of the electorate for specific political ends, the very tactics and appeals used to secure those ends almost always tend to alienate more people than they attract. As the Pat Robertson campaign of 1988 illustrated, once the religious right reached a certain level of political success, that very success set off the alarm that prevented it from going further.

America is not fertile soil for mass fundamentalist movements. The country's basic affluence and its culture of individual and collective, and political and economic, opportunity militates against the sort of stacked grievances that need to exist in order for that to occur.

5. Church/State Entanglement vs. Separation

As a fifth and final distinction to help explain the difference between cultural discord and actual cultural warfare, I offer one that may seem all too American. Insofar as I have any counsel for other nations regarding how to curb religiously based political violence, I am embarrassed to confess that it involves touting our own much heralded "separation of church and state." Certainly one mark of provincialism is prescribing one's

16. See Steve Bruce, "The Inevitable Failure of the New Christian Right," *Sociology of Religion* 55 (Fall 1994): 223-41.

own medicine for other peoples' illnesses. But in this case it seems necessary, especially since our putative separationism is misunderstood at home almost as much as abroad.

One reason for this misunderstanding is the paradox at the core of American church-state separation. While many assume that a secular state necessarily leads to a secular society, the reality is very often the reverse. Thus, the United States is fabled both for its separation of church and state *and* for being among the most religious nations in the world. While this seems a contradiction, it is not. In fact, each condition is contingent upon the other. As Rhys Williams and I have argued elsewhere,[17] the country can endorse religion's separation from the state precisely because religion is free to function elsewhere in the national experience; conversely, it is precisely because religion flowers so luxuriantly in the society at large that separation is needed to protect the state and governance processes from it. Put more pithily, having rich religious traditions, we need church-state separation; having church-state separation, we need to cultivate religion in a broad range of private and public non-governmental gardens. Northern Ireland, Israel, Guatemala, and India are only a few of a host of societies that would benefit from developing a similar combination of religious vitality and church-state separation.

Finally, the point reaches beyond religion to culture more broadly. One specific instance can be found in the 1965 *Seeger* and 1970 *Welsh* decisions of the Supreme Court which extended conscientious objector status to persons who were avowedly not religious but who held beliefs that occupied "in the life of that individual a 'place parallel to that filled by God' in traditional religious persons." In some sense, this radical allowance was precedent shattering. It is not surprising, therefore, that the Court soon dropped it as a judicial hot potato and has seldom referred to it since. But it does suggest, as Durkheim taught us all long ago, that there is a thin line between formal religion and other sacred cultural tenets, convictions, and associations.

If it is sensible to observe a distinction between government and religion, why not mark a similar gap between government and culture in its wider sense? At first blush, this may seem like extending the sublime to the ridiculous. A government without culture suggests a nation without a soul. And yet our separationism applies only to the state, not to society at large, or even to politics. While mixing religion and politics can be both

17. Rhys H. Williams and N. J. Demerath, III, "Religion and Political Process in an American City," *American Sociological Review* 56 (August 1991): 417-31.

volatile and violent, it can also animate and energize. Certainly the idea is not to expunge either religion or culture from the individual consciences of state officeholders but rather to avoid particularistic and hegemonic "entanglements" between the state apparatus and specific cultural groups, whether these are defined in terms of religion, class, race, ethnicity, gender, or any other potentially invidious reference point.

Conclusion

Does America host cultural tensions, culture battles, and cultural violence? The answer is most assuredly yes. Are its cultural wounds now deeper, more frequent, and more threatening than in the past? Not likely, since our history is as littered with examples as our current landscape. Is America engaged in a "culture war" similar to those so tragically apparent elsewhere? Clearly not. And yet this is not an all-or-nothing concept, contrary to its treatment here. Just as the United States has experienced some of its features, it would be a mistake to portray countries like Northern Ireland, Guatemala, Israel, and India as fully obsessed war-zones. The degree of cultural warfare is an important variable for every society, and one that alerts us to a range of cultural dynamics that can be fatal to ignore.

Finally, I want to say something about the extent to which contemporary American Protestantism can be described in terms of a "two-party model." In some ways, of course, it depends upon one's perspective and how much one squints. But I would suggest that the two-party model is only one interpretive option among others. For me, the more plausible interpretation is neither two-party warfare nor centrist consensus but rather a fractured pluralism with no discernible center, and without even the dubious structure of a dichotomy. I am even enough of a cynic to suggest that in some ways the particular model that obtains at any given moment is the model that best suits the dominant elites of that moment. To the extent that this is true, James Hunter (despite his overstatement of America's bipolar divisions) may be right when he says that we seem all too often a nation of sheep herded erratically by the political dogs nipping at our flanks. America is not involved in a culture war, but Americans sometimes seem to miss that fact because so many political pundits are trying to convince them that they are.

CHAPTER 3

"I Just Say I'm a Christian": Symbolic Boundaries and Identity Formation among Church-going Protestants

DAVID SIKKINK

Many researchers argue that a key feature of the religious landscape is a growing fissure between liberals and conservatives. But to what extent do ordinary church-going Protestants view the religious field through a liberal-conservative lens? Historically, research has shifted from seeing the Protestant story in terms of a single, dominant Protestant mainstream to a paradigm that sees the structure of the religious field in terms of two parties, mainline and evangelical, which often boils down to a divide between liberals and conservatives.[1] The nature and impact of this divide have become an important focus of research, though researchers differ regarding the extent to which individual Protestants actually use a liberal-conservative framework to give meaning to who they are and where they stand in the religious field. While some research shows a realignment of religious identities around a conservative-liberal axis,[2] other researchers argue that religious identities are based in more local and particular religious traditions, and go so far as to question the usefulness of the category, "Evangelicalism."[3]

1. See Douglas Jacobsen and William Vance Trollinger, Jr., "The Historiography of American Protestantism: The Two-Party Paradigm and Beyond," *Fides et Historia* 25 (Fall 1993): 3-15.
2. See, e.g., Robert Wuthnow, *The Restructuring of American Religion* (Princeton: Princeton University Press, 1988); and Wade Clark Roof and William McKinney, *American Mainline Religion* (New Brunswick, NJ: Rutgers University Press, 1987).
3. Donald W. Dayton, "The Limits of Evangelicalism: The Pentecostal Tradition,"

DAVID SIKKINK

It does seem that the older American religious identity-scheme of Protestant, Catholic, and Jew (as defined by Will Herberg in 1955)[4] is no longer definitive, and that even denominational identities are losing significance as the religious landscape is restructured.[5] Some research perspectives suggest that religious identities will likely continue to be structured around what they perceive as a moral and ideological divide between liberals and conservatives. Others suggest that the role of this bipolar division in constructing religious identities could be even stronger in the future as a consequence of a culture war in America between those of "orthodox" and "progressive" orientation, a conflict that is said to underlie political debates over issues such as abortion, homosexual rights, and school prayer.[6] Still other research adds that while the liberal-conservative dimension is important for Protestant identity formation, it is now being cross-cut by a divide between nascent and institutional religious orientations.[7] The concept of "nascent" faith, similar to current uses of the term "spirituality," refers to an inward, subjective experience of the heart that finds natural expression in life. In contrast, "institutional" faith can be thought of in much the same way the term "religion" is commonly used: a faith primarily expressed through the routines and structures of organized religious institutions and associations (e.g., congregations and denominations).[8] From this perspective, religious identity turns to some extent on the divide between a vital, personal faith and institutionalized, participant faith.

In a different vein, certain scholars are now arguing that religious identities no longer reflect normative commitments to any community of faith beyond the self, but are constructed for the self using the cultural tools of utilitarian and expressive individualism.[9] According to this per-

in Donald W. Dayton and Robert K. Johnston, eds., *The Variety of American Evangelicalism* (Knoxville: University of Tennessee Press, 1991).

4. Will Herberg, *Protestant, Catholic, Jew* (Garden City, NY: Doubleday, 1955).

5. See Steve Bruce, *A House Divided* (New York: Routledge, 1990); and Wuthnow, *Restructuring of American Religion*.

6. James Davison Hunter, *Culture Wars: The Struggle to Define America* (New York: Basic Books, 1991).

7. R. Stephen Warner, *New Wine in Old Wineskins* (Berkeley: University of California Press, 1988).

8. Robert Wuthnow, *Acts of Compassion* (Princeton: Princeton University Press, 1991), 154. See also Wade Clark Roof, *A Generation of Seekers* (San Francisco: Harper, 1993).

9. See Robert Bellah, et al., *Habits of the Heart* (Berkeley: University of California Press, 1985); and Charles Taylor, *The Ethics of Authenticity* (Cambridge, MA: Harvard University Press, 1992).

spective, religious identities, like other identities, are designed by the individual to express that person's "authenticity" (expressive individualism), or are based on a calculation of the benefits received by the individual (utilitarian individualism). These individualistic identities have an achieved, or chosen, character; that is, they can easily be taken on and put off.[10] Thus the "liberated" individual is the basic cultural unit, left adrift to make sense of his or her social world without the secure guidelines provided by a comprehensive group identity.[11] In this loose-bounded culture, religious identity is unlikely to be clearly grounded by denominational ties, or by affiliation with a liberal or conservative camp.

Religious identities articulated in the language of expressive individualism may tend to displace a concern for doctrine and truth, and to increase a concern for civility toward and tolerance of other religious and secular groups.[12] Theologian David Wells has argued that religious identities based on personal choice or preference mitigate the centrality of doctrine and truth in the construction of religious identity.[13] Philip Hammond and Robert Wuthnow have similarly contended that, in the face of cultural pluralism, both "conservative" and "liberal" religious identities are becoming highly personalized to avoid being offensive to those with different beliefs.[14] It seems unlikely that the liberal/conservative divide, to whatever degree it might have defined the identities of religious people in the past, will remain important for people more concerned with avoiding offense than they are with maintaining distinctions based on claims to absolute truth.

10. See Bellah, *Habits of the Heart;* Philip Hammond, *Religion and Personal Autonomy* (Columbia: University of South Carolina Press, 1992); and Robert Wuthnow, *Christianity in the Twenty-first Century* (Oxford: Oxford University Press, 1993).

11. See Richard M. Merelman, *Making Something of Ourselves* (Berkeley: University of California Press, 1984); and Robert Wuthnow, *Sharing the Journey* (New York: Free Press, 1994).

12. See John Murray Cuddihy, *No Offense* (New York: Seabury Press, 1978); and James Davison Hunter, *American Evangelicalism* (New Brunswick: Rutgers University Press, 1983) and *Evangelicalism* (Chicago: University of Chicago Press, 1987).

13. David Wells, *No Place for Truth* (Grand Rapids: Eerdmans, 1993).

14. Philip E. Hammond, *Religion and Personal Autonomy;* Wuthnow, *Acts of Compassion*, 152.

DAVID SIKKINK

Listening to Protestant Laypeople

This paper explores the symbolic boundaries which seem most salient to ordinary church-going Protestants. The questions that drove the initial research were of the following nature: What cultural boundaries do grass-roots Protestants use to construct religious identities? To what extent do Protestant laypeople organize their religious identities in terms of a symbolic boundary between "liberal" and "conservative" options? To what degree might other cultural factors, such as the existence of a "culture war," a divide between nascent and institutional forms of faith, or the language of self-interest and self-expression moderate the significance of the liberal-conservative distinction which supposedly has such prominence among contemporary church-going Protestants? The goal of this research was to hear the voices of grass-root Protestants coming from diverse religious positions, to ask how respondents understood their religious identities, and to see how those identities fit within the broader social world in which each person lived.[15]

To address these issues, we designed our research to uncover the markers of identity which seemed most salient to ordinary church-going Protestants, and to see how their perceptions of religious differences shaped the way they understood their own position within the broader religious field. Research protocols were specifically crafted to allow the symbolic boundaries in the religious field to emerge as we listened to how ordinary American Protestants articulated their answers to a set of questions ranging from what set them apart from other people, to what it meant to be a "true Christian."

The common format used in these interviews was to ask each respondent a series of open-ended questions about his or her religious identity, and then to ascertain how that identity was related to other labels, such as evangelical, fundamentalist, charismatic, pentecostal, and liberal. In order to probe more deeply, we asked follow-up questions about the meaning of particular labels — what it might mean, for example, to consider oneself "liberal," "charismatic," "evangelical," "fundamentalist," or "just a Christian." The goal was to derive sufficient data to map the

15. This essay is based on research conducted between July 1995 and September 1996 as part of the "Evangelical Identity and Influence" project directed by Christian Smith and funded by the Pew Charitable Trusts. Various interviews were conducted by Christian Smith, Michael Emerson, Sally Gallagher, Paul Kennedy, and me. The interpretation of the data presented in this essay is substantially my own.

topography of the American Protestant landscape as that terrain seemed to be understood by ordinary Protestants. In seeking to understand religious identity from the perspective of the person in the pew we were guided conceptually by Pierre Bourdieu's notion of how such identity operates within structured religious fields.[16]

By intention we sought to include the full spectrum of Protestantism within our study, while achieving proportionate representation for relevant theological and denominational traditions. A stratified sampling design was used to ensure that each of the major Protestant religious traditions, including conservative and liberal wings of those traditions, were represented. So, for example, respondents were included from what are typically seen as the liberal and conservative wings of the Baptist, Methodist/Pietist, Lutheran, and Presbyterian/Reformed traditions. Also selected for inclusion in our study were respondents from some of America's smaller denominations (mostly from the Holiness and Pentecostal traditions) and others from independent or non-denominational congregations. In all, 128 interviews were conducted. The number of interviews from each denominational tradition was roughly proportionate to the national population percentages for that tradition, though measures were taken to ensure that small but distinct and historically significant denominational traditions, such as the Anabaptist, Conservative Presbyterian/Reformed, Conservative Pietist/Methodist, and Liberal Episcopal traditions were represented with five interviews each. Over-sampling these smaller denominational traditions meant reducing the total number of interviews with representatives of the three largest traditions.

To achieve regional representation, researchers conducted interviews in Minneapolis; Chicago; Birmingham, Alabama; Durham, North Carolina; Essex County, Massachusetts; and Benton County, Oregon. The number of interviews conducted in each area took into account regional strongholds of denominational traditions. The majority of Lutherans were interviewed in Minnesota, for example. Sampling frames for each denominational tradition at each location were compiled using lists of local churches drawn from telephone directories. Churches in each denominational tradition were randomly selected, and individual respondents were selected randomly from church membership and regular attender lists.[17]

---

16. Pierre Bourdieu, "Genesis and Structure of the Religious Field," *Comparative Social Research,* vol. 13 (Greenwich, CT: JAI Press, Inc., 1990).

17. The sample consisted of 60% female and 40% male. The regional, denominational, and racial breakdown is as follows:

Based on these interviews, church-going Protestants do not construct religious identities primarily in terms of a liberal-conservative divide.[18] Whatever place the liberal-conservative distinction may play at the macrolevel restructuring of religion, identity formation for church-going Protestants on the grass-roots level does not turn on a symbolic cleavage between liberals and conservatives. In fact, respondents were not invested in that way of divvying up religious space much at all. Instead, most respondents used a variety of different religious images and ideals to situate themselves in religious social space. Their religious identities had numerous dimensions, rather than cohering around a single frame of reference. Usually our interviewees did not connect their own sense of religious identity with any specific denomination or broader religious movement. Finally, more often than not, our respondents expressed their religious identities in the negative by delineating various practices, ideas, or values with which they did not want to be associated.

The religious data we collected thus tended to confirm the fact that Americans now seem typically to define their identities in multiple and

---

Table A.1: Regional Breakdown of Summer 1995 Interviews by Denominational Tradition

	NC	MA	OR	MN	IL	AL	Total
White Protestant							
Anabaptist	2		3				5
Baptist (Liberal)		3	2				5
Baptist (Conservative)	9	5	10	3			27
Episcopal	2	3					5
Holiness	2	3					5
Lutheran (Liberal)			4	4			8
Lutheran (Conservative)		2		3			5
Methodist/Pietist (Liberal)	7	3					10
Methodist/Pietist (Conservative)		2	3				5
Pentecostal	4		5				9
Presby/Reformed (Liberal)		4	3				7
Presby/Reformed (Conservative)	3	2					5
Non-Denominational		3	2				5
Black Protestant							
Baptist	3	2		2	2	6	15
Methodist					4	3	7
Pentecostal	3				1	1	5
TOTAL	35	32	32	12	7	10	128

18. In this paper I limit myself to an analysis of the interviews with white respondents because this is the population group supposedly most divided along two-party lines.

conflicting fashion.[19] Identification with a religious category, whether that be a specific denomination or a liberal or conservative camp, does not appear to provide a definitive sense of "who I am" for the people with whom we talked. Nor do these identifiers reflect the kinds of clear moral stands (in Charles Taylor's sense of the term)[20] that might serve as the foundation of a neatly defined religious identity. Rather than an identity organized primarily along a conservative-liberal axis as much recent scholarship seems to suggest, our respondents pointed toward several overlapping and cross-cutting dimensions of difference, which they thought were more salient for their own identities than the liberal-conservative divide.

A Dislike of Partisan Labels

The respondents in this study were not strongly connected to any of the categories that professional researchers typically bandy about. In fact, most seemed eager to back away from almost all "divisive" labels, in favor of being "just Christians." When asked about her religious identity, for example, one respondent simply asserted, "I just say I'm a Christian."[21] In general, identity formation in our sample seemed to be based much more on self-styled, personal religious worlds than on the pre-formed categories academics use to label religious people. When asked how she would describe herself religiously, one fifty-two-year-old said: "It would definitely not be Lutheran or Baptist or whatever it would happen to be. It would be that I'm a Christian — whatever that means to whoever is listening. A child of God — period. It doesn't have to have any label, doesn't have to happen on Sunday morning in church."[22] This respondent and many others thought the standard religious categories mislabelled her personal religious world. All in all, we found that few respondents expressed a clear connection with any specific denominational tradition.

It is generally accepted that denominational allegiance is declining,

---

19. Craig Calhoun, *Social Theory and the Politics of Identity* (New York: Blackwell, 1994).

20. Charles Taylor, *The Sources of the Self* (Cambridge: Harvard University Press, 1989).

21. Oregon, August 10, 1995.

22. Minnesota, August 5, 1995.

but those with whom we talked also did not seem to identify actively with any of the major movements often thought to be more decisive in the contemporary religious field (such as the charismatic, evangelical, liberal, and fundamentalist movements). One piece of evidence for the lack of connection between personal religious identities and either specific religious movements or clear ideological positions was the way our respondents labelled themselves with strange combinations of terms. A cross-tabulation of identifiers, for example, showed that a third of the respondents thought they were both liberal and fundamentalist.

This lack of linkage between personal religious identity and larger movements within American religion was confirmed when we asked about allegiance to individual religious leaders. If there is a clear liberal/conservative divide that is central to identity formation in contemporary American Protestantism, one would expect a relatively strong connection to various religious leaders who wave either the liberal or the conservative party banners. Instead, Billy Graham was the near unanimous choice for most admired religious leader of all respondents — this was true for self-described fundamentalists, evangelicals, and liberals alike. Beyond Graham, interviewees were hard-pressed to come up with any other important religious leaders, and resorted to a hodgepodge ranging from Amy Grant to the Pope, with no particular pattern evident in those responses. The most significant religious leader for many respondents was either their local pastor or a member of their own families.

Rather than being based on a strongly held association with a religious group, religious identity for most respondents was focused on their own individual state of being. Thus when asked how respondents would describe themselves religiously, we would get responses such as: "I am an all right Christian. I could be doing better. I do my best, and do what I can."[23] Some respondents did connect themselves with certain "name brand" religious labels, but when those claims were explored the connections were often found to be more tenuous than they had first appeared. Thus, many who tentatively agreed they were "evangelical" were not sure exactly what it meant to be an evangelical. Most thought of it narrowly: to be "evangelical" was to be concerned with doing evangelism, to think one should evangelize or speak out about one's faith in some way. A fifty-seven-year-old female respondent claimed that "evangelical is people that evangelize."[24] When asked if she thought of herself as an evangelical,

23. Massachusetts, September 1, 1995.
24. Oregon, July 29, 1995.

one woman responded: "Yeah, I think I would, although I'm not the best at going out and witnessing or anything like that, but yes."[25] For these two respondents and others like them, evangelicalism was defined in the rather concrete manner of referring to a specific action of individuals; it did not define a coherent and distinct religious movement within the larger religious field. Similarly, some who took up the fundamentalist label quite readily were also concerned to limit the meaning of that term to its strict dictionary definition. Many of our respondents who adopted the fundamentalist label said that meant they adhered to the "fundamentals," but these respondents often recognized no connections between themselves and the broader historical traditions, or the current institutions, of fundamentalism. The question of religious identity seemed not to have meaning in terms of a movement, or community of faith, but was understood in categories largely restricted to the person's local world of experience.

Defining Who One Is Not

In many ways, our respondents were more articulate about who they were not than who they were. This took different forms depending on the person's location in the general religious field, but overall, religious categories seemed to function more as ways of defining the limits of one's religious identity. Labels operate, in other words, as images which mark off who one is not.

The notion of being "evangelical" was frequently used in this way. That is, evangelicalism as a social type had meaning for those who did not identify themselves as evangelicals because the explicit rejection of that term allowed them to say that they were not one of those overly emotional denigrators of tradition and liturgy that they assumed evangelicals to be. One thirty-nine-year-old Episcopalian respondent, who clearly did not see herself as "liberal," was also quite unwilling to accept the evangelical label. She argued that within evangelicalism "there's more of an emphasis on the emotional experience of religion on . . . well, perhaps a lack of emphasis on things like liturgy or traditional religious disciplines and more on a personal experience and that kind of thing."[26] Being "evangelical" in this sense defined a boundary of emotionalism or

25. Minnesota, August 10, 1995.
26. North Carolina, June 29, 1995.

lack of church structure that some respondents — and not only self-proclaimed liberals — did not want to cross.

In the same way, but often in a more powerful way, "fundamentalist" served as a dividing line for knowing who one was by knowing who one was not. People rejected the fundamentalist label because this social type was identified with "yelling and screaming," confrontational tactics, moral rigidity, and Bible-thumping. One respondent, who thought of herself as a moderate or mainline Protestant, claimed that a fundamentalist was "a person who believes in a specific belief that has not changed over the years and years, and they stick to just that belief and can't see the whole picture."[27] Self-described evangelicals seemed as focused on maintaining their distance from fundamentalists as from liberals. One United Methodist woman from North Carolina explained that evangelical means: "Not quite as conservative as fundamentalist. But people who really think the basics of the faith are important. I think evangelicals are a little more broad-minded; a little more socially concerned. This is terrible to say, I figure a little more intelligent. That's it."[28]

The image of being "charismatic" helped to shape the identities of most respondents in that most knew that they were not charismatic. Being charismatic for those people meant being "into" excessive emotion in worship services and religious fanaticism in general. One self-described liberal said that he was not into charismatic religion since "they [charismatics] are trying to draw more attention to Christianity than I'm willing to do. . . . I don't want to go and — and my wife too — we don't want to go out and be very charismatic about our religion."[29] A "Mennonite evangelical" stated that charismatics are "just really into praising the Lord, sometimes out of the context of reality. Sort of on some kind of — maybe not so reality-based, and not much intellect, not much thinking — but just the emotional expression of something that they love to feel, and not very related to real life. And not real helpful to much of anybody."[30] One self-described born-again evangelical told us, "Well, charismatics to me are people who are very . . . I've always called them charismaniacs. They are very, how do I say it, wild." Religious identity for many self-described evangelicals in our sample was often defined against an image of fanatical charismatics, which provided an outer boundary, not a positive definition, of their religious identity.

27. Minnesota, August 3, 1995.
28. North Carolina, July 10, 1995.
29. Oregon, July 28, 1995.
30. North Carolina, June 30, 1995.

The image of "liberal" was used in a similar way to set the outer bounds of religious respectability for many self-described evangelicals, charismatics, and fundamentalists. Most of the respondents who (however tentatively) claimed to be conservatives, evangelicals, or fundamentalists placed themselves against what they saw as the liberal social type. These respondents told us that a liberal Christian is someone who doesn't take the Word seriously, is morally suspect, or preoccupied with political action. For one evangelical from a Christian Missionary Alliance church, "liberal" meant "just a more loose interpretation of Scripture. Some of it doesn't apply today."[31] Another offered that liberals "just preach what they want to preach" rather than the Bible.[32] As a definition of the out-group, rather than as a definitive sense of "who I am," these images were significant for defining religious identity.

In sum, the identities of our respondents were constructed within the larger religious field against multiple and divergent images of how they thought people could be religious. How these different social types were understood usually had little to do with the historical traditions and movements of liberalism or evangelicalism or any other specific religious tradition. Few respondents articulated a clear, positive master frame when describing their own religious identities. Rather, they seemed more willing to situate themselves in contradistinction to certain clearly formed images of religious social types that differed from their own religious self-conceptions. The end-product of that process of differentiation was an identity defined by multiple and conflicting (and often negative) religious concerns revolving around several dimensions. While respondents in this study did seem quite content to place simple labels on those from whom they wanted to distance themselves, they understood that their own identities were rather more complex. They did not live within any single social type; they lived between several.

Liberal/Conservative: Culture War or Relative Location?

Though images of liberals and fundamentalists were used by respondents as oppositional foils against which to define their own positions, the liberal-conservative divide itself did not provide the primary frame within which the Protestant laypeople we studied constructed their religious

31. North Carolina, June 29, 1995.
32. Massachusetts, July 14, 1995.

identities. The notion that a liberal versus conservative battle defined an arena in which they had to declare their allegiance was often far removed from the central struggles that defined their faith. The terms "liberal" and "conservative" were used by those we interviewed, but this social typology did not so much provide a place to stand in some liberal versus conservative religious war as it let them describe where they stood relative to others within their own camp (however that was defined).

Thus, several respondents said they were fundamentalist, but on the "liberal" end of that reference group. Others said they were evangelical, but more liberal than some of their evangelical peers. One self-proclaimed conservative woman explained: "I'm a lot more conservative than most Presbyterians. . . . But then sometimes I am liberal because I believe that women can be ordained and I know that a lot of really conservative people say no, so it's hard. . . . I don't think I fall into one specific category."[33] Another self-identified evangelical defined himself not by his opposition to liberals, but instead claimed to be a liberal evangelical: "I'm definitely a conservative person compared to the world but probably more liberal compared to . . . a conservative evangelical."[34]

The salience of the liberal-conservative divide does not seem to be increasing as a result of taking up traditional or progressive positions in a broader culture war. The Protestants with whom we talked were not very heavily invested in the culture war;[35] they were not taking up oppositional "traditionalist" and "progressive" positions in order to be ready to wage local and national battles. When our respondents tried to explain their religious identities, their answers simply did not turn on a view of the world divided into two warring groups slugging it out over abortion, prayer in schools, and homosexuality. This does not mean that the people with whom we spoke were unconcerned about the current state of the nation. In fact, almost all were deeply troubled by where America seems to be heading, but this sense of dis-ease did not fit neatly into the categories of the supposed culture war. Many of our respondents were wholly unaware of the existence of a culture war. If they did know of such a thing, they usually exhibited a strong distaste for the notion.

Furthermore, even the few culture warriors among our respondents

33. Oregon, August 10, 1995.
34. Massachusetts, August 14, 1995.
35. Christian Smith et al., "The Myth of Culture Wars: The Case of American Protestantism," in Rhys H. Williams, ed., *Cultural Wars in American Politics* (Hawthorne, NY: Aldine de Gruyter, 1997).

held other beliefs or understood America's problems in ways that neutralized the extent to which the supposed culture war could serve as the primary catalyst of their religious identity. For example, while a sizable number saw the public schools as a major problem, those concerns were usually articulated in secular language. The problem was the drugs and violence that are making the schools unsafe, or the failure to focus on the basics, such as reading, writing and arithmetic. A concern that secular humanism has been infiltrating textbooks and curriculum was not part of the language we heard about the decline of the public schools. Even on supposedly key culture war issues, problems were not typically framed as a spiritual struggle, or as a struggle that ought to engage religious identity organized around conservative and liberal camps. This seems to be different from the era of the Civil Rights movement, the Vietnam War, and the early women's liberation movement (i.e., the 1960s and 1970s) when cultural factors did seem to interact with the religious field in a way that sharpened the difference between "liberal" and "conservative" options.[36] Our respondents did not view the contemporary religious field in that same bipolar way.

All of this is to say that respondents in this study did not reflect an understanding of the religious field as revolving around a war between "liberals" and "conservatives." To make a claim to being "liberal" often meant nothing more than a willingness to cross a behavioral boundary that one's evangelical or fundamentalist peers — or, at least, one's image of one's evangelical and fundamentalist peers — would not cross. Images of liberals and conservatives did have some formative power to shape religious identity, but this was mostly in terms of setting an outer boundary of identity (as described above). At those boundary lines, however, the liberal-conservative distinction had to compete for a place in the identities of those interviewed with numerous other dimensions of difference that also seemed significant. Usually the way respondents understood the liberal-conservative divide made it relatively peripheral to their core religious identities.

Religious Individualism and the Importance of Being Nice

Though multiple religious images are helpful in defining the outer bounds of religious respectability, the major religious battles that preoccupy the

36. See Wuthnow, *Restructuring of American Religion*, 145-153.

media and some religious elites are not salient for identity formation partly because religious identities seem to be constructed from the building blocks of expressive and utilitarian individualism. The claim that, for example, evangelicals lack a "binding address,"[37] or that American culture in general is dominated by a loose-bounded individualism,[38] was supported by the comments of almost all those we interviewed.

The religious identities of almost all our respondents seem to have been strongly influenced by how the notion of "the individual" is currently being constructed in American culture in general. As individualism, in both its expressive and utilitarian forms, erodes away the connections persons feel to specific communities and to particular movements,[39] it shifts the burden of identity onto individual "choice." For most respondents in this study an identity bounded to a community was thought of as a threat to the self. Having too firm an identity was considered a bad thing. This was true whether we were talking to self-styled fundamentalists, evangelicals, or liberals. "True believers," the dogmatic defenders of truth, were uniformly denigrated by our respondents, mainly because "they" created "unnecessary" conflict. Even those with more coherent religious identities tended to picture their own religious faith as a matter of individual "beliefs," "feelings," or "opinions."[40] One man, who was a self-proclaimed moderate church-goer, used this language:

> What is Christianity about? Christianity is we're worshipping the same God and so no, I don't think religious differences are very important and I don't think that . . . if they want to do it their way that's why we have had the splits in our churches and so forth. This little group wants to wave their hands so they can go ahead and have their own church and wave their hands but we're still worshipping the same God. I don't think it really makes any difference. Well, I get along better with some of the people that come in here than other people who come in here so just because I relate more easily to this group doesn't mean that these people are wrong.[41]

Even the respondents who seemed most identified with a label, who came closest to articulating a master religious frame, would claim that "each

---

37. Hunter, *Evangelicalism*, 210.
38. Merelman, *Making Something of Ourselves*.
39. Bellah, *Habits of the Heart*.
40. See Hunter, *Evangelicalism*.
41. Oregon, July 28, 1995.

individual is an individual."[42] One who was self-identified as "very conservative" was also convinced that such labels really were not necessary since religion "is a personal thing."[43]

Rather than taking on a binding address, most respondents backed away from making strong claims regarding their particular religious identity, especially as the major battle lines are conventionally drawn, and instead spoke out in favor of civility, tolerance, and a concern for what is right for each individual. A self-described conservative Christian explained that she would deal with religious difference in this way:

> I would just be careful of how I phrased things or said things until I knew how to discuss these topics with them and have a conversation and not, like, offend somebody, I guess, but I just know there is a lot of different beliefs. I don't know, I mean, until I meet God in person I won't know who's right and who's wrong so I just need to be true to what I believe in.[44]

An evangelical who claimed that she was called to bring a message of reconciliation to the world was careful to qualify that by using the language of sharing in response to pain: "I feel a responsibility to take the gospel to the world — not to coerce, but to share because we all ourselves have felt the pain of a broken relationship with God and we see pain around us."[45]

The assumption that religious identities are individual choices, and less a reflection of being bound to a community, limited the extent to which any one religious divide, such as mainline versus evangelical, could be deeply embedded in religious identities of this study's respondents. As one woman, who described herself as an evangelical, put it: "It [Christianity] is a personal belief, and it's between you and God, and it's your interpretation of the Scriptures." She went on to note approvingly that people today "are becoming more open-minded and saying, hey, maybe the Lutheran way isn't the only way of thinking. Let's look at what the Baptists have to say, let's look at what the Catholics have to say, let's look at everybody. And you read it [the Bible] and interpret it for yourself, and, you know, with God's help you develop your personal religion and your beliefs."[46] Most respondents — whatever label they

42. Oregon, August 1, 1995.
43. Massachusetts, September 1, 1995.
44. Oregon, August 10, 1995.
45. Oregon, August 1, 1995.
46. Minnesota, August 3, 1995.

might agree to wear — defined their faith largely in terms of being nice and avoiding offense.

For Some People Denominational Labels Still Count

Symbolic denominational labels, while not broadly significant, did seem helpful to a small group of respondents as they tried to make sense of themselves religiously and to define where they stood in relation to other Protestants. This was particularly true for those who came from the more historic confessional traditions. If one was to construct a macro-model of America's Protestant divisions based upon the insights and convictions of these people, one would clearly need to speak of a three-way split (at a minimum) where a denominationally rooted confessional stance would be juxtaposed both to pietistic/evangelical/conservative and to uncommitted/mainline/liberal positionings within the larger religious field.

When asked how she would describe herself religiously, for example, one woman situated herself within a confessional denomination, saying: "I'm an Episcopalian — Anglican. I'm not Protestant. I don't think of Episcopalians as Protestant. . . . I'd probably say I have more Anglo-Catholic tendencies than the other." According to this woman, being Episcopal meant owning an identity different from "a broad or liberal, sort of middle-of-the-road kind of thing."[47] It was also quite different from being evangelical. Another respondent claimed that he was a "Bible-believer" (i.e., not liberal), but he also stated clearly that he was not an evangelical or fundamentalist. Instead, he described his religious identity (somewhat inarticulately) in terms of a distinctive Mennonite tradition: "Well, I would say as a Mennonite, basically. The Mennonite church is a non-violent church. In the history of the church, they have, what's the word I'm going to use, they do not join the military, and . . . there's a word — pacifism."[48] For these and a small number of other respondents denominational identities provided an important point of clarity.

47. North Carolina, June 29, 1995.
48. Oregon, August 10, 1995.

Worship Styles

One factor which stood out as a key landmark for many of our respondents was difference in style of worship. Many respondents understood their own religious identity, and positioned themselves in the religious field, more in terms of worship practices than doctrine or creeds. But here as elsewhere persons tended to define themselves more clearly by the things from which they wanted to distance themselves than by aligning themselves too tightly with any positive practices or values. In particular, most respondents wanted to open some daylight between themselves and the "charismatics among us." This seemed to provide a clear boundary which set an agenda for how people wanted others to perceive them. Whether self-proclaimed evangelicals, fundamentalists, conservatives, or liberals, most respondents emphasized that while "excessive" emotionalism and carrying on in worship services might be fine for "them" (i.e., charismatic Christians), it would be going a bit overboard for themselves. As one woman put it,

> I think that a lot of people that are involved in the charismatic church feel really good when they get familiar to the service. I think you have to be comfortable in that type of a service. . . . I mean, you're doing a lot more but it's really an uplifting service. . . . It's very difficult to think to go into a charismatic service and leave not having . . . you know, feel uplifted so . . . but I don't know. . . . I think that charismatic is just a style of worship. . . .[49]

Part of what seemed to be going on here was not just differences in worship styles but a concern about religious respectability. That is, some people who wanted to be respected as God-believing, church-going Christians clearly did not want to be "drawing a lot of attention to their faith." It was precisely that kind of disreputable attention-grabbing behavior that these people thought they saw demonstrated in the lives of pentecostal and charismatic Christians. Thus the label "Pentecostal" provided a boundary marker for them of what was and was not respectable religious faith. One man talked about Pentecostalism in this way: "Yeah, Pentecostal we don't care for because they get kind of wild about their religion. I mean, that's how I see it. I've never gone to a Pentecostal church, but they roll on the floor and wave their hands and do all that, and we could not do that."[50] By describing the pentecostal/charismatic social type in this way,

49. Oregon, August 10, 1995.
50. Oregon, July 28, 1995.

many respondents reaffirmed their own comfort with an "orderly" worship service. One person explained:

> I've been going to the evangelical church for two years, and when I was first told about it I didn't go at first because I thought that it meant, you know, people raising their hands and what people call "holy rollers," I don't know, and that's very far from where I grew up. And I went and was really surprised because the service is not that different from the Presbyterian service.[51]

The salient dimension of difference in this area was, for most respondents, a certain understanding of what respectable people should and shouldn't do in worship services. Worship style was one of the clearest prisms through which church-going Protestants viewed the religious landscape and their place in it.

Nascent and Institutional Differences

Of all the differences discussed by respondents, however, the construction of identity in terms of a nascent-institutional religious divide came across as the most widespread. Many with a nascent orientation located themselves in the larger religious field by claiming to possess a vital, inward, spiritual faith unbounded by predefined organizational structures. Those speaking from within an institutional orientation, however, claimed that their faith was just as real, inward, and personal as those in the nascent group. Institutional types also asserted that nascent types had little religious "class," while they, in contrast, were committed to expressing their religious faith discreetly and respectably. The view from both sides of this divide proved significant to religious identities; taking a stance here was understood to be making a real claim to distinction within the religious field.

Within the categories supplied by those interviewed, the nascent-institutional division became especially significant when those orientations extended into the more public dimensions of religious faith. Nascent types felt that some kind of symbolic stance needed to be included in one's identity either through political involvement, community service, or interpersonal relations. This was juxtaposed to keeping one's faith generally

---

51. Oregon, August 10, 1995.

out of view and allowing it public expression only through quiet church-going. Persons with nascent religious identities saw themselves on a religious mission and claimed that quiescent, institutionally oriented Protestants were just going along without taking a stand.

For those on one side of this divide, the way to do religion truly was to have a vital, heartfelt faith that necessarily spilled over into all one did. The distinction between being a fanatic versus being respectable recurred in interviews. One Southern Baptist woman said: "Our pastor once told me that if anyone accused me of being overly zealous, I could tell them, well, if I'm a fanatic then that means I love the Lord more than you do. So, sometimes I might tend to be overly fanatic."[52] Often these respondents constructed their identity against an image of "churchianity," a sterile, organizational Christianity that somehow failed to engage the inner spirit of the individual, and instead was an outcome of social forces. In contrast to that demeanor, a United Methodist man stated quite adamantly:

> I don't believe that anybody should be a closet Christian. See, now there's nothing wrong with going to church . . . [but] I've been down that road where I went because that was just the proper thing to do. Everybody seemed to approve and it's a certain part of socializing. In a little town like Cloverdale with three thousand people, a church was a big part of the social life. The legal social life, I should say.[53]

This kind of nascent religious identity was often expressed in terms of a need to speak up or to take a stand for something. This was true for some self-declared evangelicals, one of whom said he was an evangelical precisely "because I speak of God and spread his good news and I speak of God through my actions and through my life and discussing topics with people."[54] But one of our self-described liberal and mainline respondents could describe himself in much the same way: "I would say that I am a practicing Christian. Because I think that there are people who call themselves Christian, but they don't practice their beliefs. I believe you have to practice what you preach. That's probably foremost. Caring, outreaching." There was, for him, no need for further qualifications since "that covers an awful lot when you say that."[55] For both of these individuals, being an authentic Christian was necessarily connected to some degree

---

52. North Carolina, July 10, 1995.
53. North Carolina, July 12, 1995.
54. Massachusetts, August 14, 1995.
55. North Carolina, June 30, 1995.

with a willingness to speak out about and to act on the basis of one's faith. The same "liberal" respondent just quoted put it this way:

> I know what I believe and I try real hard to live what I believe. But it can be kind of tough in this day and age because you just don't know how people are going to react when you make an offhanded . . . not an offhanded comment but a comment about . . . in general conversation [like] "no, you need a little guidance from God," if you need it. It doesn't bother me to say that to people anymore.

People on the other side of this divide — the institutional side — see things more in terms of religious excess. What is an appropriate, respectable expression of one's faith and what should be kept more private? Most institutionally oriented respondents thought the important things were going to church, being civil to everyone, and helping those in need. One Lutheran man said:

> I'm not really any different than those who believe in the Golden Rule . . . that's how I feel about Christianity. I still think I was born and raised to be — that everything in this life was pretty steady, steady, steady, and Christianity fits my life that same way. It's part of me. I don't want to cheat anybody, I want to be as nice as I can to everybody.[56]

Another person who said she was more fundamentalist than evangelical, viewed evangelicals in this way. Evangelicals were seen as: "Well, a lot more active than I am — going around and testifying and all, you know, to your face and all."[57] "In your face" religion separated nascent from institutional orientations, and cross-cut liberal and conservative self-identifications. This sometimes connected with the image of being charismatic. The same person just quoted distinguished her own religious identity from a charismatic identity by distancing herself from their too-ready willingness to tout their inner religious experience in public: "Expressing yourself more than I do, I mean you know . . . it's a little bit more than I . . . I don't . . . I'm not that at all." According to a forty-one-year-old United Methodist woman, a "charismatic is a radical individual. . . . Because sometimes I think the charismatics are overbearing. Very overbearing and very forceful — and I think radicals can be the same way."[58] The image

56. Oregon, July 28, 1995.
57. North Carolina, July 13, 1995.
58. North Carolina, June 30, 1995.

of charismatics allowed many of our respondents to place themselves against more nascent religious types, which, according to the institutional types, were going overboard with their religion.

Institutionally oriented respondents built their identities largely on church-going, but they also defined themselves against those who took too histrionic a public stance in matters of faith. One respondent explained that her faith had grown out of a family in which "our life centered around the church, all the activities of the church, but I don't ever remember thinking we were deprived in any way like the kids in some of those [fundamentalist] churches are now." The fundamentalists, she believed, were simply "so hard core about everything." A fundamentalist, she said, is:

> somebody that goes out and talks against this and that and the other, and they have fundamentalists who work in the legislature and such, and I don't consider myself [that]. "Christian" to me is somebody who really believes, who makes sure that their life is working toward that, but not the hard core type thing, if you understand what I'm saying?[59]

Rather than a "hard core kind of thing," this respondent thought that faith should be worked out with more subtlety: "I think if you live your everyday life as a Christian, people are going to know you're a Christian. I don't think you have to go around shouting it from the rooftops." Identity for this respondent and for numerous others turned on a symbolic boundary between expressing one's faith in the little things of everyday life and expressing one's faith in an overly public, almost aggressive manner. In distinction from those "shouting from the rooftops," institutional types took a stand which saw that kind of public faith as gaudy at best and as egoistic at worst.

The nascent-institutional divide revolved mostly around a question of style, that is, how one could and should appropriately express one's inward religious identity in one's outward, public life. The claim of many nascently oriented Protestants was that "true Christians" were those who set themselves apart from the world around them by speaking up, taking a stand, or somehow showing a religious difference that emerged from an inner spirituality. Institutional types, by contrast, were more likely to want to minimize that kind of public cleavage in matters of faith. This distinction, in turn, tended to tie back into the way people valued (or disvalued)

59. Oregon, August 14, 1995.

fanaticism and respectability in religious faith. The nexus of these concerns marked a powerful symbolic boundary within the religious identities of those interviewed.

Conclusion

This project focused on the language used by lay Protestants to construct their religious identities. I looked especially at the symbolic boundaries church-going Protestants articulated to help them understand the larger religious landscape and their place in it. Preliminary results reveal the lack of any one master frame for religious identity. Multiple and crosscutting dimensions of difference were salient in the identity construction of American Protestants across the whole spectrum of denominational affiliation and theological opinion. The meaning of identifying oneself as a fundamentalist, evangelical, charismatic, pentecostal, or liberal did not typically include a connection to any broader movements in the religious field. In fact, relatively few persons made positive claims of religious identity at all. Instead, most respondents defined the boundaries of their religious selves by appealing to a varied array of images of religious social types with which they did not want to be identified. Respondents from all across the spectrum, including most self-described evangelicals, defined their religious identities in terms of how their own faith differed from the caricatures of one or several out-groups.

Contrary to conventional wisdom, this study found that the liberal-conservative symbolic boundary was not the axis on which most religious identities turned. The liberal-conservative divide, while not always without meaning, often took a back seat to dimensions of difference within a much more circumscribed domain, helping persons to distinguish themselves from their relatively close religious peers. Other dimensions of difference proved more powerful than the liberal-conservative distinction in setting boundaries around religious identities of many respondents. For example, identities rooted in confessional denominational traditions drew powerful and competing lines across the "conservative" end of the religious field. Perhaps the single most important symbolic boundary marker pointed out by those interviewed was the fissure between nascent and institutional forms of faiths which crosscut the entire liberal-conservative spectrum.

Finally, the religious identities of study participants did show the marks of both expressive and utilitarian individualism. This mitigated the boundedness of religious identities in general and increased the extent to which almost everyone's religious identity took on some sense of "personal eclecticism."[60] Many people took stronger moral stands in favor of civility than they did in defending religious doctrines and truth. The individualistic language used in these constructions of religious identity changed the very meaning of religious identification itself. Language that expresses religious identity in terms of what is "right for me" or what "works for me" reduces the power of any single dimension of difference to define religious identity. Thus religious identity in general tends to become somewhat fuzzy as individuals mix and match, in their own persons, different characteristics of faith to which they feel varying and changing degrees of attraction and repulsion.

60. Wuthnow, *Acts of Compassion*.

CHAPTER 4

Listening to the Disenfranchised: Toward a Multiparty Conception of American Religion

FRED KNISS

The two-party theory of American religion has a long and illustrious career in a variety of disciplines among scholars who study religion. Speaking for religious historians, Martin Marty made the classic statement of the case in *Righteous Empire*, drawing the distinction between "private" and "public" Protestantism.[1] Sociology has also made frequent use of the two-party model or bipolar conceptions of the American religious terrain in order to explain religious change and conflict.

A recent instance of this notion, and one which has captured the public consciousness, is the work of James Davison Hunter. Ever since the publication of his book *Culture Wars* in 1991, the idea that America is in the midst of a fierce "culture war" has been part of our public discourse.[2] The rhetoric of recent presidential campaigns has amplified the idea in the popular consciousness, and other recent events like shootings at abortion clinics have led some to suggest that we may be observing the first literal shots in a war that is more real than metaphorical. Public metaphors like "culture war" can become self-fulfilling prophecies, especially when they become organizing principles for popular discourse. For this reason, scholars — especially those who would at-

1. Martin E. Marty, *Righteous Empire: The Protestant Experience in America* (New York: Harper & Row, 1970).
2. James Davison Hunter, *Culture Wars: The Struggle to Define America* (New York: Basic Books, 1991).

tempt to speak beyond the academy and address a larger public audience
— need to be careful that their conceptions portray an accurate picture
of social reality, capturing as much of its diversity, complexity, and subtlety as possible.

This essay takes a critical look at the common wisdom that the
American religious landscape is best described in bipolar terms. I argue
that the picture of two diametrically opposed parties is too simplistic,
drawn from unidimensional conceptions of the issues at stake. Simple and
stark bipolar conceptions have significant rhetorical payoffs, but often at
the cost of analytical rigor and subtlety. Two-party theories exaggerate the
level of conflict in society and, perhaps more importantly, ignore the
presence and impact of groups that do not fit the model. Such groups are
"disenfranchised" in a two-party system, to extend the political metaphor.
This is more than academic nit-picking. As the history of the "culture war"
notion shows, our conceptions can have real effects on people's perceptions and, thus, on their actions. Theories that hide or silence significant
segments of the religious population both misrepresent the social realities
in which we all are enmeshed and diminish the ability of disenfranchised
groups to have any real impact on society.

In the place of these bipolar, unidimensional schemes, I propose a
two-dimensional model that allows us to see the world in more complex
terms. It allows us to listen to previously disenfranchised voices as well
as to the rhetoric of the mainstream. By adding just one additional dimension to our theoretical reflection, we can produce a more refined map of
the American "moral order," the terrain upon which religious change and
cultural conflicts are often fought. This new way of mapping the moral
order opens a range of alternative approaches to our old questions, and
it also suggests some new questions that we ought to be asking about the
dynamics of American faith and society.

Bipolar Conceptions of American Religion

A number of political observers and social scientists have suggested that
post-1950s America has seen a cultural and/or religious polarization that
has increased the level of conflict in our public and private lives. Various
ways of explaining this divide have been put forward, but most share a
unidimensional, bipolar conceptualization of the conflict. For example,
Wade Clark Roof has attempted to explain the decline of liberal Protestant
denominations in terms of a cultural polarization between "locals" and

"cosmopolitans,"[3] and Dean Hoge and David Roozen have postulated a conflict between "traditional Christianity" and "scientific humanism."[4]

Robert Wuthnow, in his influential *The Restructuring of American Religion*,[5] suggests that American religion has been restructured into liberal and conservative camps, a divide that increasingly occurs within denominations rather than between them. (Others concur with Wuthnow's claim of a widening "great divide" in American religion, but debate whether this divide occurs primarily *within* or *between* denominations.)[6] The effect, according to Wuthnow, is that the general level of social conflict has been raised. Increased conflict now occurs within denominations around liberal/conservative issues, and this restructuring of religious conflict has larger parallels to the polarization of American culture in general. Wuthnow refers primarily to religious liberalism and conservatism, but he views these two camps as also sharing liberal or conservative views on moral, social, and political issues. Religion, ethics, and politics all intertwine. The ideological affinity within the two parties across these issue domains thus contributes to the macro-social polarization Wuthnow observes.

But it is James Davison Hunter who has explored the recent polarization in American culture most generally and before the largest public audience.[7] He views the situation more apocalyptically than most other analysts and has helped to bring the notion of a "culture war" into the American public consciousness. Like others, Hunter sees Americans divided into two opposing camps, but the key distinction he draws between the two camps is the issue of cultural or moral authority. The "orthodox" party adheres to "an external, definable, and transcendent authority," while the "progressive" party follows "the prevailing assump-

---

3. Wade Clark Roof, *Community and Commitment: Religious Plausibility in a Liberal Protestant Church* (New York: Elsevier, 1978).

4. Dean R. Hoge and David A. Roozen, "Some Sociological Conclusions About Church Trends," in Dean R. Hoge and David A. Roozen, eds., *Understanding Church Growth and Decline: 1950-1978* (New York: Pilgrim Press, 1979), 315-34.

5. Robert Wuthnow, *The Restructuring of American Religion* (Princeton: Princeton University Press, 1988).

6. See Wade Clark Roof and William McKinney, *American Mainline Religion* (New Brunswick, NJ: Rutgers University Press, 1987); and William McKinney and Daniel V. A. Olson, "Restructuring Among Protestant Denominational Leaders: The Great Divide and the Great Middle," paper presented at American Sociological Association Annual Meeting, Cincinnati, Ohio, 1991.

7. Hunter, *Culture Wars*. See also James Davison Hunter, *Before the Shooting Begins: Searching for Democracy in America's Culture War* (New York: The Free Press, 1994).

tions of contemporary life."[8] Hunter analyzes this polarization across a range of cultural fields and suggests that it poses a threat to the democratic order. Albert O. Hirschman, writing from further left on the political spectrum, makes a similar argument about the recent polarization of public discourse, referring to the sides as "reactionary" and "progressive." However, unlike the other analysts noted here, he views the current polarization as a normal part of the cycle of public political discourse and concerns himself more with the form of the debate than with its content.[9]

A related set of bipolar distinctions is found in the venerable body of sociological literature dealing with tensions between the individual and the community. Robert Bellah (writing alone and with various colleagues) has treated at length the polarization between "utilitarian individualism" and "civic republicanism."[10] This divide is also at the core of Martin Marty's notion of a split between "private" and "public" religion which has been so influential in both the sociological study of religion and the writing of American religious history.[11] Harold Bloom's recent controversial characterization of American religion as essentially gnostic is one current example of the ongoing life of this individual-versus-community debate.[12]

What all of these scholars share is a bipolar conception of the American religious and/or cultural scene. This conceptual logic has at least two key problems. The first and most important is that it assumes that all or nearly all individuals and groups (or at least those that matter in the public discourse) fall into one of two camps. Occasionally there are references to the fact that, of course, there are many groups who do not fit the picture and many individuals who fall somewhere between or outside the poles, but these are seldom more than passing references and seem quickly forgotten.[13] Groups that do not fit the proposed bipolar conception are left outside the explanatory model. Methodologically, this makes it diffi-

---

8. Hunter, *Culture Wars,* 44-45.

9. Albert O. Hirschman, *The Rhetoric of Reaction: Perversity, Futility, Jeopardy* (Cambridge, MA: Belknap Press of Harvard University Press, 1991).

10. See Robert N. Bellah, *The Broken Covenant: American Civil Religion in Time of Trial* (New York: Seabury Press, 1975); Robert Bellah and Phillip E. Hammond, *Varieties of Civil Religion* (New York: Harper and Row, 1980); and Robert N. Bellah, Richard Madsen, William M. Sullivan, Ann Swidler, and Steven M. Tipton, *Habits of the Heart: Individualism and Commitment in American Life* (New York: Harper and Row, Perennial Library, 1985).

11. Marty, *Righteous Empire.*

12. Harold Bloom, *The American Religion* (New York: Simon and Schuster, 1992).

13. See, e.g., Hunter, *Culture Wars,* 105.

cult to disconfirm hypotheses about cultural or religious polarization. Substantively, it leads to three subsidiary problems. First, it masks important distinctions within and between the two parties. Second, it exaggerates the level of conflict in society. And third, it ignores the presence and impact of groups that do not fit neatly into either of the two categories postulated by the model.

In the following section, I propose a multidimensional model of the American cultural battleground that addresses these problems. It takes into account the polarizations around the policy issues noted by Wuthnow and others, the authority issues noted by Hunter, and the individual/community tensions noted by Marty, Bellah, and others. This new model provides a mechanism for locating and including the ideologies and practices of groups and individuals who have been disenfranchised by bipolar or two-party theories, i.e., groups that lie outside the mainstream discourse. A two-dimensional map also enables the generation of more incisive explanations and hypotheses about the dynamic processes of religious change and conflict in America.

A New Map of the American Religious and Moral Terrain

In his *Meaning and Moral Order: Explorations in Cultural Analysis*, Robert Wuthnow tried to develop a more objective approach to cultural analysis. He did so by describing the overarching ideological system or "moral order" within which he understood American religious and political movements to pursue their various interests.[14] Wuthnow, of course, is not the only observer to posit such a system. A similar conception is present in many of the works discussed earlier. But most analysts have been rather vague about how to define the constituent elements that make up the American moral order. By contrast, the two-dimensional heuristic grid proposed here focuses specifically on those constituent elements and is thus able to produce a more nuanced "ideological map" of the American moral order. This map continues to provide categories for analysis of the dominant or mainstream ideological spectrum; but it also permits, indeed it requires, the inclusion of various peripheral positions currently disenfranchised by most two-party theories. Additionally, this multidimensional scheme allows for the analysis of relationships between the disenfranchised and the mainstream.

14. Robert Wuthnow, *Meaning and Moral Order: Explorations in Cultural Analysis* (Berkeley: University of California Press, 1987).

My two-dimensional map is organized along the lines of two over-lapping axes which represent the two central issues that necessarily con-stitute the skeleton of any "moral order." The first is the locus of moral authority, and the second is what constitutes the moral project. The first issue is concerned with the fundamental basis for ethical, aesthetic, or epistemological standards (i.e., the nature of "good," "beauty," and "truth"). With regard to these matters, the locus of moral authority may reside either in the individual's reason and experience or in the collective tradition. The second issue addresses the question of where moral action or influence should be targeted. That is, if good, beauty, and truth are to be enhanced, what needs to be changed? Relative to this second dimen-sion, the moral project may be understood either as the maximization of individual utility or in terms of the maximization of the public good. There is something of a parallel here to Max Weber's distinction between *wer-trational* and *zweckrational*.[15] That is, the issue of moral authority is con-cerned with the grounds for defining or evaluating ultimate ends, while the question of the moral project is concerned with means to those ends. The former provides the foundation for central values. The latter provides the foundation for particular policies.

Identifying these two separate and distinct ideological dimensions of the moral order can help us to distinguish some key differences between various two-party theories. For example, the restructuring theories of Wuthnow and others focus on issues related primarily to the second dimension, religious or political moral projects. Hunter, on the other hand, deals primarily with tensions over the question of moral authority. Further, the poles on both of the dimensional continua reflect the tensions between the individual and the collective that Bellah and Marty and many other analysts of American political culture have noted. While I am provisionally presenting these two dimensions as overlapping dichotomies that form four distinct ideal types, my later discussion will indicate that I really view them as spectra along which a wide variety of ideas may occur. In other words, these two dimensions crosscut and interact with each other in complex ways.[16]

15. See Max Weber, *Economy and Society: An Outline of Interpretive Sociology*, eds. Guenther Roth and Claus Wittich (Berkeley: University of California Press, 1978).

16. Jeffry Will and Rhys Williams in "Political Ideology and Political Action in the New Christian Right," *Sociological Analysis* 47 (1986): 160-68, propose a similar typology. However, by making "right vs. left" one of the dimensions, they preclude the possibility of anomalous paradigm configurations of the sort I will be discussing here.

With respect to the first issue (the locus of moral authority), the paradigm of *modernism* holds that the fundamental authority for defining ultimate values (good, beauty, and truth) is grounded in an individual's reason as applied to and filtered through individual experience. Reason is located in particular individuals in particular times and places. Thus, there is a denial of any traditional transcendent absolute authority. Authority is always subject to rational criticism and legitimation. Ethics are situational, in that determining the good requires the application of reason to particular circumstances. Since modern society is based upon reason in the form of scientific technologies and rational forms of social organization, modernists are optimistic about progress and tend to be open to change. Further, insofar as rationality is understood to be foundational to human nature, human nature is seen as basically "good." There is within modernism, therefore, an inherent trust in human beings, resulting in an emphasis upon individual freedom and civil liberties. The expressive individualism of recent decades noted (and often decried) by many of the scholars mentioned above is a product of modernism as the fundamental paradigm of moral authority.

Within religion, modernism has been the focus of much conflict during the past century. Modernism legitimized rational criticism of ecclesiastical and biblical authority. In shorthand form, one can define religious modernism as holding that: (1) religious ideas should be consciously adapted to modern culture; (2) God is immanent in and revealed through human cultural development; and (3) human society is progressively moving toward the realization of the Kingdom of God.[17] Religious conservatives have, of course, opposed this view as an attack on the "fundamentals" of religious faith and as a challenge to traditional authority.[18]

Traditionalism, in contrast to modernism, holds that the definition of ultimate values is grounded in the moral authority of the collective tradition. Rather than focusing on the free individual actor, emphasis is placed upon individuals as members of a collectivity, a social group defined by its relation to some higher authority. Authority transcends any particularities of person, place, or time. It is absolute and not open to criticism. Ethics are not seen as situational, but as absolute. Individual actions are expected to contribute to the social good.

17. See William R. Hutchison, *The Modernist Impulse in American Protestantism* (Oxford: Oxford University Press, 1982).

18. See George Marsden, *Fundamentalism and American Culture: The Shaping of Twentieth-Century Evangelicalism, 1870-1925* (Oxford: Oxford University Press, 1980).

Traditionalism stresses submission to the collectivity and restraint upon individual appetites. The nuclear family, as the smallest, most basic collectivity under a common authority, is particularly valued. Practices which are seen to threaten the family (e.g., promiscuity, homosexuality, or abortion) are thus opposed with special tenacity. In religion, traditionalism takes the form of obedience to ecclesiastical and scriptural authority. Respect for transcendent authority is paralleled by a respect for transcendent values. The goal of change, then, is not progress toward perfection, but recovery of traditional values. Modern culture is not seen as progress toward a better form of existence, but as a fall from paradise.

On the second dimension (locus of the moral project), the paradigm of *libertarianism,* like modernism, asserts the primacy of the individual. It holds that the primary moral project is the maximization of individual utility, i.e., it applies individualism to questions of economic and political relationships. The ideal economic system is the free market where free individuals acting in their own rational self-interest compete for resources. Economic growth is encouraged as a way of making more goods and services available to everyone. Growth in these terms requires unrestrained individual striving and minimal regulation by the state. Networks formed by the individual pursuit of self-interest in a free market are the bases of the social bond. Hence, only a minimal state is required, one whose function is protection of individual rights, but one that is not concerned with the provision of social services or regulation of the economy.[19] The religious counterpart to libertarianism holds that the primary moral project is the individual's salvation and moral improvement.

As libertarianism is to modernism, so *communalism* is to traditionalism. That is, communalism takes the principle of individual submission to the collective good and applies it to questions of economic and political organization rather than to questions of ultimate value. The moral project is seen in terms of the collective good rather than individual utility. A regulated market is thus valued over an unregulated free market. Egalitarianism is valued over limitless self-interested striving. The state is expected to promote these values by enforcing the redistribution of resources in a manner that promotes the collective good. (Entitlement programs are an example of public policy based upon the paradigm of communalism.) The state is also expected to curtail individual self-interested action when it threatens public goods such as environmental quality, public safety, or

19. Robert Nozick attempts a philosophical justification of this paradigm in his *Anarchy, State and Utopia* (New York: Basic Books, 1974).

public health. Communalism may be applied across generations, as when today's wage earners support Social Security payments to the elderly or when conservation policies are justified as necessary to preserve resources for future generations. In religion, communalism identifies the primary moral project as "building the kingdom of God," that is, establishing a reformed social order rather than seeking to reform the lives of people as individuals.

Dynamic Interactions between the Two Dimensions of the Moral Order

So far, I have presented the dominant paradigms of the American moral order as if they formed a fairly strict set of typologies composed of mutually exclusive categories of concern. Empirically, however, these categories occur together in various configurations and interact dynamically with each other. The ideology of any specific group will necessarily take a position on questions of both moral authority and the moral project. In American religion, mainstream and peripheral groups make use of a wide spectrum of ideas and symbols. Some of the ideas and symbols held by these divergent groups fall neatly into the given categories of one or another paradigm, but others cannot be so easily located. In fact, these not-easily-mapped ideas and symbols are often highly ambiguous. Across the board, however, we find that moral ideas and symbols rarely come packaged as simple givens, and they are rarely stable. Instead, they are constantly being contested, refined, and adapted, leading to dynamic relationships within and between the various paradigms so neatly described above.

In thinking about plausible configurations of the paradigms discussed above, one might intuitively expect the individualistic paradigms of modernism and libertarianism to occur together and be opposed to an alliance between the collective paradigms of traditionalism and communalism. In fact, American ideology has been counterintuitive in this respect. Although they may have used different terms, various writers have noted the paradoxical combination of traditionalism and libertarianism in conservative or right-wing American ideology.[20] Although many

20. See George H. Nash, *The Conservative Intellectual Movement in America, Since 1945* (New York: Basic, 1976); Seymour Martin Lipset and Earl Raab, *The Politics of Unreason: Right-Wing Extremism in America, 1790-1977* (Chicago: University of Chicago

scholars view this paradox as primarily a characteristic of post-1945 American conservatism, as far back as the 1830s de Tocqueville noted in *Democracy in America* that traditional religion in the U.S. had combined with unrestrained self-interest to promote the general welfare.[21] In contrast, the American left has combined modernism with communalism, supporting both the moral autonomy of the individual and the regulation of economic and political activity in defense of the public good. These are, of course, ideal-typical characterizations. They represent two poles on the American ideological spectrum. Clearly, there is a large ambiguous middle position; but there is, nevertheless, a clear contrast between the right and left in its "pure" forms. Recognizing the contrasts between and paradoxes within mainstream American ideological positions is important for understanding specific cases of ideological change or conflict.[22]

Figure 1 (page 82) is a graphic representation of what I call "American mainstream ideological discourse." Here the dimensions defining the paradigms are represented as spectra rather than categories. The x-axis represents the locus of moral authority and the y-axis represents the moral project. Idea systems may theoretically be located at any position on the map. Although right-wing purists would tend to be located in the northeast corner and left-wing purists in the southwest corner, the boundaries of these categories are porous. The line connecting the two extremes is the realm of mainstream discourse. There are clear, sharp, often bitterly contested differences between positions along this line, but those located within the mainstream understand the differences. There are routinized vocabularies, procedures, categories, etc., for discussing and negotiating these differences. Most negotiation takes place in the "ambiguous middle," which is where the majority of political institutions are located. This is the area both where compromises are formed and where an observer can find the seemingly incompatible elements of opposing paradigms oddly joined

---

Press, 1978); Jerome L. Himmelstein, "The New Right," in Robert C. Liebman and Robert Wuthnow, eds., *The New Christian Right* (New York: Aldine, 1983), 133-48; and Gerald M. Platt and Rhys H. Williams, "Religion, Ideology and Electoral Politics," *Society* 25 (July/August 1988): 38-45.

21. Alexis de Tocqueville, *Democracy in America,* trans. George Lawrence, ed. J. P. Mayer (Garden City, NY: Anchor Books, 1969).

22. One can speculate about the reasons for these paradoxical configurations. Perhaps there is a "need" for a balance between individual and collective values. Jerome L. Himmelstein suggests that, on the right, neither traditionalism nor libertarianism carries much appeal on its own, but each provides a corrective to the unappealing aspects of the other. See Himmelstein, "The New Right."

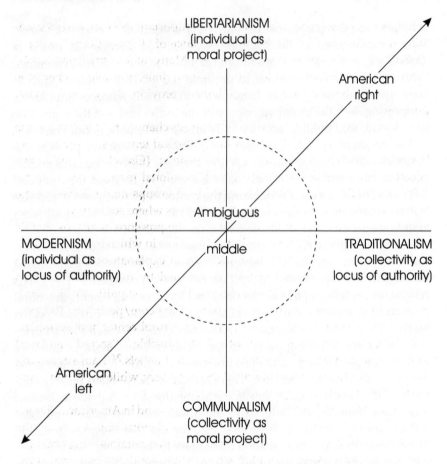

Figure 1. American mainstream ideological discourse

together — thus the phrase "politics makes strange bedfellows." Even when policies have been formulated at one or the other "purist" end of this spectrum, they tend to gravitate toward this middle in their actual implementation.

The Significance of Peripheral Groups

I argued above that bipolar conceptions of cultural conflict ignored the presence and role of peripheral groups — groups that do not fit in either of the two opposing categories. This is an important theoretical shortcoming, especially at a time when the importance of "the periphery" is being recognized in theories of social change. Many of the most influential theories of political economic change posit a dialectical relation between core and peripheral institutions. This tension provides the engine for many processes of social change.

I am suggesting that cultural or religious change and conflict operate within a similar dialectical system of ideological tensions within and between mainstream and fringe cultural groups. (Elsewhere I make this argument in some detail.)[23] The two-dimensional map proposed above helps to specify exactly how different fringe groups might be peripheral to the mainstream. Figure 2 (page 84) suggests where some fringe groups might be located on the map. Recognizing the presence of groups that lie outside the mainstream and specifying the ways in which they are peripheral allows the analyst to include them in an explanatory model and to consider how they might affect or be affected by mainstream tensions and/or polarization. Note, however, that there is a significant difference between my conceptualization and some of the core/periphery theories. Consider, for example, Shils' theory of the cultural center and periphery. For Shils, the center is the "ultimate," "irreducible," "sacred" realm of society's most important symbols, values, and beliefs.[24] I am suggesting that these values exist most purely at the periphery, while the center is the realm of ambiguity and competition over ideas.

The periphery has been especially fertile ground in American religious history. Various historians have argued that religious innovation on the periphery is the defining characteristic of American religion.[25] In particular, there has been a striking amount of activity in the southeast quadrant of the map. In many of the new religious movements in America over the past two centuries, a millenarian impulse produced a collective moral project, the establishment of a new social order, and stressed the moral authority of the collectivity, even though that authority may have been embodied in a charismatic leader.[26] The Mormons are the prime example of such a group.

23. Fred Kniss, "Toward a Theory of Ideological Change: The Case of the Radical Reformation," *Sociological Analysis* 49 (Spring 1988): 29-38.
   24. Edward Shils, *Center and Periphery: Essays in Macro-Sociology* (Chicago: University of Chicago Press, 1975).
   25. See, e.g., Edwin Scott Gaustad, *Dissent in American Religion* (Chicago: University of Chicago Press, 1973); and R. Laurence Moore, *Religious Outsiders and the Making of Americans* (New York: Oxford University Press, 1986).
   26. See Joseph Bettis and S. K. Johannesen, eds., *The Return of the Millennium*

Figure 2. Peripheral locations of fringe groups

But other less exotic religious groups are also peripheral to the American cultural mainstream as I have mapped it. Mennonites, Amish, and related groups belong here, as do many African-American Protestant groups, who have combined traditional notions of religious authority with a more "liberal" social ethic, focusing on transformation of the social order. This was most evident in the central role played by "conservative" African-American religious groups in the civil rights movement. An

(Barrytown, NY: New Era Books, 1984); and Ernest Lee Tuveson, *Redeemer Nation: The Idea of America's Millennial Role* (Chicago: University of Chicago Press, 1968).

interesting recent variation on a similar theme is the so-called "new evangelical left." Groups like the Sojourners in Washington, D.C., combine traditional notions of religious/moral authority with collectivist moral projects aimed at both establishing their own alternative utopian social order and reforming the larger secular social order. I place the Quakers halfway between the southeast and southwest points on the map. They tend to focus on collective moral projects, but also place more emphasis on an authoritative "divine spark" within individuals. They stop short of granting complete moral autonomy to individuals, however, since particular manifestations of the divine spark are to be tested and implemented within the context of the collective community. Thomas Hamm documents the Quaker move toward modernist ideas around the turn of the century.[27]

American Catholics are an especially interesting case with respect to the scheme I propose. I would argue that they are also best placed in the southeast quadrant with other groups that hold collectivist ideas about both moral authority and moral projects. However, there is enough diversity within the Catholic community that any attempt to place them in a single location is of necessity a gross generalization. If, as many argue, the history of American Catholicism is one of "Protestantization," it may be that Catholic subgroups now occupy mainstream locations as well.

I have said little about the northwest quadrant of the map, largely because few groups tend to locate there. An ideology that is thoroughly individualist will not easily sustain a coherent group identity. To the extent that groups do cohere around an ideology, they tend to move toward the collective end of at least one of the dimensions. So, for example, anarchist ideologies would be located here, but anarchist *groups* are notoriously short-lived. Some of the highly individualist therapeutic utopias of the sixties and seventies also combined individual moral authority with individualist moral projects. Many of these did not survive for long, while others moved rightward in authoritarian directions as they grew and institutionalized. The Church of Scientology is a good example of such an evolution. But just because movements in this quadrant tend to be short-lived, this does not mean such movements are either unimportant or inconsequential. For example, Hoge et al. found that "lay liberals" who reject any universal transcendent collective authority comprise a signifi-

---

27. Thomas D. Hamm, *The Transformation of American Quakerism: Orthodox Friends, 1800-1907* (Bloomington, IN: Indiana University Press, 1988).

cant proportion of Protestant Baby Boomers.[28] However, "lay liberals" are an interesting case, since many did accept the authority of more localized, relativistic moral codes which were, nonetheless, tied to a collective identity that transcended purely individual experience.

The presence of so much ideological activity in locations off the mainstream belies the notion that American religion or culture is best described in bipolar terms. It also raises significant questions for the thesis that a "culture war" is underway. The presence of active peripheral ideologies complicates easy coalition building, and mitigates cultural tension within the mainstream by exerting crosscutting pressures.

Understanding Intragroup Conflict

The "moral order map" proposed here also provides a useful heuristic tool for analyzing many of the specific cultural or religious conflicts that interest sociologists, especially those involving "sects" and "cults." These terms usually refer to groups that lie "off the diagonal" on the moral order map. The map helps us to be clearer about just how these groups differ from the mainstream. In my research, I have used this map to analyze ideological conflict among American Mennonites. For example, I have argued that Mennonites are a fringe group because they combine the paradigms of traditionalism and communalism, a configuration that places them outside the mainstream of American ideological discourse.[29] Throughout their history, they have combined an emphasis upon traditional moral and spiritual values, biblical and communal authority, and denial of individual interests in favor of the collectivity (i.e., traditionalism), with a concern for egalitarianism, social justice, pacifism, environmental conservation, mutual aid, and the like (i.e., communalism).

This ideological peripherality has been a source of conflict for Mennonites. Their combination of traditionalism and communalism has been especially uneasy within the context of twentieth-century America. Mennonite individuals and groups who are primarily concerned with traditionalism have often looked to the American right for external supportive

28. Dean R. Hoge, Benton Johnson, and Donald A. Luidens, *Vanishing Boundaries: The Religion of Mainline Protestant Baby Boomers* (Louisville: Westminster/John Knox Press, 1994).

29. Fred Kniss, "Ideas and Symbols as Resources in Intrareligious Conflict: The Case of American Mennonites," *Sociology of Religion* 57 (Spring 1996): 7-23.

links. Those most concerned with communalism, on the other hand, have looked to the American left. When these external links come to the fore, various social structural cleavages come into alignment. At particular times in Mennonite history, the internal cleavage between paradigms has aligned with external cleavages between fundamentalists and modernists in American religion and between the right and the left in American politics. Increased conflict along external cleavages results in the emergence or intensification of internal conflict.[30]

The dotted-line diagonal in Figure 2 represents an imaginary line dividing the American right from the left. Note that the right-left division becomes an internal cleavage for Mennonite ideology. It would be expected that, during times of unusual ideological dynamism within the mainstream ("unsettled times," to use the concept suggested by Ann Swidler[31]), the internal cleavage between traditionalism and communalism would become more salient and thus conflict would be more likely to emerge around these paradigms. That is, if either or both of these paradigms are objects of contention in the mainstream, then the cleavage between them would become sharper within the Mennonite community and the number and intensity of such conflicts would increase. This pattern was confirmed in my analysis of more than 200 conflict events occurring within the Mennonite Church in Virginia, Pennsylvania, Ohio, and Indiana between 1870 and 1985.[32]

There were two periods during this century when, for Mennonites, internal polarization between the traditionalist and communalist paradigms generated numerous conflicts leading to schism or expulsion of individuals and congregations. One was during the 1920s to mid-thirties. The other was during the sixties through the mid-eighties. During the former, the primary instigators of conflict were progressive communalists

---

30. James S. Coleman argues for the importance of such potential lines of cleavage within a group. The extent to which various lines of cleavage coincide will determine the extent and intensity of a conflict. Coleman refers to the process of heightened intensity as the elevation of a conflict from the level of *within* individuals to *between* individuals. I prefer to think of this as the coming into alignment of two or more structural cleavages; but regardless of how this is conceptualized, the result is a heightening of conflict. See his "Social Cleavage and Religious Conflict," *Journal of Social Issues* 12 (1956): 44-56.

31. Ann Swidler, "Culture in Action: Symbols and Strategies," *American Sociological Review* 51 (1986): 273-86.

32. Fred Kniss, *Disquiet in the Land: Cultural Conflict in American Mennonite Communities* (New Brunswick, NJ: Rutgers University Press, 1997).

who challenged the legitimacy of traditional authorities. During the latter, the modal conflict was instigated by traditionalists attempting to restore the authority of traditional sectarian standards. In each case, contenders on both sides of conflicts had ready access to ideological and material resources because of polarization in the mainstream religious and political culture. Understanding these patterns of conflict requires focusing on the interaction between, on the one hand, the internal characteristics of Mennonites that made them a fringe group and, on the other, upheaval and polarization in the mainstream.

Impact of Fringe Groups on the Mainstream

I have been making the point that bipolar conceptions of cultural conflict lead to ignoring or misunderstanding the experience of sectarian, utopian, and other peripheral groups and movements. But some may argue that this is no great loss — that fringe groups may be interesting curiosities, but they are, after all, peripheral and thus relatively insignificant for understanding large-scale cultural conflicts occurring in the mainstream. However, another implication of the moral order map I propose is that the interaction between groups on and off the diagonal has an impact on both. Thus, for example, fringe groups like the Mennonites should not only be affected by tensions in the mainstream, but should also have an impact on the larger environment. This kind of argument is much more difficult to make concisely or coherently because the effect, the impact on the sociocultural environment, is so diffuse. However, if we focus on specific characteristics of the environment, it is possible to demonstrate such effects.

Probably the best example in the case of the Mennonites is American government policy toward conscientious objectors to war. The rapid succession of wars in this century and the disastrous experience of Mennonites during the first one led to their increasingly sophisticated dealings with the government (in cooperation with other "peace churches") in developing policies relating to conscientious objection to participation in war or in the military generally. The successful insertion of such policies into the United States legal code changed at least this one aspect of the political environment, making conscientious objection to war more respectable and more accessible to many people other than Mennonites. The further institutionalization and expansion of legitimate bases of conscientious objection became, in turn, one important element of the widespread antiwar activism in the sixties and seventies. The ripple effect of Mennonite initiatives in this area was hardly minimal.

Another more recent example, and one that is missed by simple bipolar conceptions of cultural conflict, is the public discourse around abortion and capital punishment. The irony of people's positions on the value of human life has been pointed out by partisans on both sides of the abortion and capital punishment debates. That is, pro-choice parties in the abortion debate accuse pro-lifers of being concerned about saving the life of the fetus, but being unconcerned about the lives of the mothers, or of prisoners on death row, or of victims of American military interventions. Pro-life parties, on the other hand, suggest that pro-choicers are inconsistent in being willing to "kill" innocent unborn children, yet being unwilling to kill convicted murderers and rapists.

However, the seeming paradox in this debate vanishes if we consider it in light of the "moral order map" I propose. That is, the accusations of each party ignore the location of the specific issues with respect to the larger moral questions, since the issue of abortion is primarily an issue of the locus of moral authority, while the issue of capital punishment regards the moral project.

The point I want to highlight here, however, regards the impact of fringe groups on the mainstream discourse. A relatively recent development in the public debate is the entrance of Mennonites, Catholics, the "new evangelical left," and other groups located "off the diagonal" in the southeast corner of the moral order map who oppose both abortion and capital punishment and refer to themselves as "consistent pro-lifers." They have built alliances with groups on both sides of the "culture wars," thus opening space for accommodation and the lowering of tension. For example, there are emerging groups like Common Ground, a midwestern organization that brings together pro-choice and pro-life activists in cooperative efforts toward lowering rates of unwanted pregnancies and providing services such as improved prenatal care to women who find themselves in that position.

Conclusion

In this essay I have made the argument that the American religious and cultural terrain should be seen in multidimensional terms rather than in the unidimensional terms presented by bipolar theories. I argued that most unidimensional conceptualizations are overly simplistic. As an alternative,

I proposed a more complex two-dimensional map that accommodates most of the bipolar oppositions that various analysts have proposed. But adding a new dimension enables a more sophisticated analysis of specific conflicts and allows interesting distinctions to be drawn between different issues, distinctions that are blurred or ignored in unidimensional conceptualizations. A multidimensional mapping of the cultural terrain has the further benefit of highlighting the role of peripheral groups and ideologies in the larger cultural system. This enables a more complete explanation of *intra*group conflict for groups that have different locations in the "moral order" and provides new insights on the impact of fringe groups on the mainstream.

This more complex picture of cultural conflict raises some serious questions for the argument that there is a unique and significant "culture war" underway at the moment, an argument that is in tune with traditional two-party theories. Certainly there is evidence of increased polarization in public discourse, and there have been attempts on both the left and the right to frame that rhetorical polarization as a war. This strategy has been popular largely because it simplifies the issues and makes recruitment and coalition-building easier. But simplification and political expediency should not be the primary goal or motivation of scholarly analysis. The attention to empirical specificity and historical dynamics that is highlighted by a multidimensional map suggests that the polarization which seems so evident to many observers may be only one part of a picture that is much more complex than partisans would have us believe. Rather than being stacked on top of each other, many issues crosscut each other. This situation may, in fact, attenuate rather than intensify conflict. Different issues have different histories, different ideological components, and different constituencies. It behooves us as social scientists and religious scholars to remind each other and the public at large that such complexity exists and not to reinforce the simplistic apocalyptic visions of those who have particular ideological battles they feel called to fight.

CHAPTER 5

The Shape of American Protestantism:
Are There Two Parties Today?

MARTIN E. MARTY

Any attempt to assess where Americans are today with their Protestantism must begin with an effort to set the whole question into context. Forget, for present purposes, all reference to global religion and global Christianity, however important these have become for American Protestantism. The context here is North America and more particularly the United States. Of course, there are analogues in the Canadian experience, but Canada is also not part of the present focus.

Having narrowed the topic of re-form to one place, the next contextual task is setting the question in the framework of American religion. Has there ever been a Protestant center to re-form in America? You cannot re-form something if there has never been a form for it. You cannot re-form American Protestantism if there has never been any kind of form to have become de-formed or mis-formed or post-formed.

Certainly, American religion as such has had no center. Native Americans enjoyed a wild pluralism of religious options, and Catholics and diverse sets of Protestants vied to claim centrality from the late sixteenth century in the Southwest and the early seventeenth century in the Northeast. On the broadest level, it is impossible to speak of a center of American religion to be re-formed. While this broader pluralism is not the focus of this essay, it is still valid to keep an eye on this religious domain that surrounds the Christianity which surrounds contemporary American Protestantism(s).

MARTIN E. MARTY

The Diversity of the American Protestant World

As of 1990, according to the General Social Surveys,[1] Americans respond to poll-takers who ask very general questions about preference, inkling, identification, or membership as follows: Mormon, 2%; No affiliation, 7%; Jewish, 2%; Roman Catholic, 25%. The word "Protestant" appears in 64% of the identifications. But the very adjectives associated with many of the member groups of this large Protestant constituency suggest how "different" they are, how alienated from any coherent center or core Protestantism they were born to be, chose to be, or forced to be. Thus "Black Protestant, 10%" represents those segregated out of and self-segregated into bodies that never stood a chance until recently to be thought of as part of a formed center. "Nontraditional Protestants, 3%" and "'Ambiguous' Protestant, 5%" must be in a similar circumstance. One pictures groups like Jehovah's Witnesses in these clusters. That leaves "Mainline Protestant, 24%" and "Evangelical Protestant, 22%."

When one asks only slightly different questions and when different collators — Wade Clark Roof and William McKinney[2] instead of Kenneth D. Wald — are doing the interpreting and graph making, the final yield differs little. Using data from six samplings by the General Social Survey people, Roof and McKinney come up with this kind of pie: No religious preference, 6.9%; All others, 8.0%; Jews, 2.3%; Catholics, 25.0%. Whereas Wald's reckoning left us with 64% in self-described Protestant camps, Roof and McKinney's is down to 57.8%. Averaging the two, we can say that just over 60% of United States citizens identify themselves as being somehow Protestant. But Roof and McKinney divide the Protestant camp a little differently. Their figure for black Protestants is 9.1%. They classify 24.2% as "Moderate Protestants"; 8.7% as "Liberal Protestants"; 15.8% as "Conservative Protestants." Given the fact that many in the "moderate" camp of denominations are personally evangelicals, and that "liberals" fade into "moderate" spheres when the concept of "mainstream" or "mainline" Protestant comes up, we are left with two cohorts of roughly equal size. Balancing the Catholic one-fourth are two cuts of the pie: mainstream Protestants on the one hand and, on the other, "evan-

1. Kenneth D. Wald, *Religion and Politics in the United States*, 2nd ed. (Washington, DC: Congressional Quarterly Press, 1992), 71 reproduces a graph based on General Social Surveys and National Opinion Research studies from 1985 to 1989.

2. Wade Clark Roof and William McKinney, *American Mainline Religion: Its Changing Shape and Future* (New Brunswick, NJ: Rutgers University Press, 1987), 82 (graph), 285 (denominations).

gelicals" — evangelicals, fundamentalists, pentecostals, and conservative denomination members together command some sort of loyalty from one-fourth of the population. "Everybody else" makes up the fourth fourth.

When one breaks down the denominational and other commitments within the two Protestant cohorts, it may seem even more difficult than before to think of a center having existed. Certainly, until the 1930s for Methodists, the 1980s for Presbyterians, and the present and all foreseeable futures for Baptists, the North-South line prevented a center from being realized. In Roof and McKinney's "mainline" are three groups: Episcopalian, United Church of Christ, and Presbyterian, which are the heirs of the colonial era "big three." They came to offer a cultural coherence that was not visible before the birth of the nation and an ecclesiastical semicoherence that can be shaped into "mainline liberal" only in retrospect or when reporting on present circumstances.

What did the moderate Protestants have in common? They included the Methodists and Lutherans, who fought each other on every frontier; the Northern Baptists, a different ecclesial breed; Reformed, small and not easily comprehended with the others; and Christians (Disciples of Christ), who were opposed by all the others as frontier and judgmental upstarts.

If mainline is complex, think of the diversity within Roof and McKinney's "conservative" and Wald's "evangelical" camps. They conventionally get lumped together, for sociological reasons: Southern Baptists; Churches of Christ; Evangelicals/Fundamentalists; Nazarenes; Pentecostals/Holiness; Assemblies of God; Churches of God; Adventists. Many of these have little to do with each other, and to speak of them as a camp called the "evangelical one-fourth" demands handling with care.

If we shift our focus from this concern with the particular to the universal concept of "Protestantism" in general, we find that Americans do not use this label when they want to signal their loyalties. At the midpoint of the twentieth century, as the old Protestant hegemony started to be broken, and Americans in quest of a new resolution spoke conventionally of Protestant-Catholic-Jewish America, it may have seemed that Protestantism was one thing. But the element that more than any other made it appear to be one thing, anti-Catholicism, largely disintegrated during and after the Second Vatican Council (1962-1965), leaving the concept or entity called Protestantism disunited, noncoherent when not incoherent, and undefended.

Sometimes called upon to write books with "Protestant" in the title — such as *Protestantism* or *Righteous Empire*, subtitled *The Protestant Expe-*

rience in America — I found at response time that such Protestantism no longer represented a flag around which anyone rallied. And this is not only my experience. With one exception, the authors of the general histories that include the word "Protestant" — Winthrop Hudson, Franklin Littell, Robert Handy — all moved on to write on pluralism or religion as a whole in their later comprehensive works or inquiries. The exception, Jerald C. Brauer, did not write a later comprehensive work, but his energies also went into the larger complex of religion. If one principle of organization is to run up a flag to see who salutes, that principle would not serve well anyone whose flag is labeled Protestant.

After ten paragraphs designed to serve as a frame — but one that cuts the Protestantism of our topic to the size of a miniature, with borders cut off and shadings removed — it is time to come to the point of rescue. Far from being "no big deal," it turns out that, for all the Catholics and Jews and infidels, for all the "outsiders" and "marginals" and "innovators," until the middle of the present century, white Protestantism was a Big Deal. Its members and alumni ran the universities, business and corporate life, and civic and political affairs in almost all but the hugely Catholic metropolitan areas. They overwhelmingly dominated *Who's Who in America* listings, had influence on what was in the textbooks and taught in the schools, gave birth to and then dominated many if not most voluntary associations on the philanthropic and reform fronts, made the news in the dailies and weeklies, and were the subjects of most curiosity for their ecclesial endeavors — not least of all because they controlled the media that quickened and satisfied curiosities.

Given such privilege and commanding such a degree of hegemony, this kind of white Protestantism could overlook many of its theological and behavioral differences. In the nineteenth century, as the books on "evangelical" versus "nonevangelical" religion — in which "evangelical" always won hugely, and which "evangelicalism" is the antecedent of both "mainline" and "evangelical" Protestantism today — suggest: Protestantism was a Big Deal. And for strategic purposes and reflexively, especially in the eyes of foreign visitors who took note and notes, it had some sort of center. Better not to try to define it, as the would-be definers learned. Better to grasp its ethos, live with its semicoherence, and not ask too many questions about what held it together.

Where Is Protestantism Today?

The question before us is: "Are there two parties today?" My answer to the question is: "yes," or "yes, but. . . ."

There may be better names than "parties" for the parties. Not all Protestants, as we have seen, can be seen or confined or described within just the two. As hinted by reference to members of one denomination (e.g., in the mainline cluster) who see themselves in another: there is much overlap and blurring of lines. Some adherents commute from one camp to another, depending upon the moment and the issue. Not all that Protestants do is contained in them. The substance of each may differ considerably from what it was in the late 1960s and early 1970s when the "parties" concept was coined and applied, invented and patented. With so many qualifications, it is necessary to explore both the "yesses" and the "buts" to make some sense of the realities today.

The answer "yes" to the question has to be qualified. Yes, there are two parties, and the majority of active Protestants can be perceived and described as "belonging" chiefly to one or the other. Historians bring or should bring the hermeneutics of suspicion to all that follows, but here are some evidences of various sorts for the continuing validity of the two-party model.

First, public stereotypes. "Everyone thinks" of Protestants in these two large, separated, and sometimes conflicted parties. Stereotypes are not necessarily inaccurate. "Folk wisdom" about how life is organized and loyalties are developed is not necessarily lacking in wisdom. If "where there's smoke, there's fire," then in this case, "where there's pointing, there's something at which to point."

Second, academic convention has its part to play. The "vision" of history that needs "revision" is more often closer to reality than are many revisionist substitutes. We historians, in the words of Sir Steven Runciman, do our work under the watchful scrutiny of colleagues. Some of them attack inherited generalizations with all the finesse of the bull in the proverbial China shop. The more successful ones do their jabbing and revisioning through nuance, often to devastating and thus creative (for historians) effect. Still, after all the debating is done, we are more often than not left with something of the original reality, revised, more than with the wholly new outlook that a new generation of historians offers.

Academic life is not the only life, but it is an indicator. Why, one asks, does there seem to be a necessity for and an attraction to evangelical caucuses and "Christian" coalitions in academic organizations? Why hear complaints about the exclusion of evangelical academics in some secular/mainstream institutions if there is no element to define and see excluded? (Or: are they all just a bunch of whiners making these charges up?) Why do theologians of moderate and liberal camps need special invitations and definitions or explanations on the still sometimes rare occasions when they are invited to theologize at evangelical institutions? Why two orbits of scholars?

Third, one lists media perception and propagation on the religious front. Whoever deals with mass communicators knows that, for all their impulse to produce novelties, most of them cannot find significant counterevidence on any large statistical scale to the generalizations about two parties. "Why are Pentecostals so interesting and mainliners so damn dull?" is an almost formulaic question one routinely hears from reporters and producers who are doing what they can to move beyond the routine and find the unusual.

In today's America, a fourth zone should be most visible and evidence from it most compelling: commerce and the market. If evangelicalism was once the home of the Protestant ethic, the base for Protestant asceticism and resistance of materialist cultural trends, today it is the focus of consumerism on the Protestant front. It is almost inconceivable to imagine investors designing a CD industry for mainstream Protestants. The Christian Booksellers Association is a $3 billion a year industry. CBA stores will not stock mainstream Protestant books that deviate at all from approved lines. There is a $750 million Christian rock business, virtually all of it prospering off the youth of one camp. The Protestant magazine world, for all the overlap today, is still seen symbolically around the poles marked *Christianity Today* and *The Christian Century*. Tell a secular bookseller that you have a hot new item by a United Methodist theologian and she'll yawn. Tell her that you have a "how to" book by a Southern Baptist frontliner and she will have a contract ready. Try to sell the evangelical records or books at your nearby Episcopal or United Church of Christ or Reformed Church in America bookstore, and you will become aware of "two parties."

Fifth, and it's about time to notice, theological movements and definers of these find themselves delineated and delineating along "mainstream" and "evangelical" lines. Some (of us?) are typed as "crossovers" and "bridge-builders." Where would they be if there were no "over" to cross, no river banks to unite?

Finally, for present purposes, politicians and political analysts know this best of all. From Moral Majority to Christian Coalition days, or from times when ecumenical organizations of the mainline, FCC and then NCC and also WCC, dominated, there has been no secret that power flows along separate and distinct lines. From church politics, spheres of leadership, and denominational practices to the spheres of parachurch and caucuses, it is clear that there are distinct camps. World Vision attracts support from thousands of mainstreamers, but the evangelical base is clear. Not many mainstreamers would be at home in Campus Crusade.

New developments often fit into or match the framework. Thus feminism, a newly recognized reality since 1960, finds Protestant women divided along polar partisan lines; youth movements off campus are as predictably in two camps as they are on; philanthropic and relief organizations fall into two groupings; and advocacies by African-American or denominational or ecumenical organizations tend to follow the partisan lines. Note the massive feature of such organization on the missionary and missiological fronts! Add to all this the fact that the successful promoters of "culture war" analyses, when they discuss the religious dimensions of the conflict, can easily depict partisan polarization among Protestants.

Penultimately: groups and thinkers who would observe a "reforming of the center," or who would argue or work for such a re-forming, are with good reason recognized as pushing uphill, as going against the grain, and finding it necessary (in their eyes) to fight typing, stereotyping, and reflexive participation in distorting realities. They make news not for "dog bites man," but for vice versa scripting.

Some counterevidence regarding the two-party model is evident, but this evidence is not yet strong enough to cause effective displacement and replacement of the types and stereotypes. It is important to recognize some of these counterevidences. Thus we see the weakening of the denominational construct in which the two-party system was a player. It was easier to carry on the two-party battles when denomination fought denomination or when the fate of a fought-over denomination left few options to the losers.

Add to this the postmodern situation in which people pick and choose, making a pastiche, an assemblage or collage or montage of elements from many Protestantisms, Christianities, and religions. In such a time simple or neat and stable bipolarities are in trouble. As in secular politics, where the word "party" is not always alluring, so it is found that enterprising, autonomous, "picking and choosing" Protestants are less ready than were their grandparents to be confined to parties. They are, as are their political contemporaries, more frequently "independents" than party-members.

Let me add that one of the more promising blurrings of party lines occurs because of the informed and creative subversion by "the left of the right" and the "right of the left" — the place where Protestantism is most exciting. Evangelicals open to the ecumenical scene and the beckoning world and mainstreamers responsive to tradition often have more in common than the old two-party distinction would allow. So: there are counterevidences, but, in my view, they still have to "counter." And so, my summary of evidence to this point remains: "yes, there are two parties, but. . . ."

A More Nuanced Defining of Terms

Having argued as I have, it is necessary at this point to reexamine and test each word in the phrase "two-party system" as it is used in the subtitle of the Re-Forming the Center project, "Beyond the Two-Party System of American Protestantism."

I begin with the noun "party." The term "party" is an analog to the secular American political party situation. The concept of party draws its strength from politics and also meets its limits in reference to this analogical situation. Keith J. Holyoak and Paul Thagard, in *Mental Leaps: Analogy in Creative Thought*, are helpful here as they speak of three "constraints" in analogy. "Analogy," they write, "is guided to some extent by direct *similarity* of the elements involved." They want us to note that the similarity should be reasonably close: this book and your shoes "are both over a million miles from Venus," but that similarity contributes little to analogic. "The power of analogy to create similarities makes it a tool for many purposes — for solving problems, constructing explanations, and creating evocative metaphors. It also makes it a tool for argument and persuasion." Manifestly, it is thus serving those who are exploring the "re-forming the center" impulses. Note further that "the heart of analogical thinking, . . . involves establishing a *mapping*, or systematic set of correspondences, between the elements of the source and the target analog."

Second, Holyoak and Thagard continue, "Analogy is guided by a pressure to identify consistent *structural* parallels between the roles in the source [here, political party] and the target domain [here, the religious situation]. There must be considerable isomorphism between source and target."

Third, "the exploration of the analogy is guided by the person's goals in using it, which provide the *purpose* for considering the analogy at all."

Therefore, "what often matters to an analogy is the set of *causal relationships* within each analogy that bear upon the thinker's goal." This theme also has direct application to those whose goal is re-forming the Protestant center.

Holyoak and Thagard are cautious. Theirs are "not rigid rules but are diverse guiding pressures in action and observation." And they offer a check that is appropriate in our context: "The success of an analogy must finally be judged by whether the conjectures it suggests about the target analogy prove accurate and useful."[3]

The question that emerges at the analogical bottom line is this: is "party" as in "political party" the best analog for describing American Protestantism since 1960? It depends upon the users' *purpose* in using the analogy, and it must be tested as to whether *similarity* and *structure* might often be better served with other analogies. For example, I can see good reasons for employing, at least part of the time and for some purposes, concepts like "bipolar" Protestantism, because of its implied dynamism, or "zonal" Protestantism, because of the indistinctness of zonal boundaries. Thus a person is drawn to one pole or another without necessarily becoming restricted to it, signing on with it, being willing to be described as anything more than something gravitationally pulled toward it. Similarly, a person leaves one zone without being aware when one has entered the other, but a person is in one zone or another.

As for the term "two," it must be recognized that "two-ness" has an advantage over "three" or possibly "multiple," because of the deep structures in the human mind and world of anything "bi-," as in "binary consciousness," "binary symbols," "binary myths," the "binary" element in the world of all computers (1 or 0), the nature of human organization and commitment. Colloquially, "you gotta be this or that." Classic modern structuralism works on the binary principle.

For all the appeal of two, however, the historian will also watch for "ones" and "threes" and especially "manys." Protestantism is "one" in that it is not merely secular or Jewish or Islamic or Catholic or Orthodox or Mormon, etc. Protestantism may contain "threes" as in a "re-formed center." It does have "manys," as denominational yearbooks and surveys of para-church activity reveal. So historians would never exhaust what they have to say by reference simply to "two-ness," no matter how many similarities, structures, and purposes can be at least heuristically contained in "two."

And, finally, we come to the term "system." In this case, the analogi-

---

3. Keith J. Holyoak and Paul Thagard, *Mental Leaps: Analogy in Creative Thought* (Boston: Massachusetts Institute of Technology Press, 1995), 101, 4-7.

cal element is especially vivid and creative. Not much about a diffuse reality like Protestantism is able to be rendered systematic. Words like "ecumenical movement" or "denomination" or "parachurch" or "caucus" serve better in many cases, because in such cases there is some formal or official, ordained or sanctioned, authoritative or theologically justified impetus that "party" lacks.

However, the analogical element counters this by forcing one to note the "similarity" and "structure" in political parties. Parties were *not* constitutionally envisioned either. In fact, Madison, Washington, Hamilton and most other framers feared them. Nor were they governmentally licensed. One could adduce an extensive list of reservations. The Supreme Court in *Elrod v. Burns 1976* noted that "partisan politics bears the imprimatur of tradition, not the Constitution." Madison spoke regularly of the "mischiefs of faction" and Hamilton of "the danger of parties," or, negatively, of "the spirit of party." Yet parties developed and found a creative role. As historian Clinton Rossiter said somewhere: "No America without democracy, no democracy without politics, no politics without parties."

Let me register an ecclesiastical note: I have often written in favor of "church politics," based on the dynamism internal to denominations and movements. This political alternative, with its elements of bartering, compromising, winning some and losing some, is humanely preferable to the authoritarianly imposed "unum" model or the military ("shape up or ship out") replacement of politics in "schisming" denominations in our time. Baptist, Lutheran, Reformed, and Presbyterian bodies are torn when party politics breaks down and winner-take-all analogues to military life take over.

(I put that adverb "humanely" into the previous paragraph because some who are sure they speak absolutely for God are also sure that they have no reason to listen to the "other." Where there is less than fully divine self-assurance, there is room for humility that can breed humane outcomes — and never deny the pursuit of truth.)

We are reminded, therefore, that a "system" can exist in very loose forms, as voluntary, ad hoc, unstable, kinetic, dynamic, fluid, revisable, at the edge of chaos — but still, somehow, "ordered" in reality or perception.

How Fares the Two-Party Model?

Here I have to ask for the indulgence of readers unfamiliar with the background of the issue. More than I would ordinarily find congenial, I shall have to refer to my own work in this section of this essay, since it was a major element in setting up the framework within which the planners of this volume have worked. Indulgence is necessary because what follows may create the impression that I want to protect a patent; think of the position I am about to outline as fairly representative of many analyses from a quarter century ago.

A first question: *was* the "two-party system" appropriate for a description of aspects of American Protestantism in 1968-69 when I wrote *Righteous Empire: The Protestant Experience in America,* published in 1971, or its revised edition, *Protestantism in the United States: Righteous Empire,* produced in 1985 and published in 1986? That question is possibly important to historians, and certainly important for this one. One might note the publisher's concept of two parties by reference to the dust jacket of the first edition. There Dial announced that it would also publish "William R. Taylor, *The History of Evangelicalism in America.*" The publisher made clear to me when soliciting the book that I was to stay clear of evangelicalism as a topic; it would confuse readers too much to include both parties, and would leave confusion in respect to Taylor's forthcoming work. His book was never produced for the Bicentennial History "Two Centuries of American Life" series. Its absence leaves *Righteous Empire*-style Protestantism uncomplemented, and facing a void where a counterpart should have been — and it makes me seem unmindful of the presence of evangelicalism in the twentieth century.[4]

Paralleling this question and getting to its roots, its *Ur*-level: was the "two-party system," a term Jean Miller Schmidt did not use but which describes her description, appropriate before 1969 when she depicted the Protestant world of the mid-1800s to about 1910? When I plundered her thesis and assigned a name to her result I was more interested in the consequences of that development, e.g., in the Fundamentalist/Modernist controversy of the 1920s and the challenge of neo-evangelicalism/evangelicalism to ecumenical, conciliar, not-often-yet named "mainstream" — my word in 1955 — or "mainline" (later the dominant word) Protestantism.

Was there a two-party system? Jean Miller Schmidt and I must have believed the answer to have been "yes," or we would not have written book-length narratives illustrating, in her case the development, and in

---

4. Martin E. Marty, *Righteous Empire: The Protestant Experience in America* (New York: Dial, 1971); *Protestantism in the United States* (New York: Charles Scribner's Sons, 1986).

mine the eventuation, of the two-party system. The introduction to Miller Schmidt's *Souls or the Social Order: The Two-Party System in American Protestantism*,[5] which appeared as recently as 1991, and the revision of my book in 1986 suggest we both would continue to see relevance in the concept. I believe the analogy was appropriate as description in the narratives about the past; about the reality of the 1960s and 1970s, when we wrote our books; and, to be more provocative, about the present.

A second question: were and are "private" and "public" the best terms for the two parties? The term "private" has been particularly and often questioned, for example, by George Marsden. I believe it was accurate in respect to the development of evangelicalism and fundamentalism at the time of the controversies around 1925 (though the Scopes trial showed how "public" fundamentalism could become to protect its "private" world). I believe it was so in 1947 when Carl F. H. Henry in *The Uneasy Conscience of Modern Fundamentalism*[6] criticized the evangelical party for being too devoted to the "private." Private was then described as concentrating on soul-saving, individual piety, individualized virtue and vice based morality, etc. over against the (chosen word) *social* side of Protestantism, as in "Social Gospel," "Social Christianity," and other such combinations. I believe it was still appropriate in 1968-69, when evangelicals, with few exceptions, criticized "social" or "public" Protestantism for its stance, theology, and ventures.

Clearly, "private" is *not* appropriate any longer, not by any means, since a *volte-face* has occurred for many of the activities of the one broadly described party. With certain definitional nuances, to which I devote much of my "purposive" energy, "public" works for the second party. But there has been considerable erosion of validities there, too. If there are two parties, we must ask: what might be more descriptive, more appropriate today, and can a single term suffice?

In sum, at this point, I am as unready to give up the concept of two parties now, or the description of "private" versus "public" up to about 1970 as being a major characteristic of the two, as I am ready to say that new terms are needed in the new situation.

But this attitude prompts a third question: should historians, including those who invented or had an original patent on the "two-party

5. Jean Miller Schmidt, *Souls or the Social Order: The Two-Party System in American Protestantism* (Brooklyn: Carlson, 1991).

6. Carl F. H. Henry, *The Uneasy Conscience of Modern Fundamentalism* (Grand Rapids: William B. Eerdmans, 1947).

system" notion, have reason to be defensive about change in relation to it? This means: should they be a priori resistant to notions of "re-forming the center?" I cannot speak for Professor Miller Schmidt, though I could guess what her answer would be. I know what mine is. As someone perceived as participating in activities where the parties clash and meet, as a "crossover" between the two poles or a commuter between the zones (though always identified with one of them); as being a conferee often listed as "the non-evangelical at this meeting"; and, finally, as someone who has theological, ecclesiastical, and political reasons for broader commitment, I might join the conference planners and others in wishing, hoping, and working for a "re-formed center." I often observe that the most interesting place in American Protestantism is "at the left of the right and the right of the left, which is not the middle."

In sum, does the historian have reason to resist the revisioning of history in which descriptions of the late 1960s and early 1970s are seen as being criticized, threatened, rendered obsolete, or displaced? Not at all. We historians have nothing to talk about if there is *not* change.

A Commitment to Pluralism

I should add another element in my own commitment: while theologically and ecclesiastically ecumenical and thus committed to "unum" — the Corinthian letters, the Fourth Gospel, and the New Testament charter as a whole give Christians no choice but that — I am in theological celebration and ecclesiastical organization a James Madison type, finding freedom and security neither in "unum" nor "bipartisan" or "bipolar" life but in pluralist existence. I often write on the values of "crisscrossing" and multiple commitments in public religion, public theology, and the public church.

What about parties, then, in scriptural roots? The New Testament does not use any word translatable into "party," though numbers of translations do use it up to ten times, often in Acts, in reference to "the party of" the Sadducees, the Pharisees, the uncircumcised, etc. The New Testament writers do not recognize that to the "mainstream" leadership it was the Jewish-turned-Christian set of sects that was the "party" in opposition. The Greek word usually is *haeresis*, sect or choice or heresy, and sometimes simply, "those of. . . ." It is obvious that in every congregation addressed in the Pauline letters, there was a "two-party" situation, one that evoked most of the letters, but never regarded favorably in theology or ecclesiology or practical thought.

Frequently I promote the notion that citizens do well to put energies into what I call a crisscross notion associated with sociologist E. A. Ross, pundit Walter Lippmann, and others. We citizens are "knit together" by our oppositions and affective experiences. The counsel to citizens: do anything to avoid culture war polarities and simplicities, which show a lack of awareness for all whose views and postures cannot be reduced to two parties or poles. But following that up is another topic for another day. I adduce it here simply to show that there is no ideological reason for me to support adherence to the two-party model.[7]

To underscore my interpretive commitment to a multidimensional, pluralistic analysis of American Protestantism, let me revisit once more *Righteous Empire,* showing that even then my description was not confined to two-party analysis, happy as I remain with that analysis when and where it is applicable. Thus, while the "binary consciousness" and "bisociation" of analogy were a constant throughout *Righteous Empire,* the story was not restricted to the description of late nineteenth- and early twentieth-century developments.

Here are several sets of illustrations, the first of which shows that the two-party concept did not have only a single substance: "After 1776 and certainly after 1789 it was clear that the two-party system of establishment *versus* dissent within the churches was doomed."

Secondly, in respect to African-Americans, who "have always formed one of the largest of all Protestant elements," I noted that "most blacks who were religious were Protestants. From the point of view of Christian theology there should have been the experience of a single 'people of God' in America, but practically there were two such sets." It was hard to use a political analogy because blacks had no political power in the described period.

A third instance in the parade and panorama of partisans through time dealt with Civil War times: "The deepest division in the [Protestant] empire was one over which evangelicals could not have full control, nor was it stimulated by their religious enemies. . . . The evangelical empire was fatefully divided on geographical lines," North and South, as in secessionist Benjamin M. Palmer's term: "two nations" were in the empire, and a "two-nations" theory developed.

7. For those curious about following this through, there is a preliminary discussion in Martin E. Marty, *Modern American Religion Volume 2, The Noise of Conflict, 1919-1941* (Chicago: University of Chicago, 1991), in the sections entitled "A Society Riven by a Dozen Oppositions" and "A Culture of Cross-Clefts and Crisscrossings," 340-62.

One more example appears in the revised edition of *Righteous Empire*, when the "private" versus "public" division had already become less relevant. This book of 1986 told of developments after 1960 and particularly in the 1970s, and argued that: "What resulted was a sort of testing of the classic 'two-party' situation described in these chapters. The realignment that could result would disrupt a century-old pattern; that would not be the first time Protestants revised their implicit charters in respect to society." A story about Jerry Falwell's reversal followed, preceding this comment: "Not in all respects did this mean that the old 'private' Protestantism was turning 'public.'" This statement referred to poll data showing massive resistance by most Protestants to partisan organization. To this was added comment that the new "religious leadership" that "was no longer private" but "had clearly become political" was undergoing a role reversal or was adopting new roles. "Whether the new word for their location was properly 'public' was another question." There I also made distinctions between "political" and "public" and raised some theological questions about the concept of God's activity in the pluralist public, some of which remain appropriate today.

Left less developed was the question whether the weakening of ecumenical and denominational allegiances in mainstream Protestantism, and the move in this less-boundaried ecclesial element toward post-modern, highly individualized, "pick and choose" Christianity — also present in evangelicalism — did not mean that while turning local, Protestantism was also turning increasingly private. For instance, it was asked: where was this Protestantism finding a voice in presidential elections in 1980, 1984, 1988, or 1992?[8]

I cannot resist providing yet one final example from the 1960s of a bipolar role reversal I sensed might be in the works. I began item one, page one, volume one, number one of my newsletter *Context* (October 15, 1969) with the following:

> Topsy-turvy in the 1970s? Watch for surprises, if Richard R. Gilbert is right in *Presbyterian Life*. Recognizing that for two decades Billy Graham has symbolized individualism, salvation, personal spirituality, and non-committal attitudes on social thought while Harvey Cox similarly represented, during the decade past, the social activist movement, Gilbert took note of tendencies and concluded: 'It may be one of Niebuhr's typical historical ironies that a soul-saver like Billy Graham will become

8. Marty, *Righteous Empire*, 36, 27, 56-57; *Protestantism in the United States*, 262-63.

a society corrector; and a social activist like Harvey Cox will become the great celebrator of God's presence within.'

As these examples illustrate, the historian is or should be more interested in the faithfulness of her story telling and finding proper analogies for narrative structure than in ideological defense of a formalized version of one of them. This discipline-based comment tosses a ball back into the court of sociologists and cultural analysts who regularly now use the "two-party" analog. They have a different mission, vocation, methodology, and purpose than do historians.

Some elements now on the scene are likely to elicit more change in historical accountings in the future. Among these, we note:

The fact, first of all, that the two parties/poles/zones have both lost their classic twentieth-century enemies — pre–Vatican II Catholicism and Soviet Communism in the Cold War era. This has many of them looking for new, usually domestic, enemies, as in the "culture wars" and domestic secular partisan politics. What they seize upon will dictate some of the Protestant lineups in the future. As of now, many find their opposition in the other "party."

Add to this a disarray in mainstream denominations and the discovery of new energies in the company of those evangelicals who moved from a display of the "politics of resentment" to a newer "politics of a will to power." This move suggests that we might see further ironic reversals of roles in the two parties/poles/zones.

It is also important to note that changes in historians' preoccupations, motivated by feminist, racial, and ethnic concerns, toward "social history" will continue to complement or detract from the "political" or cultural history to which the two-party system idea relates. This social history focuses on nonpolitical or less political elements, e.g., child-rearing, caring and curing, adolescence and aging, quotidian life, history of spirituality.

Along with these concerns come other changes in historians' methods. Thanks to postmodern assumptions and instruments or ideologies that pull them away from "political" or "bi-" anything approaches, historians will likely develop new challenges to the picture.

A fifth foreseeable move based on present trends: we see conscious efforts, by the "evangelical left," the "mainstream traditionalizers," and others, intentionally to confuse the lines by means of "re-forming" the center or seeing that other parties should have a role in challenging the two-party description.

Finally, insofar as "two-party Protestantism" relates to political analogs, one must be sure to bring in more features than has been done conventionally when discussing the similarity and structure, and for more purposes. Thus there are to be noted the majority, the indifferent and apathetic, the independents, the third and fourth parties (Perotistas, libertarians, populists, etc.) who confuse simple bipartisanship in politics. So it also is in matters of religion. Note that the secular political parties have also undergone vast changes and role reversals since the birth of the Republican Party in the middle of the nineteenth century and the creation of the New Deal by the Democratic. So, by analogy, there can be such changes in religion. And demographic political change like the change in "solid South" as Democrat to "solid South" as Republican has religious overtones and counterparts.

Conclusion

If asked for advice to give colleagues in the historical profession, which means to publicize the strictures and alerts I use, I would include the following elements, based on experience with typologies like "private/public Protestantism."

First, be alert to historical analogies and social scientific ideal types, but do not be confined to them or constricted by them; creative narrative involves breaking the bounds and the rules.

Second, do not confuse the framework of a story, employed for purposes of promoting intelligibility and coherence, with the story itself.

Third, watch for events and unfoldings that will call into question the existing analogies, ideal types, and frameworks, and be ready to chronicle further change and even to see replacement of one historical framework by another.

Fourth, know that something "bi-" exists and often dominates in American Protestant life. Know that, as historians, when you step out of your scholarly role into activism and when you not only describe but would participate in "re-forming the center," you will quickly find out that there are two "parties," since you will be shot at by both. Still, recognize, as Alister McGrath does in *Evangelicalism and the Future of Christianity*,[9] that: "Movements to 're-form the center' have sprung up in virtually every denomination. . . . It is . . . to be expected that evangelicals

---

9. Alister McGrath, *Evangelicalism and the Future of Christianity* (Downers Grove, Ill.: InterVarsity Press, 1995), 188.

are heavily involved in such movements, with the concept of 'cobelligerence' allowing them to overlook the points of difference with collaborators who share their concern to restore orthodox belief to their wayward churches." McGrath, it should be noted, is more interested in the theological than the political dimensions, where co-belligerency is even more evident and where his observation is in place.

For all the efforts by historians to do justice to complexity, efforts in which I would assume historians as storytellers would participate, and for all the eagerness to let this "two-party system" understanding be subject to criticism and revision, I do not think it "dies the death of a thousand qualifications," as of now. "Are there two parties today" in American Protestantism? Yes, but . . . What historians do tomorrow about telling their story of it, and its corollaries, remains to be seen.

CHAPTER 6

The Presbyterian Controversy: The Triumph of the Loyalist Center

WILLIAM WESTON

The two-party view of American Protestantism is the standard explanation of the turn-of-the-century struggles in the northern Presbyterian Church between the fundamentalists and the modernists. In fact, the Presbyterian controversy is perhaps the classic site for deploying the two-party theory. From the removal of the liberal Charles Briggs in the 1890s to the exit of the conservative J. Gresham Machen in the 1930s, the Presbyterian Church U.S.A. was the scene of an articulate, colorful, and continuous battle between the left and the right. This two-party system within one of the leading mainline denominations did much to set the terms of battle throughout American religion. If, contrary to the standard account, we find in the Presbyterian struggle not only "left" and "right," but also a distinctive and powerful middle party, we will discover something important about the limitations of the two-party paradigm, and about how the center is formed. And a clear loyalist center is just what we find.[1]

1. For influential two-party accounts, see Robert Wuthnow, *The Restructuring of American Religion* (Princeton: Princeton University Press, 1988); James Davison Hunter, *Culture Wars* (New York: Basic Books, 1991); and, most relevant to this study, Dean R. Hoge, *Division in the Protestant House* (Philadelphia: Westminster Press, 1976). For a similar multi-party view of a related denomination (the Reformed Church in America), see Donald A. Luidens and Roger J. Nemeth, " 'Public' and 'Private' Protestantism Reconsidered: Introducing the 'Loyalists,' " *Journal for the Scientific Study of Religion* 26 (December 1987): 450-64, as well as their essay "Refining the Center: Two Kinds of Reformed Church Loyalists," included in this volume. For a more detailed treatment see William J. Weston, *Presbyterian Pluralism: Competition in a Protestant House* (Knoxville: University of Tennessee Press, 1997).

The conservative party was strong in the Presbytery of Philadelphia and in Princeton Theological Seminary, and their principal leaders were Machen, *Presbyterian* editor David Kennedy, Clarence Macartney, Mark Matthews, and Maitland Alexander, the last three having served as denominational moderators. The liberal party was strongest in the Synod of New York and at Union Theological Seminary, and its principal leaders included Union Seminary President Henry Sloane Coffin, Princeton University Professor Henry van Dyke, and Auburn Seminary Professor Robert Hastings Nichols. In the center of the church were the loyalists, who were undoubtedly the largest, most powerful, and least organized party. McCormick was the most important moderate seminary, and the leaders of the party included Foreign Missions Secretary Robert Speer, Princeton Seminary President J. Ross Stevenson, and Princeton Professor Charles Erdman.[2]

The Presbyterian Battle in Brief

Charles Briggs, Old Testament professor at Union Seminary in New York and one of the leading liberal churchmen of his day, first provoked the ire of the conservative wing of the church in the 1880s while leading the charge to replace the Westminster Confession with a simpler creed. The Confession was the core of the denomination's constitution, and the new creed was opposed by those who wanted to save distinctive doctrines, such as predestination, and by those who saw this "lowest common denominator" creed as a step toward union with other denominations, and thus the end of the Presbyterian Church.

Briggs was also a leading proponent of the Higher (historical) Criticism of the Bible, and when his views became widely disseminated after an 1891 lecture, conservatives brought him to trial. Briggs maintained that these charges were really designed to slow the drive for a new creed. In any event, after several trials, Briggs was indeed removed from the ministry by the General Assembly in 1893, at the same time that the Assembly

2. For general accounts of the Presbyterian Church in this period, see Lefferts Loetscher, *The Broadening Church: A Study of Theological Issues in the Presbyterian Church Since 1869* (Philadelphia: University of Pennsylvania Press, 1954); Bradley Longfield, *The Presbyterian Controversy: Fundamentalists, Modernists, and Moderates* (New York: Oxford University Press, 1991); and William R. Hutchison, *The Modernist Impulse in American Protestantism* (Cambridge: Harvard University Press, 1976).

defeated the new creed. Other liberal leaders were also swept out of the church.[3]

In the 1900s, under more accommodating leadership, the liberals had a number of successes. They got the church to revise the Confession in 1903, to reunite with the Cumberland Presbyterians in 1906, and to help create the Federal Council of Churches in 1908. The 1910s were marked by conservative reaction, attempting to narrow church doctrine in response to the broadening of the 1900s. The greatest achievement of this ideological retrenchment was the articulation of what were known as the "five points" by the General Assembly of 1910, and their reiteration by the General Assembly of 1916. In them the General Assembly proclaimed that the inerrancy of Scripture, the virgin birth of Christ, his vicarious atonement, his bodily resurrection, and his miracles were all essential and necessary beliefs for Presbyterian ministers.

In the 1920s the struggle between the liberals and the conservatives in the Presbyterian Church came to a head. The conservatives had an early success in removing the liberal Baptist Harry Emerson Fosdick from a Presbyterian pulpit, in the course of which the General Assembly proclaimed the five points a third time. The liberals, regarding the five points as unconstitutional creed making, countered with a widely distributed plea for toleration and constitutional process known as the "Auburn Affirmation," which was signed by 1,300 of the church's 10,000 ministers. The conservatives regarded the Affirmation as heretical, but did not press charges, choosing instead to make blanket denunciations of "modernists" and the "indifferentists" who tolerated them.[4]

The loyalist majority regained control of the church with the report of the General Assembly's Special Commission of 1925, which had been established in response to all the troubles. Taking a historical view of controversy in the church, it concluded that toleration would do more to

---

3. For more on Briggs see Channing Renwick Jeschke, "The Briggs Case: The Focus of a Study in Nineteenth Century Presbyterian History" (Unpublished Ph.D. dissertation, University of Chicago Divinity School, 1966); Carl Hatch, *The Charles A. Briggs Heresy Trial: Prologue to Twentieth Century Liberal Protestantism* (New York: Exposition Press, 1969); Max Gray Rogers, "Charles Augustus Briggs: Conservative Heretic" (Unpublished Ph.D. dissertation, Columbia University, 1964); Mark Massa, *Charles Augustus Briggs and the Crisis of Historical Criticism* (Philadelphia: Fortress Press, 1989).

4. The best study is Charles Evans Quirk, "The 'Auburn' Affirmation: A Critical Narrative of the Document Designed to Safeguard the Unity and Liberty of the Presbyterian Church in the United States of America in 1924" (Unpublished Ph.D. dissertation, University of Iowa, 1967).

settle the disputed issues than would schism. The limits of this toleration, however, would not simply be left up to individuals, but would be set by the church acting according to its constitution. The Commission took a middle path between liberal claims for extreme toleration and the contention of conservatives, led by Machen, that there existed two distinct religions within the church, one of which (modernism) was outside the bounds of Christianity. The Commission report was adopted in 1926 by a sizable majority of the Assembly.

The battle shifted to Princeton Seminary, which for a century had been the leading conservative Presbyterian institution. The faculty majority, led by New Testament professor J. Gresham Machen, fought to hold onto Princeton as the last bastion of conservative Presbyterianism in what they saw as an increasingly liberal church. The majority attacked the minority as being "indifferentists"; though the minority was also very conservative theologically, they were willing to tolerate liberals within the church, if not in the seminary. The battle for Princeton Seminary was waged fiercely through the 1920s, but ultimately the principles of the Special Commission of 1925 prevailed. Machen and his followers withdrew from Princeton in 1929 and established independent Westminster Theological Seminary.[5]

The final battle of this war was fought over the Independent Board of Presbyterian Foreign Missions. The Machen conservatives were increasingly disillusioned with the denomination, and began to create their own ecclesiastical institutions. In 1933 they created their own mission board, with Machen as president. The Presbyterian Church rejected working with independent missionary agencies, and the denomination ruled that ministers of the church must sever their ties to the Independent Board or be regarded as schismatics. Machen and the other Board members refused, were tried in their respective presbyteries, and lost. In 1936, all their appeals defeated, they were suspended from the Presbyterian ministry. Having expected (and, indeed, sought) this result, the Machenites immediately organized a new denomination, now known as the Orthodox Presbyterian Church, with Machen as first Moderator.[6]

---

5. For more on Machen, see D. G. Hart, *J. Gresham Machen* (Baltimore: Johns Hopkins University Press, 1994) (as well as Hart's essay in this volume); Wayne Headman, "A Critical Evaluation of J. Gresham Machen" (Unpublished M.Theol. thesis, Princeton Theological Seminary, 1974); Dallas Roark, "J. Gresham Machen and His Desire to Maintain a Doctrinally True Presbyterian Church" (Unpublished Ph.D. dissertation, State University of Iowa, 1963); and Ned B. Stonehouse, *J. Gresham Machen: A Biographical Memoir* (Grand Rapids: Eerdmans, 1954).

6. For a contrasting account, see Loetscher, op. cit.; John Hart, "The Controversy

The Presbyterian Battle as Three-party Conflict

The standard account of the Presbyterian struggle has two parties — call them liberal and conservative, modernist and fundamentalist, or progressive and orthodox — in a head-to-head conflict for control of the church. At first the conservatives won, then the tide turned, and ultimately the liberals triumphed. To the winners, the Presbyterian Church was "broadened"; to the losers, it became "apostate." The center of the denomination appears, if at all, only as a reactive mass, swayed one way and then the other.

Yet the Presbyterian case is better understood not as a two-party conflict, but as a three-party competition. The left and the right make their arguments and maneuvers, but it is the hearts and minds of the center they are competing for. There are not two visions of the church working here, but three. While the liberals seek ecumenical action and the conservatives doctrinal purity, the center has a different interest. The center of the church is led by "loyalists" who seek to preserve the institution of the church, with its practices and its doctrines and its traditional unity. The loyalists are not passive or reactive, but, on the contrary, are the decisive actors in the struggles of the church.

Loyalists tend to have an historical and institutional conception of the church, and are loyal to their *particular* denomination. Liberals also tend to have a grasp of the church as an institution, but their loyalty to the "church in general" does not keep them from exiting one denomination in favor of another. Conservatives tend to focus not on the institutional church but on its distinctive doctrines, and their loyalty to doctrine sometimes leads them to exit one denomination in favor of a new, pure one.[7]

Seen from the perspective of three-party competition, the Presbyterian battle can be summarized this way: when the Briggs liberals tried to make the entire church liberal, the conservatives appealed to the loyal-

---

within the Presbyterian Church, U.S.A., in the 1920's with special emphasis on the reorganization of Princeton Theological Seminary" (Unpublished Senior Thesis [History], Princeton University, 1978); and Gary Scott Smith, *The Seeds of Secularization: Calvinism, Culture, and Pluralism in America, 1870-1915* (Grand Rapids: Christian University Press, 1985); Ronald T. Clutter, "The Reorientation of Princeton Theological Seminary, 1925-1929" (Unpublished Th.D. dissertation, Dallas Theological Seminary, 1982); and Edwin H. Rian, *The Presbyterian Conflict* (Grand Rapids: Eerdmans, 1940).

7. These concepts of "loyalty" and "exit" are from A. O. Hirschman's *Exit, Voice, and Loyalty* (Cambridge: Harvard University Press, 1970).

ists on the grounds of the church's traditional doctrines, and thereby won the competition. When the liberals, chastened by this failure, stopped insisting that the church endorse liberalism and instead argued for toleration based on the church's constitutional tradition, this was an argument the loyalists had to consider. The Machen conservatives then blundered: instead of trying liberals through constitutional means, in which the loyalists would have supported them, the conservatives resorted to blanket denunciations of doctrinal deviants and demanded the center's support. When the loyalists did not follow, the conservatives denounced them as "indifferentists." With that, they lost the competition for the loyalists, and with it, the war.

Charles A. Briggs and J. Gresham Machen lost their battles because neither one had a clear conception of the actual structure of the parties within the Presbyterian Church. Briggs and Machen illustrate how a liberal and a conservative view of the church, respectively, can endanger the liberal and conservative parties within the church. Briggs led the liberal party over a precipice from which it took a generation to recover; Machen broke the conservative party in a schism from which it has not entirely recovered yet.

The crucial error that both individuals made was in seeing the conflict in the church as between two parties, "us" and "them," rather than the three groups that existed there. This procrustean sociology of the church forced the loyalist party to give up its mediating position in the center. When forced to choose a side, the majority chose against those leaders who forced them to choose. With the majority mobilized against it, the losing party found itself transformed from one wing of a differentiated whole to a marginal group being pressed to conform — or escape. At that point it became the losing party's turn to make a forced choice, which in either case would damage the integrity of the party as a party. A few liberals joined Briggs in exile, but most conformed; a larger number of conservatives followed Machen out of the mother church, while those who conformed to the majority felt deeply compromised because Machen had raised the stakes of the battle so high.

Had Briggs pursued a more accommodating policy, he might indeed have avoided suspension from the ministry, and even won some of his points. Without even offering to accommodate, he won several victories in his own presbytery, his seminary was behind him, and he was defended both by liberal leaders and by some respected loyalists who disagreed with him substantively. For example, Dr. Israel J. Hathaway, though a "loyal Princetonian," rose at the 1891 General Assembly to say, "I plead not for Dr. Briggs; . . . I plead for the broadest liberty of investigation in the scholarship of our Church."[8]

J. Gresham Machen's picture of the church was as polarized and unaccommodating. If one were to take his oft-repeated argument about the opposition of "Christianity" and "modernism" at face value, one would think that Machen fought a decades-long battle with modernists and naturalists for control of the Presbyterian Church, and that in the end "the Christians were driven out of the church." In fact, however, for all his talk about modernism in the church, Machen's real opponents in all the church struggles of the 1920s and 1930s were not the modernists but the theologically conservative loyalists. For all of his talk of defending Christian doctrine against the naturalists, he reserved his bitterest attacks for those who *agreed* with him on doctrine. If Machen had fought actual modernists in the church he would likely have kept the allegiance of the center and won.

Machen failed to grasp his true position in the party structure of the Presbyterian Church because of his doctrinal conception of the church. This conception had two consequences which served him ill. First, seeing the church as only an association for promoting a particular doctrine obscured the institutional nature of the denomination. In other words, Machen was not looking at the empirical organization of the church, and so was not attending to the actual groupings of idea and interest, the social structure, of the church. He did not know that there was a loyalist party because he did not know that there were any parties. Second, Machen's doctrinal conception led him to see the people who disagreed with him on doctrine — the modernists — but not to appreciate the people who agreed with him on doctrine but who disagreed with him on church policy — the loyalists. Given his conception of the church, he could only view those who agreed with him on doctrine but nonetheless opposed his actions as misguided and perverse.

In the battle for Princeton Seminary, there really were only two parties: the loyalists and the conservatives. The liberals did not even take the field. President Stevenson was a man of decidedly conservative theological views, a "conservative Presbyterian Christian"[9] whose theological

---

8. "Speech to the Detroit General Assembly, 1891, on the Briggs Case," quoted in Rogers, "Briggs: Conservative Heretic," 168; similarly, see Simon J. McPherson, "Hunting Heretics and Saving Men," January 8, 1893, Second Presbyterian Church, Chicago, n.p.; and James S. Ramsay, "A Discourse," June 21, 1891, Harlem Presbyterian Church, New York, n.p.

9. "The Greetings of a Conservative Presbyterian to the Methodist League of

position was not questioned even though there was an "underlying hostility" to him in the seminary.[10] Charles Erdman, Stevenson's ally on the faculty against Machen, was even more conservative theologically than Stevenson, and, unlike Machen and the faculty "majority," was actually an author of *The Fundamentals*, the tracts that gave fundamentalism its name. In the foreign missions fight, Machen attacked the theologically well-respected Robert Speer. By that time Machen had gone to the extreme of calling anyone who disagreed with him a "modernist" or an "indifferentist."[11]

Machen wanted a showdown over doctrine, but what he got was a fight over church order. Eventually, Machen made an all-out attack on the center, leveling the most powerful charge that a doctrinal churchman could make against fellow clergy:

> The 'heretics' . . . are, with their helpers, the indifferentists in control of the . . . Presbyterian Church in the United States of America, as they are in control of nearly all the larger Protestant Churches in the world.[12]

This seems a clear indication that Machen had given up all thoughts of trying to accommodate the center party, if he had ever had such thoughts. He had probably also given up on remaining in the Presbyterian Church in the U.S.A.

Briggs and Machen each misunderstood the tripartite structure of the Presbyterian Church, seeing it instead in bipolar terms. Though they differed from one another in many respects, this similar misunderstanding

---

Faith and Life," February 8, 1926, p. 1; #202 in Papers of J. Ross Stevenson, Speer Library, Princeton Theological Seminary.

10. Letter of Paul Martin, Secretary of the Faculty, to W. O. Thompson, December 23, 1926, p. 7, in "Correspondence Regarding Machen Case, 1925-1927," Speer Library, Princeton Theological Seminary.

11. Well before 1936, however, he issued some surprising broadsides, as in his claim that the Young Men's Christian Association was "overwhelmingly on the anti-Christian side," that the northern Methodist Church was "overwhelmingly against the gospel," or that the revered missionary leader John R. Mott was no Christian because he had some connection with Union Seminary, an institution Machen labelled the "chief center of anti-Christian propaganda in the religious life of this country." These comments appeared in a letter from Machen to James Cannon, March 18, 1925, cited by J. Ross Stevenson in a speech before the Directors of Princeton Seminary, 1925, in Stevenson's "Confidential Letters and Documents," Speer Library, Princeton Theological Seminary.

12. "Christian Scholarship and Evangelism" [1932], in Ned Stonehouse, ed., *What Is Christianity?* (Grand Rapids: Eerdmans, 1951), 130-31.

had roots in a similar structural position and experience within the church. Both men had a poor sociological grasp of the church because they were scholars and intellectuals, very involved in theological arguments affecting the church, but not experienced in the actual running of the denomination. Briggs had briefly held a pastorate and was involved in Presbyterian and international ecumenical organizations, but was not a regular on denominational boards and committees. Machen was not even that involved in the affairs of the church. It would be fair to say that both Briggs and Machen knew more about the teaching of the Bible in German universities than they did about the preaching of the Bible in Germantown Presbyterian Church.

Moreover, from these analogous positions Briggs and Machen acted according to a similar theory of religious struggle, a theory of conflict without compromise. As a result, they ended up in similar positions, namely out of the ministry of the denomination and ultimately out of the denomination altogether. Both openly courted schism rather than accept the existing diversity in the church as a permanent condition. As a result, both Briggs and Machen forced an important struggle in the church which permanently changed the character of each man's seminary — and the Presbyterian Church in the U.S.A.

The Loyalist Majority Takes Command

A crisis in the church is only settled when the loyalist majority asserts itself. The majority is difficult to mobilize. It is hard to create a collective consciousness among a group whose principal commonality is in what they do alike, more than in what they believe alike. The loyalist party becomes a party when it is attacked, when it has a common enemy to mobilize against. The loyalist Presbyterians rose against Briggs when his calls for the dissolution of all existing denominations into a union of all progressive Christians threatened their beloved church, and they put him out. The loyalists were an even more unified and self-conscious party in the struggles of the 1920s and '30s when Machen went to further and further extremes in attacking them as "indifferentists," and they put him and his works out of the church.[13]

13. Richard Reifsnyder, "Transformation in Administrative Leadership in the Presbyterian Church in the U.S.A., 1920-1983," in Milton J Coalter, John Mulder, and Louis Weeks, *The Pluralistic Vision* (Louisville: Westminster/John Knox Press, 1992).

The crux of what the loyalists mobilized to defend was the constitution of the Presbyterian Church. The constitution is more than the expression of an experience or of a doctrine, though it contains those things, too. The constitution is the foundation of the church as a particular living organization, its frame as a social body. The Briggs liberals, and to a greater extent the Machen conservatives, had a faulty sociology of the Presbyterian Church because they failed to appreciate the meaning of the church's constitution in the hearts and minds of the loyalist majority.

At critical moments in the pluralist conflict the loyalists shaped the church according to their distinctive vision. Briggs claimed that the true objective of his trial was to defeat the revision of the creed that he championed. This was true: the majority of the church rejected a revision that was designed to dissolve the Presbyterian Church into a grand union of many different kinds of churches. A decade later, when creed revision and another grand church union scheme were pursued separately, the majority accepted revision while rejecting the denomination-destroying merger plan. The loyalist party was even more fully mobilized by the Machen struggles, and its distinctive position was in the same degree more fully developed. Emblematic of this loyalist mobilization is the work of the Special Commission of 1925.

In contrast to the two strong individuals, Charles Briggs and J. Gresham Machen, who represent the liberal and conservative parties in this story, the loyalists are represented, fittingly, by a committee. Briggs and Machen were each accomplished biblical scholars in a church that made scriptural study central, and they were effective polemical combatants who rose to leadership in their parties through personal initiative. The Special Commission of 1925, on the other hand, was composed of ministers and elders who had distinguished themselves by their devotion to the specific institutions of the Presbyterian Church in the United States of America. They did not put themselves forward for the role of judge in the conflicts of the church, but had the task thrust upon them.

The Commission, appointed by 1925 Moderator Charles Erdman, consisted of eight ministers, seven ruling elders, and, as secretary, the denomination's highest administrator. Erdman himself was invited to sit in on the group's opening meetings, but he did not participate in its final deliberations.[14] The Commission was decidedly moderate-to-conservative

14. *Minutes of the General Assembly,* 1926, p. 62; Presbyterian Church in the U.S.A., "Minutes of the Special Commission of 1925," meeting of September 22 to 24, 1925 (typescript, Box M13.5 P92, Historical Department of the Presbyterian Church [U.S.A.]), 1.

theologically; one member, Mark Matthews, was a fundamentalist. In fact, Erdman later credited Matthews with first proposing the commission at the 1925 General Assembly.[15] The weight of the commission lay with men who were successful in the pastorate or in the secular professions. Few were academics, few were known for their religious polemics, and none was of the liberal party in the church. (For biographical sketches of the commission, see the appendix.)

The most striking indication of the centrality of this group to the Presbyterian Church is the line of Moderators of the General Assembly it contained. The Moderatorship is the highest honor and most powerful office in the church, and moderatorial elections were seriously contested between conservatives and moderates from the teens through the thirties. Mark Matthews was elected Moderator in 1912, and chairman Henry Swearingen won in 1921. Charles Erdman, who appointed the Commission, was elected with loyalist and liberal votes in 1925. He was succeeded by William O. Thompson in 1926, the year the Commission made its initial report, and by Robert Speer in 1927, the year of the group's final report. Cleland McAfee, brother of Commission member Lapsley McAfee, was elected in 1929, Hugh Kerr in 1930, Lewis Mudge in 1931 (concurrent with his re-election to a third five-year term as Stated Clerk), and Harry Clayton Rogers was a candidate for the Moderatorship in 1932. In addition, elders John Finney and Cheesman Herrick each served as Vice-Moderators.[16]

The work of Robert Speer and Mark Matthews on the Commission is most important. While there were no liberals on the Commission, Speer was probably its broadest, most ecumenically minded, and least denominational member.[17] As the undisputed leader of Presbyterian foreign missions, Speer would be the target of conservative attacks in the 1930s over "modernism" in the mission field. Matthews, on the other hand, was the Commission's most conservative member, an avowed and militant fundamentalist who was sent by his presbytery to the General Assembly a record twenty times in thirty-eight years to "save the Church from the

15. Quirk, "Auburn Affirmation," 284.

16. Information in this section comes from the biographical ("H5") files on each man held by the Historical Department of the Presbyterian Church (USA) in Philadelphia.

17. John H. Mackay, "Robert Elliott Speer, A Man of Yesterday and Tomorrow," pamphlet prepared for the Speer centennial celebration at Princeton Theological Seminary, 1967; in Robert Speer folder, H5, Historical Department, Presbyterian Church (USA), 8.

Modernists."[18] Whether he came down on the side of the ideologically oriented conservatives or the institutionally oriented loyalists would shape the conservative course in the church.[19]

Speer was placed on the "causes of unrest" committee. This committee came to the conclusion that, as the conservatives had argued, the real issues in the conflict concerned different views on the Bible and the virgin birth of Christ. On the other hand, they agreed with the liberals' assertion that another substantive issue concerned the authority of the General Assembly to issue doctrinal deliverances, especially as they affected the ordination of ministers.[20] Moreover, the report states flatly that there is no naturalistic, Jesus-is-merely-a-good-man party in the Presbyterian Church.[21] Whereas the liberals and conservatives thought the fight in the church was a substantive disagreement between two contending camps, the "causes of unrest" committee argued that problems had arisen because some in the denomination were certain about the church's traditional doctrines, while others were unsure. The committee report urged that those ". . . whose minds are clear and definite may well exercise forbearance and charity toward those who are less able to affirm their faith in specific doctrines."[22] On the Virgin Birth issue, the committee claimed to speak for "a third party of large force in the church" that believed in this doctrine, and yet also did not want to "harry" those "reverent men among us . . . whose response is not clear on this point."[23] This is the sort of argument that would lead Machen, a Virgin Birth expert, to tear his hair over moderate "indifferentism."

Robert Speer summed up the loyalist view of the Presbyterian church in the concluding section of the report. He wrote: "The history of our church . . . has been a history of union, then division, then reunion. And unless we now face a new and different type of divergence we can only escape the principle of constitutional comprehension and of the union of hearts, in spite of divergence, by escaping from our whole history as a

18. Dr. Ezra P. Giboney and Agnes M. Potter, *The Life of Mark A. Matthews, "Tall Pine of the Sierras"* (Grand Rapids: Eerdmans, 1943), 93.
19. "Minutes of the Special Commission," meeting of September 22 to 24, 1925, pp. 1, 6.
20. "Report of the Committee on Causes of Unrest and Possibilities of Relief" (Presbyterian Church in the U.S.A., Special Commission of 1925; Box M13.5 P92, Department of History, Presbyterian Church [USA]), 9.
21. "Report of the Committee on Causes of Unrest," 8.
22. "Report of the Committee on Causes of Unrest," 5.
23. "Report of the Committee on Causes of Unrest," 6-7.

church."[24] As the preceding section of the report had made clear, the committee did not think, as the conservatives did, that a "new and different type of divergence" existed in the church. The loyalist position was that the church could solve its problems in the traditional way, by "constitutional comprehension" and the "union of hearts."

Then there was the "constitutional procedures" committee. Mark Matthews was placed on this committee, which also took a loyalist view. Addressing the central issue in the five points/Auburn Affirmation dispute, the committee members held that

> It seems like trifling with sacred things to chance the fate of fundamental religious beliefs upon a mere vote of the General Assembly. An open and avowed change in the Constitution cannot be brought about without following a procedure which insures most careful consideration and action by the Presbyteries.[25]

The committee affirmed the authority of presbyteries, not the General Assembly, in deciding the qualifications of ministerial candidates. Most remarkable, given that Mark Matthews was a member of this committee, was the claim that "in every presbytery there must be ministers who represent both schools of thought — the strict constructionist and the liberal constructionist." The committee concluded by urging modernists and fundamentalists to try to agree on accepting ministerial candidates.[26]

The final "Report of the Special Commission of 1925" articulated the moderate, denominationally oriented position that "constitutional comprehension" and "union of hearts" had been and ought to be the Presbyterian way of settling disputes. As stated in the report:

> The principle of toleration when rightly conceived and frankly and fairly applied is as truly a part of our constitution as are any of the doctrines stated in that instrument. . . . Toleration as a principle applicable within the Presbyterian Church refers to an attitude and a practice according to which the status of a minister or other ordained officer, is acknowledged and fellowship is extended to him, even though he may hold

---

24. "Report of the Committee on Causes of Unrest," 6.

25. "Report of the Committee on Constitutional Procedure" (Presbyterian Church in the U.S.A., Special Commission of 1925; Box M13.5 P92, Department of History, Presbyterian Church [USA]), 22.

26. "Report of the Committee on Constitutional Procedure," 27-28.

some views that are individual on points not regarded as essential to the system of faith which the Church professes. Presbyterianism is a great body of belief, but it is more than a belief; it is also a tradition, a controlling sentiment. The ties which bind us to it are not of the mind only; they are ties of the heart as well. There are people who, despite variant opinions, can never be at home in any other communion. They were born into the Presbyterian Church. They love its name, its order and its great distinctive teachings. In its fellowship they have a precious inheritance from their forbears. Their hearts bow at its altars and cherish a just pride in its noble history. Attitudes and sentiments like these are treasures which should not be undervalued hastily nor cast aside lightly. A sound policy of constitutional toleration is designed to conserve such assets whenever it is possible to do so without endangering the basic positions of the Church.[27]

In short, the Commission proclaimed toleration in the church in a way that kept the authority of the constitution foremost. More than defending toleration, though, the Special Commission report eloquently expressed the loyalist's devotion to the Presbyterian Church itself.

When the General Assembly of 1926 embraced this tolerant and constitutional understanding of the Presbyterian Church, the tide turned in favor of pluralism in the church.[28] What is important to note in the context of the party structure of the church is that the commission was

27. Presbyterian Church in the U.S.A., "Report of the Special Commission of 1925," Box M13.5 P92, Historical Department of the Presbyterian Church (U.S.A.), Philadelphia, 19-20.

28. The General Assembly's adoption of the Special Commission report is still being misinterpreted. The Assembly's conclusion that it could not change the constitution of the church to define "essential and necessary articles" without the concurrence of the presbyteries is taken by some to mean that the church thinks it cannot change its constitution *at all*. This is like saying that since Congress cannot amend the United States Constitution without the concurrence of the states, the Constitution cannot be amended at all — a similarity not at all coincidental, as the constitutions of both the Presbyterian Church and United States were created together. For examples of this error (which seems to be based on a misreading of the more careful statements of Loetscher in *The Broadening Church*), see Bradley J. Longfield and George M. Marsden, "Presbyterian Colleges in Twentieth Century America," in Coalter, Mulder, and Weeks, *The Pluralistic Vision* (Louisville: Westminster/John Knox Press, 1992), 106; Jack B. Rogers and Donald K. McKim, "Pluralism and Policy in Presbyterian Views of Scripture," in Coalter, Mulder, and Weeks, eds., *The Confessional Mosaic* (Louisville: Westminster/John Knox Press, 1991), 38; and Milton J Coalter, John M. Mulder, and Louis B. Weeks, *The Re-Forming Tradition* (Louisville: Westminster/John Knox Press, 1991), 125.

responding to competition by the conservatives and the liberals for the loyalty of the loyalist majority. The conservatives competed by voting in the "five points," the liberals by the plea for tolerance and constitutional procedure in the "Auburn Affirmation."

The liberals, having been (as they saw it) burned by constitutional irregularities since the Briggs trials, had learned to make a firm alliance with the loyalists in defense of the constitutional order. This alliance lay behind the Auburn Affirmation, which was principally a protest against what the affirmationists considered to be the unconstitutional way in which the "five points" had been established. For both parties, the empirical and visible church was as important as the transcendental and invisible church: to the liberals, the Presbyterian Church was an agency for the reconstruction of society; to the loyalists, the Presbyterian Church was home.

The liberals did not win everything they wanted from the Special Commission. They did, however, ultimately get more of what they wanted because they gave more to the loyalists — namely, more recognition of the authority of the church's constitution — than conservative pugnacity did.

In contrast, the Machen group's failure to grasp the legal and emotional significance of constitutional procedure in the church led it to pursue a losing strategy in its battles within that church. For Machen, the constitution guaranteed only his liberty within the church, not his responsibility to it. When he thought that his liberties had been violated, he resorted to the southern constitutional theory of secession, neglecting the Presbyterian constitutional ban on schism.[29] The Machenites failed to bring a case against the Auburn Affirmationists in the church courts, but instead resorted to denuniciation of the Auburn Affirmation, liberalism, and "indifferentism." This strategy, not surprisingly, failed to produce constitutional changes in the church.

Conclusion

The lasting effect of the Presbyterian struggle was to break the alliance between the center and the right in the church, which had been based on a common conception of church doctrine, and forge instead a new alliance between the center and the left in the church, based on a common con-

---

29. Longfield, *Presbyterian Controversy*, 50-51.

ception of church work.[30] As a result: the conservatives were fragmented and some left the Presbyterian Church altogether; Princeton Seminary returned to a leading and moderate position in the denomination; and the liberals built upon their toleration to create, in some places, genuine pluralism.

As a result of the protracted struggle from the Briggs trial to the Machen trial, the Presbyterian Church in the U.S.A. came to adopt what might be called "constitutional pluralism." The Church is a doctrinal association, and must defend what it considers to be essential teachings. The Church is also, however, a human institution, with a form of order, i.e., a constitution, that must also be defended. An institutional church has to have some way of justifying diversity or it could not contain a variety of individuals who differ in their experiences, interests, understanding, and wisdom, as well as in their beliefs.

The long-term effect, then, of the Presbyterian struggle from Briggs to Machen was to legitimize the three-party structure itself in the mind of the church. The Special Commission successfully asserted that toleration of differing views was a tradition of the church protected by the constitution. That is, the loyalist party successfully asserted its prerogative to tolerate the liberal party and the conservative party. Party pluralism — a diversity of parties in the church — was rendered legitimate.

Appendix

Of the eight ministers on the Commission, seven were successful pastors and the eighth was an active preacher in addition to being a college president. They were:

Henry Swearingen, the chairman, who was fifty-six when the Commission was formed, and had been pastor of the House of Hope Presbyterian Church in St. Paul, Minnesota, for eighteen years. A Pennsylvanian, he had graduated from Westminster College and Allegheny Theological Seminary, both institutions of the United Presbyterian Church in his native state. For many years he served as a trustee of Macalester College and of McCormick Theological Seminary (then called the Presbyterian Theolog-

---

30. A new split between the center and the right threatens the church today; see R. Stephen Warner, "Mirror for American Protestantism: Mendocino Presbyterian Church in the Sixties and Seventies," in Coalter, Mulder, and Weeks, *The Mainstream Protestant "Decline"* (Louisville: Westminster/John Knox Press, 1990), 222.

ical Seminary of Chicago), both PCUSA schools. He was deeply involved in the Presbyterian Church in the U.S.A., serving as Moderator of the Synod of Minnesota, President of the Presbyterian Home Mission Council, and on the Executive Committee of the Presbyterian Alliance. Swearingen was also involved in Presbyterian cooperation with other churches, serving in the denomination's Department of Church Cooperation and Union, as a delegate to the Pan-Presbyterian Council and to the Universal Conference on Life and Work, and on the Executive Committee of the Federal Council of Churches.[31]

Mark A. Matthews, 58, was pastor of the largest church in the denomination, First Presbyterian of Seattle, which had some eight thousand members. Born into an active Presbyterian family in Georgia just after the Civil War, Matthews had no schooling beyond the middle of high school. He read heavily, especially in the theology of Princeton Seminary professor Charles Hodge, and was licensed to preach as a teenager. He threw himself into reform work, especially against alcohol, and while a pastor in Tennessee taught himself law and passed the bar to help the reform cause. From Tennessee he was called to Seattle, where he was a combative reformer and a very successful church builder. Though he often attacked "modernism" in the Presbyterian Church he was also committed to its institutions, serving as a trustee of Whitworth and Whitman Colleges and of San Francisco Theological Seminary.

Hugh T. Kerr, 54, had been pastor of Shadyside Presbyterian Church in Pittsburgh for twelve years. A Canadian, he had studied at the University of Toronto before enrolling in Western Theological Seminary, a PCUSA school in Pennsylvania. Before his pastorate he taught at McCormick Seminary; his son and namesake would later be a well-known Princeton Seminary professor, and another son would be a Presbyterian minister. Kerr was President of the denomination's Board of Christian Education at the time of the Special Commission, and he would later head the Western Hemisphere section of the (World) Alliance of Presbyterian and Reformed Churches.

Lapsley McAfee, 61, was in the middle of a twenty-five-year pastorate of First Presbyterian Church in Berkeley, California. Son of the

---

31. Loyalists were often involved in this sort of "life and work" ecumenism, which was organized through a federation of distinct denominations, rather than through the transdenominational para-churches that both liberals and conservatives created; see Theodore A. Gill, Jr., "American Presbyterians in the Global Ecumenical Movement," in Coalter, Mulder, and Weeks, eds., *The Diversity of Discipleship* (Louisville: Westminster/John Knox Press, 1991), 139.

founder of (Presbyterian) Park College in Missouri, McAfee was of a family well-connected in the Presbyterian Church for generations. A strong supporter of Asian missions, he died in the Philippines in 1935 while inspecting institutions formed by missionaries sent by his congregation.

Harry Clayton Rogers, 48, had been the very successful pastor of Linwood Boulevard Presbyterian Church in Kansas City for seventeen years. Reared in a strong Presbyterian family in Kentucky, he attended the church's Centre College, of which he was later offered the presidency, and McCormick Seminary, of which he became a trustee. He was also a trustee of Park and Lindenwood Colleges. He served for many years on the General Council of the PCUSA, including thirty years on its evangelism committee.

Two other moderate pastors, less prominent than those above, were Alfred H. Barr, 57, of Chicago, who had previously held long pastorates in Detroit and Baltimore, and Edgar W. Work, 64, once pastor of what became Lapsley McAfee's congregation in Berkeley, later of New York City.

A strong figure on this Commission, and chairman of the 1926 General Assembly commission that investigated Princeton Seminary, was William Oxley Thompson, 70, then completing twenty-six years as president of Ohio State University. A graduate of Muskingum College and Western Theological Seminary, Thompson regarded himself as a preacher who happened to be a college president. He was chairman of the Board of Trustees of the (Presbyterian) College of Wooster, trustee president of the Westminster Foundation, and for forty years a trustee of Lane Theological Seminary. He was President of the International Sunday School Union in 1918, Moderator of the Synod of Ohio in 1925, served on the General Council, budget committee, and Department of Church Cooperation and Union of the PCUSA, and at the time of his death in 1934 was a member of the Joint Committee on Organic Union with the United Presbyterian Church of North America.

Of the seven lay ruling elders, six were eminent men in secular institutions, and the seventh was a prominent bureaucrat of the Presbyterian Church. They were:

John M. T. Finney, a sixty-two-year-old surgeon at Johns Hopkins Hospital in Baltimore, vice-chairman. The grandson, son, and brother of Presbyterian ministers in Maryland (his father was a graduate of Princeton Seminary), Finney graduated from Princeton University and Harvard Medical School. He was an elder of the Brown Memorial Church in Baltimore, where J. Ross Stevenson had been pastor before assuming the presidency of Princeton Seminary. One of the most eminent doctors in the country, he had been President of the American Surgical Association, the American College of Surgeons, and the Southern Surgical and Gyneco- logical Association, and had been offered the presidency of Princeton University after Woodrow Wilson's resignation. Finney was a trustee of Princeton Seminary during the conflict later in the 1920s, and served as Vice-Moderator of the General Assembly under his college classmate Charles Erdman.

John H. DeWitt, at fifty-three had just been appointed a Judge of the Tennessee Court of Appeals in 1925. The son of a prominent Presbyterian minister, he attended Vanderbilt University and Columbia College of Law (in Washington, D.C.), and was an elder of Hillsboro Presbyterian Church in Nashville for thirty years. DeWitt was President of the Tennessee His- torical Association, and served as Chairman of the Judicial Commission of the Presbyterian Church in 1923.

Cheesman A. Herrick, 57, had been President of Girard College in Philadelphia for fifteen years in 1925. A graduate of the Wharton School of the University of Pennsylvania, from which he received a Ph.D., Herrick had served the Presbyterian Church as an elder of Arch Street Presbyterian Church in Philadelphia, as a member of the Board of Foreign Missions, and as Vice-Moderator of the General Assembly.

The other three secular professionals played a less prominent role in the church, if not in the world. Nelson Loomis, the General Solicitor of the Union Pacific Railroad in Omaha, had served the church's New Era Movement and the Layman's Council. Edward Duffield was the President of the Prudential Insurance Company. Nathan Moore, who descended from a long line of Presbyterian ministers in Pennsylvania and served as elder and organist in his own church, was a prominent Chicago attorney.[32]

Robert Speer was the most eminent churchman among the ruling elders on the Commission. At fifty-seven, Speer was in the middle of a forty-year term as the Senior Secretary of the church's Board of Foreign Missions. The son of a Pennsylvania Congressman, Speer was raised in a deeply Presbyterian home. After graduating from Andover he went to Princeton University, where he was a leader of the Young Men's Christian Association and the missionary Student Volunteer Movement, as well as

32. No file on Nathan Moore exists in the Presbyterian Church archives; this material was supplied by Carol R. Kelm and James Siler, Oak Park (Illinois) Historical Society, June 30 and July 14, 1992; "Nathan G. Moore Distinguished Resident, Dies," Oak Park *Oak Leaves* (Nov. 16, 1939): 72.

a varsity athlete, editor of the college newspaper, and valedictorian. He attended Princeton Seminary, leaving before graduation to work for the Board of Foreign Missions, but returned years later as President of the Board of Trustees of Princeton Seminary, where the library is now named for him.[33] Speer was also President of the Federal Council of Churches.

The final participant in the work of the Special Commission of 1925 was its secretary, Stated Clerk Lewis Mudge. At sixty, Mudge was completing the first of three five-year terms as the elected administrator of the denomination. Descended from a long line of ministers, he attended Princeton University, and at Princeton Seminary he roomed with Robert Speer. He was pastor of Pine Street Presbyterian Church in Harrisburg, Pennsylvania, when first elected Stated Clerk in 1921. A trustee of (Presbyterian) Wilson College and Princeton Seminary, he was elected Moderator in 1931.

33. Speer was also tied to Princeton Seminary through Camp Diamond in New Hampshire, where the Speer family and Charles Erdman's family spent their summers; see William R. Hutchison, "Protestantism as Establishment," in William R. Hutchison, ed., *Between the Times: The Travail of the Protestant Establishment in America, 1900-1960* (Cambridge: Cambridge University Press, 1989), 9.

CHAPTER 7

J. Gresham Machen, Confessional Presbyterianism, and the History of Twentieth-Century Protestantism

D. G. HART

I never call myself a "Fundamentalist." There is, indeed, no inherent objection to the term; and if the disjunction is between "Fundamentalism" and "Modernism," then I am willing to call myself a Fundamentalist of the most pronounced type. But after all, what I prefer to call myself is not a "Fundamentalist" but a "Calvinist" — that is, an adherent of the Reformed Faith.

> J. Gresham Machen to the trustees of Bryan
> Memorial University, June 25, 1927[1]

At its General Assembly of 1945, the microscopic Orthodox Presbyterian Church appeared to display momentous folly when it refused to join the National Association of Evangelicals. The NAE, the chief manifestation of progressive fundamentalism, looked like the wave of the future. It brought together in a loose way the individuals (Harold Ockenga, Carl Henry, Billy Graham) and institutions (Fuller Seminary, National Religious Broadcasters, Christianity Today) that would be pivotal for the post–World War II evangelical renaissance. The OPC, a denomination founded in 1936 in the aftermath of the foreign missions controversy in the Northern Pres-

---

1. Quoted in Ned B. Stonehouse, *J. Gresham Machen: A Biographical Memoir* (Grand Rapids: Eerdmans, 1954), 426.

129

byterian Church, however, was clearly living off the capital of its accomplished and articulate founder, J. Gresham Machen (1881-1937). When Machen died suddenly on January 1, 1937, only six months after the start of the OPC, the luster of the new denomination quickly faded. In that same year the OPC experienced a split, losing the Bible Presbyterians, who were led by the feisty Carl McIntire. By the time of the NAE's founding, the OPC's growth had been meager at best. It surely seemed that if Orthodox Presbyterians wanted to exercise leadership within and benefit numerically from the emerging evangelical coalition, they should have accepted the NAE's invitation. Nevertheless, the OPC followed the advice of its ecumenical relations committee and refused to join the NAE.[2]

The OPC's decision would seem to be a prime example of fundamentalist separatism. One of the reasons why the OPC remained separate was the NAE's openness to ministers from mainline denominations. From the perspective of the OPC, it seemed utterly inconsistent for the NAE to offer itself as an alternative to the modernist Federal Council of Churches, and yet allow ministers from mainline churches to be members. As historians of the new evangelicalism have argued, progressive fundamentalists like those who formed the NAE were willing to work with likeminded persons in mainline denominations in order to exert a wider sphere of influence, while separatist fundamentalists like Carl McIntire and the Orthodox Presbyterians refused to cooperate with any organization that harbored theological liberalism.[3]

2. On the founding of the NAE and the neo-evangelical movement from which it came, see Joel Carpenter, "The Fundamentalist Leaven and the Rise of an Evangelical United Front," in *The Evangelical Tradition in America*, ed. Leonard I. Sweet (Macon, GA: Mercer University Press, 1983), 257-88; Carpenter, "From Fundamentalism to the New Evangelical Coalition," in *Evangelicalism and Modern America*, ed. George Marsden (Grand Rapids: Eerdmans, 1984), 3-16; George M. Marsden, *Reforming Fundamentalism: Fuller Seminary and the New Evangelicalism* (Grand Rapids: Eerdmans, 1987), 1-93. On the reasons for the OPC's isolation from the neo-evangelical movement, see D. G. Hart, "The Legacy of J. Gresham Machen and the Identity of the Orthodox Presbyterian Church," *Westminster Theological Journal* 53 (1991): 209-25. The OPC's total membership as of March 31, 1946, was 7,555, according to the *Minutes of the Thirteenth General Assembly* (1946), 126. For concerns within the OPC about the denomination's small size, see Michael A. Hakkenberg, "The Battle Over the Ordination of Gordon H. Clark, 1943-1948," in *Pressing Toward the Mark: Essays Commemorating Fifty Years of the Orthodox Presbyterian Church*, ed. C. G. Dennison and R. C. Gamble (Philadelphia: Committee for the History of the Orthodox Presbyterian Church, 1986), 329-50; and Hart, "Legacy of J. Gresham Machen."

3. "Scripture on Cooperation: A Committee Report to the Twelfth General Assembly of the Orthodox Presbyterian Church," *Presbyterian Guardian* 14 (March 25,

This interpretation of Protestant developments in the 1940s, while it offers more nuance than the two-party paradigm,[4] nevertheless perpetuates and extends the dualistic categories that dominate the historiography of twentieth-century Protestantism. Despite differences between progressive and separatist fundamentalists, religious historians still generally divide the Protestant world in two. There are liberals who don't agree about much, and there are conservatives who may be divided about ecumenical relations, but who agree on evangelism, missions, theology, and religious practice.

Confessional Protestantism

The purpose of this essay is to make a case for the existence and importance of a type of conservatism, namely, confessional Protestantism, often overlooked in the standard accounts of twentieth-century religious history. While scholars generally regard Machen and the denomination he founded as fundamentalist because of militant opposition to liberalism, they generally overlook the particular beliefs and practices for which the OPC stood. But to look only at what conservatives opposed misses important dimensions of their identity. And when we examine the reasons why Machen and the OPC opposed liberalism, we see a set of concerns distinct from those of mainstream fundamentalism. With this distinction in mind it is possible to conclude that Presbyterian confessionalism, not fundamentalist separatism, was the concern that governed the OPC's decision not to join the NAE. In fact, at the same time that the OPC declined membership in the NAE it also refused to join Carl McIntire's American Council of Christian Churches, an organization more representative of separatist fundamentalism. From the OPC's perspective, neither the NAE nor the ACCC was sufficiently Calvinistic, and neither organization exhibited a proper (i.e., Presbyterian) understanding of the church.[5]

The OPC's porcupine-like conservatism thus raises two significant issues. The first concerns J. Gresham Machen, a figure commonly cited as the embodiment of fundamentalism *par excellence.* His association with the

---

1945): 87-88. The best assessments of neo-evangelicalism are the works by Carpenter and Marsden cited above.

4. On the two-party paradigm and its limitations, see Douglas Jacobsen and William Vance Trollinger, Jr., "Historiography of American Protestantism: The Two-Party Paradigm, and Beyond," *Fides et Historia* 25 (1993): 4-15.

5. See Hart, "Legacy of J. Gresham Machen."

Calvinistic and inerrantist theology of Princeton Seminary has been especially useful for historians who argue that the issues of the 1920s drove Princeton's Calvinists into the arms of dispensationalist fundamentalists. Closer scrutiny of Machen, however, reveals that the alliance between the Princeton theology and dispensationalism stems more from the two-party perspective of religious historians than any real similarities between Princetonians and fundamentalists. Historians have properly attributed opposition to liberalism to Princeton theology and dispensationalism. Yet, they have not recognized the tensions and antagonisms between Calvinists and dispensationalists. By examining the different rationales of those who opposed modernism — that is, identifying what they stood for positively instead of merely what they attacked — I hope not only to explain the separatist mentality of the OPC, but also to identify the distinctive thought and aims of Presbyterian confessionalists like Machen in the context of the fundamentalist controversy.[6]

The second and larger point of this study is to give some attention to confessional Protestantism more generally. Orthodox Presbyterians were not the only group to remain separate from the NAE. Others, including the Christian Reformed Church and the Wisconsin and Missouri Synod Lutherans, were also critical of the theology and ecclesiology implicit in the NAE. The OPC, therefore, represented a wider, though not necessarily large, phenomenon. Confessional Protestants, whether Lutheran, Reformed, Anglican, or Anabaptist, did not readily fit the dominant liberal and conservative parties which the Federal Council of Churches and NAE represented and which historians have used to categorize Protestant history. Consequently, while the focus of this essay is on the tradition of confessional Presbyterianism exemplified by J. Gresham Machen, its more general purpose is to add greater nuance and precision to our understanding of twentieth-century Protestantism by calling attention to Protestant confessionalism.[7]

6. For the alliance of Princetonians and dispensationalists, see Ernest R. Sandeen, *The Roots of Fundamentalism* (Chicago: University of Chicago Press, 1970); George M. Marsden, *Fundamentalism and American Culture: The Shaping of Twentieth-Century Evangelicalism, 1870-1925* (New York: Oxford University Press, 1980); Mark A. Noll, *Between Faith and Criticism: Evangelicals, Scholarship, and the Bible in America* (San Francisco: Harper and Row, 1986); 51-60; and most recently, Nancy T. Ammerman, "North American Protestant Fundamentalism," in *Fundamentalisms Observed*, ed. Martin E. Marty and R. Scott Appleby (Chicago: University of Chicago Press, 1991), ch. 1.

7. For an initial exploration of the tensions between confessional Presbyterianism and fundamentalism, see D. G. Hart, *Defending the Faith: J. Gresham Machen and the Crisis*

Machen and Fundamentalism

To argue that J. Gresham Machen was not a fundamentalist may strike some as a good example of special pleading. He was, after all, outspokenly hostile to Protestant liberalism and displayed the militancy that typified fundamentalism. In his most popular book, *Christianity and Liberalism*, Machen charged not only that liberalism was "un-Christian," fighting words in and of themselves, but also that liberalism was "the greatest menace" the church had faced, a "type of faith and practice . . . anti-Christian to the core." To add insult to injury he explained that while the church of Rome was a perversion of Christianity, "naturalistic liberalism" was an entirely different religion from Christianity.[8]

Yet militant opposition to liberalism goes only so far in defining various constituencies within American Christianity. Roman Catholics, after all, opposed modernism long before Protestants did, and yet few scholars have called conservative Catholics fundamentalists.[9] For this reason it is imperative to notice that Machen held no brief for the two most popular fundamentalist beliefs, creationism and dispensationalism, which taken together expressed uncanny certainty about the beginning and end of human history. Machen, like most confessional Presbyterians, remained an agnostic about the timing of Christ's return and grew increasingly hostile to dispensational premillennialism. In *Christianity and Liberalism* Machen called dispensationalism a "false method of interpreting the Bible," and he repeatedly rebuffed the requests of William Bell Riley to join the World Christian Fundamentals Association because of that organization's dispensationalist doctrinal plank. By the end of his career Machen feared that the Scofield Reference Bible, with its misunderstanding of the nature of sin, was "leading precious souls astray."[10]

---

of Conservative Protestantism in Modern America (Baltimore: Johns Hopkins University Press, 1994), chs. 3, 4, 6, and epilogue *passim;* and Hart, "Presbyterians and Fundamentalism," *Westminster Theological Journal* 55 (1993): 331-42.

8. J. Gresham Machen, *Christianity and Liberalism* (New York: Macmillan, 1923), 160, 52. George M. Marsden, *Fundamentalism and American Culture*, 4, states that "Militant opposition to modernism was what most clearly set off fundamentalism from a number of closely related traditions."

9. See, e.g., William D. Dinges and James Hitchcock, "Roman Catholic Traditionalism and Activist Conservatism in the United States," in *Fundamentalisms Observed*, ch. 2. For a good overview of the modernist controversy in Roman Catholicism, see Jay P. Dolan, *The American Catholic Experience: A History from Colonial Times to the Present* (Garden City, NY: Doubleday, 1985), 304-20.

10. Machen, *Christianity and Liberalism*, 49; Machen to William Bell Riley, April

Machen also showed little interest in the controversy over evolution, though it was not for a lack of initiative on William Jennings Bryan's part. In preparation for the Scopes trial, Bryan invited Machen to testify on behalf of the prosecution. Machen courteously declined, explaining that he was not a student of the Old Testament. But Machen's appeal to the rules of expertise actually concealed a perspective on creation derived from his theological mentor, Benjamin Warfield. Known for his rigorous Calvinism and doctrine of inerrancy, Warfield also believed that Christians could embrace evolutionary theories, even to the point of accepting the idea that the human form evolved from existing creatures, as long as such views allowed for a supernatural act of God in the creation of the human soul.[11]

The socio-political baggage that accompanied Protestant concerns about the creation and destiny of human life was another difference that separated Machen from mainstream fundamentalism. Creationism and dispensationalism became lightning rods in the aftermath of World War I for working-class and Southern Protestants who were alarmed by the apparent secular drift of American society. Because the terms and categories of evolution and postmillennialism had so often been used as the rationale for progressive ideals, fears about America's moral degeneracy predisposed conservative Protestants to take issue with mainstream scientific thought and theology. Furthermore, anti-German sentiments, fueled by the war, helped to unite evolution, liberal Protestant ideas about the kingdom of God, and German barbarism in the minds of most fundamentalists. Germany became the prime example of the assertion that moral and social decline followed logically from liberalism's naturalistic account of the universe and human affairs.[12]

30, 1929 and May 1, 1929; and Machen to J. Oliver Buswell, Oct. 19, 1936, Machen Archives. David Livingstone has observed the fundamentalist dogmatism on creation and eschatology in "Evolution and Eschatology," a paper presented at the Institute for the Study of American Evangelicals, Wheaton College, April 1991.

11. See Machen's correspondence with Bryan, Bryan to Machen, June 23, 1925, and Machen to Bryan, July 2, 1925. For Machen's recommendation of Warfield, see Machen to George S. Duncan, Feb. 19, 1924. For Machen's own exposition of creation, one that missed the nuances of Warfield, see his *The Christian View of Man* (New York: Macmillan, 1937), chs. 10–12. On Warfield's enthusiastic approval of a qualified evolutionary theory, see David N. Livingstone, *Darwin's Forgotten Defenders: The Encounter between Evangelical Theology and Evolutionary Thought* (Grand Rapids: Eerdmans, 1987), 116-19, 146-47.

12. See Marsden, *Fundamentalism and American Culture,* ch. 16; and William Vance Trollinger, Jr., *God's Empire: William Bell Riley and Midwestern Fundamentalism* (Madison: University of Wisconsin Press, 1990), ch. 2, *passim.*

Machen, however, viewed the war differently, and his perspective was indicative of a political philosophy that was at odds with the ideology of popular fundamentalism. Even though he served at the front in France as a YMCA secretary, Machen was ambivalent at best about United States involvement in the great war, and he criticized the Wilson administration's military conscription policy as a breach of civil liberties. Because of his studies at Marburg and Göttingen universities and friendships with German students and faculty, Machen was reluctant to endorse the Allied cause.

On the domestic front his politics were equally unusual for one thought to be a fundamentalist. For instance, Machen maintained party allegiance and voted in 1928 for the first Roman Catholic presidential candidate, the Democrat Al Smith, because of Smith's intention to repeal Prohibition. As a member of the Sentinels of the Republic, a political organization founded by Massachusetts Republicans, Machen opposed the growth and power of the federal government in such initiatives as Prohibition, the Child Labor Amendment, and the creation of a Federal Department of Education. And while Machen was a loyal son of the South, his politics were not that different from another Baltimorean, H. L. Mencken, whose conservative libertarianism poked as much fun at Southern culture as the polite society of mainstream Protestantism.[13]

Confessional Particularity

Machen's efforts to protect the autonomy and integrity of local institutions and culture from the spread of national government and cultural uniformity made him critical of both fundamentalists and liberals, both of whom desired the preservation of Christian civilization in America, even though they disagreed about the means. From Machen's perspective fundamentalists and modernists were equally guilty of confusing the spheres of church and state. In fact, Machen argued that the cruelty and vindictiveness of Yankee aggression toward the South during the Civil War and Reconstruction, as well as Protestant efforts to Americanize immigrants,

---

13. On Machen's politics, see Hart, *Defending the Faith*, ch. 6. For the context and uniqueness of Machen's political preferences, see Allan J. Lichtman, *Prejudice and the Old Politics: The Presidential Election of 1928* (Chapel Hill: University of North Carolina Press, 1979); and Lynn Dumenil, " 'The Insatiable Maw of Bureaucracy': Antistatism and Education Reform in the 1920s," *Journal of American History* 77 (1990): 499-524.

demonstrated the evils that could result from mixing religion and politics.[14]

Thus, while fundamentalism sprouted in fertile debates about Christian civilization in America during and after World War I, we must look for a different source of Machen's opposition to liberalism. Clues come from his duties as a first-time delegate to the Presbyterian Church's 1920 General Assembly. There Machen heard and reacted strongly against plans produced by the American Council on Organic Union for a merger of the largest Protestant denominations. He argued that the plan's theological rationale omitted practically all the "great essentials of the Christian faith" and relegated the Westminster Confession of Faith to merely a denominational affair. This argument turned out to be the essence of his critique of theological modernism in *Christianity and Liberalism*. Hopes for Protestant unity, he argued, exhibited a religious epistemology which possessed all the earmarks of liberalism and ultimately circumvented Christianity's explicit supernaturalism.[15]

Because Machen's opposition to church union was contemporaneous with the rise of fundamentalism, historians have usually linked the two forms of protest. But here a comparison with Canadian developments is instructive. Like Presbyterians in the United States, conservative Canadian Presbyterians also resisted the ecumenical efforts and liberal Protestant sentiments which in 1925 produced the United Church of Canada. Some of these Presbyterians had fundamentalist sympathies, but did not champion the doctrines of inerrancy or dispensationalism. Rather, conservatives took their vows to the Westminster Confession of Faith so seriously that they felt betrayed when other Presbyterians seemed eager to unite with non-Presbyterian bodies. Significantly, Canadian conservatives saw Machen as an ally. Machen regularly preached at Knox Church in Toronto, whose pastor, John Gibson Inkster, in 1926 recommended Machen for the principalship of Knox College, the Presbyterian theological school at the University of Toronto, an invitation which Machen declined.[16]

14. For these ideas, see Machen to Minnie Gresham Machen (his mother), January 28 and April 17, 1920, Machen Archives.

15. "The Proposed Plan of Union," *Presbyterian* 90 (June 10, 1920): 8, 9. See also "For Christ or Against Him," *The Presbyterian* 91 (Jan. 20, 1921): 8-9; and "The Second Declaration of the Council on Organic Union," *The Presbyterian* 91 (Mar. 17, 1921): 8, 26.

16. On Canadian Presbyterian struggles, see N. Keith Clifford, *The Resistance to Church Union in Canada, 1904-1939* (Vancouver: University of British Columbia Press, 1985), who notes that Knox Church and Knox College were centers of conservative strength. See also Machen's extensive correspondence with Robert S. Grant, an admin-

Christianity and Liberalism, Machen's most popular book, also needs to be read more in the light of Presbyterian rather than pan-Protestant developments. The manuscript stemmed from a speaking engagement sponsored by Pennsylvania presbyteries opposed to church union, and it summarized Machen's critique of the progressive and cooperative ideals fueling mainstream American Protestantism. While the central argument of the book, that Christianity and liberalism were two entirely different religions, would have broad appeal to fundamentalists, it reads more like a primer in Calvinist theology than a fundamentalist tract. Machen took issue with liberalism not because of defective views of creation, Christ's return, or even the Bible, but because it denied Christian teaching about sin and grace. To be sure, his uncompromising defense of Christian supernaturalism and the historical truthfulness of the Bible, his common-sensical handling of problems in professional biblical scholarship, and his seeming scorn for denominational officials appealed powerfully to Protestants who believed that Christian salvation was primarily individual not social, that the Bible was reliable in scientific as well as religious matters, and that the churches were becoming obstacles to the faithful proclamation of the gospel. But Machen was writing with the problems of his own communion in mind. It was, after all, modernist ministers in the Presbyterian Church who had taken vows of subscription to the Westminster Confession of Faith whom he reproached for exhibiting liberalism's worst feature, that is, the use of theological language equivocally, if not dishonestly. Consequently, conservatives who focused only on Machen's apology for the general outline of historic Christianity would be disappointed by the trajectory of his career. Rather than seeking alliances across denominational lines in order to resuscitate an earlier evangelical empire, Machen spent the remaining years of his life fighting one denominational battle after another.[17]

---

istrator in the Presbyterian Church in Canada, regarding the supply of summer interns and ministers from Princeton to the Canadian Presbyterian Church from 1921 to 1930; and Ned B. Stonehouse, *J. Gresham Machen*, 478.

17. See especially Machen, *Christianity and Liberalism*, 162-72. For a summary and assessment of *Christianity and Liberalism*, see Hart, *Defending the Faith*, ch. 3. Machen detested what he called the "sickly interdenominationalism" of fundamentalists. The best way to counteract liberalism, he felt, was not through a union of interdenominational conservatives but through historic Protestant creeds, reinforced by a strong denominational consciousness. While he affirmed "warm Christian fellowship" with fundamentalists, he said his greatest sympathies were with "those brethren, like the Lutherans, who are most insistent upon their ecclesiastical distinctness." For other

D. G. HART

Presbyterian Battles

The confessional orientation of Machen's arguments became especially clear in the aftermath of the Northern Presbyterian Church's bureaucratic efforts to cover up and recover from the instability of the fundamentalist controversy. At three successive General Assemblies, from 1925 to 1927, the church avoided a threatened liberal exodus by appointing committees to study denominational tensions. These studies concluded that the principal cause of controversy was the unfair and unfounded accusations of conservatives, especially of Calvinists associated with Princeton Seminary. This finding led to an investigation and reorganization in 1929 of the institution which many regarded as the West Point of Calvinist orthodoxy. This reorganization shifted the makeup of the Seminary's governing boards, putting conservatives in the minority. The public-relations spin that the denomination put on the affair was that the older patterns of governance were ineffective. The reorganization, consequently, was not theological or ideological; instead, it was merely an effort to make the seminary more responsive to the church and society's changing needs. Conservatives, however, had a different impression. They believed reorganization was an unconstitutional effort by tyrannical church bureaucrats to muzzle conservative dissent and, ultimately, to obscure the true state of affairs in the Presbyterian Church.[18]

The changes which occurred at Princeton Seminary in 1929 are worth highlighting because they underscore the inadequacy of two-party interpretations of twentieth-century Protestantism. Historians have had difficulty making sense of the Princeton controversy because the struggle was not between liberals and conservatives. Rather, by the lights of American Protestant historiography, both sides were conservative. The chief antagonists were Machen, who opposed reorganization, and Charles Erdman,

---

expressions of Machen's aversion to interdenominationalism, on the fundamentalist side, see Machen to J. S. Luckey, Mar. 11, 1927; Machen to Edwin H. Rian, June 3, 1930; Machen to James M. Gray, July 7, 1929; Machen to Franklin G. Huling, Sept. 6, 1925; on the liberal side, see John Rockefeller, Jr., to Machen, Sept. 20, 1926; Nov. 11, 1926; Sept. 5, 1927; and Sept. 14, 1927; Machen to Rockefeller, Oct. 28, 1926; and Sept. 9, 1927; and William Adams Brown to Machen, Mar. 31, 1924; and April 2, 1924; Machen to Brown, April 1, 1924; and April 3, 1924. The correspondence with Brown and Rockefeller concerned Machen's participation in services and projects at the Mt. Desert Parish Church in Seal Harbor, ME, where the Machens worshipped while vacationing.

18. On these developments, see Bradley J. Longfield, *The Presbyterian Controversy: Fundamentalists, Modernists and Moderates* (New York: Oxford University Press, 1991), chs. 5–7; and Hart, *Defending the Faith*, ch. 5.

a dispensationalist professor of pastoral theology and co-editor of the *Fundamentals,* who supported the changes at Princeton and insisted that the church and seminary were still orthodox. Because liberals were absent, most scholars have reduced the conflict to personalities. But the transcripts of the Princeton proceedings show that the struggle was indeed theological, even if it was not between liberalism and fundamentalism. Erdman represented the New School version of Presbyterianism, one that smoothed out the sharper angles of seventeenth-century British Calvinism to match the contours of American religion. Machen, in contrast, manifested the traditional theological and ecclesiastical concerns of Old School Presbyterianism, a tradition which had a long history of opposing American Protestant innovations, from Charles Finney's revivals to Wesleyan perfectionism. The Princeton controversy was one more episode in that rivalry. But the two-party interpretation, sensing that both Machen and Erdman were not liberal, misses the shades of Presbyterianism within a place like Princeton.[19]

More importantly, the Princeton reorganization clarified the confessional dimension of Machen's conservatism. For Machen and likeminded Calvinists in the Northern Presbyterian Church the outcome of the Princeton Seminary affair threatened the very existence of Old School Presbyterianism. Since the reunion of Old and New School Presbyterians in 1870 Princeton had been designated an Old School institution. But reorganization forced the seminary to reflect the pluralism of the denomination, thus leaving conservatives without a base. The founding of Westminster Seminary in 1929 was designed to remedy this situation. According to Machen, who spoke at the new seminary's convocation, Princeton

---

19. On Machen's role in the Princeton reorganization, see Loetscher, *The Broadening Church,* 147; Winthrop S. Hudson, *Religion in America,* 3rd ed. (New York: Scribner's, 1981), 372-73; Sydney E. Ahlstrom, *A Religious History of the American People* (New Haven: Yale University Press, 1972), 912; Marsden, *Fundamentalism and American Culture,* 192; Norman F. Furniss, *The Fundamentalist Controversy, 1918-1931* (New Haven: Yale University Press, 1954), 35; Stonehouse, *J. Gresham Machen,* ch. 21; Ronald Thomas Clutter, *The Reorientation of Princeton Theological Seminary, 1900-1929* (Ann Arbor: UMI Research Press, 1982), 166-96, 323-33; John W. Hart, "Princeton Theological Seminary: The Reorganization of 1929," *Journal of Presbyterian History* 58 (1980): 124-40; George L. Haines, "The Princeton Theological Seminary, 1925-1960," Ph.D. dissertation, New York University, 1966, 63-64; Edwin H. Rian, *The Presbyterian Conflict* (Grand Rapids: Eerdmans, 1940), ch. 3; Sandeen, *The Roots of Fundamentalism,* 255-57. Better evaluations can be found in Longfield, *The Presbyterian Controversy,* ch. 7; and D. G. Hart, " 'Dr. Fundamentalis,': An Intellectual Biography of J. Gresham Machen, 1881-1937" (Ph.D diss., Johns Hopkins University, 1988), ch. 7.

Seminary was "dead," but its "noble tradition" was still alive. Westminster would endeavor "to continue that tradition unimpaired" by propagating and defending the Westminster Confession of Faith as true and capable of scholarly defense.[20]

As the 1930s would show, Machen had more in mind than merely forming a new seminary. He also wanted to create the skeleton of a church so that when conservatives left the mainline denomination they would have a place to go. The missions controversy of the early 1930s provided Machen with the first opportunity to pursue this strategy. The infamous "Layman's Inquiry," published in 1932, raised suspicions about the soundness of the Presbyterian Church's Board of Foreign Missions. After failing to force the General Assembly to investigate the Board, Machen decided in 1933 to found his own missions agency, the Independent Board of Presbyterian Foreign Missions. This proved to be the most audacious decision of Machen's stormy career. On the one hand, it split the already small and seemingly insignificant wing of confessionalists in the denomination. Debates about the wisdom and anomaly of founding an independent Presbyterian missions agency eventually forced a showdown at Westminster, an independent Presbyterian seminary, where conservatives like Clarence Macartney and others in 1935 resigned because of their unwillingness to endorse the Independent Board. On the other hand, the anomaly of an independent Presbyterian institution was equally evident to Presbyterian officials. Even though the new missions agency could muster support for only six missionaries, the Northern Presbyterian Church vigorously opposed the Independent Board, eventually trying and suspending board members from the ministry for violating membership and ordination vows. These disciplinary actions led to the founding in 1936 of the Orthodox Presbyterian Church.[21]

The anomalies of the Independent Board can easily obscure the confessional character of that missions agency. On the surface, the board had all the marks of a fundamentalist operation, particularly in that it was adamantly opposed to the modernism of the Protestant establishment and, above all, that it was independent. But while other fundamentalists were equally alarmed by modernism within mainstream Protestant missionary endeavors, and thus established interdenominational faith missions free

---

20. "Westminster Theological Seminary, Its Purpose and Plan," in *What Is Christianity?* ed. Ned Bernard Stonehouse (Grand Rapids: Eerdmans, 1951), 232-33. On the founding of Westminster, see Hart, " 'Dr. Fundamentalis,' " 272-90.

21. See Hart, " 'Dr. Fundamentalis,' " ch. 8.

from the encumbrances of denominational creeds and machinery, Machen desired to work along distinctly Presbyterian lines. And the Presbyterian identity of the Independent Board proved to be crucial in the last controversy of Machen's life. In the fall of 1936, only four months after the founding of the OPC, the Independent Board held its annual election of officers, and, in a surprising move, failed to reelect Machen as president, a post he had held since the organization's founding. This election reflected the growing antagonism in the OPC between dispensationalists led by Carl McIntire and confessionalists led by Machen and other Westminster faculty. While the confessionalists controlled the denomination, McIntire sought control of the Independent Board. Machen believed that with this election the Board had substituted fundamentalism for true Presbyterianism. McIntire's temerity as well as the Westminster faculty's opposition to dispensationalism resulted in the 1937 secession of McIntire from the OPC to form the Bible Presbyterian Synod.[22]

The 1937 split within the OPC makes little sense from the perspective of the two-party model but does shed light on Presbyterian confessionalism. Since both Machen and McIntire were conservative, again the standard explanation of the division has been psychological. But this time it is the paranoia of McIntire, not the temperamental idiosyncrasies of Machen, that historians have highlighted. Without denying the influence of personalities — Machen and McIntire had strong and, no doubt, unusual ones — the OPC split is relatively easy to explain when Machen's confessional concerns are taken into account. As George Marsden observed almost thirty years ago, three issues divided Orthodox and Bible Presbyterians: theology, morality, and ecclesiology. The OPC stood for the unadulterated Calvinism of the Westminster standards and removed chapters on the love of God and missions that in 1903 the Northern church had added. The Bible Presbyterians, if not all dispensationalists, were clearly sympathetic to the doctrinal glue of popular fundamentalism. The church also split over the issue of Christian liberty. McIntire accused Westminster's faculty of encouraging the consumption of beverage alcohol (rumors circulated that the seminary owned a still) and endeavored to make abstinence the official policy of the church. Confessionalists, however, were unwilling to go beyond the Westminster Standards and ruled that the use

---

22. On Machen's reaction to the changes in the Independent Board, see Machen to Buswell, Nov. 27, 1936, Machen Archives. The best guide to these struggles is George M. Marsden, "Perspective on the Division of 1937," in *Pressing toward the Mark*, 301-23.

of alcohol was a matter of liberty. Just as important for the division was church polity. The OPC wanted to send out foreign missionaries fully committed to Presbyterian theology and polity. The change of leadership within the Independent Board prompted the OPC to found its own committee on foreign missions. Bible Presbyterians, in contrast, thought the theological and ecclesiastical concerns of Westminster's ethnic faculty were alien to the tradition of American Presbyterianism.[23]

OPC Confessionalism and the Two-Party Model

If this reading of the OPC's identity is correct, and if the church's eventual refusal to join the NAE reflects Presbyterian confessionalism rather than fundamentalist separatism, then it is possible to distinguish Orthodox Presbyterians from both evangelicals (including fundamentalists) and liberals. The prevailing difference between confessionalists and other Protestants is the degree to which each group has adapted Christianity to the social and religious environment of the United States.[24] Theologically, the message of mainstream Protestantism, both in its evangelical and liberal forms, has been well adapted to the realities of the American experiment, while confessionalists have generally fought to retain Old World practices. By calling upon rational, autonomous individuals to make personal decisions for Christ or to follow the moral example of Jesus, evangelicals and liberals have displayed a higher estimate of human nature than confessionalists, who have been more aware of human sinfulness and who look to the institutional church for spiritual sustenance in the ministry of word and sacrament. Evangelicals, like their Protestant cousins, liberals, have

23. Marsden, "Perspective on the Division," *passim*. Marsden also argues that the OPC division mirrored the Old School-New School split of 1837 where Presbyterians went in different directions over the Calvinism of the Westminster Standards, ecclesiastical irregularities in evangelism and missions, and the nature of Christian liberty. On that older Presbyterian division, see George M. Marsden, *The Evangelical Mind and the New School Presbyterian Experience: A Case Study of Thought and Theology in Nineteenth-Century America* (New Haven: Yale University Press, 1970); E. H. Gillett, *History of the Presbyterian Church in the United States of America*, vol. II (Philadelphia: Presbyterian Board of Publications, 1864), chs. 40–42; and Harold M. Parker, Jr., *Studies in Southern Presbyterian History* (Gunnison, CO: B & B Printers, 1979), ch. 1.

24. For the purpose of my argument about confessionalism I am not distinguishing between fundamentalists and evangelicals. Both favored revivals, tended to be Arminian in theology, and followed Anglo-American conventions regarding worldliness. Confessionalists balked at these evangelical forms.

stressed Christianity's ethical demands and have used the criteria of a highly disciplined and morally responsible life as evidence of true faith. For confessionalists, theological distinctions have been crucial. They have equated correct doctrine with religious faithfulness.[25]

Furthermore, confessionalists and other Protestants have disagreed about the nature and function of the church. Evangelicals have not had clear definitions of the church: not only do their communions minimize the distinction between clergy and laity, but they also support a variety of parachurch endeavors, both evangelistic and political, which blur differences between religious and social matters. At the same time, liberal Protestant conceptions of the church have pursued ecumenicity at the expense of confessions and creeds. Confessionalists, in contrast, have defended a high view of church office and polity, and have regarded preaching, the sacraments, and discipline as the church's essential tasks and as the best response to human suffering. Evangelicals, in this respect, departed from conservative ways by developing a theology and means of outreach that was completely at home in a nation which made the individual sovereign, regarded hierarchy and the clergy with suspicion, and thrived in the religious free market which resulted from ecclesiastical disestablishment. While liberal Protestantism has been less individualistic than evangelicalism, its theology and ecclesiology are equally well adapted to the corporate and bureaucratic trends of twentieth-century American society. Conversely, confessionalists have tried to conserve practices of Christian nurture through catechesis and church schools, and by promoting respect and recognition of the need for clergy and for the centrality of word and sacrament. To be sure, America's religious disestablishment has been beneficial to confessionalists, even to the point of allowing them to outdo the confessionalism of their Old World counterparts, who have been constrained in established churches by the sponsoring state. But the forces of modernization have ultimately proved to be more favorable to evangelicals

---

25. For good overviews in the ethno-cultural historiography of the differences between evangelicals and confessionalists, sometimes designated "pietists" and "liturgicals," in the ethno-cultural historiography, see Daniel Walker Howe, "The Evangelical Movement and Political Culture in the North during the Second Party System," *Journal of American History* 77 (March 1991): 1216-39; and Robert P. Swierenga, "Ethnoreligious Political Behavior in the Mid-Nineteenth Century: Voting, Values, Cultures," in *Religion and American Politics,* ed. Mark A. Noll (New York: Oxford University Press, 1990), ch. 7. On liberal Protestant theology, see Lloyd J. Averill, *American Theology in the Liberal Tradition* (Philadelphia: Westminster, 1967), ch. 3; and Kenneth Cauthen, *The Impact of American Religious Liberalism* (New York: Harper and Row, 1962), especially ch. 1.

and liberals than to confessionalists, who depend upon the mediating structures of family, church, and neighborhood to water the seeds of faith they have tried to plant in the New World.[26]

Theological and ecclesiastical differences have, in turn, made Protestant confessionalists uneasy about the Americanness of evangelical and liberal Protestant religiosity. First, because confessionalists have maintained strict loyalty to creedal and doctrinal expressions from the Reformation or Protestant scholastic eras, they have been suspicious of interdenominational or nondenominational forms of cooperation. Second, confessionalists have manifested a tribal culture, seeking to form an isolated world rather than proselytizing among people with different roots. Third, Protestant confessionalists have been extremely wary of various programs of assimilation into the American religious mainstream, whether the progressivist path of liberal Protestantism or the millennial biblicism of evangelicalism. Resistance to assimilation has, finally, prompted confessionalists to be equally suspicious of their American co-religionists whose practices deviate from Old World norms.[27]

Of course, Machen and his followers in the OPC came out of mainstream and evangelical Protestant backgrounds and so might be expected to display more affinities to fundamentalists than to confessionalists. Indeed, the biggest difference between the OPC and other confessional Protestants in the United States is ethnicity. For most confessional Protestants, immigration and ethnicity nurtured a separate theological and ecclesiastical identity. Yet while Machen himself came from a blue-blood Southern family in Baltimore, and while most Orthodox Presbyterians were

---

26. On evangelicalism's view of the church, see Howe, "Evangelical Movement," 1222-32; and on the impact of corporatism on liberal Protestant ideas about the church, see Ben Primer, *Protestants and American Business Methods* (Ann Arbor: UMI Research Press, 1979); Craig Dykstra and James Hudnut-Beumler, "The National Organizational Structures of Protestant Denominations: An Invitation to Conversation," in *The Organizational Revolution: Presbyterians and American Denominationalism,* ed. Milton J Coalter, John M. Mulder, and Louis B. Weeks (Louisville: Westminster/John Knox, 1992), ch. 12; and Robert A. Schneider, "Voice of Many Waters: Church Federation in the Twentieth Century," in *Between the Times: The Travail of the Protestant Establishment in America, 1900-1960,* ed. William R. Hutchison (New York: Cambridge University Press, 1989), ch. 5. Glenn T. Miller, *Piety and Intellect: The Aims and Purposes of Ante-Bellum Theological Education* (Atlanta: Scholars Press, 1990), 3-6, 444-48, makes the provocative point that confessionalism flourished more in the United States than it did in Europe.

27. James D. Bratt, "Protestant Immigrants," paper presented for the Pew Charitable Trusts project on Minority Faiths in the American Protestant Mainstream, June 1993, 2-5.

WASP, even if lower middle class, the ecclesiastical controversies of the 1920s and 1930s combined with the logic of Reformed theology and polity to give the OPC some sense of the marginalization and alienation which ethnic confessionalists also experienced. Interestingly enough, Machen and his supporters looked to other Protestant confessional groups as their closest allies. The OPC had warm relations with the Christian Reformed Church, so much so that some church leaders talked about merger for a time. And Machen himself regarded the confessional and catechetical rigor as well as the denominational self-consciousness of both the Christian Reformed and the Missouri Synod as models for his own communion. These and other pieces of evidence indicate that Machen and the OPC had more in common with Protestant confessionalists than with neo-evangelicals, fundamentalists, or the Protestant establishment.[28]

Even though the OPC had few members whom observers might describe as hyphenated Americans, during its early history the church formed the kind of ghetto that sustained ethnic confessionalists. Moving to clearly defined neighborhoods was not possible, but starting Christian schools, producing confessional literature, making the home a center of Presbyterian piety, and establishing ecclesiastical ties with like-minded Presbyterian and Reformed communions were the primary means by which Orthodox Presbyterians established a separate identity. And if one looks at the many controversies which beleaguered the OPC throughout its first ten years, what emerges is a steady and deliberate effort to create a church and nurture a piety different from the dominant forms of American Protestantism. While the OPC's ecclesiology resembled the double separatism that fundamentalists championed against the neo-evangelicals, it was decidedly different. Like fundamentalists the OPC wanted nothing to do with modernism. But Orthodox Presbyterians also opposed, albeit not quite as strongly, the theology and ecclesiology of fundamentalists and evangelicals. This opposition, I argue, was rooted in strict Presbyterianism and moves the OPC outside the standard taxonomy of liberal and evangelical into the neglected category of Protestant confessionalism.[29]

The historiography of recent American Protestantism, however, has

---

28. See Machen, "What Is 'Orthodoxy'?" *Presbyterian Guardian* 1 (1935): 54; idem, "The Christian Reformed Church," *Presbyterian Guardian* 2 (1936): 170; and Hart, " 'Dr. Fundamentalis,' " chs. 8–9 for Machen's alliance with Calvinists in the Christian Reformed Church. On union discussions between the OPC and CRC, see Henry Zwaanstra, *Catholicity and Secession: A Study of Ecumenicity in the Christian Reformed Church* (Grand Rapids: Eerdmans, 1991), 51-56, 116-17.

29. See Hart, "Legacy of J. Gresham Machen," 213-21.

obscured the tradition and nuances of Protestant confessionalism. The conflict between fundamentalists and modernists of the 1920s continues to dominate the categories scholars use, with the unhappy result that Pentecostals and Calvinists, because both profess belief in the supernatural, are lumped together like peas from the same pod. What a recognition of confessional Protestantism yields is a richer and more accurate picture of American Christianity, or as the old chestnut has it, goes to the heart of historical writing, which is to draw "distinctions between things that really differ." In the case of Presbyterian history alone, identifying the concerns of confessional Presbyterians like Machen makes sense of the seemingly petty and personal acrimony that eventually divided his denomination. This is not to say that Machen was right or that his course was always wise. But exploring the diversity of views in American Protestantism does afford the opportunity to understand ideas and movements too often flattened in the dominant historiography.[30]

Conclusion

For good or ill, the United States has experienced remarkable religious diversity. Americans have handled this diversity in a variety of ways, some commendable and some deplorable. Historians have generally celebrated America's religious diversity when it produces harmony and goodwill. And the belief of many Americans, religious historians included, has been that tolerance of such diversity will yield national unity and common purpose. In fact, religious historians have been among the greatest advocates of consensus history, a narrative which stresses stability, harmony, and continuity. Yet religious historians have generally ignored the larger pattern of human history which shows that heterogenous cultures breed antagonism and division, not consensus and goodwill.[31]

30. The aphorism about the art of history comes from Grant Wacker, "You Want It on Plain White or Pumpernickel? Reflections on Two Kinds of History," paper presented at the Institute for the Study of American Evangelicals Consultation on Advocacy and the Writing of American History, April 1994, 3.

31. See Moore, *Religious Outsiders,* Introduction. Jacobsen and Trollinger, "Historiography of American Protestantism," make a similar point about American religious history. For Moore's criticism of the consensus approach, see "Learning to Love American Religious Pluralism: A Review Essay," *American Jewish History* 77 (1987): 316-30. On consensus history more generally, see John Higham, *History: Professional Scholarship in America,* rev. ed. (Baltimore: Johns Hopkins, 1983), 221-24.

The two-party model of American Protestantism is the direct result of a consensus approach to American religious history. Though the two-party model appears to stress conflict between conservatives and liberals, the record of hostility it most often highlights is that between sectarians and ecumenicals. Thus, the desire for a religious consensus in which ecumenicity, cosmopolitanism, and cooperation prevail prompts historians to reduce religious differences and conflicts to the polarities of cooperation and separatism. The dominant interpretations of American Protestantism, from Daniel Dorchester to Martin Marty, have displayed the assimilationist impulse of the dominant WASP culture. They tend to side with groups that cooperate and implicitly disparage believers who oppose ecumenicity. Like ethnic groups, religious traditions are welcome if they shed old world identities and join the mainstream. If not, they are often written off as psychologically defective or temperamentally incapable of adjusting to life in the big city. The failure of religious historians to take seriously the peculiar views of groups like confessional Protestants stems in part from the desire to see religious hostilities minimized.[32]

Ironically, however, consensus history and the two-party model it has fostered have probably yielded as much resentment, hostility, and misunderstanding as the exclusive and divisive claims made by religious sectarians. As Machen himself argued, conservatives were not nearly as narrow-minded as liberals. By arguing for a division in the church, conservatives actually took liberal ideas seriously, so seriously that they perceived such teaching as a real threat to individual souls. But liberals, he explained, by trying to keep both parties united in the same denomination or organization, displayed real intolerance. Their insistence upon unity and cooperation revealed a failure to understand the substance of the conservative argument, which was that liberal and conservative doctrines were fundamentally at odds. This was the reason why Walter Lippmann said that the liberal plea for tolerance and goodwill was the equivalent of telling conservatives to "smile and commit suicide." Some modern-day historians confirm Lippmann's point. The religious tolerance they display

---

32. Moore, *Religious Outsiders*, Introduction, *passim*. A similar problem attends the study of political conservatism, a tradition that, while significant numerically, has not been taken seriously by the historical profession. On the reasons for this neglect, reasons which are equally instructive for religious historians who confront groups such as confessional Protestants, see Alan Brinkley, "The Problem of American Conservatism," *American Historical Review* 99 (April 1994): 409-29; and Leo Ribuffo, "Why Is There So Much Conservatism in the United States and Why Do So Few Historians Know Anything about It?" *American Historical Review* 99 (April 1994): 438-49.

toward their subjects often stems more from indifference than high-mindedness. Thus, to the extent that religious historians make coopera-tion, ecumenicity, and service to the public the criteria by which they include religious groups, individuals, and ideas in the religious history canon, they manifest not so much an admirable outlook as a general indifference to the doctrines and practices which give believers identity, and which make religious diversity and intolerance inevitable.[33]

Finally, an effort to recover the distinctiveness and history of com-munions like the confessional Protestants of the OPC is to acknowledge the realities and problems of America's religious diversity. Possible bene-fits of such study will be greater understanding of different ideas, greater reluctance to dismiss such differences with condescension or ridicule, and perhaps even the rare quality of respecting those with whom we disagree. Yet even if the study of these groups fails to produce virtue, it does provide a candid and bracing view of the American experiment and the nature of religion, one that is less inspiring than the standard story of harmony and goodwill. As R. Laurence Moore has argued, the American religious sys-tem is only working when it is "creating cracks within denominations, when it is producing novelty, when it is fueling antagonism."[34]

This antagonism stems not only from the legacy of religious dises-tablishment but also from the nature of religious conviction itself. In his obituary of Machen, H. L. Mencken wrote that "Religion, if it is to retain any genuine significance, can never be reduced to a series of sweet atti-tudes, possible to anyone not actually in jail for felony." Rather, religion, he continued, is "something far more deep-down-diving and mud-upbringing." Mencken concluded that Machen had failed to impress this "obvious fact" upon his fellow Presbyterians but was "undoubtedly right." We may not necessarily concur with Mencken's conclusion. But

33. Machen, *Christianity and Liberalism*, 167-68; Lippmann, *American Inquisitors* (New York: Macmillan, 1928), 65-66; and Moore, *Religious Outsiders*, 205. For the insults which broad-minded historians have hurled at Machen, see Sandeen, who, in *Roots of Fundamentalism*, calls Machen's position "perverse obstinacy"; and Robert Moats Miller, who in "A Compleat (Almost) Guide Through the Forest of Fundamentalism," *Reviews in American History* 9 (1981), 397, says Machen was "quite loony." Leo P. Ribuffo, *The Old Christian Right: The Protestant Far Right from the Great Depression to the Cold War* (Philadelphia: Temple University Press, 1983), xiii-xvi, has observed that students of extremism often resort to psychological categories to describe the far right. Though he focuses on political extremism, Ribuffo's observation may apply equally well to studies of fundamentalism which have attributed religious extremism to various degrees of status anxiety, paranoia, or other temperamental disorders.

34. Moore, *Religious Outsiders*, 208.

just as Machen reminded Mencken of the profound dimensions of faith, so the study of confessional Protestantism may remind religious historians of the darker and more complex aspects of the subject they study, and lead them to more sober conclusions.[35]

35. Moore, *Religious Outsiders*, 208; and Mencken, "Doctor Fundamentalis," Baltimore *Evening Sun*, Jan. 18, 1937. The point that Moore makes about the divisive character of American religion, Robert H. Wiebe, in *The Segmented Society: An Introduction to the Meaning of America* (New York: Oxford University Press, 1975), 46, also makes about American life more generally when he writes that what has held Americans together has been "the ability to live apart." Society thus depends upon segmentation.

CHAPTER 8

Evangelical and Ecumenical: Missionary Leaders in Mainline Protestantism, 1900-1950[1]

RICHARD V. PIERARD

A useful way to test the two-party thesis discussed in this volume is to look at the acrimonious struggles between conservatives and liberals which occurred in the area of foreign missions in the so-called "mainline" Protestant denominations in the years after World War I. Charges of "modernism" on the mission field were hurled with abandon, numerous new "conservative" or "fundamentalist" mission agencies were formed which competed with the existing bodies for funds and personnel, and hitherto thriving denominational agencies suffered precipitous declines in their financial support and overseas staffs. By mid-century the independent "faith" missions, societies of the newer evangelical and fundamentalist denominations, and the Southern Baptist Convention's Foreign Mission Board had considerably outstripped the older mainline or ecumenical bodies in numbers of workers overseas.

In spite of the polemics at the time (and ever since, from the conservative side) there are good reasons to doubt whether such wide-ranging erosion in the theological and spiritual character of the mainline missionaries took place during the interwar years. In fact, with just a few notable

1. The author wishes to express his appreciation to Martha Lund Smalley, Joan Duffy, and Paul Stuehrenberg at Yale Divinity School Library, New Haven, CN; Beverly Carlson and Betty Layton at the American Baptist Archives Center, Valley Forge, PA; and Gerald H. Anderson at the Overseas Ministries Studies Center, New Haven, for their assistance in this project.

exceptions, both the leadership and missionary forces of the mainline remained theologically conservative in their beliefs, remarkably evangelistic in their goals and endeavors, fully committed to carrying out the social implications of the gospel, and actively supportive of the "ecumenical project." They embodied in their lives and ministries a middle ground between the rhetorical extremes of some early twentieth-century Protestant leaders; they were, for the most part, centrists in their own denominations. Although space precludes an examination of the missionary efforts of all the mainline denominations (defined as those who belonged to the Federal Council of Churches of Christ in America), missionary leadership in two bodies which were most torn by fundamentalist-modernist controversies in these years will be singled out for closer consideration: the (Northern) Presbyterians and the Northern Baptists.

Ecumenical/Evangelical Presbyterians

The Presbyterian Church in the north, known after the reunification of the Old and New School assemblies in 1870 as the Presbyterian Church in the U.S.A., had in its early history carried on foreign mission work under the auspices of the American Board of Commissioners for Foreign Missions, which, founded in 1810, was the first American missionary society. Although primarily Congregationalist in orientation, other groups cooperated with the ABFMS. However, the Old School Presbyterians, who had little use for interdenominational voluntary societies, withdrew in 1837 and formed a separate Board of Foreign Missions under the church's control. Although the Presbyterian church divided at the outbreak of the Civil War and remained apart for more than a century, both bodies engaged in missionary activity, and the Northern Presbyterians in particular established noteworthy works in Japan, Korea, China, Thailand, India, Iran, Latin America, and Cameroon. The Korean endeavor was especially significant, as here the famous "Nevius method" (named after J. L. Nevius, an American Presbyterian in China whose colleagues in Korea in 1890 had sought his advice for developing their newly opened field) of self-support, self-government, and self-propagation was utilized, resulting in extraordinary church growth.

The towering figure in the Presbyterian missionary enterprise during the years of so much growth was Robert Elliott Speer (1867-1947).[2] The

---

2. The standard work on him is W. Reginald Wheeler, *A Man Sent from God: The Biography of Robert E. Speer* (Westwood, NJ: Revell, 1956).

son of a Pennsylvania lawyer and congressman, he graduated from Princeton in 1889 at the head of his class. While in college he was deeply influenced by D. L. Moody and A. T. Pierson (editor of the *Missionary Review of the World,* 1888-1911), and he signed the famous Student Volunteer Movement pledge, "I am willing and desirous, God permitting, to become a foreign missionary." After working for a year as an SVM traveling secretary, Speer enrolled at Princeton Seminary. However, he dropped out in his second year when he was offered a secretary's position by the Presbyterian Board of Foreign Missions.

This proved to be his life's calling, as he was to serve for forty-six years, retiring in 1937 as the board's senior secretary. He never completed a theological degree nor was he ordained, but few people had a greater impact on Protestant missions in our century than Speer. He was a man of enormous intellectual and spiritual power, the author or editor of sixty-seven books and innumerable articles, a popular conference speaker, and a denominational and ecumenical leader (he served a term as moderator of the Presbyterian church and as president of the Federal Council of the Churches of Christ in America). He also chaired the General War-Time Commission of the Churches during World War I, was involved in several important ecumenical gatherings (including Edinburgh, 1910), and for two decades headed the Committee on Cooperation in Latin America. He agreed to chair the committee that appealed for volunteers for church and foreign mission service of the controversial Inter-Church World Movement, and although he was critical of the ICWM's overemphasis on organization and fund-raising, he opposed the General Assembly of the Presbyterian Church's decision to withdraw from it.

It is quite clear that Speer had a strong commitment to ecumenism, a point his biographer W. Reginald Wheeler strongly emphasizes. A staunch Presbyterian, he was also "an active and influential spokesman and supporter of interdenominational service." He felt that the two spheres of service supplemented and enriched each other.[3] In fact, Samuel McCrea Cavert, a former secretary of the Federal Council of Churches, said at Speer's memorial service in 1947 that he was an "Apostle of Christian Unity." Cavert elaborated: "He thought of unity not as something which we achieve so much as something that we received." It was given in what God has done for us through Christ. "His basic position was not that Christians *ought* to be one but that they *are* by virtue of their common relation to Christ and that they should make this oneness *manifest*

3. Ibid., 175.

to the world." He did not feel the time was ripe for church union, but church cooperation was a major step in the direction of unity.[4]

Speer was also a strong critic of racism and an advocate of women in ministry, including their ordination.[5] At the same time, he regarded Christian unity as a necessary precondition for an effective witness regarding the social issues of the time. The churches could never bring the healing and reconciling power of Christ to bear upon economic, racial, and international problems unless they could demonstrate that power in their own relations with one another. In 1923 the Federal Council decided to join with Catholic and Jewish agencies to issue a statement condemning the steel industry's refusal to abandon the twelve-hour day. Although the action was quite controversial, Speer, who at the time was its president, told the official working on the document he would "sign that himself." He had the courage to back up his beliefs about the need for social justice.[6]

Alongside these supposedly "liberal" concerns, Speer also affirmed what can only be called an orthodox or conservative theology. This theological orientation comes out again and again in his voluminous writings. For example, in *The Deity of Christ* (1909), he declared that his belief in this cardinal doctrine rested on the following premises: (1) Christ's perfect character, as demonstrated by the supernatural claims which he made and fulfilled, the universality of his ideals, and his sinlessness; (2) the substance of his teaching, which set him apart from mere human teachers, in that he had direct knowledge of God and revealed him to us, showed humankind its spiritual possibilities including unity with one another, and set forth moral teachings of incomparable magnitude; (3) the deeds he accomplished on earth, such as the training of the Twelve and his own resurrection; and (4) his continuing influence, resulting in things as wonderful as he ever did when he was on earth, through the transformation of the world and the transformation of individual lives.[7]

4. Quoted in ibid., 181.
5. On racial issues see Speer's *Of One Blood: A Short History of the Race Problem* (New York: Council of Women for Home Missions and Missionary Education, 1924), and *Race and Race Relations* (New York: Revell, 1924). His position on women in ministry is set forth in chapter 12 of *Some Living Issues* (New York: Revell, 1930), and summarized in Wheeler, *A Man Sent from God*, 161-64.
6. Wheeler, *A Man Sent from God*, 176.
7. Robert E. Speer, *The Deity of Christ* (New York: YMCA Press, 1909). In the interests of scholarly accuracy, all direct quotations from the writings of Speer and other individuals will be presented in the essay with the original spellings and non-inclusive language.

In *The Meaning of Christ to Me* (1936) Speer labeled the death of Christ the central fact of history and the ground of our hope of salvation. He insisted the resurrection of Christ was a literal event, and it must be the center of our thought and message, since it is the proof of victory over sin and death. The free acceptance of the Lordship of Christ is the essence of discipleship. The hope of his second coming is also an integral part of our faith, as he must come again in order to complete and fulfill his first coming:

> If the supernatural return of Christ is a reality, then all ground for unbelief or doubt regarding the supernaturalism of the Incarnation is gone. This is one reason why the belief in His Second Coming is, as all who cherish that belief know it to be, the dissolution of every misgiving as to the truth of His Virgin Birth, His miracles, and His Resurrection.[8]

In a series of published lectures, *The Finality of Jesus Christ* (1933), Speer maintained that Jesus Christ did not come to found a religion but "to be the Life and Light and Lord of man." Christianity, he said, was not a human quest for truth but, rather, the supernatural self-revelation of God himself which opens all truth to the faith and obedience of humankind. It was not to be compared with other religions because "it is incommensurable and alone, like Christ, who is the First and the Last of it and of all things, the Only One."[9] After reviewing the historical development and expansion of Christianity, he then challenged various modern views which questioned the uniqueness and finality of Christ and which called for some sort of compromise with or leavening of the other religions. He concluded: "The attitude of Christianity must be that of conflict and conquest; it proposes to displace the other religions." Following this line of argument, Speer asserted that evangelism was not out of date. "Men who believe the Gospel will proclaim it, and will do so with a view to leading other men deliberately to accept Jesus Christ as their Lord and Saviour and to become His disciples."[10]

8. Robert E. Speer, *The Meaning of Christ to Me* (New York: Revell, 1936), 158-59. See also his speech at the SVM Quadrennial Convention in Indianapolis on December 30, 1923, in which he proclaimed that "[our] great central, controlling purpose should be to commit our lives absolutely and irrevocably to the Lord Jesus Christ, henceforth to do His will, and not our own, cost what it may." Manuscript of the convention speech. Box 143, Folder 2349, John R. Mott Papers, Yale Divinity School Library (hereafter YDS).

9. Robert E. Speer, *The Finality of Jesus Christ* (New York: Revell, 1933), 5-6.
10. Ibid., 374.

Speer's views were not, of course, uncontested. There were some people even within his own church who disavowed his understanding of evangelism — that is, the effort to get people to accept and confess Jesus Christ and to join the Christian church — and Speer was not afraid to confront them. He took particular aim at the idea popular in some circles in India that conversions to other faiths should be outlawed and that the ruler should "protect the ancient religious faiths" of the country. To the contrary, he argued that this froze human thought with no possibility of change. There was no reason to hold fast to something just because it was old. Moreover, since all religions had a beginning, if there could be no conversion from an old faith to a new one, then what warrant was there for any form of religion? In his opinion

> Christianity is the universal and unique and indispensable message of the salvation wrought for the world in Christ and in Him alone. He is the only way to the Father, the only Light of the world, the Way, the Truth, and the life. . . . We must make him known with the urgent desire to have Him accepted by all men and to have all men unite themselves to Him and to one another in Him. This is the missionary aim.[11]

He went on to suggest that a concept of evangelism that contented itself merely with permeating society with Christian ideals was inadequate. "The primary and effective missionary method at home and abroad is the contact of individual with individual. This is the evangelism of the New Testament and it never has been and never will be out of date." It was not enough to transform present-day interpretations of Confucianism or Buddhism or to pervade society with Christian concepts. One had to drive straight at the conversion of men and women to Christ. For Speer, this was also the most effective way to permeate and uplift the life and thought of any land. In the church at home and in all our missions, he said, Christian believers needed "to go after men and women, one by one, or in the groups and companies in which they are accessible, and to relate them to Christ and Christ to them in the elemental reality of the Gospel of the New Testament and of all time."[12] As expressed in *The Unfinished Task of Foreign Missions* (1926), he viewed the foreign mission enterprise with great hope. Significant progress had been made in the previous hundred years, and the church seemed poised on the edge of even greater

11. Ibid.
12. Robert E. Speer, "Is Evangelism out of Date?" *Missionary Review of the World* 44 (June 1931): 405-8.

success. It was the clear duty of the church to carry salvation in Christ to all the world now. "For God in Christ is our only hope and the only hope of the world, and the world needs Christ and Christ alone and Christ now."

For Speer, Christianity was the final and unique religion, and it would absorb and displace all other religions because it alone made the moral character of God the central and transcendent issue, presented a perfect ethical ideal for the individual, and articulated a social ethic adequate for both national life and world society. "As absolute, it must displace all that is partial or false. It must conquer the world. The people who have it must be a missionary people." The gospel must "enter any field in which old religions are encumbering the religious nature of man. It cannot conquer except in love, but in love it intends to conquer." The aim of foreign missions was to make itself unnecessary, that is, the missions would not be permanent agencies. Their work is to plant Christianity, foster its growth and establishment in the forms which its living principle will naturally take in a new land, and then go on to do the same work elsewhere. Missions are not the church but simply the founders and helpers of it. There was more need of foreign missions than ever, not to establish Western churches but to work away until living, indigenous churches are created. This made missions "one of the richest forms of social ministry and one of the most powerful forces in human progress." But all this was "interlace[d] with the primary evangelistic purpose."[13]

Speer's chief associate, Arthur Judson Brown (1856-1963), held similar views regarding evangelism. A veteran pastor, he joined the mission board's staff in 1895 as administrative secretary, served for seventeen years as chair of the Committee of Reference and Counsel (the executive committee) of the Foreign Missions Conference of North America, and was a prominent figure in the ecumenical gatherings of the era.[14] In two impor-

---

13. Robert E. Speer, *The Unfinished Task of Foreign Missions* (New York: Revell, 1926), 41-42, 54-55, 273-74, 279. See also *"Are Foreign Missions Done For?"* (New York: Board of Foreign Missions of the Presbyterian Church in the U.S.A., 1928), where he contended that missions are not waning, in Christ the church has the final and sufficient gospel, and we do not need to learn from other religions or assemble out of all of them the ultimate synthetic and universal religion of humankind. Jesus Christ is the universal Savior, not the Western. The foreign mission enterprise as we conceive it will not last forever, and there is no reason why we could not complete it in our generation.

14. On Brown see his *Memoirs of a Centenarian*, ed. William N. Wysham (New York: World Horizons, Inc., 1957); and R. Park Johnson, "The Legacy of Arthur Judson Brown," *International Bulletin of Missionary Research* 10 (April 1986): 71-75.

tant books, *The Foreign Missionary: An Incarnation of a World Movement*[15] and *The Why and How of Foreign Missions*,[16] he affirmed as a basic truth "that Jesus Christ is the temporal and eternal salvation of men, and that it is the duty of those who know to tell others about him." He delineated the primary motives for missions as: a genuine Christian experience of regeneration which results in the overpowering impulse to communicate this experience to others; a consciousness that the world needs Christ; a relationship with Christ which "not only lends new dignity to this earthly life but that saves [one's] soul and prepares him for eternal companionship with God"; and, finally, Christ's command to carry out the evangelization of the world. The latter "is not a request; not a suggestion. It leaves nothing to our choice. It is an order, comprehensive and unequivocal, a clear, peremptory, categorical imperative: 'Go!' "[17] Brown reiterated these points in his historical narrative of the Presbyterian mission enterprise, saying that no one was exempt from the missionary obligation because of doctrinal differences.

> No changes that have taken place or that can possibly take place can set aside the great central facts that Jesus Christ means the temporal and eternal salvation of men; that it is the duty of those who know Him to tell others about Him; that no matter how distant the ignorant may be, no matter how different in race or speech, or how unconscious of their need, or how much trouble and expense we may incur in reaching them, we must get to them.[18]

In his memoirs, Brown stated that "the heart of New Testament Christianity is not a doctrine but an event, not something that man has done but something that God has done. This is the vital difference between Christianity and other religions. They represent man's attempts to solve the problems of life and destiny by his reason. Christianity declares that they are solved by God himself in Christ." Speaking of the deity of Christ, Brown added "it would be hard to believe in the justice and goodness of

15. Arthur J. Brown, *The Foreign Missionary: An Incarnation of a World Movement* (New York: Revell, 1907; rev. ed. 1932, 1950).

16. Arthur J. Brown, *The Why and How of Foreign Missions* (New York: Young People's Missionary Movement of the United States and Canada, 1908). An edition tailored for the Episcopal church was issued in 1908, and one for the Southern Baptists in 1935.

17. Ibid., 6-11.

18. Arthur J. Brown, *One Hundred Years: A History of the Foreign Missionary Work of the Presbyterian Church in the U.S.A.* (New York: Revell, 1936), 1060.

God without his revelation in Christ." He had abandoned the traditional effort to cite miracles as a proof of Christ's deity and declared instead: "I now cite his deity as proof of his miracles." As for the Virgin Birth, Brown maintained it was something that became intelligible to him from the viewpoint of the Incarnation. He also affirmed that Christ rose bodily from the dead.[19]

On the other hand, Brown maintained that in no phase of the church's work had there been greater incentives to cooperation and union than in foreign missions. He said bluntly that it was "impossible for a divided Church to Christianize the world." Chinese, Japanese, and Indian Christians were confused by American denominationalism, and this was hindering the development of strong, united indigenous churches in these places. "So long as the unity of Christianity is thus obscured, it cannot make the strongest impression in the non-Christian world." The task of building the kingdom of God on earth "can never be accomplished until the Church addresses itself to the problem in a united way."[20]

In 1915 he devoted an entire book to the theme of Christian unity as imperative for the advance of missions. At the same time he joined together the personal gospel and its social dimensions, and insisted that in the proclamation of the Word of God no distinctions were to be made. Writing while the war in Europe was raging, he insisted that the church had an even greater obligation "to make the spirit of Jesus thoroughly pervade all human life and relationships, to clarify the distinction between the teachings of Christ and so-called modern civilization, to eliminate the pagan and selfish elements in our social, commercial, and national life, to convince men that brotherhood under the Divine Fatherhood is not only personal but international, and to exalt Christ as the only Lord and Saviour of mankind."[21]

Like Speer, Brown was an optimist. He thought the church of his own day was more virile and aggressive than at any other time in its history. "It studies the Bible more earnestly and intelligently. It gives on a far more liberal scale for the support of philanthropic, educational, and missionary work. It has developed a public conscience which is more keenly sensitive to wrong." This sensitivity, in particular, had been re-

19. Brown, *Memoirs of a Centenarian,* 122-24, 126, 141.
20. The Committee on the War and Religious Outlook, *Christian Unity: Its Principles and Possibilities* (New York: Association Press, 1921), 301-2.
21. Arthur J. Brown, *Unity and Missions: Can a Divided Church Save the World?* (New York: Fleming H. Revell, 1915), 8-9.

flected in recent outbursts against business fraud, political corruption, and the white slave traffic, things to which people had been indifferent only a few decades earlier.[22]

Other examples of conservatism among Presbyterian missions leaders could be cited as well. Cleland B. McAfee, who served from 1930 to 1936 as a senior secretary of the mission board, published *The Foreign Missionary Enterprise and Its Sincere Critics* (New York: Revell, 1935), which refuted forty-seven criticisms of foreign missions, including the increasingly popular notion that truth exists in all religions. John A. MacKay (1889-1983), a missionary in South America from 1916 to 1932 who then spent four years as Latin American secretary of the mission board and twenty-three years as president of Princeton Theological Seminary, was insistent about "the evangelistic duty of Christianity" and believed the missionary thrust should characterize theological work.[23] Similar commitments were reflected in the work of J. Christy Wilson (1881-1973), who spent twenty years in Iran and then became professor of ecumenics at Princeton, and Samuel Hugh Moffett (1916-), Korean missionary and later a Princeton professor and author of an authoritative history of Christianity in Asia. Finally, to drive the point home, as late as 1950 the Presbyterian mission board's *Manual* contained the following statement:

> The supreme and controlling aim of foreign missions is to make the Lord Jesus Christ known to all men as their Divine Savior and to persuade them to become His disciples; to gather these disciples into churches which shall be self-supporting, self-governing, and self-propagating; to cooperate with these churches as long as may be necessary in the evangelization of their countrymen and in bringing to bear on all human life the spirit and principles of Christ.[24]

The Presbyterian Mission Struggle

Since the story of the controversy within the Presbyterian Church U.S.A. over its mission program is familiar, it will be recounted here only in the

22. Ibid., 302-3.
23. Samuel Escobar, "The Legacy of John Alexander Mackay," *International Bulletin of Missionary Research* 16 (July 1992): 116-22.
24. Quoted in W. Reginald Wheeler, ed., *The Crisis Decade: A History of the Foreign Missionary Work of the Presbyterian Church in the U.S.A., 1937-1947* (New York: Board of Foreign Missions, 1950), x.

barest detail.[25] In the 1920s, under Speer's leadership, the American Presbyterian church was supporting around 1,600 missionaries and was the largest Protestant denominational effort in the world.[26] However, even with his emphasis on a simple Christocentric gospel and readiness to affirm the cardinal doctrines of New Testament Christianity (including the Virgin Birth, Christ's deity and bodily resurrection, and the command to proclaim the evangel throughout the world), Speer did not satisfy hardline conservatives like J. Gresham Machen. Machen particularly disliked Speer's concern for social issues and extensive ecumenical involvements, and strongly condemned his above-mentioned book *"Are Foreign Missions Done For?"* But Machen was also unhappy because Speer's position on Scripture held closely to the traditional language of the church, which affirmed the Bible's supreme authority in faith and life but not Princeton "inerrancy." Speer saw absolute authority as resting with Christ as he was revealed in the Scriptures and not the words of the Bible per se. He was essentially anti-creedal and opposed to doctrinal intellectualism.[27]

What brought the crisis to a head was the publication of the report of the Laymen's Foreign Missions Inquiry. The latter was the outgrowth of concerns expressed by a number of mission enthusiasts about the obviously declining interest in and financial support for the enterprise (especially among young people) and their suggestion that a reappraisal of mission motives and methods should be undertaken. In 1930 some Northern Baptist businessmen persuaded their fellow Baptist John D. Rockefeller, Jr. to finance an inquiry. A Board of Directors consisting of 35 laypersons representing seven denominations — Northern Baptist, Congregational, (Dutch) Reformed Church in America, Episcopal, (Northern) Methodist, Presbyterian U.S.A., and United Presbyterian — was formed. Not being denominational officials, the members were independent of the authority of mission boards. The inquiry was restricted to India,

---

25. On the controversy see the classic Edwin H. Rian, *The Presbyterian Conflict* (Grand Rapids: Eerdmans, 1940), and the more recent and insightful historical studies by George M. Marsden, *Fundamentalism and American Culture* (New York: Oxford University Press, 1980), Bradley J. Longfield, *The Presbyterian Controversy* (New York: Oxford University Press, 1991), and D. G. Hart, *Defending the Faith: J. Gresham Machen and the Crisis of Conservative Protestantism in Modern America* (Baltimore: Johns Hopkins University Press, 1994).

26. Gerald H. Anderson, "American Protestants in Pursuit of Mission: 1886-1966," *International Bulletin of Missionary Research* 12 (July 1986): 101, citing James Patterson, who stated that the number of missionaries peaked at 1,606 in 1927.

27. Longfield, *Presbyterian Controversy*, 203.

Burma, China, and Japan, and fact-finding teams from the Institute of Social and Religious Research carried out the first stage of the survey. The information gathered about missionary activity in these places was then turned over to a 15-person Commission of Appraisal, headed by Harvard philosopher and liberal Congregationalist William Ernest Hocking, which in 1931-32 made a nine-month tour of the areas. Upon returning home, they compiled the data from the studies and their own observations, and recommended future directions for the American missionary endeavor in a book entitled *Re-thinking Missions: A Laymen's Inquiry after One Hundred Years* (New York: Harper, 1932). The survey data was published in seven volumes the following year.[28]

The report stirred up a hornet's nest, especially its theological section ("General Principles"), which was written by Hocking. It argued that: missions should emphasize social effort apart from evangelism; missionaries should seek to link their faith with common features they could find in non-Christian religions; and there ought to be greater unity in missionary activity, both between missions and with members of other religions. The goal of missions should not be to create institutional churches on the foreign fields but to permeate the fabric of indigenous society with creative ideals and eventually to form an international fellowship in which each religion would find its appropriate place.

The Hocking Report, as many called it, evoked bitter criticism within mission circles, and only the Congregationalist mission leaders received it favorably.[29] Speer's 1933 critique, *"Re-thinking Missions" Examined*, was particularly harsh.[30] He said it was the product of a small group and thus was highly divisive. Most of the agencies represented in the Foreign Missions Conference of North America had no relationship to the venture. The report sloughed over the history of the expansion of Christianity and had no appreciation of the true motives of the early missionaries. It rooted the theological basis of mission in Protestant liberalism and reflected no understanding of the uniqueness of Christ who is *the* Way and not *a* way to God.

However, since two members of the Presbyterian Board of Foreign Missions were members of the Laymen's Inquiry, denominational conser-

---

28. Orville A. Petty, ed., *Laymen's Foreign Missions Inquiry: Regional Reports of the Commission of Appraisal* (New York: Harper, 1933). See also Kenneth Scott Latourette, *Advance Through Storm*, vol. 7 of *The Expansion of Christianity* (New York: Harper, 1945), 51-52.

29. Anderson, *IBMR*, 106-7, assesses the response to the Hocking Report.

30. Robert E. Speer, *"Re-Thinking Missions" Examined* (New York: Revell, 1933).

vatives had the opening they needed to raise questions. Machen, in fact, decided to challenge Speer and the board directly. When he received no satisfaction, he proceeded to form an Independent Board for Presbyterian Foreign Missions in June 1933. The General Assembly categorically rejected this act of insubordination and in 1935 suspended Machen and his associates from the ministry. Arthur Brown noted later that the fundamentalist-modernist controversy had sharply divided the church and its missions, but he and Speer had refused to support either party. The reason was that under the Presbyterian system the mission board was not an ecclesiastical body and had no judicial authority in matters of doctrine. He added that "of course an evangelical faith is an essential qualification for a missionary but if there is any doubt about it in a given case, the presbytery and not the board is the lawful judge."[31]

For years Speer had tried to mediate the growing differences and keep the mission work intact. As he declared in a speech before the Federal Council of Churches in 1925: "We have to quit this business of partisanship, to quit calling each other by factional names. . . . The truth of God is greater than any one party can claim or any one title but Christian can cover. . . . For my part I want no label but Christian and mean to try to call no brother-Christian by any other name."[32] But as the years of controversy dragged on, Speer became increasingly discouraged. He conceded in a letter to John R. Mott in May 1935: "I wish with all my heart that my seventieth birthday were at hand so that I could retire." (That was the normal retirement age for church officials then, and he was only sixty-seven at the time.) "I have never seen the missionary situation generally and the general religious situation in our own Church more disturbed than at the present time. . . . The Modern Missions Movement [an ephemeral liberal organization that endorsed the Hocking Report][33] on the one hand and the independent boards that are going up on the other are playing havoc with our old missionary unity. I do not foresee what the end is going to be."[34] It seems clear from the foregoing that leaders like Speer and Brown represented the strong middle that existed in Pres-

31. Brown, *Memoirs of a Centenarian*, 30-31.

32. Quoted in the *Federal Council Bulletin*, January 19, 1948, p. 3.

33. William Ernest Hocking, *Evangelism: An Address on Permanence and Change*, privately printed brochure of speech delivered to a meeting of the Modern Missions Movement, Rochester, NY, May 28, 1935. Box 203, Folder 3258, John R. Mott Papers, YDS.

34. Robert E. Speer to John R. Mott, May 1, 1935. Box 84, Folder 1510, John R. Mott Papers, YDS.

byterian mission circles. With more astute denominational leadership, the extremists on both sides (who were in the distinct minority within the church) could have been checked, and the eventual breakdown in the denominational mission enterprise could have been averted.

The Northern Baptist Controversy

The Baptist situation was somewhat different. Whereas Baptists in the South had opted for a somewhat centralized convention form of organization in 1845, their northern counterparts remained more loosely affiliated in local associations and state conventions. The national ties were maintained through voluntary societies for foreign missions, home missions, and publications, but by the 1890s many regarded this arrangement as inadequate. In response to mounting demands from the churches for a more effective kind of organization, agency leaders and representatives from various congregations met in Washington in 1907 to organize a Northern Baptist Convention. The provisional constitutional structure adopted there was formally ratified the following year.[35] The three societies now became program boards of the new denomination, which quickly embraced ecumenism by joining the Federal Council of Churches in 1908. The NBC structure would prove to be a convenient target for fundamentalists in the 1920s, especially since the New World Movement effort between 1919 and 1924 to raise $100 million dollars to help fund the denominational agencies led to confusion and suspicion among the rank and file.

It is worth noting that the second missionary agency to be formed in the United States was that of the Baptists. Adoniram Judson and Luther Rice had sailed to India in 1812 under the auspices of the American Board of Commissioners for Foreign Missions, but on the way they decided that immersion was the biblical form of baptism and resigned their appointments. Judson went on to Burma while Rice came home to raise support, and in 1814 the General Missionary Convention of the Baptist Denomination in the United States for Foreign Missions was formed in Philadelphia. It was popularly known as the Triennial Convention and functioned as a voluntary society, with individuals rather than churches as such working together. It was the first Baptist organization to operate on a national scale.

---

35. *Minutes of the Meeting for the Organization of the Northern Baptist Convention Held at Washington, D.C., May 17-18, 1907; Northern Baptist Convention Annual* (1908), 28. Library, American Baptist Archives Center (hereafter ABAC).

When the Southerners broke away in 1845, the Triennial Convention re-organized itself as the American Baptist Missionary Union. It carried on mission work in Burma, India, and the Belgian Congo, and after the turn of the century in the Philippines and Thailand. The ABMU was renamed the American Baptist Foreign Mission Society in 1910 and within a few years was integrated into the Northern Baptist Convention's structure. In the 1870s several women's societies were formed to support women missionaries and care for female converts, and by 1914 they had consolidated into one agency, the Woman's American Baptist Foreign Missionary Society. Although separated by gender, the two bodies worked together closely and finally merged in 1955.[36]

With the emergence of the fundamentalist party in the NBC at the end of World War I, foreign missionaries came under attack for alleged doctrinal deviations.[37] As part of the offensive, an attempt was made to impose a creedal requirement on the denomination, the New Hampshire Confession of Faith of 1833. Fundamentalist leader W. B. Riley moved this at the 1922 annual meeting, but Cornelius Woelfkin, a former president of the ABFMS and pastor of New York's Park Avenue Baptist Church, countered with a substitute motion, "The Northern Baptist Convention affirms that the New Testament is the all-sufficient ground of our faith and practice, and we need no other statement." This was adopted by a two to one majority.[38] Fundamentalists then demanded a full investigation of alleged "modernism" among the missionary force. The ABFMS initially rejected this proposal, but in 1924 it reluctantly agreed to permit a seven-person commission to look into "the conduct, policies, and practices of the Board of Managers of the American Baptist Foreign Mission Society and of its Secretaries in the selection of missionaries to the foreign field," and to consider what to do with those workers "who do not accept or have repudiated or abandoned the evangelical faith as held historically

---

36. *NBC Annual* (1914), 307-8. Robert G. Torbet, *Venture of Faith: The Story of the American Baptist Foreign Mission Society and the Woman's American Baptist Foreign Mission Society, 1814-1954* (Philadelphia: Judson Press, 1955), is the best account of American Baptist missions. General information about American Baptist history is found in Robert G. Torbet, *A History of Baptists*, 3rd ed. (Valley Forge, PA: Judson Press, 1973); and H. Leon McBeth, *The Baptist Heritage: Four Centuries of Baptist Witness* (Nashville: Broadman Press, 1987).

37. Donald G. Tinder, "Fundamentalist Baptists in the Northern Western United States, 1920-1950," Ph.D. diss., Yale University, 1969, 318-61; and Torbet, *Venture of Faith*, 407-21, are helpful discussions of the controversy over the NBC's foreign mission enterprise.

38. *NBC Annual* (1922), 133-34.

by Baptists." Although the commission found only a few problem cases and generally exonerated the missionaries in question (four actually did resign), it called for more careful appointment procedures and for some method of monitoring the continuing faith of an individual missionary.[39]

The mission board was attacked for its so-called "inclusive policy," that is, no specific theological test was required for those who served, other than membership in a Baptist church. But, as the chair of the society's managing board, Frederick L. Anderson, declared on May 29, 1924, this did not have the opposite meaning, namely, that any member of a church connected with the convention could be a board member or missionary. "The evangelical history and spirit of American Baptists" and their "understanding of Christ and the New Testament" restrict the choice to "those who clearly show the fruits of a regenerate life, preach, love and live the vital message of the gospel, have a passion for the souls of men, and are devoted to Christ and his purposes for the world." He went on to say that because of the ever-changing interpretations of Scripture and the diversity of views in our society, the board had sought to find the common ground on which we stand: "Guided by the facts that Baptists have always been known as evangelicals, and that the gospel is the most important message of the Scriptures, we have demanded that all our officers and missionaries be loyal to the gospel. We will appoint only suitable evangelical men and women; we will appoint evangelicals, and we will not

---

39. *NBC Annual* (1922), 133-34; (1924), 51-52; (1925), 79-94; "Open Letter to Northern Baptists from ABFMS," Oct. 29, 1923, ABFMS Group No. 1, ABAC. The fundamentalist group attempted to secure passage in 1925 of a strong resolution calling for immediate recall of missionaries who did not hold to a specified number of doctrines (including the direct creation of humanity in the image of God, supernatural inspiration of the Scriptures, and the deity, Virgin Birth, sinless life, sacrificial death, bodily resurrection, ascension, and second coming of Christ). It was instead replaced by a milder statement calling on the foreign mission board to take action to deal with those "who do not hold to the fundamentals of the faith as historically interpreted by Baptists" in the light of the New Testament as our basis of faith and in a way "as seems to them will best conserve our denominational interests and best advance the kingdom of God." *NBC Annual* (1925), 94-95, 174-75. Dissatisfied with this action and the investigating committee's final report (*NBC Annual* [1926], 554-55), the fundamentalist faction issued a statement signed by W. B. Riley, Chester Tulga, and R. T. Ketcham entitled *Foreign Mission Board Fails in Discharge of Duty* (pamphlet, 1926). It accused the ABFMS investigating committee of covering up the problem missionaries, and calling for replacing the board's leaders with "men who hold . . . biblical and historical Baptist positions" on such issues as a personal God, the integrity of the Scriptures, and the Virgin Birth, deity, blood atonement, high priesthood, and second coming of Christ. ABFMS file, ABAC.

appoint non-evangelicals." Speaking for the foreign mission board, which adopted this as its formal policy statement, Anderson defined what was understood by "gospel":

> We mean the good news of the free forgiveness of sin, and eternal life (beginning now and going on forever) through a vital union with the crucified and risen Christ, which brings men into union and fellowship with God. This salvation is graciously offered on the sole condition of repentance and faith in Christ, and has in it the divine power of regeneration and sanctification through the Spirit. The only reason we have for accepting this gospel is our belief in the deity of Christ in whom we see the Father, a faith founded on the trustworthiness of the Scriptures, and the fact that we have experienced this salvation in our own hearts.[40]

This "Evangelical Policy" was reaffirmed by the board of managers in 1933 and again during the Conservative Baptist crisis in September 1943.[41] But in spite of these efforts, independent mission societies, such as Baptist Mid-Missions (1920), Association of Baptists for World Evangelism (1927), Evangelical Baptist Missions (1928), and Conservative Baptist Foreign Mission Society (1943), continued to form and siphon off money and workers from the Northern Baptist churches. Some of them became larger than the ABFMS, which was later renamed the Board of International Ministries of the American Baptist Churches U.S.A., and now is simply known as "International Ministries." The ABFMS missionary staff experienced a forty-three percent decline between 1923 and 1939, and the agency currently has less than a quarter of the workers it had in the early 1920s.

The statements of the Northern Baptist missionary leadership were

40. Frederick L. Anderson, *Rich Harvests and Ominous Clouds* (pamphlet, 1924), 12, 14; *NBC Annual* (1925), 456; *The Truth about Our Foreign Mission Society: Report of a Special Committee Appointed to Interview the Secretaries of Our Foreign Mission Society Relative to the Present Situation* (pamphlet, 1927), ABFMS file, ABAC.

41. *The Evangelical Policy of the Foreign Mission Board* (leaflet, n.d.). On June 6, 1933, the board agreed to publish a pamphlet reaffirming the "inclusive policy," since some people misunderstood the 1924 statement to mean "folks of every shade of theological belief, however divergent from the historic New Testament Baptist faith." They failed to notice the words that qualified the expression, *"within the limits of the gospel."* ABFMS file, ABAC. This was reaffirmed, although the Conservative Baptist group regarded it as too weak. Response of the Board of Managers of ABFMS to a Proposal of the Baptist Fundamentalist Fellowship, September 21, 1943, Mission Pamphlet Series, Box 4, Folder 26, YDS. Another copy is in the ABFMS file at the ABAC, and it was also published as a leaflet entitled *Steadfastly We Affirm.*

clearly expressions of evangelical faith. Many examples could be cited in this regard, including Jesse R. Wilson, missionary to Japan and then general secretary of the SVM and secretary of the ABFMS, and Margaret Treat Doane, who in 1922 founded the Houses of Fellowship in Ventnor, New Jersey, where missionaries on furlough could stay (the forerunner of the Overseas Ministries Study Center). However, two significant figures will be chosen to illustrate the extent of evangelical beliefs among Northern Baptist missionary leaders: Helen Barrett Montgomery (1861-1934) and Kenneth Scott Latourette (1884-1968).

A Wellesley-educated daughter of a Baptist minister, Helen Barrett married William Montgomery, a successful businessman who was totally supportive of her endeavors. For fifty years she taught a large women's Sunday School class at her church in Rochester, New York. Licensed to preach as well, on occasions she conducted services in the absence of the pastor. She also authored six books for the Central Committee on the United Study of Foreign Missions, including the best-selling *Western Women in Eastern Lands* (New York: Macmillan, 1910). Long active in women's missionary groups, she helped form the united Woman's American Baptist Foreign Mission Society in 1914 and served as its president for the next ten years. In 1921-22 she was president of the Northern Baptist Convention, and in 1923 a speaker at the Baptist World Alliance meeting in Stockholm. In her spare time she translated the Greek New Testament into English, which was published in 1924.[42]

One can gain an indication of the shape of Montgomery's faith by looking at the "Declaration of Discipleship" printed in her New Testament translation:

> I desire to enroll myself as a disciple of Jesus Christ. I trust in His promise that He will reject none who come to Him. I confess my sins, and rely on His promise of forgiveness for all who repent and confess. I renounce self and will seek to follow Jesus. I claim the promised guidance of the Holy Spirit into all truth. I promise to make love the law of my life, and

42. Louise A. Cattan, *Lamps Are for Lighting: The Story of Helen Barrett Montgomery and Lucy Waterbury Peabody* (Grand Rapids: Eerdmans, 1972). It should be mentioned that Peabody, herself a former missionary and a staunch supporter of women's missionary work, was a prime backer of the separatist ABWE. See also R. Pierce Beaver, *American Protestant Women in World Mission* (Grand Rapids: Eerdmans, 1968). Torbet maintains that "the stability of the [Woman's] Society in these years was in no small measure due to the able leadership provided by Mrs. Montgomery, a woman of unusual stature in scholarship and Christian statesmanship." *Venture of Faith*, 440.

to make use of my Master's oft-repeated invitation to prayer and communion.[43]

In her study guide on prayer she maintained that the Bible contains the deepest expression of what one's prayer life should be. Its supremacy was due to its inspiration: the record was "God-breathed" and profitable for all humankind. "It is important that men should know the gospel; it is more important that they should pray the gospel. If they pray, the gospel proceeds; if they do not pray, the gospel halts." The Bible, she said, was "no loosely strung collection of truths; no unrelated mass of stories; from first to last there runs a thread of unity, because it all has been 'God-breathed' by the same inspiring Spirit."[44]

While holding a deeply personal faith, Helen Montgomery was not oblivious to the social dimension of Christianity. For example, she called attention to the fact that the mission enterprise "reduces swollen racial animosities and contempts" when people from all parts of the world sit down in one fellowship and work as one brotherhood. "Race prejudice withers and dies in the face of a religion that can draw together into one men of the most widely separated races."[45]

Kenneth Scott Latourette was professor of missions and oriental history at Yale from 1921 to his retirement in 1953, and author of numerous books on missions and the expansion of Christianity. He was deeply influenced by the Student Volunteer Movement and served as a missionary in China for two years until bad health forced him to come home. He was an ordained Northern Baptist minister, member of the board of managers of the ABFMS for three decades, Northern Baptist Convention president in 1951-52, and involved in many ecumenical bodies including the International Missionary Council, the SVM executive committee, and the Federal and World Councils of Churches. He said that at one time he was serving on thirty-three boards and committees in New Haven and New York.[46] His commitment to ecumenism was so fervent that he told this writer in a personal conversation in 1966 that he was an "ecumaniac."

43. Helen Barrett Montgomery, *From Campus to World Citizenship* (New York: Revell, 1940), 7.

44. Helen B. Montgomery, *Prayer and Missions* (New York: Central Committee on the United Study of Foreign Missions, 1924), 10-11, 45.

45. Helen B. Montgomery, *The Preaching Value of Missions* (Philadelphia: Judson Press, 1931), 9.

46. Wilbur C. Harr, ed., *Frontiers of the Christian World Mission since 1938: Essays in Honor of Kenneth Scott Latourette* (New York: Harper, 1962), 292.

His entire approach to the study and writing of Christian (as opposed to merely Church) history was ecumenical and global in nature. He saw Christianity as a force which permeated society and changed human beings not only spiritually, but culturally and physically as well. A particular interest of his was international affairs and peace; Sen. Joseph McCarthy singled out his book *The American Record in the Far East, 1945-1951* (New York: Macmillan, 1952) for special attack, even attempting to have it banned from U.S. libraries in Europe.[47]

In his memoirs Latourette testified that he "rejoiced in the Gospel — the amazing Good News — that the Creator . . . so loved the world that He gave His only Son, that whosoever believes in Him should not perish, but have everlasting life." This life "is not just continued existence, but a growing knowledge — not merely intellectual but wondering through trust, love, and fellowship — of Him who alone is truly God, and Jesus Christ whom He has sent." We can know Christ as he was on earth, and "I was convinced that the historical evidence confirms the virgin birth and the bodily resurrection of Christ." We can affirm that "Christ is both fully man and fully God," and we can rejoice in "what the Triune God has done and is doing through Him." This Good News, stated so consistently in the New Testament, is what we "are privileged — and commanded — to make known and to demonstrate to all mankind."[48]

Regarding the Northern Baptist mission board struggles, he commented that at the annual meetings he, along with the majority of the delegates, joined neither the fundamentalist nor the liberal group. "With others in that majority I was sick at heart over the distrust and seeming denial of Christian love." Eventually the fundamentalists withdrew and formed their own "Conservative" organizations, resulting in more peaceful annual conventions. Still, the majority who remained in the Northern Baptist Convention were theologically conservative, but they were willing to work with less-conservative Baptists on the principle that each Christian should interpret the Bible as "he believed the Holy Spirit directed."[49] Actually, the documents of the controversy in 1943-44 concerning the creation of the Conservative Baptist Foreign Mission Society (which Latourette preserved along with three thick folders of materials in the ABFMS files in Valley Forge) make it patently clear that the Northern Baptist

---

47. Kenneth Scott Latourette, *Beyond the Ranges* (Grand Rapids: Eerdmans, 1967), 129-30.

48. Ibid., 73-74.

49. Ibid., 122-23.

missionary leaders had not abandoned the "evangelical principle" they articulated in the 1920s.[50]

Conclusion

Although this essay has focused on only two denominations, the names of many other persons could be added to the list of "evangelical" missionary leaders in other "mainline" communions — persons who bridged the supposed gap between the liberal and conservative camps of twentieth-century Protestantism. Among those who should surely be included on such a list would be Robert P. Wilder (1863-1938), who spent much of his life working with the Student Volunteer Movement; the renowned Methodist missionary to India E. Stanley Jones (1884-1973); and John R. Mott (1865-1955), who was a lifelong Methodist and an incomparable mobilizer of both students and adults for missions and Christian cooperation. R. H. Edwin Espy, one of the general secretaries of the SVM, would later say that Mott was an "Ecumenical Evangelical" and "Evangelical Ecumenist."[51]

In short, this essay has just begun to scratch the surface of identifying missionary leaders in mainline denominations who combined theological conservatism with social progressivism, and evangelistic fervor with ecumenical zeal. Not only is the presence of these leaders at odds with fundamentalist critiques (past and present) of mainline missions, but it also runs counter to the two-party paradigm, which has characterized mainline denominations as almost wholly liberal, particularly at the leadership level. Such was simply not the case. The truth is that one really cannot square the pervasive evangelical cast of mainline foreign missions efforts in the first half of the twentieth century with the two-party thesis.

It could be that denominational mission endeavors are not good places to look for two parties. The intense desire of leaders in the missionary movement to preach the gospel and to bring Christians together to spread the message of Christ might represent an extraordinary effort to hold the center together. On the other hand, the mission leaders discussed

50. These materials include correspondence, minutes of meetings, statements by principals in the dispute, and articles from the conservative church paper, the *Watch-man-Examiner*. Box 4, Folder 26, Mission Pamphlet Series, YDS, and Conservative Baptist Foreign Mission Society 1943-50, ABFMS file, ABAC. Unfortunately, space limitations preclude an analysis of this important development.

51. *New World Outlook* 41 (September 1980): 42.

here may simply have embodied the best of American Protestantism. Perhaps mission work among real flesh and blood people does not allow much time and energy for petty differences and internal squabbling. More positively, perhaps mission work naturally fosters an attitude that affirms both concern for the soul and concern for physical and social needs.

CHAPTER 9

Wesleyan/Holiness Churches: Innocent Bystanders in the Fundamentalist/Modernist Controversy

SUSIE C. STANLEY

A writer in the Wesleyan/Holiness movement observed the controversy between fundamentalists and modernists in 1924 from a perspective that rejected both sides:

> The secular newspaper and religious press teems with the great battle now on between the so-called "modernists" and the so-called "fundamentalists." The strange thing about it is that so much error, as a rule, enters on both sides that it is hard to determine which is going the right direction.[1]

Jean Miller Schmidt classified holiness churches, along with Lutherans, the Evangelical and Reformed Church, Disciples of Christ, and several denominations in the South, as "innocent bystanders" in the controversy between fundamentalists and modernists. The above statement illustrates her contention that holiness churches were among "American Protestants who did not participate in this polemic."[2] Unlike many of the scholars

---

1. W. B. McCreary, "How Long Go Ye Limping?" *Gospel Trumpet* 38 (April 3, 1924): 6.

2. Jean Miller Schmidt, *Souls or the Social Order: The Two-Party System in American Protestantism* (Brooklyn: Carlson Publishing, 1991), 173. Schmidt identified Congregationalists, Presbyterians, Episcopalians, Methodists, and Baptists as participants in the polemic (173). Many scholars credit Martin E. Marty with establishing the two-party approach to understanding Protestant history in the twentieth century. But Marty

who later appropriated her explanation of the split within oldline Protestantism earlier in this century, Schmidt recognized that a significant segment of Protestantism did not take sides in the controversy.[3]

This essay confirms Schmidt's thesis. As will be seen here, the Wesleyan/Holiness churches were, in a very real sense, "innocent bystanders" in the Modernist-Fundamentalist controversy. They were not bystanders because they were passive, but because they had a strongly formed sense of identity that did not fit in either the modernist or fundamentalist camps.

Nevertheless, many scholars continue to categorize the Wesleyan/Holiness churches of the late nineteenth and early twentieth centuries as part of a larger fundamentalist movement. Because this is the case, the bulk of this essay will be devoted to contesting this interpretation. I need first to say something about the word "fundamentalist" and its multiple meanings. Then I will examine the positions of the Wesleyan/Holiness churches regarding a number of "fundamentalist" doctrines in order to demonstrate conclusively that the label does not fit these churches.

What precisely makes an individual or group fundamentalist? Jean Miller Schmidt focused on attitudes toward social reform, Ernest Sandeen emphasized inerrancy and dispensationalism, and Ferenc Szasz identified fundamentalists as those who rejected evolution, the study of comparative religions, and higher criticism. Finally, George Marsden has characterized

---

himself acknowledged his debt to Jean Miller [Schmidt] in the chapter notes of *Righteous Empire* when he admitted that her doctoral dissertation "provides both the quotations and the plot" for chapter 17 entitled "The Two-Party System." Martin E. Marty, *Righteous Empire: The Protestant Experience in America* (New York: Dial Press, 1970), 270. Marty reaffirms this relationship in this volume (see pp. 101-3). For her part, Schmidt has always legitimately claimed common ownership of the idea. Schmidt, *Souls or the Social Order*, xxvi.

3. Schmidt allowed for fundamentalist influence among innocent bystanders when she stated that groups might find themselves on "one side or the other in the long run." There is no doubt that fundamentalist leavening has occurred in Wesleyan/Holiness churches. Schmidt offered one example. In the early 1920s, members of the Laymen's Holiness Association abandoned the Methodist Episcopal Church and merged with the Church of the Nazarene. Former members of the Laymen's Holiness Association pushed the Nazarenes in the direction of fundamentalism (Schmidt, *Souls or the Social Order*, 191). However, at the denominational level, they were unable to secure the support necessary to change the *Manual* to reflect the fundamentalist beliefs in inerrancy and premillennialism. These issues will be discussed in more detail below.

an attitude or mind-set as the key when he defined fundamentalism as "militant opposition to modernism."[4]

Employing Marsden's definition, most members of the Wesleyan/Holiness movement would not qualify as fundamentalists because they did not assume a militant posture with respect to the issues raised by modernism. For instance, opposition to evolution was widespread, and yet Wesleyan/Holiness leaders did not play a major role in the anti-evolution campaign of the 1920s.[5] Alma White, founder of the Pillar of Fire, is a notable exception, in that she vigorously attacked modernism. Nevertheless, for other reasons explored below, fundamentalists scarcely would have embraced White as one of their own.

Assessing the Wesleyan/Holiness movement and its relationship to fundamentalism is a difficult task because neither was monolithic. The characteristic, however, which unites the Wesleyan/Holiness movement is its commitment to the doctrine of holiness or sanctification which it appropriated from Methodism. This alone was enough to separate the movement from fundamentalism, according to C. E. Brown, editor of the *Gospel Trumpet,* a Church of God (Anderson, IN) periodical:

4. Ernest R. Sandeen, *The Origins of Fundamentalism* (Philadelphia: Fortress Press, 1968); Ferenc Morton Szasz, *The Divided Mind of Protestant America, 1880-1930* (University, AL: University of Alabama Press, 1982); and George M. Marsden, *Fundamentalism and American Culture: The Shaping of Twentieth-Century Evangelicalism, 1870-1925* (Oxford: Oxford University Press, 1980), 4. In another context, Marsden described fundamentalism as a revivalist movement proclaiming inerrancy. He elaborated: "These attitudes are not ones that would be confined to just one, or even to just a few, of the submovements of American evangelicalism during the past century. Rather, such stances can be found, to greater or lesser extents, in all sorts of revivalist evangelical groups — even among many who would not call themselves fundamentalist. Many holiness and pentecostal groups, for instance, and revivalists white and black share many of these traits and hence reasonably might be called fundamentalist in a broad sense. Certainly they would properly have been called fundamentalists during the early formative stage of fundamentalism, during the 1920s, before fundamentalism had as precise a meaning as it has today. So fundamentalism, which cuts across much of evangelicalism, is, like evangelicalism itself, a broad coalition." George M. Marsden, "Fundamentalism and American Evangelicalism," in *The Variety of American Evangelicalism,* ed. Donald W. Dayton and Robert K. Johnston (Downers Grove, IL: InterVarsity Press, 1991), 25. I am more inclined to agree with Marsden's earlier assessment that fundamentalism "was quite rare on the Methodist side of American revivalism." Marsden, *Fundamentalism and American Culture,* 225. The Wesleyan/Holiness movement is a direct outgrowth of Methodism.

5. Ronald Numbers has documented Wesleyan/Holiness views on evolution and creationism. Ronald L. Numbers, "Creation, Evolution, and Holy Ghost Religion: Holiness and Pentecostal Responses to Darwinism," *Religion and American Culture* 2 (Summer 1992): 127-58.

The general holiness movement and each of the smaller holiness sects, as well as the reformation movement, [the Church of God] itself, were all conservatively orthodox, following the traditional lines in biblical criticism and theology. Nevertheless they did not often use the term "fundamentalist," whereas the evangelistic movement led by such magazines as *Moody's Monthly*, the *Sunday-School Times,* and other like papers often use the term "fundamentalist." They, however, emphasize premillennialism and generally teach against the Wesleyan doctrine of sanctification as a second work of grace. Most of the small holiness sects are premillennialistic, but they are split off from the *Sunday-School Times* and Moody institutions by their doctrine of sanctification as a second work of grace, whereas the reformation of which we write agreed with the holiness people on sanctification but rejected the doctrine of premillennialism.[6]

To Brown, the primary distinction between the Wesleyan/Holiness movement and fundamentalism was the former's belief in holiness. Even though smaller groups were premillennial, their commitment to the doctrine of holiness separated them from fundamentalists.

The reality is that only a few members of the Wesleyan/Holiness movement appropriated the fundamentalist label. In the few instances when Wesleyan/Holiness individuals referred to themselves as fundamentalist, they provided their distinctive definitions, in the process disassociating themselves from what they understood to be the general understanding of what it meant to be fundamentalist. For example, C. E. Brown, quoted above, sought to claim the label of "fundamentalist" for himself, but he defined fundamentalism as "an extension into our time of the essential foundation elements of historic Christianity, as these were reformulated and re-interpreted by the Protestant reformers of the sixteenth century." More than this, Brown rejected the notion that premillennialism was one of the "foundation doctrines."[7] Then there is Alma White, who

---

6. Charles Ewing Brown, *When the Trumpet Sounded: A History of the Church of God Reformation* (Anderson, IN: Warner Press, 1951), 355. Future references to the Church of God refer to the group with headquarters in Anderson, Indiana.

Brown did not acknowledge the Keswick movement which promoted a Calvinist version of holiness associated with the Keswick camp meetings in England. This view differed from the Wesleyan understanding of holiness because it rejected the doctrine of eradication, the removal of the sinful nature. Rather than stressing purity and power, Keswick holiness emphasized power for service. For a discussion of the Keswick movement, see Marsden, *Fundamentalism and American Culture,* 72-85.

7. C. E. Brown, "What Is Fundamentalism?" *Gospel Trumpet* 59 (February 25, 1939): 2. In my search through approximately thirty years of *Gospel Trumpet* magazines,

used the term infrequently, and who qualified it when she did. For example, on one occasion she stated: "We stand for fundamentalism," by which she meant that "We stand for vital Christianity that means holiness in living." She elaborated on her point by affirming her group's identification with "the old-fashioned kind of Methodism."[8]

All of this suggests that the Wesleyan/Holiness movement does not truly fit within the fundamentalist camp. Given that it is often assumed that this movement *does* fit within this camp, this finding substantively challenges the validity of the two-party paradigm. This essay will drive this argument home by contrasting the Wesleyan/Holiness movement with fundamentalism in four areas.[9] Rather than utilizing one characteris-

---

only two other authors adopted the fundamentalist label: R. L. B., "College Row Over Liberalism," *Gospel Trumpet* 43 (January 11, 1923): 2; and Esther K. Elsaser, "My Experience with Modern Liberalism," *Gospel Trumpet* 44 (April 3, 1924): 2.

8. Quoted in Esther Coster, "Only Woman Bishop Founded Pillar of Fire Church," *Brooklyn Daily Eagle* (December 30, 1939), in *Alma White's Evangelism: Press Reports*, 2 vols., ed. C. R. Paige and C. K. Ingler (Zarephath, NJ: Pillar of Fire, 1939-40), 2:269, 270. White's reference to Methodism hinted indirectly that Wesleyan/Holiness believers affirmed free will or Arminianism in contrast to the Calvinism of most fundamentalists. Marsden, *Fundamentalism and American Culture*, 101; and Sandeen, *Origins of Fundamentalism*, 10.

In 1928 and 1932, the General Assembly of the Church of the Nazarene clarified their position on free will to differentiate their denomination from fundamentalism. Timothy L. Smith, *Called unto Holiness: The Story of the Nazarenes: The Formative Years* (Kansas City, MO: Nazarene Publishing House, 1962), 320-21.

9. Others have challenged the paradigm with respect to the Wesleyan/Holiness movement. Donald Dayton has been the most persistent in disputing efforts to explain the Wesleyan/Holiness movement by utilizing the two-party paradigm. He has described the holiness movement as "a church tradition with a distinctive Wesleyan character and shape that was in some ways conservative, though in other ways radical, and therefore is not to be confused with reactionary fundamentalism or Calvinistically inspired orthodoxy." Donald Dayton, "Whither Evangelicalism?" in *Sanctification and Liberation*, ed. Theodore Runyon (Nashville: Abingdon, 1981), 152. In a subsequent article, Dayton offered five arguments for disassociating Wesleyanism from fundamentalism. Donald W. Dayton, "The Use of Scripture in the Wesleyan Tradition," in *The Use of the Bible in Theology/Evangelical Options*, ed. Robert K. Johnston (Atlanta: John Knox Press, 1985), 130-34. Dayton spoke for his academic colleagues in the Wesleyan/Holiness movement: "The growing consensus of the Wesleyan Theological Society is that the tradition is not well stated in the logic and ethos of the fundamentalist tradition." Dayton, "Use of Scripture," 130.

Frank Spina is representative of others who have argued that the two-party paradigm is an inappropriate interpretive framework for the Wesleyan/Holiness movement. Spina called it a "faulty paradigm" and argued "whether Wesleyanism should even be viewed under the rubric 'conservative.'" Frank Anthony Spina, "Biblical Scholarship in a Wesleyan Mode: Retrospect and Prospect," unpublished paper (July 26, 1990), 11.

tic of fundamentalism, I am adopting a multi-faceted approach to document the Wesleyan/Holiness movement's status as an innocent bystander. A discussion of biblical authority and end times illustrates the Wesleyan/Holiness movement's attitude toward biblical inerrancy and dispensationalism, two beliefs associated with fundamentalism. Opposition to the ordination of women and social Christianity reflected the implications of these fundamentalist beliefs. I will contrast these views with the Wesleyan/Holiness affirmation of ordained women and its commitment to social holiness, its distinct contribution to social Christianity. My focus will be on the Church of the Nazarene, the Church of God, and The Salvation Army (the three largest groups in the Wesleyan/Holiness movement); I will also include the Pillar of Fire, which, despite its militancy, differed significantly from fundamentalism.[10]

Biblical Authority

Sydney Ahlstrom contended that holiness sectarians "came to share the Fundamentalist's concern for biblical inerrancy."[11] An examination of statements relating to biblical authority by the churches under consideration calls for a different conclusion. They did not profess biblical inerrancy. The Pillar of Fire Church affirmed: "We believe that the Scriptures are given by inspiration of God, and that they are 'the only sufficient rule of faith and

10. Statistics for these groups are as follows:
- Church of the Nazarene — 573,834 inclusive membership (1991) and 572,152 full, communicant, or confirmed members (1991).
- Church of God — 214,743 inclusive membership (1992) and 214,743 full, communicant, or confirmed members (1992).
- The Salvation Army — 446,403 inclusive membership (1991) and 133,214 full, communicant, or confirmed members (1991). Kenneth B. Bedell, ed., *Yearbook of American and Canadian Churches* (Nashville: Abingdon Press, 1994), 254, 255, 257.
- The Pillar of Fire has not contributed statistics to the yearbook since 1949. At that time, they reported 5,100 members. Kenneth B. Bedell and Alice M. Jones, eds., *Yearbook of American and Canadian Churches 1992* (Nashville: Abingdon Press, 1992), 275. Currently, the Pillar of Fire is much smaller.

11. Sydney E. Ahlstrom, *A Religious History of the American People* (New Haven: Yale University Press, 1972), 806. James Davison Hunter is representative of those who perpetuate this viewpoint. Hunter defined "evangelicalism" broadly, including Wesleyan/Holiness churches, and then equated evangelicalism with fundamentalism, further claiming that all evangelicals are inerrantists. James Davison Hunter, *Evangelicalism: The Coming Generation* (Chicago: University of Chicago Press, 1987), 3-4, 20, 47.

practise.' The tendency is to eliminate the supernatural from the Bible. It is our business to preach the Word and not to criticize it."[12] While Alma White disparaged higher criticism in her statement on Scripture, neither she nor members of her church used the term "inerrancy" to describe their view of biblical authority. "The Doctrines of the Salvation Army" includes the following statement on the Bible: "We believe that the Scriptures of the Old and New Testaments were given by inspiration of God, and that they only constitute the Divine rule of Christian faith and practice."[13] The Church of God is non-creedal, so there is no concise understanding of Scripture which all members must accept. In 1979, the faculty of Anderson College School of Theology issued a statement of conviction which included the following affirmation relating to the Bible: "We join with the Church of God movement in the firm conviction that the Bible is the inspired Word of God (2 Tim. 3:16). Indeed, 'The Bible is our rule of faith and Christ alone is Lord; All we are equal in his sight when we obey his word.' "[14]

It must be noted that the word "inerrancy" was added to the *Manual* of the Church of the Nazarene in 1982. To quote from the *Manual:*

> We believe in the plenary inspiration of the Holy Scriptures, by which we understand the sixty-six books of the Old and New Testaments, given by divine inspiration, inerrantly revealing the will of God concerning us in all things necessary to our salvation, so that whatever is not contained therein is not to be enjoined as an article of faith.[15]

What is crucial here, however, is that inerrancy is clearly and specifically limited to "all things necessary to our salvation." Such a limited under-

---

12. Alma White, *New Testament Church* (Zarephath, NJ: Pillar of Fire, 1929), 39.

13. Milton S. Agnew, *Manual of Salvationism* (Verona, NJ: The Commissioners' Conference, 1985), vii.

14. *We Believe: A Statement of Conviction on the Occasion of the Centennial of the Church of God Reformation Movement* (Anderson, IN: Anderson School of Theology, 1979), 4. The School of Theology is the Church of God's only seminary. The quotation within the statement is by Charles W. Naylor, "The Church's Jubilee," verse 2, in *Hymnal of the Church of God* (Anderson, IN: Warner Press, 1971), 453.

15. *Manual 1993-1997: Church of the Nazarene* (Kansas City, MO: Nazarene Publishing House, [1993]), 27. J. Kenneth Grider suggested that the addition of "inerrantly" in the article may have occurred because of those within the denomination who sought to shift the denominational statement toward fundamentalism. J. Kenneth Grider, "Wesleyanism and the Inerrancy Issue," *Wesleyan Theological Journal* 19 (Fall 1984): 58. See also Paul Merritt Bassett, "The Fundamentalist Leavening of the Holiness Movement, 1914-1940: The Church of the Nazarene: A Case Study," *Wesleyan Theological Journal* 13 (1978): 74.

standing is not at all in keeping with the fundamentalist understanding of inerrancy.

Paul Bassett has explored the concept of biblical authority in the Wesleyan/Holiness context. Bassett summarized John Wesley's view of Scripture, stressing that the Bible's sufficiency was the crucial factor in Wesley's understanding of biblical authority. Bassett also outlined the view of Nazarene H. Orton Wiley, and then concluded that "the inner logic guiding the use of the Bible in the holiness movement has centered upon the Scripture's 'sufficiency for salvation.'"[16] In another context, Bassett documented the understanding of biblical authority within the Church of the Nazarene from 1914 to 1940.[17] Wiley offered a "genuinely Wesleyan third alternative" to the views of modernism and fundamentalism by stressing the internal witness of the Spirit as a source of biblical authority.[18] Several other Nazarene authors adopted a more fundamentalist position; while this became popular within the denomination during the 1930s and 1940s, fundamentalism was unable to "capture the church with its biblicism."[19]

While Bassett has concentrated on Nazarene perspectives relating to the authority of Scripture, Steve Stall summarized the views of eight leaders within the Church of God. He concluded that C. E. Brown was the only inerrantist among them.[20] Brown claimed: "The gift of inspiration conferred inerrancy and preserved from mistake."[21] John W. V. Smith, a Church of God historian, questioned Brown's self-assessment, claiming that, in conversations, Brown allowed for errors in the Bible.[22] Other Church of God leaders stressed that the authors rather than the words of the Bible were inspired. They also shared the conviction that the Bible was without error in matters of faith and practice. A. F. Gray affirmed: "No

16. Paul Merritt Bassett, "The Theological Identity of the North American Holiness Movement: Its Understanding of the Nature and Role of the Bible," in *Variety of American Evangelicalism*, 95.

17. Bassett, "Fundamentalist Leavening," 65-91.

18. Ibid., 67, 69, 82.

19. Ibid., 81, 79. J. B. Chapman and A. M. Hills were among those who adopted a fundamentalist position on biblical authority.

20. Steven Wayne Stall, "The Inspiration and Authority of Scripture: The Views of Eight Historical and Twenty-One Current Doctrinal Teachers in the Church of God (Anderson, Indiana)" (M.A. Thesis, Anderson College School of Theology, 1980), 24-27.

21. C. E. Brown, "Inspiration of the Scriptures," *Gospel Trumpet* 38 (June 13, 1918): 9. See also C. E. Brown, "What Is Fundamentalism?," 2.

22. John W. V. Smith, "The Bible in the Church of God Reformation Movement: A Historical Perspective," *Centering on Ministry* 6 (Spring 1981): 5.

mistakes are found in the Bible that are harmful to man's spiritual life."[23] Smith concluded his summary of Church of God views on biblical authority:

> It thus becomes apparent that none of the early leaders in the Church of God ever questioned either the divine inspiration of Scriptures or the absolute authority of the Bible as the only necessary "rule of faith." Despite the fact that many of them were writing in early decades of the twentieth century when the "fundamentalist" controversy over biblical inerrancy was splitting many churches apart, there is practically no evidence that any of them, with the possible exception of C. E. Brown, felt that their high view of the Bible needed to be supported by legalist definitions applied to the text such as "inerrancy" and "verbal inspiration." They simply saw no need to enter into that debate.[24]

Several Church of God writers in *Gospel Trumpet* challenged biblical literalism. W. B. McCreary listed inerrancy as one of the "cardinal truths of Christianity," yet he criticized fundamentalists for their "extremely literal interpretation" of the Bible:

> A great many prophecies, particularly from the symbolic Book of Revelation are erroneously strained to get a literal meaning out of them. Especially is this true of Revelation 20; it takes the strongest flight of imagination to interpret this chapter to mean that the saints will reign on earth one thousand years while Satan is bound. A sane, well-balanced interpretation of Scripture will do more to clear the present situation than all the wild-fire fanciful interpretations of extreme literalists.[25]

Owen F. Raney made much the same point. In an article condemning premillennialism he noted that: "Premillennialism says: The scriptures must be taken literally, and in no wise must they be spiritualized." Raney then went on to quote Romans 8:6 and 1 Corinthians 2:14, verses which admonish Christians to be spiritually minded, to refute premillennial literalism.[26] Likewise, in another article attacking pre-

---

23. A. F. Gray, *How to Study the Bible* (Anderson, IN: Gospel Trumpet Co., 1944), 80, quoted in John W. V. Smith, "Bible in the Church of God," 5.

24. John W. V. Smith, "Bible in the Church of God," 6.

25. W. B. McCreary, "How Long Go Ye Limping?", 6.

26. Owen F. Raney, "Premillennialism Affirms; the Bible Denies, Part I," *Gospel Trumpet* 64 (October 14, 1944): 7.

millennialism, Paul A. Tanner insisted: "Isaiah 11:6-7 is not to be interpreted literally."[27]

While inerrancy characterized the fundamentalist view of scriptural authority, higher criticism exemplified the modernist approach to the Bible. Paul Bassett and John W. V. Smith have argued that the Wesleyan/Holiness movement was not threatened by the issues which higher criticism raised. This was due, in part, to the belief that the internal witness of the Holy Spirit served as a source of Biblical authority. "The authority of Scripture depended to some degree upon its own self authentication, but more importantly, experience of the authenticating voice of the Living Word clinched the matter."[28]

The understanding of religion as being essentially experiential added to the lack of concern over the possibility that biblical criticism challenged scriptural authority. Experience validated Scripture.[29] As George Marsden has observed, the Methodist tradition stressed "personal experience verified by the witness of words and works. Such testimony did not have the conflict with defense of the authority of the Bible grounded in reason and science."[30]

While higher criticism did not threaten their view of Scripture, few Wesleyan/Holiness believers initially embraced it. The general superintendents of the Church of the Nazarene claimed in 1923 that there were no higher critics in their midst.[31] Most authors in the issues of *Gospel Trumpet* which I have surveyed had nothing positive to say about higher criticism. Generally, the adjective "destructive" preceded the term.[32] One writer recommended a pamphlet entitled "Is the Higher Criticism Scholarly?" in which the author answered "no" to the question posed in the title.[33] Only A. F. Gray defended higher criticism:

> The science [of higher criticism] is a legitimate one and has contributed something to our store of religious knowledge. The odium attached to

27. Paul A. Tanner, "Thy Kingdom Come *Now*," *Gospel Trumpet* 77 (October 12, 1957): 1.

28. Bassett, "Fundamentalist Leavening," 69.

29. John W. V. Smith, "Bible in the Church of God," 5.

30. Marsden, *Fundamentalism and American Culture*, 73.

31. General Superintendents' Address, Church of the Nazarene, Sixth General Assembly, *Journal . . . 1923*, 1923; quoted in Timothy L. Smith, *Called unto Holiness*, 319.

32. Earl L. Martin, "Some Conditions that Operate against Christianity," *Gospel Trumpet* 45 (October 22, 1925): 4; and E. F. Adcock, "On Dura's Plain," *Gospel Trumpet* 44 (March 6, 1924): 4.

33. "The Dispute Over Evolution," *Gospel Trumpet* 45 (July 23, 1925): ii.

the name is due to the fact that most of the critics are destructive, seeking to overthrow rather than establish the authority of the Bible.[34]

Even in his limited defense of higher criticism, Gray introduced the adjective that seemed permanently attached to higher criticism. It was not until the early 1940s that Church of God scholars such as Adam Miller and Otto Linn earned graduate degrees in Bible and began examining higher criticism as a legitimate approach to the study of Scripture rather than as a synonym for the evils of modernism. With higher education came an appropriation of the tools of higher criticism in the study of the Bible.

While belief in scriptural inerrancy is consistently mentioned as one of the characteristics of fundamentalism, it is not descriptive of the view of scriptural authority for the groups under consideration. It only appears in the statement of the Church of the Nazarene which limits inerrancy to "all things necessary to our salvation." The word is missing from other doctrinal statements relating to biblical authority. Although C. E. Brown used the term publicly in the Church of God, his overall understanding of Scripture cannot be described as inerrantist. Experience validated the truths of the Bible whose authority rested on the witness of the Holy Spirit.

End Times

In some cases, dispensational premillennialism has been declared the defining characteristic of fundamentalism.[35] C. E. Brown wrote that fundamentalism was often associated with premillennialism and that fundamentalists themselves had perpetuated this correlation.[36] As indicated above, Brown claimed he was a fundamentalist without being premillennial. He further maintained that premillennialism was "not a part of the original historical foundation doctrines of orthodox Protestantism."[37] While some fundamentalists sought to create a two-party system by using premillennialism as the determinant, one *Gospel Trumpet* author chal-

---

34. A. F. Gray, "The Divine Endorsement of the Old Testament?" *Gospel Trumpet* 44 (March 13, 1924): 3. Later in the article, Gray appeared to dismiss higher criticism by defending Moses' authorship of the Pentateuch, the traditional dating of Daniel, and the miracles in the Old Testament.

35. This was Sandeen's thesis in *Roots of Fundamentalism*.

36. Brown, "Why I Am a Fundamentalist," *Gospel Trumpet* 65 (April 7, 1945): 1.

37. Brown, "What Is Fundamentalism?", 2.

lenged this enterprise: "Some premillennialists have stated in their writings that every conservative church group believes in the premillennial reign of Christ, while every liberal group believes in the postmillennial. . . . There are, however, Christians who do not believe in any millennial reign whatsoever."[38]

The Church of God was among those groups who were amillennial. As illustrated above, Church of God authors consistently challenged the claim that premillennialism could be based on the Bible. One writer referred to premillennialism as fundamentalism's "unscriptural and unnecessary luggage."[39] Anti-premillennial articles were a standard feature of the *Gospel Trumpet*. Of the four issues considered in this paper, it was, by far, the one which received the most attention. For instance, Albert K. Kempin authored a series of thirteen articles in 1943 with the title "Why the Millennial Doctrine Is Not Biblical." The Church of God maintained that God's kingdom, initiated on the day of Pentecost, is spiritual rather than literal.[40] Dale Lehman affirmed: "We believe that the reign of Christ is present now in the hearts of men."[41] Numerous articles affirmed this understanding of the kingdom.

The Salvation Army initially was postmillennial, following the pattern of most Protestant groups until the turn of the twentieth century. William Booth, the co-founder, believed the Salvation Army's job was to convert the world to Christ in order to hasten Christ's coming.[42] The current Salvation Army doctrinal statement on end times, however, exemplifies an amillennial position: "We believe in the immortality of the soul; in the resurrection of the body; in the general judgment at the end of the world; in the eternal happiness of the righteous; and in the endless punishment of the wicked."[43]

Alma White began her preaching career as a Methodist, but she abandoned its postmillennialism before founding the Pillar of Fire. More than likely, she was influenced by her mentor William B. Godbey, who

38. Dale Lehman, "Jesus Is Coming Again," *Gospel Trumpet* 76 (July 14, 1956): 9.

39. R.L.B., "College Row Over Liberalism," *Gospel Trumpet* 43 (January 11, 1923): 2.

40. Tanner, "Thy Kingdom Come *Now*," 2.

41. Lehman, "Jesus Is Coming Again," 9. See also T. M. Mitchell, "The Millennium, Part II," *Gospel Trumpet* 65 (October 20, 1945): 7.

42. William Booth, "The Millennium: or The Ultimate Triumph of Salvation Army Principles," *All the World* 7 (August 1890): 337-43, quoted in Edward H. McKinley, *Marching to Glory: The History of the Salvation Army in the United States of America* (San Francisco: Harper & Row, Publishers, 1980), 33.

43. Agnew, *Manual of Salvationism*, vii.

was among holiness adherents within Methodism who embraced pre-millennialism.[44] The statement on end times in the list of "Doctrines of the Pillar of Fire Church" affirms: "We believe in the premillennial coming of the Lord and the Restoration of the Jews."[45] While declaring a preference for premillennialism, White differentiated her perspective from that of fundamentalists: "We are pre-millennialists and believe that Christ is coming soon. But we do not harp on Bible prophecy as do many of the modern fundamentalists."[46]

The Church of the Nazarene initially tended toward postmillennialism since many of its early leaders had been pastors in the Methodist Episcopal Church. In a discussion of eschatology in 1908, Nazarene leaders concluded: "We do not, however, regard the numerous theories that gather around this Bible Doctrine as essential to salvation, and we concede full liberty of belief among the members of the Pentecostal Church of the Nazarene."[47] Although premillennialism became increasingly popular, the Nazarene doctrinal statement on end times never reflected this position.[48]

Dispensational premillennialism is most often associated with fundamentalism. The Salvation Army and the Church of God avoided the argument between postmillennialism and premillennialism by subscribing to amillennialism. The Church of the Nazarene permitted different beliefs since one's convictions about end times were not considered a matter essential to salvation. The Pillar of Fire was the only group to officially embrace premillennialism, but its founder clarified her church's position from that of fundamentalism by stressing that her church was not preoccupied with prophecy.

---

44. Kenneth O. Brown documented the transition from postmillennialism to premillennialism among the leadership of the Christian Holiness Association, initially called the National Camp Meeting Association for the Promotion of Holiness. The leadership during the early decades of this group was predominantly Methodist. Kenneth Orville Brown, "Leadership in the National Holiness Association with Special Reference to Eschatology, 1867-1919" (Ph.D. diss., Drew University, 1988), 8, 296.

45. White, *New Testament Church*, 45.

46. Coster, "Only Woman Bishop," 2:270.

47. C. Powers Hardy, *Manual: Church of the Nazarene 1908-1958. Comparisons and Comments* (Kansas City, MO: Nazarene Publishing House, 1958), 61.

48. Smith, *Called unto Holiness*, 316-17. The current statement on the second coming of Christ reads as follows: "We believe that the Lord Jesus Christ will come again; that we who are alive at His coming shall not precede them that are asleep in Christ Jesus; but that, if we are abiding in Him, we shall be caught up with the risen saints to meet the Lord in the air, so that we shall ever be with the Lord" *Manual 1993-1997*, 33.

Roles of Women

All four of the churches under consideration granted full ministerial rights to women from their inception.[49] These groups officially noted their belief in the equality of women in the pulpit. For example, the 1870 minutes of the first annual conference of the forerunner of the Salvation Army in England recorded its commitment to placing women in every church office.[50] The 1898 Constitution of the Los Angeles Church of the Nazarene, the "mother church" of the Nazarene denomination, contained the following affirmation: "We recognize the equal right of both men and women to all offices of the Church of the Nazarene, including the ministry."[51]

On the other hand, Betty A. DeBerg examined twenty fundamentalist

49. Donald Dayton and Nancy Hardesty have played major roles in highlighting how the Wesleyan/Holiness movement has affirmed women clergy. See Donald W. Dayton, *Discovering an Evangelical Heritage* (New York: Harper and Row, 1976), 85-98; and Nancy Hardesty, Lucille Sider, and Donald W. Dayton, "Women in the Holiness Movement: Feminism in the Evangelical Tradition," in *Women of Spirit: Female Leadership in the Jewish and Christian Traditions*, ed. Rosemary Ruether and Eleanor McLaughlin (New York: Simon and Schuster, 1979), 225-54. The latter source includes a summary of six factors that "account for the Holiness movement's consistent feminist thrust" (241). These are the emphasis on experience, the fact that the doctrine of holiness was "rooted in Scripture" (244), affirmation of the inspiration and authority of Scripture, the "emphasis on the work of the Holy Spirit" (246), the experimental nature of the movement, and the sectarian nature of the movement.

A general source of information is *Wesleyan/Holiness Women Clergy: A Preliminary Bibliography*, compiled by Susie C. Stanley (Portland, OR: Western Evangelical Seminary, 1994). Regarding the history of women clergy in the Church of the Nazarene, see Rebecca Laird, *Ordained Women in the Church of the Nazarene: The First Generation* (Kansas City, MO: Nazarene Publishing House, 1993); Janet Smith Williams, "The Impetus of Holiness Women Preaching the Gospel, with Special Consideration Concerning Women in the Church of the Nazarene" (M.A. thesis, Conservative Baptist Theological Seminary, 1981); and Robert Stanley Ingersol, "Burden of Dissent: Mary Lee Cagle and the Southern Holiness Movement" (Ph.D. diss., Duke University, 1988). Regarding ordained women in the Church of God, see Juanita Evans Leonard, ed., *Called to Minister: Empowered to Serve* (Anderson, IN: Warner Press, 1989). And concerning the Pillar of Fire, see Susie Cunningham Stanley, *Feminist Pillar of Fire: The Life of Alma White* (Cleveland: Pilgrim Press, 1993).

50. *Minutes,* First Conference of the Christian Mission, Held at the People's Mission Hall, 272 Whitechapel Rd., London, June 15-17, 1879; quoted in Norman H. Murdoch, "Female Ministry in the Thought and Work of Catherine Booth," *Church History* 53 (September 1984): 355.

51. *Manual of the Church of the Nazarene* (Los Angeles, 1898), 16, quoted in Laird, *Ordained Women,* 11. Denominational officials reaffirmed that ordaining women was faithful to the gospel when laypeople raised the issue in 1922, 1934, 1939, and 1943 (144).

periodicals between 1880 and 1930, and discovered: "No matter what the position expressed concerning women speaking in church or in any other mixed assembly, all writers and editors of these magazines opposed ordaining women to traditional parish ministry."[52] In fact, and cutting across the grain of two-party analysis, modernists and fundamentalists agreed on the issue of women's ordination.[53]

Margaret Lamberts Bendroth's book *Fundamentalism and Gender* simplifies the job of comparing the role of women within the Wesleyan/Holiness movement and fundamentalist groups. According to Bendroth, fundamentalists "abhorred the use of women preachers in holiness churches."[54] Bendroth highlights the theological differences that influenced the fundamentalist view of women, stressing inerrancy and dispensationalism.[55]

Fundamentalists quoted 1 Corinthians 14:34 and 1 Timothy 2:11-12, claiming an inerrantist reading of these texts required women's prohibition from public ministry. On the other hand, Wesleyan/Holiness interpreters, such as Fannie McDowell Hunter, contended that the command to keep silence in 1 Corinthians 14:34 referred to women's questions which interrupted the worship service. Paul's intention was to maintain quiet, and his prohibition was temporary and related only to the local church in Corinth.[56] Holiness authors, such as Catherine Booth and Hunter,

---

52. Betty A. DeBerg, *Ungodly Women: Gender and the First Wave of American Fundamentalism* (Minneapolis: Fortress Press, 1990), 79. Michael S. Hamilton argues that the involvement of women in fundamentalist ministries was higher than is generally recognized but acknowledges that "fundamentalists resisted ordaining women and hiring them as church pastors." Michael S. Hamilton, "Women, Public Ministry, and American Fundamentalism, 1920-1950," *Religion and American Culture* 3 (Summer 1993): 179.

53. As late as 1977, only 17.4% of the ordained women in the United States were from ten major Protestant denominations. The majority of women clergy represented Holiness and Pentecostal churches. Constant H. Jacquet, Jr., *Women Ministers in 1977: A Report* (New York: Office of Research, Evaluation and Planning, National Council of Churches, 1978), 7.

54. Margaret Lamberts Bendroth, *Fundamentalism and Gender, 1875 to the Present* (New Haven: Yale University Press, 1993), 4-5.

55. Ibid., 30.

56. Fannie McDowell Hunter, *Women Preachers* (Peniel, TX: Berachah Printing Co., 1905; repr. *Holiness Tracts Defending the Ministry of Women*, ed. Donald Wilbur Dayton (New York: Garland Publishing, 1985), 35-36. See also Alma White, *Woman's Ministry* (London: Pillar of Fire, [1921]), 5-7; and Catherine Booth, *Female Ministry; or Woman's Right to Preach the Gospel* (London, 1859; New York: Salvation Army Supplies Printing and Publishing Department, 1975), 12-13, 17. For a brief summary of the Wesleyan/Holiness hermeneutic supporting women in ministry, see Stanley, *Feminist Pillar of Fire*, 33-35.

dismissed the passage in Timothy as irrelevant to the issue of women preaching.[57]

Fundamentalists minimized the role of women in the Bible. Priscilla "never forgot her place as a wife and did not attempt to usurp authority," and Deborah "was wise enough to call [her male assistant] Barak to stand in the front, while she stood behind him, modestly directing his work."[58] In contrast, Wesleyan/Holiness exegetes credited Deborah with choosing Barak to command the army, planning the campaign, directing the movements of the troops, and giving the order to begin fighting. As a prophet and judge she "had a God-given right to exercise all the duties and privileges of the offices."[59] Priscilla's name occurred before Aquila's three times out of five in the New Testament, indicating to Hunter that "she was the chief actor — probably being of the two, the more prominent and helpful to the Church."[60] Words such as "modestly" and "women's place" used in a restrictive manner in fundamentalist sources did not appear in these Wesleyan/Holiness descriptions of biblical women.

Fundamentalists who were dispensationalists and Wesleyan/Holiness exegetes agreed that woman and man were equal at creation and that the Fall resulted in inequality for women.[61] They disagreed on when the curse would be lifted. Dispensationalists believed that "womankind, like the rest of humanity, waited for Christ's Second Coming to lift the penalty of sin brought on by the Fall."[62] But holiness interpreters contended that Christ's first coming restored equality. Fannie McDowell Hunter claimed that "Christ re-enacted the primitive law (Matt. 19:4, 5) thus restoring to woman under the blessed spirit of Christianity equal *rights* and equal *privileges*."[63] Alma White argued:

57. Booth, *Female Ministry,* 12; and Hunter, *Women Preachers,* 38-39.

58. W. S. Hottel, "Uniform Sunday-School Lessons," *Pilot* 15 (September 1935): 313, quoted in Bendroth, *Fundamentalism and Gender,* 91; and A. B. Simpson, quoted in Leslie A. Andrews, "Restricted Freedom: A. B. Simpson's View of Women," in *Birth of a Vision,* ed. David F. Hartzfeld and Charles Nienkirchen (Regina, Sask.: His Dominion, 1986), 226-27, quoted in Bendroth, *Fundamentalism and Gender,* 27.

59. Hunter, *Women Preachers,* 14.

60. Ibid., 26.

61. For example, see White, *New Testament Church,* 275; and Bendroth, *Fundamentalism and Gender,* 45.

62. Bendroth, *Fundamentalism and Gender,* 8; see also 124. Further, "dispensational premillennialism embedded the principle of masculine leadership and feminine subordination in salvation history itself" (p. 41). This is in stark contrast to the perspective of Wesleyan/Holiness advocates of women clergy.

63. Hunter, *Women Preachers,* 94. Hunter quoted B. T. Roberts with approval: "If

There is but little hope for the human race until woman takes the place accorded her by the Creator. Then she will be a helpmeet rather than a servant or a slave. It is evident that the non-progressive old denominations with their fallen ministry will never change. And thus the Pillar of Fire Church has had to set the example of equality for the sexes, heralding a new era of religious freedom by breaking the shackles that have held woman in bondage for ages.[64]

Bendroth also highlights the fact that fundamentalists disagreed with the Wesleyan/Holiness understanding of the gifts of the Spirit: "Fundamentalists emphatically rejected the pentecostal emphasis on spiritual gifts."[65] For fundamentalists, "The spiritual gifts the apostles received then [at Pentecost] were unique and were discontinued until the final outpouring at the end of time."[66]

In contrast to this view, Wesleyan/Holiness believers recognized that the gifts of the Holy Spirit were still bestowed on men and women alike.[67] According to Salvation Army co-founder Catherine Booth, the question of women's public ministry "had been settled on the day of Pentecost."[68] And Fannie McDowell Hunter emphasized that "Joel's prediction, that 'your sons and *daughters* shall prophesy' (Joel 2:28) was not exhausted on the day of Pentecost, but was to continue to be fulfilled throughout the entire Christian dispensation."[69]

Wesleyan/Holiness adherents and fundamentalists likewise differed in their support of women's equality outside the church in the political arena. Even though prominent fundamentalists Billy Sunday and William Jennings Bryan supported suffrage, "antisuffrage statements in popular fundamentalist periodicals outnumbered prosuffrage statements by a ratio of more than ten to one."[70]

---

she was first in the fall, she was first in the restoration. 'Christ hath redeemed us from the curse of the law, being made a curse for us.' — Gal. 3:13. The *us* includes *woman*. Christ came to repair the ruin wrought by the fall' " (p. 42). Roberts founded the Free Methodist Church.

64. White, *New Testament Church*, 275, 277.

65. Bendroth, *Fundamentalism and Gender*, 4.

66. Ibid., 46.

67. For examples of this perspective, see Sarah Bishop, "Should Women Preach?" *Gospel Trumpet* 40 (June 17, 1920): 9; and F. G. Smith, "Editorial," *Gospel Trumpet* 40 (October 4, 1920): 2.

68. Booth, *Female Ministry*, 7; see also 10.

69. Hunter, *Women Preachers*, 94; see also 23-25 for Hunter's discussion of Pentecost.

70. DeBerg, *Ungodly Women*, 51.

Until all periodicals have been analyzed, it will be impossible to determine the degree of support for women's right to vote among adherents of the Wesleyan/Holiness movement. There is evidence to suggest that the Salvation Army supported suffrage.[71] Wesleyan/Holiness believers also celebrated passage of the suffrage amendment. As a writer in *Gospel Trumpet* exulted: "This is woman's day. The Suffrage Amendment to the Constitution has been ratified, and now all women in the United States can vote on anything that men can."[72] Alma White referred to the amendment's passage as one of the "crowning events in our national history," which represented "the triumph of the Cross in the liberation of women who in their inequality with the opposite sex had worn the chains of oppression."[73] White also promoted the Equal Rights Amendment, first introduced in Congress in 1923.[74] She endorsed this amendment as a means of restoring the equality present at the beginning when "God gave men and women copartnership and control of all that He had created."[75]

Wesleyan/Holiness convictions relating to the role of women differed in several significant ways from the fundamentalist perspective. No fundamentalist group sanctioned women's ordination, while The Salvation Army, Church of the Nazarene, Church of God, and Pillar of Fire all ordained women from their inception. Gifted by the Holy Spirit, women and men continued to fulfill Joel's prophecy. According to Wesleyan/Holiness believers, Christ's first coming reestablished the equal status of women, who had been subordinated to men as a result of the Fall. Women did not have to wait until Christ's second coming to achieve equality. Women's equality extended beyond the walls of the church into the political arena, evidenced by support for women's suffrage and the Equal Rights Amendment.

71. Prominent Salvationist Emma Booth Tucker's name appeared in a list of women ministers who were suffragists. Susan B. Anthony and Ida Husted Harper, eds., *History of Woman Suffrage*, vol. 4 (Indianapolis: Hollenback Press, 1902), 1080. Susan B. Anthony addressed Salvation Army audiences in California in 1896 as part of the campaign to have the state Constitution amended to give women the right to vote (486, 490).

72. "Women's Day," in "Observations of Our Times" section, *Gospel Trumpet* 40 (October 14, 1920): 3.

73. Alma White, *The Story of My Life and the Pillar of Fire*, 5 vols. (Zarephath, NJ: Pillar of Fire, 1935-1943), 5:314 and 4:237.

74. Stanley, *Feminist Pillar of Fire*, 106-14.

75. Alma White, "Equality Essential to Success," *Women's Chains* (July-August 1924): 3. White founded *Woman's Chains* for the explicit purpose of promoting women's rights.

SUSIE C. STANLEY

Social Holiness

Social Christianity generally is equated with the social gospel, which supposedly emerged from the modernist side of the fundamentalist/modernist paradigm. Timothy Smith challenged this assumption with the contention that perfectionist or holiness doctrine nourished the roots of the social gospel prior to the Civil War.[76] He documented the work of leaders of the holiness movement during this period who exhibited "sanctified compassion" which "opposed the organized evils of urban society and stretched out hands of mercy to help the poor."[77] Norris Magnuson detailed the "gospel welfare" activities of Wesleyan/Holiness groups from 1865 to 1920.[78]

More recently, the term used to describe social justice activities undertaken by Wesleyan/Holiness adherents is social holiness. Social holiness differs from the fundamentalist position, which, in its most extreme form, eschewed any social reform activities because they would impede Christ's return. Many fundamentalists believed salvation and social concern were mutually exclusive. They were pessimistic regarding the possibility of societal progress. In contrast, within most of the Wesleyan/Holiness movement temporal and spiritual salvation were inseparable, at least in the early years of the movement, and there was more hope for societal improvement. C. E. Brown, true to the primitivist impulses of the Church of God, advocated following the example of the early church, which "won its place of power in the world, first by witnessing to Jesus Christ crucified and second by implementing that witness by its care of the poor, the needy, the unfortunate, and the disinherited."[79]

Frank Stanger observed that the holiness movement raised ethics to the status that fundamentalists accorded doctrine.[80] The ethical emphasis is a direct outgrowth of the doctrine of holiness. Mary Alice Tenney contended that concern for others was consistent with John Wesley's under-

---

76. Timothy L. Smith, *Revivalism and Social Reform in Mid-Nineteenth Century America* (New York: Abingdon Press, 1957); reprint with new title *Revivalism and Social Reform: American Protestantism on the Eve of the Civil War* (Baltimore: Johns Hopkins University Press, 1980), 8, 149, 161.

77. Ibid., 176.

78. Norris Magnuson, *Salvation in the Slums* (Metuchen, NJ: The Scarecrow Press, 1977).

79. C. E. Brown, "Care of the Poor," *Gospel Trumpet* 69 (October 15, 1949): 1.

80. Frank Stanger, "Holiness and Social Justice," *The Asbury Seminarian* (July 1981): 8.

standing of holiness or perfect love, Wesley's preferred term.[81] Wesley stressed that love of God extended to one's neighbor. George Turner elaborated: "This means a concern, not only for the neighbor's eternal welfare, but also for their temporal well-being."[82] Using Matthew 25:40 as his text, one Church of God author contended that Jesus "made service to others equivalent to service to God: 'Inasmuch as ye have done it unto the least of these my brethren, ye have done it unto me' (Matt. 25:40)." The author further declared: "Love and sympathy are not merely a means of introducing the gospel; they *are* the gospel."[83] While Kenneth Jones criticized the social gospel for its neglect of the doctrine of individual sin, he encouraged pastors to avoid the extreme of preaching only personal salvation. He advocated social work, which he defined as helping the poor and relieving the oppressed.[84]

As regards the Pillar of Fire, it should be noted that from the early days of her evangelistic work Alma White distributed clothing to the poor and engaged in other acts of social holiness. During the depression, she operated a soup kitchen in Denver. Her missions throughout the country operated as communes which met the temporal needs of her followers.

In the same vein, members of the Church of the Nazarene actively engaged in social holiness activities in the early years of the twentieth century. To give but one example, Charles Jones has documented how Nazarenes in the planned community of Bethany, Oklahoma, established an orphanage and a home for unwed mothers.[85] Of course, as Timothy Smith has observed, the practice of social holiness among Nazarenes greatly declined as the century progressed.[86] The following statement by J. B. Chapman in 1922 closely resembled D. L. Moody's famous proclamation: "We are not called to act as carpenters to repair the world's tempest wrecked ship. The old ship is going to sink. We are called to man life boats and to rescue as many as possible before the old ship goes down."[87]

---

81. Mary Alice Tenney, *Living in Two Worlds* (Winona Lake, IN: Light & Life Press, 1958). See also Magnuson, *Salvation in the Slums*, 38, 178.

82. George Turner, *Christian Holiness in Scripture, in History, and in Life* (Kansas City, MO: Beacon Hill Press of Kansas City, 1977), 89.

83. K. Y. Plank, "Ye Have Done It Unto Me," *Gospel Trumpet* 65 (February 24, 1945): 5.

84. Kenneth Jones, "Our Social Gospel," *Gospel Trumpet* 65 (December 29, 1945): 8.

85. Charles Edwin Jones, "Miss Mallory's Children: The Oklahoma Orphanage and the Founding of Bethany," *The Chronicles of Oklahoma* 71 (Winter 1993-94): 392-421.

86. Smith, *Called unto Holiness*, 269-70, 318.

87. J. B. Chapman, "Editorial," *Herald of Holiness* 11 (November 1, 1922): n.p. Moody

The Salvation Army exhibited the clearest and most consistent expression of social holiness. While social holiness activities have diminished in the other groups under consideration, the Salvation Army has maintained its dual emphasis on social and spiritual redemption.[88] Edward McKinley mentioned examples of social holiness in *Marching to Glory*, his history of the Salvation Army in the United States. He chronicled their provision of cheap food and shelter depots, hotels for working women and men, industrial homes, and coal for the poor.[89] Other Salvation Army expressions of social holiness included free legal aid for the poor, crèches for children of working parents, and a poor person's bank.

McKinley differentiated the social gospel from the Salvation Army's approach by stressing the Army's lack of theory:

> Pioneer officers were little concerned with theories of social justice: they knew only that their Heavenly Commander had ordered His soldiers to take in strangers, visit the sick and imprisoned, offer drink to the thirsty, and food to the hungry; they also knew that there were souls dying all around, and that the first step in saving some of them was to lift them up so they could hear that such a thing as salvation existed. Social welfare was both Biblical and practical: salvationists needed no more elaborate arguments than these. The Army never offered a developed theory for its social welfare program. Each part evolved piecemeal, over the years, in response to immediate practical needs that were uncovered in the course of the evangelical crusade.[90]

Many fundamentalists opposed social Christianity because they believed it would hinder Christ's second coming. Wesleyan/Holiness believers, on the other hand, understood social holiness as a direct outgrowth of their understanding of sanctification or holiness. Love of God extended to love of neighbor.

---

proclaimed: "I look upon the world as a wrecked vessel. God has given me a lifeboat and said to me, 'Moody, save all you can.'" Marsden, *Fundamentalism and American Culture*, 38.

88. William Booth, *In Darkest England and the Way Out* (London: International Headquarters of The Salvation Army, [1890]). Booth outlined his program to eliminate poverty in England in this book.

89. McKinley, *Marching to Glory*, 57, 84, 85, 96, 139.

90. Ibid., 54.

Conclusion

The belief in sanctification or holiness sharply distinguished the Wesleyan/Holiness movement from the fundamentalist side of the two-party paradigm. Four other significant issues differentiated Wesleyan/Holiness churches from fundamentalism. Inerrancy did not characterize the Wesleyan/Holiness understanding of biblical authority. While a minority of Wesleyan/Holiness adherents were premillennialists, dispensationalism was not popular. Finally, while the doctrines of dispensationalism and inerrancy contributed to fundamentalism's hostility to women clergy and social Christianity, the churches examined here supported ordained women clergy and engaged in social holiness activities.

This essay has provided a broad picture illustrating significant ways in which the Wesleyan/Holiness movement differed from fundamentalism. Granted, there are exceptions, as there are with any generalization. Overall, however, the two-party paradigm fails to explain the churches that comprise the Wesleyan/Holiness movement. If we are to understand the Wesleyan/Holiness movement, we need to abandon this interpretive paradigm, and instead let the movement speak with its own voice. And in general terms, we need to develop new multi-party models that avoid distorting the identities of the groups we study, and that truly take into account the glorious complexity of American Protestantism.

CHAPTER 10

Why Restorationists
Don't Fit the Evangelical Mold;
Why Churches of Christ Increasingly Do[1]

RICHARD T. HUGHES

For the most part, evangelicals and mainline Protestants have little or no comprehension of the meaning of the "restoration vision." Whether one employs the term "restorationism" or "primitivism," most find the very concept foreign, if not incomprehensible, eccentric, and odd.

Yet, there have always existed in American religious life communities of faith that can only be described as restorationist. Though rooted in the Protestant Reformation, these people generally have denied that they are Protestants at all, claiming instead the more universal label of "Christian." And when American Protestantism seemed to fracture into modernism and fundamentalism as the twentieth century dawned, restorationists often refused to identify themselves with either camp. Instead, they were loyal to what they perceived as the most ancient forms of Christian faith and practice reflected in Christian scripture. From their perspective, liberals and evangelicals alike had courted the world's favor, and restorationists therefore judged them both as severely compromised versions of the Christian faith and, in many ways, mirror images of one another.

---

1. A portion of this essay appeared in Richard T. Hughes, "Reclaiming a Heritage," *Restoration Quarterly* 37 (Third Quarter 1995): 136-37.

Mainline Protestants, Evangelicals, and the "Restoration Vision"

What might we say of the mainline Protestant assessment of the restoration vision? The noted Methodist churchman and historian Albert Outler typified that assessment when he chanced to witness, some years ago, on a church building in Sweetwater, Texas, a cornerstone that read:

> The Church of Christ
> Founded at Jerusalem
> A.D. 33
> Organized in Sweetwater
> A.D. 1882
> This Building Erected, 1907

Outler was dumbfounded. The following summer, he shared this story with friends at the Third World Conference of Faith and Order in Lund, Sweden, but the story drew only "quizzical smiles — and, occasionally, polite incredulity."

Over the next several years, Outler repeatedly told his wife about this curious stone, but she responded with utter disbelief. Finally, Outler determined to show her the evidence. The two of them made the 200-mile trek west from Dallas to Sweetwater, only to discover that the old building with the curious cornerstone was gone. A new building now stood several miles away, but the old cornerstone was nowhere to be found. Increasingly desperate to show his wife the hard, tangible evidence for this implausible artifact, Outler located the minister and politely asked him what had happened to the stone. A majority in the church, the minister explained, did not wish the old stone in the new building, and the stone now rested in the yard of the local stone mason. Delighted, Outler located the stone, photographed it from every possible angle, then arranged for a flat bed truck to haul the stone from Sweetwater to the university museum at Texas Christian University in Fort Worth, just in case, as Outler explained, "posterity is ever interested."[2]

Though this stone reflects a worldview that characterizes all restorationist traditions to one degree or another, Outler's response of disbelief that such a stone — and such a perspective — could exist typifies the

---

2. Albert Outler, "Church History by the Cube," *Mission Journal* 20 (March 1987): 30-31.

fundamental failure of mainline Protestants to comprehend what the restoration vision is all about.

One might think that evangelicals would understand the restoration ideal better than their counterparts in mainline Protestantism, but that plainly is not the case. For many years, I indulged myself in the supposition that modern evangelicals bear a strong and special kinship to restorationists. I imagined this was true since evangelicals share with restorationists an intense allegiance to the Bible as the one and only source of Christian truth, and since so many evangelical historians have claimed Churches of Christ, Mennonites, and other restorationist traditions as part of the evangelical alliance.[3]

Recently, however, I determined to rethink my assumptions regarding the relation between evangelicals and restorationists. I began that process by reflecting on the history of my own tradition, the Churches of Christ. Before we explore that relationship in the context of the Churches of Christ, a brief introduction to the history of that tradition is in order.

Born on the American frontier in the early nineteenth century, the Churches of Christ were originally part of a wide-ranging movement that sought to unify all Christians by appealing to the Bible and to the simplicity and the ethical power of the early Christian communities. In those early years, they answered to the label "Churches of Christ," but also to the terms "Disciples of Christ" and "Christian Churches."

In that founding period, they looked to two men for leadership: Barton W. Stone and Alexander Campbell. In many ways, Stone bore the earmarks of a genuine evangelical. A child of the revivals, he stood in debt to the Great Awakening in several ways; then, in 1801, he played a key role in the Cane Ridge Revival that helped ignite the Second Great Awakening. He fraternized with the evangelical denominations and recognized their members as brothers and sisters in Christ. And yet, Stone was also profoundly restorationist, even counter-cultural in orientation. At the heart of his thought stood a New Testament ethic which he grounded in the biblical promise that the kingdom of God would finally triumph over all the world. Stone took this promise very seriously, and believed this ethic could provide the foundation on which all Christians could unite.

Equally ecumenical but less focused on ethics than was Stone, Alexander Campbell believed that unity could best be achieved through a

---

3. Cf. George Marsden, *Understanding Fundamentalism and Evangelicalism* (Grand Rapids: Eerdmans, 1991), 5; and James Davison Hunter, "Operationalizing Evangelicalism: A Review, Critique and Proposal," *Sociological Analysis* 42 (1981): 370.

progressive, rational reconstruction of the ancient Christian church, based on an almost scientific reading of the biblical text. For a variety of reasons, Campbell's influence slowly began to eclipse that of Stone. Then, in 1832, the Stone and Campbell movements joined forces and soon became the largest indigenous Christian movement in the United States.

By the late nineteenth century, however, this erstwhile ecumenical movement finally divided into two distinct denominations: Disciples of Christ and Churches of Christ. The Disciples carried Campbell's progressive and ecumenical spirit into the twentieth century and finally rejected the restoration vision altogether. At the same time, the Churches of Christ coalesced around the other side of the nineteenth-century platform: the restoration of the ancient Christian faith/church. For them, restoration embodied not only the rational reconstruction of the ancient Christian church — an emphasis they inherited from Campbell — but also a counter-cultural commitment to biblical ethics, an emphasis they inherited from Barton W. Stone.[4]

This was the tradition in which I was raised and the tradition to which I turned my attention as I began to reflect on the possible relation between evangelicalism and the restorationist heritage.

I began my reflections by reminding myself that in my own lifetime, Churches of Christ have seldom fraternized with any of the organizations one normally associates with the evangelical world. They have never sustained a connection to the National Association of Evangelicals; until recently, none of the dozen or so colleges related to Churches of Christ has ever belonged to the Coalition for Christian Colleges and Universities.[5] The truth is, in my lifetime, the formal ties that might have connected Churches of Christ to the evangelical world have been virtually nonexistent.

With that in mind, I began reading again George Marsden's book,

---

4. There are several texts that trace the history of this tradition. See, e.g., Earl Irvin West's four-volume *Search for the Ancient Order* (vol. 1: Nashville: Gospel Advocate Co., 1964; vol. 2: Religious Book Service, 1950; vol. 3: Religious Book Service, 1979; and vol. 4: Religious Book Service, 1987); Robert Hooper's *A Distinct People: A History of the Churches of Christ in the Twentieth Century* (West Monroe, LA: Howard Publishing, 1993); LeRoy Garrett's *The Stone-Campbell Movement: An Anecdotal History of Three Churches*, rev. ed. (Joplin, MO: College Press, 1994); and Richard Hughes's *Reviving the Ancient Faith: The Story of Churches of Christ in America* (Grand Rapids: Eerdmans, 1996).

5. Abilene Christian University (Abilene, TX) is the only educational institution related to Churches of Christ to join the Coalition for Christian Colleges and Universities, having done so on July 26, 1995.

Understanding Fundamentalism and Evangelicalism. I thought it would help if I compared the history of Churches of Christ to Marsden's description of evangelicals at every significant point. Marsden observed first of all that evangelicals trace their American roots to the great revivals of White-field, Finney, Moody, Sunday, and Graham.[6] I realized that though I had grown up in Churches of Christ, a denomination Marsden labels "evangelical,"[7] I had never heard of Whitefield, Finney, Moody, or Sunday until I was in graduate school. Until then, I knew little or nothing about the evangelical revivalist tradition.

In that light, I was surprised to find that Marsden identifies Alexander Campbell, one of the nineteenth-century "fathers" of Churches of Christ, as "a revivalist."[8] The truth is, Campbell was not a revivalist in any sense of the word. In fact, Campbell strenuously opposed most of the revivals of his age on the grounds that they substituted emotion for the plain word of God.

If Campbell was a revivalist, one might rightly expect to find favorable references to Charles Finney in Campbell's *Millennial Harbinger*, which he edited for virtually the duration of Finney's career. Yet, for over thirty years, only three references appear, and none of them was favorable. Two of the three, in fact, chided Finney on explicitly restorationist grounds: he had substituted "the anxious bench" for baptism and replaced the ancient gospel with his "new measures."[9]

Campbell, in fact, thought that revivals offered little more than "the machinery of 'getting religion' by animal excitement." He complained that

> the doctrine of American Revivals, so rife since the year 1734, has made Methodists of all the Protestants in America, except a few genteel Episcopalians, whose love of good breeding, more than their knowledge of the gospel, has prevented them from screaming, swooning, fainting, jerking, laughing, shouting, under "the influence of the Holy Ghost," as they express it.

Further, Campbell claimed that biblical illiteracy abounded, especially among those caught up in the revivals. "I should not be believed," he

6. Marsden, *Understanding Fundamentalism and Evangelicalism*, 2.
7. Marsden, *Understanding Fundamentalism and Evangelicalism*, 5.
8. Marsden, *Understanding Fundamentalism and Evangelicalism*, 67.
9. Alexander Campbell, "Elder Finney's Substitute for Baptism," *Millennial Harbinger*, New Series 5 (March 1841): 141; and Discipulus, "Charles G. Finney," *Millennial Harbinger*, New Series 5 (December 1841): 591-93.

wrote, "were I to tell half of what I know of the ignorance of the Book in this religious, enthusiastic, and fanatical population."[10]

Again, Marsden notes that three traditions which helped give shape to twentieth-century evangelicalism — dispensationalism, holiness, and pentecostalism — all revered Dwight Moody's lieutenant, Reuben Torrey.[11] What, then, of Churches of Christ? Did they revere Torrey as well? To answer that question, I searched the index to the most powerful paper circulated among Churches of Christ in those years, the *Gospel Advocate*, published in Nashville, Tennessee. Torrey's name never appears.

Or again, Marsden notes that "during the 1950s and 1960s the simplest . . . definition of an evangelical . . . was 'anyone who likes Billy Graham.'"[12] Yet, in my memory, Churches of Christ never much liked Billy Graham for essentially the same reasons Alexander Campbell never much liked Charles Finney. Indeed, the indexes to a variety of journals circulated among Churches of Christ for the past forty years reveal almost no references to Graham at all, and the few that did appear were largely negative.[13]

Most telling of all, Marsden observes that in the evangelical world, "denominational affiliation was ultimately a matter of free choice. . . . If you did not like one church, you could simply leave and go to the one down the street."[14] Nothing could be more foreign to the authentically restorationist mind, and certainly nothing could be more foreign to Churches of Christ, at least until recent years.

Restorationists and Evangelicals: The Basic Difference

There are many points at which one might compare restorationists, and especially Churches of Christ, with the broad evangelical tradition. One might explore worship styles, lifestyles, theology, or a host of other categories. In fact, in another essay I have compared Churches of Christ

10. Campbell, "Letter to Elder William Jones. No. VI," *Millennial Harbinger* 6 (August 1835): 355.

11. Marsden, *Understanding Fundamentalism and Evangelicalism*, 43-44.

12. Marsden, *Understanding Fundamentalism and Evangelicalism*, 6.

13. Cf. Fred B. Walker, "Billy Graham in the Nation's Capital," *Gospel Advocate* 94 (February 28, 1952): 130-31; and G. K. Wallace, " 'My Answer,' " *Gospel Advocate* 117 (September 4, 1975): 565-66.

14. Marsden, *Understanding Fundamentalism and Evangelicalism*, 17, 81.

with evangelicals from a theological perspective.[15] The present essay, however, focuses on ethics, politics, and culture since, in my view, the genius of the restoration vision finally has more to do with ethics than with theology.

Obviously, the comparisons I have already drawn are not definitive. Instead, they serve as clues to a deeper and wider gulf that separates restorationists from evangelicals. Navigation of that gulf requires a brief assessment of the cultural and political meaning of evangelicalism. We begin with John Calvin, clearly a sixteenth-century hero for most American evangelicals. Though a restorationist of sorts who liked to compare the "the ancient church" with what he viewed as Catholic corruptions,[16] Calvin concerned himself chiefly with the sovereignty of God which he longed to impose over all the earth, beginning with Geneva.

Other Reformed leaders sounded the same refrain. Martin Bucer, for example, dedicated his *De Regno Christi* to Edward VI, King of England, in 1550. Also a restorationist of sorts, Bucer argued in that book that England could become the kingdom of Christ only by restoring the faith and practice of the ancient church. Significantly, however, Bucer defined the ancient church in explicitly Constantinian terms. He described "the period of Constantine and the emperors who followed him" as a period in which "nothing [was] wanting . . . in regard to the happiness of the Church of Christ" and a period "when churches were raised up all over the world and flourished in exceptional piety."[17] In this way, Calvin, Bucer, and virtually all Reformed theologians perpetuated the old medieval vision of Christendom, though now in Protestant guise.

Joel Carpenter cast further light on this issue when he wrote that American fundamentalists also were restorationists of sorts. They, too, valued both Scripture and the Christian past. But the past they valued most was not the past of the first Christian age, but rather "the past since the Protestant Reformation." "Fundamentalists assumed that primitive Christianity had already been restored at the Reformation and revived several times since then. Their task, then, was not to recover it, but to

15. Richard T. Hughes, "Are Restorationists Evangelicals?" in Donald Dayton and Robert K. Johnston, eds., *The Variety of American Evangelicalism* (Knoxville: University of Tennessee Press, 1991), 109-34.

16. Cf. John Calvin, "Reply to Sadoleto" (1540), in Hans J. Hillerbrand, *The Protestant Reformation* (New York: Harper and Row, 1968), 154-72.

17. Martin Bucer, "De Regno Christi," in Wilhelm Pauck, ed., *The Library of Christian Classics*, vol. 19: *Melanchthon and Bucer* (Philadelphia: The Westminster Press, 1969), 209.

defend, cultivate, and promote it. . . ."[18] Carpenter should have added that the slice of the Reformation that fundamentalists valued most was the magisterial reform of Luther, Calvin, and Zwingli.

This is the context in which we must understand the genius of American evangelicalism: most evangelicals have sought "to defend, cultivate, and promote" the heritage of the magisterial reformation, to Christianize the culture in which they live, and to bring it under the sovereign sway of a distinctly Protestant God. There have been exceptions to this pattern, to be sure. J. Gresham Machen, for example, never fit this mold, as Darryl Hart points out in this volume.[19] For the most part, however, evangelicals have never fully abandoned the old Constantinian model, even in the United States. Here one finds the meaning of the title Sidney Mead gave to one of his books: *The Old Religion in the Brave New World*.[20]

Inescapably, this was the cultural significance of virtually all the revivals to which evangelicals trace their identity. In this context, the Second Great Awakening is perhaps the most notable case in point. When evangelical Protestants realized the full implications of the First Amendment to the Constitution, they sought to create through persuasion what they no longer could achieve through coercion or force of law, namely, a Protestant America. Further, since the nation's Founders sought to undermine all religious establishments, many evangelicals attacked those Founders as "infidels" whose alleged immorality would inevitably corrupt the nation. In this way, "a great tidal wave of revivalism" virtually drowned the "infidelity" that characterized the nation's founding, as Sidney Mead has pointed out time and again.[21]

Marsden confirms Mead's assessment of these events, but from a distinctly evangelical point of view. Given the nature of its founding, Marsden writes, one might expect that America might well "have adopted a genial democratic humanism, freed from explicitly Christian dogmas and institutions." However,

18. Joel Carpenter, "Contending for the Faith Once Delivered: Primitivist Impulses in American Fundamentalism," in Richard T. Hughes, ed., *The American Quest for the Primitive Church* (Urbana and Chicago: University of Illinois Press, 1988), 101.

19. See Chapter Seven of this volume: D. G. Hart, "J. Gresham Machen, Confessional Presbyterianism, and the History of Twentieth-Century Protestantism."

20. Sidney E. Mead, *The Old Religion in the Brave New World: Reflections on the Relation between Christendom and the Republic* (Berkeley: University of California Press, 1977).

21. Sidney E. Mead, *The Lively Experiment* (New York: Harper and Row, 1963), 53; and *The Nation with the Soul of a Church* (New York: Harper and Row, 1975), 122.

the fact that America had not in the nineteenth century followed the course set in the eighteenth by leaders like Franklin and Jefferson was due largely to vigorous evangelical enterprise. The United States had not drifted religiously during the nineteenth century. It had been guided, even driven, by resourceful evangelical leaders who effectively channeled the powers of revivals and voluntary religious organizations to counter the forces of purely secular change.[22]

Those revivals were so successful that Robert Baird, in his 1856 celebration of evangelical Protestantism in America, could describe the United States as "a Protestant empire" and "the most powerful of all Protestant kingdoms."[23] And Marsden concedes that by the time of the Gilded Age, "a Protestant version of the medieval ideal of 'Christendom' still prevailed."[24]

This is the context that illumines the cultural meaning of fundamentalism in the early twentieth century. If fundamentalists were evangelicals who were angry about something, as Jerry Falwell likes to suggest,[25] they were angry precisely because their long-standing domination of American culture was rapidly slipping away as the culture of modernism gained momentum.

This fact, in turn, sheds considerable light on the cultural meaning of the dispensational eschatology that most fundamentalists adopted in those years. Though there were exceptions, most evangelicals prior to the late nineteenth century had proclaimed a robust and highly optimistic *post*millennial eschatology. America, they believed, was a Protestant empire whose goodness and righteousness would hasten the millennial dawn. Indeed, this conviction had prevailed among American evangelicals for at least one hundred and fifty years, from the Great Awakening to the close of the nineteenth century. One can only conclude that postmillennial optimism lay at the very heart of American evangelicalism through the close of the nineteenth century, and grew out of evangelicals' long-standing commitment to Constantinian assumptions and their own domination of American life and culture.

Then, suddenly, evangelicals made a radical about-face. They abandoned their optimistic, postmillennial faith and adopted instead its op-

---

22. Marsden, *Understanding Fundamentalism and Evangelicalism*, 11-12.

23. Robert Baird, *Religion in America, With Notices of the Unevangelical Denominations* (New York: Harper and Brothers, 1856), 32.

24. Marsden, *Understanding Fundamentalism and Evangelicalism*, 10.

25. Marsden, *Understanding Fundamentalism and Evangelicalism*, 1.

posite: dispensational premillennialism. Why this sudden change? Clearly, the new-found premillennial theology was not central to historic evangelical thought. Rather, it served as a weapon of last resort for fundamentalists who feared that modernism would erode and perhaps even destroy their evangelical empire.

Put another way, fundamentalists would fight modernism first with the weapon of biblical inerrancy. In case they lost that fight and therefore their control of the culture, they had another weapon close at hand. Jesus himself, they believed, would reimpose his control over American life in the coming millennial age, deal the modernists a stunning defeat, and rule with his evangelical saints for a thousand years. This simply means that postmillennialism and premillennialism were but two different ways of expressing the central concern of fundamentalists: the creation and maintenance of a Protestant civilization in the United States. One way or another, the fundamentalists would finally win.

If this portrayal of American evangelicalism is even remotely correct, then it contrasts dramatically with the historic concerns of restorationists. At the most basic level, restorationists are Christians who yearn to return to the first Christian age. Some have sought to recover the Pentecost experience of the Holy Ghost, as Grant Wacker, Edith Blumhofer, and Donald Dayton have pointed out.[26] Others, like many Holiness denominations, have sought to recover ancient norms for holy living. Still others, like Alexander Campbell, have sought to reconstruct the forms and structures of the primitive church on a rational and scientific basis. Clearly, restorationists of all sorts are especially susceptible to illusions of innocence,[27] especially when they virtually identify themselves with one or another dimension of the first Christian age.

Yet, none of these concerns finally exposes the central core of the restorationist vision. That concern is simply this: the world is hopelessly corrupt, and by aligning itself with the world and its values, the church

---

26. Cf. Edith L. Blumhofer, *Restoring the Faith: The Assemblies of God, Pentecostalism, and American Culture* (Urbana and Chicago: University of Illinois Press, 1993), esp. 1-9; Grant Wacker, "Playing for Keeps: The Primitivist Impulse in Early Pentecostalism," in Hughes, ed., *The American Quest for the Primitive Church*, 196-219; Wacker, "Searching for Eden with a Satellite Dish: Primitivism, Pragmatism, and the Pentecostal Character," in Hughes, ed., *The Primitive Church in the Modern World* (Urbana and Chicago: University of Illinois Press, 1995); and Donald W. Dayton, *Theological Roots of Pentecostalism* (Grand Rapids: Francis Asbury Press, 1987).

27. See, e.g., Richard T. Hughes and C. Leonard Allen, *Illusions of Innocence: Protestant Primitivism in America, 1630-1875* (Chicago: University of Chicago Press, 1988).

corrupted itself from an early date. There was, however, a golden age when the church had not yet fallen. The church must therefore embrace the values of that golden age when the world and the church had not yet formed their alliance. If this is the heart and soul of the restoration vision, it means that authentic restorationists are inevitably radical and counter-cultural Christians. This is why, in my judgment, the genius of the restoration vision is fundamentally ethical, not theological.

In this light, authentic restorationists would find themselves bewildered when Marsden explains how "remarkable" it was that "the specifically Christian aspects" of the American heritage did not erode more than they did under the withering "winds of frankly secular ideologies"[28] issuing from the deistic founders of the American nation. Authentic restorationists would find this concept difficult to comprehend, simply because the notions of a "Christian culture" or a "Christian America" make no sense in the context of the restorationist perspective.

For this reason, authentic restorationists of the early nineteenth century were typically not among those who maligned the founders for their alleged immorality and "infidelity." On the contrary, restorationists of that period generally praised the founders for doing what evangelicals had refused to do, that is, for rejecting all attempts to Christianize, much less Protestantize, the United States. Those actions made it possible for restorationists to thrive in a way that they could not have thrived in a world controlled by evangelical Christians.

Thus, N. Summerbell, a spiritual descendant of New England's Elias Smith, criticized in 1847 those evangelicals who had "branded [Jefferson] with *Infidelity, Deism, and Atheism*." To Summerbell, Jefferson's "religious views . . . [were] as terrible to religious demagogues as were his political views to political tyrants." And when the followers of Barton Stone in Kentucky appealed to "the inalienable rights of free investigation [and] sober and diligent inquiry after [religious truth]," they implicitly praised the founders and condemned those evangelicals who still held out for a Christian establishment in the United States.[29] This suggests that Nathan Hatch's *Democratization of American Christianity* chronicles not so much the thoughts and deeds of antebellum evangelicals as the thoughts and deeds

28. Marsden, *Understanding Fundamentalism and Evangelicalism*, 11.
29. N. Summerbell, "The Religious Views of Thomas Jefferson," cited in Alexander Campbell, "Christian Union — No. XI. Unitarianism," *Millennial Harbinger* Series III, 4 (May 1847): 258-59; and J. and J. Gregg, "An Apology for Withdrawing from the Methodist Episcopal Church," *Christian Messenger* 1 (December 25, 1826): 39-40.

of antebellum restorationists; unfortunately, Hatch never makes this distinction.[30]

To put all this another way, the fundamental difference between evangelicals and restorationists is this: evangelicals subscribe to a model of Christian history that emphasizes continuity. Christian history, at least since the Reformation, is a seamless piece of cloth. This is why denominational loyalties have always been of small importance for most evangelicals. After all, evangelical Protestant churches of every stripe reflect the essence of the Reformation perspective. Further, to the extent that evangelicals seek to control the larger culture, they embrace a potential continuity between the church and the world, if only the world would submit to the sovereign rule of God.

On the other hand, the restorationist vision points to a radical tear in the fabric of Christian history. There is not the slightest possibility of continuity between the church and the world, and to the extent that Christians have made their peace with the world, the fabric of Christian history is badly torn.

Finally, however, we must acknowledge that evangelical *theology* and a restorationist understanding of what it means to live in the kingdom of God are not mutually exclusive perspectives. Surely there is no inherent tension between justification by grace through faith, for example, and kingdom ethics. On the other hand, the restoration vision and Constantinian assumptions *are* mutually exclusive understandings. Nonetheless, some evangelicals have employed an unmistakable appeal to the first Christian age, not as a tool for resistance and dissent but rather as the basis for creating a Christian political establishment. New England Puritans are perhaps the most notable case in point.[31] Yet, we must remember that when the restoration vision first emerged among England's earliest Puritans, it was nothing if not a tool for counter-cultural dissent. The Separatist Puritan tradition, eventually spawning Baptists, Quakers, and other radical dissenters who lived out of an unmistakably restorationist agenda, provides ample testimony to that dimension of the Puritan enterprise.

At the same time, living as they did when virtually everyone took for granted the notion of a Christian establishment, it was inevitable that

---

30. Nathan O. Hatch, *The Democratization of American Christianity* (New Haven: Yale University Press, 1989).

31. See Dwight Bozeman, *To Live Ancient Lives: The Primitivist Dimension of Puritanism* (Chapel Hill: University of North Carolina Press, 1988), who convincingly documents the restorationist theme in the New England Puritan experience.

some Puritans — most notably the Non-Separating Congregationalists of New England — would eventually employ the restoration vision as a tool for political power and domination. If there is a moral to this brief excursion, it is simply this: while a powerful dimension of nonconformity and dissent always lies at the heart of the restoration vision, restorationists can also employ that vision for precisely the opposite ends. When restorationists behave in this way, however, they have turned their backs on the genius of the vision they have claimed.

Scott Appleby reached similar conclusions in a recent paper that explored differences between restorationists and fundamentalists, especially in the context of Islam. Fundamentalists, Appleby argued, always seek political power in the modern world. Though their rhetoric often appeals to the founding age, their chief concern is not to conform themselves to the norms of the founding age, but instead to control the modern world. "They are clearly involved," Appleby wrote, "in constructing a synthesis between" ancient norms and the modern world. Yet, the results of their efforts "demonstrate that . . . modernity is setting the terms for religious adaptation." For fundamentalists, therefore, appeals to the founding age are rhetorical, not substantive.

Restorationists, on the other hand, care little about political control over the modern world, but care deeply about individual and social moral transformation that takes its bearings from ancient norms. For this reason, Appleby described authentic restorationism as fundamentally prophetic. Restorationists, he argued, maintain a "prophetic stance toward the very kingdoms and nation-states that the fundamentalists seek to conquer." He therefore finally concluded, "The world . . . [restorationists] seek to restore does not sit easily with the ambition of modern world-conquerors," even when those conquerors are fundamentalists.[32]

Restoration Churches: The Attraction of Evangelicalism

The relation between the restoration and evangelical traditions in America, however, is more complex than I have suggested. The picture I have attempted to paint so far is a picture based on the *beginnings* of restoration traditions, when a vision of primitive faith, undefiled by the world and its culture, still burned brightly. Such a picture would characterize not

32. R. Scott Appleby, "Primitivism as an Aspect of Global Fundamentalisms," in Hughes, ed., *The Primitive Church in the Modern World*, 17-33.

only the Churches of Christ, but Puritans, Pietists, Methodists,[33] Baptists, Latter-day Saints, Pentecostals, and a variety of holiness advocates in their earliest years. Though often evangelical in their theologies, all these movements began their careers with a distinctly restorationist orientation.

In America, however, primitivist traditions have found it difficult to retain the passion for the purity of first times, and the counter-cultural posture that passion has engendered. The allure of status and respectability in the larger culture has consistently eroded that commitment. When that commitment wanes, however, to whom can these churches turn? To ask that question is to underscore the continued power of the two-party symbolism within American Protestantism. To many participants and observers, there seem to be only two places where restorationists might migrate should they drift from their own roots: mainline Protestantism or evangelicalism. For most primitivists the mainline is not a serious option. Thus the tendency has been for restorationist churches to act as perpetual feeders of the evangelical establishment as they lose touch with their originating visions. Another way of saying this is that authentically restorationist churches are by definition sectarian. As they move away from their sectarian past and adopt a more respectable "denominational" status, however, they almost invariably tend to adopt evangelical modes of self-definition. Identification with the evangelical world seems to represent the most viable means of locating themselves amidst the limited public options that define the symbolic landscape of American religion.

Examples abound. In the late nineteenth century, American Mennonites began a flirtation with evangelicalism which intensified during the early twentieth century when fundamentalist fervor was at its height. That flirtation did not run a full course to evangelical absorption, thanks chiefly to the Mennonites' historic emphasis on non-resistance.[34] Presently the Mennonite scene is mixed, with a good number of Mennonite leaders pulling back from the cozy familiarity some used to feel toward evangelicalism, while other Mennonites seem still to be on a one-way road to evangelical identity. Similarly, Pentecostals in their earliest years were

33. Franklin H. Littell argues persuasively for the restorationist dimensions of early Methodism. Cf. Littell, "Assessing the Restoration Ideal," in Hughes, ed., *The Primitive Church in the Modern World*, 55-57.

34. James C. Juhnke, *Vision, Doctrine, War: Mennonite Identity and Organization in America, 1890-1930* (Scottdale, PA: Herald Press, 1989), 257-62; and C. Norman Kraus, "Evangelicalism: A Mennonite Critique," in Dayton and Johnston, *The Variety of American Evangelicalism*, 193-94.

distinctly restorationist and radically counter-cultural, but many moved quickly into the evangelical orbit during the mid-century. In part, this speedy transition doubtless resulted from the pragmatism that accompanied their primitivism (an unlikely pairing of qualities recently demonstrated by Grant Wacker),[35] and in part it was the result of conscious wooing by the emerging National Association of Evangelicals. Pentecostals have never fully merged with the evangelical mainstream, however, and today there is considerable ferment among Pentecostals about how close to or distant from evangelicalism they should be. The chief fear is that the homogenizing influence of evangelicalism will dilute Pentecostal distinctives. One might argue that Mennonites and Pentecostals alike were seduced by the illusion that fundamentalists were distinctly and inherently counter-cultural Christians like themselves, when in fact they were not.

There is, perhaps, no better example of the transition from restorationist sect to evangelical denomination than the Churches of Christ, to whose story we must now return. Unlike the Mennonites, the Churches of Christ did not have a strong sense of history or an established practice of counter-cultural pacifism to protect them from full colonization by evangelical ideas and ideals. Unlike Pentecostals, they did not have a distinctive, physically manifested form of piety (like speaking in tongues) to give them pause when considering the homogenizing risks of an alliance with evangelicalism. Yet the Churches of Christ did (and to some extent still do) possess a deeply ingrained suspicion of other churches and parachurches that has kept them from full formal membership within the "evangelical" domain. But these institutional quibbles have had little power to fence off the Churches of Christ either from the evangelical marketplace (books, music, magazines, etc.) or from the person-to-person, congregation-to-congregation migration of evangelical spirituality and political ideology.

But over the course of two centuries, how did this transition take place? Why has the experience of the Churches of Christ been different from that of the Mennonites and Pentecostals? There is no question that Campbell taught his followers the value of the restoration vision. Yet, like Calvin, Bucer, and other reformers before him, Campbell was only a "restorationist of sorts." After all, his restoration perspective had far more to do with a scientific reading of the biblical text than it did with the creation of counter-cultural Christian communities. Indeed, Campbell in many

35. Wacker, "Searching for Eden with a Satellite Dish."

ways was a nineteenth-century evangelical who, especially after 1837, sidled up to the evangelical establishment in his various efforts to promote a Protestant nation.[36]

On the other hand, Churches of Christ took most of their counter-cultural bearings from Barton W. Stone, who combined his vision of primitive Christianity with a distinctly apocalyptic perspective.[37] For Stone, the kingdom of God had expressed itself in the primitive church, which was therefore normative for life, faith, and practice. But the kingdom of God would come again soon in all its fullness. When that event transpired, God would rule over all the earth.

This perspective sounds remarkably like that of fundamentalists and evangelicals of the early twentieth century. Yet, there is a very significant difference. Fundamentalists embraced an apocalyptic orientation only when they saw the evangelical domination of American life and culture in jeopardy. For them, affirming the expected triumph of the kingdom of God was another way of saying that evangelical Christians would finally win the culture wars of the time, and that modernists would inevitably lose. Stone, however, never sought to dominate the culture. Instead, he consistently rejected the values of the larger culture for the duration of his career. If fundamentalists finally threw their full weight behind a Christian America, Stone rejected the notion of a Christian America and even claimed that the kingdom of God, when it manifested itself in its fullness, would finally subvert the United States along with all other political institutions.[38]

There are two notable measures of Stone's counter-cultural orientation. First, Stone freed his slaves in the aftermath of the revival, "choosing poverty in good conscience," as he put it, "to all the treasures of the world." Soon, other Kentucky Christians loyal to Stone moved to Ohio, where they also freed their slaves. These events transpired long before most southerners had seriously considered such a course of action.[39] Second, Stone shared with Mennonites an uncompromising commitment to

36. Cf. "From Primitive Church to Protestant Nation: The Millennial Odyssey of Alexander Campbell," in Hughes and Allen, *Illusions of Innocence,* 170-87.

37. Apocalyptic in this context should not be confused with premillennial. On this point, see Hughes, *Reviving the Ancient Faith,* 3, 92-93.

38. Barton W. Stone, "Reflections of Old Age," *Christian Messenger* 13 (August 1843): 123-26.

39. Barton W. Stone, *The Biography of Eld. Barton W. Stone* (Cincinnati, 1847), 44; and Joseph Thomas, *The Travels and Gospel Labors of Joseph Thomas* (Winchester, VA, 1812), 56.

the principles of pacifism and non-violence. Stone saw clearly the radical tear in the fabric of history that all restorationists discern. He therefore turned his back on the culture of his age and cast his lot with the kingdom of God, both as it was in the ancient church and as he expected it to be when the fullness of the kingdom of God finally arrived.

David Lipscomb was the great third-generation leader of Churches of Christ whose influence dominated that tradition from the Civil War to the early twentieth century. Lipscomb reflected Stone's counter-cultural views almost perfectly. Though a man of some means, he identified with the outcast and the poor, resisted racial discrimination, refused to vote, and refused to fight in wars. More important, Lipscomb grounded his counter-cultural behavior squarely in his apocalyptic orientation that prompted him confidently to expect the final triumph of the kingdom of God and "the complete and final destruction . . . of the last vestige of human governments and institutions."[40] More important still, Lipscomb thought these convictions reflected the very "key notes . . . of the Old and New Testaments." Without them, he said, the Bible was "without point of meaning."[41]

In that light, it is hardly surprising that when the *Ecclesiastical Almanac* placed Churches of Christ in the evangelical orbit, Lipscomb called the *Almanac's* report both "false and slanderous."[42] But there can be no doubt that Lipscomb's radical posture declined in popularity among Churches of Christ as the nineteenth century wore on. After all, many took their bearings more from Campbell than they did from Stone. These "Campbellites" defined the restoration vision more as a scientific recreation of the forms and structures of ancient Christianity than as a recreation of counter-cultural communities identified with the kingdom of God. Yet, Lipscomb's vision persisted with remarkable strength, especially in Middle Tennessee and the surrounding regions.

Then, between 1915 and 1960, Churches of Christ fought two great intramural wars. When those wars were over, Churches of Christ essentially had abandoned their posture as a restorationist sect and as a result began to veer off in an evangelical direction. The first of those wars centered on premillennial eschatology, which mainly served to symbolize a much deeper issue: the validity of the apocalyptic perspective, inherited from Stone and Lipscomb.

40. David Lipscomb, *Civil Government* (Nashville, 1889), 25, 27-28.
41. Lipscomb, *Civil Government*, 25, 27-28 (cf. 83-84), 96.
42. Lipscomb, "The Question Settled," *Gospel Advocate* 11 (March 11, 1869): 224.

To understand this struggle, we must first realize that in the late nineteenth century Churches of Christ suffered a disastrous division from the Disciples of Christ. In almost every city, the Disciples took the bulk of the members and the bulk of the wealth. Now relegated to the "wrong side of the tracks," Churches of Christ were left virtually to begin again, especially in urban areas.

World War I erupted in 1914, and found Churches of Christ seeking to compensate for their diminished standing. Specifically, they sought numerical growth and respectability. But it would be exceedingly difficult for Churches of Christ to gain many members or much respect in the crusading climate of World War I. After all, many of their members had committed themselves both to pacifism and to an apocalyptic outlook that judged the nation and found it wanting. Not surprisingly, leaders of Churches of Christ now took steps to scuttle the apocalyptic worldview.

This issue played itself out over dispensational premillennialism, which a small minority among Churches of Christ had embraced. The mainstream of Churches of Christ, however, rejected the premillennial vision and literally purged the church of its premillennial sympathizers. By the time they had finished their work, the entire apocalyptic vision among Churches of Christ — including the pacifist tradition — was essentially dead. While these developments actually broadened the theological gulf that existed between the Churches of Christ and most American evangelicals, they significantly narrowed the divide between the two groups on matters of ethics and political ideology. Predictably, by the 1930s, significant segments of Churches of Christ joined the Protestant crusade for old-fashioned Americanism, anti-Communism, and the maintenance of a Christian America.

The destruction of the apocalyptic vision severely weakened both the restoration vision and the counter-cultural dimensions of Churches of Christ, who increasingly made their peace with the spirit of the age. This became especially apparent in the aftermath of World War II, when the mainstream of Churches of Christ increasingly abandoned its nineteenth-century moorings in the interest of modernization, and sought, in a variety of ways, to enter the mainstream of American culture as a "respectable denomination." Many who maintained their allegiance to the values of nineteenth-century Churches of Christ saw this as nothing less than betrayal of the restoration vision. A bitter fight ensued, but when the dust finally settled in the late 1950s, the mainstream of Churches of Christ had essentially purged from their ranks those they labeled the "antis" — shorthand for the "anti-institutional" Churches of Christ.

Following the 1960s, other developments suggested that Churches of Christ were rapidly turning their backs on their restorationist heritage and moving into the emerging post-fundamentalist evangelical orbit. First, the legalism and exclusivism that had characterized many congregations for so long now gave way to the distinctly evangelical theme of justification by grace through faith. At the same time, a therapeutic gospel coupled with an emphasis on "family values," both popular among evangelical churches in the aftermath of the 1960s, increasingly dominated many Church of Christ pulpits.[43] Worship sometimes verged on entertainment, and many urban congregations adopted "church growth" strategies that had more in common with the Willow Creek Church in Chicago than with the traditional restoration heritage. In these ways, Churches of Christ were completing a journey they had begun in the early twentieth century — a journey from restorationist sect to evangelical denomination.

Conclusion

So finally we return to the church in Sweetwater, Texas, and to the cornerstone that so amazed Albert Outler. But we must recall that Outler also took note of the fact that a majority in that congregation wanted a new building without the old stone. To Outler, this was nothing less than "rejection of a tradition of rejecting 'tradition.'"[44] But it was more than that. It also symbolized the fact that this congregation — along with Churches of Christ at large — was slowly turning its back on its restoration heritage. While the cornerstone took its place in a museum in Fort Worth, Texas, many Churches of Christ began to undertake the long and arduous process of discerning who they were and what they were becoming.

While the trajectory of this narrative seems relatively clear, the full meaning of these developments remains veiled to some degree. Does this story corroborate the descriptive accuracy of the two-party model of American Protestantism, or does it merely demonstrate the self-fulfilling potential of two-party rhetoric? Do evangelicalized members of the Churches of Christ still view themselves as restorationists, or do they see themselves as members of one of only two distinct Protestant options

---

43. For an assessment of the therapeutic gospel in contemporary Protestantism, see Marsha G. Witten, *All Is Forgiven: The Secular Message in American Protestantism* (Princeton: Princeton University Press, 1993).

44. Outler, "Church History by the Cube," 31.

available to them? Does the current movement of Churches of Christ toward evangelicalism represent a transitory liaison only, or is this a permanent affair? Has the restorationist vision, for all intents and purposes, been entirely extinguished within the Churches of Christ, or will it be revived in the future? With regard to all these questions, we can only wait and see.

CHAPTER 11

The Progressive Mennonite Denominational Center: Edmund G. Kaufman and Harold S. Bender

JAMES C. JUHNKE AND ALBERT N. KEIM

Throughout the nineteenth and early twentieth centuries Mennonites were able to maintain a distinctive religious identity from the larger American religious world because of their commitment to pacifism, because of the ethnicity that held them together, and because of their general sectarian tendencies. In the decades after World War I, however, Mennonites slowly became more attuned to American culture, including American religion. One specific effect of this acculturation was that the two-party paradigm of American Protestantism, which emerged from the modernist-fundamentalist struggles of the early years of the century, made some inroads into the Mennonite community. But while two-party ways of thinking did have some impact on the American Mennonite community, this paradigm was never allowed to take deep root. For one thing, the aforementioned factors that had previously protected Mennonites from assimilation in mainstream American culture were still operative in some measure. More to the point of this essay, during these years American Mennonitism was also graced with a number of visionary leaders who helped keep this community outside or beyond the limited world of two-party rhetoric and thinking.

Two of the most important Mennonite leaders of the middle years of the twentieth century were Edmund G. Kaufman (1891-1980) and Harold S. Bender (1897-1962). Kaufman, an educator in the General Conference Mennonite Church (GCMC), was president of Bethel College (North Newton, KS) from 1932 to 1952. In his relatively decentralized church this was an excellent position from which to influence denominational developments. Edmund Kaufman came to his centrist Mennonite vision by way of a missionary term in China and studies in sociology and practical theology at the University of Chicago. Kaufman's practical, ministry-oriented disposition allowed him to move freely among the diverse membership of his church.

Bender, who became the strongest leader in the "Old" Mennonite Church (MC), was dean of Goshen College, Indiana, from 1931 to 1944, and dean of Goshen College Biblical Seminary from 1944 to 1962. Bender, who had originally planned to become a biblical scholar (completing a B.D. at Garrett Biblical Institute in 1922 and a Th.M. at Princeton Theological Seminary in 1923), later turned to church history as a less "dangerous" and more fruitful source of denominational renewal. Bender's essay "The Anabaptist Vision," first delivered as the presidential address to the American Society of Church History in 1944, became a defining document for renewal of Anabaptist/Mennonite identity in all Mennonite branches, including Kaufman's General Conference Mennonites. In his denomination, which was more centrally controlled than Kaufman's GCMC, Bender held a wide range of church offices that allowed him both to articulate a vision and to implement that vision in actual church policy.

Kaufman and Bender were committed to Mennonite denominational renewal and were convinced that the church's Anabaptist heritage needed to supply the foundation on which to build. Within their respective branches of the Mennonite community, these two men developed new and largely complementary visions of what it meant to be Mennonite. Their ideas and ideals helped prevent Mennonites from becoming hostage to either side of an allegedly divided American Protestantism. In the work of these two leaders, Mennonites discovered a normative religious stance which allowed them to bypass the critical and disruptive points of dispute over which modernists and fundamentalists had contended.

Edmund G. Kaufman and the General Conference Mennonite Church

Following in the steps of his teacher, Cornelius H. Wedel, who had served as president of Bethel College from 1893 to 1910, Edmund Kaufman embodied a Russian Mennonite tradition of "cultural engagement" with the world — a tradition quite different from the common Niebuhrian stereotype of "Christ against Culture" Anabaptism.[1] Although he was at times accused of being liberal or modernist, Kaufman considered himself to be part of a constructive, progressive, denominational mainstream. His liberal/progressive inclinations were moderated by his personal piety and by his accommodations to traditionalist elements in the Mennonite denomination.[2] Kaufman saw himself as a progressive educator who was attempting to lead his people toward wider church ministries of education, mission, and service in the world.[3]

In 1925, when Ed Kaufman returned from his missionary term in China, church membership in the General Conference Mennonite Church (GCMC) totaled about 21,500. About one third of the members were located in Kansas, products of a migration from eastern Europe to the American frontier in the 1870s. Most General Conference Mennonites were bilingual, speaking both the German of their parents and the English of America. But their rapid adaptation to the American social scene received a major jolt during World War I. Their wartime isolation as Christian pacifists reminded them of their heritage of separation from the world. They learned that as long as the nations of the world made war and conscripted men and money to fight, nonresistant Mennonites would be a people set apart from the world. At the same time, the First World War taught them the urgency of finding alternative ways to certify their claim to citizenship, to demonstrate that they were worthy contributing members of the wider national community, even if they refused military service.

Three distinct poles of Mennonite practice and opinion emerged among General Conference Mennonites as they responded to American society in the years after World War I. One pole, the *traditionalist* option, held to the German language and to the durable virtues of life in the local congregation. They tended to be non-revivalist, opposed to an educated ministry, and unconvinced of the need for aggressive new denominational

---

1. See H. Richard Niebuhr, *Christ and Culture* (New York: Harper and Row, 1951).

2. On the history of the General Conference Mennonite Church see Samuel Floyd Pannabecker, *Open Doors: A History of the General Conference Mennonite Church* (Newton, KS: Faith and Life Press, 1975); Edmund G. Kaufman, compiler, *General Conference Mennonite Pioneers* (North Newton, KS: Bethel College, 1973); Henry Poettker, "General Conference Mennonite Church," *The Mennonite Encyclopedia*, vol. 5 (Scottdale, PA: Herald Press, 1990), 329-32; and Rodney J. Sawatsky, *Authority and Identity: The Dynamics of the General Conference Church* (North Newton, KS: Bethel College, 1987).

3. See James C. Juhnke, *Creative Crusade: Edmund G. Kaufman and the Mennonite Community* (North Newton, KS: Bethel College, C. H. Wedel Series, 1995).

institutions and ministries. Among their favored virtues were humility, silence, diligence, integrity, and passive resistance to change. They depended upon traditional folkways for stability. They were not articulate about their views, and they gradually lost influence in the face of the new denominational activism.

Another GCMC pole was that of the *conservative evangelicals*, who were influenced by American revivalism, the Bible school movement, and fundamentalism. They emphasized evangelism, personal conversion, prescriptive creeds, the literal authority of Scripture, and opposition to modernism and to the social changes that alleged modernists seemed to endorse. Conservative evangelicals remained a minority among General Conference Mennonites, but they gradually gained numbers and confidence from World War I through the 1950s. Although they claimed to defend traditional values, they in fact eagerly borrowed new ideas and practices from the fundamentalist wing of American Protestantism. Among the chief representatives of this viewpoint were Peter Boehr and Cornelius Suckau, overseas missionaries, and William Gottshall, longtime president of the General Conference Home Mission Board. General Conference anti-modernists often took their cues from John Horsch, an outspoken "Old" Mennonite fundamentalist author and editor at Scottdale, Pennsylvania. In 1943 the Mennonite conservative evangelicals founded Grace Bible Institute in Omaha, Nebraska.

The third General Conference Mennonite pole was the *progressive* option, represented in institutional form by Bethel College. J. W. Kliewer, who was president of Bethel from 1911-20 and 1925-32, recruited a corps of "progressive insurgent" teachers educated at major American universities. These teachers, who had an enormous impact on the young Edmund G. Kaufman when he was a student at Bethel, promoted a socially relevant gospel, educated church leadership, ecumenical association, and openness to the new ideas. World War I perplexed these progressives, as they wanted both to embrace Mennonite nonresistance and Woodrow Wilson's democratic war aims. The war also empowered traditionalists and conservative evangelicals, who charged that modernism (in the form of these perplexed progressives) had infected Bethel College. In 1919 the Bethel board of directors conducted an investigation and purge of progressive faculty members, charging them with being unorthodox in doctrine and/or uncooperative in spirit. Kaufman, who was engaged in mission work in China at the time of the purge, was quite unhappy with the removal of teachers who had taught "a real constructive Christian view of life." He even complained to the chair of the college board, pointing out that Bethel should not forget "that we are living in the twentieth century." And yet, Bethel remained persistently progressive in the Mennonite context, even as its liberal impulses were reined in by the 1919 purge, by a conservative evangelical attempt in 1932 to create an alternative Bible school in Newton, and by the founding of Grace Bible Institute in Omaha in 1943.

Interestingly, while Bethel remained progressive, it never stopped bidding for the hearts and minds of Mennonite traditionalists and conservative evangelicals. This is telling. A prerequisite for success in denominational leadership in the General Conference Mennonite Church was to maintain contact with and the confidence of all three groups in the church (with the traditionalists being of particular importance). For example, P. H. Richert, secretary of the Foreign Mission Board and president of the Bethel Board of Directors, occupied a middle ground among traditionalists, conservative evangelicals, and progressives. He attempted, with substantial success, to keep lines of communication open among all three groups.[4] There was indeed a large middle ground, for most General Conference Mennonites were located somewhere between the three poles. Mennonite leaders maintained a commitment to their shared peoplehood. Being "Mennonite" was more important to them than labels from the American Protestant scene, such as "liberal," "conservative," "modernist," or "fundamentalist." All believed in the teaching and practice of Christian nonresistance. All had been influenced by the Pietist movement. In terms of social organization, the founding and development of *denominational* structures and projects for cooperation in missions, education, and publication was a primary means of expanding this middle ground of Mennonite/Anabaptist identity. Mennonites could be unified by common work even when they differed theologically.[5]

Edmund G. Kaufman, who presided at Bethel for two decades, well understood the interpersonal, relational nature of GCMC leadership and the importance of maintaining close contact with all three groups among the Mennonites. Kaufman's favorite image of leadership was that of a horse pulling a cart. He was the horse and the Mennonite people, including the traditionalists and the evangelicals, were the cart. The horse, Kaufman said, dared not get out too far in front, lest he get detached from

4. James C. Juhnke, *A People of Mission: A History of General Conference Mennonite Overseas Missions* (Newton, KS: Faith and Life Press, 1979), 91-94.

5. James C. Juhnke, *Vision, Doctrine, War: Mennonite Identity and Organization in America, 1890-1930* (Scottdale, PA: Herald Press, 1989), 27-31, passim.

those he was obligated to carry along. Four components of Kaufman's spiritual and intellectual character shaped the ways in which he kept in touch with his people while also being out in front of them.

Kaufman's Mennonite Vision

Ed Kaufman's personal piety was a product of spiritual formation in a Swiss-Volhynian immigrant group which bore the influences of Anabaptism, Mennonitism, Pietism, and the Amish movement. The pastors of his rural congregation (Hoffnungsfeld-Eden) at the time of immigration in 1874, Jacob Stucky and Jacob D. Goering, preached an Anabaptist gospel of suffering, discipleship, and peace, as well as a Pietist gospel of personal regeneration. In Kaufman's childhood home, the family gathered for devotions both mornings and evenings, and they knelt for prayer facing the backs of the chairs. Throughout his life Kaufman had a profound sense of the presence of God, as well as an immediate sense of living in the presence of his ancestors. But despite this deep sense of personal piety, Kaufman's family and his congregation resisted the lure of American revivalism. When Kaufman was baptized in 1909, the ritual included no references to individual conversion experiences. Christian faith expressed in daily living was more important than testifying to a crisis conversion.

Cornelius H. Wedel, president of Bethel College from 1893 until his death in 1910, was perhaps the clearest articulator of a theological rationale for this kind of non-revivalist, Kansas-style Mennonite piety. Wedel — along with other colleagues like P. H. Richert — stood squarely in the center of the tripolar General Conference Mennonite system.[6] Ed Kaufman, who had already been nurtured into this form of ecumenical Anabaptism in his home congregation, had those tendencies confirmed when he studied at Bethel Academy and College during Wedel's tenure as president. Later, during his own years as president of Bethel, Ed Kaufman would maintain and expand Wedel's general approach to Mennonite faith. Through the course he taught on "Basic Christian Convictions," which was required of all seniors, Kaufman made sure that all Bethel graduates would have been exposed to his vision of what it meant to be Mennonite. After retirement, Kaufman repackaged the contents of this course into

---

6. James C. Juhnke, *Dialogue with a Heritage: Cornelius H. Wedel and the Beginnings of Bethel College* (North Newton, KS: Bethel College, 1987).

book form so that the whole church would have access to his understanding of Mennonite faith.[7]

Of course, all three poles of the General Conference Mennonite Church — traditionalist, progressive, and evangelical — believed that theirs was the best way to be true to the historic tradition and to retain Mennonite identity. Kaufman was quite sympathetic with the traditionalists' understanding of Mennonitism, but he feared that the conservative evangelicals' view of Scripture would cut the nerve of Anabaptist-Mennonite identity. The Bible Institute theory of "literal verbally 'dictated' inspiration" put the Old Testament and the New Testament on the same level. As Kaufman understood it, this was a devastating departure from the historic Mennonite tradition which valued the New Testament more highly than the Old, and which saw Jesus as Savior and Lord, *including Lord of the Scriptures.*[8]

Kaufman was deeply committed to the Mennonite community and church. "God has preserved the Mennonites for over 400 years," he wrote in 1933. "They have been kept a small group but they have been kept for a purpose."[9] That purpose had to do with the building of community and with the witness of peace. The primary mission of Bethel College within that context was to provide well-prepared and liberally educated leaders for Mennonite communities and for the mission of the church. Kaufman did everything he could as college president and denominational leader to strengthen his church's sense of Mennonite identity. Among other things, he led in the establishment of a Mennonite museum, library and archives, and quarterly journal *(Mennonite Life)*. What is more, in all of this he never lost touch with his own Hoffnungsfeld-Eden congregation. Being Mennonite was not merely a historical or theological construct; it was being part of a living community.

Kaufman as Devout Progressivist

Kaufman's primary academic interest, especially in the first half of his career, was in sociology. His master's thesis in 1917 at Witmarsum Semi-

---

7. Edmund G. Kaufman, *Basic Christian Convictions* (North Newton, KS: Bethel College, 1972).

8. *Centennial Study Conference . . . June 20-23, 1960.* Conference proceedings, no title page, pp. D24-D26.

9. Edmund G. Kaufman, "The Training of the Mennonite Ministry," *Bethel College Monthly* (November 15, 1933): 7-8.

nary in Bluffton, Ohio, consisted of a social description of Kansas Mennonite communities.[10] His Ph.D. thesis in 1928 at the University of Chicago, published three years later by the General Conference Foreign Mission Board, was a broader study of Mennonite denominational missions and benevolence, *The Development of the Missionary and Philanthropic Interest among the Mennonites of North America.*[11] The central theoretical idea of the dissertation was the concept of the "sect cycle," which Kaufman encountered in a course under Robert E. Park. Park was a primary figure in the emerging discipline of sociology and co-author of the leading textbook in the field, *Introduction to the Science of Sociology* (1921). Kaufman was convinced that social groups undergo a natural history of evolutionary change which can be objectively described and chronicled. As different sectarian Mennonite groups emerged from social isolation into closer contact with the outside world, they created a marvelous array of missionary and benevolent agencies. Kaufman showed how this process had taken place among different Mennonite groups at different times, depending upon their location in the sect cycle process.

In 1931 Kaufman accepted a position as professor of sociology at Bethel College. He continued to teach sociology classes, and to use a sociological approach in other classes he taught, even after becoming the college president. At Bethel and elsewhere he promoted sociology incessantly. In Kaufman's mind the discipline of sociology was closely associated with the social gospel, and with the union of academic and moral forces needed to renew the church. In 1936 Kaufman wrote to Goshen College criticizing the *Mennonite Quarterly Review* for dwelling so much on history and for ignoring the "dynamic social forces" of the present and future. In response, H. S. Bender implied that he would like more sociology but that history was safer, for leaders dare not "get away too far from followers."[12] Kaufman obviously would have agreed with Bender's overall goal, but undoubtedly he thought history was not the only means to that end.

At the University of Chicago Kaufman had also imbibed a progres-

10. Edmund George Kaufman, "Social Problems and Opportunities of the Western District Conference Communities of the General Conference of Mennonites of North America," M.A. Thesis, Witmarsum Seminary, 1917.

11. Edmund G. Kaufman, *The Development of the Missionary and Philanthropic Interest among the Mennonites of North America* (Berne, IN: General Conference of the Mennonite Church of North America, 1931).

12. Edmund G. Kaufman to Edward Yoder, February 8, 1936. Archives of the Mennonite Church, H. S. Bender Collection, box 8, folder 10.

sive view of pedagogy. His teacher of religious education, William Clayton Bower, taught that creative personal and social experiences should be the means of initiating young people "into the ideals, objectives, and methods of the Kingdom of God as these emerge from the past."[13] Kaufman was greatly impressed with the "Agenda Method" which Bower used to involve students in planning curricular goals and carrying them out. Kaufman became a master classroom teacher himself and was acclaimed for his ability to draw out the students' own questions and probings, rather than merely imposing traditional answers on them. He rejected the idea of education as indoctrination, instead promoting an understanding of education which emphasized the development of Christian character through creative experience.

Kaufman's opponents among General Conference Mennonites branded him a "modernist" for having attended the University of Chicago, but they found it essentially impossible to catch him actually espousing unorthodox doctrine. In fact, when he spoke in churches Kaufman freely used evangelical-sounding language. At a 1933 GCMC session on the training of ministers, for example, Kaufman said that a minister "must have been born again as a child of God and have accepted Christ as his personal Savior," that a minister must have "a definite call from God to the particular work," and that "he must have an ever-growing vital and increasingly rich Christian experience himself."[14] Leaders of the conservative-evangelical camp were quite convinced that Kaufman was being duplicitous when he spoke this way. One such critic expressed amazement and anger over a sermon in which Kaufman preached "with tears streaming down his face even though," as the critic put it, "he didn't believe a word he was saying."[15] How could a graduate of the University of Chicago, a resister of creeds, and a teacher and defender of the liberal arts, honestly exhibit such Christian piety? Part of the answer here is surely the fact that Kaufman never did become a speculative philosopher-theologian. His degree and all his most important interests were in matters of "practical theology."

The GCMC was, during Kaufman's lifetime, the most persistently noncreedal group among American Mennonites. Until the mid-twentieth century, its only official statement of faith was a minimal one-paragraph

---

13. William Clayton Bower, *The Curriculum of Religious Education* (New York: Scribner's Sons, 1925), 219.

14. Edmund G. Kaufman, "The Training of the Mennonite Ministry," *Bethel College Monthly* (November 15, 1933): 7-9.

15. Interview with Robert Schmidt reporting on response by John C. Kaufman to a sermon which Ed. G. Kaufman preached in the Emmaus Mennonite Church.

"Common Confession" which prefaced the GCMC constitution. Between the first and second world wars, however, the GCMC experienced a growing demand for an official church statement of faith. Kaufman resisted efforts toward "creedalism," in part because the proposed statements contained fundamentalist code language which he saw as partisan and as theologically flawed. In January 1940 the General Conference Ministerial Leadership Office sent an "Information Blank" to all ordained pastors and missionaries, asking them to sign their agreement to a set of doctrinal questions, including: "Do you believe the Scriptures of the Old and the New Testament to be the inspired Word of God, the only infallible rule of faith and practice?" and "Do you believe in the Scriptural Atonement, 'The propitiation through faith in his blood'?" Kaufman signed the document, even though he never used the words "infallible" or "propitiation" to state his own theology of biblical inspiration or atonement.[16]

At the General Conference meeting in August 1941 at Souderton, Pennsylvania, Kaufman participated in the drafting, amending, and passing of a nine-point "statement of faith" to serve its seminary board. Although he disliked the fundamentalistic parts of the statement, he asked the Bethel College Board of Directors to adopt it for Bethel, in order to squelch rumors among the constituency that the college was theologically unorthodox.[17] During Kaufman's presidency (1932-52) the Bethel College Board required that all new faculty members sign this statement of faith, but Kaufman let them know that the statement could be interpreted very broadly. At the same time, Kaufman made clear in faculty recruitment that Bethel College did not have room for secular humanists. To one prospective faculty member with whom he had an extended correspondence, Kaufman wrote, "As I understand Progressive Education with a child-centered emphasis, it is purely humanistic and is on the decline. What we need is something God-centered, even for the child. Deweyism and child-centeredness leads straight to pure secularism." Kaufman said that humanism was good as an "approach," but, nevertheless, "man is not the end in himself; God is the end, even of man."[18] This critique of progressive education, written in 1940, suggested that Kaufman set some conservative limits on what he had learned at the University of Chicago.

16. Uncatalogued folder from General Conference Ministerial Leadership Office, 1940.

17. Minutes of the Bethel College Board of Directors, November 19, 1942.

18. Edmund G. Kaufman to D. D. Eitzen, February 7, 1940. Bethel Files, 1g Kaufman administration, box 46, folder 67.

Kaufman's influence in the General Conference Mennonite Church was primarily as an administrator and a teacher, not as a writer of books or as a formulator of doctrine. But in this work he consistently tried to show that the Mennonite position was something different from either fundamentalism or modernism.[19] In the final chapter of *Basic Christian Convictions*, Kaufman wrote, "Salvation means a certain way of life." Discipleship was costly, involving self-renunciation in life choices, including career and education. Growth in the Christian life *required* prayer, Bible study, and active church membership. The conclusion of Kaufman's book reflected the strongly pietistic flavor of his community's tradition. On the tripolar General Conference Mennonite map, he was located toward the progressive pole, but he had not departed from the Mennonite mainstream. In his person and his work, Kaufman provided a model of Anabaptist living that would help hold together and revitalize the center of denominational developments in the General Conference Mennonite Church.

The "Old" Mennonite Church's Flirtation with Fundamentalism

The "Old" Mennonite Church was created in 1898 as a formal connecting body for "Old," mostly Swiss, Mennonites who had come to the United States beginning in the early eighteenth century. The "Old" Mennonite Church was structured around a biannual meeting of delegates from a dozen or more regional or district conferences. It was separate from the General Conference Mennonite Church (GCMC), Edmund Kaufman's group, which had been organized in 1860 and had brought together a range of "New" Mennonites (i.e., recent immigrants), many of whom came from southern Russia. In the early 1890s the "Old" Mennonites initiated a two-decades-long institution building process which transformed their relatively loose association of churches into a fully formed denomination.[20]

By the 1920s, the Mennonite Board of Missions and Charities over-

---

19. Melvin Gingerich, "On My Desk," *Mennonite Weekly Review* (March 1974).

20. On the respective organization of the General Conference Mennonite Church and the (Old) Mennonite General Conference, see Theron F. Schlabach, *Peace, Faith, Nation: Mennonites and Amish in Nineteenth-Century America* (Scottdale, PA: Herald Press, 1988), 127-40; and Juhnke, *Vision*, 106-20.

saw several dozen missionaries, a host of city missions, several orphanages and old people's homes, and a hospital and nursing school. A Board of Education managed two colleges, Hesston in Kansas and Goshen in Indiana; a Publication Board operated the Mennonite Publishing House in Scottdale, Pennsylvania; and a number of other official committees, including the Peace Problems Committee and the Historical Committee, managed other aspects of the denomination's activities. Mennonites had never had such an extensive organizational structure, and it was largely borrowed from the broader Protestant context.

The architects of this organizational revolution, all ordained men with very limited educations, were responding to larger social changes which were beginning to affect all of the nation's rural communities. Robert Wiebe has described the general situation in his book *Search for Order* (1967), noting that the "island communities" so central to late nineteenth-century America were, by the 1920s, under acute attack from larger cultural and national forces that tended to subvert local ways of life. Mennonite institution building was in large degree a response to this broad pattern of social change. In *American Mennonites and Protestant Movements* (1987), Beulah Hostetler describes this Mennonite response as "defensive structuring," that is, an effort by the ordained leadership of the Mennonite Church to preserve their religious and cultural identity, which now seemed threatened from the outside.[21]

This institutional "defensive structuring," ironically built around numerous newer notions about how communities and institutions should organize themselves, was accompanied by an equally ironic infusion of new theological ideas coming largely from evangelical and/or fundamentalist sources outside the Mennonite world. This was perhaps most evident in the promotion of a new kind of doctrinal orthodoxy which structured doctrine into concise propositional form, separated the doctrine of salvation from ethics, and introduced the ideas of premillennial eschatology into the church.[22] The book which most clearly articulated this new doctrinal stance was the 1914 volume *Bible Doctrine,* edited by Daniel Kauffman. Kauffman (no relation to Edmund Kaufman) was one of the emerging leaders of the Mennonite organizational revolution. In 1914 he became the editor of the new Mennonite paper, the *Gospel Herald.* From this bully

---

21. Robert Wiebe, *The Search for Order, 1877-1920* (New York: Hill and Wang, 1967); Beulah Hostetler, *American Mennonites and Protestant Movements: A Community Paradigm* (Scottdale, PA: Herald Press, 1987).

22. Juhnke, *Vision,* 114.

pulpit Kauffman broadcast his views throughout the "Old" Mennonite Church.

Daniel Kauffman's vision of Mennonite faith and life would become the controlling "Old" Mennonite orthodoxy through World War II. The centerpiece was the "Plan of Salvation," borrowed almost whole cloth from American evangelicalism. Kauffman also identified seven "Ordinances": baptism, communion, footwashing, prayer–head covering for women, the holy kiss, anointing with oil, and marriage. These ordinances were more distinctively Mennonite, but they were now relegated to the function of defining the boundaries between Mennonites and other Christians. Finally, Kauffman highlighted a series of "Restrictions," which were rules to help Christians remain "nonconformed" to the world in general; these restrictions included nonresistance, nonswearing of oaths, regulation dress for men and women, and the avoidance of politics, modern amusements, alcohol, and membership in secret societies.

The greatest novelty in this new theology was that, unlike the traditional Mennonite view of salvation, which was bound up with life in the community, Kauffman now made the link between salvation and ethics sequential. "First came salvation and then came obedience." The "Old" Mennonite Church had perhaps not fully adopted an evangelical/fundamentalist version of Christian faith, but the basic framework of the church's theology had been recast in an evangelical mold.[23]

In 1921 the "Old" Mennonite Church enshrined the basic content of Kauffman's *Bible Doctrine* within a new official credo of the denomination. It was the first confession of faith written by Mennonites since the Dortrecht Confession of 1632, three hundred years earlier. Article I captured the spirit and style of the new confession: "We believe in the plenary and verbal inspiration of the Bible as the Word of God; that it is authentic in its matter, authoritative in its counsels, inerrant in the original writings, and the only infallible rule of faith and practice." Twenty-six articles followed.[24] Conspicuously missing in the changes coming out of this "defensive structuring" was any effort to invoke Mennonite history as a bearer of Mennonite identity. This was an odd gap for a church supposedly intent on holding to its distinctive past in an age of change.

23. Juhnke, *Vision*, 116.
24. John Christian Wenger, *The Doctrines of the Mennonites* (Scottdale, PA: Mennonite Publishing House, 1950), 86-89.

Bender's Resuscitation of Anabaptist History and Identity

In the 1930s and 1940s Harold Bender became the key agent for a new reconstruction of Mennonite identity, a historical reconstruction quite different from Daniel Kauffman's doctrinal approach. In 1927, while busy teaching history and sociology at Goshen College, Bender published a series of seven articles in the *Gospel Herald* entitled "What Can the Church Do for Her Historical Work?" According to Bender, the Mennonite Church should begin to write its own history: "For hundreds of years the whole of the civilized world with few exceptions thought of the Anabaptists and Mennonites as a fanatical sect of extremists, who had at various times in the past been guilty of rebellion and uprising . . . who had a totally perverted view of Christianity. . . . Mennonites are today known chiefly by the eccentricities of some of the minor groups, and are thought of as people with oddities instead of principles. The Mennonite name ought to stand the world over for certain definite ideals and principles just as the Quaker name does."[25]

A year earlier Bender had written a scathing article in the *Gospel Herald* in which he criticized the church for its lack of concern for history. "The number of books written on Mennonite history by Mennonites is so small as to be ridiculous," he wrote. It is incredible that a "denomination of over 40,000 adult members with a glorious history of over 400 years, with an average wealth above the normal, does practically nothing to further its history. . . . The church has never seriously faced the problem of properly studying and writing her history."[26] He recounted how the official Historical Committee had ignored directives to get work on Mennonite history under way. His language was so strong that the editor, David Kauffman, who was a member of the Historical Committee, sent the article back to Bender, telling him to tone it down. Bender refused, and Kauffman reluctantly printed the article. At a time when public criticism of church organizations or leaders was unheard of, Bender had gotten away with a lot. He had also established a solid rationale for the historical work through which he would seek to reconstruct Mennonite identity.

In 1931, Bender was elected Dean of Goshen College. For a while his historical activities had to be placed on the back burner, as he was im-

25. Harold S. Bender, "What Can the Church Do for Her Historical Work?" *Gospel Herald* (April 21, 1927): 58; (April 28, 1927): 90-91; (May 5, 1927): 107.

26. Harold S. Bender, "The Need for the Support of Study in Mennonite History," *Gospel Herald* (March 18, 1926): 1050-51.

mersed in a desperate struggle to save the college from the ruin wreaked by the Great Depression. But during these years he also edited the *Mennonite Quarterly Review* and completed his Th.D. degree at Heidelberg University. In addition, he established the Mennonite Historical Library at Goshen, which, by 1940, was the best repository of Anabaptist and Mennonite source materials in the world.

On the strength of his scholarship, Bender was elected President of the American Society of Church History. In December 1943 he delivered the society's annual Presidential Address, which he entitled "The Anabaptist Vision." In this academic address Bender laid out his view of the Anabaptist past and future. "Anabaptism is the culmination of the Reformation," he argued, "the fulfillment of the original vision of Luther and Zwingli . . . [the Anabaptists] enlarged it, gave it body and form, and set out to achieve it in actual experience." Anabaptists were thus not the violent heretics portrayed in conventional Reformation histories, but, actually, respectable, peaceful, and thoroughgoing reformers.[27]

According to Bender, Anabaptists embraced three essential concepts which set them apart from the remainder of the Reformation. First came discipleship, "a concept which meant the transformation of the entire way of life of the individual believer and of society." The second key Anabaptist concept was the idea of the church as a group of voluntary members based on adult baptism and committed to holy living. Third, true Anabaptists practiced the ethic of love and nonresistance in "all human relationships," which included a refusal to participate in war. Underlying all of this was the conviction that Jesus intended that the kingdom of God be built in the here and now, that is, the Sermon on the Mount was meant to be put into practice.

In good part Bender wrote this essay in response to the troubles and turmoil within the "Old" Mennonite Church that were brought about by the contradictory experience of Mennonites in the World War II years. On the one hand, Mennonite leaders were surprised and worried by the fact that nearly half of all drafted Mennonite young men chose to go into the military, in the process rejecting what many considered to be a crucial Mennonite distinctive. On the other hand, a group of younger Mennonite leaders helped organize the Civilian Public Service for 6,000 conscientious objectors. This immense project required not only massive fund-raising but also the creation of complex management systems which interfaced

27. Harold S. Bender, "The Anabaptist Vision," *Church History* 13 (March 1944): 3-24.

with government and with other peace churches, i.e., the Church of the Brethren and the Quakers. Individuals involved in this operation soon began to chafe at the rigid doctrinal formulations and isolation from other religious groups that marked the "defensive structuring" of the "Old" Mennonite Church as it had been engineered by Daniel Kauffman and his associates. These younger, more open-minded Mennonites needed a new definition of what made them Mennonite.

In response to these yearnings on the part of Mennonite leaders-to-be, and in response to the failure of Mennonites to maintain a consistent pacifist witness during World War II, Harold Bender turned to Anabaptist history, specifically to the sixteenth-century Swiss Brethren, to reestablish a theological baseline for a new Mennonite identity. "The Anabaptist Vision" essay can be understood as a synopsis or summing up of that baseline. By establishing the faith of the Swiss Brethren as normative for the twentieth century, Bender both consolidated Mennonite feelings of marginalization during the Second World War and opened up the Mennonite community to a new vision of service to society. This new vision was simultaneously more modern and more conservative than Daniel Kauffman's "Bible doctrine" model. It moved the Mennonite Church away from an alignment with American fundamentalism, and at the same time spawned a new ecumenical, but distinctly Anabaptist, sense of peoplehood among American Mennonites.

Embodying "the Anabaptist Vision" in "Old" Mennonite Faith and Practice

The new Anabaptist consensus, helped by the experience of the war and the massive American Mennonite relief work in Europe after the war, led "Old" Mennonites toward a new ecumenicity. Earlier they had kept aloof from allegedly "liberal" Mennonite events such as the Mennonite World Conference. In 1936, only two "Old" Mennonites, including Bender, had attended the fourth Mennonite World Conference in Amsterdam. Two decades later nearly all of Bender's generation of "Old" Mennonite institutional leaders attended the seventh Mennonite World Conference in Karlsruhe, Germany.

Bender's vision also led the Mennonite Church to redraft its doctrinal formulas. In 1963 the "Old" Mennonite Church adopted a new Confession of Faith that replaced the 1921 Fundamentals. There was no article on the Bible in this new statement, but there was one on "Divine Revelation." It read, "We believe that God has revealed Himself in the Scriptures of the Old and New Testaments, the inspired Word of God, and supremely in His Son, the Lord Jesus Christ."[28] The new consensus emerging in the "Old" Mennonite Church shifted the center of focus from a primary concern with inerrant Scripture to an emphasis on the Lordship of Christ. The indissoluble link between the Lordship of Christ and discipleship as the centerpiece of faith was driven home by Bender in 1950. "Christ is to be translated in the life-expression of the disciple, or in the words of the Apostle Paul, Christ is to be 'formed' in him, and He is to be Lord of all his life. This is the Anabaptist answer to Christ, and out of the understanding of the meaning of this answer derive all the major ideas of Anabaptism."[29]

Because of the stress on the Lordship of Christ the Mennonite understanding of the Bible shifted from the verbal, inerrant, plenary word of God, to "containing" the word of God. In 1959 Bender made the point succinctly in a major address at the General Conference entitled "Biblical Revelation and Inspiration." "We must speak of Jesus Christ, who is the center of Scripture and who is Himself, as no book can ever be, the supreme, final, and complete revelation of God to men. . . . In this sense the New Testament, in bringing Christ to us, contains God's Word."[30] This was a dramatic revision of the Mennonite view of the Bible. What was heresy twenty years before became enshrined in the new Confession of Faith in 1963. The change came not from a frontal assault on biblical inerrancy, but from the new understandings of discipleship rooted in a new Christology drawn from, or refracted through, the sixteenth century.

In the mid-1940s Bender became Dean of Goshen Biblical Seminary. It was an opportune time to begin the Seminary, as Civilian Public Service men and women were discharged from service. Soon a highly motivated, articulate, and experienced group of young men and women began studies in the new Seminary. Everyone took the several Anabaptist history and theology courses. In 1950 a new course entitled "Discipleship" was made a requirement for all undergraduate Bible majors and Seminary students. Steeped in this new Anabaptist vision, these students then headed off to graduate school, the mission field, or various pastorates, spreading

---

28. *Confession of Faith* (Scottdale, PA: Herald Press, 1963), 27.

29. Harold S. Bender, "The Anabaptist Theology of Discipleship," *Mennonite Quarterly Review* 24 (January 1950): 29.

30. Harold S. Bender, *Biblical Revelation and Inspiration* (Scottdale, PA: Mennonite Publishing House, 1959), 11-12.

Bender's ideas. Perhaps most strategic for the dissemination of Anabaptist ideas were the writers of the Herald Uniform Sunday school materials, the majority of whom were, by the 1950s, graduates of Goshen College and Seminary. The new historical theology was becoming part of Mennonite lay consciousness.

What smoothed the acceptance of the new theology was the enormous expansion of Mennonite relief and service activity during the late 1940s and the 1950s. Two thousand eight hundred and eighty-two persons served in Mennonite Central Committee relief work during that period, compared to 334 in the previous twenty-five years (1920-45). Soon nearly every Mennonite community in the country had members who had served abroad, usually for two or three years. The Mennonite Central Committee's sense of Mennonite identity, couched in the new language of discipleship, was made existentially real through sacrificial service. In effect, the new theological language of discipleship linked up synergistically with the real-life experiences of thousands of Mennonites, most of them young people, who returned to their communities with a life-changing service experience, and with a rich new theological language which explained and made sense of their experience. The effect was really quite dramatic. By the 1960s the Mennonite church had a generation of young people in possession of a new worldview rooted in experience and theology. For them Daniel Kauffman's old "defensive structuring" had become irrelevant.

Was Harold Bender's invoking of history merely another form of "defensive structuring"? Perhaps, but with a difference. Paul Toews once observed that Mennonites have basically responded to the inroads of the larger American culture in two ways: one, by shoring up the boundaries; two, by revitalizing the center.[31] The "defensive structuring" by "Old" Mennonites in the early part of the century was, for the most part, an effort to shore up the boundaries. Harold Bender's Anabaptist Vision was an effort to revitalize the center. And it succeeded.

By invoking the normative quality of Anabaptist history, Harold Bender and his students shifted "Old" Mennonite theology and polity from a proto-fundamentalist sectarianism to a new frame of reference rooted in sixteenth-century Anabaptist history. In the absence of such an alternative, "Old" Mennonites might quite naturally and easily have embraced resurgent post–World War II evangelicalism. Certainly many Men-

---

31. Paul Toews, "Dissolving the Boundaries and Strengthening the Centers," *Gospel Herald* (January 25, 1983): 49-52.

nonites were tempted. What diverted them was the availability of another way, the Anabaptist Vision, which not only allowed them to identify with a heroic past (in the midst of stressful social and cultural change), but gave them new, convincing theological categories which seemed appropriate to their new circumstances.

And in time, Bender's "Anabaptist Vision" also took hold among the General Conference Mennonite Church, the Mennonite Brethren branch of the denomination, and other Mennonite groups. In short, the "Anabaptist Vision" was a remarkable achievement which gave all Mennonites an opportunity to develop an alternative to the perceived polarization of American Protestantism into evangelical and liberal camps.

Conclusion

Edmund G. Kaufman and Harold S. Bender were progressive leaders in their respective branches of the American Mennonite community during the mid-twentieth century. Their work as institutional administrators, as teachers of theology, and as denominational visionaries drew upon the resources of their Anabaptist-Mennonite tradition and adapted them to fit a changing world. They were different, of course, from each other in important ways. Kaufman was a leader in the General Conference Mennonite Church, with its congregational polity and ethnic pluralism, while Bender's "Old" Mennonite Church was more culturally uniform and more episcopal in its polity. Kaufman's academic discipline was sociology, and he was interested in comparative religions and overseas missions, while Bender's primary discipline was church history. Despite these differences, the two shared a normative vision of Anabaptism which inspired Mennonite revitalization after World War II.

Although both Kaufman and Bender were "progressives" in the Mennonite context, it would be misleading to locate them at any point on a liberal-conservative or modernist-fundamentalist Protestant continuum. They belonged to multi-polar religious communities in which the forces of traditional doctrine and piety outweighed the theological influences of fundamentalist/modernist controversy. Kaufman and Bender were both more ecumenical in spirit than earlier Mennonite leaders. They attempted to create new middle ground among the forces of Mennonite tradition and piety while building up institutions for education, benevolence, and mission. They shifted the focus from boundary maintenance and defensive structuring to strategies for revitalizing the center of denominational life. In so doing, they also helped the American Mennonite community retain a distinct and constructive sense of identity that continues to exist well outside the confines of the two-party paradigm.

CHAPTER 12

Lutherans in the United States, 1930-1960: Searching for the "Center"

MARK GRANQUIST

Lutherans have long been underrepresented in American religious history. Much of this is due to the fact that Lutherans have been somewhat outside of or separate from the mainstream of American Protestantism. In part this is because Lutherans have distrusted the predominance of Reformed theology in American Protestantism, and thus have intentionally maintained a cautious distance. But there is also the matter of language: well into the twentieth century much of Lutheran religious and theological life in the United States was expressed in continental European languages. Finally, many regions of the country have been relatively unfamiliar with Lutheranism, as Lutherans have been strongly concentrated in the "Lutheran Bible Belt," a geographical area stretching from Pennsylvania through the Great Lakes states to the upper Midwest.[1]

To say that Lutherans have been somewhat outside the mainstream of American Protestantism is not to say that they have been completely isolated. In fact, they have been quite attentive to many of the larger issues facing Protestantism in the United States. But when Lutherans have become involved in such issues, it has been primarily from the standpoint of how such issues affected the internal affairs of their own denomination(s).

This essay is an examination of how one such issue in American Protestantism, namely, the fundamentalist/modernist controversy of the

---

1. The question of "Americanization" has long engaged and puzzled American Lutheran historians, especially the degree to which Lutherans in America adopted and adapted the essentially Reformed nature of American voluntary Protestantism.

first part of the twentieth century, influenced and affected American Lutheranism. The main question is: to what extent did this controversy determine the battles and mergers within American Lutheranism in these years? In addition, are the "two-party" models (fundamentalist/modernist or evangelical/mainline) adequate for understanding the history of American Lutheranism? The thesis of this paper is that the various versions of the "two-party" models do not fully explain the rather tortuous history of American Lutheranism in this century. American Lutherans are interested in, and in some ways are affected by, the fundamentalist/modernist controversies (and subsequent developments). But at their core, Lutheran battles and mergers were fought on the basis of confessional theology and polity, and the various parties to these Lutheran struggles cannot be divided along the "two-party" lines.

Lutheran Denomination Building, 1900-1960

Between 1900 and 1960, Lutherans in the United States experienced two major developments which affected them significantly: a process of mergers and affiliations which brought about an important consolidation of denominations, and the completion of a process of Americanization which brought them into the mainstream of American religious life. Many American Lutherans sought the union of all Lutheran groups, but this goal proved unattainable, and by 1962 Lutherans were consolidated into three major denominations.[2]

The first round of mergers within American Lutheranism (1917-30) brought many scattered Lutheran denominations together, so that by 1930 there were five major Lutheran groups, with six or seven additional smaller groups. Also during this period, inter-Lutheran cooperative groups developed, the most notable being the National Lutheran Council (1918-66) and the American Lutheran Conference (1930-54), which brought more unity and focus to American Lutheranism.[3] Both became

2. The most complete history of Lutheranism in America during this period is E. Clifford Nelson, *Lutheranism in North America 1914-1970* (Minneapolis: Augsburg Publishing House, 1972). See also E. Clifford Nelson, ed., *The Lutherans in North America* (Philadelphia: Fortress Press, 1975); and Abdel Ross Wentz, *A Basic History of Lutheranism in America*, rev. ed. (Philadelphia: Fortress Press, 1964).

3. For the National Lutheran Council, see Frederick K. Wentz, *Lutherans in Conference: The Story of the National Lutheran Council, 1918-1966* (Minneapolis: Augsburg Publishing House, 1968); and Osborne Hauge, *Lutherans Working Together: A History of*

loci for discussions on greater unity, and perhaps organic unity, among Lutherans.

The American Lutheran Conference in particular represented the "center" group of Lutheran denominations, which consisted mainly of Scandinavians and some Germans who emigrated to the United States in the nineteenth century. Beyond the American Lutheran Conference were two other major groups, or wings: first, the United Lutheran Church in America (ULCA), which was the most Americanized group and represented the heritage of eastern seaboard Lutheranism;[4] and second, the Lutheran Church-Missouri Synod, which was the most conservative and exclusively confessional portion of American Lutheranism.[5] Merger discussions within the centrist American Lutheran Conference often divided over the issue of including one or the other of these two wings in the discussions, and the shift in direction that this would entail. Missouri balked at any discussions which would include the ULCA, while others in the American Lutheran Conference objected to the possible exclusion of the ULCA merely to placate Missouri.[6] Eventually, by 1962 a second round of mergers resulted in three major American Lutheran denominations of roughly the same size, together representing 95 percent of American Lutherans.[7]

Of course this story, in all its detail, has been told well by denominational historians of American Lutheranism. What is less well studied, and of more general interest, is the relation of this process of Lutheran

---

the National Lutheran Council, 1918-1943 (New York: National Lutheran Council, 1943). For the American Lutheran Conference, see Fred W. Meuser, The Formation of the American Lutheran Church (Columbus, OH: Wartburg Press, 1958); and E. Clifford Nelson and Eugene Fevold, The Lutheran Church Among the Norwegian-Americans, 2 vols. (Minneapolis: Augsburg Publishing House, 1960), especially 2:287-308.

4. There is no contemporary history of the ULCA; see relevant sections in Nelson, Lutherans in North America, 373-77; and Wentz, A Basic History, 269-86.

5. On the Missouri Synod see Walter Baepler, A Century of Grace: A History of the Missouri Synod, 1847-1947 (St. Louis: Concordia Publishing House, 1947); and Carl S. Meyer, ed., Moving Frontiers: Readings in the History of the Lutheran Church–Missouri Synod (St. Louis: Concordia Publishing House, 1964).

6. So while the leaders of the American Lutheran Church (1930-60) and the Norwegians made overtures to Missouri, and snubbed ULCA, Augustana kept forcing the issue of ULCA back onto the American Lutheran Conference agenda.

7. The three denominations were the Lutheran Church–Missouri Synod, the Lutheran Church in America (LCA), and the American Lutheran Church (ALC, 1960-88). On the LCA see Johannes Knudsen, The Formation of the Lutheran Church in America (Philadelphia: Fortress Press, 1978); on the ALC see Charles P. Lutz, ed., Church Roots (Minneapolis: Augsburg Publishing House, 1985).

mergers to events occurring within the larger realm of American Protestantism, and the impact of the fundamentalist/modernist controversies on American Lutheranism. As Lutherans were seeking unity, and a truly "American" Lutheran voice, how were they using, and making sense of, arguments and events from the larger American Protestant scene?

The American Lutheran Conference

This essay will concentrate, then, on merger discussions within the American Lutheran Conference, the umbrella group representing the "center" of American Lutheran denominations, and how models and terminology from the fundamentalist/modernist controversy invaded and influenced the negotiations among American Lutherans over further steps toward Lutheran unity and union. The most important issues that divided Lutherans concerned the nature of confessional agreement necessary to fellowship, cooperation, and merger, and the nature of authority of Scripture. As American Lutheran theologians and church leaders began to discuss these issues in English, they were looking for formulations that would not only reflect their Lutheran heritage, but would also work given their American context.

To understand the dynamics of the Lutheran situation during this period, it is important to understand the groups involved (see Table 1). There were five "big players" in this situation: the United Lutheran Church in America (ULCA) on one end, and the Lutheran Church–Missouri Synod on the other; within the center three groups dominated: the Augustana Evangelical Lutheran Church (the Swedes),[8] the Evangelical Lutheran Church (the Norwegians),[9] and the American Lutheran Church (ALC, 1930-60).[10] The center groups were held together in a larger grouping called the American Lutheran Conference (ALConf), but it would be wrong to think that all the groups within the Conference were of one mind. Augustana, the Swedish Lutheran body, had strong historical ties to Eastern Lutheranism and the ULCA. The ALC, an English/German group, had equally strong ties to the Missouri Synod. The Evangelical Lutheran

---

8. On the Augustana Synod, see G. Everett Arden, *Augustana Heritage: The Story of the Augustana Lutheran Church* (Rock Island, IL: Augustana Press, 1963).

9. On the ELC see Nelson and Fevold, *Lutheranism among the Norwegian-Americans*.

10. On the "old" ALC (1930-60) see Fred W. Meuser, *The Formation of the American Lutheran Church* (Columbus, OH: Wartburg Press, 1958).

TABLE 1
Institutional Structures of American Lutherans, 1900-1960

United Lutheran Church in America (1918-62) — Eastern German Lutherans from colonial times; merged in 1918

American Lutheran Conference (cooperative body, 1930-54)	*Augustana Evangelical Lutheran Church* (1860-1962) — Swedish *Evangelical Lutheran Church* (1917-60) — Norwegian; merger of various Norwegian groups *United Evangelical Lutheran Church* (1896-1960) — Danish *Lutheran Free Church* (1897-1963) — Norwegian *American Lutheran Church* (1930-60) — German; merger of some midwestern German Lutheran groups

Lutheran Church–Missouri Synod (1847-) — German; conservative confessional midwestern Lutheran group

*Members of the National Lutheran Council (1918-66) — a cooperative body that included ULCA and churches of the American Lutheran Conference, but not Missouri.

Note: Denominational names change over time; each name given is the *last* given name of that particular group.

Church, a Norwegian Lutheran group, was formed in 1917 by the merger of three smaller groups. The Norwegians were often divided over their outside loyalties: some Norwegian groups looked strongly in the direction of the ALC and Missouri, while others were equally suspicious of such ties with Missouri. Thus, while the American Lutheran Conference was formed in 1930 as a vehicle for further cooperation and possible Lutheran union, the denominations that constituted the Conference were not united on the direction in which to proceed.[11]

The main question that convulsed the Conference was that of the direction and theological basis for the union of Lutheran denominations.[12] The Conference was determined not just to attempt to draw together its own members, but to serve as a vehicle for wider Lutheran union. The trouble was over the inclusion of Missouri and the ULCA in these wider

---

11. When addressing the 1940 convention of the American Lutheran Conference, the President of the Augustana Synod, P. O. Bersell, stated that the Conference suffered from the weakness "that our fellowship has been more exclusive than inclusive." Quoted in Nelson, *Lutheranism in North America*, 83.

12. These questions regarding the bases of unity and union have been some of the most important and influential questions in the history of Lutherans in America. For the various approaches to Lutheran unity, see John H. Tietjen, *Which Way to Lutheran Unity? A History of the Efforts to Unite the Lutherans of America* (St. Louis: Clayton Publishing House, 1975).

negotiations; while the ULCA was generally open to including Missouri in these talks, Missouri was not convinced of ULCA's "orthodoxy," and this made the inclusion of both ULCA and Missouri very difficult. The members of the Conference recognized this problem, but were divided over what to do about it. The ALC and the Norwegians sought to include Missouri by excluding the ULCA; Augustana held out for an inclusive framework that would encompass all groups (including ULCA), but the practical result of such a move would have been the self-exclusion of Missouri from such proceedings.

Discussions of closer affiliation and possible union began in a preliminary way in the 1920s and '30s, with the attempt to find a common theological ground between the groups. This resulted in the issuing of "theses" or "declarations" by various Lutheran groups attempting to spell out their understanding of the theological basis for such cooperation or union (see Table 2, p. 242). Negotiations led in 1940 to the formation of a common proposal called the Pittsburgh Declaration, which negotiators hoped would serve as the basis of union. The drafters of the declaration, however, made compromises that the denominations were not willing to accept, and the plan failed. During the 1940s a group of negotiators from the Conference and the ULCA, the so-called "Committee of 34," formulated a similar plan of union, but it too was defeated. Negotiations began to unite the five members of the Conference, but Augustana wanted to hold out for a wider union, and dropped out of the proceedings. The remaining Conference denominations set forth toward merger, and formed a new denomination called the American Lutheran Church (ALC, 1960-88) in 1960. Augustana and the ULCA, along with two other smaller groups not included in the Conference negotiations, held their own talks, which resulted in the formation of the Lutheran Church in America (LCA) in 1962. This meant that by 1962 there were three major Lutheran denominations in the United States (LCA, ALC, and Missouri).

Lutheran Confessionalism and the Two-Party Paradigm

Some have tried to force these Lutheran divisions into a modernist/fundamentalist or liberal/conservative scale, but such an attempt does not do justice to the situation.[13] The ULCA was not really modernist or liberal

---

13. For this conclusion, and the analysis of Lutheran divisions, see Nelson, *Lutheranism in North America*, 68-115.

as the terms are generally used,[14] and neither was the Missouri Synod fundamentalistic, at its core.[15] There were tendencies and sympathies in these directions by some within the respective church bodies, but such labels do not adequately define these groups. Rather, the scale of divisions between these various denominations involved the question of relations to, and understandings of, the Lutheran confessional documents of the sixteenth century (the Augsburg Confession of 1530 and the Book of Concord of 1580), and subsequent theological traditions of Lutheranism, especially the Lutheran Orthodox theologians of the seventeenth century. The debates focused on what it means to be a confessional Lutheran, and how this identity was to be formulated in the twentieth century. Concludes one scholar:

> Confessional Lutherans often did not agree with each other. . . . In America they continued the battle among themselves. There were numerous doctrinal disagreements and divergent ways of applying doctrine to practical situations.[16]

All of these American Lutheran groups officially held that, along with the Scriptures and the historic Creeds, the Lutheran Confessions were normative in the denominations and in any discussions of closer cooperation and merger. The question was how such documents were to be interpreted, and what degree of unanimity was to be required. There were really two types of Lutheran confessionalism at work in this situation and among these denominations.[17] The first was an exclusivistic Confession-

---

14. In his history of American modernism, William R. Hutchison concludes that "no branch of Lutheranism, eastern or midwestern produced any notable advocate of . . . theological liberalism" (115). Hutchison attributes this in part to "powerful confessional traditions. . . ." *The Modernist Impulse in American Protestantism* (Cambridge: Harvard University Press, 1976).

15. George Marsden suggests that the Missouri Synod, among other groups, adopted "some fundamentalist ideals while retaining other distinctive features of their European traditions." *Fundamentalism and American Culture: The Shaping of Twentieth Century Evangelicalism, 1870-1925* (New York: Oxford University Press, 1980), 195. A Missouri Synod author has suggested that "Fundamentalism and the Missouri Synod were not related closely enough for either one to exert major and lasting influence on the other." Milton L. Rudnick, *Fundamentalism and the Missouri Synod: A Historical Study of Their Interaction and Mutual Influence* (St. Louis: Concordia Publishing House, 1966), 115.

16. Tietjen, *Which Way to Lutheran Unity?*, 8.

17. For a detailed study of these two confessional traditions, sometimes labeled "Neo-Lutheranism" and "Old-Lutheranism," see Nelson, *Lutheranism in North America*, especially 70-87.

alism which predicated cooperation and union on absolute agreement on all theological issues; this approach, drawing from seventeenth-century Lutheran orthodoxy, characterized the Missouri Synod and the ALC (1930-60), along with sections of the Norwegians. The second was an ecumenical confessionalism which based cooperation and union on agreement in confessional basics, without further tests or negotiations; this approach drew heavily from certain irenic statements in the Augsburg Confession, as well as newer understandings of confessional authority (the "Erlangen School") within nineteenth-century German Lutheranism. This second approach exemplified the position of the ULCA, of the new leaders of the Augustana Synod, and of a minority among the Norwegians. The irony is that while all of these groups professed to be confessional Lutherans, they did not always trust the sincerity of each others' professions.

These confessional divisions stood behind the complicated negotiations over cooperation and union among American Lutherans in the twentieth century, with the central question being: What does it mean to be a Lutheran? Various groups at various times would issue "position papers." These declarations, theses, and statements would then themselves become the focus of further debate and negotiations (see Table 2, p. 242). The ecumenical approach characterized the ULCA's Washington Declaration of 1920 (and further documents), while the exclusivist position was embodied in the Chicago Theses of 1919, the Minneapolis Theses of 1925 (the basis of the American Lutheran Conference), and Missouri's "Brief Statement" of 1932. These documents represented long-standing theological debates within Lutheranism, and had roots in previous centuries.

The Doctrine of Scripture

But there were new features in this debate among American Lutherans in the twentieth century, and it is at this point that we see the contact with and influence from the wider sphere of American Protestantism. For suddenly, and without much warning, the question of the nature and authority of the Scriptures erupted within American Lutheranism.[18] Like many American Protestants, Lutherans tried to define and refine their notions of the author-

18. The question of biblical authority and inspiration were not really Lutheran questions in the nineteenth century. Nelson concludes: "In 1900 most Lutherans were proud of their church's solid front against the claims of critical study of the Bible." *Lutherans in North America*, 384.

TABLE 2
Inter-Lutheran Merger Documents (1900-1960)

Chicago Theses (1919)

To provide an "orthodox" basis for Lutheran union; represents the "center" of Lutheran confessionalism

Washington Declaration (1920)

ULCA counterproposal to Chicago Theses; stressed ecumenical character of confessional Lutheranism

Minneapolis Theses (1925)

Intended as middle way between ULCA and Missouri; basis for the formation of the American Lutheran Conference (1930-54)

Brief Statement (1932)

Missouri Synod statement on basis for unity

Savannah Declaration (1934)
Baltimore Declaration (1938)

ULCA statements on confessionalism and the question of Scripture

Sandusky Declaration (1938)

ALC statement directed to Missouri; restates "Chicago" and "Minneapolis"

Pittsburgh Agreement (1940)

Product of ALC/ULCA negotiations, but failed as means to unite these two groups

Plan(s) of the "Committee of 34" (1950)

Proposals to unite all eight members of the National Lutheran Council; defeated by member denominations

United Testimony (1952)

Statement of belief of four American Lutheran Conference bodies (Augustana having withdrawn); led to organic merger of these groups into the "new" American Lutheran Church (1960-88)

Note: Adapted from table "Documents of Lutheran Unity — 1919-1940," E. Clifford Nelson, *Lutheranism in North America, 1914-1970,* p. 71. Most of these documents can be found in a collection of Lutheran sources: Richard C. Wolf, *Documents of Lutheran Unity in America* (Philadelphia: Fortress Press, 1966)

ity of the Bible, and to state more carefully the ways in which the Bible was the inspired Word of God. Many American Lutherans, in their attempt to construct such a definition in English (rather than in the immigrant languages), used the terminology, derived from fundamentalism, of "verbal inspiration" and "inerrancy." For example, the Minneapolis Theses of 1925 stated that the Scriptures are "the divinely inspired, revealed, and inerrant Word of God . . . the only infallible authority in all matters of faith and life."[19] Other Lutherans thought this attempt was misguided and mistaken, in that it was attributing a type of authority to the Bible that Lutherans had never traditionally held. In 1930 one Lutheran theologian wrote:

> Lutheranism takes its own position. . . . it cannot follow fundamentalism in many of its contentions. The general attitude of fundamentalists is to exalt the Bible in a legal way. . . . There is a lack of the appreciation of the living Word of God within the Bible.[20]

It is in this point of disagreement that the history of American Lutheranism seems most closely to parallel the larger divisions within American Protestantism,[21] but there are certain uniquely Lutheran aspects to the American Lutheran debates.

Lutheran ideas about Scripture and the inspiration of the Bible are a particular tradition within Protestantism, distinctive and separate from the Reformed tradition which produced the fundamentalist/modernist debates over the question of scriptural authority. Lutheran theology, going back to Martin Luther himself, has traditionally held that the authority of the Scriptures rests in their identity as the Word of God, but that the Word of God is not limited to the Scriptures.[22] The Word of God is most properly Jesus Christ himself, and then secondarily the means by which the reality of Christ is presented to humanity. Thus the Bible is the Word of God in a christological sense, in that it witnesses to the Word, namely, Jesus Christ. But preaching, too, and other means of spreading the gospel can be con-

---

19. "Minneapolis Theses," in Wolf, *Documents of Lutheran Unity,* 340.

20. John A. W. Haas, "What Is Lutheranism?" in Vergilius Ferm, ed., *What Is Lutheranism? A Symposium in Interpretation* (New York: The Macmillan Company, 1930), 192.

21. Nelson states the issue this way: "The Modernist-Fundamentalist controversy of the mid-twenties forced the issue of biblical criticism. Was the choice that lay before Lutherans . . . limited to two alternatives, either to repristinate an orthodoxist view of Scripture . . . or to abandon the Lutheran confessions? Some concluded these were the only options, and as far as Scripture was concerned, they found it impossible to disassociate themselves from a fundamentalist viewpoint: the verbally-inspired inerrancy of the Bible." *Lutheranism in North America,* 83.

22. On Luther's understanding of Scripture, see Jaroslav Pelikan, *Luther the Expositor: Introduction to the Reformers' Exegetical Writings* (St. Louis: Concordia Publishing House, 1959); and Willem Kooiman, *Luther and the Bible* (Philadelphia: Muhlenberg Press, 1959).

sidered the Word of God, insofar as they "push" or communicate the reality of Jesus Christ.

Luther, being less systematic than Calvin or other reformers, created some ambiguity for Lutherans with his various ideas of the Word of God, and the authority of Scripture. He was strongly insistent that, taken as a whole, the Bible is the true and authoritative Word of God, yet he could be very critical of parts of the Bible. Luther doubted the canonicity of the Epistles of James and Jude,[23] and wished in print that the book of Esther had never been included in the Bible.[24] At times Luther even suggested that the gospel writers had at times made mistakes in their facts. The Lutheran Orthodox theologians who followed Luther in the late sixteenth and seventeenth cenuries went a great distance in "systematizing" the Lutheran doctrine of Scripture, but they did not remove all the inconsistencies.[25]

Thus it was that, when the question of the inspiration and authority of the Scriptures erupted within American Lutheranism in the twentieth century, there was more than one "Lutheran" position on the question. The main point of contention, as Lutherans moved into using English in their theology, was whether or not terms like "inerrancy" or "verbal inspiration" were the correct English equivalents of Lutheran positions on the question. Did Luther and the later Lutheran theologians teach, in emphasis or in fact, that the Bible is the "inerrant" or "verbally inspired" Word of God? Some Lutherans, most notably in the Missouri Synod and the ALC, suggested that such was the case.[26] Other Lutherans, mainly in the ULCA and some in Augustana, sought to concentrate on Luther's idea of the christological authority of the Scriptures, and saw that such an idea was not incompatible with the higher criticism of the biblical text.[27]

23. Martin Luther, "Preface to the Epistles of St. James and St. Jude" (1545).

24. Martin Luther, "Tabletalk" (1534) #3391a. See also "Bondage of the Will" (1525), *Luther's Works,* American edition, 33:110.

25. For the developments in Lutheran Orthodoxy, see Jaroslav Pelikan, *From Luther to Kierkegaard: A Study in the History of Theology* (St. Louis: Concordia Publishing House, 1950); and Robert D. Preus, "The Word of God in the Theology of Orthodoxy," *Concordia Theological Monthly* 33 (1962): 469-83.

26. For a detailed account of the discussions between the ALC and Missouri Synod on the one hand, and the ULCA on the other, over the question of the authority of Scripture, see E. Clifford Nelson, "A Case Study in Lutheran Unity Efforts: ULCA Conversations with Missouri and the ALC, 1936-40," in Herbert T. Neve and Benjamin Johnson, eds., *The Maturing of American Lutheranism* (Minneapolis: Augsburg Publishing House, 1968), 201-23.

27. On the new openness in Augustana toward criticism, and the repudiation of fundamentalist Biblicism, see Arden, *Augustana Heritage,* 284-97.

An additional reason for some Lutherans to adopt the language of biblical inerrancy or verbal inspiration came from their fear of higher biblical criticism, which had been moving into some American denominations and Divinity Schools. Many American Lutherans, especially in the American Lutheran Conference and the Missouri Synod, saw higher criticism as a direct threat to their traditional understanding of scriptural authority.[28] They also saw the initial tentative openings to higher criticism in the ULCA as a rejection of the Lutheran theological and confessional traditions. So in their writings and their official doctrinal statements some American Lutherans included phrases describing the Scriptures as "inerrant," "infallible," and "verbally inspired." But they insisted very strongly that such words were *not* a new import to Lutheranism from fundamentalism, but, instead, were the very doctrines taught by the Lutheran orthodox theologians, the Lutheran confessions, and by Luther himself. One of the leading theologians of the ALC, Johan Michael Reu, came to maintain:

> In this country the slogan has been proclaimed, "Lutheran theology in its classical period knew nothing of a verbal inspiration." If [this slogan] . . . include[s] the rejection of the inerrancy of the original documents, it cannot be supported by Luther's views. . . .[29]

Other Lutherans, especially in the ULCA and some in Augustana, were cautiously open to higher criticism, as long as the *christological* authority of Scripture was maintained. Taking their inspiration from Luther's example, they insisted that, used properly, higher criticism could clarify the biblical record and strengthen the Christian faith. Augustana pastor C. A. Wendell wrote in 1930 that for Luther:

> The Bible may be externally rough and rude, but . . . "precious is the treasure, Christ, which lies therein." That is the secret of Luther's love for the Bible . . . not its literary beauty, not its philosophical insight, not

---

28. In this battle, Missouri Synod Lutherans felt a common purpose with the Fundamentalists, while not in agreement with them on other issues. See Rudnick, *Fundamentalism and the Missouri Synod,* especially 67-79.

29. Johan Michael Reu, *Luther and the Scriptures* (Columbus, OH: Wartburg Press, 1944). This work represents Reu's complete conversion to inerrancy; earlier he had held that the Bible is inerrant only in regard to salvation. This earlier "liberal" view had almost scuttled the formation of the ALC in 1930. See Nelson, *Lutheranism in North America,* 86.

its historical or scientific value, not its alleged "inerrancy from cover to cover," but Christ who dwells within.[30]

These Lutherans rejected inerrancy as an unnecessary and un-Lutheran addition of modern origin.

The Lutherans who were open to higher criticism were, however, very cautious in making their pronouncements, for fear of sending the wrong signals. In the late 1930s the ULCA held up publication of a New Testament commentary by one of its teachers because of its mildly positive stance toward higher criticism; it was feared that publication of this work would upset merger negotiations, as well as a number of pastors and members within the ULCA itself.[31]

The dispute among twentieth-century American Lutherans over the formulation and wording of a doctrine of the authority of Scripture raises the question of whether it is helpful to view these disputes in light of the fundamentalist/modernist controversy. There is no doubt that American Lutherans were interested in and influenced by this growing rift within American Protestantism; there is no question that the use of inerrantist language derived in part from such interest and influence. But it is quite another story to explain Lutheran divisions on the basis of such a two-party schema; for a further examination of this question we must return to a larger-scale view of the relationship of American Lutherans to the fundamentalist/modernist controversy.

Lutherans and Fundamentalists

As a general rule, American Lutherans in the first half of the twentieth century were a conservative and cautious group, and they were wary of new movements within American Christianity. There were no groups of

---

30. C. A. Wendell, "What is Lutheranism?" in Ferm, ed., *What is Lutheranism?* 238.

31. The books in question were commentaries on the Old and New Testament written by ULCA Professor H. C. Alleman, originally published in 1936. Nelson suggests that Alleman was "one of the first American Lutheran Biblical scholars to employ the historical critical method" and that "the ULCA found it expedient to withhold temporarily [the Old Testament volume for fear] . . . that the offending book might upset inter-Lutheran relations." The books by Alleman became an issue in the 1936-40 discussions between ALC and ULCA. Nelson, "A Case Study . . . ," 211-12 and 265-66, n. 32.

individuals which could be defined as "liberals" or "modernists" in the larger sense of the term. Even the ULCA, which Missouri and others branded as liberal, came nowhere close to endorsing the liberal theology of American Protestantism. For example, ULCA leader John A. W. Haas followed up his criticism of fundamentalism (note 21) with a critique of modernism:

> Lutheranism is far more adverse, however, to modernism. It is willing to use modern forms of thought and established modern results, but it considers the fundamental error of modernism to be the constant correction of the body of evangelical truth, by the changing conceptions of science and the varying contentions of philosophy.[32]

There were some cautious attempts to employ higher criticism of the Scriptures, but none of the other theological aspects of modernism.

On the other hand, although Lutherans of all stripes expressed varying degrees of sympathy with specific fundamentalist positions, not even the most conservative Lutheran groups (Missouri and ALC, especially) can be considered simply fundamentalists.[33] In fact, there were leaders within the Missouri Synod who attacked parts of the fundamentalist program quite severely, and sought to stem these influences (particularly "unionism," premillennialism, and social activism) within the Synod. Milton Rudnick observes:

> Among doctrines which Fundamentalism had allegedly distorted as a result of its Reformed orientation were those of the means of grace, especially Holy Baptism and Holy Communion. Again and again it is stated that liberalism originated in the Reformed hermeneutical principle, and that since most Fundamentalists operated with this principle the Missouri Synod could not enter into fellowship with them.[34]

While they appreciated the fundamentalist stance on the question of scriptural authority, they were profoundly opposed to other parts of the fundamentalist platform. Missouri strongly resisted fundamentalism's social activism, that is, the attempt to impose (Reformed) Christian morality

32. "What Is Lutheranism?" in Ferm, *What is Lutheranism?* 193. Nelson gives other examples of ULCA's attitude toward Liberalism and Modernism. *Lutheranism in North America,* 87-88.

33. This is the conclusion of Rudnick, *Fundamentalism and the Missouri Synod,* 103-16; other historians generally agree with him. See also n. 16.

34. Rudnick, *Fundamentalism and the Missouri Synod,* 87.

on the American nation.[35] To give but one example, the Missouri Synod adamantly opposed Prohibition. And the fundamentalist approach to unity also seemed wrongheaded. Missouri called the attempt to forge unity on the basis of a few common beliefs "Unionism," and insisted that unity could only be achieved by means of total doctrinal agreement. Missouri leaders saw the creeping influence of fundamentalism as a dangerous encroachment of Reformed Christianity into their Lutheran Synod.

Of course, there were some individual Lutherans, including pastors and professors, who did become active in the fundamentalist movement, but these personal decisions did not necessarily reflect synodical or church decisions. For example, one eastern Lutheran teacher and pastor, Joseph Seiss, was an active leader in the millennialism movement of the late nineteenth century.[36] ALC professor Leander S. Keyser was "closely affiliated" with fundamentalism, and in the 1920s he was an "active participant" in the World's Christian Fundamentals Association.[37] Then there was Missouri Synod professor and popular national radio speaker Walter Maier, who was sympathetic to the fundamentalists, and who attracted many of them as listeners because of his scathing denunciations of liberalism. Still, while Maier was sympathetic to the fundamentalist movement, he was not a fundamentalist in the classic sense of the term.[38] In keeping with other Lutheran confessionalists, Maier insisted that *all* Christian doctrines were fundamental, not just the five that the fundamentalists selected. He was happy to make common cause with them to defend biblical authority, but this was a strategic move to counter liberalism, and not a meeting of the minds.

Some have argued, however, that although conservative groups like the ALC and Missouri had their theological differences with fundamentalism, they did share with fundamentalism the same modes of

35. On Lutheran attitudes toward social legislation, especially prohibition, see Nelson, *Lutherans in North America*, 417-18. Only Augustana and the Norwegians supported Prohibition as a means of moral reform.

36. On Seiss, see Ernest R. Sandeen, *The Roots of Fundamentalism: British and American Millenarianism, 1800-1930* (Grand Rapids: Baker Book House, 1978), 95-96. Sandeen suggests that later Lutheran disinterest in millennialism came about because of "the surge of Scandinavian and German immigrants whose confessional and liturgical orientation and lack of English language swamped the syncretistic tendencies of the more Americanized part of the denomination" (p. 163).

37. Donald Huber, *Educating Lutheran Pastors in Ohio, 1830-1980* (Lewiston, NY: Edward Mellen Press, 1989), 172.

38. Rudnick, *Fundamentalism and the Missouri Synod*, 90-102.

thought.[39] The point of contact between these conservative Lutherans and fundamentalism was an opposition to modernity and liberal Christianity and a desire to combat these groups by returning to certain traditional theological "nonnegotiables." In other words, while they had their differences with fundamentalists, these Lutherans employed a similar strategic response to the "acids of modernity."

But this argument misses a key difference between conservative Lutherans and fundamentalists. The theory behind the publication of *The Fundamentals* (beginning in 1909) was to define certain theological essentials to which all Christians must assent. However, for the fundamentalists, agreement on these essentials was enough: different Christians could maintain their own views on such other doctrines as Baptism, the Church and the Sacraments, and the work of the Holy Spirit. This sort of approach was totally antithetical to exclusivist confessionalists such as members of the ALC and the Missouri Synod, who insisted on absolute agreement on *all* theological points before cooperation and union could even be considered. It is telling that, despite their close relations and sympathies, the ALC and the Missouri Synod were never able to achieve such unanimity. It is hard to see any American Lutherans as being more than mildly sympathetic to some of the stated aims of fundamentalism; it is impossible to call these exclusivistic confessionalists "fundamentalists" either in doctrine or approach.

This is not to say that those American Lutherans who adopted inerrantist language to define the authority of the Bible used the term "inerrancy" differently than their fundamentalist counterparts; on this one point the two groups did agree. But agreement on this one point does not mean that these confessional Lutherans had substantially adopted the agenda of fundamentalism, that they were deeply influenced by fundamentalism, or that they substantially agreed with the fundamentalists. The exclusive confessionalists, in Missouri and the other groups, had little use for either the content of fundamentalism or its approach to Christian unity. These confessionalists did share the language of inerrancy with other American Protestant groups, but solely for their own purposes, and because they believed the term captured the meaning of the older Lutheran traditions.

39. For such an argument, see Leigh D. Jordahl, "The Theology of Franz Pieper: a resource for fundamentalistic thought modes among American Lutherans," *Lutheran Quarterly* 23 (May 1971): 118-37.

Conclusion

It seems clear from our examination of American Lutheranism that the "two-party" system (fundamentalist/modernist) is not adequate to explain or define the growth and divisions within this ecclesial family. Although some American Lutherans expressed some sympathy with either fundamentalist or modernist goals, no group within American Lutheranism can be seen as being either truly modernist or truly fundamentalist. Lutherans found, at times, that their own choices and allegiances brought them into contact with the wider world of American Protestantism, but these contacts did not, in form or content, fundamentally shape any Lutheran denomination.

The main question that divided American Lutherans was the nature and degree of confessional loyalty, and how Lutheran confessional documents could or could not be understood as defining and creating a larger Lutheran union. Disputes centered on the degree to which Lutheran groups needed to agree theologically before cooperation or union was possible. The exclusivistic confessionalists (such as ALC and Missouri) sought further definitions beyond the Confessions, and absolute agreement on all theological issues. Ecumenical confessionalists, such as those in ULCA and Augustana, understood agreement on the confessional documents to be sufficient, and that no additional documents or subscriptions were necessary for unity. The divisions were essentially over the *degree* of confessional agreement necessary for cooperation and unity.

In their search for further clarification and elucidation of the Lutheran Confessions, especially in English, the exclusivist confessionalists did engage in one important and significant borrowing from American fundamentalism, namely, the adoption of the language of "inerrancy" and "infallibility" to express their ideas of scriptural authority. Yet such borrowing did not mean that these Lutherans had become fundamentalists; the terms "inerrancy" and "infallibility" (whether wisely chosen or not) were used by Lutherans to express their understanding of the older traditions of Lutheranism, going back to the Lutheran Orthodox theologians, and perhaps even to Martin Luther himself. Their use of these terms did not signal a Lutheran acceptance of the Reformed, Princetonian view of Scripture which was the norm in most fundamentalist circles. But it is significant to note that even the adoption of common inerrantist statements by the ALC and the Missouri Synod was not enough to ensure or engender a closer cooperation or union between these groups. The fact that they agreed on a common wording to express their understanding of the authority of Scripture was not enough to overcome the rest of their differences. It is significant that when the "merger dust" settled in the early 1960s, there were three rather than two Lutheran denominations, and the divisions did not run along a clear liberal/conservative line.

Modernism has had a very limited appeal to American Lutherans, and it would be hard to suggest that any one of these denominations was liberal in any sense of the word. They were conservatives of various types and understandings; at times they borrowed some of the language of fundamentalism for their own purposes. Yet the model of fundamentalism held no promise for them; they did not see the particular doctrines that were so important to fundamentalism as crucial to their own program, nor did they agree that cooperation or union was possible on the basis of these doctrines. A confessional understanding of Lutheran history with multiple disputes and tensions goes much further in explaining the course of American Lutheranism in the twentieth century than any forced application of the two-party model.

CHAPTER 13

Refining the Center: Two Kinds of Reformed Church Loyalists

DONALD A. LUIDENS AND ROGER J. NEMETH

The notion that American Protestantism is divided into two parties, one more or less conservative and the other more or less liberal, became part of the academic discourse after Martin Marty used these categories in his historic volume *Righteous Empire: The Protestant Experience in America*.[1] But the idea that American faith might tend to split along liberal-conservative lines had been around for some time before Marty wrote. In *Righteous Empire,* Marty quotes the late nineteenth-century religious leader Josiah Strong, who described a divide in American faith that was "not to be distinguished by any of the old lines of doctrinal or denominational cleavage." Strong's description of two Protestant parties stressed their "spirit, aim, point of view, [and] comprehensiveness." He said, "the one is individualistic; the other is social."[2]

Following this lead, Marty dubbed one Protestant party the "private party" and the other the "public party." The private party "accented individual salvation out of the world, personal moral life congruent with the saved, and fulfillment or its absence in the rewards or punishments in a life to come." The public party, he said, "was more exposed to the social order and the social destinies of men," and it took greater cognizance of the public and political facets of faith. The public party accordingly "pursued a Social Christianity" which strove for some transformation of the world.[3]

1. Martin E. Marty, *Righteous Empire: The Protestant Experience in America* (New York: Harper and Row, 1970).
2. Ibid., 177.
3. Ibid., 179.

While Marty spoke of two Protestant parties as representing a broad divergence of practice and belief that transcended denominational lines, the two-party model has also been used to describe divisions within individual denominations. For example, in 1976, Dean Hoge tested the two-party thesis on a sample of Presbyterians by using several theological indices to measure Marty's parties. Hoge identified two basic parties within the denomination, each a polar opposite of the other on a variety of theological issues. He concluded that Marty's categories represented an accurate rendering of divisions within the Presbyterian Church. In fact, Hoge argued that the public and private parties described by Marty had, at least in the denomination he studied, become increasingly polarized during the 1960s, resulting in the "collapse of the middle."[4]

In 1986, we decided to test the applicability of Marty's two-party model and Hoge's elaboration of that hypothesis to another denomination, The Reformed Church in America (RCA). We published our findings in an article entitled "Public and Private Protestantism Reconsidered: Introducing the Loyalists." Expanding on the theological indices developed by Hoge's 1976 study, we performed a factor analysis of responses from a national sample of RCA members. Our findings suggested that, while a Private Pietist party was alive and well in the RCA, the Public Party (at least in its ideal form) was a marginal entity within the denomination. These findings confirmed to a degree the descriptions offered by Marty and Hoge, which both maintained that private pietists have historically dominated Protestant denominational life.[5]

However, we also found a distinctive third party in addition to the two hypothesized by Marty and Hoge. This third party, which was characterized by a strong institutional focus, had significant support among lay respondents. In contrast to Hoge's findings, a "center" was found to exist. It was to some degree an amorphous center, but it was hardly "collapsed." This third group held a theology similar to that of the Private Pietists, but what most characterized it was a strong allegiance to the denomination and to its traditions and agencies. Accordingly, we labelled this group the "Loyalists." The Loyalists were the most institutionally committed members of the RCA, and more than any other group they

---

4. Dean Hoge, *Division in the Protestant House* (Philadelphia: Westminster Press, 1976).

5. Donald A. Luidens and Roger J. Nemeth, "Public and Private Protestantism Reconsidered: Introducing the Loyalists," *Journal for the Scientific Study of Religion* 26 (1987): 450-64.

comprised the organizational core of the denomination. Because of their dedication to institutional structures, we argued that the fate of the Loyalists would be critically important to the future vitality of the RCA.

The 1991 study presented here is a partial replication and expansion of our earlier study of the RCA. Using a larger and more comprehensive survey of RCA membership, we revisit both Marty's two-party model and the three-party division we had found among RCA members in 1986. Findings from our factor analysis offer partial support for the existence of two polar (though not necessarily opposite) groups: a large "Private Pietist" party and a smaller and less cohesive "Public Party" (which we call "Up-Scale Moderates") do exist. Moreover, we continue to find evidence of a significant centrist grouping distinguished by its high level of allegiance to the denomination. But this centrist group, which we had labeled "Loyalists" in 1986, now appears to be composed of its own "two-party" system. On the one side we find institutionally committed activists, and on the other we find affectively associated inheritors of the church. We label these two different groups "Institutional Loyalists" and "Hereditary Loyalists" respectively.

This four-party map of the RCA is considerably more complex than that proposed by Marty and raises serious questions about how a simple two-party scheme can misrepresent the experience of many members of the RCA and other mainline denominations. Before discussing these findings in more depth, however, we need to introduce the RCA, explain how its membership was surveyed, and describe the indices which we used to sort people into our four parties.

Focus of Study and Initial Findings

The Reformed Church in America (RCA), formerly the Dutch Reformed Church, was first established in New Amsterdam (New York City) in 1628.[6] As one of the oldest and smallest of the so-called mainline Protestant denominations, the RCA reports a total membership of just under 325,000,

---

6. The RCA should not be confused with the Christian Reformed Church, which split from the RCA in the mid-nineteenth century. The RCA has been placed among the Methodists, Lutherans, American Baptists, and Disciples of Christ in a "middle position" between the more liberal and more conservative branches of American Protestantism. See Wade Clark Roof and William McKinney, "Denominational America and the New Religious Pluralism," *Annals of the American Academy of Political Social Science* 480 (1985): 24-38.

nearly two-thirds of whom are active communicant members.[7] Although its membership has traditionally been concentrated on the East Coast and in the Midwest, the RCA's current parishioners live in every region of the United States and Canada, and in rural and urban areas in roughly the same proportions as the general population.

The RCA is similar to most other mainline denominations in that it experienced initial increase and subsequent decline in membership over the past four decades. After twenty years of dramatic membership growth following World War II, the RCA reached a high point in the mid-1960s and then began a period of decline which lasted until about 1990. Since then the number of active communicants has remained around 200,000. Concomitant with contracting numbers, the RCA has become more ethnically diverse. Ongoing since colonial days, the ethnic diversification of the denomination has resulted in only about one-half of the current membership reporting any Dutch heritage.[8]

Data for this study come from a 1991 nationwide survey of the beliefs and practices of RCA lay members.[9] A systematic sample was drawn from congregational membership registries based on congregation size and location in the RCA's seven regions. From the 9,718 mailed questionnaires, 4,518 (46%) were returned in useable form. Comparisons with other RCA studies indicate that the sample is representative of the denomination with regard to age, gender, regional distribution, and rural/urban residence.

In our 1986 study, we had argued that the future of the RCA (and, by extension, the future of other mainline denominations) would be dependent upon the fortunes of the Loyalist center. While it was clear that the Public Party was marginalized, and that the Private Pietists made up a significant segment of the membership, the Loyalists were the ones who ran the congregations and other denominational structures, and they

7. *1994 Directory and 1993 Financial Statements of the General Synod of the Reformed Church in America* (Grand Rapids: Reformed Church Press, 1995), 129.

8. Roger J. Nemeth and Donald A. Luidens, "The RCA in the Larger Picture: Facing Structural Realities," *Reformed Review* 47 (Winter 1993-94): 85-113.

9. Since the RCA does not maintain a national membership registry, this study required the development of a multi-stage sampling design. The initial step of sampling involved requesting current membership lists from each of the 963 RCA congregations. This resulted in names and addresses of all communicant members from nearly 600 churches (representing about 60 percent of all congregations and over two-thirds of the denomination's total membership). The second stage of the sampling involved taking a probability-proportionate-to-size sample of members based on the RCA's seven "Regional Synods" and on congregation size. See Leslie Kish, *Survey Sampling* (New York: John Wiley, 1965), for a fuller discussion of this sampling design.

would bring cohesion and direction to the institutional church. Consequently, we made the status of the Loyalist center a major focus of our new study.

Our initial task was to ascertain the contours of the three RCA subgroups we had identified earlier. Did Personal Pietists, Public Activists, and Loyalists continue to co-exist in the RCA? Indices parallel to those used in the 1986 study, complemented with additional measures of belief and personal background, were constructed to make this assessment. Factor analysis[10] of the data demonstrated that, with some important refinements, the three parties were still very much present in 1991. These findings are presented in Table 1 (see the appendix on pp. 269-70 for a listing of the items and reliability scores for the indices used in the factor analysis).

The findings presented in Table 1 differ from those of the 1986 study in two significant ways. First, instead of there being three discernible groups (Personal Pietists, Public Activists, and Loyalists), there are now four (Pietists, Institutional Loyalists, Hereditary Loyalists, and Up-Scale Moderates). Second, the position of primacy which Loyalists had enjoyed in 1986 has given way to the Personal Pietist party. On the basis of responses to the various indices, it would appear that the four groups are roughly distributed as follows: about 45% are Personal Pietists; 25% are Institutional Loyalists; and the remaining 30% are evenly split between Hereditary Loyalists and Up-Scale Moderates.

Consider first the shift from three factors to four. Table 1 shows that Factor 1, the strongest factor in this analysis, represents Marty's private party. Its members score strongly on items measuring support for traditional tenets of Calvinism[11] (although less strongly for the *creeds* from

---

10. Factor analysis is a procedure by which measures are grouped on the basis of statistical correlation. The "strength" of a factor is dependent upon how strongly the individual measures correlate with the overall "factor." Since we did not want to assume any determined structure to the data, a principal component analysis with VARIMAX rotation was performed. See Jae-On Kim and Charles Mueller, *Introduction to Factor Analysis* (Beverly Hills, CA: Sage Publications, 1978). Using a scree test with an eigenvalue of unity as a demarcation point, we found the first four components significant in accounting for the total explained variance. The order of the factors indicates how cohesive, overall, each of them is. Thus, Factor 1 would be expected to be the most cohesive and would include all those items which score strongly in relation to it (in this study, the weakest acceptable factor score was +/-.60).

11. During the 1986 survey of the RCA, it was found that many members had no personal knowledge of the major documents of the denomination, commonly referred to as "the creeds and standards." These included the Apostles' Creed and the Heidelberg Confession as well as the *Book of Church Order*, which governed the denom-

Refining the Center: Two Kinds of Reformed Church Loyalists

TABLE 1
Factor Analysis of Variables and Indices
Created from the 1991 Survey of RCA Laity
(Rotated Factor Matrix)

	Factor 1 Pietists	Factor 2 Institutional Loyalists	Factor 3 Hereditary Loyalists	Factor 4 Up-Scale Moderates
Calvinism Index	**.74**	.17	-.05	.21
Midwest Region	**.75**	-.07	.19	-.04
Personal Piety Index	**.69**	.39	.08	.09
Age of Members	-.10	**.81**	.06	-.07
Loyalty Index	.24	**.72**	.06	.17
Creedal Assent Index	.32	**.65**	.13	.20
Lifetime Member of the RCA	.07	.11	**.78**	-.08
Dutch Descent	.47	.11	**.64**	.05
Distance from Member's Hometown	-.01	-.30	**-.60**	-.49
Political Conservatism Index	.22	-.04	-.16	**-.80**
SES Index	-.01	-.30	-.21	**.63**

which those tenets were extrapolated) and on practices of personal piety. In addition, these Pietists hail disproportionately from the most traditional regional section of the denomination, the Midwest.

On the other end of the scale, indicated by the far weaker Factor 4, are RCA members who are notable for their greater wealth and higher educational attainment (SES) and for their relative political liberalism (as indicated by the negative score on the Conservatism Index). This group appears to be the remnant of what we formerly identified as the Public Activist party. In the 1986 study it was noted that fewer than one-fourth of the denomination were part of this group. In 1991, on a seven-point scale of political opinion, only eighteen percent of the respondents placed themselves anywhere to the left of center; of that eighteen percent, four percent were self-styled "left" or "far left," while the rest were barely left of center. Clearly there has been a political move to the right within the denomination.

---

ination's polity. In 1991 it was decided to include an index measuring support for eight items which had been extrapolated from those creeds; the latter items, which received widespread recognition and support from respondents, are referred to as the "tenets" of the creeds and standards (see the appendix on pp. 269-70 for both sets of measures).

Because of their socioeconomic standing and their weakly liberal perspectives, members in what remains of the Public Party have been relabeled "Up-Scale Moderates." While maintaining greater liberality on social and political issues than others in the RCA, this party does not display any activist urgency. The Public Activist Party in the RCA is thus in significant eclipse, if it really continues to exist at all. It appears to be neither "public" nor "activist" to any significant degree.

But what should be made of the two groups that reside in the center? It would appear that they represent different sets of loyalists. In one group (Factor 2) we find long-standing members, who express strong allegiance to their congregation and to the denomination, and who cherish the historic creeds and standards of the RCA. We call these folks "Institutional Loyalists" because they are concerned with the structural integrity and continuity of the denomination. In the other group (Factor 3) we see a rather different kind of Loyalist. These people are lifelong members of the RCA (of varying ages), who also disproportionately claim Dutch descent. They seem to be a geographically sedentary group; most live within close proximity to their childhood hometowns. Members of this group have accordingly been labeled "Hereditary Loyalists," for it would appear that their affection for the denomination is, in large measure, a consequence of "having been brought up in it." It is not necessarily a matter of active involvement or volitional conviction.

Therefore, the "center" of the RCA, the category of members which we called "Loyalists" in 1986, is really more complex than we had first thought. On the one hand the center is comprised of institutionally committed activists, and on the other it is held together by affectively associated inheritors of the church. One might call this a two-party model of the center. But it would be wrong to construe these two groups as aligned against each other in the manner typically implied by the classic two-party model. Hereditary Loyalists may at times frustrate their Institutional Loyalist friends with the seeming laziness they display toward denominational programs and institutional life, and Institutional Loyalists may seem a little too much the denominational team players and cheerleaders to suit the tastes of Hereditary Loyalists. But they would hardly see each other as partisan adversaries.

While the Loyalists *appear* to have fractured into two groups between our 1986 and 1991 studies, caution must be exercised when attempting to interpret this apparent shift. It could signal either an actual split in the loyalist camp, or it could simply be that the less refined measures we used in 1986 were unable to discern the distinction between the two groups.

Thus, what might appear to be a split could actually be an artifact of the more refined measures we used in 1991. If the split is real, however, then there has been an actual shift in the faith and practice of RCA members in a few short years. In either event, the big winner in the current division of the denomination seems to be the Private Pietist party, which has gained increasing ascendancy.

A fuller description of the four parties in the RCA yields a clearer understanding of their distinctive characteristics. The items and indices which composed each factor were combined to form indicators of each of the four groups. These indicators were then correlated with a wide array of other descriptive and attitudinal variables to draw the fuller portraits we present below (see Table 2 for the following discussion).

Personal Pietists

As stated above, the three items which comprised Factor 1 are respondents' region of the country (the Midwest), support for the Calvinism Index, and support for the Personal Piety Index. Because of the different waves of Dutch immigration to the United States, the RCA has a long history of regionally related differences in the beliefs and practices of its membership. The more recent nineteenth-century immigration to midwestern states brought members who were considerably more Calvinist and pietist than were their contemporary RCA members living on the East Coast. These regional differences persist and manifest themselves on many issues related to faith and practice. The examination of other variables associated with RCA Pietists further illustrates the makeup of this group.

Pietists strongly affirm the importance of religion — an importance which is evident in much of their lives (see Section C: Religious Attitude Items). For instance, Pietists are particularly noteworthy for their high levels of involvement in a range of religious venues: regular church and Sunday school attendance complemented by high levels of giving and readership of religious publications (see Section B: Religious Behavior Items). Evangelism and missions head the list of congregational priorities for the Pietists, while preaching and Christian education are also endorsed, but at a lower rate (see Section E: Congregational Practice Preferences).

For Pietists, religious commitment has decidedly conservative political and social implications. Indeed, their willingness to support Christian

TABLE 2 — SECTION A
Attitudes, Behaviors, and Backgrounds of Four Parties
(All correlations reported are at least ±.20 and significant at .01 level)

	Pietists	Institutional Loyalists	Hereditary Loyalists	Up-Scale Moderates
Section A: Factor Items				
Calvinism Index	*	.29	.24	-.25
Midwest Region	*	.28	-.20	
Personal Piety Index	*	.49	.26	-.26
Age		*		-.22
Importance of Congregational Membership	.26	*		-.21
Importance of Denominational Membership	.20	*	.22	-.29
Creedal Assent Index	.35	*	.32	-.30
Dutch Descent	.42	.28	*	-.22
Distance from Hometown			*	.23
Political Conservatism Index	.25			*
Socio-Economic Status Index	-.24	-.34	-.24	*

*Indicates that variable loaded on this factor.

candidates and to get involved in politics is consistent with the broader "Christian Right" movement of the last two decades (see Section C).[12] In a similar vein, they express uniform opposition to abortion, homosexuality, and increased roles for women in and outside the church (these items were combined in the Political Conservatism Index, Section A: Factor Items; see also Section C). "Liberal" ecumenical organizations like the National Council of Churches (NCC) and the World Council of Churches (WCC) receive strong negative ratings from Pietists (see Section C).

This heightened conservative agenda, which is widely held by RCA Pietists, begs the question: Are they any more "private" than other groups in the Reformed Church? The answer, clearly, is no. Ironically, it would appear that while the "Public Activists" have become the quiescent "Up-Scale Moderates," "Private Pietists" have become more socially aware and politically engaged. Their defining characteristic continues to

12. See also Roger J. Nemeth and Donald A. Luidens, "The New Christian Right and Mainline Protestantism: The Case of the Reformed Church in America," *Sociological Analysis* 49 (Winter 1989): 343-52.

TABLE 2 — SECTIONS B, C, AND D
Attitudes, Behaviors, and Backgrounds of Four Parties
(All correlations reported are at least ±.20 and significant at .01 level)

	Pietists	Institutional Loyalists	Hereditary Loyalists	Up-Scale Moderates
Section B: Religious Behavior Items				
Church Attendance	.49	.33	.21	-.20
Sunday School Attendance	.37			
Average Weekly Giving	.30			.28
Tithing to the Church	.32	.25		
Reads RCA Publications	.38	.38	.20	
Reads Other Religious Publications	.40			
Section C: Religious Attitude Items				
Importance of Religion in Their Lives	.48	.40		
Support for NCC/WCC	-.43			-.33
Role of Women in Church	-.39	-.22	.27	
Section D: Political Opinion Items				
More Likely to Vote for "Born Again" Candidate	.38			
Active to Defeat Candidates They Do Not Agree With	.44			

be their personal and public devotionalism; however, this pietism is increasingly expressed through an activist, conservative political and social agenda.

Despite their enthusiastic religious commitment, it is apparent that Pietists are more concerned with personal religious faithfulness than with membership numbers or with the institutional survival of their church or denomination. They are not likely to be officers in their own congregations or in the denomination, and they are only moderately affirming of their congregations and the RCA as a denomination. Moreover, despite their strong support for evangelism and mission outreach, Pietists place very little emphasis on "church growth"; apparently they see church growth as an institutional preoccupation rather than as a matter of personal outreach.

Pietists are not concentrated in any particular age group, nor are they necessarily lifelong RCA members; indeed, a sizable proportion of this group are newcomers who have joined the RCA for reasons of personal

Table 2 — SECTIONS E AND F
Attitudes, Behaviors, and Backgrounds of Four Parties (All correlations reported are at least +/-.20 and significant at .01 level)

	Pietists	Institutional Loyalists	Hereditary Loyalists	Up-Scale Moderates
Section E: Congregational Practice Preferences				
Importance of Church Growth		.50	-.26	
Importance of Fellowship		.20		
Importance of Preaching	.23	.23		
Importance of Music		.21		
Importance of Missions	.37	.39		
Importance of Evangelism	.45	.35		
Importance of Christian Education	.26	.22		
Importance of Pastoral Care		.27		
Importance of Neighborhood Outreach		.24		
Section F: Miscellaneous Items				
Own/Access to High Technology		-.34		.46
Number of Close Friends in Congregation	.25	.38		
Size of Community			-.21	.23

conviction and the attraction of specific congregational programming rather than for their affinity with the traditions of the RCA. In this respect, they represent a radical departure from the RCA's history. They are found in small and large congregations and in all sizes of communities. In matters of education and income, they tend to be lower on these scales than are the Up-Scale Moderates to be described below.

Institutional Loyalists

Factor 2 comprises one of the two loyalist groups making up the center of the Reformed Church. The items having most significance with regard to this factor are age, the Loyalty Index (measuring congregational and denominational loyalty), and the Creedal Assent Index. This institutional focus has earned Factor 2 persons the title of "Institutional Loyalists." Institutional Loyalists are more likely to be older, to rate their congregational and denominational memberships as being extremely important, and to have knowledge of and express general support for the official creeds and standards of the RCA. However, they demonstrate less support for the specific *tenets* of the creeds (see Section A and Appendix A). Members identified as Institutional Loyalists are also likely to hold (or to have held) leadership positions in their congregations or the denomination. If any single group can be identified as the "organizational bedrock" of the Reformed Church, it would clearly be the Institutional Loyalists.

In many ways, Institutional Loyalists strongly resemble the Pietists. They tend to be highly involved in acts of personal devotion as well as acts of collective worship (along with prayer, Bible reading, and family devotions, church attendance and tithing are much in evidence in this group; see Table 2, Sections A and B). Like Pietists, Institutional Loyalists feel that religion is extremely important in their lives (Section C).

However, in other ways Institutional Loyalists differ from the Pietists. They are more likely to be longtime RCA members, although they are not necessarily lifelong members; their commitment to the RCA and their home congregations is paramount. They think that "church growth" is an essential task if the church is to survive into the future — and the institutional survival of the church is of greater importance for these people than matters of dogmatic purity (Section E).

In addition to this strong support for church growth, Institutional Loyalists want their churches to perform strongly on all kinds of other activities. Indeed, *every* proposed agenda item (from preaching and music to pastoral care and outreach to neighborhoods) is affirmed by Institutional Loyalists (Section E). Institutional Loyalists want it all! The church clearly occupies a central place in their lives and activities. As a further indication of their personal integration into the daily life of their congregation, Institutional Loyalists are "networkers": they consistently demonstrate the highest proportion of close friends being a part of their congregations (Section F: Miscellaneous Items). On the denominational level, Institutional Loyalists are consistently the strongest supporters of RCA institutions and agencies and are the most regular readers of denominational literature (Section B).

Among the group characteristics associated with Institutional Loyalists are that they tend to be from lower-middle-class backgrounds, with many retirees on fixed incomes. They are very unlikely to own or have access to high technology equipment such as personal computers and fax machines (perhaps a reflection of their older ages). They hold centrist positions or have no uniform position on most political and social issues. Geographically, they are likely to be found throughout the United States, in small and large communities, and to be members in congregations of all sizes (Section F). They are, indeed, the centrist backbone of the RCA.

In sum, Institutional Loyalists are theological traditionalists, but they are not doctrinaire. They are more concerned with preserving the denomination and its institutional structures than they are with insuring its theological purity.

Hereditary Loyalists

Factor 3 identifies the second centrist group. Items loading on this factor are lifelong membership in the RCA, Dutch ancestry, and how closely one lives today to where he or she grew up. Because of these largely parochial characteristics, we call people in this group "Hereditary Loyalists." Like Institutional Loyalists, Hereditary Loyalists are notable for their affinity with the RCA; furthermore, like both Pietists and Institutional Loyalists, they are relatively orthodox in matters of personal piety and public worship. However, unlike the other loyalist group, Hereditary Loyalists are not particularly active in the life of their congregations or of the RCA. Indeed, other than in church attendance, they report the lowest level of church participation of any of the four groups. Many of these non-activists, however, would undoubtedly protest strenuously if their names were removed from congregational roles: We've always been members and we always will be, say Hereditary Loyalists.

Hereditary Loyalists are found in all age groups and in all sizes of congregations. They tend to come from lower-middle-class backgrounds and smaller communities in the Midwest. Perhaps this could be expected given the higher percentage of members of Dutch descent found in midwestern states.

The RCA's creeds and standards are generally familiar to and supported by Hereditary Loyalists. At the same time, even more than was the case with Institutional Loyalists, Hereditary Loyalists exhibit only weak support for the *tenets* of those creeds and standards. On other matters of theological and political opinion, Hereditary Loyalists are only slightly to the right of center. In general, they are not a very politicized group.

The fact that a high percentage of Hereditary Loyalists are of Dutch descent suggests the possibility that the Reformed Church might be for them a way of identifying with their ancestral ethnicity.[13] This hypothesis receives partial support from the fact that Hereditary Loyalists have little discernible enthusiasm for, or antipathy against, denominational agencies and councils and the larger interdenominational organizations of which the RCA is a part (e.g., the NCC or WCC). Moreover, they are not particularly committed to their own congregations; it is the denomination which commands their allegiance, and that largely for reasons of personal biography.

Up-Scale Moderates

Two items load onto the final factor identified in Table 2: high rankings on the Socio-Economic Status Index and relatively low rankings on the Political Conservatism Index (Section A). RCA members in this group have moderate (perhaps even slightly liberal) views on issues such as women's rights, women's roles in the church, homosexuality, capital punishment, abortion, and school prayer. They are predominately from the middle to upper middle class, and they are likely to have college educations. Accordingly, they are significantly more likely than their fellow parishioners to own or have access to the technology of the upper middle class, including personal computers and fax machines (Section F). We call this group "Up-Scale Moderates."

Relative to other RCA members, Up-Scale Moderates report less frequent engagement in acts of personal piety such as reading the Bible, praying, and conducting daily devotions (Section A — Piety Index). They are also in less agreement with many of the RCA's creeds as well as with the items in the Calvinism Index. Up-scale Moderates place little importance on their congregational and denominational memberships, and they do not look favorably on church growth efforts. While they are able because of their higher economic status to give more to their church, and in absolute dollars they are relatively strong givers, they are also unlikely to tithe.[14]

---

13. See Roger J. Nemeth and Donald A. Luidens, "The Persistence of Ethnic Descent: Dutch Clergy in the Reformed Church in America," *Journal for the Scientific Study of Religion* 34 (June 1995): 200-213 for a discussion of the persistence of Dutch ethnicity in the RCA. For an ethnic group such as the Dutch-Americans, one that has experienced tremendous assimilation and acculturation, ethnic identity has become increasingly a matter of choice (or, as Gans calls it, "symbolic ethnicity"). For many Hereditary Loyalists, the RCA continues to function as a symbolic culture-carrier.

14. See Donald A. Luidens and Roger J. Nemeth, "Social Sources of Family Contributions: Giving Patterns in the Reformed Church in America," *Review of Religious Research* 36 (December 1994): 205-15, for further elucidation of this anomaly.

Demographically, this group is more likely to be younger, to live in larger cities, to live on either the east or west coasts, and to live far away from where they were raised. In all respects, Up-Scale Moderates are a unique entity within the RCA. They represent, disproportionately, the cultural skills and financial strength of the denomination, yet they are the most heterodox on all behavior and belief scales.

What happened to the liberal, Public Activist party in the RCA? Where did it go? While the data to answer these questions definitively are lacking, a study of Presbyterian baby boomers is suggestive. Dean Hoge, Benton Johnson, and Donald Luidens found in the early 1990s that most of the liberals who had been raised in the Presbyterian Church during the 1950s and 1960s had not only left the United Presbyterian Church, but left organized religion entirely. While they still claimed to be faithful Christians, they did so without being members of a congregation.[15] We suspect the same exodus has been true for the liberal members of the RCA.

Four Clusters and Two Kinds of Centrists

The Pietists of Marty's two-party model are most evidently alive and well in the RCA in 1991. However, they are no longer strictly "private" in their focus, increasingly active in promoting a conservative political and social agenda. As Marty and Hoge suggest, they represent the bulk of believers, strongly engaged in acts of personal and public piety, committed to theological orthodoxy, and moderately supportive of the denomination and its agencies. Doctrinal purity overrides other church-related commitments and is especially valued over merely preserving the institution.

On the other end of the denomination's community are Up-Scale Moderates, a tepid reflection at best of the Public Activist party described by Marty. Up-Scale Moderates are less convinced than their peers of the importance of theological purity and more in tune with the cultural and social forces which characterize the contemporary age. While no longer "liberal" in any distinguishable way (except, perhaps, in matters related to the status of women), these Moderates are reluctant to impose theological or social absolutes on their fellow believers. Their human and material

---

15. Dean R. Hoge, Benton Johnson, and Donald A. Luidens, *Vanishing Boundaries: The Religion of Mainline Protestant Baby Boomers* (Louisville, KY: Westminster/John Knox, 1994).

resources are significant, and they would be sorely missed by the rest of the RCA, despite their atypical profile and minority status.

Beyond these "polar" parties (if one can call them that), does an identifiable center exist within the RCA? The findings presented here suggest that the answer is yes. Indeed, there appear to be two parties to that center. Both of these groups are loyal to the RCA and warmly committed to it, but they root their allegiance to the denomination in quite different patterns of behavior and belief. The Hereditary Loyalists' identification with the RCA seems to have more to do with family traditions, parochialism, and ethnic identity than with their support for the institutions, creeds, and standard beliefs of the denomination. At least for the current generation, this group is likely to continue to support the RCA with its giving and its membership. It does not, however, appear ready to contribute the time and energy needed to sustain the organization over the long haul. Nor is it certain that future generations from this group will maintain this need to identify with the RCA or its Dutch heritage.

If the RCA were to look to the future and ask, "On what rock will we build this denomination?" the group that must be at the heart of that future is the Institutional Loyalists. Although they may lack the enthusiasm for theological purity exhibited by the Pietists, they are the most committed to the maintenance of the RCA's traditions and the deliberate growth of the denomination through aggressive outreach to new members (who, ironically, are most likely to be Pietists with little commitment to the denomination and its traditions). Regardless of how the RCA's position may change on any particular social or political issue, this group has demonstrated its ideological flexibility and its enduring commitment to the RCA by devoting its time, energy, and resources to the denomination.

That the long-term survival of the RCA and similar denominations is a pressing matter is supported by the ongoing changes experienced in the RCA since 1986. In the mid-1980s, the Loyalists (more inclusively defined than in the present study) were the dominant group in the RCA. It would appear that the division which we now see within this Loyalist cadre means that the position of denominational primacy may have been yielded to the Pietists. This ascendancy of the Pietist party may weaken the hold that the Loyalists — both Hereditary and Institutional — will have on the denomination's tiller, and denominational continuity could be severely jeopardized as a consequence. While the religious faithfulness of Pietists is not under suspicion, it is clear that they have significantly less commitment to institutional preservation. Potentially more damaging to the RCA, their earnest quest for theological purity could serve as a pretext for considerable institutional havoc.

It is likely that, even though the characteristics and size of the groups might vary, most mainline Protestant denominations have a centrist group similar to what we have found in the RCA — a core of devoted members whose commitment to the organization transcends particular individual leaders, issues, or positions.[16] For the RCA that group is the Institutional Loyalists, who bring high levels of involvement in and support for their congregations and the denomination, strong devotion to the denomination's traditional creeds and standards, and (most problematic) their older ages. While their older (but not yet elderly) status allows them to occupy positions of leadership in the church today, it also means that a new generation of committed members must be curried, a generation able and willing similarly to devote themselves to the institutional survival of the church. If denominations like the RCA are not able to reproduce such a group of institutionally active Loyalists in the next generation, their future may be gravely in doubt. The RCA will not likely ever divide in half along the lines of the two-party model, but it may well dissolve as an institution if the denomination should lose its critical mass of people who see the denomination itself as the central focus of their religious identity.

---

16. For a historical analysis of such a group in the Presbyterian tradition, see William J. Weston's essay in this volume (pp. 109-28) and his *Presbyterian Pluralism: Competition in a Protestant House* (Knoxville: University of Tennessee Press, 1997).

APPENDIX

Items Comprising Indices Used in Factor Analysis

Calvinism Index = Indicated agreement or strong agreement with the following statements:

1. I regard the Bible as totally authoritative for my faith.
2. I regard the Bible as totally authoritative for my actions.
3. The church should bring Christ to the whole world.
4. Even though there is suffering in the world, God is still in charge.
5. I believe in a divine judgment after death where some shall be rewarded and others punished.
6. Jesus Christ brings me into a new covenant with God.
7. Humans are by nature sinful.
8. Our salvation is determined by God even before we are born.

Cronbach alpha =.86

Piety Index = Indicated frequency or importance of the following:

1. How often do you read the Bible? (greater than once a week)
2. How often do you pray privately? (once a day or more)
3. How often, if at all, are family devotions held in your home? (once a week or more)
4. In general, how important would you say that religion is to you? (extremely or quite important)
5. In general, how important is prayer in your life? (extremely or quite important)

Cronbach alpha =.77

Loyalty Index = Indicated the importance of each of the following:

1. In general, how important would you say your Congregational Membership is to you?
2. In general, how important would you say your Denominational Membership is to you?

Correlation Coefficient =.61

Creedal Assent Index = Indicated how important each of the following are to their faith:

1. Apostles' Creed
2. Belgic Confession
3. RCA Book of Church Order
4. Canons of the Synod of Dort
5. Heidelberg Catechism
6. Our Song of Hope

Cronbach alpha =.89

Socioeconomic Status Index = Indicated high levels on each of the following:

1. What is your family's approximate total income *before* taxes?
2. What is the highest level of formal education that you have *completed?*

Correlation Coefficient =.41

Political Conservatism Index = Indicated their level of agreement with each of the following:

1. Imposing the death penalty for all persons convicted of murder.
2. Passing the Equal Rights Amendment.
3. Banning all abortions.
4. Allowing homosexuals to teach in public schools.
5. Permitting prayer in public schools.

Cronbach alpha =.70

The Woman's Christian Temperance Union: A Woman's Branch of American Protestantism

NANCY G. GARNER

The two-party paradigm utilized by historians and church leaders to describe twentieth-century American Protestantism (most often described as fundamentalist vs. modernist or conservative vs. liberal) focuses on the important theological conflicts over evolution and higher criticism of the Bible. Emphasis on these particular divisions within Protestantism has given the impression that all Protestant organizations can be neatly situated within this dualism. But when one considers the case of the Woman's Christian Temperance Union, the most significant organization of U.S. Protestant women in the early twentieth century, the paradigm becomes irrelevant. One looks in vain for references to the conservative/liberal debate within WCTU records. These women ignored the debate while conducting work that defies easy categorization. Labels such as progressive or conservative fail to describe satisfactorily a WCTU that supported prohibition, labor legislation, the censorship of motion pictures, Americanization of immigrants, child welfare legislation, Sunday blue laws, and the ordination of women. Seeming at first glance to be a mixture of conservative evangelicalism and the social gospel, the WCTU is neither. Instead, it is a prime example of how Protestant women's organizations refuse to fit neatly into the fundamentalist/modernist controversy.

Focusing on the two-party paradigm obscures other important divisions within twentieth-century American Protestantism which have not received the attention they deserve. Prime among these are the powerful separators of race, class, and gender. The two-party paradigm only attempts to describe the white male Protestant world and, as such, has distorted our historical knowledge of the diversity within Protestantism.[1] African-Americans, women, and other ethnic and racial groups are left out. Thus, too little scholarship on Protestantism has included the Woman's Christian Temperance Union. As historians broaden their view of Protestantism beyond the confines of the white, male-dominated Church, we are challenged to see beyond the two-party paradigm and encounter a much more complex and multi-faceted organism.

WCTU as "Woman's Church"

The creation of the Woman's Christian Temperance Union in 1874 was a direct challenge to the institutional sexism enshrined within Protestantism. While women made up a large part of Protestant congregations, they had no real authority within their churches. Denied or discouraged from entering seminaries and the ministry, it is not surprising that WCTU participants did not experience the same theological debates as their male counterparts. Few women dealt directly with issues of evolutionary theory and critical analysis of the Bible. Issues that were important to women in their traditional roles as wives, mothers, and sisters were, however, being largely ignored by both their churches and government. In 1874, many white, middle-class women focused on male alcohol use as a symbol of their inability as women to control the economic well-being of their families. When they perceived that laws governing alcohol use and saloons were not being effectively enforced and their churches were not strongly denouncing alcohol, they formed their own adjunct women's church in the WCTU, and began to combine and develop an approach to politics that would remain firmly rooted within their uniquely feminine vision of the gospel. At the same time, they consciously fashioned an exclusively female branch of Protestantism where women held positions of religious power and authority. Because they were so self-consciously a women's organization, and because the two-party paradigm of Protestantism only attempts to categorize a largely white male theological debate, the paradigm quickly becomes an irrelevant and inadequate tool with which to analyze and

---

1. Douglas Jacobsen and William Vance Trollinger Jr. assess and criticize the historiography of the two-party paradigm (without, however, considering the exclusion of women) in their article "Historiography of American Protestantism: The Two-Party Paradigm, and Beyond," *Fides et Historia* 23 (Fall 1993): 4-15.

explain the success and failure of the WCTU, and thus very limited in its power to address the whole of twentieth-century American Protestantism. Put another way, to understand more fully both the WCTU and Protestantism, we must add a feminist analysis to our historiography.

The Woman's Christian Temperance Union was organized in late 1874 in Cleveland, Ohio, after the national grass-roots Woman's Crusade against alcohol had spread across the country during the winter of 1873 and spring of 1874. Over 50,000 (mostly) Protestant church women had invaded taverns and saloons, praying and singing in an effort to shut them down.[2] At a national Sunday school teachers' institute in Lake Chautauqua, New York, that August, women who were energized and inspired by their crusade experiences called for the convention in Cleveland at the Second Presbyterian Church to organize a National Woman's Temperance Union.[3] The WCTU reached its peak of membership in the late 1920s.[4]

From the beginning, its organizers proclaimed its Protestant Christian foundation. Jennie F. Willing of Bloomington, Illinois, the first convention's temporary chair, opened the meeting by asserting that theirs was "simply and only a religious movement."[5] Mary Johnson of Brooklyn, New York, made it clear that God had called them as women to do his work: "We meet as women of Galilee, who have been following the blessed Master. We have seen the multitudes in sin and suffering upon whom He has compassion, and have looked to Him for strength, and He has given it. Ours is a most solemn call. Our God is upon our side."[6]

By 1877, the WCTU in Cleveland was conducting what the national WCTU annual report referred to as a "Woman's Church," where 50,000 people had attended services throughout the year.[7] The report specified that there was no male pastor, but a "shepherdess" who held that "sacred office."

2. Jack S. Blocker, Jr., *"Give to the Winds Thy Fears": The Woman's Temperance Crusade, 1873-1874* (Westport, CT: Greenwood Press, 1985), 7-26.

3. Ruth Bordin makes it clear that the original organizers of the WCTU utilized their "church network contacts" in forming the new organization. Ruth Bordin, *Woman and Temperance: The Quest for Power and Liberty, 1873-1900* (Philadelphia: Temple University Press, 1981), 35.

4. Jack S. Blocker, Jr., "Progressivism Anticipated: Temperance Women, Home Protection and Women's Rights, 1873-1933," paper delivered at the Conference on Women in the Progressive Era, National Museum of American History, Smithsonian Institution, Washington, D.C., March 10-12, 1988.

5. *WCTU Minutes, 1874 Convention,* 6.

6. Ibid., 11.

7. *WCTU Minutes, 1877 Convention,* 196.

It is emphatically a company of believers, whose spiritual and temporal interests are in the hands of seven women — deaconesses they might well be called — members of the Woman's Temperance League, of Cleveland. In this spiritual home believers are baptized, the Lord's Supper is administered, and the dead have been buried. Pastors of the various churches cordially officiate on these occasions, but their sermons are with the "Woman's Kingdom."[8]

Importantly, this embryonic "Women's Church" was careful not to supplant or compete with established Protestant churches. They were also careful to avoid denominational allegiances.[9] The Woman's Christian Temperance Union became an adjunct or "helpmeet" to Protestant churches, rather than taking the more radical step of establishing an alternative women's church. WCTU members remained within the fold, criticizing the patriarchy of the church from within while exercising the religious leadership and authority denied them in traditional Protestant churches.

A Theology of Difference and Equality

Frances Willard, the well-known national president of the WCTU from 1879 to 1898, placed the WCTU directly within a paradigm of a Protestant church divided more profoundly by sexism and its resulting gender differences than by theological debates. She asserted that the women of the WCTU were practicing a religion of compassionate action, based on their understanding of God's "mother-heart," rather than a religion she characterized as dead theology, most often practiced and propagated by men.

Willard effectively illustrates the contradictory pro-woman stance that typified the WCTU's arguments for increased women's power in both the church and government. Within WCTU ideology one can find strands of both feminism, which argues that men and women are equal, and the nineteenth-century cult of domesticity or evangelical domesticity, which argued that women were spiritually and morally better than men. Both arguments were utilized, sometimes within the same breath, by WCTU members challenging the exclusion of women from positions of authority.

In her book *Woman in the Pulpit*, Willard argued that male clergy

---

8. Ibid.
9. *WCTU Minutes, 1916 Convention*, 101.

(especially under Catholicism) had so denigrated women as to shun marriage and family life and deny them to male and female religious. Male clergy had introduced hierarchies and perversely translated God's message of love, life, and compassion into dogma, creeds, formulas, exegesis, and martyrdom. Confidently asserting that God had both a male and female nature, she proclaimed: "The mother-heart of God will never be known to the world until translated into terms of speech by mother-hearted women. Law and love will never balance in the realm of grace until a woman's hand shall hold the scales."[10] God should be represented in his church by both male and female clergy, since the essentially opposite natures of men and women complemented each other (the cult of domesticity or evangelical domesticity).[11] Both male and female were necessary to express God's nature as well as human nature.

In fact, Willard went so far as to argue that if God chose to be incarnated into human form in the nineteenth century, she would come to earth as a mother. Willard argued that mothers symbolize the very incarnation of God because their essential nature is so close to God's. The pain and sacrifice necessary to give birth and raise children is similar to the pain and sacrifice of the Lamb of God to save God's people, giving birth to new spiritual life. A mother's intercession on behalf of her children mirrors Christ's intercession on behalf of Christians. Thus, the mother-

---

10. Frances Willard, *Woman in the Pulpit* (Chicago: Woman's Temperance Publication Assoc., 1889), 46-47.

11. Many historians have described evangelical domesticity, under a variety of terms. These include the following scholars: Susan Earls Dye Lee, "Evangelical Domesticity: The Origins of the Woman's National Christian Temperance Union under Frances E. Willard" (Ph.D. dissertation, Northwestern University, 1980); Keith Melder, "Ladies Bountiful: Organized Women's Benevolence in Early Nineteenth-Century America," *New York History* 68 (July 1967): 231-54; Carroll Smith-Rosenberg, *Religion and the Rise of the American City: The New York City Mission Movement, 1812-1870* (Ithaca: Cornell University Press, 1971), 118-24, 203-24; Ronald W. Hogeland, "'The Female Appendage': Feminine Life-Styles in America, 1820-1860," *Civil War History* 17 (June 1971): 1010-1114 (Evangelical Womanhood); Anne M. Boylan, "Evangelical Womanhood in the Nineteenth Century: The Role of Women in Sunday Schools," *Feminist Studies* 4 (October 1978): 62-80; Nancy F. Cott, "Passionlessness: An Interpretation of Victorian Sexual Ideology, 1790-1850," *Signs* 4 (Winter 1978): 219-36; Barbara Leslie Epstein, *The Politics of Domesticity: Women, Evangelism, and Temperance in Nineteenth Century America* (Middletown, CT: Wesleyan University Press, 1981), 67-87 (Domesticity); Lori D. Ginzberg, *Women and the Work of Benevolence: Morality, Politics, and Class in the Nineteenth-Century United States* (New Haven: Yale University Press, 1990), 11-35 (female moral superiority); and Colleen McDannell: *The Christian Home in Victorian America, 1840-1900* (Bloomington: Indiana University Press, 1986), 127-36, 143-49.

preacher is not a freak of nature; instead, she vividly portrays the very nature of God.[12]

Frances Willard, as well as other WCTU members, also asserted that God had made both men and women equal. As biblical feminists, they argued that women were equal believers with men and that gender should make no significant difference within the religious sphere.[13] Willard wondered at theologians who asserted that Jesus was an equal member of the Trinity with God the Father, but who claimed that women were subordinate to men, even though Paul declared that woman's relation to man was the same as Christ's relation to God the Father.[14] Willard declared that there was no record of a "woman's meeting" in the New Testament because both the regenerated hearts of Christian believers and those of their ministers are "of the common gender." Christian believers should not have to segregate themselves by sex, since their hearts were of one gender.[15]

Willard argued early for inclusive language when she objected to a preacher who kept referring to his congregation only as "brethren." She claimed that every time the New Testament referred to "brethren," both men and women were meant, and ministers should make that clear by including the "sisters" when they referred to their congregation.[16]

12. Willard, *Woman in the Pulpit*, 65-67.

13. "Biblical Feminism" is a term introduced by Letha Dawson Scanzoni and Nancy A. Hardesty in 1974 with the first publication of their book *All We're Meant to Be* (Waco, TX: Word Books, 1974). WCTU members and other nineteenth-century evangelical woman's rights activists never used the term. Biblical feminists can be distinguished as a subset of Christian feminists who believe that the Bible is the authoritative word of God and, when correctly interpreted, will not support patriarchy. The term is defined in the first chapter of Letha Dawson Scanzoni and Nancy A. Hardesty, *All We're Meant to Be: Biblical Feminism for Today*, 3rd ed. (Grand Rapids: William B. Eerdmans Publishing Company, 1992), 1-20. Recent surveys of Christian feminist interpretations are included in Reta Halteman Finger, "Feminist Biblical Hermeneutics: Scripture as Friend and Enemy," *Update: Newsletter of the Evangelical Women's Caucus* 11 (Winter 1987-88), 1-4, 15; Anne E. Carr, *Transforming Grace: Christian Tradition and Women's Experience* (San Francisco: Harper & Row, 1988), 95-113; and (specifically compared to a Reformed perspective) Douglas Schuurman, "Reformed Christianity and Feminism: Collision or Correlation?" in Mary Stewart Van Leeuwen et al. (eds.), *After Eden: Facing the Challenge of Gender Reconciliation* (Grand Rapids: William B. Eerdmans Publishing Company, 1993), 117-46.

14. Willard, *Woman in the Pulpit*, 29.

15. Ibid., 34-35.

16. Ibid., 34-35.

Salvation and the Social Order

Focusing on challenging their exclusion from positions of power in both church and government rather than on theological debates, WCTU members created religious positions of authority for themselves. They also began work that was identical to that advocated by the liberal social gospel movement, but which was unconnected with that movement theologically. Rather than coming to an understanding of the social gospel through the works of theologians such as Walter Rauschenbusch, WCTU women combined a focus on piety and the needs of the world that flowed from their insistence that women's concerns for the welfare of families and children be addressed by both the church and the state. Thus, they avoided the dichotomy between the conservative theological insistence on individual salvation and the more liberal emphasis on societal welfare.

The Woman's Christian Temperance Union's adjunct women's church boldly called its own female evangelists, who had been ignored and denied by the male-dominated Protestant churches. A few examples from across the nation confirm Frances Willard's assertion that women serving in the Evangelistic Department would rather be commissioned by their churches; denied this, they were given "their rightful recognition of women as participants in public worship and as heralds of the Gospel" by the WCTU.[17] As mentioned earlier in this essay, the Cleveland WCTU was characterizing itself as a "Woman's Church" just three years after the founding of the organization. They performed the functions of a church: preaching, burying, and administering communion. The national and state WCTUs employed evangelists, some of them ordained ministers. They traveled across the nation, not only preaching temperance sermons, but also preaching the gospel. Rev. Mary Moreland, Superintendent of the Illinois WCTU, reported that, during the fall of 1911, she had preached twenty-seven gospel sermons, conducted twelve prayer meetings, and taught twelve Bible classes.[18] Kansas WCTU members were urged in 1884 to lead church prayer meetings (and, in fact, warned to guard against letting men take control), to read Scripture from the pulpit, and to preach the gospel not only to women, but also to men.[19] A group of WCTU women in Galena, Kansas, organized forty-six revival services in 1887, in the absence of a resident minister.[20]

17. Willard, *Woman in the Pulpit*, 56.
18. *Illinois WCTU Minutes, 1912 Convention*, 135.
19. *Kansas WCTU Minutes, 1884 Convention*, 76.
20. *Kansas WCTU Minutes, 1887 Convention*, 98.

The women did not confine their "evangelistic work" to the walls of the church. WCTU members expanded this category of work to include prison reform, ensuring the observance of the sabbath, lobbying to include Bible study in public schools, and cooperation with women's missionary societies, among other concerns. This is specifically where they translated their religious ideas into a political agenda that amounted to their uniquely feminine version of the Social Gospel. Arguing that "men have always tithed mint and rue and cummin in their exegesis and their ecclesiasticism, while the world's heart has cried out for compassion, forgiveness, and sympathy," Frances Willard urged WCTU members to "Do Everything." So they plunged into social reform issues, organizing over thirty separate departments of work.[21] Historian Mary Sudman Donovan has argued that Episcopal church women were practicing the social gospel before male ministers developed its theology.[22] In a similar way, the Woman's Christian Temperance Union anticipated and participated in the Social Gospel movement, but yet remained outside of it. In fact, Mrs. Thomas Nicholson, president of the Foreign Missionary Society of the Methodist Church, noted in 1925 that: "As I look back I can say that in my work in the missionary society, the sense of the completeness of the Gospel of Christ I learned in my early contact with the WCTU. We know today that we must preach a complete gospel to the peoples of the world. Individual salvation is not enough."[23]

Thus, WCTU women established Americanization work with immigrants, advocated movie censorship, lobbied for women's and children's labor laws, and worked for child welfare reforms, as well as their primary work for prohibition legislation. This seemingly contradictory combination of "liberal" and "conservative" stances makes more sense when it is understood outside of the fundamentalist/modernist paradigm of Protestantism.

WCTU Decline

The decline of the WCTU, which began in the 1930s, is also more easily explained by something other than a two-party dichotomy of Protestant-

---

21. Willard, *Woman in the Pulpit,* 46-47.

22. Mary Sudman Donovan, *A Different Call: Women's Ministries in the Episcopal Church, 1850-1920* (Wilton, CT: Morehouse-Barlow, 1986).

23. *Our Messenger,* December 1925, 3.

ism. Again, if we focus on the WCTU's challenge to the sexism within church and state that called the organization into being, it is easier to understand how the WCTU's decline can be traced to their abandonment of that challenge.

The WCTU's boldest assertions of religious authority occur in the earliest years of the organization. Gradually, there are more mentions of Bible studies and prayer meetings in Evangelistic Department reports, rather than a listing of sermons and revivals. The 1929 WCTU handbook's description of the Evangelistic Department encourages the distribution of Bibles, stewardship, sabbath observance, and the study of the Bible in public schools.[24] By 1945, the aims of the Spiritual Life Department, which had replaced the Evangelistic Department, were "to deepen the spiritual life of our members" and "to help people, through acceptance of the Christian way of life, to practice total abstinence and to work for the abolition of the liquor traffic."[25]

At the same time that the WCTU Evangelistic Department was muting or even silencing its call for women's religious authority and encouraging its members in traditional women's church activities, its pro-woman reform stance was also declining. The Child Welfare Department of the 1910s and 20s, which had worked on a national and state level to lobby for women's and children's labor laws, passage of the Sheppard-Towner Act that would improve maternal and infant health care, and the establishment of state child health bureaus, was eventually reduced to holding mothers' meetings by the 1930s and '40s. Those meetings emphasized motion picture censorship and total abstinence from alcohol as the key to a better future for childhood. The WCTU's earlier interest in reforming society to protect the interests of women and children by lobbying for labor, child welfare, and prison reform legislation had disappeared.

Why did the Woman's Christian Temperance Union's pro-woman, and at times even feminist, stance disappear? One reason is that churches had become "feminized" during the nineteenth century, with female membership outnumbering male membership. As religious and moral values were delegated to women, allowing men to be free to compete aggressively in the developing capitalist economy, men found the church increasingly irrelevant, while women were seen as spiritually superior. As fewer and fewer men attended church, there were more leadership opportunities

24. *Handbook of the National WCTU, 1929*, 33-35.
25. *Handbook of the National WCTU, 1945*, 26.

available for women in evangelical Protestant churches.[26] And there is strong evidence that men flocked to fraternal organizations in the late nineteenth century, in part to reassert their religious authority in temples that excluded women.[27] But in the early twentieth century conservative Protestants like Billy Sunday constructed a "muscular Christianity" in an effort to reclaim male membership.[28] In a religious world anxious to regain male members, an organization which claimed more religious authority for women was threatening. The brief opportunity for Protestant women to gain a lasting place in the pulpit was gone. The WCTU gradually forsook its biblical feminism and developed their evangelical domesticity into an ideology of organized motherhood that justified their entrance into politics, a sphere which seemed less threatened by women's authority than

26. Barbara Welter, "The Feminization of American Religion, 1800-1860," ch. 6 in *Dimity Convictions: The American Woman in the Nineteenth Century* (Athens: Ohio University Press, 1976). Ann Douglas argues that we don't have enough statistical evidence to support the contention that more women than men were church members and suggests that liberal ministers reported that fewer men were joining the church because of their anxieties about the proliferation of women's church and charitable societies. Ann Douglas, *The Feminization of American Culture* (New York: Anchor Press, 1988), 99. However, historian Mark Carnes argues that many men distanced themselves from evangelical churches and resented women's increasingly dominant role in the churches: Mark C. Carnes, *Secret Ritual and Manhood in Victorian America* (New Haven: Yale University Press, 1989), 77-78. See also Janette Hassey, *No Time for Silence: Evangelical Women in Public Ministry around the Turn of the Century* (Grand Rapids: Academie Books, 1986).

27. Carnes, *Secret Ritual and Manhood*, 79.

28. Douglas Frank describes Billy Sunday's preoccupation with manhood in his book *Less than Conquerors: How Evangelicals Entered the Twentieth Century* (Grand Rapids: William B. Eerdmans Publishing Company, 1986), 188-93, 236-68. However, Frank fails to assess the significance of Sunday's emphasis on manhood, as Betty A. DeBerg has pointed out. DeBerg more successfully analyzes fundamentalists' anxiety about a female takeover of the church and their efforts to restrict women's authority in their churches and their efforts to recruit men. Betty A. DeBerg, *Ungodly Women: Gender and the First Wave of American Fundamentalism* (Minneapolis: Fortress Press, 1990), 75-98. Gail Bederman explains that as the corporation became more important in the business world, aggressive competition was not as important as it had been under an earlier entrepreneurial capitalism. A "tamed" business world was no longer so incompatible with religious values, allowing men to become more moral and religious. At the same time, women's extended private sphere was threatening male dominance in the church and in government. Protestant churches sought to regain male membership and strengthen male authority with a series of revivals aimed at men only. Gail Bederman, "'The Women Have Had Charge of the Church Work Long Enough': The Men and Religion Forward Movement of 1911-1912 and the Masculinization of Middle-Class Protestantism," *American Quarterly* 41 (September 1989): 432-65.

religious institutions. To do this, they capitalized on the exalted image of motherhood that was part of the cult of domesticity.

However, WCTU rhetoric surrounding the image of motherhood shifted from emphasizing the power and authority wielded by the priestess of the home to emphasizing the grave responsibility mothers had to instill moral values in their children. While they gained the prestige and acceptance associated with saintly motherhood in the late nineteenth and early twentieth centuries, they also placed the responsibility for the moral standards of society almost solely upon women. S. H. Wallace, a Kansas City, Kansas, WCTU leader, noted in 1905 that "the children must be taught right principles in the home. They should early in life be pledged to total abstinence from all intoxicants. . . . If the home life is what it should be, municipal life will take care of itself."[29] This led the members of the WCTU to focus not only on political and structural solutions to societal problems, but ultimately to seek to reform themselves and other women. The implication of this belief that "the hand that rocks the cradle rules the world" is that coercive governmental solutions to society's ills should only be temporary since the ultimate and final solution to societal problems is individual. Individual mothers must be equipped and dedicated to raising up the next generation free of alcohol and committed to God-ordained American middle-class standards of behavior.

This led the WCTU to encourage and teach individual mothers through their literature and also by organizing Mothers' Meetings, "where she will receive real information and help."[30] WCTU members, while they recognized certain societal evils that could be attacked through public action, such as child labor laws and the Sheppard-Towner Act, felt that the major solution was the reformation of home and family life. They claimed God-ordained power as mothers, but in doing so they made every woman a mother, either in fact or as symbol. Women who were so strongly identified with a role, and an important one at that, could not easily see themselves as individuals, nor would it be important to them. The WCTU celebrated women's power as mothers, but also called upon them to sacrifice individual aspirations for their children and society's future.

Just as their rhetoric surrounding motherhood shifted from a celebration of mothers' power to an emphasis on the responsibilities of motherhood, the focus of the WCTU's political agenda shifted as well.

29. *Our Messenger*, September 1905, 3.
30. *Our Messenger*, June 1923, 3.

Instead of working for progressive governmental reforms, assuming that society needed to change to improve poor living conditions for women and children, WCTU women of the 1930s increasingly worked to reform the individual.

The WCTU's evangelical domesticity had served them well as an effective strategy during the late nineteenth and early twentieth centuries. It allowed them to address real problems in society, such as child labor and poverty, without calling for a total restructuring of economic and societal structures. WCTU women were reluctant to completely forsake a system that allowed them the benefits of their privileged white, middle-class status. They were also loathe to give up their moral authority. However, claiming that authority on the basis of their gender had become problematic with the reassertion of Christian manhood.

Their only other pro-woman option would have been to choose biblical feminism, which called for a radical egalitarianism. That would have threatened the largely white middle-class members' class status and would have required them to align themselves with all women, regardless of race and class. While the story of the WCTU's "Work among Negroes" is the subject of another essay, suffice it to say that white WCTU members were undecided as to whether they should act as patronizing "mothers" or equal "sisters" to their African-American membership.[31] The same conflicted attitude appears in their reports on Americanization work with immigrant women. White, middle-class WCTU members constantly reminded themselves that under God all are one, but they also conducted their work with women of other races and classes as if they must educate "women of the other." Only with careful training and education could women of color and alien citizenship be allowed to advance to a social position just a step below "native" white middle-class women on the pedestal of elevated white motherhood.

The members of the WCTU finally rejected feminism, and began to claim authority, not on the basis of their gender, but simply on their status as righteous Christians. They retreated to a stance that called for the reform of society through individual improvement. When they abandoned their pro-woman stance, they also abandoned their unique brand of feminine social gospel and their claim to be a Woman's Church. By the 1950s, the Woman's Christian Temperance Union had reduced itself from a vital

31. See Nancy G. Garner, "For God and Home and Native Land: The Kansas Woman's Christian Temperance Union 1878-1938" (Ph.D. dissertation, University of Kansas, 1994), 238-87.

women's branch of American Protestantism to simply another temperance organization.

Conclusion

This feminist historical analysis which highlights the Woman's Christian Temperance Union's recognition and challenge to gender divisions within Protestantism is much more satisfactory than an analysis which would attempt to force the WCTU into the two-party paradigm. In fact, the WCTU itself found no relevance in the debate between theological conservatives and liberals. If scholars strive to adequately analyze and explain the whole of twentieth-century Protestantism, the case of the Woman's Christian Temperance Union (among others) challenges them to broaden their analysis beyond theological debates alone and to focus also on questions generated by gender, race, and class.

CHAPTER 15

Black Protestantism as Expressed in Ecumenical Activity

MARY R. SAWYER

In contrast to white Protestants in the United States who are distributed across a dozen or more Protestant "families," African-American Protestants, with but few exceptions, are concentrated in three groups: Methodist, Baptist, and Pentecostal. Over 80 percent of black Christians, some 19 million altogether, are members of the eight largest traditional black denominations: African Methodist Episcopal; African Methodist Episcopal Zion; Christian Methodist Episcopal; National Baptist Convention, U.S.A., Inc.; National Baptist Convention of America, Inc.; Progressive National Baptist Convention; National Missionary Baptist Convention of America; and the Church of God in Christ. At least 1.2 million African Americans are estimated to be affiliated with smaller Baptist bodies, scores of small Holiness and Pentecostal communions, and independent congregations. Another 1.2 million are members of predominantly white denominations. Two million African Americans are Roman Catholic.

These populations collectively constitute the "Black Church." There does not exist a singular structural entity that is *the* Black Church in the same sense that there is a Roman Catholic Church or United Methodist Church. Rather, the expression "Black Church" connotes a unity of the body of black believers, a unity forged out of a common experience of oppression and out of a common ethnic identity. It is a unity that transcends the divisiveness of doctrine and polity, and that circumvents the two-party dichotomy of liberal and conservative.

Black churches have never fit neatly in either the conservative/private or the liberal/public category. They are, more accurately, "both/and." On balance, the Black Church is liberal on matters of social concern (e.g., racial justice, poverty, and peace) and conservative on matters of individual morality (e.g., abortion, homosexuality, and premarital sex). Even those constituents of the Black Church who evidence what might be referred to as fundamentalist characteristics invariably also assert the imperative, in gospel terms, of pursuing racial justice.

In fact, it was precisely the issue of racial discrimination and injustice that initially caused black congregants to break away from the predominantly white Methodist and Baptist bodies in the late 1700s and throughout the 1800s. This discriminatory treatment came to have theological significance: black Christians understood that whites who named themselves Christian were failing to honor the "fundamental" Christian tenets of the parenthood of God and the kinship of all people. Thus, the pursuit of racial justice — of true and full kinship — has been a core characteristic of the black religious tradition throughout the history of the Black Church.

While some scholars have described the pre-1960s church as escapist and otherworldly, there is much evidence to the contrary. For example, black ministers played a key role among free blacks in protesting slavery in the antebellum period. Moreover, leaders of slave revolts were often Christian preachers who were motivated by biblical imagery of a prophetic and liberationist character. And in the decades immediately following emancipation, radical black ministers advocated emigration to Africa as an alternative to perpetual consignment to an oppressive caste system in the United States.

Admittedly, with the institutionalizing of the system of Jim Crow segregation, the conservative, passive side of black Christendom — which was always present in tandem with the liberating, activist side — became pervasively dominant. In a climate of extreme violence and intimidation, black ministers were called to shepherd their flocks in a way that enhanced the odds of sheer survival. The Black Church — the one institution controlled by black Americans — provided the organizing matrix for black life, including moral guidance, basic education, recreation, economic institution building, and leadership development. Already evangelical, the character of many black churches did become increasingly otherworldly, especially in the South, as congregations focused on enduring the conditions of this life while anticipating the rewards of the life to come. This emphasis on the primacy of one's personal relationship with God was particularly evident in the development of black Pentecostalism in the late 1800s and early 1900s.

But in the midst of the socially compelled religious conservatism of the grassroots Black Church in these years, there emerged a radical, politically active expression of black religiosity in the form of the Fraternal Council of Negro Churches. As the precursor of the black ecumenical movements of the second half of this century, the Fraternal Council warrants examination in some depth. Its continuity with more contemporary movements will then be established through an overview of several of those movements in the last section of this essay.

The Early Years of the Fraternal Council of Negro Churches

Neither the existential unity of the body of black believers nor their structural concentration in three Protestant families has obviated the need for or the inclination toward ecumenical — that is, cooperative, interdenominational — activity among the constituent parts of the Black Church. The Fraternal Council of Negro Churches, like its various successors, can be used as a prism which reveals the overarching theological consistency of black Protestantism.

The Fraternal Council of Negro Churches was organized in 1934 by a bishop of the African Methodist Episcopal Church, the Right Rev. Reverdy C. Ransom, whose socialist and nationalist inclinations were well known. Initially gathering together fellow black members of the predominantly white Federal Council of Churches, Bishop Ransom soon established an ecclesiastically diverse *black* "council of churches" that included not only the three black Methodist denominations and two National Baptist conventions, but also such religious bodies as the African Orthodox Church; the Church of our Lord Jesus Christ of the Apostolic Faith; Church of God in Christ; the Pentecostal Church; Freewill Baptists; Primitive Baptists; Church of God, Holiness; Church of God and Saints of Christ (Black Jews); the Bible Way Church of Washington, D.C.; the Metropolitan Community Church of Chicago; and the Central Jurisdiction of the Methodist Church. Also included were black contingents from predominantly white denominations, including Episcopal, Presbyterian, Congregational, Disciples of Christ (Christian), and the Conference of Community Churches.

The constituency of the Fraternal Council was always considered to be the total membership of the participating denominations, some eight to nine million as of the mid-1940s. But in this ecumenical format, the Fraternal Council also became the religious-political champion of racial uplift for all of black America. Within its parameters, individual salvation gave way to corporate responsibility, prophecy displaced acquiescence, and attention was turned to the quality of life in this world, rather than the next.[1] This emphasis was made clear in the statement of purpose issued by the Council at the conclusion of its organizing conference, held in August 1934 in Chicago, Illinois:

> While not acting under the authority of our different communions, we as officials and leaders feel that the present plight of our race in this country calls for the united strength, wisdom and influence of its religious leadership. We start with the distinct understanding that in this proposal for the Federation of Negro Churches, the question of religious doctrine, creed, polity or any interference with denominational independence, authority or control is not to enter into our deliberation. We propose that the Negro religious denominations shall cooperate on all questions touching the spiritual, moral, social, political, economic and industrial welfare of our people.[2]

In this statement the Fraternal Council established that its interests were neither doctrinal consensus nor structural merger (even though it periodically served as a forum for advocacy of the latter). In fact, the wide range of smaller black denominations and sects to which invitations to participate were extended included Holiness and Pentecostal bodies which had not previously enlisted in any ecumenical endeavors, and which would not be interested in merging into a single black church structure. Church unity clearly was an objective of the founder, as it was of other participants, but that unity was to come through cooperative action: not the cooperative action of conventional mission work or evangelism, but, instead, cooperative social action directed toward the achievement of racial justice.

That the official organizing meeting of the Council was convened in Chicago and attended predominantly by northern ministers pastoring urban churches was no coincidence. Since 1917, Bishop Ransom had been pleading in the *AME Review* for interdenominational cooperation and coordination of services to blacks in northern urban ghettos who had migrated from the South during the War and Depression years. However,

---

1. The following discussion draws on an article previously published in *Church History* 59 (March 1990): 51-64. For a more extended discussion of the Fraternal Council and other black ecumenical organizations, see Mary R. Sawyer, *Black Ecumenism: Implementing the Demands of Justice* (Valley Forge, PA: Trinity Press International, 1994).

2. Reverdy C. Ransom, ed., "The Fraternal Council of Negro Churches in America," *Year Book of Negro Churches, 1935-36* (Wilberforce, OH, 1936), 24-25.

positions taken by the Council in subsequent meetings demonstrated concern not only for the problems engendered by urban life, but for the plight of sharecroppers in the South. At the same time, their deliberations pointed to a keen awareness that the twin scourges of racism and economic discrimination were part of a larger global dynamic.

The Fraternal Council met a second time in Cleveland, Ohio, in August of 1935. The nearly 200 delegates who attended this session issued "A Message to the Churches and to the Public" which, as a statement of the ecumenical and theological orientation of the Council, merits quoting at length:

> For more than three hundred years Americans of African descent have embraced every creed and form of religious belief that would admit them to membership in their churches. They had nothing to do with the bitter religious controversies and divisions that gave birth to the numerous communions and sects that divide American Protestant Christianity. They have produced no Martin Luthers, John Calvins, or John Wesleys. They have never been called upon to suffer persecution for conscience sake because of religious belief. They have simply divided and followed the many divergent paths where their white fellow Christians had paved the way. But these religious divisions have left us weak and almost helpless of power to protest and defend ourselves in the social, industrial, economic and political framework of American society. . . .
>
> In the United States we have about four million Jews who always stand together when the interests of Jewry are at stake. We have here, five million Negroes organized into many different churches, each acting separately and apart, so far as the interests of the race as a whole are concerned. Neither the Baptists nor the Methodists, however numerous, however strong they each may be within themselves, are powerful enough to face the pitiable plight that confronts our people without the reinforcement and cooperation of the others. . . .
>
> The hour is at hand when the Negro church should unite to fearlessly challenge the faithless stewardship of American Christianity by submitting it to the test of political, social, and economic justice, a justice that accepts no peace on the basis of submission, compromise, or surrender.
>
> Shall the American Negro, whose broadest boast is the patriotic devotion and loyalty with which he has defended our flag in all wars, be less devoted and loyal to the cross of Christ when all that it stands for in human relations is either openly denied or menaced, in social, economic and political denial with which it is flouted or assailed?
>
> Those who have joined the Fraternal Council have found joy in the

larger freedom and fellowship. We call upon ministers and lay members in all the churches to cross the boundary lines of their denominationalism to join in the common task of working in the present to secure the future peace and justice not only of our race, but of all underprivileged and oppressed.[3]

In addition to its cogent appeal for black cross-denominational unity, this statement is noteworthy for its explicit critique of white churches. Theologically, that critique is predicated on justice for the "underprivileged and oppressed," language that anticipates by over thirty years the National Conference of Black Christians (NCBC) and the black theology movement to which NCBC gave birth. The securing of justice is clearly posited as the appropriate measure of faithfulness not only of the white church, but of the black church as well.

The statement was attended by a series of resolutions addressing a wide range of pragmatic issues, including the exclusion of farm laborers and domestic workers, who constituted more than half the black population, from the new Social Security Act; the "condition of virtual serfdom" of black sharecroppers; the exclusion of blacks from labor organizations; and discrimination in the administration of government relief programs. Regarding Italy's threatened assault on Ethiopia, one resolution read: "While by sympathy, principle, and ideals we are Americans to the core, we cannot be deaf to the cry that comes from a menaced nation in the land of our fathers' fathers." And regarding evangelism, the Council proclaimed that: "We urge our ministers to study their Bibles with particular reference to the . . . teachings of Jesus regarding social justice and brotherhood. . . . We also urge that our people be encouraged to organize whenever they can."[4]

In an "Address to the Country" issued the following year, in 1936, the Fraternal Council spoke to many of the same issues, but included appeals for blacks themselves to utilize their potential political and economic power. The Council also added this word of clarification, which in important respects anticipated the philosophy of cultural pluralism that emerged from the black consciousness movement of the 1960s and early 1970s:

3. "A Message to the Churches and to the Public from the Fraternal Council of Negro Churches," reprinted in Reverdy C. Ransom, *The Pilgrimage of Harrriet Ransom's Son* (Nashville: A.M.E.C. Sunday School Union, n.d.), 297-300.
4. *1972 Heritage Brochure: Facts about the National Fraternal Council of Churches, U.S.A., Inc.,* assembled and issued by the Washington Bureau, National Fraternal Council of Churches, July 1972, 8-10.

We would not . . . have it understood that by urging organization along racial lines we are urging antagonism to the white people of our country. Far be it from that. We are offering the only method of cooperating with white people. The Negroes cannot hope to cooperate individually, but only collectively. We are of very little power today because we act as individuals. We must act as a body in order to cooperate with other bodies working in the same field.[5]

It must be noted that, beyond issuing resolutions, there is little evidence of program activity in the first few years of the Council's life. Part of this was due to the lack of money. The Council accepted no funds from white churches or foundations, but, instead, was entirely dependent on offerings received at its meetings and dues paid by denominational representatives (one dollar per year per representative, according to its original constitution). Given that these were the years of the Great Depression, offerings and dues were hard to come by. Just to maintain an organizational structure throughout the Depression years was an accomplishment of no small magnitude.

William H. Jernagin's Leadership of the Fraternal Council

The Fraternal Council really came into its own in 1938, when the presidency of the Council passed from Bishop Ransom to Rev. William H. Jernagin. In addition to pastoring Mount Carmel Baptist Church in Washington, D.C., Jernagin served for over thirty years as president of the National Sunday School and Baptist Training Union of the National Baptist Convention, U.S.A., Inc. For more than a decade he sat on the Executive Board of the Baptist World Alliance; he was also a representative to the Federal Council of Churches before the Fraternal Council came into existence. Beyond his denominational and ecumenical experience, Jernagin had sterling credentials as an activist. His opposition to the enactment of Jim Crow laws in Oklahoma led ultimately to the 1915 Supreme Court decision outlawing the "grandfather clause" which had so effectively disenfranchised blacks following Reconstruction. Years later, in the 1950s, a test case brought by Jernagin and Mary Church Terrell led to the Supreme Court decision outlawing segregation in public accommodations in Washington, D.C. In 1954, Jernagin succeeded Terrell as chair of the Coordinat-

5. Monroe N. Work, ed., *Negro Year Book* (Tuskegee, AL, 1937-38), 215.

ing Committee for the Enforcement of the D.C. Anti-Discrimination Laws. Jernagin's political activism and prominence are further attested by the fact that the FBI maintained a "main" file on him, as well as a "cross-referenced" file on the Council, from the early 1940s into the 1950s.

In 1940, Jernagin became chair of the Fraternal Council's executive committee, holding that office for six years. While serving in that capacity, Jernagin proposed and established the Washington Bureau. He then served as the first director of the Bureau. As a result of conflicts with the executive secretary, who was the appointed administrator of the Council, Jernagin moved to sever the Bureau from his administrative oversight. Thereafter, the Bureau reported directly to the executive committee, which Jernagin chaired. The autonomy of the Bureau was thus assured. Jernagin officially resigned in 1947 on complaint that he himself had had to raise the funds to support the Bureau's work and that his request to the executive committee for staff support had been ignored. However, he maintained his relationship to the Bureau in the capacity of advisor and consultant, and for all practical purposes continued to direct its program. In 1952, Jernagin again became chair of the executive committee, retaining that position until his death in 1958, at age 89.

In short, from the late 1930s to the late 1950s the Rev. William Jernagin *was* the Fraternal Council. Under his leadership the Fraternal Council shifted from a conciliar approach to a more autocratic model. But it also moved from simply issuing public pronouncements — though it continued to do that — to pragmatic activism. Thanks to Jernagin, the Washington Bureau was for twenty years the voice of the Black Church on executive and legislative matters pertaining to the struggle of black Americans to secure their civil rights. From 1943 to 1964, the Bureau's staff met and corresponded with presidents Roosevelt to Johnson; testified before House and Senate Committees on such issues as the FEPC, anti-lynching and anti-poll tax bills, desegregation of interstate travel, housing and education aid, civil rights for the District of Columbia, and the 1957 and 1964 Civil Rights Acts; protested incidents of discrimination in the armed services; published the monthly "Capitol Letter" as a means of informing local church constituencies; cooperated with A. Philip Randolph on labor issues and with Clarence Mitchell on the NAACP's legislative program; and organized civil rights conferences, prayer vigils, and pilgrimages.

The Lasting Legacy of the Fraternal Council

What is particularly striking is how active the Fraternal Council's Washington Bureau was in the years prior to 1954 (which is often seen as the beginning of the civil rights movement). For example, in 1943, at the height of World War II, the Bureau was instrumental in arranging for black churchmen to visit soldiers in overseas war zones. The next year the Bureau sponsored the "National Conference of Christians for Religion, Democracy, and Building a Community of World Brotherhood," from which a "Manifesto" for action was issued to the nation and the government; this Manifesto asserted that, "We are in the process of defeating master racism abroad, but master racism is in the process of defeating us at home."[6] After the war's end, the Bureau sponsored three church observers at the organizing meeting of the United Nations. And in 1948 the Fraternal Council organized a National Prayer March in Washington attended by nearly 200 ministers from seventeen states. The "Statement on Negro Citizens and Human Rights, addressed to the Country," issued by the participants on that occasion, read in part as follows:

> We believe in the necessity of a strong Navy, a well equipped Army and ships and planes to protect our national borders and the peace of the world against international violators of human rights; but we also believe these things to be most important in the absence of the Good Neighbor principles. We therefore urge that our national leaders shall look wisely to the spending of more millions for education, good homes and other vehicles of goodwill, and that they do more in legislation and in practice to conquer the prejudices against sections, races and groups, and thereby establish a sense of security among all our citizens.[7]

One of the most ambitious projects of the Fraternal Council and its Washington Bureau was the creation of "Committees of One Hundred" in major cities. These committees consisted of ministers who could be called on to lobby for the passage of legislation that advanced the cause of social justice. In fact, such calls were issued and ministers did travel to Washington to lobby their representatives. This model was later to be adopted by Partners in Ecumenism, which for several years devoted a

---

6. Cited in Spurgeon E. Crayton, "The History and Theology of the National Fraternal Council of Negro Churches" (master's thesis, Union Theological Seminary, 1979), 42.

7. 1972 Heritage Brochure, 21.

portion of its annual meetings to active legislative lobbying. A Committee of One Hundred was organized in Washington, D.C., and apparently functioned as an adjunct of the Bureau. Rev. Jernagin himself was officially registered as a lobbyist for the Fraternal Council following passage of the Legislative Reorganization Act of 1946. A Women's Auxiliary, headed by Jernagin's wife, was organized in 1950.

Significantly, the Council did not restrict itself to domestic issues, but was concerned with international affairs as well. For example, the 1950 Report of the Committee on the State of the Country asserted that:

> The hope of everyone, the dream, the deep and abiding desire of all is for Peace. Yet it would appear that our method of arriving at such is altogether foreign to our deepest yearnings. The church, aware of the armament race of the nations of the world, a race in which this our nation seems to be outstripping all others, would point out that peace, World Peace, is not to be attained by the production of more and better weapons of war, but by rising to great stature, great moral and spiritual stature in world and domestic character. We cannot but deplore the decision of the government to proceed with [humanity's] most devastating and utterly destructive . . . experiment in self-annihilation.[8]

The dynamism of the Council and its concrete contributions were given eloquent testimony by a 1945 article in the *Pittsburgh Courier*, which described the Council and its Washington Bureau as "mobilized Christian theology in action." According to the *Courier*, the work of the Bureau was "one of the most revolutionary developments of our time," with "its dramatic technique of organizing Negro preachers." The black preacher, "the all-time leader of a patient flock of believers, is gradually realizing that the 'keys to the kingdom' can be found in militant social action." Thanks to the Bureau, "a growing number of ministers think that the church cannot be reborn unless it is through a movement of the disinherited and dispossessed."[9]

This theologically grounded activism continued into the 1950s, providing support for the emerging civil rights movement. On September 22, 1954, the Fraternal Council sponsored a "Lincoln Thanksgiving Pilgrimage" at the Lincoln Memorial in celebration of the Supreme Court decision setting aside the "separate but equal" doctrine in pubic education. The

8. Ibid., 35.
9. "Fraternal Council's Bureau Growing in Social Action," *Pittsburgh Courier,* May 26, 1945.

Council also presented a citation to Thurgood Marshall, and voted to contribute $20,000 to the Freedom Rally Fund of the NAACP. In 1956, Jernagin led a movement which culminated in a National Prayer Day for "victims of Montgomery, Alabama's Bus Protest." That event, observed on March 28, resulted in several thousand dollars being raised to help with the "Montgomery problem." The Council participated in the 1957 Civil Rights Conference, resolutions from which called for establishment of a U.S. Civil Rights Commission and aid to dislocated persons in Hungary and the Middle East. The Conference also commended and expressed support for Martin Luther King, Jr., and other participants in the emerging civil rights movement of the South. In 1963, the Council co-sponsored a city-wide mass meeting in observance of the centennial anniversary of the signing of the Emancipation Proclamation.

One of the Council's last major acts was its decision to support and participate in the 1963 March on Washington. That it would do so was consonant with the precedent for nonviolent protest established in 1948 and continued throughout the 1950s. But by the early 1960s the Washington Bureau had begun to concentrate on issues indigenous to the District of Columbia. The fact is that, with the advent of the national civil rights movement, the Fraternal Council had been eclipsed. Those who might have been expected to support the organization were attracted to more activist and better-known organizations, notably the recently constituted black ecumenical organization known as the Southern Christian Leadership Conference. In short, the heyday of the Fraternal Council had passed.

At no time in its history did the Council even begin to fulfill Bishop Ransom's vision of a mass movement led by a united Black Church. Although hints of mass action were to be found in the prayer vigils and the organized lobbying, the reality was that the Council's preeminent strategy was to position itself within the system and to agitate for change through resolutions, legislation, and lobbying of persons in positions of power.

And yet, external impediments and internal shortcomings notwithstanding, the Fraternal Council of Negro Churches represents an important effort on the part of the Black Church to overcome denominational divisions in order to improve the social, economic, and political status of the black populace. More to the point of this essay, the existence of the Fraternal Council challenges the one-sided image of the Black Church in the first half of the twentieth century as being strictly accommodationist and escapist. Rather, the Council provides confirmation of the claim that while the Black Church has historically been conservative on matters of individual morality, it has been liberal and, at times, even radical on matters of racial justice and (to a lesser degree) on matters of economic justice.

Black Ecumenism, 1960s to 1980s

While the Fraternal Council was eclipsed by the advent of the civil rights movement, it had already been seriously undermined by the formation of the predominantly white and "liberal" National Council of Churches. Particularly after the 1954 Supreme Court decision declaring unconstitutional the doctrine of "separate but equal," expectations for integration were running high, and many members of the Fraternal Council came to regard a separate black organization as both inappropriate and unnecessary in view of the existence of the new National Council. But within a decade this position had been rejected by the Church leaders.

In addition to the Southern Christian Leadership Conference (SCLC), the 1960s and 1970s saw the emergence of half a dozen other national black ecumenical organizations and numerous movements at the local level. In keeping with the founding purpose of the Fraternal Council, a key reason these organizations came into being was because of deep dissatisfaction with white religious organizations. But the motivation for their conception also contained an affirming and celebrative dimension. In the 1960s a new black awareness was fostered which sought to preserve and enlarge upon those aspects of black culture involving heritage, ethnic pride, African origins, artistry, and moral integrity. As a consequence of this black consciousness movement and the social change which attended it, Black America underwent a metamorphosis in which the overtly religious component of black culture participated. What ensued was a transformation in existing religious institutions and symbols, a transformation, as C. Eric Lincoln put it, from the "Negro Church" of passivity and escapism to the "Black Church" of empowerment and liberation.[10] In reality this "new" Black Church was, of course, the embodiment of the black religious tradition which from the beginning had affirmed political struggle toward the ends of justice, freedom, and equity. And, in keeping with the historic example of the Fraternal Council, nowhere was this revitalized character of the Black Church more in evidence than in the black ecumenical movements.

10. C. Eric Lincoln, *The Black Church Since Frazier* (New York: Schocken Books, 1974).

The civil rights movement, especially in the early years, was in large part a movement of the Black Church.[11] The flagship organization of the civil rights movement, the Southern Christian Leadership Conference, or SCLC, was headed by a black Baptist minister — the Rev. Dr. Martin Luther King, Jr. — and governed by a board of directors comprised overwhelmingly of black ministers. The lifeblood of SCLC was its local affiliates, which often consisted of the pastors of black churches in a given city or community. Moreover, the local nonviolent protests and movements of the South were invariably organized in local churches and carried out by the lay members of those churches. They were primarily Baptist, secondarily Methodist, and not without a Pentecostal presence; in short, local movements, in keeping with SCLC leadership, were ecumenical.

The civil rights movement was succeeded by the black power movement, a largely secular reaction to the pacifist ideology and perceived slow pace of SCLC. The seemingly radical and sometimes harsh rhetoric of this movement generated a backlash among white religious bodies, including members of the National Council of Churches, as well as among conservative black churchpersons. The concern on the part of progressive black ministers to interpret the demands of black power in theological terms gave rise to a new organization called the National Conference of Black Christians (NCBC), which functioned actively from 1966 to 1972. While NCBC gave attention to urban economic problems and to relations with Africa, its primary involvement and contribution was the development of what came to be known as "black liberation theology."

Black liberation theology in turn provided the impetus and framework for yet other ecumenical efforts, including the Black Theology Project, organized in 1977, and Partners in Ecumenism (PIE), an entity within the National Council of Churches which was organized in 1978. But among the most important of these ecumenical efforts was the Congress of National Black Churches (CNBC). Founded in 1978, the Congress of National Black Churches, like the older Fraternal Council of Negro Churches, was organized on a conciliar model; that is to say, membership was determined on a denominational, rather than individual, basis. To date, membership has included the three major black Methodist denominations, the four national black Baptist conventions, and the largest black Pentecostal denomination, the Church of God in Christ.

Social justice, rather than structural merger or doctrinal consensus,

---

11. See Aldon D. Morris, *The Origins of the Civil Rights Movement: Black Communities Organizing for Change* (New York: The Free Press, 1984).

has been the primary concern of the Congress of National Black Churches. But its agenda of social transformation has consistently been presented within a framework of evangelism, or, as one of its early task forces was entitled, "evangelism in the black perspective." As defined by the Congress's founder, AME Bishop John Hurst Adams, "evangelism in the black perspective . . . encompasses the social mission of the Black Church. It is the whole church responding as a caring community to the redemptive needs of the whole person and the whole society."[12] Another member of the Congress, Baptist minister Thomas Kilgore, put it this way: "evangelism in the black perspective" involves the need to "wed traditional evangelistic goals of soul-winning with social and political action in whatever materials and resources we may develop."[13]

In important respects, the Congress was the mirror image of yet another black ecumenical organization that had come into existence in 1963 precisely with the objective of wedding evangelism with social action. The National Black Evangelical Association (NBEA), under the leadership of William Bentley, Tom Skinner, and a dozen other individuals, consisted primarily of members of the "evangelical" wing of American Protestantism who, until the advent of the black consciousness movement, had cut themselves off from the heritage and traditions of the historic Black Church. From its founding to the present time, NBEA's agenda has continued to focus on the defining and implementing of a holistic ministry to the black community that is inclusive of social concerns as well as spiritual affairs. In the process, it has influenced the National Association of Evangelicals in a positive direction, particularly in its attention to the social reality and destructiveness of racism.[14]

In advancing its agenda, members of the National Black Evangelical Association have pointedly rejected the fundamentalist versus liberal debate that characterized much of the white evangelical establishment. In effect, it functioned as a black caucus within the evangelical wing of American Protestantism, and hence was also an interdenominational caucus, drawing members from independent, Bible, Holiness, and Pentecostal churches, as well as Methodist, Baptist, Presbyterian, Mennonite, and Quaker bodies. As much as anything, the National Black Evangelical

12. John Hurst Adams, interviews, Washington, D.C., January 17 and 22, and March 19, 1985.

13. CNBC Minutes, December 16-18, 1980, Houston, TX.

14. Concerning the NBEA see William H. Bentley, *The Meaning of History for Black Americans* (Chicago: NBEA, 1979) and *National Black Evangelical Association: Bellwether of a Movement, 1963-1988* (Chicago: NBEA, 1988).

Association has served as a refuge for black pastors who had termed themselves evangelicals, embraced white evangelical perspectives, attended white evangelical schools — and then found themselves left to minister to African Americans with white evangelical models that were devoid of sensitivity to the cultural, social, and religious distinctions of the black community.

This overt emphasis on developing an "evangelism in the black perspective" by two different organizations — one more connected to what might be referred to as the white liberal expression of Protestantism and the other more connected to what might be referred to as the white conservative evangelical expression of Protestantism — attests to the inability of the two-party system of white Protestantism to impose itself in any enduring way on expressions of Protestantism anchored in the black experience. In other words, these understandings of Christianity and its mandates, which were forged by black believers in the fires of oppression and exploitation necessarily transcend the theological bifurcations of the ruling caste. While black individuals or congregations may drift toward one or another of the camps that allegedly divide white Protestantism, those black Christians who remain connected, or reestablish contact, with the heritage and tradition of the Black Church find those bifurcations rendered meaningless. While black Protestantism has always emphasized a Bible-centered and personal faith, black piety has also been strongly ethical and communal in orientation. In fact, the motto of the Black Church might well be, "We've come this far by faith," that is, *we* as a *people* have come this far by faith. Sin is understood to be both individual and corporate; redemption is personal and social. Insofar as racism is a denial of the divinity in all persons, it is an affront to God and therefore a condition compelling evangelical outreach and missionary efforts toward conversion — conversion which, if successfully achieved, will be manifested in efforts of social reform, if not social transformation.

If there is a theme common to black ecumenical efforts, it is precisely this. From SCLC, with its appeal to the moral conscience of America; to NCBC and the Black Theology Project, with their gospel-grounded emphasis on redistribution of power and economic resources; to Partners in Ecumenism, which sought to bring white churches into the work of addressing black social conditions; to the Congress of National Black Churches and the National Black Evangelical Association, with their overt theme of "evangelism in the black perspective" — in all of these organizational efforts the preeminent assertion was and is the parenthood of God and the kinship of all people. All are to be brought into the fold; more than this, all are to be brought into the fold with standards of justice and respect prevailing.

In this "evangelism in the black perspective" — in the holding together of the conservative and the liberal, in the holding together of the concern for the status of one's soul and concern for the status of one's socioeconomic well-being — black ecumenical organizations are representative of the Black Church as a whole. Even those units of the Black Church that were and are more evangelical and even fundamentalist have upheld the Christian mandate for equality. What might be termed "fundamentalism" in black churches has thus been qualitatively different from fundamentalism in white churches, to the point that evangelization has often been understood to mean a responsibility to convert white Christians from their racial prejudices and biases to a more authentic and inclusive expression of Christianity.

Accordingly, as noted in the introduction of this essay, it is inaccurate and inappropriate to characterize the Black Church (or any segment of the Black Church) as either "conservative" or "liberal." More than this, in its melding of the personal and social dimensions of the gospel the Black Church is a shining "city on a hill" from which all Christians could learn much.

CHAPTER 16

Keeping the "Fun" in Fundamentalism: The Winona Lake Bible Conferences, 1895-1968

MICHAEL S. HAMILTON AND
MARGARET LAMBERTS BENDROTH

"At least those who love the Lord can learn some lessons from Winona Lake," Bob Jones, Jr., grumbled in response to news of the Bible conference's closing in 1968. The demise was, in his eyes, a teaching opportunity, for it proved an axiom of fundamentalist theology, which Jones repeated with grim satisfaction: "Compromise of Truth means destruction to a Christian work."[1]

Matters of personal piety aside, the story of Winona does add substantially to the narrative of early twentieth-century Protestantism. The Winona Lake Bible Conference, which convened every summer from 1895 to 1968, was one of fundamentalism's most important rallying grounds. All of the movement's pulpit stars, from Bob Jones and Billy Sunday to William Jennings Bryan and J. Gresham Machen, made regular pilgrimages to the "playground of the Christian world" in northern Indiana.[2]

---

1. Jones, *Cornbread and Caviar: Reminiscences and Reflections* (Greenville, SC: Bob Jones University Press, 1985), 110. Interestingly, Jones traces liberal infiltration to the 1930s (cf. 101f), while two other observers (also based at Bob Jones University) mark that decade as the beginning of fundamentalist hegemony at Winona, a process they argue was not completed until the 1950s. See David O. Beale, *In Pursuit of Purity: American Fundamentalism Since 1850* (Greenville, SC: Unusual Publications, 1986), 5; and Mark Sidwell, "The History of the Winona Bible Conference" (Ph.D. dissertation, Bob Jones University, 1988).

2. The phrase comes from Vincent H. Gaddis and Jasper A. Huffman, *The Story*

But so did many others not easily pegged as fundamentalists, such as Presbyterian moderate Robert Speer and Lutheran radio evangelist Walter Maier. Indeed, the Winona program probably never met Bob Jones's standard of fundamentalist orthodoxy. Well into the 1930s Winona kept alive a dying Protestant discourse about the social gospel, eschatology, evolution, and the Bible. Even in the heyday of doctrinal controversy Winona represented a type of ecumenical fundamentalism that was not defined by anti-modernity, dispensational theology, rationalist approaches to Scripture, or the battle plans of publicists and theologians. In Winona, for a time, something of the old evangelical order survived.

After the 1930s Winona's cultural program declined while its Bible Conference program expanded under a new, more self-consciously fundamentalist leadership. But rather than promoting a narrowly anti-modernist agenda, Winona's leaders worked to make the Bible Conference an institution dedicated to issues that a wide variety of evangelicals could support with enthusiasm: Bible study, personal holiness, and the necessity of an individual "born again" conversion.

The story of Winona tempers, but does not completely contradict, the standard outline of the fundamentalist-modernist controversy. Winona was not torn apart by the conflict, and, indeed, for some time after seemed untouched by its divisive spirit. But in due time, the same changes that shattered some other Protestant institutions reached Winona Lake, as the nineteenth-century evangelical synthesis of individualistic piety and social vision narrowed to exclusively spiritual concerns.

Perhaps even more important, however, Winona Lake also demonstrates that fundamentalism came in two versions. One type, described by Ernest Sandeen and George Marsden, stressed doctrinal correctness. Its rationalist approach to the faith never inspired widespread popularity, appealing more to those schooled in the details of fundamentalist

---

of Winona Lake (Winona Lake, IN: Rodeheaver Co., 1961), 9. On the history of Winona see also Sidwell, "The History of the Winona Lake Bible Conference," and Thomas Kane, *All about Winona* (Winona Lake, IN: Winona Assembly and Sunday School Association, 1904).

Because of financial difficulties Winona went through several reorganizations; with each new incarnation, the Bible Conference took greater central focus. Organized first as the Winona Assembly and Sunday School Association, it reopened in 1915 as the Winona Assembly and Bible Conference. In 1937 it underwent yet another reorganization and came under more direct fundamentalist control as the Winona Lake Christian Assembly, Inc.

dogma.[3] The second type, emphasizing conversion and spiritual nurture, was irenic and ecumenical. Joel Carpenter has located it within a cluster of independent, interdenominational parachurch organizations, such as Bible institutes and evangelistic ministries. Carpenter's fundamentalists are both separatists — that is, argumentative, doctrinally concerned, and sectarian — and evangelizers, conciliatory pietists who minimized denominational doctrinal differences.[4]

Winona Lake's revivalist, populist ethos fits this latter description far better than the former. The Bible Conference maintained a consistent level of denominational diversity, but sought to unite all Protestants behind a common evangelical vision, centered in the continual need for spiritual revival. Winona Lake stood for a type of fundamentalism that flourished in interdenominational parachurch organizations that *always* promoted evangelism, missions, Bible study, prayer, and Keswick-style holiness, and *often* promoted (and was nearly always friendly to) the doctrines of inerrancy, premillennial dispensationalism, and opposition to modernist theology.

A Fundamentalist Chautauqua

Popular fundamentalism flourished in places like Winona. Its guests could check their institutional and theological baggage at the door, and enjoy a leisured but thoroughly Christian summer vacation. Winona's directors offered a consistent menu of relaxation and inspiration, designed for laypeople and clergymen who yearned for a break from doctrinal controversy.

3. Sandeen identified fundamentalism as the direct descendant of the premillennialist prophecy conference movement, having also taken on the doctrine of biblical inerrancy as formulated at Princeton Seminary. Marsden, whose definition of fundamentalism is most commonly cited, describes it as "militantly anti-modernist Protestant evangelicalism." Marsden's definition also included the movement's roots in revivalism, the holiness movement, Scottish commonsense realism, and the 1920s controversy over modernism in several northern denominations; yet it still makes militant opposition to modernism the litmus test for the movement, even when he admits that this was "not necessarily the central trait of fundamentalists." See Sandeen, *The Roots of Fundamentalism: British and American Millenarianism, 1800-1930* (Chicago: University of Chicago Press, 1970); and Marsden, *Fundamentalism and American Culture: The Shaping of Twentieth-Century Evangelicalism* (New York: Oxford University Press, 1980), 4, 231, n. 4.

4. Joel Carpenter, *Revive Us Again: The Reawakening of American Fundamentalism* (New York: Oxford University Press, 1997).

As one speaker reflected in 1920, "There are griefs enough at home. We leave them there and [are] happy at Winona."[5] Winona folks were "plain people . . . without frills, theological or otherwise," an enthusiast explained. At Winona, even the stodgiest doctors of divinity soon found "the dust of their theology washed off in the waters of the lake."[6] Its leaders were not after "religious or educational vagaries," another supporter explained, but were "hard-headed, tender-hearted, far-sighted, faith-filled men."[7]

Winona's easy blend of inspiration and fun was evident from its inception. Solomon C. Dickey, Winona's founder, was Indiana's superintendent of Presbyterian home missions, and an admirer of both the Chautauqua movement and the Northfield Bible Conferences headed by D. L. Moody. After conferring with Moody and John Heyl Vincent, the Methodist Sunday school visionary and founder of Chautauqua, Dickey decided that his conference would include the best features of both. It would be educational, entertaining, and deeply spiritual. More than a camp meeting but not quite Coney Island, it was to be "a resort that will serve the needs of the whole man, aiding him physically, socially, mentally and spiritually."[8]

True to this aim, Winona endeavored to keep the "fun" in a rapidly polarizing, increasingly militant fundamentalist movement. At its peaceful shores the faithful could enjoy a vigorous program of summer sports, from swimming and boating to croquet and tennis. A full Chautauqua program, complete with musical performances, temperance lectures, trained pets, and Shakespearean drama, ran all season, capped by the two-week Bible conference in mid-August. The second-largest Chautauqua in the country, Winona sponsored an endless variety of specialized summer schools, from Bible classes and ministers' meetings to an agricultural institute, conservatory of music, and a Chautauqua Literary and Scientific circle.[9] Laurence

---

5. Ira Landrith, "The Bible Conference," *Winona Echoes* (1920): 94.

6. Kane, *All about Winona*, 24; "Winona Herald, 1917," 18.

7. William Charles Covert, "Winona: Her Solidity, Sanity, Optimism," *Interior* 29 (September 1904): passim.

8. Sol Dickey, "Foreword," in "Winona Year Book and Programs, 1909" (Winona Lake, IN, 1909), 3. The springs that fed Winona Lake were said to be medicinal. According to one report, Winona water "produced highly beneficial results in cases of rheumatism, kidney, liver and stomach troubles" (Kane, *All about Winona*, 12).

9. The Bible Conferences and the Chautauqua program were not separate entities. According to the Winona Year Book of 1910, "The resident on the grounds who passes out of one directly into the other will find them controlled by the same spirit, yet

Moore's observation that Chautauqua popularized the "idea that churches owed their members some good times" certainly holds true for Winona. Both were artful minglings of piety and play, reflecting the growing acceptance of spiritual leisure in a work-driven Protestant culture.[10]

The fun even spilled over into the Bible Conferences. J. Gresham Machen, who first spoke there in 1915, noted that the "rough house element" pervaded all. "Practically every lecture, on whatever subject, was begun by the singing of some of the popular jingles, often accompanied by the blowing of enormous horns or other weird instruments of music," Machen later related. "And the lectures themselves, if they were to be successful, had to be a good deal after the manner of stump speeches." Although he became a regular Winona visitor, Machen counted his first talk a failure, taking dubious comfort in the compliment that at least his talk had not been marred by applause. All of which led Machen to conclude, albeit mournfully, that "there may be a few — though a very few — people even at Winona who are content to consider a serious subject in a serious way."[11]

Winona's program relaxed the body, rested the soul, and gently stirred the emotions. Musical performances and songfests regularly uplifted the faithful; higher life meetings at Winona's "Round Top" thrilled them with quiet awe. Virginia Asher, an evangelistic associate of Billy Sunday, convened twilight meetings for women at Winona's shoreline, addressing the gathering while standing in a small boat. As night fell she drifted off into the darkness, while she sang "The Light of the World Is Jesus" in her clear, lilting soprano.[12]

---

directed to a somewhat different spirit. The Assembly represents the inclusion of all life in religion; the Conference the intensification of religion in all life. The Assembly generalizes on Christianity; the Conference specializes on it" (21). By 1907 "Bible Day" became part of the Chautauqua program ("Year Book of the Winona Assembly and Schools, 1907").

10. Moore, *Selling God: American Religion in the Marketplace of Culture* (New York: Oxford, 1994), 149-55.

11. Ned Stonehouse, *J. Gresham Machen: A Biographical Memoir* (Grand Rapids: Eerdmans, 1955), 232-33. As a side note, Bob Jones, Jr., reported that his mother found visits to Winona an exercise in endurance. "The backwaters of the lake bred mosquitos. The climate, she declared, was the worst imaginable — one day was insufferably hot without a breath of air; the next was damp, cold, and rainy. . . . Between trying to fight mosquitos and keep house in an inconvenient and inadequately furnished summer place and keeping a sharp eye on this active boy, she had her hands full, and it is no wonder that she looked on the annual visit to Winona as a penance and not a vacation" (*Cornbread and Caviar*, 87-88).

12. Interview with Edna Louise Asher Case, Billy Graham Center Archives; Lena S. Sanders, *The Council Torchbearer* (Roanoke, VA, 1936), 11.

All of this contributed to Winona's spectacular success, as did the continuing appeal of populist revivalism. By 1904 the conference grounds included 200 cottages, three large hotels, well-stocked general stores, and its own water, sewer, and electrical system. Attendance flourished; by 1905 it reached 12,000 (including 2,000 clergymen), and in 1915 an estimated 20,000 came on a single day to hear Billy Sunday and William Jennings Bryan share a platform.[13]

Winona's Inclusiveness

Presbyterians had been the strongest early supporters of Winona — in 1896 the General Assembly met there, and its bylaws specified a two-thirds Presbyterian majority on the Bible conference board of directors — but they never monopolized the platform. Reflecting the religious diversity of its northern Indiana setting, Winona attracted a steady trickle of Lutherans and Christian Reformed visitors, as well as numerous United Brethren, Baptists, and Methodists (both North and South), and Disciples of Christ.[14] Methodists and United Brethren built cottages on Winona property, and all were free to worship at Winona's federated church, supplied by a Presbyterian pastor but open to full and affiliate membership by all Protestants.[15] Ecumenical pastors' conferences and denominational rallies remained an important feature in Winona's summer program. In 1932 it hosted sixteen different rallies, from Mennonites and Quakers and Congregationalists to Methodists and Baptists, both north and south.

Year after year Dickey, as well as his successor, evangelist William Biederwolf, introduced the conference with a plea for tolerance. "If any

13. Dickey, "Short History of the Winona Movement," in "Winona Year Book," 1904, 26-27; "C.L.S.C. Round Table," *Chautauquan* 38 (1905): 199; "Sunday Record Day at Winona," *Indianapolis Star,* August 29, 1915. Winona relied on gifts and subscriptions to meet its costs. It had no endowment, and the weekly cost of admission to all attractions was $5.00 in 1905. According to one account, four-fifths of Winona's 500 stockholders had only one share (Kane, *All about Winona,* 24).

14. For a denominational profile, see Clifton J. Phillips, *Indiana in Transition: The Emergence of an Industrial Commonwealth, 1880-1920* (Indianapolis: Indiana Historic Bureau and Indiana Historical Society, 1968), 437-68.

15. See, e.g., "Winona Bible Conference," *Quarterly Review of United Brethren in Christ* 11 (October 1900): 381-82. The Winona property is now owned by the Grace Brethren, and houses Grace College and Theological Seminary. By 1906 the federated church included 16 different denominations in its membership. See Gaddis and Huffman, *The Story of Winona Lake,* 48.

speaker does not speak as you thought he would, or should," Dickey urged in 1915, "please remember . . . that it may be perhaps, in God's plan, to get us out of a rut . . . of thought or method." "We love our brethren even though we do not see all things just alike," Biederwolf, a self-declared fundamentalist, reminded the faithful in 1930. "Others may contend with [a] belligerent and unkindly spirit; Winona is content with a positive message. She is the champion of no particular 'Ism' but 'Evangelism.' "[16]

In these years, Winona contended for a faith that was triumphantly inclusive, reflecting the zeal for federation in the Protestant church at large. The big problem with modern secularism, Southern Baptist moderate E. Y. Mullins explained in 1909, was its fragmentation. To illustrate his point, Mullins listed sixteen different modern truth claims, and showed how the gospel eclipsed each one.[17] As Sol Dickey declared that same year, "If there is any one word which marks Winona it is the word 'Federation,' " and he predicted that denominational divisions "will soon be so low that we can step over them."[18] John P. Hale, the president of the Interdenominational Council of Churches in Indiana, put the issue in more practical terms to the Winona faithful: "We ask Christian ministers to preach the New Testament teaching that the church is one, and that it takes all parts of it to make a whole."[19]

Dickey and Biederwolf repeatedly assured their audiences that all conference speakers upheld two central principles of orthodox belief, the deity of Christ and the inspiration of Scripture. But no doctrinal statement appeared until 1928, and even then the board of directors phrased it in

16. Dickey, "Opening of the Conference," *Winona Echoes* (1915): 7. Biederwolf, "Opening Remarks," *Winona Echoes* (1930): 6.

17. Mullins, "Christ's Response to Modern Thought," *Winona Echoes* (1909): 102-3. See also John Balcom Shaw, "The Good and Bad in Modern Evangelism," *Winona Echoes* (1909): 35.

18. Dickey, "Opening Remarks," *Winona Echoes* (1909): 6. Dickey noted that his audience included representatives from 20 different denominations and 100 foreign missionaries.

19. Hale, "Federation in Indiana," *Winona Echoes* (1911): 286. See also Peter Ainsley, "Federation and Union," idem, 278-79. The Interdenominational Council included Baptists, Congregationalists, Disciples, Free Baptists, Friends, Methodists, Moravians, Presbyterians, Reformed, United Brethren, and United Presbyterians. See also William Biederwolf, "The Unity Which Jesus Taught," *Winona Echoes* (1910): 120-28; Charles Sheldon, "The Food and Fire of Life," *Winona Echoes* (1912): 63-64; William H. Roberts (president of the Federal Council of Churches), "Church Unity and Cooperation," *Winona Echoes* (1911): 259-64; Ralph McAfee, "The Cooperative Idea in Religion," *Winona Echoes* (1928): 228-29.

broad terms that they hoped would unify rather than divide their diverse constituency. The brief document, written so that "there may be no possible misunderstanding" as to Winona's stand on doctrines "essential to the Faith delivered by the inspired writers of the Holy Scriptures," included statements on the infallibility and authority of Scripture, the Trinity, virgin birth, substitutionary atonement, resurrection, personality of the Holy Spirit, and the necessity of being "born again." It also included a statement on the "coming judgment for all mankind" that was neither pre- nor post-millennial. In its brief and simple definition of orthodoxy, the 1928 doctrinal platform marked no significant departure from the previous thirty years.[20]

In fact, Winona's directors took pains to place this document within an interdenominational context. Beginning in 1923, each summer program schedule opened with a doctrinal endorsement from a Bible Conference Committee, composed of representatives from a wide variety of denominations. As the decade of controversy progressed, the list diversified, illustrating Winona's continuing commitment to evangelical ecumenicity as a means of combatting potentially divisive issues.[21]

The regular presence of missionaries in the summer program, both as speakers and attendees, underlined this concern. In 1904 the conference began sponsoring an interdenominational Summer School of Missions, which met separately from the Bible Conference. Beginning in 1923, however, foreign missions became a regular part of the daily program. The innovation was apparently well received: the highly successful 1926 Bible conference included furloughed missionaries from every state in the union.[22] Speaking from a historically ecumenical tradition, they were among the most outspoken in criticizing Protestant infighting. In 1931 Isaac Malik Yonan, a missionary in the Middle East, decried the "unwholesome controversies in the church of America," noting that they had been "received with jubilation by the religious leaders of Islam. Anything that

20. See William Biederwolf, "Opening Remarks," *Winona Echoes* (1928): 51-53.

21. In 1925, e.g., the Bible Conference Committee included representatives from Methodists (north and south), Disciples of Christ, United Lutherans, the Reformed Church in America, Congregationalists, Presbyterians (north and south), Northern Baptists, United Brethren, Evangelicals, Church of the Brethren, and "Protestant." The Committee stated that "Winona is not controversial. Its spirit is not belligerent. It fosters no particular Ism. But it stands absolutely four-square to fundamental doctrines of evangelical Christianity and tolerates nothing on its platform in the slightest degree subversive of them." See "Winona Lake Bible Conference, Thirty-First Annual," 2.

22. "Winona's Greatest Conference," *Winona* 1 (September 1926): 4.

weakens and discredits the missionary message," he warned, "is turned into a weapon of attack."[23]

The strong presence of British evangelicals on the Winona platform also moderated the pull toward militant fundamentalism. Beginning in 1904 and continuing through the end of the 1920s (with a brief hiatus during World War I), Winona's program was consistently transatlantic. British preachers like J. Campbell Morgan and Graham Scroggie remained perennial favorites, even though they often used the occasion to chide their American audience's tendency toward theological oversimplification. In 1902, for example, J. H. Johnston Ross denounced the "mental imbecility in this asking for a 'simple gospel,' when these great slabs of holy scripture are waiting for study and exposition to men. There is in the New Testament no going down to the adult idiocy that so many people affect."[24]

Speakers on the Winona platform often availed themselves of its tolerant inclusiveness. Although all supported the inspiration and infallibility of the Bible, few openly campaigned for inerrancy and some explicitly rejected it. In 1902, A. C. Zenos argued for study of the Bible that incorporated elements of "higher criticism," rejecting pious arguments that such literary and scientific analysis would be detrimental to faith. "If your face is set toward the truth, if you are seeking for that which is sound and correct in the matter of Bible knowledge," Zenos countered, "you will come to it in due time."[25] Camden Coburn, an archeologist from Allegheny College (PA), gave ten lectures at Winona between 1913 and 1918, detailing findings in Palestinian excavations that supported the authenticity of Scripture. However, Coburn was hardly an orthodox fundamentalist him-

23. See James Alan Patterson, "The Loss of a Protestant Missionary Consensus: Foreign Missions and the Fundamentalist-Modernist Conflict," in *Earthen Vessels: American Evangelicals and Foreign Missions,* ed. Joel Carpenter and Wilbert Shenk (Grand Rapids: Eerdmans, 1990), 73-91; Yonan, "Christianity and Islam," *Winona Echoes* (1931): 261.

24. Ross, "Does God Speak Now?" *Winona Echoes* (1902): 16. British speakers included J. H. Jowett, Gypsy Smith, James Orr, John Thomas, James McNeill, Stuart Holden (vicar of St. Paul's in London), J. Rhys Davies, Erskine Blackburn, and Frederick Norwood. On a comparison of British and American fundamentalism, see Ian S. Rennie, "Fundamentalism and the Varieties of North American Evangelicalism," in *Evangelicalism: Comparative Studies of Popular Protestantism in North America, the British Isles, and Beyond, 1700-1990,* ed. Mark Noll, David W. Bebbington, and George Rawlyk (New York: Oxford, 1994), 333-50.

25. "Sermon by Rev. Prof. A. C. Zenos," in *Addresses Delivered at the Winona Bible Conference,* vol. 3 (Winona Lake, 1902), 256.

self. His more relaxed view of the Bible is evident in the way he referred to an erroneous rendering of a Roman official's name in Acts by quipping that "it is a good thing that infallible spelling is not necessary to piety or to inspiration."[26]

There was also George L. Robinson, a professor of Old Testament History and Biblical Archeology at McCormick Seminary who was one of Winona's most popular speakers (*Winona Echoes* reprinted fourteen of his talks between 1911 and 1930). Robinson also did not hold to a fundamentalist "party line" on biblical inspiration. "Let us not deceive ourselves into thinking that the term 'inerrancy' can be applied to our present Scriptures," he argued in 1924. "That could apply in any case only to the original documents concerning which we are altogether uninformed. . . . The only true infallibility of the Bible is its inerrant power to save; and in this sense, and in this sense only, it is inerrant."[27]

Winona also avoided a party line on premillennialism, and deliberately invited a range of eschatological opinion. Perhaps they took a cue from the rapid and untimely demise of the Niagara Bible and Prophetic conferences, which collapsed under the weight of the conflicting interpretations that its premillennial doctrine seemed to attract. In 1918 the directors organized a special forum on prophecy, to run concurrently with the Bible conference program. "Bible students who have made Prophecy a life study will address this conference," the advance publicity promised. "It will not be a debate, but various views on the meaning of the Scriptures on this head will be presented. The list of speakers will include both Pre and Post-Millennialists, and the character of the advocates of both beliefs guarantees sanity and scholarship." The speakers, advocating "Premillenarian, Postmillenarian, Futures and Neutral views," included J. C. Massee, William Bell Riley, and James M. Gray, as well as George Robinson, Daniel Heagle, and A. F. Wesley.[28] Although Winona consistently tilted toward premillennialism, appearances by Dutch Calvinist amillennialists John J. Hiemenga and John Kuizenga in 1927 and 1925 suggest that the issue was far from closed.[29]

26. Coburn, "New Light on Paul and His Time," *Winona Echoes* (1915): 49.

27. Robinson, "The Inspiration of the Scriptures," *Winona Echoes* (1924): 217-18.

28. "Interesting Features Not Scheduled in the Foregoing List," *Winona Herald* (Winona Lake, 1918): 15-16. It is perhaps noteworthy that Bob Jones targeted this particular event as a reason for the "original declension" of Winona. See his *Cornbread and Caviar*, 110-11.

29. See, e.g., Hiemenga's strong amillennial argument in "The Struggle of the Ages," *Winona Echoes* (1927): 105-10.

All of this suggests that Winona, in its first decades, hardly conformed to a militant, doctrinal fundamentalist profile. It was irenic and committed to revival, and emphasized a simple, basic Christianity as the foundation of orthodox alliances and Christian service, not as an occasion for separation and division. To an increasing degree the fundamentalist-modernist theological controversy affected its character, but it did not impose its battle lines.

In 1931 Robert Speer addressed the Winona assembly for the first time. A thorough ecumenist, during the 1930s Speer was a controversial figure in the growing Presbyterian schism over foreign missions. Machen reportedly considered him "the most dangerous and injurious man in the Presbyterian Church."[30] Though his own theology was thoroughly orthodox, Speer valued the unity of the church far more than theological uniformity. His message, entitled "What is Christianity?", would have been thoroughly unpalatable to the exclusivist faction in his own denomination; it was, however, in tune with Winona's historic aversion to doctrinal controversy. Speer emphasized the fundamental unity of all Christian believers and the centrality of Christ. He touched on the necessity of evangelism, and the danger of elevating creeds over authentic religious experience.[31] It is perhaps one of the oddities of history (or of the traditional way of doing history) that the symbolic liberal Robert Speer, whose name in some circles became synonymous with the perils of theological inclusivism, was more comfortable at Winona than the symbolic conservative leader J. Gresham Machen.

Closer Ties to Fundamentalism

Notwithstanding Speer's popularity at Winona in the 1930s (he spoke there each summer from 1931 to 1935), the conference as an institution was growing more recognizably fundamentalist. Evangelist William Biederwolf, who had taken over direction of the conference in 1922, had been educated at Princeton University, Princeton Seminary, and in Germany and France. His early ministry efforts combined soul-winning with

---

30. On Speer, see Bradley J. Longfield, *The Presbyterian Controversy: Fundamentalists, Modernists, and Moderates* (New York: Oxford, 1991), 181-208. Winona had a long-standing connection with Princeton Seminary, and with Presbyterianism in general. Cornelius Woelfkin appeared there regularly in the early 1900s, as did Charles R. Erdman. Lewis Mudge, another Presbyterian moderate, also spoke in 1931.

31. Speer, "What Is Christianity?" *Winona Echoes* (1931): 221, 231.

civic reform, prohibition, and patriotic activities. Before he came to Winona Lake, however, he had also developed a keen interest in dispensationalist versions of biblical prophecy and premillennialism. By the time he came to Winona he was calling himself a fundamentalist and moved almost exclusively in fundamentalist circles. Under financial pressures that threatened to close the summer program, Biederwolf reorganized the Winona Lake Christian Assembly along more tightly drawn fundamentalist lines, and he made sure that every board member was a thoroughgoing fundamentalist. In 1937, he expanded the doctrinal platform, added an anti-evolution plank, and made the entire statement unchangeable and irrevocable. He also extended the authority of the statement, prohibiting anyone who purchased or rented Winona property from teaching any contrary doctrine.[32]

J. Palmer Muntz, who succeeded Biederwolf in 1939, was no less a fundamentalist. He grew up attending fundamentalist Bible conferences, and received his education at the University of Buffalo, Moody Bible Institute, and Northern Baptist Theological Seminary. He pastored a large Baptist church in New York and presided over the fundamentalist Conservative Baptist Fellowship. He had assisted Biederwolf for several years, and was personally committed to the typical set of fundamentalist doctrines, including premillennial dispensationalism.

In Winona's early years, the Chautauqua drew the crowds; the Bible conference was its adjunct. Then in the 1920s, as Winona's Chautauqua joined others around the country in decline, the Bible conference moved to the center of the program and flourished under fundamentalist leadership. In the decade after 1938, it expanded from ten days to seven weeks in length. At its peak it annually drew from 100 to 140 speakers who delivered over 500 sermons, Bible lessons, and inspirational talks to between 60,000 and 100,000 visitors. During its peak years, the conference consistently turned a profit, and its momentum propelled it through the 1950s with little change. But in the early 1960s the Bible conference quickly collapsed, the victim of high debt, old facilities, and changing American vacation patterns.[33]

The 1937 statement of faith was consistent with fundamentalism in

---

32. Sidwell, "The History of the Winona Lake Bible Conference," 171-72.
33. Winona Lake Bible Conference programs for 1938 and 1948; Sidwell, "The History of the Winona Lake Bible Conference," 209; Gaddis and Huffman, *The Story of Winona Lake,* 11; Leslie Flynn, "Pastor at Large," *Christian Life* (June 1950): 3; Lance Zavitz, "Practical Christianity at Work, Play," *Buffalo Evening News* (July 1948).

both form and function. Significantly, however, the statement avoided two fundamentalist touchstones. It did not use the word "inerrant" to describe the Bible, and it was silent on the millennial question. It merely asserted that Christ would return visibly to judge the human race, language that was pleasing to premillennialists, but that could nonetheless be affirmed by those who did not hold premillennial views. Winona's leadership designed the creed to keep theological liberals off the board of directors and to keep liberal doctrines from being taught during the conference, but not to insure that conference speakers personally subscribed to all its provisions. Lutheran radio evangelist Walter Maier, for instance, continued to be a popular speaker at Winona, and was warmly welcomed by the conference leadership, as long as he did not propound his belief in baptismal regeneration.[34]

As the Bible conference settled more comfortably into fundamentalist hands, however, sermons on social reform, other than prohibition, became extremely rare. This signifies the final departure of the last remnants of social gospel interest from Winona's meetings. After 1937, the Winona Lake Bible Conference could hardly have been less overtly political.

Sermons on Bible prophecy, on the other hand, became a Winona Lake staple. In the mid-1930s the first prophecy conference and first Jewish school of missions were held at Winona Lake as separate meetings. Muntz made them an integral part of the Bible conference, usually as the last week or two of the overall program. These meetings provided long drinks of dispensational premillennialism for those who thirsted for that sort of thing. The speakers at the prophecy conference were uniformly premillennialists — or nearly so. Muntz thought it was funny when he discovered one year that one of his prophecy speakers held amillennial views. He did not, however, mind having amillennialists on the platform during other segments of the Bible conference.[35]

Fundamentalists built their movement on a structure of entrepreneurial, special purpose parachurch organizations. The Winona Lake conferences provided fundamentalists with an ideal setting in which to publicize their work, raise funds, and recruit workers. Speakers promoted the causes of the Oriental Missionary Society, the International Christian Leprosy Mission, the American Association for Jewish Evangelism, Youth for Christ, the Bible Meditation League, and a host of other agencies. They found it in their own best interest to adopt cooperative attitudes, appealing

34. Sidwell, "History of Winona Lake Bible Conference," 188.
35. Ibid., 350-51.

to the evangelical beliefs that the entire audience would have in common. Furthermore, the parent corporation that sponsored the Bible conference, the Winona Lake Christian Assembly, was itself such an organization. Its leaders had to publicize, promote, and raise money just like all other fundamentalist entrepreneurs. Despite the nonmilitant tone of the meetings themselves, Biederwolf discovered that positioning the Bible conference in opposition to liberalism could increase the flow of financial gifts. In 1935 he encouraged Muntz to include in a newsletter mention of a board dispute over the membership of a theological liberal: "The incident about that modernistic preacher being put on the Board etc. was the thing that brought in all the money we got thus far," he reminded Muntz. "I wonder if it is wise to leave it out."[36]

Winona's Continuing Breadth of Spirit

In other ways, however, the Winona Lake Bible conference failed to conform to the supposed patterns of fundamentalism. For one thing, it was anything but sectarian. Winona's range of denominational affiliations was quite broad, and grew even broader after the consolidation of fundamentalist leadership in 1937. The 1932 conference hosted sixteen denominational rallies, mostly mainline groups. By 1950, at the height of the conference's popularity, twenty-two denominational groups had sufficient representation to sponsor rallies. The mainline denominations, Congregationalists, Presbyterians, Methodists, Baptists, Disciples of Christ, and Lutherans, were still present, joined by a welter of immigrant, Holiness, fundamentalist, and Pentecostal denominations. Conference organizers simultaneously called on platform speakers to tone down denominational distinctives and encouraged the attenders to maintain their denominational affiliations.[37]

Winona's speakers were rarely militant in advice or tone. The closest they came to calling for crusades were appeals for greater efforts in evangelism. They rarely spoke on modern social conditions; when they did, it was almost always to underscore a religious point. Outright attacks on theological modernism were few and far between. The vast majority of Winona addresses were either explications of Bible passages and Christian

36. Biederwolf to Muntz, 5 July 1935, correspondence files, Bible Conference collection, Grace College and Seminary Archives.
37. Programs of the Winona Lake Bible Conference, 1934, p. 17 and 1950, p. 75.

doctrine, exhortations to higher levels of faithfulness and holy living, or calls to support foreign missions and evangelization. In 1938 evangelist J. C. Massee preached a two-sermon series on "The Transcendent Greatness of Jesus Christ," the goal of which was to inspire personal humility and awe for God's power and purposes. In 1943 Bible teacher Coretta J. Mason chided all Christians — she did not single out liberals — for the spiritual indifference of their churches. In 1945 evangelist Mervin E. Rosell delivered two messages, one encouraging his listeners to elevate love and forgiveness to the top of their hierarchy of Christian values, the other challenging young men to go abroad as missionaries. Urvin V. White taught that it was through forgiving their enemies that Christians became "More Than Conquerors." Marian Leach preached that faith in God would yield a transformed life, a life not free from problems, but a life lived above its circumstances. In 1946, prophecy chart artist Roy L. Brown reminded his hearers that the imminent return of Christ required that every Christian become an evangelist: "If we are not fishing for men, we are not following our Lord."[38]

Not surprisingly, Winona's sermons were as ecumenical as its crowds. Despite the fact that the conference leaders were thoroughgoing, self-professed fundamentalists, they never insisted that speakers adhere to all fundamentalist doctrines. Moreover, they put pressure on their speakers to mute the differences between evangelical traditions to the point of virtual silence. For instance, it was not unusual to find attacks on Pentecostalism in America's fundamentalist press, but this sort of thing never happened at Winona Lake. When Baptist W. H. Rogers preached a sermon on "The Holy Spirit and the Christian" in 1938 he did not mention tongues, but he did warn his listeners to avoid the peril of quenching the Holy Spirit, by which he meant failing to use any gift given by the Spirit. He then closed his address with a mystical account of a direct encounter with the Holy Spirit that was surprisingly congenial to Pentecostal spirituality.[39]

---

38. J. C. Massee, "Transcendent Greatness of Jesus Christ in Heaven" and "The Transcendent Greatness of Jesus Christ in the Universe," both in *Winona Echoes* (1938); Coretta J. Mason, "The Potter and the Clay," in *Winona Echoes* (1943); Mervin Rosell, "Heaven's Wonderful Heart Throb" and "God's Global Go!" in *Winona Echoes* (1945): 260-74; Urvin V. White, "More Than Conquerers," in *Winona Echoes* (1945): 293-306; Marian Leach, "The Believer's Position — Psalm 1," in *Winona Echoes* (1945): 190; Roy L. Brown, "The Truth on Canvas: The Christ of the Scriptures," *Winona Echoes* (1946): 9-28; quotation on p. 9.

39. Rogers, "The Holy Spirit and the Christian," *Winona Echoes* (1938): 258-66.

Conversely, speakers felt free to criticize fundamentalism by name. In discussing Jesus' opponents, Rogers called the Pharisees "Fundamentalists in theology, and rigid traditionalists in teaching . . . moral, religious, zealous, self-denying, and self-righteous, destitute of the sense of sin and need. They were hearers and not doers of the Word." William Ward Ayer, a prominent Baptist pastor and radio preacher, once lamented, "There has never been a time when the devil has been so successful in sprinkling ashes on the church of God. He has choked the flames of love and evangelistic power in many places. He has changed many Fundamentalists into unloving and acrimonious folk."[40]

Fundamentalism is often associated with moral prohibitions, but the Winona conferences had only a very basic set of behavioral rules. In the 1930s a nightly curfew went into effect at 10:45 p.m., and on Sunday people were to refrain from commerce, swimming, and games. "No smoking" signs hung in most buildings, and the town and conference grounds were dry. Many fundamentalists believed that movies and the theater were inherently immoral, but the Chautauqua program regularly scheduled Hollywood movies and various kinds of dramatic productions. The major behavioral dispute of the decade seems to have been swimming attire. Swimmers were expected to be "properly robed while going to and from the beach," but in December 1937 Biederwolf angrily directed the "Public Decorum Committee" to "keep naked men and women from running all over the park" and to consider separating male and female bathers to avoid a "panorama of nakedness" at Winona's shores. The committee stepped up enforcement of the "properly robed" rule the next year, but never tried to segregate swimming beaches. The swimming problem was apparently peculiar to Biederwolf, for it vanished when the more genial Muntz took over in 1939. Muntz's philosophy was to let Winona's guests and residents establish their own behavioral rules. When asked why the conference organizers did not publish a list of rules prohibiting nonfundamentalist behaviors, Muntz replied, "We don't have to say anything about it. The people who like to do those things just wouldn't enjoy life here."[41]

Winona was also easygoing about the place of women. Almost all meetings were mixed-sex gatherings. The only exceptions were the daily

40. Rogers, "In the Last Days," *Winona Echoes* (1938): 267; Ayer, "Beauty for Ashes," *Winona Echoes* (1947): 35-36.

41. "Rules and Regulations," *Winona* 4 (Program number April 1930): 4; ibid. 12 (April 1938): 7; *Winona* 13 (April 1939): 6; Zavitz, "Practical Christianity."

"Minister's Hour" scheduled concurrently with the "Women's Hour." These meetings for women only were very popular, and usually featured a female evangelist, Bible teacher, or missionary speaker. Most of the "Women's Hour" talks were as appropriate for men as for women, but frequently the speakers used them as occasions to develop distinctly female variants of conservative Protestant spirituality. In 1946 Ruth Stull, a well-known author and former "jungle" missionary, gave a talk developing the concept of the church as the bride of Christ: "As the Bride, there is loving to be given, loving to be received, and childbearing to be expected. Her love has wings? Yes, for the Bride there are the wings to comfort and protect, there are wings on which to mount up for loving and high service, and there are the wings on which to go to the Bridegroom."[42] The same women who delivered "Women's Hour" sermons also addressed a few mixed gatherings at the Bible conference every year. Their talks were often broadcast on the radio and reprinted with the other sermons preached at the conference.

Conclusion

As this brief survey suggests, Winona did become more fundamentalist in orientation after 1937. However, fundamentalism had never been a tightly uniform movement, nor was its identity fixed in stone; in fact, in these years fundamentalism was experiencing its own transitions. And the end product, at least at Winona, was a humble (but still quite convinced) form of fundamentalism that emphasized evangelism and personal spirituality more than doctrinal correctness. This form of fundamentalism allowed for a range of denominational loyalties and theological opinions because it emphasized a goal far more pressing for ordinary Protestant believers, that is, maintaining the integrity of supernatural religion in an increasingly materialistic culture.

Is twentieth-century American Protestantism best understood as a two-party system? The story of Winona provides a mixed answer to the question. Even in its early days, Winona flourished within a generally fundamentalist ethos; doctrinal issues dear to the hearts of fundamentalist spokespersons, such as dispensationalist-style prophecy interpretation, received far more attention on Winona's platform than they did at tradi-

---

42. Stull, "Her Love Has Wings," *Winona Echoes* (1946): 131. All *Winona Echoes* were published in Grand Rapids by Zondervan.

tional camp-meetings or Chautauquas in other parts of the country. In its later stages, Winona's fundamentalist leadership used the Bible Conference to unite a broad range of Protestants who believed that personal conversion, piety, and the Bible ought to be at the center of the Christian life. Of course, in doing so, they presumed the right to speak for all Protestants, and helped bring into being modern evangelicalism, which seems to function for some as a sort of party in American Protestantism.[43]

Still, the Bible conference's basic evangelical, ecumenical orientation kept it largely free of the polarizing pressures that split some churches in the 1920s. Winona consistently resisted enforcing a monolithic piety or practice. There was room for variation in spirituality, theology, and church affiliation. The Winona faithful retained multiple loyalties to different leaders, organizations, and denominations. They could, and often did, choose to remain members of denominations led by persons opposed to fundamentalism. This kept the lines in American Protestantism fluid and shifting, as people in the pews defined their own interests independently of formal party alignments. And, in the final analysis, it is at this grass-roots level that the two-party paradigm of American Protestantism is found most wanting.

43. Martin Marty's description of "individualistic" or "Private" Protestantism fits Winona's style of Christianity, though those labels are reductionistic in a number of ways. See Marty, *Righteous Empire: The Protestant Experience in America* (New York: Harper and Row, 1970), 177-79.

CHAPTER 17

"Avoid Provoking the Spirit of Controversy": The Irenic Evangelical Legacy of the Biblical Seminary in New York

STEVEN M. NOLT

Once ignored or slighted in the annals of religious history and historiography, evangelicalism, particularly its twentieth-century American manifestations, has recently received critical academic attention. As interpretations have matured and the work of revision has begun, scholars are increasingly uncomfortable with the singular image of a militant, confessionally oriented evangelicalism bent on battling for doctrinal truth against the minions of modernism and liberalism. While in some cases sources support such an interpretation of American evangelicalism, an interpretation in keeping with the "two-party"[1] paradigm, a closer look at the evidence reveals a more moderate and irenic form of evangelicalism at work in America.

The story of the Biblical Seminary in New York (BSNY) provides a window into this kind of centrist evangelicalism.[2] The philosophy, cur-

1. The classic presentation of this framework is "The Two-Party System," pp. 177ff. of Martin E. Marty, *Protestantism in the United States: Righteous Empire* (New York: Charles Scribner's Sons, 1986).

2. Prior to 1921 the school operated under several different names, including the Bible Teachers' College and the Bible Teachers' Training School. In 1921 the institution adopted the name Biblical Seminary in New York. Because most of this essay deals with events after 1921, the Biblical Seminary title and BSNY acronym are used throughout.

In 1987 Virginia Lieson Brereton produced "The History of the Biblical Seminary

riculum, and composition of this significant training center suggest currents of American Protestant life flowing outside the two-party framework during the early and middle decades of the twentieth century. The school not only provided an alternative evangelical academic setting during its years of operation but also bequeathed a rich legacy to the wider Protestant community. Current fascination with "inductive Bible study," holistic reading and canonical approaches to biblical criticism, and "child-centered" patterns in Christian education are but three of the latter-day legacies of BSNY. An unobtrusive seminary in the nation's largest city, BSNY charted a moderate course which still influences American evangelicalism and, more generally, American Protestantism.

A Distinctive Seminary

Chartered in 1900, Biblical Seminary in New York emerged from the ideals and activity of educator and Semitics scholar Wilbert Webster White (1863-1944).[3] White's conservative Presbyterian upbringing provided him with a traditionally orthodox Christian worldview and a high regard for formal education. After studies at the College of Wooster and Xenia Theological Seminary, White went to Yale, where in 1891 he earned a Ph.D. degree in Hebrew. White often named his graduate advisor and cousin-by-marriage William Rainey Harper (1856-1905) as one of the most significant influences on his thought and work.[4] While inspired by Harper's painstaking scholarship and educational insights, White was

---

in New York, 1900-1965" (unpublished, available from New York Theological Seminary). The monograph is useful, but it is also uneven and loosely documented. Additionally, the book gives little attention to the school's post-1935 history. Much BSNY archival material is now housed at the Asbury Theological Seminary Archives, Wilmore, KY (hereafter ATSA).

3. White's biography, philosophy, and theology are presented (somewhat glowingly) in Charles R. Eberhardt, *The Bible in the Making of Ministers: The Scriptural Basis of Theological Education: The Lifework of Wilbert Webster White* (New York: Association Press, 1949). See also Wilbert W. White, "The Way There Before Oct. 29th, 1900," n.d., in Literary Productions, Memoirs, Wilbert W. White papers (hereafter WWW papers), 30:14, ATSA; and Brereton, "The History of the Biblical Seminary," 1-17.

4. For his part, Harper apparently had great respect for White, as his correspondence illustrates. Correspondence, William R. Harper, 1886-1890, WWW papers, 1:20, ATSA. In a January 11, 1887, letter Harper mused that White could easily obtain a teaching position at Yale after graduation, or immediately at Chicago's McCormick Theological Seminary, if he wished.

also troubled by the assumptions and implications of Harper's dis-passionate higher criticism. In imitation and reaction, White tried to cultivate Harper's intellectual rigor without abandoning his own or-thodox, evangelical sense of theology.

White taught at his alma mater in Xenia until his activity in the Keswick higher life movement drew criticism from the school's strictly Calvinist administration. Frustrated with denominational boundaries, White joined the staff of Dwight L. Moody's Bible Institute in Chicago.[5] Although White found the training facility's spiritual atmosphere con-genial, he had little patience with the school's low academic standards and dearth of faculty scholarship. In 1896, after only two years in Chicago, White took an international YMCA teaching assignment.[6] Instructing scores of American missionaries in India confirmed White's suspicion that stateside theological education suffered from a deep divide which left some graduates with a confusing assortment of critical tools while others possessed piety without intellectual depth.

While on a speaking tour of Britain, White received encouragement and £2,000 from the Scottish evangelical leader Lord Overtoun to establish an academically respectable, evangelically oriented seminary. Returning to the United States, White opened a school in Montclair, New Jersey, with the assistance of local ministers and his energetic brother-in-law, the ecu-menical leader and Montclair resident, John R. Mott (1865-1955).[7] In 1902 the school relocated to New York City, ultimately establishing its campus on East 49th Street in midtown Manhattan.

Although the upstart institution began as a non-degree Bible school, faculty and trustees envisioned a full-scale graduate seminary.[8] By 1916 the school received provisional rights to grant degrees in Sacred Theology, and five years later it became an independently accredited institution.

---

5. Reuben A. Torrey to White, April 5, 1894, Correspondence, R. A. Torrey, WWW papers, 2:15, ATSA.

6. White's brother, J. Campbell White, leader of the Layman's Missionary Move-ment, was then a YMCA executive.

7. C. Howard Hopkins discussed White's and Mott's relationship in *John R. Mott, 1865-1955: A Biography* (Grand Rapids: William B. Eerdmans, 1979), 84, 88, 94, 216, 248, 253, 680.

8. Their grand dreams are clear in a 1910 decennial anniversary address, "The Bible University," by adjunct faculty member Robert W. Rogers, BSNY Literary Pro-ductions, Historical, Biblical Seminary in New York papers, 83-M-014 (hereafter BSNY papers), 7:9, ATSA. Brereton discusses the school's sense of academic mission in "The History of the Biblical Seminary," 133-42.

BSNY moved quickly to shed its Bible school aura and professionalize its program. For example, in 1925 the school forged an arrangement with New York University (NYU) whereby Biblical Seminary students could apply their credits toward NYU graduate degrees in education.[9] Three years later, BSNY itself began awarding doctoral degrees and added approved programs in religious education.

To a large extent Biblical Seminary reflected White's theological and ecclesiological commitments. Disdaining narrow "sectarianism," New York Biblical eschewed denominational affiliations and precise confessional formulae.[10] No more than one-third of the school's trustees could come from any one church body,[11] and faculty represented diverse Protestant backgrounds.[12] By mid-century, the 100- to 150-member student body regularly included more than thirty denominations, including several "mainline" churches and many smaller evangelical groups.[13] Students represented Episcopal churches, Presbyterian churches, various Lutheran synods, Evangelical Congregational Churches, Free Methodists,

9. Material from typescript "The Book of the Chronicles of BTTS and BSNY, 1881-1933," BSNY papers, 1:1, ATSA; BSNY Proceedings, Charters and Constitutions, New York University Affiliation, 1903-1930, BSNY papers, 1:5, ATSA; Eberhardt, *The Bible in the Making of Ministers;* and Brereton, "The History of the Biblical Seminary."

10. Wilbert W. White, "Where We Stand," unpublished booklet (1924-30), 28-31, BSNY Literary Production, Historical, BSNY papers, 8:5. White argued that students could transcend denominational differences by focusing on the Bible and yet remain loyal denomination workers.

11. The diversity was real throughout the period. Trustees in 1967 included American Baptist, American Lutheran, Christian and Missionary Alliance, Congregational, Episcopal, Evangelical Free Church, Lutheran Church in America, Mennonite, Methodist, Reformed Church in America, and United Presbyterian members.

12. A list of prominent faculty members through the years bears this point: White and Dean G. McKee (Presbyterians), Caroline L. Palmer (Congregationalist), Herman Harrell Horne (Baptist), Howard T. Kuist (Evangelical Church), Emily J. Werner (Lutheran), Helen Garber (Brethren Church), and Robert A. Traina and Dewey M. Beegle (Free Methodists).

13. As early as 1912 and 1913 the school had received endorsements from bodies such as the United Evangelical Church and the Primitive Methodists. White also took pride in the seminary's attracting evangelical Lutherans of various stripes. See "The Book of the Chronicles of BTTS and BSNY, 1881-1933," BSNY papers, 1:1, ATSA; "BSNY Scrapbook Materials, Evangelicals and BSNY, 1937," BSNY papers, 9:27, ATSA; "BSNY Scrapbook Materials, Lutherans and BSNY, 1920-1929," BSNY papers, 10:2, ATSA. On the attendance of Mennonites at the school, see Steven M. Nolt, "An Evangelical Encounter: Mennonites and the Biblical Seminary in New York," *The Mennonite Quarterly Review* 70 (October 1996): 389-417.

Primitive Methodists, Swedish Baptists, Mennonites, United Brethren, and the Church of the Nazarene.[14]

While the seminary's statutes upheld "the Holy Scriptures as the only infallible rule of faith and practice" and "the Deity of Christ" and "His atoning sacrifice as the sole ground of men's salvation," it was otherwise vague, calling only for commitment to "the associated elements of apostolic and evangelical Christianity." The seminary would teach "in such a way as to avoid provoking the spirit of controversy and to foster unity among all the students" so as to produce "constructive, nondisputatious" alumni.[15]

In contrast to many of the doctrinally driven evangelical schools which sprang up in the wake of the modernist-fundamentalist excitement — including Dallas, Westminster, and Faith — systematic theology took a back seat at BSNY in a curriculum dubbed "biblio-centric." While BSNY faculty generally opposed dispensationalism, issues surrounding Calvinism, Arminianism, and Pentecostalism were generally adiaphora. Students recall BSNY president and longtime professor Dean G. McKee (1904-87) teaching historical theology in such a way that virtually all post-Reformation options seemed worthy. Irenic in spirit, academic in tone, and innovative in method, the institution reflected White's efforts to connect the worlds of Yale, Moody, and the YMCA; as one administrator put it, the goal was to combine in one school "the qualities of the scholar, the saint, and the servant."[16]

---

14. A variety of lists are available. See, e.g., BSNY Lists, Faculty and Students, 1930-32, BSNY papers, 11:6, ATSA. Several early compilations of students seem heavily weighted toward Presbyterians. This is likely due to these lists' inclusion of correspondence and extension program students (the totals are too high to represent residents only). White's initial channels of advertising the correspondence program were largely through New Jersey and New York Presbyterian circles. Considering only the resident students since the later 1920s, a much more diverse crowd takes shape than earlier compilations suggest. Throughout its history, the school was also noted for its significant female enrollment. For White's comments on the importance of theological education for women, see his "Concerning the Biblical Seminary in New York: Some Institutional Confidences," 27, in BSNY Subject Files, Historical, BTTS, 1899-1901, BSNY papers, 5:15, ATSA; and Brereton, "The History of the Biblical Seminary," 157.

15. BSNY Proceedings, Charters and Constitution, New York University Affiliation, 1903-30, BSNY papers, 1:5, ATSA. This commitment also kept BSNY from holding a communion service until the 1943-44 school year. Interview with BSNY alumnus Jacob J. Enz, February 17, 1995, Elkhart, IN.

16. Walter E. Bachman, "Standards and Ideals of the Curriculum of the Biblical Seminary in New York," unpublished paper, 1930, BSNY Literary Productions, Manuscripts, BSNY papers, 8:9, ATSA.

Indeed, the school was difficult to label theologically. It was, as one faculty member observed, "regarded as too conservative for the liberals and too radical by the conservatives."[17] White himself was hard to situate with regard to controversies in his own Presbyterian denomination. He associated with moderate progressives such as Robert Speer, Charles Erdman, and J. Ross Stevenson: all lectured at Biblical during its early years, and Stevenson served on the school's board of trustees for nine years. Yet other contacts pointed in differing directions. For example, White supported the fundamentalist League of Evangelical Students at Princeton in 1928, about the same time BSNY hosted a conference on closer institutional relations with General Theological Seminary and Union Theological Seminary. Historian Virginia L. Brereton is convinced that no one thought of BSNY as liberal, but White complained to Mott that he received just such a label from Charles Trumbull and other fundamentalists. In the end, the school's orientation is hard to position, largely because its rigorous inductive epistemology rejected the assumed theological markers of the day: higher criticism, inerrancy, dispensationalism, and the like.[18] At bottom, it was the seminary's approach to Scripture and teaching which provided its distinctive edge and gave its evangelical agenda a unique identity.

Inductive Bible Study

White, his colleagues, and his successors championed inductive English Bible study, initially modeled after the methods of White's mentor, William Harper.[19] Harper had incorporated inductive teaching methods into his

17. Howard T. Kuist, "The Premises of a New Strategy for Theological Education, 1937," BSNY Literary Production, Manuscripts, BSNY papers, 8:12, ATSA.

18. See various references in "The Book of the Chronicles of BTTS and BSNY, 1881-1933," BSNY papers, 1:1, ATSA; BSNY Lists, Board of Trustees, 1900-1932, BSNY papers, 11:2, ATSA; Paul Woolley to White, 2 August 1928, in BSNY Scrapbook Materials, Evangelicals and BSNY, BSNY papers, 9:27, ATSA. White to John R. Mott, 31 August 1933, Correspondence, John R. Mott, 1897-1942, WWW papers, 1:36, ATSA. Brereton, "The History of the Biblical Seminary," 125. See also the discussion in Eberhardt, *The Bible in the Making of Ministers*, 205-18.

19. An early exposition of the approach is White's sermon "What the Bibliocentric Curriculum Really Means," delivered November 26, 1912, at a New York City Swedish Baptist Church. Literary Production, Speeches, WWW papers, 32:20, ATSA. See also Wilbert W. White, *Why Read the Bible? How to Read the Bible, What to Read and Why* (New York: Grossett and Dunlap, 1931). A secondary discussion is Eberhardt, *The Bible in the Making of Ministers*, 127-42. Unfortunately, Mark A. Noll, *Between Faith and*

Semitics classes at Yale and, later, at the University of Chicago. Inverting conventional pedagogical practices, Harper refused to begin courses with a discussion of grammar. Instead, he taught pronunciation and basic vocabulary, then set students to reading. Pupils uncovered grammar inductively by working with the language.[20]

White theorized that the same approach would improve Bible study. While American evangelicals had long endorsed and even celebrated inductive thought and methods, White believed few applied it in their study of the Scriptures.[21] Coming to the text with doctrinal commitments in mind, students frequently read with an eye for passages which supported established dogmatic categories. Because they were working with the text itself and assembling and categorizing verses as discrete data, many thought of their approach as inductive.[22] To White's mind, however, such

Criticism: Evangelicals, Scholarship, and the Bible in America, 2nd ed. (Grand Rapids: Baker Book House, 1991), the only volume to approach a complete description of academic evangelical thought about the Bible, does not discuss BSNY's approach, philosophy, or methods, except for a non-indexed, passing reference on p. 61. Noll does mention one BSNY alumnus, Asbury Theological Seminary's George A. Turner (p. 97). However, because Noll's selection of influential evangelical scholars is weighted toward those who attended Harvard (thus, Turner), a number of more creative BSNY scholars (and their circle at Asbury, Union-Richmond, and Princeton) remain unnamed.

20. William Rainey Harper, *Elements of Hebrew by an Inductive Method* (New York: Charles Scribner's Sons, 1881), 5. By 1890 the widely used textbook was in its twentieth edition.

21. On the powerful place of Baconian induction among nineteenth-century American evangelicals, see Marsden, *Fundamentalism and American Culture,* 55-62. Both Harper and White were thoroughly trained in the Scottish "common sense" philosophy so prevalent in nineteenth-century American higher education. White retained a "common sense" confidence that science and religion must ultimately harmonize, as seen in his *The Resurrection Body according to the Scriptures* (New York: George H. Doran, 1923), esp. ix. Neither Harper nor White studied in Europe, and both seemed largely unaware of European-style Idealism. What was unique in Harper's and White's presentation of induction was not the approach per se, but the thoroughgoing manner in which they employed the principle. See James P. Wind, *The Bible and the University: The Messianic Vision of William Rainey Harper* (Atlanta: Scholars Press, 1987), 62-66.

22. Timothy P. Weber, "The Two-Edged Sword: The Fundamentalist Use of the Bible," in *The Bible in America: Essays in Cultural History,* ed. Nathan O. Hatch and Mark A. Noll (New York: Oxford University Press, 1982), 101-20, discusses this paradox in fundamentalist ideology and practice.

Cf., e.g., Reuben A. Torrey, *How to Study the Bible for Greatest Profit* (Chicago: Fleming H. Revell Co., 1896). While the section on studying the Bible by books is presented as an inductive approach, Torrey's assumptions ultimately suggest certain categories under which students should group verses, a sort of preunderstanding White would have considered deductive.

methods were clearly deductive. In contrast, he argued that systematic theology and dogma functioned like grammar and could and should only arise from a close reading of the text itself. Thereafter doctrine always remained in a real sense tentative and open to further consideration.

White eschewed dispensationalism, Calvinist systematics, and precise theories of inspiration as "eisegetic," deductive accouterments which hindered direct Bible study.[23] Yet White also differed from the higher critics (who also operated in a less than inductive mode) in that he expected the Bible to present a coherent, though not necessarily systematic, message once the critical inductive task was complete.[24] Practitioners of higher criticism sought to suspend faith and adopt a thoroughgoing hermeneutic of suspicion, which in turn drove their questioning and probing. In contrast, students who were guided inductively allowed the text itself to raise the issues for debate. The difference was subtle, but significant.

Biblical Seminary also championed English Bible instruction. Although trained as a Semitics scholar, White followed Harper's call for biblical study in the vernacular.[25] Building on educational theory which stressed cognition in one's native tongue, Harper argued that vernacular study allowed students to probe the text more thoroughly as literature.

---

23. In refuting dispensationalism White insisted that "The Bible is not a riddle, but a revelation." See Wilbert W. White, *The Divine Library, Its Abuse and Use, or How to Study the Bible* (n.p., n.d.), 3, 10. His unease with dispensationalism is evident in his passionate attempt to present the book of Revelation in an inductive manner. A commentary on the Apocalypse of John, though unfinished at the time of his death, was a lifelong project for which he amassed an enormous amount of material (especially given the fact that his teaching was in Hebrew and Old Testament). See Subject Files, WWW papers, 7:18-25, 8:1-17, 9:1-16. Also, Wilbert W. White, *Thirty Studies in the Revelation of Jesus Christ to John* (New York: Fleming H. Revell Co., 1898), 16-17.

24. Despite their interest in questions of biblical criticism, White and Harper operated fundamentally out of a hermeneutic of belief, not one of suspicion. See Paul Ricoeur, *Freud and Philosophy: An Essay on Interpretation* (New Haven, Conn.: Yale University Press, 1970), 54-56, for a discussion of the importance of this distinction. Wind, *The Bible and the University*, 61 and 76, distinguishes Harper's approach from that of the "Chicago school" often associated with Harper.

25. Widely known for his tireless efforts to revive the study of Hebrew in America, Harper also launched the English Bible movement, requesting a chair in that name from Yale in 1890. The importance of English Bible study was a regular theme in Harper's editorials in *The Old Testament Student*. A sampling of early examples are 5 (March 1886): 290-91; 5 (April 1886): 323-24; 6 (January 1887): 129-35. See also William Rainey Harper, *The Trend in Higher Education* (Chicago: University of Chicago Press, 1905), 235, 247-50, 265.

Indeed, he argued that half the theological curriculum should be given to English Bible study.[26] Like his mentor, White endorsed English Bible study while demanding concurrent attention to Greek and Hebrew. With the easy availability of improved translations (White was an enthusiastic member of the American Revised Version Committee), vernacular and original language study meshed better than ever and afforded splendid opportunities for reviewing textual criticism in the classroom.[27]

In practical terms, inductive English Bible study began by approaching a text without commentaries or other secondary sources in hand. During repeated readings of the passage students made copious written "observations" and carefully analyzed its literary structure. Examining the relationships between and within portions of the text, students compiled lists and constructed charts and tables to aid in organizing the material. Students gradually moved from the particulars to generalizations, summing the text into meaningful interpretive conclusions.[28] The process was time-consuming, and both teachers and students were bound to follow their material to its conclusions without *a priori* commitments to dogma or lesson plans. Longtime faculty member Robert A. Traina detailed the method most clearly in *Methodical Bible Study: A New Approach to Hermeneutics*, which employed a highly developed, logical system of "inductive-inferential reasoning" to move from observation to application.[29]

Indeed, Traina and others always insisted that the inductive approach was first and foremost an epistemology and not simply a heuristic

---

26. Wind, *The Bible and the University*, 6, 47, 81-103, 178.

27. White's concern was also pastoral. As a graduate assistant to Harper, White had compiled survey results of seminary alumni in which nearly ninety percent lamented their lack of English Bible study and reported difficulty in preparing text-based sermons. See "Bible Study in the Pastorate: Figures and Facts," *The Old Testament Student* 6 (January 1887): 133-34.

28. So committed was the administration to the method that professors were to destroy their class notes and lectures each year, rewriting syllabi each summer after a careful inductive study of course contents.

29. Robert A. Traina, *Methodical Bible Study: A New Approach to Hermeneutics* (New York: Ganis and Harris, 1952). The book is still in print and currently available from Zondervan. Traina's epistemology is clearly presented in a two-part essay, "Inductive Bible Study Reexamined in the Light of Contemporary Hermeneutics," in *Interpreting God's Word for Today: An Inquiry into Hermeneutics from a Biblical Theological Perspective*, ed. Wayne McCown and James Earl Massey (Anderson, IN: Warner Press, 1982), 53-109. In these essays Traina also compares the inductive approach to other major twentieth-century hermeneutical systems.

method.[30] As such, it offered a way of thinking about the Bible's authority which moved beyond the apologetics of deductive inerrancy. Wilbert White had long rejected as a "modern abuse of the Bible" what he termed the "Super-logical" approaches of both classical inerrantists such as J. Gresham Machen and dispensationalists like Charles G. Trumbull.[31] An inductive epistemology took a different tack. Instead of ascribing particular status to revealed, inspired Scripture, an inductive orientation accepted only what the text claimed for itself. BSNY faculty argued that those claims were purely "instrumental," that is, the canonical witness pointed simply to "the instrumental worth of Holy Scripture in forming responsible Christian character."[32]

Bypassing metaphysical and ontological arguments for scriptural authority, inductive examinations of the text itself pointed to its encounter with human beings; contact with the text produced Christian lives, which in turn provided the Bible with an existential authority. Indeed, inductive study proponents insisted that such authority was all the Bible itself claimed, and thus they refused to demand any sort of preunderstanding on the part of readers.[33] The Bible was, in the words of one inductive-instrumental advocate, simply "a means to an end."[34] Taken together, the BSNY approach to interpretation and authority contrasted sharply with the classical inerrantist position, built on a deductive ontology, and with dispensationalism, which viewed the Bible as a collection of data requiring an external grid to make sense of it.[35] Indeed, when BSNY

30. Interview with Robert A. Traina, March 14, 1995, Wilmore, Kentucky. BSNY had long maintained that induction was primarily an epistemology, a point long-time faculty member Louis Matthews Sweet (1869-1950) tried to make in *To Christ through Evolution* (New York: George H. Doran, 1925), 7: "The author's position is frankly theistic, no less frankly Christian, no less frankly evangelical, but the whole purpose of his writing is to show that one may be all these and maintain the open mind and, what is quite as necessary, the balanced judgement."

31. Wilbert W. White, "The Modern Abuse of the Bible, or Some Modern Abuses of the Bible," handwritten notes on a page dated January 16, 1930, Subject Files, Method, General, Bible Misuses, 1927 [sic], WWW papers, 14:5, ATSA. White named Machen and Trumbull specifically.

32. Howard Tillman Kuist, *These Words upon Thy Heart: Scripture and the Christian Response* (Richmond: John Knox Press, 1947), 19.

33. E.g., John 20:31 does not presume the necessity of any particular belief before one engages the text. Interview with Robert A. Traina, March 14, 1995.

34. Donald G. Miller, *Fire in Thy Mouth* (New York: Abingdon Press, 1954), 59-82, esp. 67.

35. See Mark A. Noll, ed., *The Princeton Defense of Plenary Verbal Inspiration* (New York: Garland Publishing, 1988); Benjamin B. Warfield, "The Inerrancy of the Original

professor Dewey M. Beegle (1919-95) outlined the seminary's inductive-instrumental approach in *The Inspiration of Scripture,* some evangelicals were aghast.[36] Others, however, especially those in the Wesleyan-Holiness tradition, found the gauge of existential faithfulness and discipleship congenial, if not obvious.

If some fundamentalists and evangelicals were unsure of the merits of BSNY's inductive approach, the school also had its supporters and admirers, including a number of "mainline" leaders. For example, A. Ross Wentz (president of Lutheran Theological Seminary, Gettysburg, Pennsylvania, and secretary of the Association of Theological Schools) praised BSNY in a lengthy 1937 article in the journal *Christian Education.* He suggested that the seminary's curriculum should be seen as a model for other theological schools.[37]

BSNY's firmest base of support, however, was a wide assortment of evangelicals who were more interested in Bible study than apologetics, and more concerned with daily discipleship than with systematics. Some, like White himself, were evangelicals whose encounters with the Keswick holiness movement had redirected their theological outlook and priorities. Others, like longtime BSNY instructor Robert Traina, found that the school's approach complemented his Free Methodist upbringing and understanding of faith with its logical, but ultimately experiential and practical, orientation.

Autographs," in *The Princeton Theology, 1821-1921,* ed. Mark A. Noll (Grand Rapids: Baker Book House, 1983), esp. 268-74; Cornelius Van Til's introduction to Benjamin B. Warfield's *The Inspiration and Authority of the Bible* (Philadelphia: The Presbyterian and Reformed Publishing Co., 1948), 3-68; and Edward J. Young, *Thy Word Is Truth: Some Thoughts on the Biblical Doctrine of Inspiration* (Grand Rapids: William B. Eerdmans, 1957), esp. 86-87. On the connection between dispensationalism and inerrancy, see Marsden, *Fundamentalism and American Culture,* 58-60; and C. Norman Kraus, *Dispensationalism in America: Its Rise and Development* (Richmond: John Knox Press, 1958), 60-68, 73-75, 131-32.

36. Beegle, *The Inspiration of Scripture* (Philadelphia: The Westminster Press, 1963). Beegle, a Free Methodist and graduate of BSNY, was a faculty member from 1951 to 1966. The volume was one of the most hotly debated in conservative evangelical circles in the 1960s. Carl F. H. Henry and Frank E. Gaebelein found the inductive-instrumental approach disturbing. See "Yea, Hath God Said . . . ?" and "Books in Review," *Christianity Today* 7 (April 26, 1963): 26-28, 39-41, 45-47. A revised version of the book appeared as *Scripture, Tradition, and Infallibility* (Grand Rapids: William B. Eerdmans, 1973). Harold Lindsell took this edition to task in *The Battle for the Bible* (Grand Rapids: Zondervan, 1976), 169-83.

37. Abdel Ross Wentz, "A New Strategy for Theological Education," *Christian Education* 20 (April 1937): 291-318.

The seminary's students were among the most enthusiastic supporters of BSNY's inductive orientation, since many found the approach deeply formative. In the mid-1940s Stanley Shenk, a Mennonite student from Virginia, transferred to BSNY after a troubling experience at Eastern Baptist Seminary, where he found that professors "rammed Second Isaiah down our throats." After coming to Biblical, however, Shenk discovered that inductive study often raised a host of critical questions about composition and authorship, but without the prerequisite acceptance of secular notions drawn from evolutionary religious theory.[38] By allowing the text to present the questions, students did not need to exchange their faith for suspicion at the classroom door. Moreover, the emphasis at Biblical was always on finding the central message of Scripture after completing critical inquiry. Shenk discovered Christian faith that "was conservative in interpretation and doctrine, and yet relaxed and tolerant." Students and faculty "accepted the supernatural framework of Christianity" without being "dogmatic [or] intrusive."[39]

About the same time, Mary Creswell (later Mary Creswell Graham), a young Presbyterian from California, went to BSNY "eager to learn God's Word." However, she soon realized that she had "also taken along my 'template' for interpreting Scripture." The inductive approach came as a shock to her. "The professors at seminary never told us students what they believed personally and never criticized us, but taught us how to study Scriptures and make our own conclusions. After one year at seminary I was in 'pieces,' and had to return to be put back together." She had come to the seminary with the idea that "if a person did not hold the Pre-millennial view, that person was not a Christian." At Biblical Seminary the combination of an interdenominational setting and an open, inductive spirit ushered Creswell into a wider evangelical world. "I learned that those who disagreed with me had their reasons, based on Scripture," she recalls. "And I came to respect other viewpoints. What a great world of Christian fellowship I have now."[40]

BSNY graduated scores of loyal alumni who took the school's approach with them to pastorates, further graduate study, and mission as-

38. Interview with Stanley C. Shenk, February 3, 1995, Goshen, IN.

39. Stanley C. Shenk journal, p. 6374, Hist. Mss. 1-734, Stanley C. Shenk papers, Archives of the Mennonite Church, Goshen, IN. See also Shenk's "A Tribute to Good Old Biblical," *Newsletter: Inductive Bible Study Network* (Spring 1991): 1-2.

40. Mary L. Creswell Graham to Steve Nolt, February 15, 1995, and March 25, 1996. Graham notes that she had been in official interdenominational settings before, but that these had been intra-Calvinist and intra-dispensationalist affairs.

signments around the world. The institution's modest size and irenic spirit (i.e., not "provoking the spirit of controversy") kept it, for the most part, out of the evangelical spotlight. In an evangelical world often marked by heroic polemics and dramatic crusades, promoting inductive study and the instrumental authority of Scripture seemed less exciting. Still, the school, its faculty, and alumni influenced a surprisingly broad slice of American Protestantism through a number of academic, congregational, and parachurch channels.

The Popular Diaspora of BSNY's Inductive Bible Study Method

The inductive approach to Bible study had long given Biblical Seminary its distinctive edge, but the influence of the method soon moved beyond the school's classrooms. In part, inductive study's emergence in other evangelical colleges and Bible schools stemmed from the gradual placement of BSNY alumni in schools around the country. Before long, Biblical graduates were integrating the approach into their own classrooms, and instructing hundreds of students. One BSNY alumna, Mary Creswell Graham, editor of the Inductive Bible Study Network *Newsletter,* has traced the influence of BSNY's philosophy to scores of professors in dozens of institutions who carry on some form of the BSNY tradition in academic settings such as Asbury Theological Seminary, Regent University, and Wheaton College.[41]

However, the inductive approach to Scripture study did not remain behind ivy-covered walls. It soon became a widely practiced method among lay students and local study groups nationally, with the evangelical student organization InterVarsity Christian Fellowship (IVCF) playing a remarkable role in popularizing the process. The connection is not accidental, as IVCF's early staff included many Biblical Seminary graduates. BSNY's bibliocentric, nondoctrinal commitments fit well with the outlook of InterVarsity's young leadership, especially its founding general secretary, C. Stacey Woods. An Australian of Plymouth Brethren background, Woods was committed to the lay study of the Bible, and unconcerned with the specifics of North American fundamentalist agendas. In

---

41. See copies of *Newsletter: Inductive Bible Study Network.* Issues record dozens of connections between BSNY, InterVarsity Christian Fellowship, and teaching faculty at numerous evangelical liberal arts colleges, Bible schools, and seminaries.

1940 Woods brought InterVarsity to the United States.[42] One of his first staff recruits was Jane Hollingsworth (1919-93), who was just completing a master's degree at BSNY. Beginning in 1942, Hollingsworth held a variety of positions within the organization, but her most important contribution, observers agree, was to bring "inductive Bible study into the Fellowship." IVCF's charter required weekly Bible study meetings of each chapter, and Hollingsworth "brought the skills and method." She was not alone: institutional chroniclers cite at least ten BSNY alumni (nine of whom were women) among InterVarsity's leadership during the movement's first two decades. One longtime IVCF staff person has noted that general secretary Woods's "openness to reach into a seminary like Biblical . . . might have been questioned by others because it had no written doctrinal statement." Yet Woods's interests in biblical study, women's ministry, and moderate approach kept the IVCF-BSNY channels open.[43]

The inductive method was a practical boon to IVCF chapters, since commentaries and other study helps were rare among students. Additionally, the method built on commonly discovered truths, not predetermined doctrinal formulations, a critical element in a movement trying to build a broad-based, interdenominational evangelical coalition. While some students absorbed the method in direct training sessions and IVCF camps, many read the organization's publications, which explained the approach. Hollingsworth herself authored the first InterVarsity study guide, *Discovering the Gospel of Mark*. In 1945 she and Alice Reid (another BSNY alumna) produced the second guide, *Look at Life with the Apostle Peter*.

By 1955 staff member Rosalind Rinker was transferring her experience at Biblical even more directly into her presentations to InterVarsity groups. Using mimeographed typescript pages of biblical texts, she encouraged students to observe, mark, and diagram Scripture as literature. The resulting program, "Mark I and Mark II Manuscript Bible Study," became an important means of introducing the inductive method.[44] In 1964 another former BSNY student and longtime InterVarsity worker, Barbara Boyd, began developing a student leadership clinic eventually known as the Bible and Life Training courses. The middle third of the training program was devoted to teaching "the principles and joy of

42. Keith Hunt and Gladys Hunt, *For Christ and the University: The Story of InterVarsity Christian Fellowship of the U.S.A., 1940-1990* (Downers Grove, IL: InterVarsity Press, 1991), 56-90.
43. Ibid., 96-99, 105, 175. But see p. 424, n. 24 on the limits for married staff women. See 126, 427-28 on fundamentalist opposition to Wood and InterVarsity.
44. Ibid., 176, 260.

personal inductive Bible study." The program "became a key discipling tool" in the 1970s and beyond, leaving an indelible mark on the organization and permanently associating InterVarsity with inductive study.[45]

In addition to the direct work of the organization, the publications of InterVarsity's press made literature about inductive Bible study available to a host of local Bible study groups. Devotional guides intended to structure daily "quiet times" began with inductive study exercises.[46] Longtime staff member James Nyquist's *Leading Bible Discussions* (1967) offered a detailed description of inductive study in a small group setting, while books such as *How to Understand Your Bible* (1974) and *Small Group Leaders' Handbook* (1982) focused on other aspects of making the approach a weekly reality for groups across the nation.[47] In the 1990s, InterVarsity Press's new LifeGuide Bible Studies series continued to popularize the method.[48] Through InterVarsity's organizational efforts, promotions, and publications, countless individuals have been introduced to the method.

The Academic Diaspora of BSNY's Approach to Scripture

While BSNY's inductive method of study spawned a host of grassroots Bible study programs, its epistemology and orientation also had implications for academic study. While Wilbert White had long argued against what he felt were the deductive assumptions of inerrantists and historical-critical liberals, he spent less time creating academically respectable alternatives. Several of his BSNY successors, however, attempted just that. One of the most creative Biblical Seminary instructors was Howard

---

45. Ibid., 256-58, 312. The inductive study method spread from American Inter-Varsity circles to other wings of the global International Fellowship of Evangelical Students network (146-47, 426 n. 10). In 1969 staff members Boyd and Keith Hunt employed a "biblio-centric curriculum" model in their design of a new School of Discipleship Training program. Like the BSNY pattern, the system graphically placed Bible book studies in a central "hub" with other courses emanating outward in circular fashion; students began with Bible courses and then moved to relevant applied studies, back to the hub, and so on (257).

46. *Growing Your Christian Life* (Downers Grove, IL: InterVarsity Press, 1962), iv.

47. James Nyquist, *Leading Bible Discussions* (Downers Grove, IL: InterVarsity Press, 1967); T. Norton Sterrett, *How to Understand Your Bible* (Downers Grove, IL: InterVarsity Press, 1974); and Steve Barker et al., *Small Group Leaders' Handbook* (Downers Grove, IL: InterVarsity Press, 1982).

48. See the introductory pages of each volume of the LifeGuide Bible Studies series, which specifically compare induction and deduction.

Tillman Kuist (1895-1964).[49] A popular speaker at summer Bible conferences, Kuist was also a well-loved teacher, whose warm piety won the
affection of many students. Kuist later left BSNY to teach at Union Theological Seminary, Richmond, Virginia, and in 1943 assumed the Charles T.
Haley Chair in Biblical Theology at Princeton. Kuist took his BSNY-
developed perspective with him as he moved from school to school, pref-
acing courses with discussions of White and inductive epistemology.[50]
While at Princeton he often returned to New York to teach weekend
courses, maintaining his ties with BSNY.

Kuist outlined his approach to biblical studies most fully in *These
Words upon Thy Heart: Scripture and the Christian Response*. Like White, Kuist
downplayed redaction criticism and arguments over date and composition, favoring an analysis of the text as a literary unit accepted by the
church. Kuist presented an artistic approach to Scripture which he called
the "re-creative" method of criticism. Drawing on John Ruskin's "Essay
on Composition" and Theodore Meyer Greene's *The Arts and the Art of
Criticism*, Kuist suggested that scholars approach the biblical text as an
artistic composition.[51] How the present text received its current form was
much less important than how it actually stood and functioned today. As
Brevard S. Childs, one of Kuist's later students at Princeton, said: "Kuist

---

49. No published biography of Kuist exists, although a biographical sketch ac-
companies the Howard Tillman Kuist papers, 88-MF-004, Golda Meir Library, University of Wisconsin-Milwaukee. The papers are available on microfilm at ATSA. Also
telephone interview with James M. Kuist, April 12, 1995; and with Kuist student
Howard H. Charles, February 3, 1995, Goshen, Indiana.

50. The debt his teaching owed to BSNY is evident from the text of a 21-page
summary of lectures for his course "Old Testament Book Studies," taught during the
spring semester of 1939, at Union Theological Seminary, Richmond, Virginia. Kuist
devoted the entire first class to a lecture on Wilbert White, the founding of BSNY, and
the inductive English Bible approach. See "Old Testament Book Studies" course transcript, personal papers of David R. Bauer, Asbury Theological Seminary, Wilmore, KY.

51. Kuist, *These Words upon Thy Heart*, esp. 38-39, 56-60, 71, 79, 92, 98-107, 142.
Ruskin's essay (from his 1857 *Elements of Drawing*) appeared as an appendix in the
book. Theodore Meyer Greene, *The Arts and the Art of Criticism* (Princeton: Princeton
University Press, 1940). Further testimony to Kuist's interest in artistry and theology
is his essay "Reflections of Theology from *Gone with the Wind*," *The Union Seminary
Review* 50 (October 1939): 1-13. A secondary discussion of Kuist's method is Eberhardt,
The Bible in the Making of Ministers, 153-57.

See also Howard T. Kuist, "The Training of Men in the Christian Tradition," *The
Union Seminary Review* 52 (April 1941): 3-24; "The Use of the Bible in the Forming of
Men," *The Princeton Seminary Bulletin* 38 (June 1944): 4-14; and *How to Enjoy the Bible*
(Princeton: The Theological Book Agency of Princeton Theological Seminary, 1939).

realized that the historical-critical method was killing the text, and he insisted that the meaning was in the text itself. You didn't have to rearrange the text to fit your own reconstruction, the structure and meaning became clear in the text itself. By a sheer illumination of reading, a holistic reading, he turned the corner."[52]

When Kuist had first arrived at Princeton, however, few colleagues or students were interested in his approach. The long shadow of the 1920s modernist-fundamentalist controversy still lay over the institution, and Kuist's reticence to debate historical-critical assumptions and his efforts to shift the debate away from redaction criticism left him with few supporters. While Childs thought Kuist was "a breath of fresh air" and his "inductive approach very freeing," Childs realized that Kuist "was a very isolated character at Princeton." In the classroom many students' questions were openly hostile, and some quietly mocked Kuist's pious outbursts of joy in the midst of a lecture. At the same time, Kuist had almost no dogmatic training, and little knowledge of nor interest in contemporary intellectual activity in Britain or the Continent, deficiencies which hindered his scholarly and classroom effectiveness.

Still, Kuist's approach influenced students, who went on to help shape new approaches to biblical studies, particularly the Biblical Theology Movement and canonical criticism. While neither of these movements sprang directly from Biblical Seminary, the school's orientation is visible in aspects of both. The so-called Biblical Theology Movement of the postwar years shared with Kuist a concern to give priority to the message of Scripture and to view that message in terms of biblical motifs. Since the bibliocentric curriculum at BSNY shied away from systematics in favor of biblical studies, theology soon took on a distinct shape. Administrators insisted that students could find a "common meeting ground" around the Bible, rather than in "a theological viewpoint, such as the Modernist or [the] Fundamentalist."[53] Theology at BSNY typically amounted to exercises in drawing out biblical themes within and across the testaments. While such efforts could be crude, some faculty and students became rather sophisticated.

Not surprisingly, several BSNY graduates, most notably Donald G. Miller, went on to play key roles in the Biblical Theology Movement of the postwar years. In his influential homiletics text *Fire in Thy Mouth,*

---

52. Telephone interview with Brevard S. Childs, January 11, 1996.

53. Paul C. Warren, "Denominational Loyalty in an Interdenominational Seminary," BSNY Literary Production: Manuscripts, BSNY papers, 8:18, ATSA.

Miller tried to bring the insights of Biblical Theology and inductive-study sermon preparation into the parish.[54] BSNY graduates and Kuist students from other schools initially found the Biblical Theology Movement congenial. The movement's "major thrust was directed against the misuse of historical criticism by theological liberals." In place of a fragmented text, Biblical Theology proponents reasserted the importance of the fresh proclamation of the biblical message. Moreover, some scholars hoped the movement would offer a way through the modernist-fundamentalist deadlock of the previous decades, another common interest of BSNY-oriented evangelicals. Eventually, however, the Biblical Theology Movement became almost wholly Neoorthodox in orientation. With James D. Smart, G. Ernest Wright, and others assuming leadership and charting the direction of the enterprise, it was soon caught up in battles for contemporary "relevance," and essentially collapsed in the early 1960s.[55]

In 1970, Brevard Childs published *Biblical Theology in Crisis*, a book which documented the movement's rise and demise. The volume was also an initial presentation of an alternative understanding of biblical studies which Childs had been formulating for some time, an understanding reflecting, in some part, his encounter with Kuist.[56] Eventually known as "canonical criticism," Childs's new approach proposed to focus "attention on the final form of the text itself" and treat "the literature in its own integrity." Unlike traditional historical-critical methods, canonical criticism refused "to bring extrinsic, dogmatic categories to bear on the biblical text by which to stifle the genuine exegetical endeavour." Instead, "the approach seeks to work within that interpretive structure which the biblical text has received from those who formed and used it as sacred scripture."[57]

---

54. Miller, *Fire in Thy Mouth*. See also his essays, "The Minister and His Bible," *The Princeton Seminary Bulletin* 44 (Summer 1950): 13-26; "Art Form and the Genius of the Bible," *The Union Seminary Review* 54 (June 1943): 28-46; "Neglected Emphases in Biblical Criticism," *The Union Seminary Review* 56 (August 1945): 327-58; and *The Authority of the Bible* (Grand Rapids: William B. Eerdmans, 1972). Miller and Balmer Kelly were co-founders of the journal *Interpretation: A Journal of Bible and Theology*, an early forum for the Biblical Theology Movement. See the editorial "Criticism, and Beyond," *Interpretation: A Journal of Bible and Theology* 1 (April 1947): 219-25.

55. Brevard S. Childs presented the history of the Biblical Theology Movement in *Biblical Theology in Crisis* (Philadelphia: The Westminster Press, 1970), 13-87. Childs tied Kuist to the movement's interest in understanding the biblical message from within the text, or from the Bible's own perspective (45 n. 52).

56. Ibid., 91-219.

57. Brevard S. Childs, *Introduction to the Old Testament as Scripture* (Philadelphia: Fortress Press, 1979), 73. See also *The New Testament as Canon: An Introduction* (Philadel-

While there was no direct cause-and-effect relationship between Kuist's re-creative, wholistic reading of accepted Scripture and Childs's highly developed and nuanced canonical approach, Childs himself says there may have been an "unconscious connection": "In retrospect, things from Kuist aided me; I took over later, I'm sure, some of his insights."[58]

"Child-centered" Christian Education

Given the pedagogical significance the BSNY faculty and alumni attached to the methods and epistemology of inductive study and thinking, it is perhaps natural that one of the school's greatest bequests would come in the area of Christian education. A so-called "child-centered" approach to Sunday school instruction and curriculum emerged from the work of Christian educators and theorists influenced by Biblical Seminary. Their efforts at places such as Wheaton College and through publishers such as Scripture Press changed the way many thought about passing on the faith.

From his Yale days with Harper, Wilbert White had a keen interest in pedagogy, and he brought that interest to BSNY. Impressed with nearby Columbia Teachers College, White sought to implement creative, experimental educational methods in the seminary curriculum.[59] Biblical's administrators encouraged all faculty, not just those teaching Christian education, to study pedagogy.[60] Herman Harrell Horne (1874-1946), a Harvard Ph.D. and educational philosopher teaching at NYU, served as an adjunct BSNY faculty member and advisor, and brought depth to the school's educational experimentation.[61]

Biblical's style of teaching drew on its foundational inductive theory. Learning inductive study, proponents believed, took place through obser-

---

phia: Fortress Press, 1984); *Canon, Theology, and Old Testament Interpretation: Essays in Honor of Brevard Childs* (Philadelphia: Fortress Press, 1988). Certainly, canonical criticism is far more complex than the oversimplified description given here.

58. Telephone interview with Brevard S. Childs, January 11, 1996.

59. Brereton, "The History of The Biblical Seminary," 14-15.

60. E.g., New Testament professor Howard T. Kuist authored *The Pedagogy of St. Paul* (New York: George H. Doran Co., 1925), which discussed the apostle's writings in relation to modern educational theories.

61. See Herman Harrell Horne's *Jesus, the Master Teacher* (New York: Association Press, 1920) and *The Philosophy of Education, being the Foundations of Education in the Related Natural and Mental Sciences* (New York: Macmillan, 1927), for the variety of his religious and secular writings.

vation and experience with a text: asking questions, comparing related texts, organizing findings, and making concrete applications. In the realm of Christian education the parallels were obvious. Students began with observations and concerns from their own life experiences, asked pertinent questions, looked to the Bible for guidance, and drew practical applications. The role of experience at the beginning and end of the process suggested something of a parallel with the educational theory of John Dewey, who argued that education was a way of living, rather than preparation for future living.[62] Although the students and faculty at BSNY did not accept all of Dewey's ideas,[63] the inductive epistemology they employed did shift the focus of children's Christian education away from a preestablished set of doctrinal facts demanding memorization, to a child-centered (and, in part, child-directed) curriculum similar to what Dewey advocated. This contrasted with the standard fundamentalist approach to child training, which stressed memorization of catechismal devices.

By 1928, BSNY's undergraduate and graduate programs in Christian education accounted for a sizable portion of the school's enrollment, and dozens of BSNY graduates went on to replicate its Christian education philosophy and program at other institutions. The most prominent was Rebecca R. Price (1910-72), a 1934 Biblical graduate. Price received her NYU doctoral degree three years later through the BSNY cooperative arrangement. Beginning in 1936, when she became the first professor of Christian education at Wheaton College (IL), Price was one of the leading theorists on the subject. As a Wheaton professor, she brought Biblical's inductive study methods to the classroom. Her course on the Gospel of Mark was widely regarded as one of the best Bible courses on campus.

More significant was her presentation of BSNY-style child-centered educational theory. The department soon reflected Price's perspective, since the faculty additions were either her students from the Wheaton graduate program or fellow BSNY graduates.[64] Two of Price's best charges were Mary E. (1910-82) and Lois E. LeBar. In 1945, with the sisters just

---

62. John Dewey, "My Pedagogic Creed (1897)," in *John Dewey on Education: Selected Writings* (New York: Random House, 1964), 427-39.

63. Indeed, at least one BSNY student attended a public debate on educational psychology between Horne (of NYU/BSNY) and William Kilpatrick (representing Dewey). Students knew that Horne, White, and other BSNY faculty rejected the anti-supernaturalist elements of Dewey's thought. Reported by Mary C. Graham, May 12, 1996.

64. Paul H. Heidebrecht, "The Educational Legacy of Lois and Mary LeBar," unpublished paper, 1991, 15-18.

finishing their advanced degrees, Price invited them to join the faculty. Although they left briefly to complete doctoral studies at NYU, following in Price's footsteps, the LeBars continued teaching at Wheaton until the 1970s.[65]

Meanwhile, in 1952 Price left Wheaton for Pasadena, California, where she began a similarly oriented and influential Christian education program at Fuller Theological Seminary.[66] Thereafter, the LeBars effectively defined the Wheaton programs that shaped the educational outlook of hundreds of Christian education majors. Mary LeBar also continued teaching Price's popular inductive study course on Mark.[67] About half of the LeBars' graduating majors took positions as directors of Christian education in local churches, while others assumed teaching posts in a variety of Bible schools, colleges, and seminaries.[68]

The influence of the inductive educational ideal spread far beyond the Wheaton campus not only through the department's graduates, but also through the LeBars' extensive writing of Sunday school curriculum and teacher education materials. The sisters had begun writing for Scripture Press before coming to Wheaton, and they continued their relationship with the firm.[69] Begun in 1933, Scripture Press was one of the leading publishers of Sunday school materials in the nation. The sisters produced or revised materials annually, in addition to preparing curriculum for vacation Bible schools. As one historian noted, "Though she never earned a national reputation for writing children's literature, Mary's [and, one might add, Lois's] contribution to the education of thousands of young children in evangelical churches can hardly be overestimated."[70]

The Scripture Press materials reflected the LeBars' educational commitments. In her widely used teacher manual, *Patty Goes to the Nursery Class*, Mary offered a yearlong plan of Sunday school units organized around attitudes and feelings rather than doctrines, with "the aims of each

65. At NYU they studied with, among others, William Heard Kilpatrick, an ally of Dewey.

66. On Price's significance, see Margaret Lamberts Bendroth, *Fundamentalism and Gender, 1875 to the Present* (New Haven: Yale University Press, 1993), 86-87; and Marsden, *Reforming Fundamentalism*, 45, 127-28, 145.

67. The longevity and continuity of this course is intriguing. Julie Gorman, chair of the Christian Education Department at Fuller Theological Seminary, took the course from Mary LeBar at Wheaton and now teaches this course at Fuller, where Rebecca Price introduced it in 1952. See *Newsletter: Inductive Bible Study Network* (Winter 1993): 4.

68. Heidebrecht, "The Educational Legacy," 24-43.

69. Lois wrote for Scripture Press until 1969; Mary, until 1975.

70. Heidebrecht, "The Educational Legacy," 20.

unit . . . stated from a child's viewpoint."[71] Indeed, "A teacher's check list" for class evaluation measured lessons against the experience of each child. According to Mary, play and discovery were more important than didactic presentation of truth. Young children inductively learned spiritual principles from "The kinds of toys we furnish and the suggestions we give [for play activities]." Teachers were facilitators of a child-directed process: "The interpretation we give to happenings and interest of Patty" set the agenda and constituted teachable moments.[72]

For her part, Lois LeBar complemented her younger-age curriculum writing with college-level Christian education texts, such as *Children in the Bible School* and *Education That Is Christian*.[73] In an essay on curriculum published by Moody Press, Lois presented her philosophy of education, which set evangelicals' interest in propositional truth within a framework of inductive, experiential learning. "Evangelicals teach 'thus saith the Lord' with a ring of authority," she noted, yet "pupils fail to hear the voice of God speaking to them." LeBar continued, "Thus the pupils' self-activity is necessary" in order to "discover insights that they can use and appropriate in their own lives." She summarized her theory by emphasizing that: "Initially, continuity of experience is more important than continuity of content." True to her inductive epistemology, Lois insisted that only "later in the process" should a teacher expect that "truth becomes organized systematically in doctrine and theology."[74] Meanwhile, the sisters' graduates, who had been deeply immersed in the theory of inductive, experiential learning, filled positions at evangelical publishing houses. By the late 1950s the "influence of the inductive Bible study method . . . in the structure of the lesson plans" was clear, particularly at Scripture Press.[75] BSNY was continuing to shape Christian education in America.[76]

---

71. Mary E. LeBar, *Patty Goes to the Nursery Class* (Chicago: Scripture Press, 1945, rev. 1952), 7. See outline of units and themes on 8-9.

72. Ibid., 62 and 107.

73. Lois E. LeBar, *Children in the Bible School* (Westwood, NJ: Fleming H. Revell Co., 1952) and *Education That Is Christian* (Westwood, NJ: Fleming H. Revell Co., 1958).

74. Lois E. LeBar, "Curriculum," in *An Introduction to Evangelical Christian Education*, ed. J. Edward Hakes (Chicago: Moody Press, 1964), 91-92. On Lois's ideas compared with Dewey's, see Robert W. Pazmiño, *Foundational Issues in Christian Education* (Grand Rapids: Baker Book House, n.d.), 147.

75. Heidebrecht, "The Educational Legacy," 40.

76. The LeBars' interest in inductive learning process also fueled their late 1960s efforts to radically rethink Christian education in active evangelical congregational life. Lois suggested that only such an approach could yield effective answers. "Let's banish

STEVEN M. NOLT

Conclusion

The Biblical Seminary in New York no longer exists as such. The institution underwent a radical reorganization and theological reorientation in the mid-1960s, changed its name to New York Theological Seminary, and by 1970 was a very different school.[77] In its own day, however, Biblical Seminary was remarkable for presenting and representing a faith which often defied neat categorization. Born of Wilbert White's desire to wed scholarship and evangelical faith, BSNY employed radical induction to make an end-run around the epistemological battles which pitted fundamentalists and liberals in exhausting struggle with each other. Rejecting the deductive ontology of the former and the hermeneutic of suspicion championed by the latter, the Biblical Seminary in New York offered an alternative and centrist approach to Scripture and Christian faith. Its irenic legacy can still be felt today.

---

from our minds preconceived ideas of how things have been done," she wrote, "and let's explore all the unexamined possibilities" (Lois E. LeBar, *Focus on People in Church Education* [Westwood, NJ: Fleming H. Revell Co., 1968], 15). Along with fellow Wheaton professor Lawrence O. Richards, the LeBar sisters co-hosted two conferences on congregational revitalization in the summers of 1967 and 1968. Held at Wheaton's Honey Rock Camp in Wisconsin, the meetings included teachers, pastors, and youth workers who suggested sweeping structural changes in evangelical Christian education, congregational forms, and mission. The discussions and results, including the leadership contributions of the LeBars, are recorded in a series of articles by Lawrence O. Richards in *United Evangelical Action* 26 (August 1967): 4-5, 16; (September 1967): 12-14, 23-24; (October 1967): 16-18, 33-35; (November 1967): 14-16, 34-35; 27 (Fall 1968): 22-24, 29, 50; (Fall 1968): 30-36; (Winter 1968): 16-24. Few of the revolutionary ideas were implemented by American evangelicals, but the suggestions derived from an inductive assessment of the church in American society found their way into popular evangelical youth ministry textbooks of the 1970s. Lawrence O. Richards, *Youth Ministry* (Grand Rapids: Zondervan, 1972); *A Theology of Christian Education* (Grand Rapids: Zondervan, 1975).

77. Brereton, "History of the Biblical Seminary," 156-60. Interview with Robert A. Traina, March 14, 1995. In 1966 Traina left for Asbury Theological Seminary, Wilmore, KY, where he continued to promote the traditional BSNY approach. See also George Dugal, "Old Line Seminary Picks Liberal," *The New York Times* (March 10, 1969): 30; John Evensong, "New Leader, New Motif for New York Seminary," *Christianity Today* (28 March 1969): 42; and Robert W. Pazmiño, *The Seminary in the City: A Case Study of New York Theological Seminary* (Lanham, MD: University Press of America, 1988), vii, 44-45. George W. Webber, president of New York Theological Seminary after 1969, discussed the school's post-1970 orientation in *Led by the Spirit: The Story of New York Theological Seminary* (New York: Pilgrim Press, 1990).

CHAPTER 18

The Two-Party System and the Missionary Enterprise

SAMUEL ESCOBAR

Since Protestantism embraces such a wide spectrum of trends and movements around the world, we know that any effort to develop a comprehensive typology is bound to be limited and imprecise. The historical study of Protestant missionary practice and theory during the past two hundred years brings to light those limitations and imprecisions. From its beginnings among the Moravians in central Europe, the missionary enterprise has clearly exhibited Protestantism's paradox of unity and disunity. American Protestantism is no exception to this rule.

This volume, which focuses on "Re-Forming the Center," offers an appropriate forum for exploring some kinds of missionary activity and reflection where the paradox of unity and disunity can be illuminated and to some degree resolved. In particular the disunity defined by the two-party model of Protestantism has indeed been crossed and blurred by some mission agencies and individuals who were able to set aside "pugnacious and competitive formulas of identity,"[1] even when the divisions and confrontations of the two parties in the United States seemed to many as acute as ever. What is more, a convergence of sorts — if not a full unity — has been called forth at times by a missionary vision that was embraced by individuals and institutions from both sides of that supposed divide.

This essay is an initial exploration into the kind of American missionary effort in which the lines of the two parties were crossed, particularly during the years since 1960. Two case studies will serve my purpose: first,

---

1. Douglas Jacobsen and William Vance Trollinger Jr., "Evangelical and Ecumenical: Reforming a Center," *The Christian Century* (July 13-20, 1994): 684.

the InterVarsity Christian Fellowship (IVCF) of the USA, an organization that works primarily with college-age students and that has been active in the promotion of missions and recruitment of missionaries; and, second, the Latin America Mission (LAM), a missionary sending agency based in the U.S.A. During the period under consideration, developments within organizations such as these helped prepare the way for what missiologist David Bosch called "an era of convergence" between evangelicals and ecumenicals during the years after 1974.[2] Efiong S. Utuk has gone even further. In his review of developments in evangelical missiology between 1966 and 1974 he concludes that "the new fact of our time" in missiology is not "the widening gulf between evangelicals and conciliarists," but rather "an emerging consensus on many missiological questions . . . as well as the fact that 'evangelicals' are becoming more 'ecumenical' than ever, while 'ecumenicals' are becoming more 'evangelical.' "[3]

The two organizations examined here moved toward this convergence from what would typically be seen as the evangelical zone of American Protestantism. However, these groups were able to make such a move largely because they found affinities with some prominent members of the supposed other party, mainline Protestantism. Of special importance here is the influence of John A. Mackay, president of Princeton Theological Seminary from 1936 to 1959 (see note 28). What we find is that as persons from one or another of the supposed two parties drew closer to the center, the boundary separating those two spheres seemed almost to disappear.

InterVarsity Christian Fellowship

The InterVarsity Christian Fellowship (IVCF) of the USA identifies itself as an evangelical movement dedicated to the evangelization and discipling of college and university students. It was officially launched as an American entity in 1941.[4] Its origins go back to a movement with the name Inter-Varsity Fellowship (IVF) that was organized in Great Britain in 1928 on the basis of prior student-led groups or "unions," such as the Cambridge Inter Collegiate Christian Union (CICCU), which had existed since 1887. The IVF

2. David J. Bosch, " 'Ecumenicals' and 'Evangelicals': A Growing Relationship?", *The Ecumenical Review* 40 (1988): 464.

3. Efiong S. Utuk, "From Wheaton to Lausanne: The Road to Modification of Contemporary Evangelical Mission Theology," *Missiology* 14 (1986): 218.

4. Keith and Gladys Hunt, *For Christ and the University: The Story of InterVarsity Christian Fellowship of the U.S.A./1940-1990* (Downers Grove: InterVarsity Press, 1991), 86.

sent volunteer promoters to other English-speaking countries such as Canada, Australia, and New Zealand; the movement entered the United States from Canada. An important factor in the formation of the British IVF had been the dissatisfaction of evangelical students with developments within the ecumenically oriented Student Christian Movement (SCM).

But the American IVCF had broader roots than just the British IVF. In particular, there was a relationship with the Student Volunteer Movement for Foreign Missions (SVM). SVM was a spontaneous movement of college students that developed during the nineteenth century in the United States, reaching official status in 1888.[5] The organization played a significant role in the growth of American missions abroad. In fact, the early SCM in Europe and the American SVM became a training ground for the leadership of the ecumenical movement that developed after the Missionary Conference at Edinburgh in 1910. It produced persons like John R. Mott, Robert P. Wilder, and Robert Speer, who were at the same time pioneers of ecumenism and enthusiasts of Christian mission. These were Protestants in whose lives and careers there was an inseparable blend of evangelical and ecumenical elements. Mott's biographer puts it this way: "Mott and others inherited the best of Moody's outlook. The warm-hearted spirit and enthusiasm of Evangelical Christianity shaped their deepest personal predilections; at the same time they possessed an ecumenical viewpoint that would have pleased their mentor in Northfield."[6] SVM leaders were inclusive in their appeal for cooperation in mission; because of their denominational origins they also had a high sense of churchmanship. In these aspects their stance was different from what would later become the position of the so-called evangelical "party."

This genuine youth initiative became a ferment within the large Protestant bodies in North America. From the first 6,000 volunteers that went to the mission field inspired by SVM, 85 percent came from mainline denominations: Presbyterian, Methodist, Baptist, and Congregational. The movement flourished until the 1920s, but it then entered a period of decline associated with the heated theological debates of the modernist-

5. For narrative, analysis, and bibliographies about the SVM and similar movements see Samuel Escobar, "Recruitment of Students for Mission," *Missiology* 15 (1987): 529-45; Wilbert Norton, "The Student Foreign Missions Fellowship over Fifty-Five Years," *International Bulletin of Missionary Research (IBMR)* 17 (1993): 17-22; and Timothy C. Wallstrom, *The Creation of a Student Movement to Evangelize the World* (Pasadena: William Carey International University Press, 1980).

6. James F. Findlay Jr., quoted in C. Howard Hopkins, *John R. Mott: A Biography* (Grand Rapids: Eerdmans, 1979), 29.

fundamentalist controversy.[7] Persons of more evangelical or fundamentalist convictions who remained within the SVM tended to become pessimistic about the future of the organization.

In 1936, fifty-three students from fourteen colleges and Bible institutes formed a committee to start a new organization that would continue the original aims and the spirit of the SVM, because they felt SVM was abandoning those ideals. This process eventually led to the formation of the Student Foreign Missions Fellowship (SFMF), which merged with the IVCF in 1945. The director of the Missions program of IVCF was also the chairperson of the SFMF.[8] Some older leaders of the SVM such as Robert Wilder agreed with these developments. James Patterson says that "Wilder himself, in the 1930s, passed the SVM torch to Inter-Varsity Fellowship and thus indirectly to the Student Foreign Missions Fellowship and the Urbana triennial missionary conventions."[9] Thus, for many, IVCF in the USA and Canada came to be seen as that organization which best embodied the aims and missionary spirit of the SVM.

The first full-time Missions Secretary of IVCF after its merger with SFMF was J. Christy Wilson, and his career exemplifies the way party lines were easily crossed within the frame of the missionary vocation. Wilson's parents had been Presbyterian missionaries in Iran; when they returned to the States, their home was frequently visited by well-known promoters of mission such as Mott, Speer, and Wilder, who left a deep impression on the young Christy. As a student Wilson would later become actively involved in the SVM, but he also witnessed its decline at the time of the liberal-fundamentalist debates. Though he was attracted to the SFMF and the IVCF, he first went to study theology at Princeton Seminary. Upon graduation he became the first American IVCF missions secretary.[10]

It was under Wilson's leadership that IVCF organized its first mis-

---

7. Time and space do not allow for a more detailed treatment of the historical frame within which the evangelical student movement developed. Several authors deal with many aspects of the influence of the fundamentalist-liberal controversies on the missionary enterprise, the decline of ecumenical missions, and the growth of fundamentalist and evangelical missions in Joel Carpenter and Wilbert Shenk, eds., *Earthen Vessels* (Grand Rapids: Eerdmans, 1990).

8. Norton, "Student Foreign Missions Fellowship," 18, 20; David Howard, *Student Power in World Evangelism* (Downers Grove: InterVarsity Press, 1970), 97-108.

9. James A. Patterson, "The Legacy of Robert P. Wilder," *IBMR* 15 (1991): 30.

10. Wilbert Norton, "Climbing the Urbana Tree," *His Magazine* 34 (1974): 34-37. Later Wilson would respond "to the call for teachers to staff the schools in Afghanistan." Before departing on that venture, however, "he topped his training for the task by taking the Ph.D. in Islamics at Edinburgh University."

sionary conference, in Toronto in 1946. More than five hundred students attended. The next missions conference, held in 1948, was moved to the campus of the University of Illinois at Urbana. The so-called "Urbana missionary convention" has since that time been a rallying point for university students interested in missions, and it has been a prime recruiting ground for mission boards looking for missionary candidates. While the name "Urbana" has become a symbol of missionary enthusiasm, the conference has also become an important forum for missiological reflection and critical thought.[11]

The steady growth in the number of students who attend the Urbana conventions, in spite of the general decline of missionary fervor within American Protestantism, is evidence of the continued interest of a new generation of (primarily evangelical) students in Christian mission.[12] However, the influence of the Urbana conventions has always reached beyond the confines of any narrowly defined evangelical party. Two of the twelve denominations most heavily represented among the attendees at Urbana 90 were the Presbyterian Church in the U.S.A. (5.48 percent) and United Methodists (2.08 percent). In addition, mission boards from several mainline denominations have always been present among the agencies, trying to recruit prospective missionaries.[13]

IVCF's Theological Ethos and Self-Critical Missiology

Due to its historical development, the ethos of IVCF in its formative period was different from the ethos of most "evangelical" American youth movements. First, it was shaped more by the British experience than by the American one. This helped to avoid the excesses of "separationism" typical of those forms of American evangelicalism that had been foundationally shaped by the traumas of the modernist-fundamentalist debates. A decisive role here was played by the Australian C. Stacey Woods, the first General Secretary of IVCF, and the Britishers David Adeney and Eric Fife, who were influential in the formation of IVCF's missionary program.

11. See table of Urbana themes and attendance records in Norton, "Student Foreign Missions Fellowship."

12. For a careful analysis of trends as expressed in figures of evangelical involvement in missions, see Robert T. Coote, "Good News, Bad News: North American Protestant Overseas Personnel Statistics in Twenty-Five-Year Perspective," *IBMR* 19 (1995): 6-13.

13. Samuel Escobar, "The Significance of Urbana '90," *Missiology* 19 (1991): 332-38.

Second, and not unrelated to the first, IVCF developed a theological disposition that focused on major theological questions rather than on minor cultural and contextual issues that had become so crucial in the development of the intolerant and separatistic ethos that is associated with fundamentalism. Third, this understanding of theological issues made it possible to incorporate into the IVCF persons who were concerned about missions and who were members of the historic Protestant churches. Besides Anglicans such as John R. W. Stott, speakers at the Urbana conventions always included mainline missionaries, evangelicals active in the ecumenical world, and progressive missiologists. Fourth, IVCF's aim to be an "indigenous" ministry on secular college campuses forced it to take seriously the context within which it had to accomplish its mission. Because of this it had to learn how to deal with secular challenges to the Christian faith.[14] These four factors contributed to the shaping of a more open and irenic spirit in the IVCF, which allowed for a self-critical stance on missionary issues that had not been possible within the fundamentalist missionary establishment.

In his historical overview of mission theology, Rodger Bassham says that "during the 1960's the range of concerns and issues involved in the discussion of evangelical mission theology broadened considerably."[15] The Urbana convention in 1961 represented a distinct turning point in this process. Alongside the inspirational part of the program, this conference also included a critical educational component that dealt with crucial and controversial issues for which there was no other evangelical forum. The publication of Eric S. Fife and Arthur F. Glasser's *Missions in Crisis*[16] as a study book for that convention set the tone for what was to be a decade of theological growth and ecumenical awareness in IVCF. The significance of this book and of the conference itself has to be understood against the background of the growing triumphalism that permeated the evangelical missionary enterprise in the fifteen years after the end of World War II. That postwar evangelical missionary activity had been shaped by the ideology of the Pax Americana and the Cold War; according to historian

---

14. In reference to this point, Harvey Cox offers a surprisingly positive analysis of IVCF's ability to minister in the secular frontier of the campuses. See *The Secular City* (Harmondsworth: Penguin Books, 1968), 233-34.

15. Rodger C. Bassham, *Mission Theology, 1948-1975: Years of Worldwide Creative Tension Ecumenical, Evangelical, and Roman Catholic* (Pasadena: William Carey Library, 1979), 186-87.

16. Eric S. Fife and Arthur F. Glasser, *Missions in Crisis* (Chicago: InterVarsity Press, 1961).

Richard V. Pierard, "evangelicals from the U.S. had bought heavily into the war-induced revival of civil religion, and most of them engaged in a syncretic confusion of Christianity and Americanism."[17]

By 1960, however, the missionary enterprise was being challenged by several new factors such as the closing of China, the growth of a Third World nationalist awareness after the Bandung Conference (1955), and the emergence of indigenous "evangelical" churches in the Third World. Questions posed by the new situation were tackled realistically by the authors of *Missions in Crisis*. They were concerned by the fact that, in response to international tensions, "many have felt that they should identify the Church with the political program of the West in its cold war with the communist powers." They also pointed out the failure of organizations such as the World Evangelical Fellowship and the fundamentalist International Council of Christian Churches to penetrate the hearts and capture the imagination of Christians overseas. What was the explanation? The authors of the study thought that these organizations were "too closely identified with American cultural imperialism, too American-controlled, too American-financed, and as a result too emotionally involved in the ideological East-West conflict of these times."[18]

Another influential factor in the development of this new self-critical evangelical missiology within IVCF was the inclusion in IVCF's meetings of leaders from other parts of the world. Voices from members of the "younger churches" of the world were heard from the platform at the Urbana conferences, and in many cases these were the articulate voices of university graduates who came from the ranks of student movements similar to IVCF (many from within the family of the International Fellowship of Evangelical Students).

It is worth mentioning at this point the role played by Paul Little in exporting IVCF's new view of missions. Little, a well-known student evangelist, had been the director of the Urbana conventions for several years before becoming the organizational architect of the Lausanne Congress on Evangelism in 1974. Little's experience with the Urbana conferences added much to both the efficient organization and the spirit of Lausanne. His lecturing trips put him in touch with evangelical leaders and university students all over the world. This was reflected in his selection of speakers for the Urbana platform, and this unique network of

17. Richard V. Pierard, " 'Pax Americana' and the Evangelical Missionary Advance," in Carpenter and Shenk, eds., *Earthen Vessels*, 165.

18. Fife and Glasser, *Missions in Crisis*, 61, 142.

contacts was later to be reflected in the program of the Lausanne Congress.[19]

As a member of the Program Committee for the Lausanne meeting in 1974, I witnessed firsthand the effort of Paul Little and others (such as Anglican Bishop Jack Dain) to allow the widest possible range of participation. This ecumenicity included men and women from mainline churches and organizations. This broader vision constantly clashed with the narrow vision of fundamentalist members of the committee, but the broader view prevailed.

IVCF's self-critical posture was also reflected at the Lausanne Congress. It was there, for example, that evangelist Billy Graham acknowledged his past mistake of identifying the gospel with American culture. Now, Graham said, "when I go to preach the Gospel, I go as an ambassador for the Kingdom of God — not America. To tie the Gospel to any political system, secular program or society is dangerous and will only serve to divert the Gospel."[20] A new evangelical missiology was in the making, one that detached evangelical missions from the trap of American civil religion, and IVCF had played a crucial role in its development.[21]

Within the IVCF orbit there had always been leaders, teachers, and spokepersons who had remained loyal to their mainline denominations at the same time that they were active and influential in the more conservative missionary sectors. The unique ethos of IVCF allowed for this; eventually this openness influenced evangelicalism at large, as evinced by the Lausanne movement. In many ways, the missions department within IVCF cultivated a wider ecumenism more successfully than many other avowedly ecumenical organizations. Relatively unrelated to the strictures of church order and ecclesiastical polity, this grassroots ecumenism has proven very fruitful in the past and still holds a transforming promise for the future. A similar situation can be seen in the history of the Latin America Mission.

19. It is ironic that Paul Little is not even mentioned in the most recent official biography of Billy Graham, which has an important chapter about Lausanne. See William Martin, *A Prophet with Honor: The Billy Graham Story* (New York: William Morrow and Co., 1992).

20. J. D. Douglas, ed., *Let the Earth Hear His Voice: International Congress on World Evangelization, Lausanne, Switzerland* (Minneapolis: World Wide Publications, 1975), 30.

21. For analysis and evaluation of the Lausanne movement see James A. Scherer, *Gospel, Church and Kingdom: Comparative Studies in World Mission Theology* (Minneapolis: Ausgburg, 1987); Valdir Raul Steuernagel, "The Theology of Mission in Its Relation to Social Responsibility within the Lausanne Movement" (Ph.D. thesis, Chicago: Lutheran School of Theology, 1988); and John R. W. Stott, "Twenty Years after Lausanne: Some Personal Reflections," *IBMR* 19 (1995): 50-55.

The Latin America Mission (LAM)[22]

American mainline missionaries to Latin America cooperated in the development of national churches whose outlook, doctrinal stance, and practice could all easily be characterized as "evangelical" in the broadest sense of that term. Indeed, this missionary disposition in Latin America marked the mainline American Protestant missionary establishment itself. As a result the divisive revisionings of Protestant theology that took place during the controversial thirties and forties in the United States never really reached Latin America. Instead, the division in Latin America was between Protestant and Catholic forms of Christian faith. This tension existed in mainline missions, but was exacerbated within conservative circles as attitudes toward Roman Catholicism were becoming in the United States a litmus test of authentic evangelicalism.

The Latin America Mission (LAM) was founded by Harry and Susan Strachan on July 24, 1921, at Stony Brook, Long Island. It was first incorporated as the Latin America Evangelization Campaign (LAEC), a name that describes well the intention and experience of the founders. Like all Protestant missionaries in Latin America, the Strachans had the conviction that, despite the pervasive institutional presence of Roman Catholicism and the deep religious faith of the masses, most Latin Americans were almost completely ignorant about Christianity.[23]

Harry had been born in Canada but later returned to Scotland, the land of his family. Susan was Irish. They met at Harley College in East London, an independent training school for missionaries directed by H. Grattan Guinness. From Harley both went as missionaries to Argentina under the auspices of the Regions Beyond Missionary Union (RBMU). Susan arrived in 1901 and Harry in 1902. They were married in 1903. During the following years RBMU went through a financial crisis, and its mission work in Peru and Argentina merged with a South American Evangelical Mission to form the Evangelical Union of South America

---

22. I am in debt in this section to veteran LAM missionaries and executives W. Dayton Roberts and Clayton L. Berg for their valuable comments and information. With regard to the Strachan family and the history of the Latin America Mission I depended heavily on the manuscript "Harry Strachan: An American Don Quixote," now partially incorporated into a book: W. Dayton Roberts, *One Step Ahead* (Miami: Latin America Mission, 1996). I have used the manuscript and quote it here with the author's permission.

23. See John A. Mackay, *The Other Spanish Christ* (New York: Macmillan, 1932), for an informed Protestant perspective about this point.

(EUSA) in 1911. The Strachans remained in Latin America working with this new organization.

Harry was a born evangelist; besides specific responsibilities in the city of Tandil near Buenos Aires, he traveled extensively, experimenting with a great variety of evangelistic methods. He was also a visionary and had great dreams of evangelization campaigns that would reach all of Latin America with the methods that had proved fruitful in Argentina, such as city crusades, tent revivals, and horse-drawn wagons turned into bookmobiles. Funds from the mission were scarce, but Strachan managed to get local support for survey trips to Brazil, Chile, and Peru.

During the years of World War I, there was no chance that the British branch of EUSA could attend to Strachan's funding requests for his new and ambitious projects. While on furlough in the United States in 1918, he connected with the Canadian branch of EUSA, seeking unsuccessfully to obtain from them the financial help he needed for his new evangelistic ventures. Disappointed, Strachan returned to the New Jersey and New York area, where he finally did find, among relatives and friends, a group of people ready to support him. In particular, Robert C. McQuilkin of the *Sunday School Times* played a key role in gathering support and encouraging him.

With this new source of support behind him, Strachan eventually resigned from the EUSA and decided to found his own organization, which he called the Latin America Evangelization Campaign. (Its name would later be changed to the Latin America Mission.) The mission statement of the new organization expressed well its ethos and the guiding principles that shaped these initial decades of the work: "This is an independent, interdenominational work on faith lines, which has been founded under the guidance of God, to reach the unevangelized millions of Latin America by a forward movement of aggressive evangelism, carried out in cooperation with the missionaries of all denominations working in the field."[24] Strachan's first order of business under the umbrella of this new organization was a trip to survey the conditions of the Protestant churches in eighteen Latin American countries.

The Strachans decided to establish their base in Costa Rica. Almost from the start their evangelistic work was defined by its holistic approach, which included medical and educational work, literature distribution, radio programming, and leadership training. While Harry concentrated on evangelism, Susan started many projects in response to the acute social

---

24. Roberts, "Harry Strachan," 52.

needs she confronted every day. The Strachans' missionary experience thus confirms Van Engen's observation that: "On the mission field many interdenominational fundamentalist and evangelical mission agencies found themselves far more socioeconomically and politically active than they would have considered being in North America. Was it because the North American environment had forced them into a 'fundamentalist reduction' that could be overcome in other parts of the world?"[25]

Strachan aimed to have the best possible preachers associated with the work of the LAM — preachers who could communicate with all the social classes — and many of these he found in the mainline churches. However, Strachan did not agree with the "ecumenical" stance and the methods of the Committee of Cooperation in Latin America (CCLA).[26] The result, as W. Dayton Roberts has observed, was that not "every segment of Protestantism [was] happy with the new campaign movement. As time went on, there would be increasing coolness on the part of some missionaries. There was a strong current of ecumenical Protestants who would prefer the methodology of non-controversial lectures, dialogical publications and comity agreements to the abrasive conflict of evangelicals and public campaigns."[27] But Strachan continued to welcome preachers such as John A. Mackay, Gonzalo Báez-Camargo, and Pablo Burgess, who had connections with the CCLA. This accounts for what Roberts describes as Strachan's ambivalent relationship with the ecumenical sector of Protestantism, a relationship that was to be characteristic of the mission as a whole and that would produce enemies of the mission within the fundamentalist sector of American Protestantism.

But the Strachans not only had to struggle to make their way among other Protestants. Many times Strachan found himself in open confrontation with the conservative sectors of the Roman Catholic Church, which resented the presence of Protestant missionaries in Latin America. All in all the Strachans often found themselves and their mission caught in the

---

25. Charles E. Van Engen, "A Broadening Vision: Forty Years of Evangelical Theology of Missions," in Carpenter and Shenk, eds., *Earthen Vessels,* 211.

26. Protestant missions and missionaries who labored in Latin America were excluded from the World Missionary Conference held in Edinburgh in 1910 because of pressure from European Protestants (especially Anglicans) who were sympathetic to Roman Catholicism. American Protestants were, however, reluctant to accept this kind of "High Church" ecumenism, and spokespersons such as John R. Mott, Robert Speer, and other mission leaders decided to form the Committee of Cooperation in Latin America, in order to help coordinate Protestant efforts in the region.

27. Roberts, "Harry Strachan," 56-57.

middle between a variety of antagonistic, or semi-antagonistic, Latin American and North American Christian groups.

LAM's Broadening Vision

Harry Strachan died in 1945. He was succeeded in the direction of the mission by his wife and later on by his son R. Kenneth, who had been born in Argentina in 1910. The career of Kenneth Strachan (d. 1965) provides an interesting example of the kind of mediating role that was chosen by the leadership of LAM, in an effort to respond to the missionary demands of Latin America.

Ken Strachan grew up in Latin America. His preparation for ministry began with the education he received in the conservative atmosphere of Wheaton College (Illinois), which was followed by his immersion in the fundamentalist dispensationalism of the Evangelical Theological College of Dallas, Texas (later to be known as Dallas Theological Seminary). He graduated in 1939 with a Bachelor of Theology degree and returned to Costa Rica to work in his father's mission.

After the initial years of intense missionary work, Ken went back to study at Princeton Theological Seminary for his Th.M. degree. Under men of the caliber of President John A. Mackay, Ken grasped a new vision.[28] He became aware of the importance of the church in God's plan

28. Because of the important background role played by John A. Mackay and Princeton Seminary in the histories of both IVCF and LAM, it is appropriate here to make that connection a bit more explicit. During the mid-twentieth century, Princeton was one of the main places where evangelical-ecumenical dialogue and encounter took place. This was the case largely for two reasons. The first reason was the school's links with the missionary movement. It was this concern for missions that prompted evangelical interest in the seminary. The second reason was the person of John Alexander Mackay (1889-1983) who was president of the institution from 1936 to 1959. Mackay came to this position, after twenty years of involvement in missionary work, first as an educator and youth evangelist in Latin America, and later on as a mission executive in the Board of Foreign Missions of the Presbyterian Church in the USA. Mackay was very self-consciously an evangelical-ecumenical bridge builder.

Mackay had been an active participant in the development of the ecumenical movement, especially in the International Missionary Council, of which he was honorary chair between 1947 and 1957. He took a leading role in the preparations for the Amsterdam Assembly of the World Council of Churches (1948), where he preached the opening address (which was later published as "The Missionary Legacy to the Church Universal," in the *International Review of Mission* 37 [October 1948]). He also served as an elected member of the World Council's Central Committee from 1948 to

for humankind, and of the message and deep significance of the Reformation. He also discovered the Hispanic spirituality of the sixteenth century and became familiar with the scholarly study of missions. W. Dayton Roberts has obseved: "Until this time his thinking had been more traditional than original and his writing mediocre. Princeton seemed to stimulate his thought into new channels and mature his powers of expression as well as of reasoning."[29]

Ken Strachan's basic missionary outlook reflected the vision and conviction of the generation of evangelical missionaries represented by his father, Harry, that was at the core of LAM. That vision was decidedly evangelistic, yet it had a continental breadth, and looked for cooperation on a wide basis. Ken's own missiological stance had developed from reflection on his experience, but he also gained insights through the study

---

1957 and was active in the formation of the Federal and National Council of Churches in the U.S.A.

During this illustrious ecumenical career, Mackay never lost his evangelical zeal, as is evident in his writings. In addition to works cited see John A. Mackay, *A Preface to Christian Theology* (New York: Macmillan, 1941), *Christianity on the Frontier* (New York: Macmillan, 1950), *Ecumenics* (Englewood Cliffs: Prentice Hall, 1964), and *Christian Reality and Appearance* (Richmond: John Knox Press, 1969). When he came to work in the United States he was able to move beyond the borders of the two parties freely, even in times of acute controversy. He put his unique administrative and diplomatic skills at the service of the ecumenical enterprise, but he also shared the fire of his Evangelical zeal with the broader ecumenical world. His deep sense of the significance of our century as the "ecumenical era" moved Mackay to invest time and energy in the great ecumenical conferences of the mid-century, but he always insisted that ecumenism remain faithful to the missionary vision which had given it birth. He reminded all that "Evangelistic fellowship on the missionary road preceded ecclesiastical fellowship in the home sanctuary. Christian churches who took seriously their missionary obligation and crossed the frontiers of non-Christian lands began to transcend the barriers by which they had been themselves divided in their own home countries" (see John A. Mackay, "The Missionary Legacy to the Church Universal," 370).

Mackay left his mark on Princeton. He had become president at a time when the school was still divided by bitter theological controversies, and when "an alternative was needed which moved beyond both Fundamentalism and Modernism." He committed himself to work for what he called "the restoration of theology," giving a central place to the Bible and insisting that a missionary thrust should be at the soul of that theological work. This was the evangelical ecumenism in which key leaders of both IVCF and LAM were schooled between the fifties and the seventies and which they built into their respective organizations. This was a centrism that clearly transcended the two-party system.

29. W. Dayton Roberts, *Strachan of Costa Rica: Missionary Insights and Strategies* (Grand Rapids: Eerdmans, 1971), 36.

of missiologists such as Roland Allen, Hendrik Kraemer, and Donald McGavran.[30] As he developed his views, Strachan became a frequently invited speaker in evangelical circles in North America because he knew the Latin American situation so well and could articulate evangelical perceptions of missionary problems so clearly.

Strachan's broadening missionary concern, however, was also characterized by an attitude of practical ecumenism that would not miss opportunities for dialogue and cooperation. As such, it contained the seeds of new developments that would push his missiological views beyond the limitations of the fundamentalist ethos. His main concern was rooted in his observations of separatistic missionary behavior in the field, as he eloquently observed:

> There are places where missionaries, especially those with separatistic inclinations, have allowed themselves to be pushed off into little eddies wholly outside the main stream of life around them, leaving them unhappy and almost devoid of influence. We are not entering into people's lives; we live comfortably on the outskirts of hunger, immorality, misery and sorrow; we stand on the shores, almost in a spectator attitude, while the tide of humanity sweeps past.[31]

Strachan's own change of mind in relation to "separationism" had come as a result of a long process of study and heart searching. In 1957 he was invited to a consultation sponsored by the International Missionary Council in Puerto Rico. In response, Roberts says, "He made a full and careful study of what the Bible teaches — by historical implication, apostolic example and specific admonition — about 'separationism,' or the doctrine that Christians ought to withdraw from fellowship with those who do not adhere to the fundamental doctrines of the Christian faith or who associate with those who do not." His conclusions were in open contrast with the practice of fundamentalist and conservative missions. He concluded that "such a doctrine of separation can have no other logical end than continued divisions and . . . it tends to become spiritually sterile and to breed pharisaical self-righteousness and bigotry."[32]

Strachan attended the meeting of the IMC in Puerto Rico, and contacts established at that point allowed him to play a key role in the 1958

30. Roberts, *Strachan of Costa Rica*, 83.
31. R. Kenneth Strachan, "Eddies and the Main Stream," *His Magazine* (February 1960): 11.
32. Roberts, *Strachan of Costa Rica*, 7, 80.

Caribbean crusade of Billy Graham. The participation of the Protestant churches from Puerto Rico in that crusade was virtually total — an unusual demonstration of cooperation in mission. Because of the role he played, Ken Strachan's name became a respected commodity in ecumenical circles. Roberts writes: "Ken's insights were being increasingly sought and appreciated by ecumenical leaders and others outside his more customary and conservative circles. Men like John Mackay and Lesslie Newbigin were seeing in him a natural bridge between their own evangelical position within the historic denominations and that of the independent conservative groups."[33]

Cooperation was key for Evangelism in Depth (EID), which was LAM's most significant contribution to missionary strategy and missiology. Ken coined the name and articulated the famous "theorem" which summarizes his findings: "The growth of any movement is in direct proportion to the success of that movement in mobilizing its total membership in the constant propagation of its beliefs."[34]

The movement was geared to renew, motivate, and mobilize Christians and churches in a concerted effort to impact a whole nation with the gospel. Having evangelism as a center, the program included specific steps to respond to social needs and to touch the structures of society. EID was made possible in part because under Ken's guidance the mission had already taken specific steps to incorporate Latin Americans into the administrative structures and the strategic planning of the mission's work. EID also tried to take seriously lessons learned from the growth of the Pentecostal movement in Latin America, which was both holistic in approach and significantly indigenous in leadership. In all these aspects LAM was pioneering missiological changes that most other evangelically identified missions were reluctant to implement. After the initial EID effort in Nicaragua (1960) there were similar nationwide movements in Costa Rica (1961), Guatemala (1962), Honduras (1963-64), Venezuela (1964), Bolivia (1965), the Dominican Republic (1965-1966), Peru (1967), and Colombia (1968).

In 1963 (at the request of Lesslie Newbigin), Ken Strachan wrote an article for the *International Review of Mission*, entitled "Call to Witness," which described the way EID had taken form in his mind and the lessons he had learned from his experience with the program. Victor Hayward

---

33. Roberts, *Strachan of Costa Rica*, 96-97.
34. W. Dayton Roberts, *Revolution in Evangelism: The Story of Evangelism in Depth in Latin America* (Chicago: Moody Press, 1967), 95.

from the staff of the World Council of Churches wrote a response, and Strachan a rejoinder.[35] In the decade that followed, this "debate" became one of the most quoted pieces of missiological literature.

It is evidence that ecumenical leaders, who had previously been reluctant to take evangelical missiological ideas and concerns seriously, were now willing to do so, thanks in part to Strachan and his work with LAM. But within the American missionary establishment, and especially within the very conservative Interdenominational Foreign Missions Association (IFMA), the overtures of LAM to the ecumenical world caused concern and resistance. Nonetheless, as Glasser has observed, the IFMA representatives "were never quite able to persuade LAM's leaders that Scripture endorses IFMA's posture of deliberate isolation from major segments of the church."[36]

Evangelism in Depth and LAM had enough impact on the life of churches and even on public life to attract the attention of journalists, sociologists, and historians. It has been evaluated critically by mainline scholars and sociologists.[37] More recently, David Stoll has explained some of the scholarly attention shown to LAM in terms of the "paradoxical results" of the EID program:

> For one the mission alienated fundamentalists with its sociological frame of reference, talk about the need for Christians to address social needs, and tolerance of different opinions. For another, LAM became aware of the need to decolonize missionary work. By incorporating Latin Americans into its program on an equal basis with North Americans, it internalized the tensions between the two in a creative new way.[38]

This "creative new way" pioneered by Strachan involved a complex double move on the part of LAM. This erstwhile conservative organization had decided to go against the stream and move simultaneously both

35. *International Review of Mission* 53 (1964): 91-215. For a more mature elaboration of Strachan's missiological position see his posthumous work *The Inescapable Calling* (Grand Rapids: Eerdmans, 1968).

36. Arthur F. Glasser and Donald A. McGavran, *Contemporary Theologies of Mission* (Grand Rapids: Baker, 1983), 117.

37. See, e.g., Rubem Cesar Fernandes, "Fundamentalismo à direita e à esquerda," *Tempo e presença* [Rio de Janeiro] 29 (1981): 13-25; and Ray S. Rosales, *The Evangelism in Depth Program of the Latin America Mission* (Cuernavaca, Mexico: Centro Intercultural de Documentación, 1968).

38. David Stoll, *Is Latin America Turning Protestant? The Politics of Evangelical Growth* (Berkeley: University of California Press), 120.

toward an ecumenically defined center and away from the hegemonic missiological dominance of North America over Latin America.

Like Ken Strachan himself, the team of missionaries that accompanied and followed him after his death in 1965 — people like Horace Fenton, Dayton Roberts, Wilton M. Nelson, and Clayton L. Berg — are examples of evangelical ecumenism. These leaders as well as other missionaries who served with LAM had several things in common. Many of them came from "evangelical" congregations within mainline denominations. Besides having studied in bastions of evangelicalism, such as Wheaton or Dallas, several of them had also graduated from Princeton Seminary; others were Fuller Seminary graduates. During the key decade before the milestone Lausanne Congress of 1974, Horace ("Dit") Fenton, Strachan's successor as director of the mission, participated in many evangelical forums, and was also a spokesman for evangelicals in dialogues with the ecumenical world.[39] He always combined a clear evangelical stance with a disposition to tackle the most difficult questions that came from the missionary frontier. As he once wrote:

> In my thinking there is one basic question that above others challenges us, and it is this: Can we, as evangelicals, engage in positive, helpful criticism of our own methods and programs — learning from our failures as well as from our successes? The answer to that is not clear; we are often a defensive lot, spending most of our time justifying positions we have taken and attacking nonevangelicals who disagree with us.[40]

Different from other faith missions, LAM recruited candidates among IVCF alumni and attracted support from mainline churches.[41] Among the members of the Board of LAM there have always been members or ministers from mainline denominations. Of the fifteen members listed in LAM's *The Latin America Evangelist* in 1978, ten were from main-

---

39. Fenton was a frequent speaker in IVCF events. See also his important contribution, "Mission and Social Concern," to the 1966 "Congress on the Church's World Wide Mission" that took place in Wheaton (see Harold Lindsell, ed., *The Church's Worldwide Mission* [Waco, TX: Word Books, 1966]). Fenton also interpreted the 1966 Wheaton Congress for the ecumenical journal *International Review of Mission* (1966), and contributed a chapter to the dialogical volume *Protestant Crosscurrents in Mission: The Ecumenical-Conservative Encounter*, ed. Norman Horner (Nashville: Abingdon, 1968).

40. L. Fenton, "Some Questions the Quarterly Must Help to Answer," *Evangelical Missions Quarterly* (1974): 28.

41. Roberts, *Strachan of Costa Rica*, 73.

line churches: Presbyterian, Reformed Church in America, and American Baptist. Five of them had also participated actively in IVCF. Church membership as well as theological training connected these leaders, missionaries, and supporters of LAM with the ecumenical world. This was in real contrast with other "evangelical" missions that had membership, leadership and support exclusively from fundamentalist or conservative circles.[42] In all of this LAM kept the vision of Ken Strachan alive and even expanded it.[43]

42. In a personal communication to the writer, Clayton L. Berg, former President of LAM (1976-1989), estimates that half of the missionary force and membership of the Board came from mainline Protestant churches.

43. Building bridges and fostering cooperation out of renewed missiological convictions in LAM went hand in hand with a number of adjustments and structural changes inside the mission itself. The late 1970s and 1980s were a time of testing for LAM. American and Latin American missionary strategists, including Dayton Roberts, Rubén Lores, and Orlando Costas, played an important role in the decentralization and latinoamericanization of LAM's structure, a process that eventually gave birth to the Latin American Community of Evangelical Ministries (CLAME). Dayton Roberts describes the process as an effort to deal with the missiological question of "how to structure a missionary bridge over the gap between Old World resources and Third World Opportunities." But as Stoll has observed, various offshoots of the mission became institutional frameworks for the implementation of very different agendas.

Moreover, tensions were created by the changing political scenes in both Latin America and the United States. Especially in the case of Central America, Protestantism became polarized by the political turmoil of the Sandinista revolution in Nicaragua and United States policies against it. A resultant radicalization of the left and the right affected several of the CLAME institutions, especially the Biblical Seminary in San José. While it might be quite safe, in a setting like the Lausanne Congress, for a person like Billy Graham to detach his evangelism from the interest of the Pax Americana, it was not necessarily safe at all for someone to do the same thing in Costa Rica during the eighties. Such an act could bring open persecution from conservative evangelical sectors. This was precisely the experience of LAM theologian John Stam. The chronicle of his life illustrates well the difficulties of pursuing a centrist missiological course in polarized society.

Since 1982 there are two organizations claiming to represent two "parities" in Latin American Protestantism. Conservative evangelicals organized CONELA (Confraternity of Latin American Evangelicals), affiliated with the World Evangelical Fellowship, while mainline denominations closely related to the World Council of Churches organized CLAI (Council of Latin American Churches). There are Pentecostals on both sides, but none of these two organizations has been able to attract a significant majority of Latin American Protestants. The Latin American Theological Fraternity (FTL) founded in 1970, which is not a church-related organization, has provided a permanent forum for encounter and dialogue of leaders from a wide spectrum of Protestantism. In 1992 the FTL brought the Presidents and Secretaries of

Conclusion

By moving beyond the confines of narrow fundamentalist or separatist positions, the movements and persons we have considered opened avenues for the renewal of evangelical missiology and the missiological revitalization of the ecumenical movement. Overcoming "separationism" as a formula of identity, the persons discussed here adopted that "more humble and less strident understanding of what it means to be evangelical [that] has always been present in the broader evangelical movement."[44] They held on to their evangelical piety and theology, but they also contributed to realistic policies and serious theological work with regard to a holistic balance between evangelism and social concern, the passing of leadership to national leaders in the young churches, the purification of the gospel from imperialist accretions, and the exploration of new patterns of missionary cooperation in an age of global Christianity.

Carpenter and Hutchison have rightly interpreted developments within evangelicalism from the sixties to the eighties as part of a cyclical process of maturation.[45] There is truth in Carpenter's assessment that the fundamentalist legacy to the missionary enterprise of the post-1945 period was separation and isolation from the Protestant mainstream. Therefore, "when a post-fundamentalist, 'neo-evangelical' theological movement appeared in the 1950's and 1960's, it virtually had to reinvent evangelical missions theology."[46]

In this reinvention of the 1950s, 1960s, and 1970s, an evangelical theological consensus emerged which was open to circumscribed ecumenical cooperation in missionary work. The evangelical leaders who helped formulate this new missionary vision were those who kept the door open for dialogue and dared to cross party lines for the sake of the gospel. In doing this they often found with surprise how much they had

---

CONELA and CLAI to dialogue about the future of mission in Latin America. Several missionaries of the Latin American Mission, such as René Padilla, Tito Paredes, Guillermo Cook, and John Stam have played an important role in the bridge-building work of the FTL.

44. Jacobsen and Trollinger, "Evangelical and Ecumenical: Re-forming a Center," 683.

45. Carpenter and Shenk, eds., *Earthen Vessels;* William B. Hutchison, *Errand to the World: American Protestant Thought and Foreign Missions* (Chicago: University of Chicago Press, 1987).

46. Joel Carpenter, "Propagating the Faith Once Delivered: The Fundamentalist Missionary Enterprise," in Carpenter and Shenk, eds., *Earthen Vessels,* 131.

in common with important sectors within the ecumenical world, and sometimes even with Roman Catholic traditions.[47]

The case studies examined here also illustrate the principle that all sectors of American Protestantism involved in the overseas missionary enterprise were transformed by their interactions with global Christianity. Perhaps this shows that the true center of North American Protestantism may ultimately lie outside North America, in the transcendence of North American Protestantism's North Americanness, as much as it may lie in any balanced approach that seeks to avoid the reductionistic extremes of the two parties.

47. There is a surprising number of coincidences in documents such as the *Lausanne Covenant* (an evangelical document from 1974), the *Evangelii Nuntiandi* (a Catholic document from 1974), and the statement *Mission and Evangelism — An Ecumenical Affirmation* (an ecumenical document from 1982). See James A. Scherer, *Gospel, Church and Kingdom: Comparative Studies in World Missions Theology* (Minneapolis: Augsburg, 1987), 40-41.

CHAPTER 19

Youth Ministry at the Center:
A Case Study of Young Life

RONALD C. WHITE, JR.

"I'm not a problem. I'm a man." So blare the words beside the picture of a young African-American teenager on the cover of *Focus on Youth*. The year is 1968. Opening the magazine, one is confronted with a solid black page containing a single quotation from the National Advisory Commission on Civil Disorders: "What white Americans have never fully understood — but what the Negro can never forget — is that white society is deeply implicated in the ghetto. White institutions created it, white institutions maintain it, and white society condones it."[1]

Focus on Youth is the magazine of Young Life. The first page of the magazine defines Young Life as a "nonsectarian organization to communicate the Christian faith to the adolescent." One might naturally assume that this evangelistic statement of purpose signals a wholesale identification of the organization with the alleged "evangelical party" of American Protestantism. But neither the cover design nor the articles, graphic pictures, dialogue, questionnaire, and reading list contained in the magazine seem to fit the evangelical stereotype. The articles probe the nature of prejudice; as the editorial on page two begins: "In the United States recently we have been acting as a nation caught in a giant social eclipse — our Black-White dilemma." But it's not just the content that is significant here; it's also who is doing the talking. For example, Cameron Wells Byrd's "Tell It Like It Is" is an edited version of an address he delivered to the Youth Division of the National Council of Churches. The final article,

---

1. *Focus on Youth* 2 (July, 1968): 1, 3. Young Life has had several magazines with different names since the original *Young Life* in 1943.

RONALD C. WHITE, JR.

"Racism and the Renewed Life," is by George D. Kelsey, Professor of Christian Ethics at Drew University, who, an inset says, is "familiar to Young Life leaders who have learned from him at the Young Life Institute."[2] What is going on here?

This essay examines Young Life as a case study regarding the possibility of re-forming the center.[3] I argue that, in its second generation (i.e., the 1960s and 1970s), this parachurch youth ministry was propelled by two centrifugal forces well beyond the evangelical vision on which the organization was founded in 1941. The result was a transformed youth organization which in part bridged the ostensible two-party division within American Protestantism. These two centrifugal forces were: (1) an evolving understanding of the church; and (2) the challenge of urban ministry, which included an engagement with the Black Church. Together these concerns forced Young Life to develop a much larger understanding of both the church and American culture.

The eruption of these forces within Young Life coincided primarily with the years when William S. Starr was president of the organization, 1964 to 1977. As Young Life celebrated its first quarter century of ministry, the reins of leadership passed from founder Jim Rayburn to Bill Starr. Starr brought to the presidency of Young Life a prophetic sensitivity to the new forces swirling through both the church and American society. This was an age far different from the era of World War II and the 1950s in which Young Life was born and grew into adolescence. During this time, Starr plotted a course for Young Life that might not have been predicted from his own roots. As a result, the course of Young Life in its second generation is quite different from other "evangelical" parachurch youth ministries with which it has often been grouped.[4]

2. Ibid., 2, 31.

3. This chapter is part of a larger historical study first suggested by the Louisville Institute for the Study of Protestantism and American Culture. I gratefully acknowledge that Phase I and Phase II of the project have been funded by the Lilly Endowment and the Louisville Institute.

4. A benefit of participation in the Re-Forming the Center conference was the opportunity to test hypotheses. Martin Marty, the keynote speaker at the project's June 1995 conference, offered the opinion that Young Life seemed to him distinct among parachurch youth ministry organizations in its efforts to reach out to the churches.

The Youth Ministries Movement

Before proceeding to describe and analyze Young Life, it is necessary to place this movement in its larger historical context. I say "necessary" because youth ministry is invisible in the standard histories of American religion. The fact that youth and youth ministry have been so overlooked suggests that vital elements of the American religious mosaic have been ignored. Most people have the general religious direction of their life set during their youth. This study seeks both to help fill the historical gaps in our knowledge of youth ministry and to provide evidence that one particular youth organization, Young Life, largely transcended the bipolar distinctions assumed in the two-party model of American Protestantism.

Youth ministry, as a national movement, grew from the vision of Francis E. Clark, a Congregational pastor in Portland, Maine, in 1881. Exactly one hundred years after Robert Raikes founded the Sunday School to reach out to poor children in England, Clark decided there must be more for young people than the pink teas, oyster suppers, and literary guilds sponsored by the churches of his day. This was also the time when adolescence was first being discovered as a social phenomenon within American culture. The notion of "youth" was, in late nineteenth-century America, a much more inclusive category than it is today, including persons ranging in age from twelve into the twenties or even up to thirty-five. (This is still the designation of youth in most countries of the world today.) Building on the motto "For Christ and the Church," and obviously filling a need in American religious culture, Christian Endeavor exploded across the country. In 1895, 55,000 youthful delegates gathered for the annual Christian Endeavor convention in Boston.

Denominations were not long content, however, to leave the field solely to this interdenominational movement. Soon, the Methodists (1889), Baptists (1891), Lutherans (1895), and others formed their own denominational youth organizations. Many denominations, however, including the Presbyterians and the African Methodist Episcopal and African Methodist Episcopal Zion churches, kept Christian Endeavor as their youth organization. But by the time of Clark's death in 1927 Christian Endeavor had lost some of its vitality and the denominations had picked up the slack. As denominations copied business methods of incorporation in the early twentieth century, many of the denominational youth organizations, which had been begun as auxiliary movements almost outside denominational structures, now became domesticated and bureaucratized. As all of these youth societies progressed, it was also discovered that members didn't want to drop out of the organizations. Soon, many of the "youth" were in their thirties and forties and were crowding to the sidelines the true adolescents in their midst.[5] All of this contributed to the gradual decline of Christian Endeavor.

Youth ministry entered a new phase in the 1940s. Concerned about the fragmentation and competition in church youth work, and convinced that youth societies continued to function too much as auxiliaries to the churches rather than as fully integrated parts of the church, denominational leaders sought to revive their own denominational youth fellowship programs. For example, the Methodists reinvented the Epworth League as the Methodist Youth Fellowship in 1941; the Presbyterians, which began to grow critical of Christian Endeavor in the 1930s, started the Westminster Fellowship in 1943.[6]

Emerging almost simultaneously was a fresh cluster of new, independent, interdenominational youth ministry organizations. Young Life (incorporated in 1941), InterVarsity (1941), Youth for Christ (1945), Campus Crusade for Christ (1951), and the Fellowship of Christian Athletes (1954) were all launched in the crusading ethos of the World War II era. (In every case there was a start-up period of trial and error that went back at least several years.) These movements were different in form and strategy from both Christian Endeavor and the denominational youth programs. Some years after their beginnings, these independent groups would come to be called "parachurch" organizations, defined by David Barrett, editor of the *Almanac of the Christian World*, as "almost a church, resembling a church." Resembling churches, organizations such as Young Life would soon begin to create their own new patterns of ministry within the American religious ecology.[7]

---

5. G. Stanley Hall's *Adolescence* (New York: D. Appleton, 1904), articulated in a scholarly way some of the popular conversation at the end of the nineteenth century about a stage of life between childhood and adulthood. A central chapter in this study was about the ways religious conversion was particularly associated with this age group. Some of Hall's ideas about conversion and the young would be discredited by later scholars, but they received much credence at the time.

6. Mary-Ruth Marshall, "Precedents and Accomplishments: An Analytical Study of the Presbyterian Youth Fellowship of the Presbyterian Church in the United States, 1943-1958" (Ph.D. Dissertation, Presbyterian School of Christian Education, 1993), 98-99.

7. I am indebted to Darrell L. Guder for sharing with me an unpublished paper, "Para-Parochial Movements: The Religious Order Revisited." He cites Barrett's definition.

The Early Years of Young Life

Young Life began as a novel idea "hashed out" by a young seminarian and a veteran Presbyterian pastor. Jim Rayburn, a third-year student at Dallas Seminary, took a part-time position at the First Presbyterian Church in Gainsville, Texas. Clyde Kennedy and Jim decided that Jim's territory would not be the church building or program. Instead he headed for the local high school. His desire was to befriend high schoolers on their own territory.

The methods of Young Life were being born. Jim wanted to communicate with teenagers unwilling to participate in the churches. Rayburn "looked for books on youth work, but there were none." Utilizing what he would call "friendship evangelism," Rayburn recruited seminary classmates and lay volunteers to reach out to high schoolers at football games, school plays, and drug store soda fountains across Texas — wherever teenagers gathered. Young Life as an organization was incorporated in the state of Texas in 1941.[8]

Young Life leap-frogged the country from Dallas to Chicago to Seattle to Memphis to Los Angeles in the 1940s and early 1950s. The message focused on the presentation of a winsome Christ. The method was rooted in relationships with kids. Rayburn's oft-quoted biblical mandate was from the apostle Paul: "Walk with wisdom toward them that are without." Within the organization, this was translated into the watchword: "Winning the right to be heard." The proposition undergirding Young Life's contact work on high school campuses, at camps, and in clubs held in the homes of teenagers[9] was that every kid had a right to hear the story of Jesus the Christ in an attractive and compelling way in language that teenagers could understand. Reading between the lines was the conviction that traditional church programs didn't get the message through to kids. As

---

8. The basic story of the origins of Young Life can be found in the following books: Emile Cailliet, *Young Life* (New York: Harper & Row, 1964); Char Meredith, *It's a Sin to Bore a Kid: The Story of Young Life* (Waco: Word, 1978); Jim Rayburn III, *Dance, Children, Dance: The Story of Jim Rayburn, Founder of Young Life* (Wheaton, IL: Tyndale House, 1984); and John Miller, *Back to the Basics of Young Life* (Colorado Springs: Privately Printed, 1991). See also *Young Life Magazine* 19 (June 1962): 3-4. Sources for this chapter are also taken from interviews with nineteen staff members of Young Life conducted in May 1994, at the Young Life headquarters in Colorado Springs.

9. The acquisition of Starr, Silver Cliff, and Frontier Ranches in Colorado from 1946 to 1951 accelerated a camping program that would spread throughout the United States and Canada.

Rayburn said in his studied Southwestern drawl: "It's a sin to bore a kid with the Gospel."

Differences of ecclesiology have been seen as flashpoints in the standard two-party paradigm of American Protestantism. During the first half of the twentieth century, it is assumed that the liberal, public party advanced a churchly and increasingly ecumenical vision for religion in America. By contrast, the conservative, personal party supposedly charted a course that was both more individualistic and more sectarian. According to this story line, the conservative party was finally forced to found the National Association of Evangelicals in 1942 as a means of opposing what they saw as the growing hegemony of the Federal Council of Churches (formed in 1908), which represented mainline Protestantism. It would be expected, given this scenario, that the new parachurch youth movements formed in the 1940s and early 1950s would naturally find themselves part of the NAE orbit. Youth for Christ certainly seems to fit this expectation in both its leadership and constituency. Young Life, however, is a much more complicated story.

Bill Starr's Pilgrimage

Young Life's changing understanding of the church is reflected in the pilgrimage of William S. Starr. Bill grew up around the railroad yards of St. Paul and Chicago. The major church influence on him as a young person was his mother's Evangelical Free Church congregation in St. Paul. In 1943 Starr became the youngest commissioned officer in the Navy. While in the Navy he was influenced by the Navigators, a parachurch ministry to service personnel, which emphasized the memorization of Scripture.[10] After World War II, Bill attended Wheaton College (Illinois). At Wheaton he met a group of students who were collecting money to purchase a plane ticket for a fellow named Jim Rayburn to come from Texas to speak to them about how to reach young people. Starr had led a High-C club in St. Paul, but when he met Rayburn he knew that this

---

10. Dawson Trotman launched the Navigators in 1933, and it was incorporated in 1943. Typical of the charismatic founders of parachurch organizations, his relationship to the church was somewhat uneven. Raised and nurtured in a Presbyterian church in Southern California, he became disenchanted with mainline denominations rather early in his career. See Betty Lee Skinner, *Daws: The Story of Dawson Trotman, Founder of the Navigators* (Grand Rapids: Navigators, 1974). This is an empathetic biography written to extol the founder.

visionary Texan could be a mentor in his desire to reach teenagers in a fresh way.[11]

Starr began his ministry with Young Life in Portland, Oregon, in 1950. In Portland he pioneered the concept of a committee of local church people to help support Young Life. In 1953 he moved to Spokane, Washington. In Spokane he visited over one hundred pastors (and kept notes on all these visits). His goal was to get to know the pastors and tell them about Young Life. In the process Starr underwent a "shaking experience." He began to see things from their perspective. He found himself understanding the pastors' questions, their concerns, and their criticisms. He was told he was the first person from a parachurch organization who had ever come to talk with them.

His special friend in Spokane was Russell Hubbard, Bishop of the Episcopal Church. Bishop Hubbard was so appreciative of Young Life that he would introduce Bill at Young Life–sponsored parents' meetings in Spokane. From time to time Starr found himself slipping away from the Covenant church to worship at the Grace Episcopal Cathedral on Spokane's South Hill.

In 1956 Starr was appointed Midwest Regional Director of Young Life. In locating in Park Ridge, a Chicago suburb, it was suggested by his predecessor that Starr attend the Park Ridge Bible Church, a strong supporter of Young Life in the community. In this congregation Starr found himself struggling with what he called "the framework of fundamentalism." He became aware that the church lacked a sense of worship as central. What's more, legalism stood in the place of ethics. Starr started attending St. Mark's Episcopal Church on Wednesday mornings and early Sunday mornings. He found these experiences of worship to be "like a breath of fresh air."

In the Chicago area Starr became even more conscious of the lack of communication between churches. Church pastors and leaders did not care enough to get to know each other. He continued visiting churches and realized how the spectrum of his visits was widening. For example, while leading the Young Life club at New Trier high school he visited both the Winnetka Bible Church and the Congregational Church in Winnetka — congregations on opposite ends of the church spectrum in the commu-

---

11. The biographical materials on Bill Starr are mostly from interviews with him on March 27-29, 1995, and November 21, 1996. In 1996 he retired after ten years as the founding President of the Southwest Leadership Foundation in Phoenix. See Meredith, *It's a Sin to Bore a Kid*, 52-53, 63-64, and 105-112.

nity. On the one hand, Starr's experience was that some liberal churches on Chicago's northshore were extremely negative about Young Life's evangelistic mission to teenagers. On the other hand, he found himself "increasingly much more at home" with various mainline congregations, who cared about their own youth and were able to affirm what Young Life was doing in their local high school.

While in the Chicago area, Starr also came to reevaluate his own approach to youth evangelism. One particular incident stands out. A Jewish girl from New Trier who made a Christian commitment at a Young Life meeting was later committed to a mental hospital by her parents. Through his own anguish and tears over this incident, Starr underwent a transformation. As a result of this event, he made a vow "never to impose the Christian faith" on anyone again.

Starr was present in 1962 when Rayburn convened the Chicago Fellowship as an effort to reach out to the churches. Individuals from fifteen denominations gathered at the Union League Club to talk about how to reach young people. John Mackay, recently retired President of Princeton Seminary, gave the keynote address. Alvin Rogness, President of Luther Seminary, and Bishop Hubbard from Spokane and Sam Shoemaker, two prominent Episcopal ministers, were in attendance. The goal of the conference was to "finally explore together . . . the exerting of a new impact by the Church on today's young people."[12]

Starr was appreciative of Rayburn's initiative in convening the Chicago Fellowship, but he later came to believe that the rationale for this gathering was based too much on the premise of expanding Young Life's influence with the churches. However well intentioned that approach might be, Starr would ultimately come to see it as too self-serving. In its place, Starr gradually came to emphasize that Young Life was more a method than an organization. The best way to share that method would be to give it away to the churches.

In 1964 Starr was elected to succeed Rayburn. After a quarter century he became only the second leader of the Young Life organization. The move to headquarters in Colorado Springs made it possible for Bill and Ruth and their family to make another move he had long been contemplating. He joined the Ascension Lutheran Church, a congregation in the then American Lutheran Church. Later, he would find that mainstream church leaders responded with surprise when they found out that

12. This quotation is from an audiotape of Jim Rayburn's address to the Chicago Fellowship in 1962.

the leader of a parachurch ministry was a member of the Lutheran church.

A cluster of experiences in the 1960s and 1970s continued to deepen Starr's appreciation for the church in both its depth and diversity. In the early 1960s he met with exchange students from Latin America at a summer conference at Frontier Ranch. These Catholic students, Starr said, "jarred my little system" that had taught it was the responsibility of Protestants to convert Catholics. This experience helped put into place for Starr a cardinal principle of ministry he would carry with him for life: the essential aspect of faith is acknowledgement of Jesus as the Christ. While "evangelicalism" in theory would affirm this same essence, evangelical practice usually added a powerful "and" which appended certain theological beliefs (i.e., the substitutionary view of the atonement) and certain behavioral practices to the gospel.

Starr's new understanding of Jesus as the Christ led him to explore the further question: where is the presence of Christ? Two diverse experiences in Europe helped clarify Bill's emerging views.

The first was visiting Rod and Fran Johnston in France. The Johnstons were Young Life's first missionaries in Europe. In Starr's conversations he became increasingly uncomfortable with the Johnstons' exclusion of Catholics. Rod and Fran were a celebrated couple supported by thousands of American high schoolers. What was he to do with his response? Starr felt alone in his questions and affirmations.

The second experience was meeting Darrell Guder in Germany. Guder was an American Presbyterian, educated at UCLA, who had completed a Ph.D. at the University of Hamburg. He was a good friend of Helmut Thielicke. Guder was a theologian and missiologist who had worked with both university students and the Lutheran Diaconic movement in Germany for ten years. Starr was deeply impressed with Guder, and as a result of this visit Guder was invited to join Young Life's training department. An intellectual and churchman, Guder did not fit the mold of the usual youth ministry leader, but he quickly became a mentor and friend in Starr's search for a more viable working relationship between Young Life and the churches.[13] One fruit of Guder's wide-ranging involvement in both Lutheran and Reformed circles was a proposal by the Church of Württemberg inviting Young Life to help revitalize its ministry with youth.

13. Darrell Guder directed theological studies in Young Life from 1975 to 1985. He is presently the Peachtree Professor of Evangelism and Church Growth at Columbia Theological Seminary, Decatur, GA.

RONALD C. WHITE, JR.

A unique partnership thus began in 1975 which saw an official German church asking an American parachurch youth organization for help in training its leaders for a ministry of incarnational witness with German youth. Among the joint activities sponsored by Young Life and the Church of Württemberg was a series of theological dialogues. The first was held in Germany in 1975. At the second dialogue, held at Trail West in Colorado in 1980, the Church of Württemberg brought a delegation of local church leaders, and Young Life brought a team of American theologians, church leaders, and its own staff. Included in the German delegation was Peter Stuhlmacher, Professor of New Testament and Dean of the Faculty of Theology at Tübingen. Stuhlmacher presented a paper on the primitive mission of the New Testament church. In the ensuing discussion he related this New Testament understanding of the church's mission to Young Life's theology of "incarnational evangelism."[14]

Young Life and the Churches in America

Was it possible for Young Life in the United States to duplicate the partnership model operating so effectively in Germany? There were a number of problems involved. Even when Young Life had the best intentions, most American denominations did not know what to do with parachurch agencies. The German church, by contrast, had a more inclusive sense of ministry that allowed for a diversity of forms. The result was that no American denomination stepped forward, as had the Church of Württemberg, to admit its own need and to ask Young Life for help or partnership in ministering to its own youth.

Finally, however, one church did step forward as Young Life expanded its ministry in 1960s and 1970s. To the surprise of many, it was Roman Catholics who welcomed Young Life most warmly in different areas of the country. How was one to understand this openness? From the vantage point of the Re-Forming the Center discussions, one interpretation could be that Catholics, not caught up in the Protestant residue of the Fundamentalist-Modernist controversy, were free to accept what Young Life could offer.

Struggling with how to reach their own teenagers, Catholics were

14. The dialogue with the Church of Württemberg made a lasting impression on the author, who was pressed into service at the last moment as the respondent to Stuhlmacher's essay.

370

eager to learn from Young Life staff members who were obviously effective. In 1978, Michael Warren, Associate Professor for Religious Education at St. John's University, edited *Resources for Youth Ministry*. Published by Paulist Press, the volume contained "reports" from people doing youth ministry. Jeffrey Johnson's chapter, "Young Life Ministry: Room for Catholic Youth Ministers," encouraged Catholics to learn from Young Life. Johnson observed: "Rooting themselves in what they call 'relational ministry' and the ministry of friendship with teens, Young Life ministers are traveling the route that must be followed by any successful ministry to youth." Could this approach work in Catholic parishes? Johnson believed it could. "If Catholic parishes followed this single foundational aspect of Young Life ministry they would be well on their way toward fostering a renewed ministry to young people." Warren also included a chapter by Bill Starr entitled: "Young Life Focus: Friendship."[15]

Another promising model of working with churches was developed by Charlie Scott, Young Life's Regional Director in Florida. In 1977, the pastor of Charlie and Mary Scott's home congregation, Maitland Presbyterian Church, asked Scott to take charge of a high school group which attracted only four or five high schoolers each week. Scott decided to invite his unchurched Young Life kids. On the first Sunday over sixty showed up. "The church's senior pastor and most of the congregation were thrilled to see this large influx of teenagers." In 1980, Bob Alexander, pastor of the Leesburg First Presbyterian Church, told Charlie that two things were needed for the community: Young Life for the unchurched and a youth minister trained in Young Life methods for his congregation. Scott and Alexander decided that it would be best to "fill both needs" with one person. Scott recruited a person to lead both the youth group in the Leesburg church and the Young Life club at the local high school in an experiment in partnership.[16]

Within a year, six more churches in Florida "asked for people trained in Young Life to be part of their church staff." A program called "Church Partners" was developed, and it grew to include more than sixty churches throughout Florida. What is significant here is which churches were in-

15. Jeffrey Johnson, "Young Life Ministry: Room for Catholic Youth Ministers," in Michael Warren, ed., *Resources for Youth Ministry* (New York: Paulist Press, 1978), 45-46, 59ff.

16. Interview with Charlie Scott, April 1989; Charlie Scott, "Partners Together: The Church and Young Life," *The Church and Young Life: Partners in Ministry* (Colorado Springs: Young Life, n.d.), 49.

volved. Scott reported: "Most of the churches are in the mainline denominations — Episcopalian, Presbyterian and Methodist churches." Young Life had traveled a long way from its origins at Dallas Seminary. Its success was so great that the demand for "Church Partners" finally outstripped the availability of trained staff for placement.[17]

But all of these efforts still did not provide a systematic answer regarding how Young Life could and should relate to the larger church. In the nineteenth century Young Life probably would have been recognized as a voluntary society. These societies were voluntary associations of individuals organized to do a specific task: education, reform, and mission. Understood in this sense, Young Life was an association of individuals organized to do a specific task: evangelism with youth. But the American churches have never quite figured out the precise relationship they should have with such organizations. For example, New and Old School Presbyterians had quarreled in the 1830s about the role of voluntary societies. And Methodists, concerned about the domination of the voluntary societies by Congregationalists and Presbyterians, had begun founding their own denominational societies in the 1830s. These same tensions are still evident today when mainline churches squabble over how to treat Young Life or World Vision or other parachurch organizations. Some want to force their perceptions of these parachurch movements into the conservative side of the conservative/liberal or personal/public divisions of the two-party typology. But for groups like Young Life, this simply will not work.

One way that Young Life tried to establish a more constructive relation between itself and the larger church was through an expanding conversation about the nature and mission of the church nurtured by Starr and his successor, Bob Mitchell. In particular, Young Life invited a range of prominent theologians to teach or lecture at its Institute for Youth Ministry. The Young Life Institute had been founded by Rayburn in 1954. In 1977 a partnership was created with Fuller Theological Seminary which allowed the Institute to be accredited and the name was changed to the Institute of Youth Ministry. Under the leadership of Paul King Jewett, Professor of Systematic Theology at Fuller, the first Dean of the Institute, a distinguished faculty of seminary and college professors from across the country was recruited to teach. While other parachurch youth ministry organizations had their own institutes, most of these focused on practical training. The theological focus of the Institute for Youth Ministry was unique.

17. Scott, "Partners Together: The Church and Young Life," 49.

At the Young Life Institute prominent theologians were invited to think out loud in guest lectures and faculty seminars about the nature of evangelism, the meaning of the church, and the relationship of Young Life and the church. Emile Cailliet, I. John Hesselink, Hendrik Kraemer, John Mackay, Richard Mouw, Bernard Ramm, Robert S. Paul, and Leonard Trinterud contributed their reflections out of their quite different church and missionary experiences. A related but little known story is that Starr used to visit the World Council of Churches offices in Geneva on visits to Europe to continue some of these conversations. Starr became friends with Emilio Castro, who was at the time serving as Secretary for Evangelism of the WCC. A fruit of this friendship was a special Dialogue on Young Life and the Church. Castro came to Colorado to meet with a group of American theologians and Young Life staff members as he was on his way to the World Council of Churches Assembly in Vancouver in 1983.

Young Life's Urban Ministry

The various official or internal histories tell us that Young Life expanded to Chicago and Los Angeles, but actually the growth was to such middle- and upper-class suburbs as Winnetka and Park Ridge, South Pasadena and San Marino. Starr observed: "We were building a donut organization. In the middle of the donut was the inner city, and we were building our ministries around it."[18]

Into the middle of the donut came a collection of Young Life leaders who would challenge Young Life's own self-understanding of its mission to teenagers. Harv Oostdyk, a staff person in Morristown, New Jersey, first crossed into the unfamiliar territory of Newark, New Jersey. He began to reach out to young people on the streets of Newark. He convinced Vinnie Pasquale, a former narcotics addict, to go with him and a group of teenagers to Frontier Ranch in the Colorado Rockies.[19]

Oostdyk and Pasquale "talked up" the idea of reaching out to young people in New York City. Bill Milliken, a college freshman from Pittsburgh,

---

18. Tom Austin, *Urban Warriors: A History of Young Life Urban Ministries (From 1960 to 1988)* (n.p.: National Urban Office of Young Life, 1988). Much of what follows is from this internal history. The text contains no page numbers. See also George F. Sheffer, Jr., "History of Young Life Urban Ministry," a twenty-three-page internal Young Life paper.

19. In addition to Austin and Sheffer, the information for what follows comes from Cailliet, *Young Life,* 99-106, and Meredith, *It's a Sin to Bore a Kid,* 75-81.

joined the conversation. On June 17, 1960, Milliken drove to Newark to visit with Oostdyk and Pasquale. The next morning they "grabbed a basketball and started across the George Washington Bridge to look for some kids to shoot baskets," not knowing what might happen. Milliken and Pasquale rented a cold water flat on the Lower East Side. Young Life's urban ministry was beginning. Soon Dean Borgman, a former paratrooper, would join up. Borgman was working on a doctorate at Columbia University, but he also wanted to work with kids. Milliken and Borgman started a Young Life club at an Episcopal Church on the Lower East Side. Milliken contacted kids in a public housing project and organized them as "The Cross Carriers." Oostdyk moved into Harlem and started an apartment ministry in cooperation with Eugene Callendar, minister of the Church of the Master. In the early 1960s volunteers started arriving from all over the country to join this new effort.[20]

Oostdyk, whose family owned a large trucking operation, was the entrepreneur of Young Life's Urban Ministry. He wanted to found an Urban Training Institute. To do so he secured grants from the Rockefeller Foundation, the Lilly Endowment, and the First National City Bank. When Callendar became Director of the Urban League in New York City, Oostdyk worked with him to start Street Academies in several city neighborhoods. But at Young Life headquarters in Colorado Springs the question was being raised: "Is what they're doing in New York City actually Young Life work?" Some veteran leaders were asking how street academies were part of Young Life's traditional focus on evangelism.

Young Life was being pulled into urban ministry just as the senior staff was overseeing a rapid expansion among suburban white youth. Bringing these two dimensions of the movement together could create problems. One big challenge was adapting Young Life camps to inner-city teenagers. One June week in the 1960s four teenagers from the Lower East Side and eight from Harlem arrived at Starr Ranch. Counselors found themselves breaking up fights and asking kids to turn over drugs; nevertheless, some remarkable transformations took place in the lives of these urban teenagers.

In 1966 George and Marty Sheffer moved to inner-city Chicago to start urban work there. In the early 1960s, while working in Dallas, the Sheffers found themselves working with Hispanic and black teenagers along with suburban white teenagers. George had been one of Rayburn's first recruits at Dallas Seminary more than a quarter century before. His

20. Sheffer, "History of Young Life," B-9.

booming voice was powerful within Young Life circles. When west Chicago burned for two days in April 1968, after the assassination of Martin Luther King, Jr., Sheffer was warned by his young black friends not to come into their neighborhoods. "Because I was a white man," Sheffer related, "my black friends could not acknowledge me without terrible risk that their homes would be burned."[21] Sheffer observed: "Uncertainty, hostility, rejection, riots, physical beatings, and many 110 hour work weeks are experiences we had read about but had not experienced during our first forty years of life."[22] But out of the ashes of the riots Sheffer renovated a burned-out building and made it the center of his expanding ministry.

Among all the Chicago staff, Charles Campbell had the most "street smarts." Sheffer had been put on to Campbell, recently released from prison, by the prison chaplain. He described this new Christian as "gifted and extremely intelligent." Campbell and his wife Joan opened their South Side apartment to kids. It looked like Sheffer had found a neighborhood black leader who could lead the Chicago Young Life urban ministry. But one evening, as Campbell and his wife were returning to their apartment, he was murdered. It was rumored that he was killed because he had stumbled into a bribery ring among guards at a jail where he had gone to visit the inmates. A promising career ended abruptly.

Young Life's new commitment to urban ministry exposed the soft underbelly of parachurch ministries which focus solely on evangelism. As Young Life was drawn into the urban world, it was not prepared for what it would encounter. Drug addicts who were converted at Starr Ranch went back to New York or Chicago or Jacksonville streets that were more conducive to drugs than discipleship. In ministering in the city Young Life had to face up to the whole meaning of social justice. Befriending urban kids led to street academies, which in turn led to involvement in the whole structure of urban life.

Young Life learned quickly that there was no way to go it alone in the city. In the suburbs it was possible to start clubs with little or no cooperation from local churches (even if this was not Young Life's ideal means of operating). In the city this was impossible. Young Life staff found themselves needing to work with African-American churches if they wanted to have a ministry there at all.

African-American churches have never fit neatly within the two-party paradigm. They have not had the luxury of dividing the Christian faith into

---

21. Ibid.
22. Ibid., B-10.

private and public spheres. Marginalized by the mainstream white society, black churches have occupied a much more central role within their own communities. In this regard, their preachers have exercised a greater leadership role than have most white preachers and pastors.

The holistic approach to ministry of these African-American churches produced ferment and change within Young Life. The challenge of the day became "walk your talk," and white staff members sought to win the right to be heard by walking a "walk" that was consistent with their "talk." Young Life had always prided itself on its relational ministry. Now African-American staff members were to challenge that point. They pointed out that Young Life's incarnational approach to ministry could not be understood simply in relational terms — it needed to be enlarged. This enlarged understanding of both sin and salvation is what stood behind the famous "I am a man" issue of *Focus on Youth* (mentioned at the beginning of this essay). The racism in which African-American teenagers were caught encompassed education and jobs, as well as more relational concerns. African-American staff challenged white staff about the wider dimensions of what it meant to "walk your talk." What was really being suggested was that Young Life, however unintentionally, had bought into structures of institutional racism that were so often unrecognized by white America.

African Americans, whether young converts, Young Life staff, or supportive church leaders, became a presence to be reckoned with. Some of the African Americans invited to assume senior administrative positions within Young Life were church leaders who first came to know Young Life in urban centers. But when African-American leaders spoke up, Young Life, like many other predominantly white organizations, often did not know how to hear or how to respond. Even while they were assuming leadership roles within Young Life, African-American staff members sometimes felt like second-class citizens. Nonetheless, Young Life was trying to open itself up to African-American leaders and their understandings of ministry. Starr believed that African Americans had much to teach Young Life about both urban ministry and the church. But no one could predict what the result of this new partnership would be.

Tensions within the Organization

By the late 1960s, Young Life had a tiger by the tail. The organization had originally set out simply to reach teenagers. But for the first two decades nearly all those teenagers had been middle-class, suburban, and white. The ministry's new venture into urban America was both challenging and threatening to that older base of support. Some urban workers, in Young Life staff meetings, found themselves challenging a vision of ministry which seemed to them too private and too individualistic. A movement where everyone had once known each other on a personal level had now become a diverse organization with differing visions for the future. Starr was urged by Rayburn and others to "cut loose the urban ministries before they kill us." The new president was at the eye of a storm.[23]

The first problem, at least according to the business leaders who sat on the board of directors, was financial. Bill Taylor, a Chicago businessman, had come to Colorado with Starr in 1964 to bring sound financial management to a visionary mission. He told the mission in the spring of 1967 that they were in "technical bankruptcy." There was not enough money to cover bills, and all the properties were fully mortgaged. Charisma might be great with teenagers, but it did not balance the books. More specifically, a voluntary society like Young Life could relatively easily venture into suburbia where middle-class parents supported with their dollars a mission to their own sons and daughters. But urban ministry could not be supported by the contributions of urban parents.

One answer to this problem had been the entrepreneurial model championed by Harv Oostdyk. He promoted many schemes to raise money, including tapping foundations. But Oostdyk raised as many problems as he did dollars. In 1970, according to Starr, Young Life "just about came apart at the seams." Oostdyk's urban programs were making inroads in education, housing, and employment — and losing money. "Oostdyk was very creative and brilliant," observed Starr," but it was getting impossible for us to keep up with him. One of the most painful things I ever had to do was to ask Harv Oostdyk to leave the organization."[24]

The third problem was the picture of the young black teenager on the cover of *Focus on Youth* in 1968. A firestorm erupted. Young Life in Mississippi, one of the oldest Young Life areas in the South, disappeared almost overnight. Starr rushed to Memphis, the site of the assassination of Martin Luther King, Jr., to talk with members of the committee there who were also thinking of leaving Young Life. Letters and phone calls protested Young Life's meddling in racial politics. Some board members were upset, but friends rallied. The next issue of *Focus on Youth* contained

23. Austin, *Urban Warriors*, ii, 5.
24. Ibid., iii, 1.

letters from Seminary Presidents McCord (Princeton), Rogness (Luther), Hubbard (Fuller), and Come (San Francisco) commending Young Life for its "courageous," "effective," and "prophetic" ministry with young people. Starr's commitment and his entreaties with key supporters won the day. What surprised the Board was that financial contributions actually rose in the aftermath of the "I am a man" episode.[25]

But rumblings about urban ministry continued. They were heard within the Young Life Board itself. Longtime board member Robert Stover presented a plan to divide Young Life into three separate organizations: suburban, urban, and international. The tensions and misunderstandings, fueled by financial uncertainty over funding urban ministry, were becoming so great that many questioned whether Young Life could be held together.

Starr spoke to these tensions in a *Focus on Youth* issue dedicated to the "Greening of the City" in the summer of 1971. He asked a question: "Why have we multiplied our urban efforts when it costs so much more in dollars and energy to make an imprint in the city than it does in the suburbs?" He admitted that there had been a struggle within Young Life "to embrace the city and its tensions." "There have been those who were convinced that an urban ministry would destroy us." Starr then stated his own conviction: "I am unwilling to divide Young Life and have one suburban and one urban. Separation would be in direct contradiction to the message we preach."[26]

In 1977 Starr resigned as President of Young Life. He came to the conclusion that "he was too far out in front and that there wasn't enough of a following." Starr had led Young Life into hitherto uncharted waters, but by the mid-seventies there were questions about his leadership. Many board members and staff did not understand why Young Life should be "wasting its time" trying too hard to relate to the church. The commitment to urban ministry was threatening Young Life with turmoil and division.[27]

---

25. *Focus on Youth* 2 (October 1968): 2.

26. Bill Starr, "Green in the City," *Focus on Youth* 4 (Summer 1971): 3.

27. Starr, Interview. In the 1980s Starr, in addition to his duties with the Southwest Leadership Foundation, resumed his association with Young Life, working part-time in the area of church relations (hosting an annual national event for church leaders) and working with Young Life in Europe.

Conclusion

In this brief case study we have seen Young Life develop from its small evangelistic beginnings into a multifaceted, ecumenically minded youth ministry organization. Some brief concluding remarks about how this relates to the two-party system and efforts to re-form the center are in order.

First, Bill Starr and Young Life did not set out to build bridges. In a sense they had to be pushed toward the center. Bridge building occurred as Young Life sought the support of local churches and was invited by both individual congregations and a German state church to give itself away. Bridge building was also forced on a suburban "donut" organization when it moved into the city and found the very nature and shape of its ministry (i.e., incarnational evangelism) challenged by the city's problems and its people. African-American churches brought to Young Life a more holistic understanding of the gospel and a new understanding of partnership as the way forward in the city.

Perhaps this is the way the center is always formed and re-formed. It is formed and re-formed by necessity because it is necessity that moves us beyond the relatively narrow ideologies of either a two-party system or a denominational worldview. That is to say, necessity forces individuals and groups to cooperate with each other and in so doing builds a center up on the foundation of our common realities.

Second, the history of Young Life reminds us that the price of leadership in voluntary societies is high. If Young Life was being pushed by external realities, Bill Starr did his best to pull the organization forward as his own understanding of Christ and the church broadened toward the center. In any attempt to re-form the center the persons involved will be moving from some particular starting point — be that more conservative, or more liberal, or more some other position that does not fall neatly on any left-right continuum — toward the middle. For the leader of an organization, it is important not to get too far ahead of that organization's core constituency in this process. To lead involves risks. Starr's leadership gifts were obvious and appreciated by many within and without Young Life. But his broader ecumenical engagement with the churches, although supported by some senior colleagues, was never fully understood by either influential board members or the rank-and-file club leaders. Even though parachurch movements are often characterized by strong leaders at the top, over time the base of the organization must also own the vision or problems will develop.

RONALD C. WHITE, JR.

In the history of Young Life, we have a case where a leader of an organization could only convince the base of the wisdom of his ideals *to some degree*. The situation even today remains somewhat fluid because of this. Will Young Life solidify its new centrist identity or will it fall back to its earlier, more "evangelical" identity? The jury seems still to be out on that issue.

Finally, the story of Young Life may well illustrate the "learning curve" that any organization must go through if it is to change its identity and move toward the center. Such learning never follows a smooth course of development. It is always a matter of fits and starts. But these sometimes uneven and often awkward adjustments may represent the only practical means of moving ahead. The model of Young Life gives us hope that the more ragged histories of many of our institutions may, in fact, reflect an uneven, but progressive, learning curve that is ultimately bending toward the center.

CHAPTER 20

Hispanic/Latino Protestantism in Philadelphia[1]

EDWIN DAVID APONTE

Religion is a crucial aspect of the life and culture of Hispanic communities. This is true both of the roots of these communities in Latin America and their present-day developments in the United States. Latinos/as now comprise the second largest racial/ethnic group in the United States, and even conservative estimates predict they will be the largest such group by early in the twenty-first century.[2] Any consideration of the nature of American religious faiths can thus hardly afford to ignore this significant group. At present, however, most studies of Hispanic religion in the United States use interpretive models that do not allow us to see the complexity which actually exists within the Latino/a community. This needs to be rectified so that the full spectrum of Hispanic faith can be considered in any re-conceptualization of American religion in general.

One way in which the complexity of Latino/a faith is truncated is by

1. Research for this study was sponsored by the Pew Charitable Trusts, and was undertaken by the department of religion and the Institute for Public Policy Studies at Temple University. See Edwin David Aponte, David Bartelt, Luis A. Cortés, Jr., and John C. Raines, *The Work of Latino Ministry: Hispanic Protestant Churches in Philadelphia* (Philadelphia: The Pew Charitable Trusts, 1994). I am indebted to Rhys Williams and Peter Cha, who read and commented on an earlier draft of this essay. I am also appreciative of the helpful critiques from members of the Chicago-Area Group for the Study of Religious Communities at the Winter 1995 meeting. Their comments were useful in my revising this essay. Any remaining shortcomings are solely my own.

2. See, e.g., Angela L. Carrasquillo, *Hispanic Children and Youth in the United States: A Resource Guide* (New York: Garland Publishing, 1991); Rodney E. Hero, *Latinos and the U.S. Political System: Two-Tiered Pluralism* (Philadelphia: Temple University Press, 1992).

the prevalence of studies in which the focus is exclusively on Roman Catholicism.[3] While it is true that the majority of Hispanics in the United States are Roman Catholic, a significant portion of the population is Protestant.[4] This observation is not meant to endorse anti-Catholic polemics, nor is it meant to diminish the very significant role that Hispanic Catholicism has had in shaping contemporary Latin American and Latino cultures.[5] However, when Latino/a religion is discussed solely in terms of Roman Catholicism, only a partial picture of Hispanic life and culture is obtained, a fact that is rarely acknowledged.[6]

3. David Maldonaldo, "Hispanic Protestantism: Historical Reflections," *Apuntes* 11 (Spring 1991): 3. Also see L. H. Gann and Peter Duignan, *The Hispanics in the United States: A History* (Boulder, CO: Westview Press, 1986); Thomas Weyr, *Hispanic U.S.A.: Breaking the Melting Pot* (New York: Harper and Row, 1988).

4. While not without its difficulties, the National Survey of Religious Identification (NSRI) indicates that 23% of the Hispanics surveyed are Protestant. See Barry A. Kosmin and Seymour P. Lachman, *One Nation Under God: Religion in Contemporary American Society* (New York: Crown Trade Paperbacks, 1993), 127, 138. This is consistent with other estimates.

5. In illustration of this last point, see María Teresa Babín, "A Special Voice: The Cultural Expression," in Arturo Morales Carrión, ed., *Puerto Rico: A Political and Cultural History* (New York: W. W. Norton, 1983), 345. Babín comments on this significant influence of Hispanic Catholicism on the culture of Puerto Rico: "the psychological and ethical standards of the Puerto Rican people reveal a deep belief in God and a Christian faith that gives the concepts of love, life, and death a special meaning. . . . Even Puerto Ricans who have adopted other faiths may reveal in their conduct and innermost sentiments the indelible imprint of Catholicism." The literature on the dominance of the Catholic Church in Latin American culture is substantial. See Robert Ricard, *The Spiritual Conquest of Mexico* (Berkeley, CA: University of California Press, 1966); Americo Castro, *Iberoamérica: Su Historia y Su Cultura* (New York: Holt, Rinehart and Winston, 1971); Virgilio P. Elizondo, *Galilean Journey: The Mexican American Promise* (Maryknoll, NY: Orbis Books, 1983); Andrés Guerrero, *A Chicano Theology* (Maryknoll, NY: Orbis Books, 1987); Justo L. González, *Mañana: Christian Theology from a Hispanic Perspective* (Nashville: Abingdon Press, 1990); Jeanette Rodriguez, *Our Lady of Guadalupe: Faith and Empowerment among Mexican-American Women* (Austin, TX: University of Texas Press, 1994). It is beyond the scope of the present study to examine how this Catholic influence specifically manifests itself within the various Hispanic Protestant groups.

6. A few examples will suffice. In *Latinos and the U.S. Political System* (pp. 46, 48), Hero's only mention of the role of religion in Latino culture is Catholicism as an assimilating factor. See also Matt S. Meir and Feliciano Ribera, *Mexican Americans/American Mexicans: From Conquistadors to Chicanos* (New York: Hill and Wang, 1993), 227. The historical survey of Mexican Americans by Meir and Ribera has a short reference to Protestantism as engaging in recent "intensive proselytizing," while allowing that some Protestant churches "have dealt with economic and political as

Another way in which understanding of Latino/a Christianity becomes truncated, particularly Hispanic Protestantism, has to do with the interpretive models brought to bear on the subject. In particular, the "two-party" typology, which is so dominant in the analysis of "Anglo" religion in the United States, needs to be held at bay. This model contrasts American Protestant groups which emphasize individual salvation and pietistic expressions of faith to groups that focus their religious concern on issues of the larger society and how Christian faith might have an impact on the larger cultural context. Perhaps the most often quoted description of the two-party approach comes from Martin Marty's survey history of American religion, *Righteous Empire:*

> One party, which may be called "Private" Protestantism, seized that name "evangelical" which had characterized all Protestants early in the nineteenth century. It accentuated individual salvation out of the world, personal moral life congruent with the ideals of the saved, and fulfillment or its absence in the rewards and punishments in another world in a life to come. The second informal group, which can be called "Public" Protestantism, was public insofar as it was more exposed to the social order and the social destinies of men. Whereas the word "evangelical" somehow came to be a part of the description of the former group, the word "social" almost always worked its way into designations of the latter. They pursued a Social Christianity, the Social Gospel, Social Service, Social Realism, and the like.[7]

---

well as religious concerns of Mexican Americans." Most telling is the revised work of the historian Edwin Scott Gaustad in his *A Religious History of America* (New York: HarperCollins, 1990). See pp. 334-36 where the entire short discussion focuses on Hispanic Catholicism.

7. Martin E. Marty, *Righteous Empire: The Protestant Experience in America* (New York: Dial Press, 1970), 179. Also see Marty's revision *Protestantism in the United States: Righteous Empire* (New York: Charles Scribner's Sons, 1986), 179. The definition is unchanged except for some orthographic editing and the adoption of inclusive language.

Marty has refined his own position during the years since 1970, advocating a more nuanced understanding, while retaining a basic two-party distinction. See Chapter 5 of this volume. See also Martin Marty, "Public and Private: Congregation as Meeting Place," in James P. Wind and James W. Lewis, eds., *American Congregations: New Perspectives in the Study of Congregations*, vol. 2 (Chicago: University of Chicago Press, 1994), 154-55. Commenting on the currency of this paradigm Marty states: "It suffices for us to recall that the critics of congregation life by the late 1950s had seen such trends toward privatization becoming virtually complete. . . . It is not difficult to see why especially around mid-century and *again today* [emphasis added] one could treat and can treat the congregation as living behind the 'wall of private life.' "

This model contrasting the private and the public — "souls or the social order," as Jean Miller Schmidt has put it[8] — is still used in many historical and sociological studies of American Protestantism to sort individuals and organizations into two broad groups. While these categories may have some historically specific validity with regard to certain Protestant groups, they are not universally applicable. In particular, the two-party paradigm is a construct derived from white Protestant history, and its applicability to other ethnic/racial Protestant churches is questionable at best. Recently James Wind and James Lewis have commented on the cultural bias inherent in the use of such concepts and on the need to bring other interpretive schemes to bear on the study of American religion. They write: "For far too long American religious historiography has focused on the white Protestant mainstream, ignoring much of the rich tapestry that is American religion. Recently scholars have pointed out the deficiencies of this privileging of a Protestant center and have urged that the story of American religion be reinterpreted."[9]

When the distinctive character of a Latino/a congregation as a *Latino/a* community is ignored, or instead squeezed into the two-party model of white Protestantism, analysis is short-changed and interpretations are predetermined. To be specific, Hispanic Protestants have often been blithely categorized as religious conservatives. What is more, it is usually assumed within the two-party formulation that if a group shows some of the characteristics of one party, it naturally follows that essentially all the traits of that party will be found to cohere in that group. Thus one does not need to look too closely at the group under investigation because one already knows what one will find. But the two-party categories are not sufficient to represent either the tensions or genius of Hispanic Protestantism.

The present study contends that a close analysis of one specific Latino Protestant context reveals a different and more complex reality than that anticipated by the two-party model of American Protestantism. Moreover, it is argued that an historical sketch of Hispanic Protestantism in Philadelphia provides a case study for understanding Hispanic Protestantism in the United States as a whole. While each Hispanic community has reacted

---

8. Jean Miller Schmidt, *Souls or the Social Order: The Two-Party System in American Protestantism* (Brooklyn, NY: Carlson Publishing, 1991).

9. James P. Wind and James W. Lewis, "Introduction," in James P. Wind and James W. Lewis, eds., *American Congregations: New Perspectives in the Study of Congregations,* vol. 1 (Chicago: University of Chicago Press, 1994), 11.

in its own distinctive, innovative, and contextual way to the particular social and historical dynamics it has experienced, certain shared problems and common patterns of response are evident and can be illustrated in the story of the Hispanic Protestant churches in Philadelphia.

Methodology

An ethnographic approach was employed in this study as the best means of capturing the nuances of the socio-cultural context of Latino/a religion in the United States.[10] The qualitative research approach used here consisted of in-depth focus interviews and participant observation, supported by archival materials when available — materials which were, more often than not, identified during the interviews. The need to take this historical, archival material seriously has pushed this study toward what anthropologist James Clifford has called "the rapprochement of ethnography and history."[11] Both the history and contemporary experience of the Latino/a community need to be understood if one is to grasp the inner dynamics of Hispanic Protestantism.

Field work was conducted between October 1991 and March 1993. The city of Philadelphia was chosen as the site for this study because it is a major metropolitan area in which there is a substantial population of Hispanics, and yet it is small enough to be able to survey the entire community. The majority of Philadelphia's Latino/a population is Puerto Rican. However, this is not simply a Puerto Rican case study. None of the congregations examined had a 100 percent Puerto Rican membership, and the participants themselves recognized and commented on the fact that their community included a diversity of Latin American peoples. Therefore, there is good justification in using the pan-ethnic designations "Hispanic" and "Latino/a," which indeed were employed by the study participants themselves.

The primary source of information for this study is to be found in interviews conducted with 33 pastors and lay ministers from congrega-

10. An additional reason for this qualitative rather than quantitative approach was the issue of access and entrance into the community. The Latino community in Philadelphia as a whole is suspicious of quantitative studies, and it was determined that the greatest chance for success and participation lay in using a qualitative research approach.

11. James Clifford, "Notes on (Field)notes," in Roger Sanjek, ed., *Fieldnotes: The Making of Anthropology* (Ithaca, NY: Cornell University Press, 1990), 54.

tions representing every type of Latino/a Protestant denomination and association present in Philadelphia. These focus interviews were complemented by participant-observation at church services and other congregational activities. These visits provided the opportunity to observe firsthand the worshiping communities in Hispanic Protestant Philadelphia and to correlate some of the information obtained through prior interviews with pastors and lay ministers. All in all, an ethnographic approach was adopted that is similar to that now being used in a number of other contemporary studies of Hispanic-American religion. Isasi-Díaz, in particular, writes regarding her own use of ethnography in the construction of *mujerista* theology as follows:

> The meta-ethnography I use in doing *mujerista* theology does not attempt to aggregate the information gathered in interviews, but rather to interpret it. First, I present the different accounts as they were actually voiced by Hispanic women. I then attempt to bring together the single accounts by pointing out some of their commonalities and differences. This results in what meta-ethnography calls "knowledge synthesis," a synthesis which is both inductive and interpretive. This knowledge synthesis (or interpretive synthesis) uses an emic approach that is holistic and considers alternatives.[12]

The History of Hispanic Protestantism in Philadelphia to the 1970s

There are indications that there may have been Latino/as in Philadelphia as early as 1900,[13] but we know for sure that there was a small Hispanic presence in Philadelphia in the years immediately following World War I. Edwin Bach's *Americanization in Philadelphia,* published by the Philadelphia Chamber of Commerce in 1923, stated that the city's "foreign born white population 21 years and over" had included 318 persons from Mexico, and 366 from Central and South America in 1920. Mention is also

12. Ada María Isasi-Díaz, "*Mujerista* Theology's Method: A Liberative Praxis, A Way of Life," *Listening* 27 (Winter 1992): 45.

13. I am indebted to Victor Vasquez, a doctoral candidate in history at Temple University, for sharing results from his ongoing research into the history of the Latino community of Philadelphia. Vasquez has uncovered evidence of the probable early presence of Puerto Rican tobacco workers in the city, as well as the possibility that the Pennsylvania Railroad employed Mexicans in one of its work projects before World War I.

made of "the foreign-born employees of the Pennsylvania Railroad," who, Bach says, included Mexican, "Porto Rican" [*sic*], Cuban, and Costa Rican workers, as well as persons from other South and Central American nations.[14] Puerto Ricans, the largest subgroup of Latinos in Philadelphia, first came to the greater Philadelphia area in large numbers as agricultural workers in the years immediately following World War I as part of the contract-labor migration from the island to the United States.[15]

The early Latino/a community in Philadelphia remained relatively small into the 1940s. But after World War II dramatic growth occurred in the Hispanic population of Philadelphia,[16] mainly due to increased Puerto Rican migration driven by deteriorating economic conditions on the island, the decreased cost of regular air travel, and employment opportunities in Philadelphia's industries.[17] Mexican migrant workers who had been a part of the agricultural economy of southeastern Pennsylvania for some time were also settling in Philadelphia on a permanent basis. As the century progressed, the breadth of the Philadelphia Hispanic community slowly increased in the light of new migrations of Cubans, Dominicans, and other Latin Americans into the area.

While the majority of Latinos/as moving into the Philadelphia region were Catholic, there was also a significant Protestant presence. The recollections of surviving participants emphasized an absence of denominational partisanship within this early Protestant community in the face of the shared context of larger challenges, i.e., the difficulties of urban life

---

14. Edwin E. Bach, *Americanization in Philadelphia: A City-Wide Plan of Co-ordinated Agencies* (Philadelphia: The Americanization Committee, Philadelphia Chamber of Commerce, 1923), 63, 77.

15. Hector L. Colón-Colón, *Iglesia Metodista Unida "La Resurrección": Estudio de Una Congregación en Crecimiento Buscando Servir a Una Comunidad en Transición* (Unpublished Paper, Eastern Baptist Theological Seminary, 1983), 7.

16. This postwar wave of emigration was not restricted to Philadelphia, but was simultaneously occurring in other cities of the United States. See Hero, *Latinos and the U.S. Political System*; and Clara E. Rodriguez, *Puerto Ricans: Born in the U.S.A.* (Boulder, CO: Westview Press, 1991). The overall growth of Philadelphia's Hispanic population parallels the three major waves of Puerto Rican migration to New York City. This trend is summarized by Rodriguez as follows: the time of the *pioneros*, 1900-1945; "the great migration" of 1946 to 1964; and the revolving door migration, 1965 to the present.

17. Arthur Siegel, Harold Orlans, and Loyal Greer, *Puerto Ricans in Philadelphia: A Study of Their Demographic Characteristics, Problems and Attitudes* (Philadelphia: Commission on Human Relations, City of Philadelphia, 1954), 2-7; Commission on Human Relations, *Philadelphia's Puerto Rican Population: A Descriptive Summary Including 1960 Census Data* (Philadelphia: City of Philadelphia, 1964), 2.

in general, as well as the presence of a much larger Roman Catholic Hispanic population.

The full picture of early Hispanic Protestantism in Philadelphia is yet to be uncovered, but it does seem clear at this point that the role of one particular congregation was crucial. What would become the First Spanish Baptist Church began in September 1929 as a relatively informal Bible-study group in the Hispanic community by a Baptist student at the Philadelphia School of the Bible.[18] Through a succession of leaders,[19] this group maintained its existence and eventually organized itself as a mission church under the name *Primera Iglesia Evangelica* (January 20, 1934).[20] Unfortunately, no written records survive from the years 1937 to 1944,[21] and no participants from that time could be found to interview.

In 1944, however, the Rev. Enrique Rodríguez became pastor. Under his leadership the mission church was reorganized as the First Spanish Baptist Church (July 14, 1946). The significance and influence of Rodríguez's pastorate cannot be underestimated. While serving as the minister of the First Spanish Baptist Church, he essentially functioned as the pastor of the entire Hispanic Protestant community of Philadelphia. Enrique Rodríguez's ministry at First Spanish Baptist Church is remembered as having a lasting influence on almost all the denominational, independent, and Pentecostal congregations that would later emerge from the early Philadelphia Hispanic community.

One Pentecostal interviewee who had attended the Baptist congregation during these years indicated that, in those early days when the First Spanish Baptist Church was the only Hispanic Protestant congregation in Philadelphia, all *evangélicos* (i.e., Protestants) participated in the congregation while continuing to affirm their differing doctrinal positions. Baptists and non-Baptists, Pentecostals and non-Pentecostals were all members of this one church. The surviving participants whom I interviewed were emphatic in stating that they were aware of the doctrinal differences that existed among them. Nevertheless, in the social context of that time they had all found it useful and acceptable to be involved together in the First Spanish Baptist Church. This situation continued until

18. Luis Cortés, *Seeking the Welfare of the City, Jeremiah 29:5-7: A Study for Hispanic Church Planting and Development* (Unpublished Report, Eastern Baptist Theological Seminary, Philadelphia, 1982), 12.

19. Joan D. Koss, *Puerto Ricans in Philadelphia: Migration and Accommodation* (Unpublished Ph.D. dissertation, University of Pennsylvania, 1965), 65.

20. Cortés, *Seeking the Welfare of the City,* 12.

21. Cortés, *Seeking the Welfare of the City,* 13.

other Hispanic Protestant congregations began to be established in the 1950s.

The second major phase of Hispanic Protestantism in Philadelphia extends from around 1952 into the early 1970s. These years could be seen as a time of consolidation, during which time the size of the Latino community of Philadelphia as a whole grew significantly, with both the community and the churches establishing a more abiding presence in the city. Hispanic Protestantism built upon its small beginnings and extended its sphere of influence as other congregations appeared in addition to First Spanish Baptist and took root in the community. Greater denominational diversity appeared as more congregational options became available, each seeking to institutionalize their presence in a relatively permanent form.

Perhaps the most significant development here was the introduction of Pentecostal faith into the Latino/a community. Interviewees indicated that two separate small Pentecostal congregations were organized in the early 1950s, each with its own pastor. While the Hispanic population was increasing during this period, there was some question whether the small number of Pentecostals could support two congregations. Eventually these two congregations merged to create a more effective Pentecostal presence among Hispanics in Philadelphia. In 1952, the Rev. Victor Ulloa was called as the pastor of the new united congregation, Iglesia Sinai (which was associated with the Assemblies of God). Ulloa had come from New York City where he had attended a Bible institute and was associated with the prominent Iglesia Juan 3:16.

Under Ulloa's pastorate of over thirty years the congregation grew and became widely influential, not only in Philadelphia but throughout southeastern Pennsylvania and southern New Jersey. During this time Sinai Church helped establish independent Latino/a Protestant churches in the Pennsylvania cities of Lancaster, Reading, Allentown, and Bethlehem, as well as in Atlantic City, Vineland, and Camden, New Jersey. Occupying a place of respect in the Hispanic Protestant community, Iglesia Sinai ran one of the two larger Philadelphia *institutos*, i.e., the community-based Bible institutes where the majority of formal theological education in the Hispanic Protestant community took place. The *instituto* at Iglesia Sinai drew (and continues to draw) numerous students from beyond the congregation, even from non-Pentecostal congregations.

Other Pentecostal congregations soon began to appear within Philadelphia's Hispanic neighborhoods. One of the most prominent was the Second Missionary Church of Philadelphia founded by the Rev. I. Padron in 1958. As was the case at both the First Spanish Baptist Church and

Iglesia Sinai, the tenure of the founding minister was lengthy. Padron served the Second Missionary Church for 20 years.[22] Second Missionary Church was to become the home of Philadelphia's other major Hispanic Bible *instituto*. Like other Hispanic Protestant churches established during this period, Second Missionary Church used its Bible institute to help consolidate its social position in the Latino/a community.

A significant non-Pentecostal congregation that was established in this period was Iglesia Evangelica Bautista (Evangelical Baptist Church). Iglesia Evangelica Bautista is affiliated with the General Association of Regular Baptists and does not view itself as being aligned with either the Pentecostal churches or historic Protestant denominations. The congregation was founded in either 1954 or 1955 (memories were not precise), and in 1956 established Timothy Academy, a private Christian school. Although Timothy Academy was originally a work of Baptist Mid-Missions, in 1974 ownership was transferred to Iglesia Evangelica Bautista. The regular activities of the church have included worship, prayer meetings, a "Word of Life" club for youth, and regularly scheduled pastoral counseling opportunities.

The orientation of faith evident in these three examples indicates the general sense of piety that would ultimately come to inform almost all of the other congregations that appeared during this period. Virtually all of these churches emphasized the reality of the supernatural, the importance of individual salvation, participatory worship, the need for a personal life of devotion, and a radically changed sense of morality.[23] These characteristics were present in Pentecostal and non-Pentecostal contexts. That is, they shared a common ethos even if their denominational affiliations would normally lead one to assume that would not be the case. At the same time, however, these congregations all found themselves increasingly called upon to address the social conditions of their members. Often this was handled on a "private" case-by-case basis, but this was not always possible. Thus while the churches emphasized a personal, pietistic faith, the needs of church members set within the larger social context of urban Philadelphia never let them build a fixed barrier between "private" faith and everyday "public" life.

---

22. Miguel A. Diaz, *Strategy for Church Growth, Second Christian Missionary Church, Philadelphia, Pennsylvania* (Unpublished Paper, Eastern Baptist Theological Seminary, 1991), 1.

23. Cf. Marty, *Protestantism in the United States*, 179.

The Philadelphia Protestant Hispanic Community since the 1970s

The areas of Hispanic settlement in the city have shifted over the years, and Latinos/as are presently concentrated in only a few of Philadelphia's many neighborhoods. All of these areas are characterized by high rates of unemployment and poverty, blatant discrimination and racism, inadequate and expensive housing, and a drug culture that fosters crime. The community as a whole is confronted with health concerns of crisis proportions, including high rates of infant mortality, teenage pregnancies, and HIV/AIDS. Preventive health care is nearly nonexistent. In addition to these problems there is a great deal of concern about how family units can maintain themselves in a community where only a third of the families are maritally intact. There is also concern for the increasing number of youth in the Latino/a community who are growing up in an unfriendly, threatening, and dangerous environment, and who seem to be ignored by the Philadelphia public education system. Performance on standardized achievement tests is low, and the high school dropout rate is high. All these factors combine to produce an environment of discouragement, despair, and defeat in the community. This is the social context in which the Latino/a Protestant church has to struggle to survive and to make a constructive contribution to the life of the Hispanic community.

Along with the surrounding community, Hispanic Protestantism in Philadelphia has experienced expansion and transition since the early 1970s. In particular, various Hispanic congregations have entered into a new, more explicit engagement with the "public" sphere. This has required older Hispanic congregations to reevaluate their previous case-by-case approach and to view the social issues confronting their individual members as part of larger systemic problems that need to be addressed publicly. For many churches, this kind of public stance is no longer seen as necessarily entailing a compromise of personal faith. The supposed two-party divide makes no sense here. In recent years, several of the historic, establishment denominations (traditionally called the "mainline") have also tried to expand and/or consolidate their presence in the Hispanic community. This has been prompted in part by demographic trends showing an increase in the Hispanic population, combined with a decrease in the traditional white membership base of these "mainline" city congregations. Many of these churches share the common ethos found in other Hispanic Pentecostal and non-Pentecostal congregations. Here too, then, we see Hispanic dynamics at work that do not fit neatly into the standard two-party categories.

Perhaps the most startling new development within Hispanic Protestantism, however, has been the appearance of numerous parachurch ministries designed to deal with social ills. Some of these parachurch efforts are connected to local congregations; others are not. Shepperd House, founded in 1989, is a free-standing parachurch organization which focuses on drug rehabilitation. This program provides four to six months of residence rehabilitation for its clients which includes group sessions, job skills training, and required chapel attendance. Shepperd House is a Pentecostal parachurch agency whose executive director readily uses the language of individual salvation and divine intervention to describe how God delivered him from drug addiction and subsequently gave him the vision for this community-based rehabilitation program. Shepperd House and similar Pentecostal drug rehabilitation programs are explicitly trying to address one of the most prominent social problems in Latino/a Philadelphia. At the same time, those running Shepperd House and other Latino parachurch agencies like it are adamant in saying that they are not simply providing a social service. This is a "ministry" to the community, they say, and it flows directly from their personal faith in God.

Proclaimers of Hope Ministries/Bethel Temple Church provides a different example, one connected to a local congregation. Led by an English-language-dominant second-generation Latino pastor, this church, which now reports a membership of about 200, was organized as the result of mission efforts of the independent fundamentalist Bethel Temple Church. Bethel Temple Church, with its largely "Anglo" membership, had relocated to the northeast section of Philadelphia, but continued to hold title to its original property in an area of the city known for its high crime rate, gang activity, and drug trafficking. They allowed a new Hispanic congregation, Proclaimers of Hope, to use the facility.

In traditional theological terms Proclaimers of Hope Ministries would be classified as "conservative" or even "fundamentalist" with its strong emphasis on individual salvation, rigid behavioral norms, and suspicion of "the world." The activities of Proclaimers of Hope Ministries include regular Bible studies, Sunday school, open air meetings, and church services, all of which might be expected of a conservative or fundamentalist congregation. However, the church's ministries also include year-round youth activity programs, academic tutoring, clothing and food banks, summer street festivals, support programs for recovering addicts and their families, transitional housing, and group homes. This second group of activities, all considered forms of "ministry" by members of the church, focuses specifically on the social needs of the urban area in which the congregation is found. The Latino pastor of Proclaimers of Hope Ministries/Bethel Temple Church also hopes someday to obtain control of several abandoned properties in the neighborhood (currently used as crack houses) and either rehabilitate them or construct new buildings on the sites for affordable, intergenerational housing. He views this as an important long-term way of transforming the neighborhood. (Proclaimers of Hope has been so successful that members of white suburban churches from Pennsylvania and other states now come to the church to learn how to do urban ministry.)

Another parachurch Hispanic Protestant ministry which has appeared in the Latino/a community is Esperanza Health Center. This inner-city, non-profit health care agency was founded in 1989 and is driven by a concern for holistic community health care as an integral part of its proclamation of the gospel. Programs run by the Center deal with a range of medical and social ills. Esperanza's integrative model addresses the medical, psychological, and spiritual needs of its patients, seeking to treat not just the symptoms but also the causes of their distress. Drawing upon their personal encounters with God and their interpretation of the Bible, Esperanza Health Center views its clients as people whom Jesus himself would have served, that is, those most in need. While the professional staff at Esperanza Health Center try not to impose their beliefs (profession of faith in Jesus is not, for example, a prerequisite for receiving health care), they are very open with anyone who inquires about his or her personal belief in God and the religious motivation that compels them to engage in this type of social ministry to the Latino community. In their own words, the ultimate goal of the Center is "whole person evangelism."[24]

Alongside these more or less indigenous ministries that have developed, one also needs to look at the variety of contemporary "mainline" denominational ministries now operating within the Hispanic community of Philadelphia. The experience of the Episcopal Church serves as a window through which to view this facet of Hispanic Protestantism. At the time of my field research, Christ and Saint Ambrose parish was the only existing Hispanic Episcopal congregation in the city of Philadelphia. This church had been formed in 1968 through the merger of two older congregations: Christ Church (founded 1871) and St. Ambrose (founded 1894).

---

24. Carolyn Klaus, "Introduction to Esperanza Health Center," transcript of an address given in June 1992 on the occasion of the Rev. Billy Graham's visit to Esperanza Health Center, 3.

Membership had declined in these formerly white urban congregations as the neighborhoods around the churches became predominantly Hispanic during the 1970s. Rather than relocating out of the city, the two congregations merged and re-focused the new ministry on the needs of the local community. In 1992 membership was reported at approximately 150 with Sunday attendance averaging about eighty. Puerto Ricans, Cubans, Nicaraguans, Dominicans, Salvadorans, and Mexicans/Chicanos are all represented in the congregation, reflecting changes in the composition of the Philadelphia Latino/a community in general since the early 1970s.

In contrast with many other Latino Protestant churches in Philadelphia, Christ and St. Ambrose embraces the cultural Catholicism which is present in the Latino community rather than calling for a complete break from this background. This intentional connection with Catholicism includes use of the rosary in prayer, devotion to the saints, and veneration of the Virgin Mary. The congregation has also been involved in joint ministry efforts with several other churches from across the theological spectrum. Worship is a creative blend of the Episcopal service and Latino/a cultural expressions of faith and music. Many features found in Hispanic Pentecostal services were present in this context, such as the specific choruses sung and the indigenous instruments used.

Energized by its understanding of relationship with God and its creative worship life, the parish offers a preschool/kindergarten program, classes in English as a Second Language (ESL), and preparation for the G.E.D. exam. For its Wednesday night meetings the congregation regularly brings in speakers on such topics as education, how to pay fuel bills, or the spread of AIDS in the community. The congregation has also established a community development program to work for decent affordable housing in the neighborhood, and the priest has forged relationships with local gang members to the point where they feel protective of the parish and its property. Once again, a closer look at Hispanic congregations show that the use of predetermined neat categories such as "two parties" is difficult to employ in this context.

In many ways Christ and St. Ambrose Episcopal Church might be considered a success story, but some other "mainline" initiatives within the Philadelphia Hispanic community have failed. One such example is found in the brief and merging histories of Good Samaritan Episcopal Mission and St. Barnabas Episcopal Church. Good Samaritan Mission (Misión Buen Samaritano) and St. Barnabas originally were separate entities. St. Barnabas had been a predominantly African-American congregation, but the local neighborhood had become primarily Latino/a by the 1980s. As a result, the Philadelphia diocese decided St. Barnabas should be merged with the nearby store-front ministry known as Buen Samaritano Episcopal Mission. The intention of the merger was to establish a second Hispanic congregation at St. Barnabas alongside the older African-American congregation, both using the same building and thereby consolidating resources. The grassroots understanding was that eventually the two churches would merge into one congregation. While the specific accounts of what happened vary, this initiative did not succeed. A diocesan decision was made to close down the combined congregation in 1991. The Episcopal Diocese clearly had not understood the local situation on its own terms.

One last group of organizations deserves mention here: the Hispanic Clergy Association of Philadelphia and Vicinity, and its affiliated bodies, Nueva Esperanza Development Corporation and the Hispanic Century Fund. The Hispanic Clergy Association was founded in 1982 as a professional support group for Latino/a Protestant ministers in the Philadelphia area who felt marginalized to some degree by the Metropolitan Christian Council of Philadelphia (the local, supposedly "ecumenical" council of churches).[25] The Hispanic Clergy Association provides continuing education events, sponsors retreats for clergy and their families, publishes a newsletter, and provides a forum for discussing concerns particular to Latino urban ministry. It is a truly "ecumenical" body (although some of its members would not want to claim that specific adjective) made up of ministers from local Baptist churches, different kinds of Pentecostal groups, some independent congregations, and various Presbyterian, Methodist, and United Church of Christ Hispanic parishes.

Perceiving a connection between the preaching of the gospel and the social condition of their people, the Hispanic Clergy Association established Nueva Esperanza, Inc. in 1988 as a non-profit development corporation to support community-based development projects ranging from home rehabilitation, to job training, to community education about how to finance home ownership, to the construction of a laundromat (in an area where most residents lived in apartments and there was no other laundromat nearby).

---

25. These ministers seem to have been doubly marginalized. First, they were marginalized because of their ethnic identity. Second, they were marginalized to some degree because the "mainline" leaders of the council tended, in good two-party fashion, to see these Hispanic ministers as too "evangelical" and thus not really part of the council's "ecumenical" mix.

In 1992 the Hispanic Century Fund was established as a separate foundation to fund other projects that would be of benefit to the Latino community as a whole, including a Latino community college. These projects were seen by Latino/a participants as part of the proclamation of the gospel fully consistent with the preaching of individual salvation.

"Private" and "Public" in Hispanic Protestantism

As can be seen from the above survey, the Hispanic Protestant churches of Philadelphia play an important role in the community in ways that defy the boundaries defined by the two-party model. In a situation of growing social instability and decreasing public resources many Hispanic Protestant churches have stepped into the gap. Rather than constructing walls between personal piety and the larger social setting, Hispanic Protestant churches have become agents of stability and hope in neighborhoods where the people, in keeping with all who are oppressed, face a host of social ills: high unemployment, family distress, poor housing, inadequate schools, generational stress, insufficient medical care, high rates of pregnancy and death, gang activity, and rampant drug trafficking. The Hispanic Protestant churches have thus demonstrated that in the *barrios* of North American cities effective Latino organizations do indeed exist that address in multifaceted ways the religious and social needs of the community.

The Hispanic Protestant churches, in accordance with their own individual ("private") understandings of personal salvation and the mission of the church, have entered the public arena on their own terms. They provide needed social services in a situation of increasing retreat from the public sector by government and private secular agencies alike. Because of the pressing needs in the Latino community, numerous Hispanic Protestants have learned how to reconcile "social ministry" ("public" Protestantism) with a continuing emphasis on personal salvation ("private" Protestantism). This twofold emphasis, which defies the neat labels derived from the history of white, Anglo-American Protestantism (as it has usually been told), indicates that Hispanic Protestant churches are seeking to maintain their identities both as communities of "born again" Christians and as socially committed members of their local communities.

The recent history of Latino Protestantism in Philadelphia shows that conscious choices have been made to engage in types of social ministry that would (or could) have been avoided a generation ago. This has not taken place without a great deal of introspection. In fact, some congregations, wishing to be true to a purely individual understanding of ministry, have taken the path of further withdrawal from "the world." But this has not been the majority response. In Philadelphia, many Hispanic Protestant churches have now come to the realization that a theology of individual piety and social withdrawal does not make sense for a people already marginalized by the larger society. As a result, they have concluded that preaching a message of personal salvation is not compromised by, nor is it at odds with, addressing the social condition of the community.

The Boundaries of Community

While the liberal versus conservative two-party model does not help us understand Latino/a Protestantism in a place like Philadelphia, there is another bipolar distinction that does play a significant role in Hispanic faith and life. That is the distinction between who really is a participant in the local community and who is not. There is an ambivalence toward groups outside the Latino community. This dynamic can be seen most clearly in those Hispanic congregations that have a formal relationship with the old, established "mainline" denominations that clearly have their centers of gravity outside the Hispanic community.

During the last few decades, numerous "mainline" churches have stated their desire to have Latino congregations be part of their denominations. However, it appears that when Hispanic congregations are established (through new church plants and affiliations), most of the "mainline" denominations simply do not know how to proceed. Hispanic congregations are formally included, but functionally marginalized. This is perhaps most clearly seen in the ways that "mainline" denominations try to measure the successes and failures of various Hispanic ministries and congregations. The methods and measures that have been used have typically been derived from the experience of middle-class "Anglo" suburban congregations, and are not suitable as means of evaluating the effectiveness of Latino/a urban ministries. And yet, those denomination-wide (i.e., white, suburban) methods of evaluation are often used to evaluate Hispanic urban efforts; when those ministries do not seem to measure up to expected standards of success, funding is often called into question.

This problem has been compounded by what the Hispanic community tends to see as fits and starts of attention given by various denominational judicatories to the Hispanic congregations within their folds. Although there have been some individual exceptions, on the whole the relations between "mainline" Protestant denominations and their Hispanic congregations have been poor. Virtually all the Hispanic denominational pastors with whom I spoke (and who wished to remain anonymous) felt out on a limb with regard to their denominations. These pastors have accordingly been forced to act independently, in part because they feel misunderstood by their denominations; however, this independence has only reinforced stereotypes within the church bureaucracies. Some of these pastors have felt themselves placed on display as token Hispanics at denominational gatherings; at the same time, they have been allowed little input into denominational policies regarding ministry in the city. Hence, they often feel like less than full partners in ministry.

A radically different situation prevails within the Pentecostal wing of Hispanic Protestantism, where entrance into ministry is more accessible and local leadership predominates. Within the Pentecostal tradition there is a strong emphasis on personal religion, which has had a potent appeal among Philadelphia's Latinos/as. This emphasis is most often expressed in terms of salvation understood as a personal, intimate experience of God.

Another aspect that adds to the complexity of this Latino Protestant community is its shared sacred rhetoric. Elements of the style of worship nurtured in Pentecostal contexts seem to strike a particularly responsive chord among Philadelphia's Latinos/as, in that allowance is made for expressive communal participation in worship through culturally familiar avenues. In fact, such worship is encouraged. In this regard, it seems that Pentecostals have either influenced how Hispanic Protestant churches as a whole have structured their worship, or Pentecostals have simply adapted Latino/a cultural forms of worship. Either way, one can visit Hispanic congregations of different traditions and find in all these churches common elements of worship that are more or less Pentecostal in origin and/or nature.

Based on these observations, it would not be out of line to claim that, because of its influence on the indigenous ethos, Pentecostalism is actually the "mainline" faith of the Hispanic Protestant churches of Philadelphia. The reality of this Hispanic Pentecostal "mainline" calls into serious question the two-party model. Within the two-party typology of liberal versus conservative, the "mainline" has traditionally been identified with so-called "liberal," public Protestantism. In Hispanic Philadelphia, however, the Protestant Pentecostal "mainline" is dominated by people who are committed both to social involvement in the community and to a form of Christian faith that is basically very conservative and that strongly emphasizes the need for personal salvation. The dualities of this self-identity call into question the central assertion of the two-party model. The complex relations that exist between Pentecostal and non-Pentecostal Hispanic churches do the same. More nuanced ways of describing the Protestant landscape are needed if the complex self-understandings and practices of the Hispanic churches are to be understood.

Hispanic Protestantism and the Restructuring of Religion in the United States

While focused on only one city, the present study provides a window into understanding other Hispanic Protestant communities across the United States. Without minimizing differences, it can be stated that there indeed are parallels between Latino/a Philadelphia and other urban Latino/a communities in the United States. Hispanic Protestantism in the United States cannot be understood adequately by using the dominant two-party categories of liberal and conservative, or of "mainline" and those outside the mainline. Part of the richness of Hispanic Protestantism is that it creatively draws on many sources that cross the two-party division while seeking to be relevant to its own social, cultural, historical context.

In the largest picture of things, Hispanic Protestantism is part of the religion of those on the margins of the dominant society in the United States, of the disenfranchised[26] and "outsiders" who nevertheless are playing a significant multi-functional role in the making of America.[27] Indeed, these Hispanic Protestant religious communities which emphasize both

26. On this point I am grateful for the helpful comments of Rhys Williams: "I am wondering if the real story here is the religious responses one finds among the disenfranchised. When a community is abandoned or exploited by the private sector, perhaps the only institutional resource left is the so-called 'third sector' — of which the churches are such a prominent component" (unpublished response, at the Chicago-Area Group for the Study of Religious Communities Winter meeting, February 1995).

27. On this theme, see R. Laurence Moore, *Religious Outsiders and the Making of Americans* (New York: Oxford University Press, 1986), 208. Moore writes: "What we have tried to suggest is that 'mainline' has too often been misleadingly used to label what is 'normal' in American religious life and 'outsider' to characterize what is aberrational or not-yet-American. In fact, the American religious system may be said to be 'working' only when it is creating cracks in denominations, when it is producing novelty, even when it is fueling antagonisms. These things are not things when properly understood, are going on at the edges or fringes of American life. They are what give energy to church life and substance to the claim that Americans are the most religious people on the face of the earth."

personal piety and social responsibility are reshaping contemporary and future American society. The religious organizations of Hispanic Protestantism in Philadelphia — its congregations, agencies, and parachurch ministries — have shaped Latino/a society far more than is generally recognized. David Watt has stated that: "In the United States, religious organizations play an important role in shaping society in general and politics in particular. Their relationship to American public life is a matter that attracts much attention."[28] This clearly is true, but contrary to Watt's observation, Latino/a efforts in this domain have not as yet attracted much attention because the Latino/a community is still seen as culturally marginal by so many citizens of the United States.

In seeking to make Latino/a faith more visible, it would be wrong to portray the Latino Protestant community as a monolith. It is not. Yet, it is possible to make some general statements regarding a common Hispanic Protestant ethos or worldview. It does seem, for example, that the Latino/a Protestant ethos provides congregations with a rationale for engaging culture and society, for entering the public sphere, while maintaining the centrality of a personal encounter with God through Christ. Within Latino/a communities, religion is defined in a personal and christocentric manner that easily crosses denominational and congregational boundaries. A personal and individual relationship with God through Christ is central to the community's own self-understanding, and from this core all other perspectives and behaviors, both private and public, radiate. Unless this is understood by the outside observer, a full appreciation of the community is not possible.

One common way in which this community-wide understanding of faith is manifested is in the strongly held view that the gospel must be preached, that evangelism must take place. At this point there are differences within the Hispanic Protestant community as to what this actually means in practice. For nearly all segments of the community this means an obligatory personal encounter with God. Some Hispanic Protestant pastors insist on an identifiable point of conversion, including a clear break from both earlier sinful practices and any vestiges of cultural Catholicism. Other pastors appear more comfortable having people experience a gradual apprehension of *evangelico* faith as they simultaneously hold on to parts of their cultural Catholicism.

28. David Harrington Watt, "United States: Cultural Challenges to the Voluntary Sector," in Robert Wuthnow, ed., *Between States and Markets: The Voluntary Sector in Comparative Perspective* (Princeton: Princeton University Press, 1991), 244.

However conversion occurs, becoming part of the Hispanic Protestant church involves a great deal of commitment on the part of those who join. This call to committed service is an important element in the Latino/a Protestant ethos. The commonly held expectation is that church will not be simply a one-service-a-week affair. The commitment made to God through conversion involves coming to church several times a week to participate in the events there. The days are filled with meetings for men, women, and youth. Meetings are held for prayer, prison visitation, rallies, special services, regular Bible study, G.E.D. classes, and music lessons. Other gatherings explain how to become a homeowner and how to become a citizen. Even if the individual member cannot meet the ideal, there is common consensus on what the ideal is for the committed Christian. Becoming part of one of the *iglesias evangelicas* entails a huge commitment of time and resources.

It is possible that what is occurring through this call to commitment is that the Hispanic Protestant churches are constructing their own everyday life-worlds by expanding their activities throughout the week. The otherworldly christocentric focus of the faith is not forgotten but in an aggressive way informs the this-worldly activities of day-to-day life. Thus, the presence of church-centered activities throughout the week offers Latino/a adults, youth, and children an alternative to the life-world of the streets with its own destructive demands. This church-centered alternative need not be automatically interpreted as escapism, as a retreat from the world. From the perspective of those struggling through life in marginalized areas of the United States, church-centered existence can be a positive, life-affirming, and world-changing option.

The pressures of the larger society do, however, tend to raise the question of choosing between an escapist posture and a socially engaged lifestyle. But this issue is complex and ambiguous. David Watt has said:

> It seems clear that privatized religious groups are, because of the on-going penetration of life-world by system, increasingly jettisoning their reluctance to enter the public fray; it is also true that whenever religious groups in the contemporary United States do try to speak authoritatively about public matters, they cause controversy. That is because such claims strike large segments of the American population as a violation of a long-standing, informal religious settlement. According to that settlement, religion's primary contribution to public life is the fostering of private virtue.[29]

29. Watt, "United States," 266.

Watt's way of putting things helps to make clear some of the perplexing dynamics at work here, but his formulation of the problem may still be too "Anglo" to unravel the processes at work in Hispanic Protestantism. Rather than being a recent phenomenon, for example, it seems that from its early stages, at least some parts of Hispanic Protestantism in Philadelphia were attempting "to enter the public fray" because of the social position of their members. This did cause controversy and consternation both within the community and without. If this was the case, however, what we see in the present is not a reentering into the public sphere, but just one more example of always having been there — despite the "long-standing, informal religious settlement" of the religious establishment which would push the Hispanic church away from its engagement with society into the realm of "private virtue" alone. Indeed, it may be that what we observe is an ongoing effort of the *iglesia evangelica* not to succumb to the bifurcation of life inherent in any "informal religious settlement." Hispanic Protestants had no part in negotiating that informal settlement, and they continue to feel a need to hold on to both public and private dimensions of faith and community. This will undoubtedly continue to be an area of tension as Latino/a Protestantism becomes a larger entity within the society of the United States.

Within the study of American religion it is commonly held that the historic "mainline" is fracturing and that the religious landscape is realigning itself. There is considerable debate as to when this phenomenon began and what factors precipitated it.[30] Generally speaking, historic American "mainline" Protestantism has experienced a decline in membership, while at the same time there has been substantial growth in churches outside the traditional mainline, especially within Pentecostalism. Robert Wuthnow[31] has described this phenomenon as part of the restructuring of American religion that has occurred since World War II.

In many settings discussions about the restructuring of American Protestantism continue to be dominated by issues of "institutional development, disembodied theological debates, and the experience of trans-

30. On the variety of interpretations see Wade Clark Roof and William McKinney, *American Mainline Religion: Its Changing Shape and Future* (New Brunswick, NJ: Rutgers University Press, 1987); Roger Finke and Rodney Stark, *The Churching of America, 1776-1990: Winners and Losers in Our Religious Economy* (New Brunswick, NJ: Rutgers University Press, 1992), 237-75.

31. Robert Wuthnow, *The Restructuring of American Religion: Society and Faith Since World War II* (Princeton: Princeton University Press, 1988).

planted European immigrants,"[32] but that is too narrow a focus. Around the specifically religious restructuring of North American society a larger cultural restructuring is taking place. In this cultural restructuring the crucial questions of alliance and division will likely be heavily influenced by issues of race, ethnicity, gender, and class (including access to power). In seeking to understand this situation, Hispanic Protestantism represents a case study of significant proportions. Despite the continuing scholarly neglect of this important community of faith, Hispanic Protestantism is well positioned to have a major effect on general trends in religion and public life in the United States as demographic shifts are rapidly making Latinos/as the largest racial/ethnic group in the country. Rather than using the old two-party model as a map for the future of American Protestantism, we ought to turn to the Hispanic Protestant community, and similar ethnic churches, to see what models derived from those sources might be able truly to enlighten our understanding of the new America that is coming into being.

32. Robert H. Craig, *Religion and Radical Politics: An Alternative Christian Religion in the United States* (Philadelphia: Temple University Press, 1992), 229.

CHAPTER 21

Mapping Faith:
Choice and Change in Local
Religious Organizational Environments

NANCY L. EIESLAND

We all use maps to help us navigate through the geographies of place, and
we all use maps to help us negotiate the geography of ideas and practices
as well. In the religious realm, the two-party/sector/pole map of the
geography of American religion has often determined how historians,
sociologists, and pundits have surveyed the complex world of American
Protestantism. However, in this essay I demonstrate that a map of American religion which focuses primarily on the two-party axis (whether those
two parties are designated as liberal and conservative, or as mainstream
and marginal, or as evangelical and mainline) leaves too much of contemporary religion unmapped for it to remain the default grid for interpreting
American Protestantism.

   Forces just now coming into play will clearly reshape our maps of
religious life in ways that differ significantly from the recent past. New
patterns of religious life are beginning to take shape locally. These patterns
include multilayered, spatially distant religious loyalties that cross back
and forth across the gulf represented in the two-party map. I argue that
these emergent patterns are related, in part, to the changed urban landscape in which many Americans now map their lives locally. Finally, I
highlight the tension that can exist within congregations when some
people operate with relatively fixed religious and spatial maps while
others work with dynamic religious and spatial maps. For this latter group,
there is no one map; rather, many maps need to be consulted.

   In the second half of the twentieth century, the maps of most metropolitan areas have been literally redrawn. Cities broke through the barriers that had previously restrained them. Subdivisions sprouted like mushrooms after a summer rain. They expanded into rural areas, engulfing small towns in their wake. Small towns, once perceived by residents to be distant physically and culturally from the city, became "exurbs" or suburbs to the new outer, or edge, cities that were developing.[1]

In the 1970s, the U.S. Census reported that for the first time more people were living in the suburbs than in other settlement spaces. Then 37.1 percent of the population was suburban, in comparison to 31.5 percent in the central city and 31.4 percent in rural areas. By 1990 even more rural areas had been absorbed by metropolitan deconcentration. The population in suburbia had grown to 46 percent, compared to 40 percent in central cities and 14 percent in rural areas.[2] As more and more Americans came to work and live in the urban margins, older center/periphery maps of metropolitan regions were rendered obsolete. Increasingly, metropolitan maps resemble not the donut of a center city with neat concentric suburban circles around it, but a kind of pepperoni pizza with multiple-edge cities scattered almost randomly on the doughy landscape.

Since the first large-scale wave of suburbanization in the post–World

1. Exurb here refers to an existing small town which is pulled into a metropolitan orbit by metropolitan deconcentration. The coinage of labels for these new decentralized formations has been something of a growth industry. Robert Fishman in "Megalopolis Unbound," *Wilson Quarterly* (Winter 1990), notes that "the new city's construction has been so rapid and so unforeseen that we lack even a commonly-accepted name for what we have created." Mark Gottdiener and George Kephart,"The Multinucleated Metropolitan Region: A Comparative Analysis," in Rob Kling, Spencer Olin, and Mark Poster, eds., *Postsuburban California: The Transformation of Orange County since World War II* (Berkeley: University of California Press, 1991), characterize these formations as "deconcentrated" and "polynucleated." Robert Fishman in *Bourgeois Utopias: The Rise and Fall of Suburbia* (New York: Basic Books, 1987) identifies them as "techno-city" and "techno-burb." Mark Baldassare's *Trouble in Paradise: The Suburban Transformation of America* (New York: Columbia University Press, 1986) names them "transformed suburbs." Rob Kling, Spencer Olin, and Mark Poster, in "The Emergence of Postsuburbia: An Introduction," have coined the term "postsuburban region" for the phenomenon. Other terms that are circulated include outer cities and new urban villages. I have elected to use "exurb," the term used by A. C. Spectorsky in *The Exurbanites* (New York: Berkley, 1957). The term "edge city," taken from Joel Garreau's *Edge City: Life on the New Frontier* (New York: Doubleday, 1991), refers to concentrations of business, retail, and light industrial development outside of historic city centers. The Gwinnett Place Mall Corners is an edge city to which Dacula is an exurb.

2. U.S. Bureau of the Census, *Census of Population and Housing, 1990* (Washington, DC: U.S. Printing Office, 1990).

War II era, middle-class people's homes have been located miles from their jobs.[3] Now, however, instead of a commute from the suburban home to work in the central city, many individuals travel back and forth between edge cities in their daily trek to and from work. The growth of edge cities and the pervasiveness of commuting have enabled and required each person to make his/her own decisions about where to live, where to work, where to go to school, where to shop, and where (and if) to worship within the expanding matrix of separate places that make up the metropolitan region.[4] Furthermore, this new kind of commuting lifestyle has diffused interpersonal relations so that people no longer rely as extensively on those most geographically adjacent to them to fulfill their needs for intimacy and sociality.[5]

3. Kenneth Jackson notes in *Crabgrass Frontier: The Suburbanization of the United States* (New York: Oxford University Press, 1985) that the first wave of suburbanization occurred between 1815 and 1875, when the first railroad suburbs were developed. However, large-scale suburbanization did not occur until 1945. He argues that these postwar suburbs shared five common characteristics, including peripheral location, low density, architectural similarity, easy availability, and economic and racial homogeneity (see 238-41). He writes, "The creation of good, inexpensive suburban housing on an unprecedented scale was a unique achievement in the world" (245).

4. See Daniel V. A. Olson, "Fellowship Ties and the Transmission of Religious Identity," in Jackson Carroll and Wade Clark Roof, eds., *Beyond Establishment: Protestant Identity in a Post-Protestant Age* (Louisville, KY: Westminster/John Knox Press, 1993). Olson demonstrates that religious institutions flourish among mobile individuals. This counters evidence that geographic mobility in the short run deters religious participation. See Robert Wuthnow and Kevin Christiano, "The Effects of Residential Migration on Church Attendance in the United States," in Robert Wuthnow, ed., *The Religious Dimension: New Directions in Quantitative Research* (New York: Academic Press, 1979); and Roger Finke, "Demographics of Religious Participation: An Ecological Approach, 1850-1980," *Journal for the Scientific Study of Religion* 29 (1989): 45-58. See also R. Stephen Warner, "Work in Progress Toward a New Paradigm for the Sociological Study of Religion in the United States," *American Journal of Sociology* 98 (1993): 1044-93. In the case of Gwinnett County, the rates of participation did appear to decline at the peak of the area's demographic boom, but quickly rebounded to represent relatively high rates of religious participation in the 1990s.

5. Robert N. Bellah, Richard Madsen, William M. Sullivan, Ann Swidler, and Steven M. Tipton, in *Habits of the Heart: Individualism and Commitment in American Life* (Berkeley: University of California Press, 1985), write: "While mobile professionals in the United States do indeed engage themselves in complicated networks of intimate relationships, these networks are often not tied to a particular place. One may maintain close friendships with a host of people scattered all across the country" (186). See also Claude Fischer, *To Dwell Among Friends: Personal Networks in Town and City* (Chicago: University of Chicago Press, 1982).

Mapping Religious Change in the Exurbs

This move to suburbia and beyond has presented religious organizations with unique challenges. As their members moved to suburbs and edge cities, many religious leaders initially expected that traditional religious affiliations would be reinforced in these new settlement spaces. An article in the March 22, 1950, issue of the *Christian Century* highlighted the views of many religious leaders: "The residents of Suburbia are, by and large, Protestant in tradition and by natural addiction. They want to have Protestant churches in their communities and will support them generously. They send their children to Protestant church schools, and more often than not maintain a church membership for themselves."[6] However, choice was a fundamental factor in the move to suburbia and beyond, and this freedom to choose would to a large extent undermine the expected compulsion of suburbanites to adhere to traditional patterns, including religious ones.

As choice became increasingly important to people's relationships with religious organizations, religious special purpose and support groups, megachurches, independent congregations, and evangelistic organizations which offer pluralism within and across religious organizations became the embodiment of those choices.[7] In religious life too, residential proximity became less significant in the choices of affiliations than had been the case earlier.

6. Quoted in James Hudnut-Beumler, *Looking for God in the Suburbs: The Religion of the American Dream and Its Critics, 1945-1965* (New Brunswick, NJ: Rutgers, 1994), 6-7. In *Edge City,* Garreau claims that edge cities have few religious organizations. He writes: churches "are not anathema to Edge Cities. One Houston developer approves of one next to the Galleria as a 'noncompeting low density use.' If, in fact, one argues that a city is always a monument to the worship of something, it is clear that Edge City worships a prevailing god not the same as the one celebrated in the design of Jerusalem, Rome, Mecca, Kyoto, and Beijing" (64). Though Garreau's anecdotal accounts do not depict the edge city as a location for religious development, Gwinnett Place Mall Corners and numerous other edge cities are growing centers for religious organizations.

7. See Robert Wuthnow, *The Restructuring of American Religion: Society and Faith since World War II* (Princeton: Princeton University Press, 1988) and *Sharing the Journey: Support Groups and America's New Quest for Community* (New York: Free Press, 1994). In *The Restructuring of American Religion,* Wuthnow argues that the increased organizational pluralism brought about by the growth of special purpose groups, specialized ministries, coalitions, home fellowships, and support groups did not take the place of membership in denominationally affiliated congregations (120-21). They did, I argue, however, alter the meaning and the context for congregational membership, allowing for multilayered religious participation in which church membership was not necessarily privileged.

Researchers have highlighted how these religious changes are related to education[8] and income.[9] Lately, particular attention has been paid to generational consideration,[10] especially the impact of the baby boom cohort, relative to religious choice. Kirk Hadaway and David Roozen write: "All of the evidence suggests that boomers' relationship to the church is fundamentally different from that of previous generations of Americans — that it is, to use the varied terminology of recent scholarly discussion, more 'voluntaristic,' consumer-oriented, and captive to the subjective, expressive dimensions of cultural individualism."[11] Penny Long Marler and Roozen describe the generational change as one from tradition to consumer choice.[12] Writing about baby boomers, Wade Clark Roof notes: "Increasingly within the Protestant, Catholic, and Jewish mainline, people identify themselves by adding on layers of experiential meaning to older, less relevant religious and denominational labels." He summarizes the views of social scientists who have focused on generational changes: "Choice, so much a part of life for this [baby boom] generation, now expresses itself in dynamic and fluid religious styles."[13]

However, relatively little research has focused directly on issues of alterations in settlement space that occurred at the same time as these other changes. In this essay, while I do not ignore the generational, educational, and income differences between oldtimers and newcomers, the focus is on the divergent ways in which people in the exurbs literally map faith locally.[14]

The exurb of Dacula is located in Gwinnett County, Georgia, which

8. Nancy T. Ammerman, *Baptist Battles: Social Change and Religious Conflict in the Southern Baptist Convention* (New Brunswick, NJ: Rutgers University Press, 1990).

9. Dean R. Hoge, Benton Johnson, and Donald A. Luidens, *Vanishing Boundaries: The Religion of Mainline Protestant Baby Boomers* (Louisville: Westminster/John Knox, 1994); and Wuthnow, *Sharing the Journey*.

10. C. Kirk Hadaway and David A. Roozen, "Denominational Growth and Decline," in David A. Roozen and C. Kirk Hadaway, eds., *Church and Denominational Growth* (Nashville: Abingdon Press, 1993); and Wade Clark Roof, *A Generation of Seekers: The Spiritual Journeys of the Baby Boom Generation* (San Francisco: Harper Collins, 1993).

11. Hadaway and Roozen, "Denominational Growth and Decline," 243.

12. Penny Long Marler and David A. Roozen, "From Church Tradition to Consumer Choice: The Gallup Surveys of the Unchurched American," in C. Kirk Hadaway and David A. Roozen, eds., *Church and Denominational Growth* (Nashville: Abingdon Press, 1993).

13. Roof, *A Generation of Seekers*, 5, 201.

14. For further analysis of religious organizational change in exurban locales, see Nancy L. Eiesland, *A Particular Place: Exurbanization and Religious Response in a Southern Town* (New Brunswick: Rutgers University Press, forthcoming).

had the dubious distinction during the 1980s of being the fastest growing county in the nation for several successive years.[15] This former small town has become a haven for young families who work in the office parks of the edge cities rimming central city Atlanta but who also value Dacula's bucolic setting and quality public schools.[16] The area's demographic alterations have resulted in the development of (at least) two populations of local residents — oldtimers and newcomers.[17] As will be addressed in detail below, oldtimers and newcomers use different maps to navigate physical space and religious geography.

Dacula's Hinton Memorial United Methodist Church, which plays prominently in this study, is a historic congregation of approximately 85 members.[18] Oldtimers and newcomers who are associated with this congregation use their different spatial and cognitive maps to organize their religious lives in ways that differ from each other. As a result, they interpret

15. The report developed by researchers at Dun and Bradstreet examined the growth of the nation's counties with at least 100,000 inhabitants: Gwinnett County, according to these findings, had experienced the fastest rate of population growth (50.4 percent) anywhere in the nation in the preceding five years. This report was picked up in national print media (e.g., *American Demographics, The New York Times, Time Magazine,* and *The Wall Street Journal*), bringing the county to national attention.

16. While Dacula, Georgia, is hardly a microcosm of the United States, the Sunbelt, the South, or even Gwinnett County, the concerns and experiences of Dacula oldtimers resemble those of many small towns whose patterns of life have been altered by the sociospatial changes of urban residential and industrial deconcentration in the past three decades. The demographic changes in Dacula represent the changes that are occurring in the region and the differences that are still evident between this small town in the process of exurbanizing and Gwinnett County at large. While the city population of Dacula has increased only 28.8 percent in the past decade, the population in the local zip code area has grown by 40.2 percent during the same time period.

17. I am not claiming that the families discussed here are strictly representative of oldtimers and newcomers. Rather, the stories of these families highlight general patterns — diverse as the specifics are. The stories presented here about the networks of Vernon and Marie England and Todd and Faith Penner are cultural representations of the transformations that have accompanied and, to a large extent, comprise the organizational alteration in this exurban location. Furthermore, the terms "oldtimers" and "newcomers" do gloss diversity within the groups. For example, oldtimers include a small but culturally important population of African-American residents. This diversity is not represented fully in this essay. It should be noted that the terms "oldtimer" and "newcomer" here do not represent an individual's age, but rather tenure in the community. Though oldtimers were likely to be older than newcomers, age variation existed within each group.

18. The names used for individuals are pseudonyms. However, the towns and churches are actual names of communities and congregations in Georgia.

the meaning of their religious participation in the life of this local congregation in rather different ways as well.

Oldtimers: Vernon and Marie England

Vernon England, a short, balding man, leaned over the back of my pew to whisper in my ear, "How do you like them apples?" He showed me a copy of the Hinton Memorial UMC Sunday bulletin on the back of which was printed the week's selection of "chuckles" — a sampling from Reverend Luther Dawson's file of *Reader's Digest* funny stories and aphorisms. The one that Vernon highlighted with his thumb was "Jogging is a good way to meet new people — orthopedists, podiatrists, cardiologists, and ambulance drivers." The chuckle recalled a conversation that Vernon and I had had earlier that morning about his doctor's orders to get more exercise. Vernon, a 68-year-old retired watchmaker, had said that he could not think of many more useless activities than running when you had no place to go.

Vernon and Marie England have lived in Dacula since childhood. The stories of their families fashion their local map. Vernon's father was a Baptist preacher at a church two miles away from Dacula, and Marie's father owned an auto repair shop and later a jewelry store in downtown. Vernon and Marie went to school together at Dacula's elementary and high schools. They married in Vernon's father's church when Vernon was nineteen years old and Marie was eighteen. The photo of the event taken in front of the clapboard structure, which hangs in a collage with nearly fifteen other family photos in the couple's living room, shows Vernon grinning mischievously and Marie stone-faced — an apt portrait of the couple even today.

Home and neighborhood are largely coextensive for Vernon and Marie. Home, though centered in their split-level, is intimately connected to Dacula's businesses, clubs, schools, and community activities. Their recreation revolves around local friends, family, and community events. Most of the couple's friends have over the years relocated to the same area in the southern end of town. Most of these friends are "Saturday night church friends," i.e., a group that has been going out every Saturday night for years. All have to get back early enough to go to services on Sunday morning; most attend Hinton Memorial UMC, but several go to other congregations in the area. The church friends from Hinton Memorial also get together once a month on Tuesday morning (when they have the seniors' discount) for the breakfast buffet at Shoney's in a thriving suburb nearby.

Vernon and Marie's active involvement in Dacula Methodist Church (as Hinton Memorial UMC was then known), which is just a quarter mile from their home, dates to the early 1950s. Marie had attended congregational events while Vernon was in the military during World War II and had helped to found a Ladies Aid of mostly Methodist "war widows" during those years. After Vernon's return, the young couple visited several churches before settling on Dacula Methodist, which is the only church in which they have held membership. Vernon characterized their participation in congregational events before the birth of their children as sporadic. "We'd be there pretty often but — I don't know — it didn't seem all that important," he explained. The birth of their eldest son Elliot, however, initiated a period of scrupulous family religious participation. "You start to thinking that you want your children to have good values and friends, so you start getting more involved," Marie explained.

Though Marie's religious background was Methodist, Vernon jokes that he is still a closet Baptist (though he admits that he has not been inside a Baptist church for ten years except for funerals). The couple attended an adult membership class while the children underwent confirmation. Marie recalls that the children were particularly faithful in their attendance: "Back then we had six month pins, one year pins, five year pins, and ten year pins for perfect attendance. And if we went somewhere, we had to take them to church, so they'd get their pins. I think Elliott got his ten year pin." Ellen, the couple's daughter, was a pianist at the church until she was a teenager.

The Englands also became involved in the youth programming of the congregation. Vernon recalls: "We had ball teams and all when Elliott was young. Then later Elliott coached and Tom would play. I guess Elliott was about 14. They played within the church league for a long time. And we had the Cub Scouts, which was pretty good. I don't think they had the Boy Scouts, but we had the Cub Scouts." Vernon remembers his role in the youth activity and his ongoing contact with those youngsters:

> I'd take as many as I could pile in, sitting in the car, in the trunk, on the hood, and take them up to Lake Lanier and come back to get another load and another load to have a campout. Boy, we had great times. But the thing about it is some of them still call me, from all over the country. Wanting me to tell . . . two of the stories especially, that I used to tell, so they could record it for their children. I found an old book, in a

falling-down log school over here in the woods. I was hunting. And it was completely . . . just rotted. But I opened it, and I could still read two stories in the center. And the book disintegrated. But I memorized those two stories, but I tell you what, they still want me to record it for their children. It was good.

Vernon was also active on various boards in the church, serving most consistently on the Trustee's Committee but also assisting on the Pastor-Parish Relations Committee and the Administrative Board from time to time. Beginning in the mid-1950s, he was appointed to the Pleasant Hill Cemetery committee, which is composed of both church and town leaders, and oversees the upkeep of the grounds. He served on the cemetery committee for more than forty years. Marie was active in the United Methodist Women and could always be counted on to prepare food for funerals or to visit the sick, though she steadfastly refused to take more formal jobs, such as being Sunday school teacher or committee member. The family's religious involvement centered solely around Hinton Memorial.

Everything in Dacula, Marie maintained, seemed to revolve around congregational life at Hinton — even time. Marie remembers Hinton's church bell that rang the noon hour and on Sundays to set the watches of local residents. Vernon recollected: "We'd have bonfires, and weenie roasts on special occasions, or before football games or something. There were lots of important things around here then, that's right. And you knew everyone around back then, all your neighbors. There was just always activity." The community changes have, according to Vernon, undermined their church's prominence in the community.

Nonetheless, the Englands have responded to the arrival of increased numbers of newcomers with appreciation for the vitality and financial support they contribute to the church, but also with some bewilderment at their lack of loyalty. Marie comments, "It's hard. You'll see one couple for a few Sundays then you won't see them again until they come to join the church. I think that we've got to have some way to find out if they are serious." Vernon also finds the habits of some newcomers puzzling: "Some of them you never see together. One will bring the kids one time and the other the next time. The other thing is that you don't know what some of them are. They are all the time changing their denomination." Though the Englands understand the busyness of a dual-income couple and the ne-gotiations of an interdenominational marriage, they also expect that loy-alty to a single congregation should undergird a family's religious life.

Vernon and Marie England map their lives and their faith within an interarticulated system of relationships and organizational ties that is centered in Dacula. Though they have had numerous opportunities to relocate in pursuit of employment advancement, the couple has opted to stay in Dacula, where they have buried their dead and reared their young. Their religious participation at Hinton Memorial has been stable. The loyalties and deeply embedded community ties of the Englands epitomize the maps of many Hinton Memorial and Dacula oldtimers.

Newcomers: Todd and Faith Penner

On a sultry summer morning in 1993, the Penners stood at the front of Hinton Memorial's sanctuary holding their two children to receive the baptismal charge. Faith Penner held their eight-month-old daughter, Alisa, who wore a flowing lace baptismal gown. Todd held the couple's four-year-old son Andrew, who like his father was dressed in a suit and tie. This Sunday father, son, and daughter were being baptized, and the couple was joining the church. In his prayer, the pastor, Rev. Luther Dawson, asked for strength that would enable Todd to follow the dictates of the Lord all his life, to be successful in balancing the demands of work and family, and to find peace in God in the midst of his stressful lifestyle. After the baptisms, the congregation stood to recite with the Penners the rite of membership from the Methodist hymnal. Dawson charged the congregation to care for and protect the faith of the Penners. The Penners vowed to support the congregation with their time, talents, and finances.

The Penners, who are in their mid-thirties, had been living in the Dacula area for four years when they joined Hinton Memorial UMC. They resided two and a half miles south of Dacula. Todd and Faith had met during college at the University of Florida, Gainesville. Not long after the couple began dating, Faith's parents were killed in a plane accident. In the aftermath of the tragedy, Faith turned to Todd for support, and eventually the couple moved in together. They married within a year and relocated to Gwinnett County, where Todd had lived as a child. Faith worked for several years at a bank in downtown Atlanta. Todd, a marketing analyst and engineer for an oil company, works in an Atlanta edge city office park, approximately forty minutes from their home. However, at the time of my research, they were preparing to relocate to Nashville, his corporate headquarters, in order for Todd to take a promotion. This would be the first move that Todd's career has required the family to make.

413

The anticipated move has increased Faith's worry about Todd's work habits. "He works too hard," she said. "He's never home before seven or eight and then it's the weekend in the office sometimes, too." These tendencies especially disturb her because she characterizes Todd's father as a workaholic whose "addiction to work destroyed his family."

The couple's original choice to reside in Dacula had been dictated by Todd's desire to have a home with a "buffer zone" around it, rather than living in a tightly packed subdivision, and by Faith's desire to reside some distance from Todd's work to help him "really get away." When they decided to purchase, the couple could only afford property on the far outskirts of Atlanta. Faith, who now works full-time caring for her children, said that she loved their home, but preferred not to be "stuck" there.

Faith, like many women who elect to become stay-at-home moms in the exurbs, in actuality stays at home hardly at all, especially on weekdays. Unlike homemakers in the suburbs in a previous era, today's exurban homemakers are much more likely to view their home as one hub in a network of activities rather than as a haven from the hustle and bustle of life. Faith Penner said, "I never wanted to be a housewife. Todd knew that when I married him, but it just made sense for me to be with the kids now." Housekeeping, in particular, was not a priority for her, saying laughingly that if I looked in her Jeep, I would get a better sense of how she kept house.

Distance, eclecticism, and convenience characterized the Penners' religious choices. Their day care provider, The Child's Place, is run by a Church of God (Cleveland, TN) congregation in Duluth, an exurb approximately ten miles from Dacula. It was recommended to the Penners by one of Faith's former co-workers. They were very satisfied with the care at the center and laughed about the "fundamentalist" songs, such as one action chorus about stomping on Satan, that Andrew sometimes came home singing. The couple also allowed Andrew to participate in a children's cantata at the church, entitled "Bullfrogs and Butterflies."

Since late 1992, Faith has attended a weekly Grief Relief support group meeting at yet another church — Hebron Baptist Church, a megachurch located only one half-mile from their home. The weekly sessions, which are led by a licensed psychologist, begin with prayer and expound a twelve-step model of dealing with personal loss. Each session includes an opportunity to share the pain and anger of loss. Faith found one session, during which group members took turns screaming into a pillow held by a partner, to be especially therapeutic. "You start out feeling really stupid.

But then you feel something let go inside of you. You're not alone," she shared. Grief Relief provided a close-knit group of mostly women who shared each other's burdens and provided consistent support for one another. Faith and Todd attended a few worship services at Hebron Baptist and did not like the experience, but they were not pressured to join: "They seem OK with me just coming for the meetings. I really get a lot out of them; it's when I feel closest to God."

Like the Englands nearly three decades earlier, the Penners had decided to join Hinton Memorial UMC partially in response to their perceived need for assistance in teaching their children about values. The couple's difficulty in balancing family and work had made Reverend Luther Dawson's baptismal prayer for Todd especially apropos, as far as Faith was concerned. Faith reported:

> I said "Now, Todd, how are our kids going to learn about the Bible and values?" "Well, I'll teach them," he said. But I said, "What are you doing to teach them?" His point was that he didn't feel like you had to go to church to be spiritual, and I agree with him. But we were doing nothing for Andrew and Alisa to give them a foundation. He was too busy. When you have the responsibility of your own kids it all comes full circle and you want to instill that in your kids.

Faith, who had been reared in the Baptist church, believed that a religious "foundation" was especially important. Faith said: "Up until I was about eighteen years old, we went three times a week. Sunday [morning], Sunday [evening], and Wednesday. If that foundation is there you will eventually come back." During her teen years Faith ceased to attend, finding the strictures of attendance at her parents' Baptist church too difficult. She felt that Baptists were "too extreme" because of their emphasis on being saved and attending church so often. "I think what's important is that you believe in God," she said. She explained that she believed that it was not as important where one went, meaning the denominational affiliation of the church, as much as that one went somewhere. She explained:

> My sister became a Presbyterian over the last year. Her husband is a Catholic. But she's really interested in religion. Like Jehovah's Witnesses came to meet her, and I think she's met with them three times, trying to find out what they really believe. So I'm learning a little bit about the Jehovah's Witnesses from her. Maybe she'll try that if it helps her.

Though Todd also held the opinion that going to church was good for a family, he was not fond of religious people. Faith recalled that getting

Todd to attend any church was difficult in the beginning because of his view that too many religious people were just hypocritical and because his parents had never set a model of church attendance for himself and his brothers. She said, "I was raised in the church pretty much and Todd really wasn't. His parents were but they never went to church and really never taught him things." Todd attributed his parents' lack of church participation to their childhood experiences. "Both my parents when they were growing up were Baptist. My mother's father was a farmer, and they had six kids. They went every Sunday and Wednesday. My father was the same way. It wasn't an option. So they told me that they weren't going to make us go to church. Most of the people I knew who went to church were a bunch of hypocrites." Faith interrupted, "But I can't ever recall when your parents went to church. I never saw them set an example." Todd responded, "Well, we said grace at the table. There were people that I knew at school and stuff who said that if you don't go to church, you go to hell. On the other side, they did a lot of things that were not Christian or whatever. More than I ever thought about doing."

Initially Faith began to attend Sunday morning religious services in the area on her own with Andrew. Finally, she persuaded Todd to attend Hebron Baptist with her. The experience was, she said, a dismal failure. Todd hated the congregation's large size and felt that services were too orchestrated. The altar call made him particularly uncomfortable. "He'd just stand up there and beg until he got the right number of people down there crying," Todd said. Several months after their experience at Hebron, Faith convinced Todd to accompany her to Hinton Memorial. She explained how she made her decision to visit the church:

> So I saw these two little old quaint churches. One out here — Brooks — was no longer a Methodist church. I've never seen a church change denomination, but that's now something like New Life Baptist, I believe. And I noticed that they've got a fence up around the cemetery where all the Methodists are buried, and it's a national historic site, so they can't do anything with it. So then we were left with one quaint, little, old church, so we tried here. And the people at Hinton are very friendly, and they make you feel welcome.

Todd was much more favorably impressed by the service at Hinton Memorial UMC than he had been at Hebron Baptist. "It was just good, solid common sense," he said. "I like it being small. Sitting in [the pastor's] Methodism class, I found that I believed that too." The couple became regular attenders about six months before Alisa's birth. Faith said, "Once we got out and going we both enjoyed it. When I didn't go I felt like I was missing something. It took me a while to get Todd interested in going all the time. Now he's primarily the one who's interested." Todd explained his change of heart:

> They just teach — I know it's not popular — family values. I praise Vice President Quayle for getting up there and not being afraid to say that we need more of that. I think if some more of our leaders were that way, we might have a better country. You're supposed to be ashamed, you're not supposed to mention that you believe in those old-fashioned things, like taking care of your family and working hard. We'll go down just like the Roman Empire did. It's coming, unless we change ourselves. Anything goes today, and if you don't believe that you're a real queer duck, you know?

Todd was quick to say that his views were not like those held by fundamentalist Christians, but that he wanted the church to teach the traditional moral codes. Asked what he felt he was affirming in his baptism, Todd replied: "I believe in a God — nobody's any better than anybody else. It's just like let's just call it even and get on with life. Everything in moderation." These are also the values that he hopes Alisa and Andrew garner from their attendance at vacation Bible school, Sunday school, and United Methodist Tots. Todd explained:

> I hope that they learn about God — that there is a Supreme Being — what ever you want to call it. They may grow up to call it Allah, for all I know. If he grows up to be atheistic, I don't care. He truly tries to believe but he just can't, I think God is compassionate enough to understand that. I would rather have him say that than be a hypocrite. I want him to know right from wrong. He's got to be fair and decent. Take care of his family first.

Todd and Faith's concern about instilling values in their children prompted their return to church. But they also reported that Sunday morning attendance has been good for them as well. Faith believed that it had made the couple less selfish in their interactions with one another and more patient with their children.

They were, however, somewhat distressed at the level of participation that some members at Hinton expected. "They put us on a committee — I think nurture — right after we started coming. I called up [the pastor] and said that we would not do it," said Faith. Faith and Todd attended worship services most Sundays, bringing their children early for Sunday school. Faith and the children were occasionally present for Wednesday night suppers, and Faith often brought Andrew to children's events. Sometimes, the couple could also be called upon to serve as impromptu ushers. The ability to choose their own degree of involvement in the programming of the congregation without being sanctioned by other members for their choices (despite some sense of pressure for greater participation) was an important factor in their ongoing connection with Hinton Methodist Church.

As they prepared for their move to Nashville, they expressed their concern about finding religious services that would meet their needs. Faith said, "I hope that I can find another group like Grief Relief if I need it and someplace where the kids are taken care of by people who have religious values." Todd also remarked: "I don't care about the denomination, but we need to find a church that's good — small and solid." Faith Penner's choice to attend Grief Relief meetings at Hebron Baptist Church, the couple's decision to place their children in the Church of God's The Child's Place, and their attendance at Hinton Memorial United Methodist Church created an eclectic mix of religious involvement, structured by the perceived needs of her exurban family and not by geographical proximity or by communal and organizational allegiance.

Conclusion

The religious and spatial maps used by oldtimers and newcomers at Hinton Memorial UMC and in the Dacula area in general diverge from each other. For oldtimers like Vernon and Marie England, Dacula is the context in which they have sought to fashion a decent life based on commitment and cohesion. For newcomers like Todd and Faith Penner, Dacula is part of a larger and diverse metropolitan region with multiple edge cities and exurbs, clusters of malls, office developments, and entertainment complexes that have arisen where major highways cross and converge. The Penners have recourse to multiple spatial and cognitive maps of the area. Their lives are governed by complex patterns of multidirectional travel and an assumption of choice. Their religious lives are characterized by a relatively eclectic mix of loyalties and participation which often traverse the divide between the two supposed Protestant parties or which simply have no point of reference to either of those parties.

The multilayered and diffused religious participation of newcomers created organizational dilemmas for congregations in this changing community. Some religious organizations, like Hebron Baptist Church, responded by offering specialized services, such as the Grief Relief group, that allowed area newcomers to participate in the congregation at different levels of commitment. Though the Penners were invited to join the church, their decision not to do so did not mean that other services were cut off.

Other congregations, like Hinton Memorial UMC, have found grappling with the meaning of these multiple religious ties more difficult. Some longtimers, like Marie England, perceived the multiple commitments of newcomers as a lack of loyalty to Hinton. This perception sometimes created hard feelings as some oldtimers felt as though the religious organization, for whose survival they had sacrificed, was held in low esteem by the newcomers who simply "shopped around" for the most trendy programming. Others oldtimers, however, disagreed, noting that the "subcontracting" relationships of many newcomers helped the financially strapped congregation not to lose members simply because they were unable to offer certain specific services. Individuals could find those services elsewhere while continuing to maintain a certain kind of loyalty to Hinton.

For their part, newcomers were sometimes put off by the participation assumptions of some oldtimers whose networks were more localized and overlapping than their own. Faith Penner, for example, saw attendance at committee meetings as a drain on her limited personal and family time, not as desirable opportunities for socializing.[19] Oldtimers at Hinton Memorial UMC, accustomed as they are to assuming commitment and cohesion as principles within the congregation, are finding themselves increasingly needing to relate to fellow congregants who have developed a pastiche of religious organizational ties quite different from their own. For newcomers, there is no one map; there are many maps. The multilayered involvement of these newcomers has thus plunged the congrega-

---

19. Wade Clark Roof writes about this phenomenon in *A Generation of Seekers:* "They [baby boomers] want good programs, inspired worship, and meaningful ways of serving their faith. But what does the church offer? All too often, as [one baby boomer pastor] said, 'We stick them on a committee.' Churches and other religious institutions expect them to 'fit in' to existing programs and structures. Consequently, returning boomers often experience a gap between what they are looking for and what is offered to them by organized religion" (184). Though Roof sees this experience as a sign of the lack in many congregations of "any sensitivity to their deeper concerns, or a structure designed to help people to grow spiritually," an equally plausible explanation is that many religious organizations continue to take for granted overlapping networks.

tion as a whole into a vertiginous era defined by the multiple religious maps new members and attenders bring into the church with them.

In local congregations, especially in exurban locations like Dacula, the meaning of membership, commitment, and loyalty is being re-negotiated. This eclecticism and dynamism at the local level argues against maps of the religious geography which attend primarily to two parties. While numerous religious spokespersons and many denominational officials may continue to try to chart the relevant topography of American religion as if that geography is defined by the two parties (i.e., conservatives and liberals, fundamentalists and modernists, or evangelical and mainline churches), many individuals are now charting their own different ways of making sense of, and acting within, the American religious scene. And the new maps these people are using take little or no thought of such bipolar divisions.

CHAPTER 22

Narrative Theology and the Pre-Enlightenment Ethos of the American Protestant Center

MARK ELLINGSEN

Some developments in American Protestantism since 1960 seem to confirm the two-party analysis. One thinks of the schisms between moderates and fundamentalists in the Southern Baptist Convention and in the Lutheran Church–Missouri Synod. In the socio-political realm, one hears much talk these days of a politically influential religious right adopting a posture in direct tension with the ecumenical establishment, most prominently represented by the National Council of Churches and its constituent denominations. These "two-party" dynamics are sometimes portrayed in terms of a "culture war" in American society between so-called "progressives" and the "orthodox."[1]

Despite these religious and socio-cultural dynamics, certain developments seem to tell a different story. I have in mind, on the one hand, the interaction among theologians on both sides of the supposed two-party divide regarding their assessments of certain new (though in some ways really quite ancient) approaches to theological hermeneutics, particularly narrative hermeneutics. On the other hand, I would point to some usually overlooked survey data regarding the American public's attitudes toward biblical authority.

It seems clear to me that, if two theological parties stand out as particularly visible among the numerous divisions within American Prot-

1. See James Davison Hunter, *Culture Wars: The Struggle to Define America* (New York: Basic Books, 1991), esp. 108-16.

estantism, it is differences in hermeneutics and the nature of biblical authority that form the core dispute which defines those parties against each other. But I must pause here because some analysts have maintained that the dividing lines between the so-called parties are not so much theological as they are sociological, relating to lifestyle standards, power, church politics, or administrative style. Because this is so, I find it necessary first to examine what the disputants themselves have said about the issues that divide them.[2]

Biblical Authority and Hermeneutics: *The* Theological Issue

A number of recent analyses of the two-party controversy and relevant data pertaining to the theological commitments of churches normally said that to belong to one or the other of the two parties indicates that the way in which biblical authority is construed does, or at least has in the past, divide much of American Christianity into two parties.[3] This certainly

---

2. Among those pointing to these other factors as dividing the disputing parties, especially in the Southern Baptist Convention, are W. Randall Lolley, telephone conversation, September 7, 1992; and Nancy Tatom Ammerman, *Baptist Battles: Social Change and Religious Conflict in the Southern Baptist Convention* (New Brunswick, NJ: Rutgers University Press, 1990), esp. 87-167. For similar observations regarding factors occasioning the two-party conflict in general, I cite G. W. Bromiley, private interview, Fuller Seminary, March 14, 1985 (who identifies church practice as the real issue dividing the evangelical movement from the mainline churches); Panel (including William McKinney, Charles G. Newsome, Mark Noll, and Barbara Wheeler) dealing with the two-party paradigm for the Evangelical Theology Group at the AAR/SBL Annual Meeting, Chicago, November 19, 1994 (which distinguished the two parties almost exclusively in terms of their respective attitudes toward evangelism and institutional maintenance without regard to differences in their view of biblical authority). Also see Donald G. Bloesch, *The Future of Evangelical Christianity: A Call for Unity amid Diversity* (Garden City, NY: Doubleday & Co., 1983), 11, 13.

3. George Marsden, *Fundamentalism and American Culture: The Shaping of Twentieth-Century Evangelicalism, 1870-1925* (Oxford: Oxford University Press, 1980), esp. 5; Ernest Sandeen, *The Roots of Fundamentalism: British and American Millenarianism, 1800-1930* (Chicago: University of Chicago Press, 1970). Sociologists of religion and opinion surveys typically distinguish two parties in American Christianity by means of differing attitudes toward biblical inerrancy. See James Davison Hunter, *Evangelicalism: The Coming Generation* (Chicago and London: The University of Chicago Press, 1987), 20-24; Ammerman, *Baptist Battles*, 80ff. Also see Hunter, *Culture Wars*, 120-27.

seems to be the case when viewed from the "right."[4] There are in fact numerous analyses offered by prominent evangelicals and fundamentalists which identify biblical authority in some form or other as the one issue that ultimately divides them and other like-minded Christians from those whom they perceive to be representatives of the more "liberal" segment of American Christianity.[5] The observation made by Gerald Sheppard some years ago still seems on target: Inerrancy is for a good number of evangelicals the language of social identification that distinguishes them from all non-evangelical persons and institutions.[6]

In this regard, Sheppard reminds us that "inerrancy" seems often to function in more of a sociological manner than theological. That is, it is not so much the case that all evangelicals hold a particular view of biblical authority in contradistinction to another wholly distinct party of American Christianity, as it is the case that one cannot remain within the evangelical community very long without identifying oneself with the term and re-

---

4. It might be argued that we should not allow the judgments of participants from one side of the two-party divide to determine our assessment of the issues at stake. In response, I would simply contend that we need to take the words of the disputants in this conflict seriously. Furthermore, it may well be possible to gain insight, even about the center, from those who specifically have placed themselves not at the center, but at one of the poles of American Christian faith.

5. For example, consider the assessments of these evangelicals: Carl F. H. Henry, *God Who Speaks and Shows: Fifteen Theses, Part Three*, Vol. IV of *God, Revelation and Authority* (6 vols.; Waco, TX: Word Books, 1976-83), 179; David A. Hubbard, *What We Believe and Teach* (pamphlet, reprinted 1981), 5; Mark Noll, "Evangelicals and the Study of the Bible," in *Evangelicalism and Modern America*, ed. George Marsden (Grand Rapids: Wm. B. Eerdmans, 1984), 118; Francis Schaeffer, *No Final Conflict: The Bible without Error in All That It Affirms* (Downers Grove, IL: InterVarsity Press, 1975), 8; Harold Lindsell, *The Battle for the Bible*, 14th printing (Grand Rapids: Zondervan, 1981), 210.

For a similar assessment by a prominent fundamentalist, see Jerry Falwell, ed., *The Fundamentalist Phenomenon* (Garden City, NY: Doubleday & Co., 1981), 7-8.

That fundamentalists in the Southern Baptist Convention understand the controversy within the Convention as a dispute over biblical authority is evident in the analysis provided by Clark Pinnock, "What Is Biblical Inerrancy?," in *The Proceedings of the Conference on Biblical Inerrancy 1987* (Nashville, TN: Broadman, 1987), 77, who claimed that the dispute in the Convention "is a fight over how inerrancy is to be defined. . . ." Ammerman, *Baptist Battles*, 80ff., cites similar views maintained by SBC fundamentalists like Paul Pressler and W. A. Criswell. For a similar assessment by SBC moderates, see James Flamming, "Response," in *The Proceedings of the Conference on Biblical Inerrancy 1987*, 143-44; James Robison, *The Unfettered Word* (Waco, TX: Word Books, 1987), cited in Ammerman, *Baptist Battles*, 84-85.

6. Gerald Sheppard, "Biblical Hermeneutics: The Academic Language of Evangelical Identity," *Union Seminary Quarterly Review* 32 (1977): 84, 90, 92.

maining in dialogue in some way with the concept of biblical inerrancy. But even if, for the sake of argument, we would grant the point that differences between the two parties over the nature of biblical authority and hermeneutics do have a strongly sociological character, I would still contend that finding a theological way in which both sides could remain in dialogue about these concepts would be ecumenically significant. It would be significant because ultimately no other topic divides the parties theologically in the sense of being an ecumenical *Grundverschiedenheit* that justifies their separation.

However, I am not willing to cede the argument to the sociologists that quickly. Ultimately, I do not think lifestyle and socio-ethical (public policy) differences among American Christians authorize the two-party analysis. For example, while many evangelicals may abstain from alcohol, that is an expectation in many mainline Methodist and Baptist churches too. On public policy issues I would further argue that there is actually a remarkable commonality in the statements that come from church bodies on both sides of the so-called two-party dividing line. Granted, one can offer counterexamples such as the coalition built between the Roman Catholic Church and the Religious Right on sexual issues and parochial education.[7] However, proponents of the two-party analysis would seem to have lost their case if Roman Catholicism and the Religious Right were to be seen as together forming one of the parties. Evangelicals and fundamentalists insist that theological differences divide them from Roman Catholicism. (In fact, some evangelicals and fundamentalists do not even see themselves as one party, since some fundamentalists do not regard evangelicals as even distant allies.) Consequently, the two parties of American Christianity very noticeably break down into three parties (or, as I will imply below, even more parties) at odds with each other.

Setting two-party analysis aside, I would still argue that overcoming theological tensions between the Protestant mainline and evangelical movements does seem a worthy task in view of the obvious tensions that seem to exist between them. The preceding discussion has provided some warrant for the contention that such tensions can only be resolved by finding suitable middle ground on the question of biblical authority and

---

7. The full arguments with thorough documentation for these claims are available in two books of mine, *The Evangelical Movement: Growth, Impact, Controversy, Dialog* (Minneapolis: Augsburg Publishing House, 1988); and *The Cutting Edge: How Churches Speak on Social Issues* (Geneva and Grand Rapids: WCC Publications and Wm. B. Eerdmans Publishing Co., 1993).

hermeneutics. Happily, precisely those kinds of developments have been transpiring in the broader Protestant academy in recent years.

Two developments seem especially pertinent. The first is that a path has been opened toward a new middle ground as a result of the "liberalization" of the evangelical movement. I speak here of the gradual endorsement by a growing number of evangelical scholars of the historical-critical approach to the biblical text and the increasing use by evangelicals of Neo-Orthodox theological models for appropriating the results of that new scholarship. One thinks, for example, of the controversies surrounding the theological developments on the Fuller Seminary campus nearly since its founding, as well as the emergence of ecumenically oriented evangelical leaders like Ron Sider, Jim Wallis, Donald Dayton, Cecil Robeck, and others associated with the so-called Catholic evangelical movement.[8]

The second development is to be found in the rise of postliberal narrative theology within the larger academy — a theological method that has also been appropriated by a number of prominent evangelicals. The

8. For the best analysis of these developments at Fuller, see George Marsden, *Reforming Fundamentalism: Fuller Seminary and the New Evangelicalism* (Grand Rapids: Wm. B. Eerdmans Publishing Co., 1987). See the Fuller Theological Seminary *Statement of Faith* (1979), III, which affirms only that the Bible is the "written word of God, the only infallible rule of faith and practice." Such an endorsement of the "limited infallibility" of Scripture, insulating the Bible's infallibility from questions concerning its historical accuracy, is typical of Neo-Orthodoxy and its claim that the Bible recounts a special "salvation-history," and so is not necessarily historically reliable. See Karl Barth, *Church Dogmatics*, Vol. I/1, ed. G. W. Bromiley and T. F. Torrance (4 vols.; Edinburgh: T. & T. Clark, 1935-69), 373-78; Oscar Cullmann, *Christ and Time*, trans. Floyd V. Filson (London: SCM Press, 1951), 99. Fuller's concept of the Bible as "written word of God" conforms precisely with the wording of Barth, *Church Dogmatics*, Vol. I/1, esp. 111ff., and his discussion of the "threefold form" of the Word of God.

With regard to evangelical involvement in ecumenism, see, for example, the "Open Letter," prepared by evangelicals participating in the WCC Vancouver Assembly, in *TSF Bulletin* 7 (September-October 1983): 18-19; *Evangelical-Roman Catholic Dialogue on Mission* (1977-84); *Roman Catholic-Pentecostal Dialogue* (1976); *The Chicago Call: An Appeal to Evangelicals* (1977); Donald W. Dayton, "Yet Another Layer of the Onion: Or Opening the Ecumenical Door to Let the Riffraff in," *The Ecumenical Review* 40/1 (January 1988): 87-110; Stan Grenz, *Revisioning Evangelicalism* (Downers Grove, IL: InterVarsity Press, 1993).

The argument by Douglas Jacobsen and William Vance Trollinger, Jr., "Evangelical and Ecumenical: Re-Forming a Center," *The Christian Century* (July 13-20, 1994): 683, that Billy Graham has always practiced an ecumenical posture could be taken as support for claiming that the developments in the evangelical movement noted above are in fact indicative of an already existing middle ground between the two parties in American Protestantism.

remainder of this essay will briefly outline the rudiments of this theological model, describe some evangelical reactions to it, and indicate how,
theologically as well as sociologically, this model represents a most promising theological formulation for expressing and marshalling the spiritual
yearnings of the American Protestant center.

Postliberal Narrative Theology and the Protestant Center

Postliberal biblical narrative theology had its modern origins largely
within the mainline Protestant orb. It developed on the campus of Yale
University among the students and spiritual heirs of H. Richard Niebuhr
and was built on the New Critical literary analytic predispositions being
articulated by important figures in the institution's English Department.
In describing this theological model, I refer to the work of George Lindbeck, Hans Frei, and to some extent Brevard Childs.[9] The fundamental
common commitment of all of the various proponents of the postliberal
biblical narrative approach is that the Bible as a whole is to be construed
as a kind of realistic narrative. As such, the truth of faith need not await
scientific and historical findings before laying claim to being authoritative.

The postliberal narrative model is not to be confused with so-called
"story" approaches to theology which have become standard fare in many
mainline denominations. The postliberal version does not advocate the
mere retelling of secular stories as the best way to communicate the
gospel.[10] Rather, the postliberal biblical narrative approach advocates the

---

9. George A. Lindbeck, *The Nature of Doctrine* (Philadelphia: Westminster Press,
1984); Hans W. Frei, *The Identity of Jesus Christ* (Philadelphia: Fortress Press, 1975);
Hans W. Frei, *Types of Christian Theology*, ed., George Hunsinger and William C. Placher
(New Haven: Yale University Press, 1992); Brevard S. Childs, *Introduction to the Old
Testament as Scripture* (Philadelphia: Fortress Press, 1979); Brevard S. Childs, *The New
Testament as Canon: An Introduction* (Philadelphia: Fortress Press, 1985), esp. 544ff. (for
his views on the differences and commonalities with his colleagues' views). For a more
detailed discussion of the biblical narrative approach and the commonalities among its
adherents, see my *The Integrity of Biblical Narrative: Story in Theology and Proclamation*
(Minneapolis: Fortress Press, 1990), esp. 15ff.

10. By a "Story" approach to theology I have in mind efforts to correlate secular
stories with the biblical accounts, often subsuming both under an ontology which is
said to be of a "story" character, such as is exemplified in the thought of Paul Ricoeur,
Time and Narrative, trans. Kathleen McLaughlin and David Pellauer (3 vols.; Chicago,
University of Chicago Press, 1984-88), Vol. 2, 29-60, 156-60; Vol. 3, 158-59, 179; Robert
McAfee Brown, "My Story and The Story," *Theology Today* 32 (1975): 171; James Wm.

use of biblical accounts and images (interpreted as realistic literature, rather than as primitive symbols for expressing some foundational religious experience) as world-constituting norms for Christians. In the Bible, the faithful learn who they are.

The Bible's stories and their related images portray a "world" in which the faithful come to see themselves as participants in God's historic drama. This worldview, in turn, helps orient these Christians in their daily interactions with everyday reality. Such an approach, as Frei and other proponents of this model have demonstrated, bears marked affinities with pre-Enlightenment theological models evidenced in Luther's, Calvin's, and Augustine's uses of Scripture.[11]

McClendon, Jr., *Ethics*, Vol. 1: *Systematic Theology* (Nashville: Abingdon Press, 1986), 35, 37-38, 40, 62, 105, 108, 147, 154, 169, 171, 172, 174, 183, 212, 225, 242-43, 256-57, 301, 310, 314, 328ff.; Johann Baptist Metz, "A Short Apology of Narrative," *Concilium* 5/9 (May 1973): 84-85, 93-96; Edward Schillebeeckx, *Jesus, Die Geschichte von einem Lebenden* (Freiburg/Basel/Wien, 1975), 69; Leonardo Boff, *Kleine Sakramentenlehre* (Düsseldorf, 1976), 15, 16ff., 32, 41ff.; James H. Cone, *God of the Oppressed* (New York: Seabury Press, 1975), 30-31; Sallie M. TeSelle, *Speaking in Parables* (Philadelphia: Fortress Press, 1975), 125, 138, 139.

This approach has also come to dominate the discipline of Homiletics. See, e.g., Eugene Lowry, *Doing Time in the Pulpit* (Nashville: Abingdon Press, 1985), 40, 58, 74-77, 83-84, 87; David Buttrick, *Homiletic: Moves and Structures* (Philadelphia: Fortress Press, 1987), esp. 10-11, 113, 116, 118, 259, 261, 269-70, 278-80, 321-23, 333-63, 375, 414-18, 435-36.

For a more detailed comparison of biblical narrative and story models of theology, see my *The Integrity of Biblical Narrative*, 53-60.

11. For detailed arguments and documentation for this case, see Hans W. Frei, *The Eclipse of Biblical Narrative* (New Haven: Yale University Press, 1974), 2-3, 17-50; Ellingsen, *The Integrity of Biblical Narrative*, esp. 43-51. The biblical narrative commitment to interpreting present reality as a figure of the biblical world is evident in Augustine, *The Confessions* (399), Bk. XIII; and Martin Luther, *The Gospel for Christmas Eve* (1521), in *D. Martin Luthers Werke, Kritische Gesamtausgabe* (Weimarer Ausgabe), Vol. 10 (56 vols.; Weimar: Hermann Böhlaus Nachfolger, 1906-61), 58-62 (English translation: *Luther's Works*, Vol. 52, ed. Jaroslav Pelikan and Helmut Lehmann [55 vols.; St. Louis: Concordia Publishing House; Philadelphia: Fortress Press, 1955-86], 9-10).

Elsewhere, in his *Sermon on John 2:13-15* (1538), in *D. Martin Luthers Werke*, Vol. 46, 726 (English translation: *Luther's Works*, Vol. 22, 218), Luther reflects the commitments of the biblical narrative model when he bypasses questions about the gospel's historical accuracy, despite apparent conflicts in favor of attention to the canonical text. Likewise, his argument for the Resurrection of Jesus in *Commentary on I Corinthians* (1533), in Weimarer Ausgabe, Vol. 36, 492-530 (English translation: *Luther's Works*, Vol. 28, 68-98), parallels the biblical narrative approach. In accord with this theological model, the Reformer makes no effort to argue for the historical credibility of Jesus' Resurrection, but concentrates solely on the Word and its logical implication that Christians cannot remain Christian if they deny the Resurrection. Though John Calvin,

MARK ELLINGSEN

Given the affinities between the postliberal biblical narrative model and many pre-Enlightenment hermeneutical approaches, it is hardly surprising to discern affinities between this hermeneutic and the homiletical hermeneutic which characterizes those religious traditions that have never become enmeshed in the two-party controversies of American Protestantism. I refer here especially to historically ethnic Protestant traditions like the African-American Christian community and the Lutheran and Free Church traditions. (Though not drawing their membership from any particular ethnic group, the holiness movement, at least in its nineteenth-century origins, might also be identified as a tradition belonging to this non-Enlightenment, non-two-party "middle ground.") These churches represent a third way of sorts, fitting neatly in neither party. While one branch of Lutheranism (my own Evangelical Lutheran Church in America) and a number of historic African-American denominations belong to the established ecumenical mainstream councils, one can hardly claim that these bodies are at the forefront of theological liberalism. Likewise, while many of these traditions are functionally evangelical in theology and piety, most would not want to wear the evangelical label uncritically.[12]

Typically, these traditions of the Protestant center have proceeded with the supposition, shared by postliberal biblical narrative theology, that the Bible is authoritative in a general sense and that taken as a whole it provides a framework for interpreting our reality. Modern scientific or rationalist models do not function as frameworks for interpreting the Bible in these Christian subcultures. Moreover, members of these traditions who have not been unduly influenced by the fundamentalist par-

Institutes of the Christian Religion (1559), IV.viii.6, alludes to something like the divine dictation of Scripture, he employs a hermeneutic at many points in _ibid._, I.vi.3; II.xi.1, and in his _Commentary on a Harmony of the Evangelists_ (Lafayette, IN: Calvin Publications, n.d.), 12, which suggests the sort of figural interpretation typical of the postliberal biblical model.

12. For fuller discussions and documentation of such assessments of these traditions, see my _The Evangelical Movement_, 66-71, 147, 149; Donald W. Dayton, "The Holiness and Pentecostal Churches: Emerging from Cultural Isolation," _The Christian Century_ (August 15-22, 1979): esp. 788-89; Milton G. Sernett, "Black Religion and the Question of Evangelical Identity," in _The Variety of American Evangelicalism_, ed. Donald W. Dayton and Robert K. Johnston (Downers Grove, IL: InterVarsity Press, 1991), 142-45. Concerning the largely conservative character of African-American churches, see the conservative attitudes toward women's ordination in these churches reported in C. Eric Lincoln and Lawrence H. Mamiya, _The Black Church in the African American Experience_ (Durham, NC: Duke University Press, 1990), 292-93.

adigm do not insist that the Bible be construed as a rationally reliable set of "truths."

As we have seen, very similar commitments have been endorsed by proponents of the postliberal biblical narrative model. As those commitments have a certain pre-Enlightenment character, and as they converge with the hermeneutical commitments of the great pre-Enlightenment Christian tradition, it is valid to conclude that the traditions of the Protestant center, in endorsing these same commitments, are themselves to some extent pre-Enlightenment in their outlook.[13] It is little wonder, then, that the postliberal biblical narrative model of theology might resonate well with this Protestant center.

Recent survey data, in fact, indicate that the postliberal theological model does resonate with an American Protestant center that extends far beyond the bounds of the "middle ground" traditions we have just examined. Proponents of two-party analysis, however, have overlooked these survey data. Were they to attend to this information, particularly with regard to the public's views concerning biblical authority, such analysts might be forced to reconsider their assessments.

For example, consider the results of a June 1993 Gallup poll.[14] The poll revealed that 38 percent of the American public believed that the Bible is the actual Word of God, the absolute truth. It seems fair to conclude that at least a sizable portion of this group reflects a conservative evangelical or fundamentalist form of Protestant piety. A big surprise in the survey was that only thirteen percent regarded the Bible as a merely historical document: The number of theoretical atheists and/or card-carrying Christian liberals seems not to be very large. This leaves a significant group of Americans in the middle. According to the poll, forty-four

13. For relevant documentation of these points, especially pertaining to the view of biblical authority in these traditions, see my *The Evangelical Movement*, esp. 141-42, 166-67, 168-71. For further documentation to make the case of the convergence between the biblical narrative model and the characteristic (pre-Enlightenment) hermeneutic of these traditions, see George A. Lindbeck, "The Church's Mission to a Postmodern Culture," in *Postmodern Theology: Christian Faith in a Pluralist World*, ed. Frederic B. Burnham (New York: Harper & Row, 1989), 42-43; Paul Merritt Bassett, "The Theological Identity of the North American Holiness Movement: Its Understanding of the Nature and Role of the Bible," in *The Variety of American Evangelicalism*, esp. 76ff.; Theophus H. Smith, *Conjuring Culture: Biblical Formations of Black America* (New York: Oxford University Press, 1994), 250-54.

14. *Gallup Poll Monthly* (September 1993): 24ff. The poll also revealed that 47% of the public believes that God created humanity in its present form only 10,000 years ago, 35% believe in God-guided evolution, and only 11% believe in pure evolution.

percent of the public believe that the Bible is the inspired Word of God, but that it is not accurate in all details. This large sector of the American public (and this may well be an actual majority if, as is my hunch, some of the people who placed themselves in the Bible-is-absolutely-true group actually belong here) holds a position on the authority of the Bible which is "neither fish nor fowl," one that does not readily accommodate itself to the stereotypes of either of the two parties of American Protestantism. It is truly a position of the center.

When one analyzes the essence of the poll's results theologically, the way in which the postliberal biblical narrative model represents the opinions of the American pews is striking. Proponents of this theological model insist on the full authority (plenary inspiration) of the biblical accounts. When the Bible as a whole is construed in this way (i.e., as a kind of realistic narrative one should take at face value), then the text itself becomes the sole authority we have for understanding the characters portrayed in it, just as the "absolute truth" for understanding a novel's characters is only given by the text itself. In a similar vein, the postliberal biblical narrative model assumes it would be no more valid to dismiss a portion of the Bible as unessential to the work as a whole than it would be arbitrarily to skip two chapters of a novel.

It seems evident, then, that the inspired and authoritative character of the Bible as accounted for by the postliberal biblical narrative model is consistent with the plurality opinion of the American public regarding the authoritative character of the biblical text in its entirety. Likewise, the biblical narrative model's insistence that the authority and meaning of the Bible is not mitigated by historical-critical or scientific findings echoes the currently prevailing sentiments of the American public that the Bible is not necessarily accurate in all its details. Of course, sometimes even with a fictional novel the reader becomes so wrapped up in the story that the account takes on the sense of reality itself. Little wonder then that some Americans, reading the Bible with literary analytic suppositions akin to those of the postliberal biblical narrative model, sometimes assume that large segments of the biblical text are to be taken as if they were intentionally written to provide us with accurate scientific information about the world. The Gallup poll reflects this predictable conclusion, but that does not mean that all who respond in this manner would want to locate themselves at the extreme conservative end of the spectrum.[15] The ability of the postliberal biblical narrative model of theology to represent the

15. See n. 14, above, for relevant data.

plurality of the American public's opinions on biblical authority, far more comprehensively than any of the other contemporary theological alternatives, strongly suggests its rightful claim to function as the theological foundation of the American Protestant center. That center is larger than either of the so-called "two parties"; in fact, it is probably larger than the two combined.

Granted, it could be argued that data gained from polls are always inconclusive and that to make the case for an American Protestant center which is best represented by the postliberal biblical narrative model of theology can only be a tenuous conclusion. Polls, after all, often reflect the disposition of the pollsters and are thus to a certain degree dependent on the latest religio-social fashion, which might change within the year. To be sure, other recent survey data indicate compatible results with the 1993 Gallup poll we have considered.[16] Nevertheless, if we rely on polling data alone, the existence of a postliberal narrative theological center of American Protestantism remains too undefined to undermine the two-party paradigm.

To support these contentions we must turn to recent developments in the academy related to how the postliberal biblical narrative model has been received by different segments within American Protestantism. Here we see more concretely the blurring of lines that is taking place between evangelical theology, on the one hand, and mainline theology, on the other. An analysis of this dual reception process also provides insight as to why conflicts between the two American Protestant extremes have become more virulent in recent years, despite the existence of a significant middle ground of Protestant conviction.

Conservative and Liberal Receptions of Postliberal Biblical Narrative Theology

The postliberal biblical narrative model of theology has generally been regarded as a legitimate alternative within the mainline theological establishment. How could things have been different with the model's origins in one of the bastions of that establishment elite, Yale University? Still, some criticism of the model has been voiced. The most characteristic critique, offered by David Tracy and other like-minded analysts, is that

---

16. See, e.g., survey results of the Barna Research Group reported in "Evangelical Beliefs on Decline, Pollster Says," *The Christian Century* (December 14, 1994): 1185.

postliberal biblical narrative theology essentially relegates the doing of theology to "the Christian ghetto."[17] It is interesting to analyze the underlying suppositions of this critique. Essentially these critics seem discontent with the notion that theology revolves around the task of a religious community articulating its own self-understanding. Rather, they insist that theology is to be subsumed under a more foundational, transcendental scheme which validates all the ontic possibilities of human existence.[18]

Interestingly enough, critics of the postliberal biblical narrative model from within the evangelical movement have operated with a somewhat similar set of suppositions. They too have been enticed by the continental Enlightenment tradition to adopt an objectivist approach to the biblical text. This disposition has been heightened by the impact of *The Westminster Confession of Faith*, whose use of the language of inerrancy either encourages the endorsement of the concept or its militant repudiation, on the theological perspectives of many American Protestants.

Rather than concentrating on these criticisms of postliberal biblical narrative theology, I would like to examine in greater depth its positive reception, especially within the evangelical world. Since the model is largely recognized as a mainline theological option, its positive reception by evangelical scholars would place the postliberal biblical narrative model in a very strong position from which to claim standing as *the* centrist Protestant position. Within the evangelical domain we do see a number of prominent scholars speaking strongly in favor of the model. What is more, even the premier theological spokesman of the movement, Carl Henry, has engaged in dialogue with the postliberal biblical narrative model, articulating some appreciation for it.[19]

---

17. David Tracy, "Lindbeck's New Program for Theology: A Reflection," *The Thomist* 49 (1985): 465; Gary Comstock, "Two Types of Narrative Theology," *Journal of the American Academy of Religion* 55 (Winter 1987): 126; Lynn M. Poland, *Literary Criticism and Biblical Hermeneutics: A Critique of Formalist Approaches* (Chico, CA: Scholars Press, 1985), 120-37; Rowan D. Williams, "Postmodern Theology and the Judgment of the World," in *Postmodern Theology: Christian Faith in a Pluralist World,* ed. Frederic B. Burnham (New York: Harper & Row, 1989), 101.

18. See David Tracy, *Blessed Rage for Order: The New Pluralism in Theology* (New York: The Seabury Press, 1978), 55-56. For this observation, I am indebted to Frei, *Types of Christian Theology,* 3, 24.

19. Gabriel Fackre, *The Christian Story: A Narrative Interpretation of Basic Christian Doctrine,* rev. ed. (Grand Rapids: Eerdmans, 1984), 2-10, though at some points (6-7, 14-16, 26-30, 38-39), Fackre shows more affinities to the story approach to theology; Paul E. Larsen, *The Mission of a Covenant* (Chicago: Covenant Press, 1985), esp. 3-4, 12-13; Frank W. Spina, "Canonical Criticism: Childs versus Sanders," in *Interpreting God's Word*

Some of the convergences between the postliberal biblical narrative model of theology and the classic evangelical view of Scripture are obvious. The commitment of this mainline model to interpreting Scripture as a piece of literature, rather than as a sourcebook for the history of the early church, bears a striking similarity to evangelical commitments to the authority of the canonical text. The evangelical movement (at least as articulated by the International Council on Biblical Inerrancy) has likewise maintained that it is the canonical text, not precanonical sources, that ultimately is authoritative.[20] These commitments to the authority of the canonical text entail that all Scripture is seen as the Word of God, as there is no precanonical or extracanonical authority to stand over the text ruling against the authority of certain portions of it. The postliberal biblical narrative model also endorses the Bible's plenary authority. Its supposition that the Bible in toto is to be regarded as akin to a realistic novel entails that all portions of the book should command the reader's attention if the whole book is to be understood rightly. Just as one cannot truly understand a novel if one skips certain chapters, the same is true with Scripture.

The postliberal biblical narrative project, taken as a whole, effectively endorses the adequacy of human language for communicating divine

---

for Today, ed. Wayne McCown and James Massey (Anderson, IN: Warner, 1982), 188-89; Gerald T. Sheppard, "Canon Criticism: The Proposal of Brevard Childs and an Assessment for Evangelical Hermeneutics," *Studia Biblica et Theologica* (1976): 3-17; Douglas Jacobsen, "Re-visioning Evangelical Theology," *The Reformed Journal* (October 1985): 21; Roger E. Olson, "Whales and Elephants: Both God's Creatures But Can They Meet? (Evangelicals and Liberals in Dialogue)," *Pro Ecclesia* (Spring 1995); Carl F. H. Henry, "Narrative Theology: An Evangelical Appraisal," *Trinity Journal* 8 (1987): 3-19; Henry, *God, Revelation and Authority*, Vol. IV, 457-458; Henry, "Where Will Evangelicals Cast Their Lot?", in *Twilight of a Great Civilization: The Drift Toward Neo-Paganism* (Westchester, IL: Crossway, 1988), 73 (where Henry goes so far as to refer to one proponent of the narrative model, myself, as an "Evangelical brother").

For earlier and more detailed discussions of the convergences between the characteristic evangelical view of Scripture and the postliberal biblical narrative model, see my *The Evangelical Movement*, 355-87; "Dürfen Philosophische Theorien über Geschichte den Leib Christi Spalten?", *Evangelium/Gospel* (June/August 1985): 82-109.

20. International Council on Biblical Inerrancy, *The Chicago Statement on Biblical Hermeneutics* (1982), XVI. These commitments also seem evident in the appeal to a "grammatical-historical" interpretation of Scripture by Henry, *God, Revelation and Authority*, Vol. IV, 104, 392; Harold Lindsell, *The Battle for the Bible*, 14th printing (Grand Rapids: Zondervan, 1981), 37.

These commitments may be compared with Hans W. Frei, *The Eclipse of Biblical Narrative* (New Haven, CT: Yale University Press, 1974), esp. 1ff.; Childs, *Introduction to the Old Testament as Scripture*, 72-83, 485-86.

revelation, which is another typically evangelical position. Hans Frei, for example, has asserted that the written text is actually God's linguistic presence among God's people. A similar point has been made by Brevard Childs. He claims, much as many evangelicals do, that history per se is not a medium of revelation but only functions as revelation in the final form of the biblical text where normative history reaches its proper end as it is properly interpreted.[21] What else is this but an implicit affirmation of the verbal authority of Scripture? Is not the verbal inspiration of the Bible implied by these commitments?

Confidence in the adequacy of the Bible's use of human language for conveying divine revelation has led proponents of the postliberal biblical narrative model to share with the evangelical community a focus on the Bible's literal sense, its commonsense meaning. At least this is the case with regard to biblical texts that are written in literary genres that imply a realistic narrative. The leading mainline proponents of the postliberal biblical narrative model, like their evangelical counterparts, endorse the possibility of identifying the plain, descriptive meaning of such texts, irrespective of the interpreter's existential suppositions.[22]

When the biblical text is considered in light of these suppositions, proponents of the postliberal biblical narrative model arrive at other conclusions that are remarkably compatible with the evangelical mainstream. Virtually all of them, for example, affirm the unity of the Bible by arguing that a commonsense reading of the biblical text shows quite clearly that

21. Hans W. Frei, "Theology and the Interpretation of Narrative: Some Hermeneutical Considerations" (lecture presented at Haverford College, Haverford, PA, 1982), 18; Childs, *Introduction to the Old Testament as Scripture*, 76.

22. Frei, *Types of Christian Theology*, 15, 44; Frei, *The Identity of Jesus Christ*, xv, xvii; Frei, "Theology and the Interpretation of Narrative," 26; Childs, *The New Testament as Canon*, 28-29; Lindbeck, *The Nature of Doctrine*, 116, 101-2, 68. Cf. *The Chicago Statement on Biblical Hermeneutics*, VII, IX; Carl F. H. Henry, *God Who Speaks and Shows: Fifteen Theses, Part Two*, Vol. III of *God, Revelation and Authority*, 369, 359; Lausanne Congress Group Report, *Authority and Uniqueness of Scripture Report*, in *Let the Earth Hear His Voice*, ed. J. D. Douglas (Minneapolis: World Wide Publications, 1975), 996.

There are some points at which the major proponents of the biblical narrative model appear to compromise these commitments. My various books cite these particular texts and note that these qualifications are nothing more than either acknowledgments of the need for interpreters to work with certain formal presuppositions concerning the character of the biblical text (as narrative) or are remarks regarding how the biblical text is existentially appropriated as distinct from seeking its descriptive, literal meaning. See my *The Integrity of Biblical Narrative*, 34ff.; *A Common Sense Theology: The Bible, Faith, and American Society* (Macon, GA: Mercer University Press, 1995), 29-38.

the narrative accounts of Jesus' life, particularly his death and resurrection, are at the center of Scripture. (Other portions of Scripture embodying other kinds of literary genre, like the Epistles and Wisdom literature, are deemed as commentaries on this overarching narrative.)[23]

The numerous points of convergence between the postliberal biblical narrative model of theology and the characteristic evangelical view of biblical authority are striking indeed. We have already noted four such points: (1) the authority of the canonical text; (2) the Bible's unity; (3) the verbal and plenary character of its inspiration/authority; and (4) the possibility that a normative, literal meaning of certain pericopes can be identified. But the shared concerns of the postliberal biblical narrative model and evangelical views of the Bible are not exhausted by these points. Another point of contact is the postliberal biblical narrative model's insistence that the truth and authority of the biblical text, construed as literature, are not contingent upon verification by historical and scientific research. This claim seeks to establish Christian faith as a kind of distinct "language-game" (to use conceptions of Ludwig Wittgenstein on which these theologians draw) with the Bible serving as that language's lexicon. In this understanding, the Bible functions as an infallible guide within this language-game insofar as its authority and factual implications are uncritically accepted.[24]

The logic employed by many prominent evangelicals when arguing for the inerrancy of Scripture is very similar. For example, like the biblical narrative model, the International Council on Biblical Inerrancy claims that it is "not proper to evaluate Scripture according to standards . . . that are alien to its usage or purpose."[25] This kind of theological move (i.e.,

---

23. Childs, *Introduction to the Old Testament as Scripture*, 671; Frei, "Theology and the Interpretation of Narrative," 21-22. Cf. Henry, *God, Revelation and Authority*, Vol. IV, 468; Robert K. Johnston, *Evangelicals at an Impasse* (Atlanta: John Knox Press, 1979), 72; Lausanne Congress Group Report, *The Report of the Study Group on the Role of Hermeneutics in the Theology of Evangelization Report* (1974), in *Let the Earth Hear His Voice*, 1006; Church of God in Christ, *Official Manual* (Memphis, TN: COGIC Publishing House, 1973), 40. At least one prominent Anabaptist evangelical, John Howard Yoder, in "The Use of the Bible in Theology," in *The Use of the Bible in Theology: Evangelical Options*, ed. Robert K. Johnston (Atlanta: John Knox Press, 1985), 111, is even willing to speak of the entire canon as "narrative in its framework."

24. For their acknowledgment of indebtedness to categories of analytic philosophy such as language-game, see Frei, *The Eclipse of Biblical Narrative*, viii; Lindbeck, *The Nature of Doctrine*, 20; cf. Ludwig Wittgenstein, *Philosophical Investigations*, trans. G. E. M. Anscombe (New York: Macmillan Co., 1958), 2-5, 20-21.

25. International Council on Biblical Inerrancy, *The Chicago Statement on Biblical Inerrancy* (1978), XIII.

assigning the biblical accounts their own unique language-game status) is reflected among evangelicals who, like Carl Henry and even B. B. Warfield, claim that, because the biblical authors were not intending to teach ontology, their lack of scientific accuracy cannot imply the errancy of Scripture.[26] In fact, all evangelicals who, like Henry, operate with the method of presuppositionalism maintain that arguments for Christian truth are valid only if employed in the context of an initial presupposition (or faith) that God/Christ exists and has been revealed in Scripture. (It is on this basis that biblical inerrancy is then endorsed.) This is precisely the logic of the postliberal biblical narrative model of theology in drawing upon the notions of Wittgenstein, i.e., that the Bible, like every other language-game, has its own presuppositions which cannot be challenged by extraneous criteria.[27]

To the extent that even its arguments on behalf of the authority (and truth) of Christian faith parallel those of esteemed evangelicals, the postliberal biblical narrative model of theology seems well positioned to lay claim to represent the American Protestant center. It is an accepted mainline theological alternative which can also function legitimately as a valid evangelical theological option insofar as it converges with many prominent evangelical commitments. To be sure, proponents of this model do not expressly endorse the concepts of biblical infallibility or inerrancy. However, that seems not necessarily to preclude the model as a legitimate evangelical alternative. At least it seems not necessarily precluded if the

---

26. Henry, *God, Revelation and Authority,* Vol. IV, 201-2; B. B. Warfield, "The Antiquity and Unity of the Human Race," in *Princeton Theology 1812-1921,* ed. Mark A. Noll (Grand Rapids: Baker, 1983), 290-91; Gerhard Maier, *Das Ende der historisch-kritischen Method* (Wuppertal: Verlag Rolf Brockhaus, 1974), 71.

27. John P. Galbraith, *Why the Orthodox Presbyterian Church?* (Philadelphia: The Orthodox Presbyterian Church, n.d.), 3; Christian Reformed Church, *The Nature and Extent of Biblical Authority* (Grand Rapids, n.d.), 13-14, 23; Evangelical Congregational Church, *The Inspiration and Authority of the Bible* (Myerstown, PA, n.d.), 5-6; G. W. Bromiley, "The Church Doctrine of Inspiration," in *Revelation and the Bible,* ed. Carl F. H. Henry (Grand Rapids: Baker, 1958), 213; Francis Schaeffer, *The God Who Is There* (Downers Grove, IL: InterVarsity Press, 1968), esp. 87ff.; Robert Preus, "Notes on the Inerrancy of Scripture," *Concordia Theological Monthly* 38 (June 1967): 365, 372, 374-75. Henry, in *God, Revelation and Authority,* Vol. III, 384, even explicitly appeals to the philosophical models of Wittgenstein in arguing that Christian faith has its own proper methods of verification. For his use of the method of presuppositionalism, see his *God Who Speaks and Shows: Fifteen Theses, Part One,* Vol. II of *God, Revelation and Authority,* 307-8, 310, 319; ibid., Vol. III, 247, 428. There are some indications that even *The Chicago Statement on Biblical Inerrancy,* XV, Exp., employs this method.

evangelical community would concur with the former president of the theologically conservative Lutheran Church — Missouri Synod, Ralph Bohlmann, who in 1983 claimed that inerrancy is a necessary concept, though the term itself "is perhaps expendable."[28] Even evangelicals like Henry who employ the presuppositional methodology effectively relegate the term "inerrancy" to second-order status. It is a kind of logical conclusion drawn from prior presuppositions about God and God's means of revelation. Without employing the term, the postliberal biblical narrative model seems to treat the canonical text in essentially the same way. The Bible is inerrant in the sense that Scripture is regarded as being incapable of deceiving the Christian community or leading it away from the gospel and truth.

Evangelical Criticism and Postliberal Response

Despite the convergences, many evangelicals, particularly those who are most conservative, remain wary of the postliberal biblical narrative model. For example, despite his careful attention to and interest in the model's resources, Carl Henry has raised concerns. In an article which expressly responds to the postliberal biblical narrative model, Henry notes that there seems to be in the model an apparent dearth of interest in "all objective historical [referential] concerns," which he thinks implies a "revolt against reason" and a weakening of "universal truth claims."[29] These commitments bespeak the perdurance of a kind of foundationalism implicit in his theology and in the theology of many other evangelical theologians. (In an odd turn of events, it is also essentially the same critique as put forth by liberal theologian David Tracy.[30] I shall explore that point further in my conclusions.)

More pertinent here is the need to respond to Henry's misperception that the biblical narrative model neglects historical concerns. At one point in his article Henry claims that "it is difficult to find a categorical statement [by narrative theologians] that if Christ's body disintegrated in the tomb Christian faith would be impaired."[31] But in fact, a core

---

28. Ralph A. Bohlmann, "Lutherans and Inerrancy," *The Lutheran Witness* (March 1983): 34.

29. Henry, "Narrative Theology: An Evangelical Appraisal," 11, 19.

30. See n. 17, above, for pertinent references.

31. Henry, "Narrative Theology: An Evangelical Appraisal," 13.

commitment of Frei's version of the postliberal biblical narrative model is that evidence against the historicity of the resurrection would discredit Christian faith.

The character of the biblical text construed as realistic narrative entails a most significant claim. The Bible is a reality-constructing book. We may even rightly speak of the Bible's "tyrannical authority" in this regard.[32] The faithful are compelled to identify with the characters of the biblical text. They are called on to place themselves in biblical history, to interpret the issues and events of their contemporary lives in the context of the biblical world. In a sense, the biblical narratives function like an immigrant's native culture, shaping who he or she is (attitudes, manners, way of looking at life) while living in a foreign new land.[33]

The interconnections which Henry seeks between the canonical text and ordinary historical reality seem largely addressed at this point by proponents of the postliberal biblical narrative model. Canonical text and ordinary historical reality overlap not in objective science, but in the lives of the faithful who have been overwhelmed by the historical world of the biblical accounts. As a tyrannical authority, the world of scriptural history is irreplaceable and unsubstitutable. There can be no other Jesus than the One depicted in the canonical text.[34] On this point, Frei argues that Jesus is "most fully Himself [specific and unsubstitutable in his identity] in the Resurrection." In short, Jesus cannot be properly conceived unless he is regarded as the Risen One.[35] This line of thought has factual implications.

Frei and those who agree with him are not asserting that the resurrection accounts are making historical claims, i.e., that one must have historical evidence before believing in the resurrection. However, "because it is more nearly factual than not, reliable historical evidence *against* the

32. This phrase is employed by the literary critic Erich Auerbach, *Mimesis*, trans. Willard Trask (Princeton, NJ: Princeton University Press, 1953), 14-15, who heavily influenced framers of the biblical narrative model; cf. Frei, *The Eclipse of Biblical Narrative*, 3; Hans W. Frei, "The 'Literal Reading' of Biblical Narrative in the Christian Tradition," in *The Bible and the Narrative Tradition*, ed. Frank McConnell (New York: Oxford University Press, 1986), 72; Lindbeck, "The Church's Mission to a Postmodern Culture," 38; Childs, *Introduction to the Old Testament as Scripture*, 143.

33. See Lindbeck, *The Nature of Doctrine*, esp. 32-41, 64-66, 68.

34. Frei, *The Identity of Jesus Christ*, 139, 50; cf. Hans W. Frei, " 'Narrative' in Christian and Modern Reading," in *Theology and Dialogue: Essays in Conversation with George Lindbeck*, ed. Bruce Marshall (Notre Dame, IN: University of Notre Dame Press, 1990), 161.

35. Frei, *The Identity of Jesus Christ*, 49-50, 145.

resurrection would be decisive."[36] This claim that Christianity's truth could be disconfirmed by historical evidence that Jesus' body had been stolen or decayed is in accord with the centrality to Christian faith of Christ's resurrection.[37] It is also in accord with a literal reading of the canonical text. Only if the facticity of the resurrection is challenged are the claims of faith bankrupt (1 Cor. 15:17-19). Such a claim is not made by proponents of the postliberal biblical narrative model pertaining to the factual implications of other biblical accounts.

In short, there is much evidence to counter Henry's critique of the postliberal biblical narrative model for failing to offer "categorical statements" that faith would be impaired if Jesus had not risen.[38] This criticism has also been addressed quite specifically by Hans Frei:

> Of course I believe in the "historical reality" of Christ's death and resurrection, if those are the categories which we employ. But they weren't always the categories employed by the church. . . . If I am asked to use the language of factuality, then I would say, yes, in those terms, I have to speak of an empty tomb. In those terms I have to speak of the literal resurrection. But I think those terms are not privileged, theory-neutral, trans-cultural, an ingredient in the structure of the human mind and of reality always and everywhere for me, as I think they are for Dr. Henry.[39]

The tyrannical authority of the biblical narrative also entails for this model other connections with ordinary historical reality. While other biblical accounts are not fully significant in themselves, they do have their own literal meaningfulness as they function as "figures" or "types" pointing to Christ.[40] As such, as long as Christ's resurrection and the historicity of Christ's personhood are not discredited by hard evidence, the actual facticity of these other accounts is of no *ultimate* significance for faith.

To be sure, other biblical accounts are still significant for faith insofar as they contribute to the Christian worldview by depicting the Christ who has risen and still lives — i.e., they help comprise the Christian's "native

---

36. Ibid., 151. Also see my *The Evangelical Movement*, esp. 380; references to my other books in nn. 9 and 22.

37. See n. 23, above, for references.

38. See n. 31, above. Also see references to my books, cited in nn. 36, 22, 9, above, which provide such "categorical statements."

39. Hans W. Frei, "Response to 'Narrative Theology: An Evangelical Appraisal,'" *Trinity Journal* 8 (1987): 23-24.

40. Frei, *Identity of Jesus Christ*, 51, 139.

culture" to which we earlier alluded. Living under the Bible's "tyrannical authority" is like being so totally immersed in a culture that that culture's norms and myths are seen as self-evidently true. This way of construing the status of all the Bible's historical accounts on grounds of the postliberal biblical narrative model of theology seems most amenable to evangelical pieties. The facticity of biblical accounts other than Christ's resurrection is never even considered by one caught up by the Bible's "tyrannical authority." Biblical truth is never questioned; it is self-evident for faith.

This train of thought in no way need result in mere fideism, by which the claims of faith have no contact with ordinary historical reality. Self-evident cultural norms are not entirely free from the judgments of history, but their truth is largely determined by how well they function in promoting the quality of life of the members of that culture. It is on this basis, for example, that we have been prone in the last decade to speak of the errors of Marxism in contrast to the validity/truth of democracy. George Lindbeck has very literally adopted these insights and the image of a "culture" for understanding the status of the biblical accounts. Given this cultural metaphor, he argues, reliable social scientific evidence adduced against the ability of the biblical narratives to help the Christian community cope with reality would count against Christianity's truth.[41]

Lest the postliberal biblical narrative model's commitment to the validity of how the faithful assume the truth of the biblical accounts be deemed "a reflection of the revolt against reason," careful analysis of these operating assumptions in comparison with those of modern science readily alleviates this concern. Science, after all, proceeds with certain assumptions, just as the Christian assumes the truth of the biblical accounts. Just as scientists employ their assumptions (i.e., theories) without absolute proof in dealing with ordinary reality, and they continue to accept these theories as long as they are helpful in coping with data, so likewise Christians on grounds of their theological model properly assume the truth of the biblical accounts until they no longer help them cope with

41. Lindbeck, *The Nature of Doctrine*, esp. 131, 68. Even Brevard Childs does not rule out some sort of dialogue between the biblical canon and objective historical concerns. Insofar as he contends that the canon witnesses to the history of revelation, in *Old Testament Theology in a Canonical Context* (Philadelphia: Fortress Press, 1986), 6, 16, it would seem to follow that historical evidences which implied that Scripture did not accurately represent the historical development of the formation of the canon, while not decisively disproving the truth of Christian faith, would seem to count against its authority.

ordinary reality.[42] The operating assumptions of the postliberal biblical narrative model of theology is no more bereft of a proper use of reason than natural science is.

Even Henry's concern that historical referents are clouded by the postliberal biblical narrative model can be quickly dispatched. Frei's remarks, previously cited, indicate a readiness to account for the referential function of biblical language on grounds of his literary analytic theological suppositions.[43] However, George Lindbeck has made another important contribution to this subject by deploying Thomas Aquinas's views on religious language as a tool for conceptualizing how to describe the sense in which biblical narratives refer extra-textually.[44] Aquinas's awareness of the imperfect character of human language for depicting God entails that when we speak of God, we are merely affirming that there are certain concepts, unavailable to us, that are appropriate to God. To understand what is entailed by saying that God is good or to evaluate reports of divine miracles based on our human concepts of miracle or by means of our historical-critical tools is rather like evaluating a good marriage in an Eastern culture by the standards of a good marriage in American society.

With this construal of religious language, proponents of the postliberal biblical narrative model are enabled to claim an extra-textual referential function for the biblical texts while accounting for why these narratives cannot be verified by means of ordinary historical or scientific tools. Because these narratives are about God, our intellectual tools are inadequate for adjudicating the truth of their referential claims. This is why they must be evaluated only by means of literary analytic tools. Yet the extra-textual referentiality of these biblical accounts is by no means compromised.

---

42. For this analysis I am, of course, indebted to the work of Thomas S. Kuhn, *The Structure of Scientific Revolutions*, 2nd ed. (Chicago: University of Chicago Press, 1986), 4, 9-10, 36ff., 145. For an endorsement of Kuhn's model, see Lindbeck, "The Church's Mission to a Postmodern Culture," 50-51. For more detailed discussions of these issues, see my *A Common Sense Theology*, 42-44; *The Integrity of Biblical Narrative*, 59-60.

43. See nn. 29, 39 for pertinent references.

44. Lindbeck, *The Nature of Doctrine*, 66-67; cf. Thomas Aquinas, *Summa Theologica* (1265-73), I, Q.13, Art. 3. For a more detailed analysis, see my *A Common Sense Theology*, 42-44; *The Integrity of Biblical Narrative*, 41-43.

Conclusion

On every point raised by Henry, including his concern about the postliberal biblical narrative model's treatment of the historical referentiality of the canonical text, we have discerned the ability of this model to respond. It does not appear guilty of "a flight from history" or a "revolt against reason."[45] In view of these considerations, as well as the widely acknowledged, previously noted points of convergence between it and characteristic evangelical approaches to biblical authority, can it not fairly be deemed a legitimate evangelical theological option? As such, does the postliberal biblical narrative model of theology not lay a strong claim to representing the American Protestant center, insofar as it is the most viable mainline theological approach on the present scene which might also be acceptable to evangelicals?

Generally speaking, the points that I have been raising in response to evangelical critiques of this theological model were published prior to the critiques. Why, then, were they overlooked by many evangelicals like Henry? Why has this model not been more widely endorsed than it has already been within the evangelical movement? And why do liberal theologians like Tracy and others continue to indict the biblical narrative model as fideistic, when, as we have observed, it offers a most reasonable (scientifically credible) approach?

Perhaps the failure of these critics to take these other features of the postliberal biblical narrative model into account is a function of their misreading. Hans Frei has suggested that the critics' failure to appreciate how the biblical narrative model might in fact address their concerns is that they operate with a certain common supposition, which clearly differs from the pre-Enlightenment suppositions of his own theological model regarding the autonomy of the canonical text. It is helpful to explore these intuitions further in closing, as they shed more light on the nature of the American Protestant center previously identified by recent polls and also help account for the continuation of conflicts between the Protestant right and left in America.

According to Hans Frei, both Tracy and Henry (and like-minded theologians of both parties) share common philosophical assumptions rooted in the continental Enlightenment. Both share a common propensity, typical of theology since the eighteenth century, to subordinate the biblical text to a set of foundational, universally valid and philosophically derived

---

45. See n. 29, above, for the source of these quotations.

principles which function to correlate/explicate the biblical narrative and to evaluate the meaning and truth of its claims. Thus Tracy subsumes theology under a more foundational, transcendental scheme which validates all ontic possibilities of existence, and Henry calls for a unity of faith and reason in which "universal truth-claims" and unambiguous "historical referents" prevail. In both cases, the Bible's authority is necessarily evaluated by these other criteria.[46] This is a very different set of assumptions than the pre-Enlightenment ethos of the postliberal biblical narrative model of theology, which refuses to subordinate the canonical text to any interpretive scheme. Little wonder that the Protestant right and left would challenge these assumptions.

This analysis indicates that the two (most visible) parties in American Protestantism have more in common than is generally recognized. Despite all their differences, proponents of extremes on both the right and the left tend to interpret Scripture in light of certain philosophical assumptions regarding the nature of reality, giving priority to scientific and historical-critical models of truth. Awareness of the common Enlightenment suppositions which both of these parties affirm helps explain why two-party conflicts have been exacerbated during the past twenty-five years, even while the centrist position of the postliberal biblical narrative model was being developed and gaining recognition.

Given the commonly shared Enlightenment suppositions of both sides of this conflict within American Protestantism, it follows that whenever such Enlightenment suppositions are uncritically accepted only two options will be left. Either the Bible is seen as rationally and scientifically credible, or it is not! Generally speaking, as is notably evident in the present conflict within the Southern Baptist Convention, the two parties may also share in common the Puritan/Reformed tradition that introduces into the conversation a preoccupation with biblical infallibility.[47] This in turn forces participants to take sides on the question for or against the Bible's historical/scientific accuracy. Such a concern, however, has not been at the heart of a number of other non-Puritan traditions such as confessional Lutheranism, the Free Church tradition, and large segments of African-American Christianity. This is precisely why these traditions

---

46. Frei, *Types of Christian Theology,* esp. 23-25, 166. See nn. 18, 33, for appropriate references for Tracy and Henry.

47. *The Westminster Confession of Faith* (1647), I.9, is the Puritan document which introduced this consideration into the theological discourse of traditions influenced by the Puritan heritage.

better represent the American Protestant center than either liberalism or conservative evangelicalism. The polling data discussed above seem to suggest that a centrist pre-Enlightenment view is also that of the plurality of Americans in the pew, insofar as most of these believers are ready to accept the Bible as authoritative without the canonical text first needing to pass the Enlightenment bar of reason and criticism.

So why is this already existing center not more visible and accepted? I submit that the voice of this center has been effectively silenced by the dominance of Enlightenment suppositions among America's religious, cultural, political, and media elite, who seem only able to hear and attend to the two parties which share their core suppositions. They see the situation as a fight over power and dominance, but the real center is not suited to be heard in the institutions of power. With the center's potentially mediating voice effectively stifled, however, controversies in American Protestantism and in American society have quite expectedly become sharper and meaner.

My proposal is that in order to overcome these socio-religious controversies, American Protestants (if not American society) would be well served by appropriating insights of postliberal biblical narrative theology and its critique of an uncritical appropriation of the suppositions of the continental European Enlightenment. Similarly, we might start listening to the theology of the American pew more carefully. There is a center already in existence, but in order to see that center we will need explicitly to reject the Enlightenment theological and philosophical paradigms that have so dominated the American academy this century and into which too many Protestant leaders have been nurtured. That is to say, the American Protestant center of the present and future ironically seems to lie in our pre-Enlightenment past.[48]

---

48. My recently published book *A Common Sense Theology* outlines the broader socio-cultural implications that the reinvigorating of this center might have.

CHAPTER 23

"Two-Party" Rhetoric amid "Postmodern" Debates over Christian Scripture and Theology

GERALD T. SHEPPARD

My argument, in brief, is that a contemporary description of Protestantism in the United States in terms of two competing parties (i.e., "liberals" versus "conservatives") is misleading for two reasons. First, it depends too heavily on an assessment pertinent only to certain highly visible segments of Anglo-American Protestantism, specifically those who identify themselves as "mainline" or "mainstream," on the one hand, and as "evangelical," on the other. Second, it presupposes that we still live in the same "modern" situation that predominated from about the beginning of the nineteenth century until the late 1960s. But we no longer live in the era of modernity or according to its dominant episteme or "form of knowing."

Many social historians and philosophers now agree that, at a minimum, "we are living in a borderline era between modernity and a new, as yet inadequately theorized social situation."[1] These scholars see signs that our culture is undergoing a significantly new and systemic reorientation away from the older modern paradigm toward a significantly altered postmodern perception of reality. The magnitude of this shift is comparable in scope to the changes that took place in much of Europe between the Renaissance and the gradual emergence of the Classical Age during the second half of the seventeenth century, as well as between the

---

1. Steven Best and Douglas Kellner, *Postmodern Theory: Critical Interrogations* (New York City: Guilford Press, 1991), 261.

Classical and the Modern Age, which began to gain dominance around the beginning of the nineteenth century. Michel Foucault, who pioneered efforts to describe the effects of that earlier change from the Renaissance to the Classical Age, has spoken of an epistemic transformation extending across a wide spectrum of society.[2] Included in that process were Protestant biblical interpreters who began to perceive new ways of understanding for what had formerly been called "history," "literal sense," "author's intent," and the "scope" of biblical books.[3] Theologians, similarly, had to rethink the relation of theology to biblical studies, the sciences, medicine, and other domains of practical analysis. In our own day, all those same areas of concern are once again being reconceptualized.

If a postmodern analysis of our present situation has any validity at all, then the two-party model describes only the last strident voices of a now nearly obsolete older modern Protestantism, a modern Protestantism that was, like the entire modern project, prone to see the world in terms of oppositional dualisms (e.g., sacred versus secular, private versus public, civilization versus nature, and, in the case of biblical scholarship, historio-grammatical exegesis versus historical [or "higher"] criticism).

For many, if not most, biblical and theological scholars today, these kinds of dualisms fail to name the elements of the most significant real choices facing Protestants, precisely because major changes have already transformed the deep structures of how we view the world, including the Bible. While scholars cannot take credit for being the architects of these postmodern changes, they do properly serve the larger society by trying

---

2. Besides Foucault's many publications on these themes, an introduction to his more general theory can be found in *The Order of Things: An Archaeology of Human Sciences* (New York: Random House, 1970).

3. My own work in this area includes "The Geneva Bible and English Commentary, 1600-1645," in *The Geneva New Testament: The Annotated New Testament, 1602 Edition, with Introductory Essays,* ed. G. T. Sheppard (New York City: Pilgrim Press, 1989), 1-4; "Between Reformation and Modern Commentary: The Perception of the Scope of Biblical Books," in *William Perkins' A Commentary on Galatians (1617), with Introductory Essays,* ed. G. T. Sheppard (New York City: Pilgrim Press, 1989), xlii-lxxi; "Joseph Hall's Solomon's Divine Arts among Seventeenth-Century Commentaries, 1600-1645," and "The Role of the Canonical Context in the Interpretation of the Solomonic Books," in *Solomon's Divine Arts: Joseph Hall's Representation of Proverbs, Ecclesiates, and Song of Songs (1609), with Introductory Essays,* ed. G. T. Sheppard (Cleveland, OH: Pilgrim Press, 1991), 1-10 and 67-107; and "Christian Interpretation of the Old Testament between Reformation and Modernity," in *William Perkins' A Commentary on Hebrews 11 (1609), with Introductory Essays,* ed. John Augustine (New York: The Pilgrim Press, 1991), 46-70.

to describe the strengths and weaknesses of this new perception, and the new choices facing us within this reconstituted vision of reality. For these reasons, the two-party model misguides us by looking back nostalgically at older modern possibilities, just when we need to be the most sensitive to elemental changes in how we perceive reality within a postmodern, global culture and society.

What remains most useful about the two-party model is how it describes the survivals of modernity in a late modern situation. Because modern "conservatives" and "liberals" both "see" the world and the biblical text "objectively" through a similar set of spectacles, to use a commonplace premodern expression, they essentially agree enough to disagree. They thus situate themselves in symbiotic juxtaposition to each other, like "worthy" opponents who have squared off against each other face to face, while their lack of historical self-awareness allows them to assume that in that contest they are merely continuing a public struggle that has gone on through all human history. The apperceptive capacities of modern conservatives and liberals, in other words, predetermine what options they can "imagine" as "valid" responses to current social, moral, hermeneutical, political, and/or theological issues in the commonly construed world they together have envisioned. For this reason, the Protestants who best fit within the two-party model may represent only anemic apologetic voices from an older modern age. They thrive on the polarities of an outdated set of choices and goad each other into asserting the most extreme dualistic positions.

Emerging Protestant Postmodernisms

However, a rich variety of promising "postmodern" possibilities have been taking shape since the late 1960s within the very same segments of Protestantism that the two-party model tries to interpret: the upper strata of Anglo-American Protestantism. Many of these more recent approaches explicitly use older modern historical criticisms, but in a manner unanticipated by the modern period from which they were derived. One sign of the infancy of these newer efforts since the 1960s is the problem scholars have with labels for their work.

For example, in the early 1970s Brevard Childs occasionally employed the label "canonical criticism" for his own new approach — a term he borrowed from James Sanders. However, Sanders began to use canonical criticism as a method to rediscover a consistent factor in the process of tradition history, before and after the Bible, by which one could explain why the same normative tradition might properly lead to greatly different interpretations of it in varied times and circumstances. Sanders called this factor "the canonical hermeneutic," while acknowledging that not every interpretation found in Scripture itself met that standard. For that reason, since the mid-seventies Childs has stopped using the term "canonical criticism" due to its misconstrual as merely one more form of modern "criticism" that needed to be added to all the other available modern "methods," and he began to speak of his own work as based on a "canonical *approach*," oriented more toward an effort to describe "the shape" or "the scope" of a scriptural text, rather than describing the factors that went into the process of its composition. From Childs's perspective, the scriptural text itself must determine which modern historical criticisms will prove the most helpful in illuminating it as a scriptural text. In other words, every scriptural text has its own unique and unpredictable lines of continuity and discontinuity between the words and traditions of that text and the particular prehistory that informed it. Based on the specific nature of that continuity and discontinuity, different historical criticisms, as well as other methods, may prove essential or not to postmodern scholars as they read a scriptural text *as Scripture*.

But postmodernism is not one thing; Childs's approach is not the only option. Other postmodern scholars have put their primary emphasis on either social-scientific assessments or literary approaches, some with a particular stress on intertextuality and/or semiotics. A great variety of social-scientific approaches use biblical or prebiblical texts to reconstruct patterns of behavior, if not "ideal types," which persist across the centuries. So, the prophets depicted in the Old and New Testaments seem to fit well an anthropological model of ecstatic religion, while the "conquest" stories in Joshua may provide evidence in support of an internal revolt, abetted by some liberated Hebrew slaves, among Canaanite peasants in ancient Palestine. These and other social-scientific studies, at a minimum, criticize the older modern models for writing a "history" about persons and events that neglected socio-economic, cultural-anthropological, and political factors integral to the social construction of reality in ancient Israel and the original Jesus movement.

Literary approaches in contemporary biblical studies have provided a robust and equally diverse set of options, often directly departing from an older modern priority given to the historical dimensions of texts. Some strategies openly espouse a "synchronic" analysis of one variety or another, while others prefer evidence of intertextuality over signs of extra-textual reference. Ideological criticism, especially feminist close readings of biblical texts, have proliferated since the 1970s. Sophisticated linguistic and philosophical hermeneutical theories now inform a wide range of textual descriptions. While some historically conservative scholars have tried to find in signs of a text's fastidious, aesthetic "coherency" evidence for a single traditional "author," others raise political, cultural, gender-related, or racial issues with or without attention to religion and theology. In general, almost all of the newer literary assessments go well beyond the "historicism" and "formalism" so widespread in older modern literary theory. Again, most of these strategies participate in a postmodern impulse to expose the limits of modern theory, without necessarily rejecting the continuing value of modern criticisms as essential aids in the new questions we now ask of biblical texts.

From the academic discipline of theology, rather than biblical studies, we can see similar tendencies to displace the dominance of older modern theory. The late theologian Hans Frei offered in the opening decades of the 1970s a self-consciously "postmodern" reformulation of how to interpret biblical narratives, with an attack upon all consistently referential, modern theories of interpretation. While many scholars have rushed to describe his work as support for a "narrative theology," Frei himself disavowed that label. Later, the "socio-linguistic" proposal of George Lindbeck built partly on Frei's work, but employed a more rigid model of language theory than Frei himself had advocated. In sharp contrast to the two-party model, Lindbeck resists labeling his proposal simply "conservative," though it allows for an orthodox confession of Christian faith. By resisting all "foundationalist" assumptions, as well as "first order truth claims," Lindbeck breaks free of the modern way of framing the major theological questions. Likewise, David Tracy has pursued his theological work by declaring his preference for "literary approaches" over historical-critical interpretations of Scripture, while tacitly affirming the validity of historical criticisms. Some theological efforts by biblical scholars also seek to minimize attention to the "diachronic" dimension of biblical texts, while others, such as Phyllis Trible's "rhetorical criticism," seek initially to use older modern historical criticisms, and then go "beyond" them literarily and theologically.

Finally, we can examine a number of "postmodern" proposals recently put forth by representatives of marginalized Protestant groups, including Hispanics, African Americans, other non-Anglo-American communties, and a plethora of lower-class Anglo-American churches. These efforts in academic publications have usually crisscrossed the lines drawn between conservatives and liberals. As one example, Cornel West's two-volume collection of essays, *Prophetic Thought in Postmodern Times: Beyond Eurocentrism and Multiculturalism,* proposes a radical political position that on some levels sounds "liberal," but on other levels decidedly does not. In particular, the "prophetic" theme which he employs conveys a densely confessional claim far closer to the premodern Christian tradition than to older modern reformulations of it.[4] Similarly, Eldin Villafañe's *The Liberating Spirit: Toward an Hispanic American Pentecostal Social Ethic* makes eclectic appeals to modern criticisms while aiming at "a deeper understanding of the 'mystery of iniquity,'" expressed in terms outside the conventional modern categories of conservative and liberal.[5] Consequently, we ought not to be surprised if contemporary historians of Protestantism in the United States would have trouble knowing whether West and Villafañe belong accurately to either of the "two parties." Obviously, these two examples barely touch the surface of an extensive array of postmodern contributions by marginalized church communities and their theologians.

In sum, the landscape of Protestantism in the United States since the late 1960s has been irrevocably altered. At the present moment, a wide diversity of emergent postmodern proposals (some of which do not explicitly refer to themselves as postmodern) has already begun to take the center stage away from older modern debates, though they have not yet displaced entirely the highly polarized voices of older modern dissent. For the reasons listed above, I think the two-party model fails to do justice to the most promising varieties of contemporary Protestantism in the United States.

The Two-Party Model in Socio-Historical Perspective

At the outset, the "two-party" label invites a question about what is meant by the term "party." This word may remind us of familiar tensions in American politics of the United States, such as the conflict between the Democratic and the Republican "parties," or between labor "parties" and

---

4. Cornel West, *Prophetic Thought in Postmodern Times: Beyond Eurocentrism and Multiculturalism,* 2 vols. (Monroe: Common Courage Press, 1993). See also his *Prophetic Fragments* (Grand Rapids: Eerdmans, 1988).

5. Eldin Villafañe, *The Liberating Spirit: Toward an Hispanic American Pentecostal Social Ethic* (Grand Rapids: Eerdmans, 1993), 181.

management. Often in academic discussions, the term "parties" implies two "cultures," and we might think of the situation in Canada, where the Quebec party opposes other parties dominated by the rest of a predominantly English-speaking Canada. In Canada these two cultures within one nation operate so separately from each other that they have been called two "solitudes."[6] The two parties may conflict with each other on new issues, even before either party fully rationalizes why they supposedly disagree with each other.

Certainly in the United States the contemporary liberal and conservative counterparts to the older fundamentalist-liberal divisions of the 1920s have nurtured an insularity from each other as they have also sought to take up positions at odds with each other on new issues that would ensure that their division and insularity would remain. Even some issues that at first glance seem blatantly theological may be better understood in this sociological manner as rhetorical strategies in support of a social identity rather than being explicitly theological in nature. So, for example, the social, cultural, and political consequences of affirming "inerrancy" may be far more clear than how that concept actually contributes to a doctrine of Scripture.[7] My point is simply that the two "parties" may survive as "parties" long after the logic that gave rise to them has become otiose.

The two-party model requires us to consider carefully the identification of each of those positions with modernity. Jean Miller Schmidt has stated that: "For all its diffuseness and apparent imprecision, the concept of modernization has seemed to me . . . to be a fruitful interpretive framework for looking at the relationship between public and private in American religion."[8] She concludes that the two parties can be distinguished by how each of them has responded to modernity and to each other. But not being a two-party partisan herself, she also challenges the caricatures each party draws of the other. She reminds us, for example, that modern

---

6. This expression, borrowed from a poetic line of Rilke about two lovers and applied to the Canadian situation, occurs in a significant novel, Hugh MacLennan's *Two Solitudes* (Toronto: Macmillan, 1945).

7. For this argument in more detail, see my "Biblical Hermeneutics: The Academic Language of Evangelical Identity," *Union Seminary Quarterly Review* 32 (Winter 1977): 81-94.

8. Jean Miller Schmidt, "Reexamining the Public/Private Split: Reforming the Continent and Spreading Scriptural Holiness," in Russell E. Richey, Kenneth E. Rowe, and Jean Miller Schmidt, eds., *Perspectives on American Methodism: Interpretive Essays* (Nashville: Abingdon Press, 1993), 245.

social gospelers ultimately sought to invigorate traditional Christian faith and, conversely, that conservatives were as deeply invested as liberals in some modern ideas and social practices.[9]

In the current scholarly emphasis on the social history of religious institutions, however, two-party rhetoric still trades upon the notion of a trajectory of conflict that supposedly goes back to the bitter acrimony of the fundamentalist-liberal split. In an effort to nuance that trajectory, Robert Wuthnow has argued for a significant change in the relationship between fundamentalists and liberals, and their counterparts, in the years following World War II. He says that from that time until "well into the 1950s" we can observe them "burying the differences of the past and focusing on concerns about which there was greater consensus."[10] However, the ferment around controversial social issues since the 1960s partly explains the resurgence of a sharp division between what we call today "the two parties."[11] At a minimum, the social history of the two parties pertains primarily to groups that were "mainstream" together in the 1920s and were fully influenced by modernity, unlike many other Protestants who were socially marginalized due to racism, class prejudice, or a self-chosen insularity based on ethnic nationalism, theological peculiarities, a rejection of things modern, or other reasons.

Within this view of modernization and the two parties, we benefit greatly by giving attention to neglected groupings of Protestant churches within the United States, especially "submodern" Protestants like Pentecostals. It is certainly not an accurate social-historical description to label all Pentecostals (including African-Americans, Hispanics, Koreans, and others) "fundamentalists." One interesting sign of the nonfundamentalist impulse of Pentecostals is the remarkably large numbers of them who prefer now to attend "liberal" or "mainstream" denominational seminaries instead of going to the conservative evangelical ones. Even the more "fundamentalistic" wing of Pentecostalism represented by the Assemblies of God waited until 1961 to include in its "Statement of Fundamental Truths" an affirmation of the virgin birth, substitutionary atonement, and the bodily resurrection of Jesus Christ — three of the so-called five tenets of fundamentalism. This revision occurred at a timely moment, one year after the denomination's General Superintendent, Thomas F. Zimmerman,

---

9. Schmidt, "Reexamining," 246.

10. Robert Wuthnow, *The Restructuring of American Religion* (Princeton: Princeton University Press, 1988), 12.

11. Wuthnow, *The Restructuring of American Religion*, 12, 132-72.

was elected president of the National Association of Evangelicals (1960-62).[12]

Likewise, Pentecostals have held contradictory positions, combining premodern and complex weddings of *ad hoc*, intuitive ideas informed by modern points of view. For example, a primarily submodern Anglo-Pentecostalism in 1914 began to describe "speaking in tongues" in thoroughly modern and extrabiblical language as "the initial physical evidence." Pentecostal interpreters of "the last days" often used fundamentalist dispensational charts while ignoring the anti-Pentecostal logic behind their theological assumptions about the "Church Age."[13] A chart that derives from a particular modern fundamentalist hermeneutic at variance with Pentecostalism might still be used by Pentecostals for an entirely different reason. The colorful charts of the dispensationalists seemed to shed light on esoteric verses of some very difficult biblical books (Daniel, Ezekiel, and Revelation). The illustrative power of the charts themselves won over Pentecostals who usually could not have cared less about the fundamentalist justification for these charts on the basis of a nuanced, peculiarly modern theory of ecclesiology in relation to eschatology. Donald Dayton has examined these dynamics on a much wider scale to show how divergent forms of nineteenth-century Protestantism belatedly *became* "fundamentalist" or "evangelical."[14] Consequently, the modernism of both fundamentalists and liberals often reached the lower classes and racially marginalized groups in a piecemeal fashion, with astonishing indirection, and by amalgamations with folk culture in ways

12. Cf. Timothy B. Cargal, "Beyond the Fundamentalist-Modernist Controversy: Pentecostals and Hermeneutics in a Postmodern Age," *Pneuma* 15 (Fall 1993): 163-87; and my "Word and Spirit: Scripture in the Pentecostal Tradition," *Agora* 1 (Spring 1978): 4-5, 17-22 and 2 (Summer 1978): 14-19. See also Douglas Jacobsen, "Knowing the Doctrines of Pentecostals: The Scholastic Theology of the Assemblies of God, 1930-55," published in the papers for a conference on "Pentecostal Currents in the American Church" (Pasadena: Fuller Theological Seminary, March 10-12, 1994), and my "Biblical Interpretation after Gadamar," *Pneuma* 16 (Spring 1994): 121-41.

13. For a more detailed argument, see my "Pentecostalism and the Hermeneutics of Dispensationalism: The Anatomy of an Uneasy Relationship," *Pneuma* 6 (Fall 1984): 5-33.

14. Donald Dayton, *Discovering an Evangelical Heritage* (New York: Harper and Row, 1976). Note recently his debate with George Marsden in *Christian Scholar's Review* 23 (September 1993). Here I would disagree with Marsden's assumption that the essence of fundamentalism was "anti-modernism." See his argument with Dayton on this matter on 37 of his "Response to Don Dayton," in the *Christian Scholar's Review* cited above.

modern theorists could not possibly anticipate.[15] Two-party rhetoric implies a consistency to the influence of modernization greatly at odds with the experience of these other Protestant groups.

Developments since 1960

We need to consider again why controversial issues since the 1960s have energized the present polarization of some Protestants in terms of two parties. Why do the best examples of "conservatives" within the two-party scheme so often appear today more like the fundamentalists of the 1920s and 1930s than they do the "evangelicals" and "neoevangelicals" after World War II and into the 1950s? One factor has been the erosion of modern ways of thinking since the 1960s. We are still just beginning to sense the shock wave of social and intellectual disequilibrium that has accompanied this major transition. Today, a great variety of "postmodern" proposals have already begun to appear, and many things we once thought we knew now require careful redefinition (e.g., "parties," "institutions," "church," "Scripture," "politics," "preaching," "history," "revelation," "tradition," "literal sense," "interpretation").

In practical terms, the loss of an older modern consensus in the 1960s eroded the very foundation upon which some more subtle mediating positions between the alleged two parties had previously flourished (e.g., neoevangelicalism, "young evangelicals," the biblical theology movement, neoorthodoxy). So, for example, Sydney Ahlstrom argued that H. Richard Niebuhr's *Radical Monotheism and Western Culture* offered "a requiem for the neoorthodox period, and an opening into the secular theology and non-religious interpretation of Christianity for which the 1980s would be remembered."[16] At the same time, divisive social issues have more and more demanded that churches take stances on public issues that have serious political and economic ramifications. These issues played into the self-interest of the two hardiest survivors of the older

15. For an interesting discussion of how subjugated and/or marginalized people adopt and adapt the ideologies of the ruling elites for their own purposes, see Michel de Certeau, *The Practice of Everyday Life* (Berkeley: University of California Press, 1984).

16. Sydney E. Ahlstrom, *A Religious History of the American People* (New Haven: Yale University Press, 1972), 961. For a more detailed argument on these points, see my essay "How Do Neo-orthodox and Post-neoorthodox Theologians Approach the Doing of Theology Today?" in John Woodbridge and Thomas Edward McComiskey, eds., *Doing Theology in Today's World* (Grand Rapids: Zondervan, 1991), 437-59.

modernist options that were still alive in the 1960s. The issues themselves provide an opportunity for each of the two parties to gain social status and political strength by identifying with one position or its perceived antithesis in a polarized conception of the public good, particularly in matters such as abortion, homosexuality, feminism, and the role of religion in presidential politics. Wuthnow states, "Increasingly, it appears, both sides take their cues from each other and allow political considerations to dictate their choice of means and ends. Genuine alternatives often seem to be drowned out by these strident voices."[17] If the decline of the Modern Age undermines tolerance for the subtlety of mediating positions, then we are left without a full continuum and find, instead, only the polar extremes.

New ways of describing a postmodern perspective, with implications for interpreting the social and political alliances which are pertinent to churches as well, come from the work of certain postmodern French philosophers since the 1960s. With the failure of so many Marxist countries and the criticism of Freud and all metanarratives generally, Giles Deleuze, Jean Baudrillard, Jean-Francois Lyotard, and others now think French culture can be best described beyond the older modern paradigm in terms of various competing decentralized groups. They theorize this situation by appeal to a postmodern disequilibrium interplaying with the micropolitics of desire, which spins off a variety of independent movements with no necessary relation to one another.[18]

According to Ernesto Laclau and Chantal Mouffe, the survival of each micropolitical group requires alliances or "hegemonies" with other groups.[19] Different kinds of temporary or long-term hegemonies occur between, for example, marginalized ethnic groups, feminists, post-Marxists, gay and lesbian liberationists, labor unions, religious activists, diverse church organizations, political parties, and so forth. No one universal theory can explain the specifics of the structures of oppressive power felt by each of these groups, but each group must establish its own coalitions of discourse and action with other groups. While Laclau and Mouffe see contemporary society as "a heterogeneous ensemble of isolated practices," they seek to identify "nodal points" of temporary alignment

17. Robert Wuthnow, *The Struggle for America's Soul: Evangelicals, Liberals, and Secularism* (Grand Rapids: Eerdmans, 1989), 18.

18. For an excellent critical overview of their proposals, see Best and Kellner, *Postmodern Theory*, 77-180.

19. Ernesto Laclau and Chantal Mouffe, *Hegemony and Social Strategy: Toward a Radical Democratic Politics* (London: Verso Books, 1985).

that disclose, in Foucault's terms, "regularity in dispersion."[20] As this theory pertains to the topic of this essay, we may note that Protestants are responding to the present situation by participating in multiple parties, religious and otherwise, organized around disparate lines or themes from ecology to evangelism. Laclau and Mouffe offer some suggestions regarding a model for interpreting the interplay between the various coalitions formed by different Protestant groups with other groups that fall outside of the characteristics assigned to the two-party description we have challenged.

At stake are the continuities presupposed by the two parties and their familiar historic alliances. For example, just when some "conservatives" think same-sex sexuality might provide a reliable litmus text to distinguish conservatives from liberals, we confront both the orthodox theology of most Metropolitan Community Church pastors and, then, "Evangelicals Concerned," with its constituency of self-avowed "evangelicals," and even fundamentalists, in support of gay partnerships. Then, internationally, we find "Other Sheep," a mission agency in support of gay and lesbian Christians throughout Latin America under the leadership of a self-labeled "evangelical," Tom Hanks, who previously served as an Old Testament professor, with sponsorship from the "conservative" Latin American Mission, at Seminario Bíblico Latinoamericano in Costa Rica. Clearly the possible hegemonies between different parties today cross lines and entail a rich variety of implicit treaties, partial covenants, working relationships, tacit cooperations, orchestrated conflicts, and outright opposition.

The Literal Sense of Scripture in Modern Guise

At least in theory, the debate over the literal sense of Scripture belongs to a central theme in the identity of Protestantism, namely, the principle of *sola Scriptura* or the claim that the literal sense of Scripture provides a sufficient norm for Christian faith and practice. The debate over the use of historical criticism in determining the literal sense played a key role in the modern fundamentalist-liberal split, and, not surprisingly, it continues to play a similar role in current representations of two-party Protestantism. This topic raises the most rudimentary questions about how Protestants interpret Scripture.

20. Foucault, *The Order of Things*, xiii-xix, 344-87.

The implications of an older modern form of knowing when applied to the classical Christian pursuit of the literal sense of Scripture can be clearly seen in Frederic Farrar's impressive Bampton Lectures of 1885, *History of Interpretation*. What Farrar shares emphatically with the preceding centuries is a conviction that the "literal sense" alone provides the normative basis for doctrinal arguments. However, Farrar and Protestants since the nineteenth century had begun to take for granted a peculiarly modern transformation of this premodern principle for reading Scripture. So, Farrar states what seemed obvious in the modern period: "the aim of the interpreter should be to ascertain the specific meaning of the inspired teacher, to clothe it in terms which will best convey that meaning to the minds of his contemporaries."[21] On this basis, he finds a review of the history of interpretation to be "a melancholy one," because we discover "that past methods of interpretation were erroneous."[22] Likewise, the Rabbis offer little of enduring value because they "were children of an imperfect and abrogated dispensation"; in the Talmud Farrar finds nothing of value "apart from a few moral applications and ritual inferences in matters absolutely unimportant."[23] After a few glimmers of insight from the Reformation before the modern period, scholars at the dawn of the seventeenth century regressed into dogmatic controversy: "The whole of this epoch was retarded."[24] In every case, he judges a premodern pursuit of the literal sense according to its ability to anticipate the insights of modern historical criticism. Within the modern period itself, Farrar declares, "the notion of verbal infallibility could not possibly survive the birth of historic inquiry, which showed in scripture as elsewhere an organic growth, and therefore a necessary period of immature development." Yet, Farrar confesses with no uncertain sound, "the Bible is still the divinest of all books and the Lord Jesus Christ is still the Son of God, the Saviour of the World!"[25]

These modern apperceptions of "history," "author's intent," "meaning," and "literal sense" had immediate consequences for Protestants — more, for example, than they did for many Roman Catholics.[26] Yet, it is a

21. Frederic W. Farrar, *History of Interpretation* (1886; reprint, Grand Rapids: Baker Book House, 1961), 4.

22. Farrar, *History of Interpretation,* 8-9.

23. Farrar, *History of Interpretation,* 429, 10.

24. Farrar, *History of Interpretation,* 359.

25. Farrar, *History of Interpretation,* 430.

26. See, e.g., from the Roman Catholic side, how Raymond Brown tries to distinguish "the literal sense" (what a text "meant" according to "the author" when it was written) from a "canonical sense" (what it "means" according to "the living

thoroughly modern reformulation of a premodern traditional Christian claim, retaining the same words but hearing them differently, and in a different order of priority. It obviously lies behind the fundamentalist-liberal debate of the 1920s, with roots back and branches forward. Moreover, this debate itself is not accurately a conflict between intellectual "liberals" and anti-intellectual fundamentalists, since many fundamentalists rose well above that critique.[27] Yet, from a postmodern perspective, the modernist reformulations by both parties now appear to have offered us false options.

Liberals were, of course, frequently accused by fundamentalists of "modernism," because modern historical criticism set before us new conflicting choices not so clearly seen in previous centuries of biblical interpretation. At their best, fundamentalists could accuse liberals of violating the same Protestant principle they used to justify their historical inquiries. If the Bible had once been chained to the pulpit of priests, it now seemed tethered *de facto* to the desk of professional academics. Only they, the modern "objective" scholars, could reconstruct the "original" or "genuine" texts of the Bible, amid the "secondary" and "non-genuine" additions of later editors. Only they could read between the remaining lines of a reconstructed text to find evidence of an author's "theology" from the traces of it left in a "source" he or she had written. In this way, speculative and previously unknown "biblical traditions" (in most cases they were more accurately "prebiblical" traditions) came to replace the Bible itself as the primary testimonies of faith shared between a liberal Protestant pulpit and the pew. Nonetheless, the fundamentalist effort to legitimate the Bible on a similar historical basis could be easily discredited by most liberal scholars. Fundamentalists were, in essence, wiped off the social register of elite Protestant seminaries.

But scholars on the supposedly "conservative" side were also in the business of using premodern terms and notions in radically new modern ways. This is particularly evident in the repeated effort by Princeton scholars at the turn of the century to defend "the scope" of biblical books

---

teaching office of the Church"). In these terms, the normative sense of Scripture for Christian faith is determined by the magisterial Church tradition with, in spite of, and beyond "the literal sense"; see Raymond Brown, *The Critical Meaning of the Bible* (New York: Paulist Press, 1981).

27. See Mark A. Noll, *Between Faith and Criticism: Evangelicals, Scholarship, and the Bible in America* (San Francisco: Harper & Row, 1988), 23; George Marsden, *Fundamentalism and American Culture: The Shaping of Twentieth Century Evangelicalism 1870-1925* (New York: Oxford University Press, 1980), 212-21.

in terms of an historical author's intent. "Scope" was heard in premodern periods as a text-oriented description of what we today might call the "unity" or "shape" of a whole biblical book. One could speak of a "scope" of land or hear "scope" as "purpose" almost in the sense of compass and map.[28] However, by the late nineteenth century, both the Princeton scholars and their "liberal" rivals heard the term as designating an element in the "intentionality" of a reconstructed historical author. Historical "authorship" of biblical books took on a force in the Modern Age that it had never attained before. Both conservatives and liberals alike tried to use "scope," in the sense of "aim" or "purpose," in order to mark a mechanism that orchestrated a plethora of inner thoughts. As a result, even fundamentalists began to distinguish between a biblical author's "revelatory" and "non-revelatory intentions."[29]

At a minimum, modernization contributed significantly to what all the main participants in the two parties found thinkable and unthinkable, imaginable and unimaginable. What had become in the modern period perceptively axiomatic, accompanied by a triumphalist sense of discovery, often caused modern interpreters to view the premodern past as stupid, stubborn, and dogmatically paralyzed. But when words do not signify the same things, those who have unconsciously changed in their forms of knowing may easily develop a false sense of superiority over persons dead and buried. One sign of such modern false superiority is the common description of biblical interpretation before the modern period as "pre-critical." One postmodern contribution ought to be that we, at least, forego such a pejorative label and speak instead of "premodern criticism." Again, my main argument is that fundamentalists and liberals essentially agreed upon the terms of the modern debate. A common historical, referential grammar supported their conflict on political, ethical, and doctrinal matters. One side or the other could thus be deemed right or wrong. Conflict over "truth" made sense.

28. For the premodern use of "scope" see Sheppard, "Between Reformation and Modern Commentary," xlii-lxxi. For evidence of "the modernized conservative" view of Princeton scholars, see Marion Ann Taylor, *The Old Testament in the Old Princeton School (1812-1929)* (San Francisco: Mellen Research University Press, 1992), 64-69 (Hodge), 115 (J. Alexander), 212-13 (Green), and 281-86.

29. For example, see C. I. Scofield's note on Eccl. 9:10, "Verse 10 is no more a divine revelation concerning the state of the dead than any other conclusion of 'the Preacher' (Eccl. 1,1) is such a revelation," in *The Scofield Reference Bible* (New York: Oxford University Press, 1909).

GERALD T. SHEPPARD

"Conservative" Protestantism Is Not the Same as Premodern "Orthodoxy"

In his 1970 essay on "The Two-Party System," Martin Marty cites favorably a statement by Josiah Strong, made in 1913, that "there are two types of Christianity, the old and the older. The one is traditional, familiar, and dominant. The other, though as old as the Gospel of Christ, is so rare that it is suspected of being new, or is overlooked all together."[30] I want to challenge this statement, but do so humbly and self-conscious of how indebted I am to Martin Marty's work throughout the span of my own theological training.

In my view, Strong's statement illustrates well a twofold modern historical fallacy by its appeal to "the old and the older." First, "the old" surely includes premodern "traditional" Christianity, which he assigns inaccurately to his own contemporary, modern fundamentalist-evangelical Protestants. Second, "the older" type of Christianity implies the use of historical criticism to rediscover a "lost" gospel at variance with both "traditional" Christianity and perhaps Scripture itself. What follows is a criticism of each of these premises. Each, in my opinion, relies on modern assumptions that can no longer remain uncontested, and, therefore, the two-party model they support ought no longer to be cited as representing viable options for Protestantism in the United States.

Do "conservatives" in Anglo-American Protestantism represent what is "traditional" and "famliar" in historic Christianity? Strong assumes that most contemporary Protestants of his day accept what is "old" and "traditional," and for the purpose of this essay, the "old" includes the premodern. But an assumption that such continuity exists between premodern and modern conservative Protestants presupposes some theory about how one writes a history of resemblances. What follow are two examples of the kinds of problems that stand in the way of any simple assumption of a direct continuity between "traditional" premodern interpretation and modern "traditional" fundamentalism or conservative evangelicalism.

First, we find in 1 Corinthians 11:4 in the Geneva Bible of the sixteenth and first half of the seventeenth century a statement irrelevant to most modern Protestants: "Every man praying or prophecying having *any thing* on *his* head, dishonoureth his head." The italics mark English words

---

30. Martin Marty, *Righteous Empire: The Protestant Experience in America* (New York: Harper and Row, 1977), chap. 17 ("The Two Party System"), 177.

without Greek equivalents that were added, nonetheless, to make better English sense of the verse. The problem raised by this verse in the seventeenth century is that men always wore hats on public occasions or when they preached in a church. Since preaching was, in William Perkins' words, *"the art of prophesying,"* the question of the literal sense of this verse touched directly on a matter of common practice.

While the grammar and lexical values of the words of the verse are undisputed, its "literal sense" may not be. Its "literal sense" was heard only when the relation of its testimony to the revealed subject matter of Scripture became clear. A marginal note addresses this matter in "historical" terms by explaining: "It appeareth, that this was a politike Lawe serving onely for the circumstances of the time that Paul lived in, by this reason, because in these our dayes for a man to speake bare headed in an assembly, is a sign of subjection."[31] In premodern commentary the phrase "circumstances of the time" or "circumstances of the place [text]" signified how the historical past tense sheds light on the literal present tense of the biblical text. In this case, the testimony of the text touches on the matter of public "subjection," expressed in circumstances no longer directly pertinent to the seventeenth century. In principle, other direct commands by Paul are not *legalistically* binding but must be related to the nature of the gospel itself in order to know their scriptural import. By contrast, fundamentalists have commonly sought to handle such problems by appeal to "accommodation" within the historical intentionality of Paul, in contrast to this premodern effort to hold text as testimony together directly with its subject matter. Of course, Geneva's notes did not undo an assumption that women ought to be subordinate to men, but did warn against "no measure of this inequality" and also cited a contradictory ideal "that mutuall conjunction may be cherished." In its own setting, these positions were not merely traditional but explored frontiers that would be perceived differently by later generations of interpreters.

A second example can be found in the work of the aforementioned and famous Cambridge teacher/pastor, William Perkins. During the 1590s, he offered a series of sermons on Hebrews 11, subsequently published in 1609. In Hebrews 11:32, Perkins confronted a serious problem. This verse celebrates Jephthah as a symbol of faith. Perkins immediately moves from the verse in Hebrews to the narrative account in Judges 11 where Jephthah makes a vow to offer as a burnt offering whatever living thing might cross

---

31. *The Geneva Bible: The Annotated New Testament 1602 Edition, with Introductory Essays*, ed. G. Sheppard (Cleveland: Pilgrim Press, 1989), 85.

the threshold of his house when he returned home after God gave him victory in battle. According to a common reading of Judges 11, when his own daughter appears at the door, he fulfills his vow by killing her. The idea that such an action is an example of faith deeply troubled Perkins, who devoted much of his time and labor counseling people in "cases of conscience," using Scripture and his own resources of "pastoral care," including what we today call "psychotherapy."

Perkins argues in two ways against the possibility that the literal sense of Scripture celebrates Jephthah for killing his own daughter. On a historical and grammatical level, he accepts a rabbinic suggestion regarding Jephthah's vow that "the words, in the originall, may as well be translated thus: It shall be the Lord's (or) I will offer it." Here he openly speculates ["may well be"], then supports this possibility of "or" instead of "and" in grammar by opining, "this latter translation is more suitable to the circumstances of the place." Within this historical speculation, Jephthah promised to offer an animal as a sacrifice but was willing only to require of a human being the Nazarite vow ("It shall be the Lord's"). Even this possibility causes Perkins to express hesitancy, "I speake not here, how well or ill Iephte did in making her a Nazarite."

Accompanying all this historical detail is a second factor: he refuses to find "the literal sense" apart from the gospel to which it bears witness. From what he already knows of the gospel, he states emphatically concerning Jephthah's possible oath and killing of his own daughter: "God would never accept of such a vowe," "this faith and such a vow cannot stand together," and a "godly Iephte . . . could not think that God would be pleased, with such an abominationable sacrifice."[32] We see here that a tension engendered by a knowledge of the gospel itself leads to historical speculation in search of the literal sense. His comments are not "precritical," or merely intuitive, ahistorical, literalistic, or methodologically undisciplined. He is not a fundamentalist because he neither presupposes modern historicism nor does he locate the literal sense by appeal to subtleties in the "author's original intent." My point here is to note how the intertextual warrants have functioned in the premodern period, for both Jews and Christians, in a radically different way from that adopted by modern fundamentalists, for whom they usually became merely accurate references to historical events or to the intentionality of an historical "author."

---

32. *William Perkins' A Commentary on Hebrews 11 (1609), with Introductory Essays,* ed. John Augustine (New York: The Pilgrim Press, 1991), 174-75.

What ought to be clear in my presentation thus far is my dependence on both older "liberal" modern historical criticism and on what I would call postmodern perspectives that follow from reformulations within the left wing of modern studies since the late 1960s. To be clear from the start, I do not think we are going to discover any neatly formed center among postmodern critics. What we may find, however, is that beyond the free play of postmodern deconstruction, certain new possibilities for biblical interpretation and Christian living may emerge that would allow the incidental politics of our lives to be transfigured into more constructive means of moral endeavor by a language of faith and revelation toward acts of love, justice, forgiveness, and grace.

A Postmodern Rediscovery of the Gospel

We recall Strong's other assumption that modern liberals defend a position "as old as the gospel of Christ" but "so rare it is suspected of being new." I will respond to that notion by looking at John Dominic Crossan's impressive study *The Historical Jesus: The Life of a Mediterranean Jewish Peasant*, which relies almost entirely on older modern historical criticism. Crossan begins his book with a chapter entitled "The Gospel of Jesus." There Crossan offers us a collection of all the "authentic" words of the historical Jesus.[33] However, among those words we do not, in fact, find that Jesus ever calls what he is teaching a "Gospel." We should realize that it is historically inaccurate to do so, even as it is historically inaccurate to call a reconstruction of Q a "Gospel," on a par with the four Gospels. Though Crossan has spoken somewhat loosely and anachronistically to identify these sayings with "the Gospel," he has at least been careful enough to call it "The Gospel *of Jesus*," rather than "of Christ." He knows that this same historical reconstruction gives no evidence that the historical Jesus ever overtly identified himself as "the Messiah" or as "Christ." On this same basis, we can argue against Crossan that modern historical criticism does not *historically* lead us back behind the New Testament Gospels to an older "Gospel of Jesus," much less to the "Gospel of Christ." We ought to recognize that, historically speaking, the disciples were not "Christians" prior to their testimony to the resurrection of Jesus Christ.

Insofar as Strong's description of "the Gospel of Christ" could be

---

33. John Dominic Crossan, *The Historical Jesus: The Life of a Mediterranean Jewish Peasant* (San Francisco: HarperCollins, 1991), xiii-xxvi.

identified with Crossan's "The Gospel of Jesus," it cannot historically represent a "type" of Christianity Strong seeks to describe. Also, from a postmodern perspective, there is no universal reason by which we might be able to derive scriptural revelation from historical criticism, much less prove on the basis of historical criticism alone that Scripture itself has a capacity to testify to God's revelation. This last claim would be vulnerable to historical criticism insofar as it depends on certain implicit historical assertions, but no Jesus as reconstructed by historical criticism could ever substantiate a Christ of faith. This matter is not merely a technical issue, but reflects a major shift in our understanding about what older modern critical methods can and cannot do.

This problem has recently been directly engaged by scholars in the so-called "third quest for the historical Jesus." We find currently an intense debate over whether Q, a sayings source underlying Matthew and Luke, can be called a "Gospel" in any sense at all. James Robinson has perhaps made the best, very speculative argument in support of that possibility. The term occurs only as a verb at some later stage in the redactional history of Q, now found preserved in Luke 7:22, as a quotation from Isaiah 61:1. In a rigorous refutation of Robinson's proposal and the tendency by scholars in the United States to speak of Q as a "Gospel," Frans Neirynck shows how the identification of any book as a "Gospel" belongs only to the second century, so that the extrabiblical "Gospel of Thomas," for instance, has that title only as a secondary addition, much as the canonical Gospels of the New Testament.[34] Hence, we may argue that "Gospel," like "Torah," when it was first attached as a label for scriptural books did not denote a genre, but instead the ephemere of the specific revelation to which these books were assumed to bear witness.

What is gained by a postmodern perspective is a fresh appreciation for these differences and their inability, in and of themselves, either to establish or refute categorically an appeal to revelation. The semantic transformation of originally prebiblical traditions into a new and later context of Scripture raises a whole set of issues that cannot be addressed by historical criticism alone. Postmodern criticism must allow for the possibility that when these prebiblical traditions become biblical traditions, they might deliver on the promise implicit in Jewish or Christian

---

34. See James Robinson, "The Sayings Gospel Q," in *The Four Gospels* (Festscrift for Frans Neirynck, Vol. 1; Leuven: Leuven University Press, 1992), 361-88; and F. Neirynck, "Q: From Source to Gospel," *Ephemerides Theologicae Lovanienses* LXXI/4 (December 1995), 421-30.

scripture itself. They might offer us what "history" alone could never give us.

For Protestants, after the Modern Age, a rediscovery of Scripture as sufficient human testimony to the gospel offers far greater hope to Christian faith than any modern reconstruction of the historical Jesus, conservative or liberal. This observation does not invite us to ignore historical criticisms, but to recognize that their illuminating power will inevitably be relative to our specific preunderstanding regarding what "text" we want to interpret and why. While historical criticisms remain a necessity, their relevance is unpredictable since hermeneutical relevance is determined more by the practical implications of a choice of a text and context than by a universal theory of etymology. Yet because historical criticisms inform the very lexicon of grammatical possibilities, their absolute necessity in any high and serious biblical interpretation remains ensured. We must now both benefit from the insights of historical criticism and push them to their limits. Today, Jewish scholars such as Michael Fishbane and Jon D. Levenson have similarly renegotiated the relation between modern historical criticisms, rabbinic commentary, and a future for Jewish interpretation beyond the modern paradigm.[36] So, too, Wilfred Cantwell Smith's recent *What Is Scripture? A Comparativist Approach* moves well beyond the options of a "two-party" Protestantism in his appeal to world religions as evidence regarding how premodern Jews and Christians have profoundly read their scriptures scripturally rather than merely historically.[37]

In general, a postmodern perspective doubts all historical apologetics, both liberal and conservative, for "the Gospel" and for Christian scripture, whenever those defenses seek security in foundationalist arguments or theories based on a universal theory of "history," "hermeneu-

---

35. For a perceptive discussion of this problem even in the modern period regarding an author or an author and his/her work, see Michel Foucault, "What Is an Author?" 141-60, trans. Josué V. Harari in *Textual Strategies: Perspectives in Post-Structuralist Criticism,* ed. Josué V. Harari (Ithaca: Cornell University Press, 1979). With an application to the book of Isaiah, see G. Sheppard, "Isaiah as Scroll and Codex within Jewish and Christian Scripture," in *Society of Biblical Literature: 1996 Seminar Papers* (Atlanta: Scholars Press, 1996), 204-24.

36. Among their writings, see Michael Fishbane, *The Garments of Torah: Essays in Biblical Hermeneutics* (Bloomington: Indiana University, 1989) and Jon Levenson, *The Hebrew Bible, the Old Testament, and Historical Criticism: Jews and Christians in Biblical Studies* (Louisville: John Knox Press, 1993).

37. Wilfred Cantwell Smith, *What Is Scripture? A Comparative Approach* (Minneapolis: Fortress Press, 1993), 18.

tics," "ontology," or even practical reason alone. Perhaps Calvin, who flirts with various proofs for the credibility of Scripture, now sounds almost postmodern when he finally admits that we have "no great certainty" until "the Spirit shining upon it, enables us there to behold the face of God."[38] A postmodern reformulation of Calvin's claim suggests that we read Scripture scripturally for a revelation from God that transfigures our lives and politics, in preference to either a pious interpretation of a reconstructed historical Jesus or a metaphysical theory of the transcendent.[39] Neither does Calvin's statement nor this reformulation of it, as an alternative to the older modern conservative and liberal options, offer a flight merely into pneumatic exegesis. Such claims follow rather than precede our having already negotiated well the literary and historical dimensions of the literal sense of Scripture in the hope that another, equally historical possibility might loom on an otherwise familiar hermeneutical horizon, one requiring of us spiritual as well as historical criticism.

38. John Calvin, *Institutes of the Christian Religion*, trans. Henry Beveridge (Grand Rapids: Eerdmans, 1966), vol. I, 86.

39. Cf. Paul Lehmann, *The Transfiguration of Politics: Jesus Christ and the Question of Revolution* (London: SCM Press, 1975).

Conclusion

The central theme of this volume is simple and straightforward: the two-party paradigm of American Protestantism needs to be dethroned from its place of prominence so that we can formulate more nuanced and accurate understandings of the past and present state of Protestantism in America. Our argument is that the two-party paradigm is inadequate as a descriptive frame for telling the grand story of American Protestantism. What is more, when applied to particular Protestant individuals and groups, the bipolar model often contorts those narratives into plot lines largely alien to the data themselves. The question we asked our contributors was how to portray the American Protestant past and present, in its particulars and in a general sense, more accurately and fairly than the two-party paradigm made possible.

In this regard, it should be noted that the goal of this project was never to deny the possibility that a two-party model might best explain certain Protestant events, controversies, and developments. In some specific cases a binary interpretation may, indeed, be the best interpretation. Moreover, it was never our goal to include only those scholars who have little to no use for the two-party explanation of American Protestantism. As a result, some of the essays in this volume defend a continued, if more nuanced, use of the two-party model (most notably Martin Marty), while other essays seek to incorporate the old two-party categories into somewhat expanded taxonomies of classification (e.g., Fred Kniss, Donald Luidens and Roger Nemeth).

But most of the essays in this volume have endeavored, in one way or another, to dismantle the two-party paradigm, in the process retelling old stories that have been distorted by its bipolar categories, or revealing new stories that have been hidden in the long shadows cast by the paradigm. Discovering appropriate case studies for examination proved to be relatively simple (in fact, while this volume is quite lengthy, it could easily have contained twice as many essays), thanks to the overwhelming, almost hegemonic influence that the two-party model has had in recent years on the historical and sociological study of American Protestantism. In other words, one can select almost any American Protestant topic, and find an academic analysis of that story that employs two-party terms.

It could be suggested that the kind of criticism of the two-party paradigm contained in this volume is really an exercise in overkill. That is to say, one might very well ask: Doesn't everyone already admit that the two-party model is, at best, a limited tool for exploring the dynamics of American Protestantism? Well, yes and no. Based on the numerous conversations we have engaged in related to this project, it would seem that many (most?) historians and sociologists of religion would agree that the description of American Protestantism presented by the two-party model is much too simple to do justice to the complex realities of American Protestant history and life. On the other hand, it is striking how readily and how quickly historians and sociologists, even those of us who would disavow the bipolar model, will slip into two-party terminology. The two-party paradigm has become a kind of default language that permeates many or most examinations of twentieth-century American Protestantism.

Not surprisingly, supporters of the two-party model have seen in the pervasiveness of bipolar language proof positive that, when it comes right down to it, American Protestantism is divided into two camps. To state their case more forcefully, if one cannot talk about Protestantism without slipping into liberal versus conservative categories of analysis there must obviously be a good deal of truth in such bipolar categorizations. But this assumption misses the fact that, in constructing historical or sociological accounts, scholars (and, even more so, journalists) are almost irresistibly drawn toward organizing their material into simple, clear protagonist-antagonist plots. In his address at the June 1995 Re-Forming the Center conference, Randall Balmer referred to this penchant for bipolar narrative as "the disease of dualism." As Balmer pointed out, this particular approach is so rampant in the literature of the field precisely because "dualism and conflict make for good copy: gather a couple of quotations from each camp and you've got a story — a story uncluttered with mediating voices, uncomplicated by perspectives that suggest the issue isn't quite so simple as polemicists on both sides would have us believe."

The appeal of uncluttered, uncomplicated stories notwithstanding, it seems clear that historians and sociologists should exercise great caution before forcing their data into a two-party grid. In many cases, where the story is complicated and only drastic contortions can make it fit within a bipolar narrative, this is the most obvious sort of advice. There are, however, some stories that seem to cry out for a two-party interpretation. One thinks, for example, of recent developments within the Southern Baptist Convention. If there's a two-party tale to be told, it would seem to be the SBC in the years since 1979. But even here we must remember that only one of the two supposed sides in this dispute is truly happy with a hard-and-fast two-party interpretation of what has happened in their denomination in the past two decades. "Fundamentalist" leaders certainly have argued that the Southern Baptist Convention has split into two clear liberal versus conservative camps. By contrast, Southern Baptist "moderates" hold a more complicated understanding of recent events, i.e., one particular party among several (i.e., the "fundamentalist" party) seems intent of late on removing all diversity from the convention, thus colonizing the entire denomination under its party banner. To adopt a purely two-party interpretation of Southern Baptist developments is thus to agree with the perceptions of one particular group — and in this case, the "winners" — against all others.[1] Perhaps it is precisely in these kinds of "pre-interpreted" bipolar situations that historians and sociologists need to be most cautious in their use of the two-party paradigm.

A good example of the need for such caution can be found in the northern Presbyterian controversies of the 1920s and 1930s. From the beginning this series of events has been explained in bipolar terms, i.e., liberals and conservatives fighting it out for the heart and soul of Presbyterianism. In fact, as William Weston has noted in these pages, this early twentieth-century Presbyterian controversy has been "perhaps the classic site for deploying the two-party theory."

But as Weston, D. G. Hart, and Richard Pierard retell the story in this volume, each in his own way, the picture of the Presbyterian conflict changes. Before our very eyes the so-called conservative party divides into two antagonistic subgroups (i.e., fundamentalists and confessionalists); the so-called liberal party includes all sorts of folks who, in many ways, do not fit the liberal stereotype; and, in the allegedly barren middle region between conservatives and liberals, we now see a huge group of denom-

---

1. Barry Hankins, "History Is Written by the Losers: Historiography in the Southern Baptist Controversy, 1979-1996," Biennial Meeting of the Conference on Faith and History, Calvin College (Grand Rapids, 1996).

inational loyalists. All of a sudden it becomes clear that it is a historical distortion to reduce this controversy simply to a battle between "modernists" and "fundamentalists." Northern Presbyterians of the 1920s and 1930s cannot be shoehorned into two-party categories that have any sort of definitional integrity. Baldly stated, the two-party model proves inadequate even when applied to what might be referred to as the paradigmatic example.

While a few contributors to this volume do not completely agree with this conclusion, research associated with the Re-Forming the Center project (presented at several conferences at Messiah College and in a host of other academic settings)[2] has made it abundantly clear to us that, as Randall Balmer announced at the 1995 Re-Forming the Center conference, "It is time to declare that the two-party paradigm is dead, or at least dysfunctional; if nothing else, the postmodern context cries out for a new paradigm."

*   *   *

Of course, this last point, the call for a new paradigm, raises a critical question: Where do we go from here? Perhaps we should start by being very clear as to what we are not saying. We are not calling for a return to the one-party consensus narratives which so dominated American religious history earlier in this century. That sort of interpretation has its own serious distortions, particularly in its effort to explain American Protestantism in terms of a mainstream and its periphery. In fact, and as we have argued elsewhere, the two-party paradigm was a needed corrective to the consensus approach to American religious history.[3]

The point here is that matters are considerably more complex than accounted for by either of these interpretive models. But the question remains: If the one-party and the two-party models are rejected because they fail to do justice to past and present Protestant realities, where do we go from here? While we do not claim to have a comprehensive proposal for the future study of American Protestantism, or anything approaching a comprehensive proposal, we do offer a few modest suggestions as to

2. See the Appendix for a complete listing of programs organized by the Re-Forming the Center project.

3. For more on the consensus approach to American religious history, and the two-party paradigm as a response, see Douglas Jacobsen and William Vance Trollinger, Jr., "Historiography of American Protestantism: The Two-Party Paradigm, and Beyond," *Fides et Historia* 25 (Fall 1993): 4-15.

how historians and sociologists might proceed. As Balmer intimated above, any new interpretive approaches will need to take into account certain postmodern insights. One of these insights is that scholars must be extremely wary of meta-narratives, or grand explanatory theories. For one thing, such meta-narratives, in their sweeping, even all-encompassing generalizations, often distort more than they illuminate. Let's take the case at hand. No one can dispute that American Protestantism is terribly diverse and complex and, often, just plain baffling. Yes, there are patterns in American Protestant life and history, but these patterns overlap and combine, conflict and diverge, and intensify and fade in a host of complicated and unpredictable ways. In short, American Protestantism does not lend itself to any sort of grand interpretation, particularly a simple unipolar or bipolar interpretation. As a result, the only way to make a comprehensive interpretive model of American Protestantism "work" is to "weed out" data that do not fit, and/or to "reshape" and squeeze the data into the contours of the paradigm.

It is important to recognize that meta-models such as the two-party paradigm of American Protestantism are part of the larger structuralist vision that has dominated academic discourse for much of this century. (In this regard, see especially Gerald Sheppard's essay in this volume.) This structuralist pose discredits the importance of the "subjective," and disallows the importation of our own hopes, dreams, and experiences into our work as scholars. In reality, however, and as postmodernists have emphasized, all of us do bring our subjectivities with us into our research and writing. As a result, each of us sees things from different vantage points. While a certain kind of "objectivity" is required in scholarship, the simultaneous reality is that such "objectivity" will neither eliminate our own subjectivity nor guarantee that we will agree on one way in which to view, understand, and explain Protestantism in twentieth-century America. There are many interrelated Protestant stories that need to be told, and they will, necessarily, be told from many different viewpoints. Better understanding our own particular grids of perception, we will need to allow our theorizing and categorizing to become more complex, fluid, and "fuzzy" than is currently the case. Protestants and Protestant groups often cannot be squeezed into neat definitional boxes, and we must eschew the temptation to do so. At the very least, we must acknowledge the limits of all our definitions and categories.

In the same vein, we must reject the notion that we can describe American Protestantism as falling along a single line spectrum that stretches from conservative to liberal, or from orthodox to progressive, or from any one pole to any other pole. American Protestantism is far too complex to fit onto this simple linear scale of difference. This is true *even* for spectra that allow for fluid and fuzzy categories, and *even* for spectra that have many more stopping points along the way than the simple left and right of the two-party model. Whatever new interpretive paradigms we might develop must either be multi-dimensional in nature, or they must very clearly delineate the limited range of data with which they are dealing.

Perhaps most important, any effort to develop a large-scale interpretive model, fluid and fuzzy and multi-dimensional as it may be, must always take into account that what is happening at the grassroots level, in congregations or in small groups, might be very much at odds with developments at the "top" level, whether that "top" is viewed in national perspective or in organizational terms. In other words, to borrow a slogan at the heart of what used to be called the "new social history," we must think about American Protestant history from the "bottom up," as well as from the "top down." In this regard, it should be noted that the two-party paradigm, in keeping with most meta-narratives, has been primarily an effort to account for and explain the ideas and behaviors of religious elites and the organizations they lead. While one could legitimately argue that the bipolar model does not even work at this level, it works much more poorly when it comes to grassroots analysis. As Nancy Ammerman aptly noted in her response to the proceedings of the 1995 Re-Forming the Center conference, "It sometimes amazes me that this two-party image has been so powerful, both among pundits and among scholars, [given that] it . . . describes so little of how most people experience their religious choices and activity." In this volume, the essays by David Sikkink and Nancy Eiesland, in particular, drive home this crucial point.

Of course, some critics will charge that this effort to incorporate grassroots, "views from the pews" perspectives negates the possibility of creating coherent explanatory narratives. We disagree, but would also grant that incorporating such perspectives will mean that our narratives and analyses will need to be more tentative, contingent, and humbly constructed than is often now the case. Something is lost when the scope of one's scholarly interpretation must be limited in this fashion. Nonetheless, it is also quite exciting to begin thinking about American Protestantism in ways that are consonant with the messy realities of lived experience, past and present.

*   *   *

All of this is to say that, for the sake of descriptive accuracy and adequacy, we are convinced that we need to go beyond the two-party paradigm toward developing and employing more multifaceted and nuanced interpretive schemes of American Protestantism. It seems to us that this is an end sufficient unto itself. But we would be remiss if we did not conclude this volume with some acknowledgment of the *prescriptive* concerns that have also informed the Re-Forming the Center project.

On one level the prescriptive concerns that have compelled us to put together this particular collection of essays are rather modest. We are concerned that the current two-party model exercises a negative impact on American Protestantism in the form of self-fulfilling prophecy. Too much talk of two parties does have the potential to create (artificial) bipolar division and conflict. Our hope is that the development of more complex models of Protestant history and life will defuse some of these "false" polarities, and prevent others from developing in the future. In other words, our agenda has not been so much to promote "good" ends as it has been to reduce the potentially "negative" impact of current two-party language. In this regard, we believe that the essays included in this volume do begin to paint a different picture of the American Protestant experience, one that is less negative in its impact on American Protestantism than the reigning bipolar paradigm.

But, to be honest, our deepest prescriptive concerns involve more than merely seeking to overcome the potentially negative impact of two-party thinking. The editors and many of the contributors to this volume are people of faith who earnestly desire that Protestantism develop a more constructive presence in American society. What do we mean by a "more constructive presence"? Of course, there is no one answer to that question, as different persons would answer that query in different ways. But we think we speak for the majority of the contributors to this volume, and the majority of participants in the Re-Forming the Center project, when we say that we would like American Protestants to articulate faith commitments in more positive, less oppositional forms and formulas; to fight less with each other while becoming more at home in our own religious particularities; to be more attuned to the needs of the communities in which we live, and less concerned about our competitive positions in the American religious marketplace; to be more educative and less dogmatically proclamatory in the manner in which we address political and social issues; and, to be more faithful to the gospel mandate to love God with all our hearts, and to love (all) our neighbors as ourselves.

All of this may make us sound like glassy-eyed idealists woefully overinvolved with the subject matter we seek to study. But of course, as noted above, objective scholarship does not exist, and we have been quite self-conscious of our own biases throughout this project. More than this, we have tried to be careful to ground our idealistic hopes for the future of American Protestantism in a rigorously realistic assessment of the past history and present state of Protestantism in the United States. We have sought to include in this volume essays that provide just that sort of realistic assessment, and that meet the standards of analytical accuracy and fairness required of good scholarship. We are thus postmodern in our rejection of absolute objectivity when it comes to history and sociology, but we strongly resist the notion that the prescriptive concerns of a project such as this necessarily turn analysis into pious fiction.

But as regards our prescriptive concerns, nagging questions may rightfully remain about our use of the term "the center" in the title of this book, and in the title of the larger project of which this is a part. Doesn't the term "the center" imply that there is also a periphery, and hasn't "the center" been used to marginalize the stories of countless groups and individuals? Isn't such a notion out of synch with the multipolar understanding of American Protestantism that we seek to foster?

We freely acknowledge that there are problems with the term "the center." There is no question that it can conjure up images of nineteenth-century "Protestant America," in which all non-Protestants and even some Protestants (including, for example, African Americans, members of peace churches, Pentecostals, and various "ethnic" church communities) were deemed to be outside the religious and cultural mainstream. Let it be said that we have no sympathy with this sort of marginalization, in either its academic forms or in its churchly and/or societal practices. In particular, we abhor the anti-Catholicism that has so often served as a pan-Protestant rallying point in the past. Furthermore, we are adamantly opposed to efforts to reestablish a Protestant hegemony (or even a Christian hegemony) in the United States that would facilitate the kind of marginalization that has taken place in the past. Such goals could not be further from our understanding and use of the term "the center."

We also do not think of "the center" as simply the region between the two Protestant poles. Now there are people who, in many ways, can be seen as doing significant work in the area between the evangelicals and the mainline, people aptly referred to by project participant Peggy Shriver as "bridge people." For example, many of the missionaries discussed by Samuel Escobar and Richard Pierard in their essays in this volume might well be described in these terms. But the problem with concentrating exclusively on people or groups that bridge the region between liberals and conservatives is that all those individuals and groups who fall outside or beyond the traditional two parties continue to be ignored or dismissed. To put it another way, to think of the center as the area "in between" means that we are still thinking of American Protestantism in the terms established by the old, flawed, two-party paradigm. In responding to the sociological essays in this volume, Nancy Ammerman made just this point: "So long as we stay within the two-party metaphor, our only model for moving forward is 'bridging' or re-centering. When we begin to hear a broader range of voices, however, we may discover new models and new language that need no longer explain their experience in the terms dictated by these modern poles."

Of course, one might argue that, given these problems, we should simply dispense with "the center." In a certain sense we agree. We have, in fact, sometimes used the term "middle ground" as an alternative way of expressing our concern.[4] But this admittedly more winsome phrase ultimately suffers from many of the same limitations as "the center," including the fact that it can be construed in a manner that marginalizes numerous people and groups. Peggy Shriver suggested the notion of a Protestant archipelago, a circle of islands connected together under the water, and Randall Balmer proposed an evolving geography of religious tectonic plates in creative collision. Both metaphors hold promise. Still, for now we retain "center," albeit a center that is construed in a non-hegemonic, multi-polar, multi-dimensional, and nonhierarchical fashion.

All of this, however, pushes us well beyond the confines of this particular volume. While these larger prescriptive concerns have informed our work, this book has sought to concentrate only on the question of how we can better describe and understand Protestantism in twentieth-century America. In this role, we believe that the essays speak for themselves. Let's put the two-party paradigm of American Protestantism to rest. It's time to move on.

---

4. We have been especially influenced in our use of the term "middle ground" by Richard White's *The Middle Ground: Indians, Empires, and the Republics in the Great Lakes Region, 1650-1815* (New York: Cambridge University Press, 1991).

Persons Involved in Programs Organized by the Re-Forming the Center Project

The first Re-Forming the Center national conference, **Reclaiming a Nonpartisan History of American Protestantism, 1900-1960**, was held at Messiah College, June 2-4, 1994. Presenters included Margaret Lamberts Bendroth and Michael Hamilton, "Ecumenical Fundamentalism at the Winona Lake Bible Conference"; Nancy G. Garner, "The Woman's Christian Temperance Union: A Woman's Branch of Protestantism"; Mark Granquist, "Lutherans in the United States, 1930-1960: Searching for the 'Center'"; Barry Hankins, "If the Hat Doesn't Fit, Why Wear It?: Southern Baptists and the Two-Party System"; David Edwin Harrell, Jr., "Bipolar Protestantism: The Straight and the Narrow Ways"; D. G. Hart, "Conservatism of a Different Sort: The Presbyterian Confessionalism of J. Gresham Machen"; Richard T. Hughes, "From Dissent to Accommodation: The Restorationist Vision of Churches of Christ"; James Juhnke, "The Progressive Mennonite Denominational Center in the Mid-Twentieth Century: The Vision of Edmund G. Kaufman"; Albert N. Keim, "Harold S. Bender's Anabaptist Vision: The Use of History to Revitalize a Tradition"; David E. Kucharsky, "The *Christian Herald:* A Stable Center in a Turbulent Age"; Edgar V. McKnight, "A. T. Robertson: Baptist Evangelical"; Donald Matthews, "'The Spiritual Option' — The Black Church at the Turn of the Century"; Richard V. Pierard, "Missionary Leaders: Upholding Evangelical Principles in the Ecumenical Mainstream"; Susie C. Stanley, "Wesleyan/Holiness Churches: Innocent Bystanders in the Fundamentalist/Modernist Controversy."

At the Biannual Meeting of the "Conference on Faith and History" (held at Messiah College, October 7-8, 1994) the following project-related papers were presented: Jonathan Dorn, "Remapping the Social Gospel: The Institutional Church Movement in the South End of Boston, 1880-1920"; William R. Glass, "The Development of Fundamentalism in the South, 1900-1950"; Paul Harvey, "Southern Baptists and the Social Gospel: White Religious Progressivism in the South, 1900-1925"; Jeffrey A. Mackey, "A. B. Simpson and William Stringfellow in the Metropolitan Crucible of Ministry, New York City, 1900-1960"; Edward Queen, "The Southern Baptist Convention, 1900-1960: A One Party System but a Multiparty Democracy"; Dale Edward Soden, "Mark Matthews: At Two Ends of the Spectrum."

A panel session entitled "Beyond the Two-Party Paradigm of Protestantism" was organized for the Evangelical Theology Group of the American Academy of Religion at the Annual Meeting held in Chicago, November 19-22, 1994. Members of this panel were William McKinney, Martin E. Marty, Clarence G. Newsome, Mark A. Noll, and Barbara G. Wheeler.

The Re-Forming the Center project organized a session entitled "Breaking the Mold: Protestant Leaders Who Transcend the Two-Party System" at the 1995 Spring Meeting of the American Society of Church History held at the University of Miami, FL, April 21-22, 1995. Presenters included Guy Alchon, "Mary van Kleeck, Constructive Evangelical: The Women's Colleges, the YWCA, and the Institutionalization of Social Christianity, 1900-1940"; Rudy V. Busto, "Beyond the Center: A Mexican American Pentecostal Eschatology from the 1950s"; and Stephen A. Graham, "A New Paradigm for American Protestantism: E. Stanley Jones and the Kingdom of God."

The second national Re-Forming the Center conference, **Are There Two Parties Today?: American Protestantism, 1960 to the Present**, was held at Messiah College, June 1-3, 1995. Presenters at this gathering were Edwin David Aponte, "Hispanic Protestantism in Philadelphia: A Case Study beyond the Two Parties"; N. J. Demerath, III, "So You Want to Talk Culture Wars?"; Nancy L. Eiesland, "Making Faith: Religious Choice and Change in Local Religious Organizational Environments"; Mark Ellingsen, "Narrative Theology and the Pre-Enlightenment Ethos of the American Protestant Center"; Samuel Escobar, "The Two-Party System and the Missionary Enterprise"; Julie Ingersoll, "From Women's Lib to Feminism: A Brief History of the Evangelical Women's Caucus"; Fred Kniss, "Relocating the Disenfranchised: Expanding the Two-Party Theory"; Martin E. Marty, "Re-Forming the Center: Are There Two Parties Today?"; Gerald T. Sheppard, " — 'Two-Party' Rhetoric amid a 'Postmodern' Debate over

Christian Scripture and Theology"; William H. Swatos, Jr., "Methods, Meanings, and Parties"; and Ronald C. White, "Bridging the Divide: Parachurch Youth Ministry." A panel on recent developments within ecumenical associations included Donald Argue, Myron Augsburger, Eileen Lindner, Leonard Lovett, and Mary Sawyer. A panel of persons discussing recent denominational developments included Dennis C. Dickerson (AME), Donald Luidens and Roger J. Nemeth (RCA), Kerry Strayer (Mennonites), and Mark Wilhelm (Lutherans).

The Re-Forming the Center Project helped organize two sessions at the 1995 Annual Meeting of the Society for the Scientific Study of Religion (October 27-29, 1995) held in St. Louis, MO. One, entitled "Re-Slicing the Protestant Pie: Beyond the Two-Party Paradigm," included Bradley Hertel, "Optimizing Categorization of American Protestant and Other Religious Bodies along a Orthodoxy Continuum"; David Sikkink, "Dimensions of Difference in American Protestantism: Relative Positions in Bounded Social Space"; and Donald Paul Sullins, "An Organizational Classification of Protestant Denominations." The other was a panel session entitled "Women and the Two-Party Paradigm of Protestantism"; it included Nancy Eiesland, Julie Ingersoll, Christel Manning, Jean Miller Schmidt, and Barbara Brown Zikmund.

The third project conference, held at Messiah College (May 31-June 1, 1996), was entitled **Re-Forming the Center: Where Do We Go from Here?** and was organized around discussion of a position paper ("Re-Forming What Center?") written by Douglas Jacobsen and William Vance Trollinger, Jr. Participants included Margaret Lamberts Bendroth, David Daniels, Nancy Eiesland, Gabriel Fackre, Douglas Frank, David Edwin Harrell, Harold Heie, Patrick Henry, Cheryl Johns, Fred Kniss, James Lewis, Henry Lederle, Elizabeth H. Mellen, Michelle Moe, Donald Musser, Thomas Schmid, Don Shafer, Peggy Shriver, Ronald J. Sider, Susie Stanley, Phil Thorne, H. Dean Trulear, Mary Stewart van Leeuwen, Barbara Wheeler, and Mark Wilhelm.

Index

INDEX